Library of
Davidson College

The RCN in Transition, 1910–1985

This book is about the life of a navy, going back to its roots in the nineteenth century and looking ahead to its prospects in the twenty-first.

The RCN is portrayed as a resilient institution, often starved for resources, capable of basic change, and on the brink of important new developments. Leading naval historians and defence policy specialists record Canada's naval problems, the navy's pragmatic search for solutions, and its future potential. The essays contain much new or little-known material and open up areas of discussion that will be of fundamental importance in the critical years to come. No other book places the navy's most recent problems in a comprehensive historical perspective. Those problems include unification—a unique Canadian experience.

The

RCN in Transition

1910–1985

edited by W.A.B. Douglas

The University of British Columbia Press
Vancouver 1988

THE RCN IN TRANSITION, 1910–1985

© The University of British Columbia Press 1988
All rights reserved

This book has been published with the help of a grant from the Canada Council.

Canadian Cataloguing in Publication Data

Main entry under title:

The RCN in transition, 1910—1985

   Includes bibliographical references and index.
   ISBN 0-7748-0312-6

   1. Canada. Royal Canadian Navy – History. 2. Canada – History, Naval – 20th century. I. Douglas, W.A.B. (William Alexander Binny), 1929–
FC231.R69 1988   359'.00971   C88-091515-3
F1028.R69 1988

ISBN 0-7748-0312-6
Printed in Canada

CONTENTS

Abbreviations vii

Introduction: The Canadian Navy in the Modern World 3
  W.A.B. Douglas
1 Naval Mastery: The Canadian Context 15
  Paul Kennedy
2 Strategy and Maritime Law:
  "Free Seas" and the Canadian Navy 34
  Barry D. Hunt
3 Historical Strategy and Its Uses in Large and Small Navies 49
  Donald M. Schurman
4 MARCOM Education: Is It a Break with Tradition? 61
  Richard A. Preston
5 The End of Pax Britannica and the Origins of the
  Royal Canadian Navy: Shifting Strategic Demands of
  an Empire at Sea 90
  Barry Morton Gough
6 Hard Luck Flotilla: The RCN's Atlantic Coast Patrol, 1914–18 103
  Roger Sarty
7 Inshore ASW in the Second World War:
  The U-Boat Experience 126
  Michael L. Hadley
8 Inshore ASW: The Canadian Experience in Home Waters 143
  Marc Milner
9 Canada and the Wolf Packs, September 1943 159
  Jürgen Rohwer and W.A.B. Douglas
10 The *St Laurent* Decision: Genesis of a Canadian Fleet 187
  S. Mathwin Davis
11 Canada and the Cold War at Sea, 1945–68 209
  Joel J. Sokolsky
12 International Naval Co-operation and Admiral Richard
  G. Colbert: The Intertwining of a Career with an Idea 233
  John B. Hattendorf

13	Economic Considerations in the Development of the Canadian Navy since 1945 *Dan W. Middlemiss*	254
14	Canadian Naval Responsibilities in the Arctic *Harriet Critchley*	280
15	Ships: Managing the Need *J.M. Treddenick* and *C.G. Galigan*	292
16	Canada and Maritime Defence: Past Problems, Future Challenges *R.B. Byers*	316
17	The Future of Naval Warfare *G.R. Lindsey*	334

Notes	355
Contributors	391
Index	399

ABBREVIATIONS

A	Mid Ocean Escort Force escort group (American)
ABDA	Australian British Dutch American alliance
ACE	Allied Command Europe
ACLANT	Allied Command Atlantic
ACNS	Assistant Chief of Naval Staff
ACNS(P)&(A)	Assistant Chief of Naval Staff (Plans) and (Air)
ADC	Aide de Camp
ADM	Assistant Deputy Minister
AIRCOM	Air Command
ASEAN	American and South East Asian Nations
ASV	Air to Surface Vessel radar
ASW	Anti-Submarine Warfare
AWPPA	Arctic Waters Pollution Prevention Act
B	Mid Ocean Escort Force escort group (British)
BdU	*Befehlshaber der U-boote* (Commander, U-boats)
BT	Bathythermograph
BX	Coastal Convoy, Boston to Halifax
C	Mid-Ocean Escort Force escort group (Canadian)
CAF	Canadian Armed Forces
CANCOMAIRLANT	Canadian Air Commander, Atlantic
CANLANT	Canadian Atlantic area
CANMARLANT	Canadian Maritime Command, Atlantic
CASAP	Canadian Submarine Acquisition Program
CC	Prefix for Canadian submarines in the First World War
CEU	Combat Equivalence Unit
CFE	Canadian Forces Europe
CINCEASTLANT	Commander-in-Chief, Eastern Atlantic
CINCHAN	Commander-in-Chief, Channel
CMR	Collège Royal Militaire de St Jean
CNO	Chief of Naval Operations (United Nations)
CNS	Chief of the Naval Staff
CNTS	Chief of Naval Technical Services
COMNAVSOUTH	Commander, Naval Forces South [Europe]
CONCOMARLANT	Canadian Maritime Commander, Atlantic
CPF	Canadian Patrol Frigate

CRAD	Chief, Research and Development
CSC	Canadian Services College
CTOL	Carrier Take Off and Landing
CU	Jamaica to United Kingdom convoy
DATAR	Digital tracking and remoting
DDE	Destroyer Escort
DDH	Helicopter-Destroyer
DDP	Department of Defence Production
DE	Destroyer Escort
DELEX	Destroyer Life Extension
DEW	Distant Early Warning
DGLEM	Director General Land Engineering and Maintenance
DGRET	Director General Recruiting and Training
DND	Department of National Defence
DNPI	Director of Naval Plans and intelligence
DNPO	Director of Naval Plans and Operations
DOD	Department of Defence (USA); Director of Operations Division (Canadian navy, Second World War)
DPC	Defence Planning Committee
DPDSA	Defence Production and Development Sharing Arrangements
DPED	Director of Professional Education and Development
DPMS	Defence Program Management System
DROTP	Director of the Regular Officer Training Plan
EDP	Emergency Defence Plan
EEZ	Exclusive Economic Zone
EG	Escort Group (usually assigned to support groups)
EW	Electronic Warfare
FAT	*Federat Apparat* (spring-loaded) torpedo
FFG	Guided Missile Frigate
FFH	Helicopter Frigate
FFS	Free French Ship
FMC	Forces Mobile Command
FOAC	Flag Officer Atlantic Coast
FUMB	*Funkmess Beobachtungsgerät* (Radar observation equipment)
FUMO	*Funkmess Ortungsgerät* (Radar detection equipment)
FW	Focke Wulf
GNP	Gross National Product
GSR	German search radar

GUS	Mediterranean to United States convoy
HE	Hydrophone effect
HF/DF	High Frequency Direction Finding
HMCS	Her Majesty's Canadian Ship
HX	Fast convoy, Halifax or New York to United Kingdom (First and Second World Wars)
HS	Slow convoy, Halifax or Sydney, Nova Scotia, to United Kingdom (First World War)
IBERLANT	Iberian Atlantic Area [Portugal]
ISA	International Seabed Authority
KMF	Fast convoy, United Kingdom to North Africa
KMS	Slow convoy, United Kingdom to North Africa
LUT	*Lagan unabhängiger* (independent) torpedo
MAD	Mutual Assured Destruction
MARAIRMED	Maritime Air Mediterranean
MARCOM	Maritime Command
MARE	Maritime Engineering
MARS	Maritime Surface or Subsurface
MCF	Maritime Contingency Force
MIT	Massachusetts Institute of Technology
MKF	Fast convoy, North Africa to United Kingdom
MKS	Slow convoy, North Africa to United Kingdom
ML	Motor launch
MOEF	Mid Ocean Escort Force
MOPS	Maritime Officer Production Study
MP	Member of Parliament
(N)	Following rank in Canadian Armed Forces: Navy
NAORPG	North Atlantic Ocean Regional Planning Group
NATO	North Atlantic Treaty Organization
NCC	Naval Constructor in Chief
NDHQ	National Defence Headquarters
NL	Coastal convoy, Quebec to Labrador
NORAD	North American Air (now Aerospace) Defence Command
NORPATS	Northern Patrols
NOTC	Naval Officer Training Centre (HMCS *Venture*)
NRC	National Research Council
NSHQ	Naval Service Headquarters
ODB	Officer Development Board
OG	United Kingdom to Gibraltar convoy
ON	Fast convoy, United Kingdom to North America
ONS	Slow convoy, United Kingdom to North America
OPEC	Oil Producing Economic Consortium
OS	United Kingdom to West Africa convoy

ABBREVIATIONS

OTC	Officer Training Corps (Canadian army university training scheme for reserve officers)
POM	Planned operation and maintenance
QS	Coastal convoy, Quebec to Sydney, Nova Scotia
RAF	Royal Air Force
RCAF	Royal Canadian Air Force
RCMP	Royal Canadian Mounted Police
RCN	Royal Canadian Navy
RCNVR	Royal Canadian Naval Volunteer Reserve (Second World War)
RE	Reserve Entry
RMC	Royal Military College of Canada
RN	Royal Navy
RNCC	Royal Naval College of Canada
RNCVR	Royal Naval Canadian Volunteer Reserve (First World War)
RNR	Royal Naval Reserve
ROTP	Regular Officer Training Plan
SAC	Strategic Air Command
SACEUR	Supreme Allied Commander Europe
SACLANT	Supreme Allied Commander Atlantic
SALT II	Strategic Arms Limitation Treaty (II)
SC	Slow convoy, Sydney or Halifax, Nova Scotia, to United Kingdom
SCEAND	Senate Committee on External Affairs and Defence
SDI	Strategic Defence Initiative
SHINPADS	Ships Integrated and Processing Display System
SL	West Africa to United Kingdom convoy
SLBM	Sea Launched Ballistic Missile
SLCM	Submarine Launched Cruise Missile
SLOC	Sea Lines of Communication
SLT	Second Language Training
SOSUS	Sound Surveillance System
SOUP	Submarine Operational Update Program
SPANS	Sealift Procurement and National Security Study
SQ	Coastal convoy, Sydney to Quebec
SSBN	Ballistic Missile Nuclear Submarine
SSGN	Guided Missile Nuclear Submarine
SSN	Nuclear-powered submarine
STANAVFORLANT	Standing Naval Force Atlantic
STANFORCHAN	Standing Force Channel
STOL	Short Take Off and Landing
STOVL	Short Take Off and Vertical Landing

TAS	Torpedo, Anti-Submarine (British and Canadian specialization for naval officers)
TG	Task Group
TRUMP	Tribal Update and Modernization Program
TU	Task unit
U	*Unterseeboot* (Submarine)
UC	United Kingdom to Caribbean convoy
UGS	United States to Mediterranean convoy
UK	United Kingdom
UN	United Nations
UNCLOS	United Nations Conference on the Law of the Sea
UNTD	University Naval Training Division
URTP	University Reserve Training Plan (RCAF)
USCG	United States Coast Guard
USN	United States Navy
USS	United States Ship
UT	Tanker convoy, United States to United Kingdom
UTPM	University Training Plan, Men
UTPO	University Training Plan, Officers
VCNS	Vice-Chief of the Naval Staff
VHF	Very High Frequency
VLR	Very Long Range aircraft (usually applied to modified Consolidated Liberator B-24)
VSTOL	Vertical and Short Take Off and Landing
VTOL	Vertical Take Off and Landing
WLEF	Western Local Escort Force
XB	Coastal convoy, Halifax to Boston
XK	Gibraltar to United Kingdom convoy

THE RCN IN TRANSITION, 1910–1985

INTRODUCTION:
THE CANADIAN NAVY IN THE MODERN WORLD

W.A.B. Douglas

The Canadian navy, which was seventy-five years old in 1985, has survived several major crises in its short life and has gone on to make remarkably important contributions, both in war and peace, to national and alliance aims. This book records a selection of proceedings from a conference, held to mark the seventy-fifth anniversary of the naval service, that attempted to place those crises and contributions in their past, present, and future context. Some revisions have been made in the light of subsequent events, but the reader should bear in mind that the original papers were written in 1985.

The 1968 unification of the armed forces, a troublesome landmark in Canadian military history, set the limits for an earlier conference marking the seventieth anniversary of the naval service. Held at Royal Roads Military College, near Esquimalt, British Columbia, it was a naval occasion of some moment, and it led to a well-received book, *The RCN in Retrospect, 1910–1968*, edited by J.A. Boutilier.[1] The success of the 1980 conference, the increasing number of books and articles relating to Canadian naval matters, and changing interpretations of Canadian naval history that resulted from new research in the field all gave rise to the second conference in 1985.

Addressing the theme "The Canadian Navy in the Modern World," the conference undoubtedly produced more questions than answers. One issue of central importance was whether, and to what extent, transforming an independent navy into the "sea element" of unified forces has affected Canada's defence capabilities. The locale of the meetings, the Maritime Warfare School at the Canadian Forces Base, Halifax, lent weight to this concern. The book that has resulted will, I hope, help readers to do some "thinking in time" and draw their own conclusions about the transition from Royal Canadian Navy to Maritime Command.

It was during the heyday of the Royal Navy that the RCN had its beginnings, and Canadian naval fortunes can certainly be related to Paul Kennedy's important book, *The Rise and Fall of British Naval Mastery*.[2] His paper on "Naval Mastery: The Canadian Case" sets the framework in which the other papers should be read. As a foil to Kennedy, who writes from the standpoint of a relatively detached observer, Canadian historians concerning themselves with issues of a general nature stay closer to home. Does the navy's role, for example, reflect a national policy? Have new developments led to a damaging break with tradition in the way we educate our naval officers? Can the teaching of history in small navies, as opposed to large navies, foster useful alternate approaches to an understanding of national naval needs?

Barry Hunt, who has examined law of the sea through the eyes of that thoroughly pragmatic sailor, Admiral Sir Herbert Richmond,[3] discusses the concept of "free seas" in Canadian terms. The dichotomy between coastal and oceanic aspirations, not entirely new to Canadian governments, has become more pronounced since Canada became a leader among coastal states. Richard Preston, the foremost authority on Canadian military education,[4] draws attention to obvious departures from traditional naval methods and values in recent years. "The proof of the pudding," the calibre of the product, suggests that in spite of fears and reservations expressed by some senior officers, the professionalism inherited from the Royal Navy has not been lost, and something has been gained in other respects.

The teaching of naval history provides less cause for satisfaction. Donald Schurman, who has studied this problem for twenty years or more,[5] gave a controversial paper on the need for naval history as a vital ingredient in the education of strategic planners. Canadians must study outside present alliance constraints and feed on materials outside the Great Power syndromes on which Corbett and Mahan based their judgments. True, some naval history is studied in the navies of the small countries to which he made reference, but currently, and deplorably, there is not much serious attempt to relate that history to the strategic planning process. The utilization of history, he emphasized, is not a live process. This is what has led, in Schurman's view, to a lack of clear, flexible thinking about options in this equipment-dominated world. He thought that Canadians needed this flexibility of approach.

There is, for example, a distinct connection between fisheries protection forces—together with the Department of Marine that preceded the RCN—and subsequent naval development. Standard interpretations used to relate the Naval Service Act of 1910 to European competition in naval armaments, and dismissed as anomalies earlier attempts to establish a navy. Barry Gough adds another dimension to recent modifications of these previously accepted views with his use of British sources, to show how imperial concerns preceding the Dreadnought race of the early 1900s also influenced policy in Canada. It is a useful contribution to Canadian historiography, and work now being done in the field promises to elaborate still further on this thesis by comparison with antipodean examples. The navies of Australia and New Zealand offer just the kind of variety in naval experience that will help us to understand the role of small navies and could provide fruitful sources of comparison and contrast. The fact is, the roots of the RCN are still a matter of speculation, and the more we learn about the roots, the more we will know about the growth they support.

The tactical and strategic imperatives governing the formation and employment of a Canadian naval service are nevertheless apparent. The end of Pax Britannica, Barry Gough discerns, was a matter of great strategic importance, because the Americas became "the zone of United States dominance." Roger Sarty's account of Canadian naval responses to a German submarine threat during the First World War reveals what this meant. The story he tells is one of a nascent navy composed almost entirely of small and slow armed vessels. Their patrols on the east coast, demanding, unglamorous, and generally thankless though they were, played a vital part in the protection of shipping. In the Second World War RCN coastal forces, a little better equipped but equally overburdened, had a similar role. In both wars the odds seemed to favour the far more professional German naval forces in the region, and U-boats for the most part survived Canadian naval attacks.

Michael Hadley observes that alliance commitments to oceanic naval operations left a "defence gap" at home that actually invited U-boats to our coastal waters; in the eyes of German sailors, inshore antisubmarine warfare (ASW) was generally conspicuous by its absence. Marc Milner confirms the RCN's inability to solve the tactical ASW problem. Two things can be said of this. In the first place, U-boat successes in Canadian waters were not exceptional, after the terrible spring and summer of 1942, and that was enough to frustrate Karl Dönitz's aim, in what he thought was one of the "soft" spots in his war against Allied seaborne trade. In the second place, schnorkel submarines on their lone patrols in the western Atlantic created a tactical problem similar to that experienced by surface and air forces against true submarines in the post-war years. Analysing the methods developed in a "hot" war, even if they were not completely successful, can be useful to latter day anti-submarine warriors. Now as then, for inshore ASW, numbers count.[6]

Canada's contribution to alliance warfare overseas, in both wars, at first took the form, so far as the RCN was concerned, of seamen and airmen for the Royal Navy. At the beginning of the First World War *Niobe* and *Rainbow* made a gesture, in the case of *Rainbow* a very brave gesture, in support of the Royal Navy's needs in the Atlantic and Pacific. After *Niobe* had completed patrols against German merchant shipping in 1914, however, and *Rainbow* had returned from a foray against the powerful armed cruiser *Leipzig*, the RCN took no major part in the "blue water" operations of that war. On the other hand, from 1914 to 1918, and from 1939 to 1945, Canada did have a surprisingly large shipbuilding industry and merchant marine. Kenneth Mackenzie, in a preliminary discussion of the subject (not included in this collection), left the impression that until we understand the relation of merchant naval activity to national policy in wartime, we will not be able to grasp the oceanic dimensions of our naval responsibilities. A full history of Canada's shipping industry, and of our ocean resources as a whole, is badly needed.

The operational history of ocean convoy, by contrast, constantly yields new insights. *The RCN in Retrospect* touched upon equipment and training crises that had to be overcome before the RCN could make an adequate contribution to the naval war of 1939–45 and, for the first time, related Canadian convoy operations to the intelligence war.[7] Analysis of convoy operations leading up to the withdrawal of wolf packs from northern convoy routes in May 1943 did not place the RCN in a favourable light. By the autumn of 1943 improved training, equipment, and experience fostered professionalism among Canadian elements of the Mid Ocean Escort Force and in Eastern Air Command of the RCAF. The account in this volume is the first to make extensive use of both British intelligence and German naval documents covering the convoy battles of September 1943, and it is also the first analysis prepared by two historians from both sides, in close co-operation. The positive experience of that co-operation is noteworthy; it is to be hoped that other historians will follow this example.

The battle for convoys ONS-18 and ON-202 illustrates how a navy, in its formative years, could respond to the needs of the times. Equally, it shows how the odds thus went against battle-hardened submariners, with the latest equipment, fighting in a desperate cause. In passing, it is worth observing that trade protection is the need that has most frequently manifested itself throughout the history of "blue water" operations.

The Second World War remains the most significant event in Canada's naval past, and its study will give good value for a long time to come. The navy's role in post-war years was not so spectacular, but its importance is sufficient to demand a much greater literature than now exists. *The RCN in Retrospect* made a beginning with some valuable papers on post-war engineering developments and operations in the Korean War. Internal problems of the post-war navy were brought out by Louis Audette's account of the Mainguy Report of 1949 and Keith Cameron's comments on the unification crisis of 1968. The papers in this collection open up the field for further analysis. They do not focus on the Korean War, or on unification, but they do consciously address themselves to the navy before and after the changes brought about by unification.

Joel Sokolsky and Dan Middlemiss place naval developments after 1945 in their broad political, military, and economic context. Complementing their work is a study by S. Mathwin Davis of the decisionmaking process behind the first ship designed and built to RCN specifications for a Canadian fleet. This was one of the most important decisions in Canadian naval history and, described by a naval architect intimately involved with warship design and procurement, reveals much about the nature of the RCN.

The navy of this period has to be seen in the framework of the North Atlantic Treaty Organization. Sokolsky argues that until the mid-1960s Canadian naval forces were well suited to their responsibilities; since then they have become increasingly inadequate, not only in quantity but also in concept. It is possible that naval policymakers, preoccupied with keeping a fleet of aging ships ready for sea, have not placed great emphasis on developing concepts. As Sokolsky notes, however, they have not lost sight of the need to maintain close contact with allied navies.

Readers may still wonder why, in a book about the RCN, an entire chapter is devoted to the career of an American Admiral. The fact is that an asset of incalculable importance during these difficult post-war years has been the intellectual idea of international naval co-operation. Too easily taken for granted, improvements in this area have compensated for the shift from British to American naval dominance that began at the turn of the century and have vastly reduced the difficulties in joint operations that in the Second World War were so damaging to Allied interests, as the RCN found out in the western Atlantic. John Hattendorf gives Admiral Richard B. Colbert, USN, major credit for promoting international naval understanding. Senior Canadian officers who heard his paper certainly responded with instant recognition of the man and the idea.

The technological revolution put the RCN on its mettle after the Second World War. With almost no previous experience the navy managed to build, on the foundation laid between 1939 and 1945, an evidently useful fleet for Canadian purposes. Davis's paper sheds light on the process by which the RCN established a design team and saw the *St Laurent* class of destroyer escort through to completion. Much more, though, needs to be said about technology and the navy.

Commodore E.C. Ball, a retired naval engineer of wide experience, and Commander Marc Garneau, Canada's first astronaut, gave a most illuminating paper at the 1985 conference containing a great deal of technical data that could not be included in this collection, but the argument they put forward deserves a comprehensive summary here.

Whatever the limitations of the post-war navy, Ball and Garneau say, it has reacted successfully to bewildering technological and organizational change, including unification. They use a model developed in 1974 by Harold Leavitt, of Stanford University, with four variables: people and their skills, tasks they perform, technology with which they work, and the organization by which their actions acquire legitimacy and authority.[8]

The variables operated amid increased centralization and swift rotation of personnel in the government between 1953 and 1985. "Personal agendas of strong minded individuals, no doubt well meaning within their own perspectives and value systems," became the determining factors in technical decisions. The Department of National Defence tended "to concentrate all resource allocation authority at the top and to neglect the high level attention required by the policy environment." The Department of Defence Production, reorganized as the Department of Supply and Services, became responsible for total government procurement and "entered into an unwanted but inevitable state of tension with ... National Defence." "Ingenious cooperation borne of common sense and good will" did not prevent "failures marked by bitter recrimination and even shattered careers."

And yet, as Captain J.H.W. Knox pointed out in his contribution to *The RCN in Retrospect*, "An Engineer's Outline of RCN History," this was a period of remarkable technological advance in the navy. Ball and Garneau emphasized the design and construction of four classes of destroyer-escort and destroyer: seven *St Laurent*, 1953–4; seven *Restigouche*, 1958–9; four *Mackenzie* (or repeat *Restigouche*), 1962–3; and four *Tribal*, or DDH-280 class, 1972–3. There was also a series of innovative developments, some described elsewhere, that demonstrate the adaptation of naval organization to changing technology.[9]

In the forefront of material developments, for instance with notch ductile steel hulls, cupro-nickel water-piping systems, cathodic protection, and inorganic zinc silicate primers, the navy is also studying non-metallic fire resistant materials for ships and has adopted unmistakeably Canadian standards for living conditions. Design teams are anticipating further change, for example to accommodate women crew members. These are, in their way, assertions of sovereignty: small ones perhaps, but enough to do away with the sometimes awkward compromises in RCN ships before and during the Second World War.

With solid state devices, real time digital data processing led to improved hull design, propulsion control systems, sensor accuracy and sensitivity, weapons control, and command and control of ships and fleets. The navy's best technical officers uncovered and resolved design problems, identified new requirements such as variable depth sonar, helicopter haul-down, and data links between ships at sea. Indeed, data links, and the concept of a ship as an integrated system, can be traced back to 1952, when DATAR, standing for Digital Tracking and Remoting, was demonstrated in HMC ships *Digby* and *Granby*. Ball and Garneau dwell on that development:

> [The name was] chosen to catch the attention of decision makers and to establish a place in history for instrumentation of combat data, just as RADAR and SONAR revolutionized their respective fields. While the name didn't catch on, the concepts did, and their impact has eclipsed the advances of the developments it was aimed to rival. The demonstration of the DATAR development system was sufficient to cause both the USN and the RN to evaluate the concept in depth, to expend substantial resources in exploring it, and ultimately to supplant the older analogue techniques. To a generation nursed in mother's arms while she works the keyboard of her home microcomputer, this revolution will seem an obvious step of no great consequence, but when it is realized it took place in 1952 and comprised the first digital data link, and pushed the state-of-the-art in circuit design and electronic devices, then this naval development has to be seen as a major stepping stone in the development of digital computers and computer-based systems.

Approval of the system had to await the DDH-280 class (and the caution manifested by this twenty-year delay, Ball and Garneau concede, turned out to be well advised), when the design team, in face of resistance to a full-blown digital command and control system, argued successfully that the minimum system necessary to operate a data link should be installed. This led to the development of CCS-280, the first comprehensive Canadian command and control system actually employed in operational vessels.

From the lessons learned with CCS-280, naval engineers developed a conceptual design for a comprehensive distributed digital system, SHINPADS (Ships Integrated Processing and Display System). To design SHINPADS, key junior personnel were given computer training then challenged to design a single display to meet all the needs of the eight different existing computer and display systems in the ship design. This "bypassed the older guardians of the status quo," removed many of the barriers between different sections of a design authority, and ensured that an integrated combat system design would be contributed by combat systems engineers, while the design of a comprehensive propulsion and power system, with its appropriate controls, would be the domain of maritime systems engineers. "The sheer size of the design teams of the USN and RN," maintain Ball and Garneau, "inhibited this kind of organization."

Adapting to radical changes in technology, according to the Leavitt model, demands appropriate changes in organization. Canadian naval success in developing the ship as an integrated system, say Ball and Garneau, is a classic demonstration of the model. How was Canada, a relatively small country only modestly endowed with human and scientific resources, able to acquire and sustain the talent to achieve such results?

Like the Royal Navy and the USN, the RCN borrowed from civilian ranks of professional engineers, naval architects ad technicians, and engineering technologists. The median age of technical staff in 1955 was about forty years. In 1960, although some senior personnel thought attrition would break up the design team, the headquarters staff in Ottawa found new talent by instituting an engineer-in-training program that was in the forefront of a new wave of public service activity. The Engineers Career Committee, and later the Technical Officers Career Committee, was strongly supported by the Public Service Commission. After unification the committee was expanded to include both engineers and naval architects, and it led to the formation of a Technologist Training Program, with postgraduate training opportunities for civilian engineers.

For technical personnel in uniform, the navy turned to its engineering, electrical and ordnance branches; they had to adapt to new skills, change tasks, and settle the boundaries between their spheres of responsibility. Ships had too many technical officers. If they did their job well, they were underemployed. If they left the ships, the systems began to deteriorate. Operational officers needed technical qualifications. "No longer were we equipping the man but we were manning the equipment." This, supported by the resentment of professionally trained technical officers that their way to the top was blocked, so long as line officers believed they were unsuitable for command, led to the

General List concept.[10] Then unification forced the navy "against its will and against all reason other than uniformity with the army and air force, to totally reverse the process." Technical officers again formed their own corps.

> Fortunately [note Ball and Garneau], the navy was in the midst of reaping the harvest of a considerable investment in personnel development ... New graduates from MIT and the USN Postgraduate school were readily appointed to assist in the design and construction of the DDH-280 class ... Although several officers spent many months at sea on trials and development assignments ... the state of the systems in ships without technical officers deteriorated, and technical officers serving on ships were seen as role models.

To solve the problem, Lieutenant-Commander (now Vice-Admiral) Brian Hotsenpiller, career manager for naval officers in headquarters, created the "Combat Systems Engineers." This met and, according to Ball and Garneau, still does meet resistance from some quarters, but the new subclassification was given substance by the approval of a formal training program. The example and leadership of dynamic and influential officers in command of ships and schools, moreover, breathed spirit into the scheme.

Between 1982 and 1984 a massive investigation of the career structure and training of naval engineers revealed the lack of a well-defined role for the naval engineer in headquarters. Design of warships was not supposed to be the engineer's responsibility, but producing documents for the acquisition of warships could only be done successfully if warships were designed. It is a conundrum that remains to be worked out. Whatever is decided, the unity of the navy and of naval engineering seems to feature as strongly as ever. And the many Canadian-designed and -developed systems in the new Canadian Patrol Frigate are testimony to the marriage of civilian and military technological expertise, a marriage that has survived powerful undermining influences ever since the Second World War.

What the future holds for technology in the Canadian navy is uncertain. There is room for optimism because naval engineers adapted so well between 1953 and 1985. They adapted, according to Ball and Garneau, by recognizing and responding to constant change. And they were well-equipped for the task. Commander (now Captain) Garneau, a most impressive representative of the new breed of naval engineer, is himself proof of the potential the navy has for leadership in the field. The danger that he and Commodore Ball fear is that the Department of National Defence will not use that potential, that the bulk of design work ultimately will be done outside Canada for lack of the skill to do it at home. They conclude with a plea to remember the intimate connection between organization, people, tasks, and technological change, and not to lose the flexibility that marked the period 1953–85. It must be said that many would take a less optimistic view of the situation and argue that the navy has already lost its design capability. To this argument Ball and Garneau respond in terms that are calculated to challenge the doubters. "Time and time again, officials of the Department of National Defence in Canada have lent credence to the idea that we have no warship design capability in [the department]! It is at best an error, an error which has contributed greatly to the high mid-career attrition of naval engineer officers. At worst it is a deliberate fraud, perpetrated to protect the concept of 'low risk' contracting."

Technology provides a useful bridge between the navy before and after unification. Technological problems facing the RCN were not, evidently, very different from those facing Maritime Command, and the same can be said of political, economic, and strategic policy, except in matters of scale. Huge increases in defence costs, together with the reduction in defence spending between 1970 and 1985, means that the magnitude of difference in scale takes on its own significance, and that there is far less margin for error in planning and decision making. Rod Byers, in his discussion of past problems and future prospects, takes the navy to task for not explaining its problems adequately, and he argues that until decisionmakers and planners learn to put their needs into their proper strategic context, the navy will continue to be on the short end of government handouts. When he presented this paper, his critical observations on the quality of naval staff work aroused sharp reactions from a naval audience and an eloquent rebuttal from the Chief of Defence Staff, an airman. Readers can draw their own conclusions on this controversial matter. They may also find food for thought in Professor Byers's suggestion that the traditional role of the RCN is more one of sea denial than "naval presence." Few will disagree, however with his conclusion that the real challenge of the future is to bridge the commitment-capability gap.

Should Canadian naval commitments extend to the Arctic? Commander G.G. Freill, in the paper he delivered at the 1985 conference, strongly and eloquently advocated establishing and maintaining an arctic capability in the Canadian navy. This has always been a matter of priorities; his argument, representing the position of the Naval Officers Association of Canada, provoked lively discussion among the delegates, including the Commander of Maritime Command. Some of what he had to say has been overtaken by events, but the question is still a central one, a subject of bitter contention brought into sharp focus by the defence White Paper of June 1987. One of Canada's distinguished arctic sailors, Captain Thomas Pullen, is a strong advocate of the Polar 8 icebreaker to establish and maintain a Canadian presence in the northwest passage.[11] The White Paper urges the necessity of a naval presence with nuclear-powered submarines that can also operate in other ocean areas if necessary. Professor Harriet Critchley lays out the considerations that have to be taken into account in this important debate, showing that the two positions are not necessarily contradictory, with a comprehensive summary of the writing and research now being done in that field.

The importance of such ideas is one thing; the will to implement them is quite another. Jack Treddenick, looking at the fundamental problem of acquisition and maintenance of ships, paints a gloomy picture about the future of Canadian naval procurement. The high cost of ships, especially when considered as integrated systems, makes even the most optimistic forecast, under present budget allocations, inadequate to meet the navy's needs. In the past our defence policy has reacted to crises in order to correct such shortfalls. That in turn has created domestic crises. It has been a dangerous luxury. In the future, as the military historian Desmond Morton has suggested, the crises could be terminal and the luxury a fatal one.

A paper given at the 1985 conference by George Kamoff-Nicolsky (not included in this collection because it covers some of the same ground as the other papers addressed to political and strategic factors of naval planning) drew attention to the nature of the threat. Third World interests, he pointed out, have created the need and opportunity for a global Soviet maritime presence. The result has been a steady growth of activity, far beyond the waters in which Russian navies have traditionally operated, and it is in the light of such considerations that the strategic assessments offered by Joel Sokolsky and Rod Byers need to be seen. Add to this George Lindsey's sober but wide-ranging predictions about the future of naval warfare, and the future of Canada seems pretty closely linked with the future of the Canadian navy. Of the five possible types of future naval fleets he envisages, two are appropriate to the Canadian case: a multinational force of escort ships and maritime patrol aircraft; and a national force of ships, aircraft, and submarines devoted mostly to coastal operations.

Finally, amid the rapid changes of our times, just about the only thing that remains constant is the human factor. We know too little about it and often give it too little consideration. James Boutilier offered an innovative and interesting sketch of Canadian sailors based on interviews with men who had served in the lower deck. This is an important initiative, although the findings are still tentative, and the emphasis on policy in this collection prevented the inclusion of his paper. Much more is needed about the social history of the navy, and until we have such history it will never be possible to understand completely how the service has evolved. What can be said on the basis of historical experience, though, is that whatever success has been achieved in the transition from RCN to Maritime Command must be attributed to the effective leadership, high morale, and loyal service of its personnel. They have been tested to the limit with worn-out ships and equipment, and high attrition rates among the best personnel are likely to increase if the situation does not improve. So long as Canadians do not lose sight of this reality and give their sailors the support they deserve, they will be in a fair way of getting the navy they need to serve their interests best.

Apart from the contributors and other participants, I would like to thank the many people who helped bring this book to completion. I would especially like to thank Elsie Roberts, who has been an invaluable help all through the preparation of the book. Laura Coles, the manuscript editor, and Jane Fredeman attended with care to the minutiae of military terminology; Christine Rowe and Roger Sarty in particular proofread and indexed the final manuscript.

Chapter 1

NAVAL MASTERY: THE CANADIAN CONTEXT

Paul Kennedy

This paper is an attempt to describe briefly the role of the Canadian Navy within the broader context of western and, in particular, British naval mastery during the present century. It is, therefore, much more of a discussion of Canadian sea power from without than from within. While this in isolation would appear a one-sided approach, the other contributions to this collection will clearly address the balance. It also ought to be stated here that this paper will consider Canadian naval strategy, not only in the strictly operational sense but also (indeed more) in relation to such larger background factors as geopolitics, economic change, and the indigenous political culture. Again, this may seem to some to be painting the canvas with too broad a brush, but it is done with the conviction that introductory papers ought to place the themes which are to follow within a wide and comprehensible framework.

The starting point for this analysis is the author's book *The Rise and Fall of British Naval Mastery*, which first appeared in 1976.[1] The term "naval mastery" was used there, it was explained, simply because the rival term "sea power" lacked quantification:

> almost any state can claim to have or have had a certain amount of sea power. It can also exist at almost any level: a Mediterranean power of classical times, a Chinese pirate chief, or a Latin American state can be found to have possessed command of the sea for a period in their local area. By the use of the term "naval mastery," however, there is meant here something stronger, more exclusive and wider-ranging; namely a situation in which a country has so developed its maritime strength that it is superior to any rival

power, and that its predominance is or could be exerted far outside its home waters, with the result that it is extremely difficult for other, lesser states to undertake maritime operations or trade without its tacit consent ... Naval mastery is also taken to imply that the nation achieving it will usually be very favourably endowed with many fleet bases, a large merchant marine, considerable national wealth, etc., all of which indicates influence at a global rather than at a purely regional level. All these definitions are suggesting a measure of maritime supremacy which only a few nations have ever achieved and which has marked them off from lesser rivals.[2]

Great Britain possessed such a naval mastery in 1815 and for a period before and after that significant date; the aim of the book was to analyse the circumstances which explained the rise and decline of that power's maritime supremacy. Precisely because it focused upon "circumstances," the book did not concern itself too much with individual admirals and battles, still less with "the finer points of tactics, ship design, gunnery, navigation and social life in the navy."[3] It did focus, however, upon economic themes, arguing that "Britain's naval rise and fall has been so closely bound up with her economic rise and fall that it is impossible to understand the former without a close examination of the latter."[4] More controversially, perhaps, it suggested that the "sea power" about whose influence Mahan had written in his seminal work[5] was historically and geographically specific: that is, it exerted its greatest influence upon world affairs between the early sixteenth and the later nineteenth centuries and then found itself in turn influenced by the rise of the near-autarkic, continent-wide superpowers of the twentieth century.[6] Even at its strategical and naval zenith, however, Great Britain had never been able to act as a purely maritime power but, because of its proximity to the European landmass, had always endeavoured to maintain the continental balance-of-power when that was threatened by a new challenge. Western sea power and British naval mastery over the past two centuries were therefore intimately connected with economic change, geopolitics and industrialization, and land-power and the European balance. To view it in isolation, merely as a series of (usually successful) British naval encounters from Blake to Nelson, or to Cunningham, was to ignore both its full potential and its many natural limitations.

This rather abstract and generalizing argument may seem to be taking us a long way from the story of the Royal Canadian Navy, but in fact it is setting the scene for what follows. When one examines in more detail the reasons for the steady rise of British naval mastery, it becomes clear that North America (and later, Canada) play an important contribution. Obviously, the well-situated "offshore island" of Britain had a better chance in wartime of maintaining links with North America than the hybrid land-cum-sea power of France or The Netherlands, but this easier access for British colonists, shippers, and regiments to defend and expand overseas settlements brought its own benefits: profitable export markets, flourishing shipping lines, additional seamen in wartime, and an assured flow of raw materials.[7] This is not to ignore the importance of European factors, as the extreme navalists tended to do,[8] but the Elder Pitt was perfectly correct in explaining to the Prussians at the time of the Seven Years War that "we must be merchants while we are soldiers ... our trade depends upon a proper exertion of our maritime strength ... trade and maritime forces depend upon each other, and ... the riches which are the true resources of this country depend upon its commerce."[9]

And when the relatively favourable diplomatic and geopolitical circumstances which attended British strategy in that war had been replaced by the far more threatening context of the War of American Independence or by the critical scene of 1809–12, Canada (as British North America) was an important contributor to the British strategical effort: a source of supplies in naval goods, the location of vital bases for the Atlantic trades, an entrepôt for smuggling goods into New England, a producer of seamen. Ships, trade, colonies—Mahan's revered and interacting trilogy—were what Canada both provided and symbolized. To be sure, these elements needed to be linked to other aspects of grand strategy, like the funding of continental armies against Napoleon, but no one can doubt that the maintenance of British naval mastery would have been much more difficult without the possession of this trans-Atlantic dominion.[10]

In the same way, when we turn to the area which concerns us more, the role of Canada's contribution within the context of twentieth-century Western naval mastery, the important thing to understand is the way that part fits into the whole. It was in the late nineteenth century that British statesmen and the British public reluctantly began to readjust to the steady erosion of their country's formerly unchallenged industrial, colonial, and naval supremacy. The growth of new world powers, the impressive development of new industrial competitors, the 'scramble' for African and Asian colonies, made the world a lot less comfortable a place for the British than it had been in Palmerston's time.[11] It was partly in defensive reaction to these new dangers, and partly because of contemporary notions of Social Darwinism, Pan-Anglo-Saxonism and Imperial Federation, that both British and Dominion circles began to urge a policy of closer imperial co-operation and of the takeover by self-governing parts of the Empire of some of the defence obligations and costs which Joseph Chamberlain's "Weary Titan" found itself burdened with at the onset of the twentieth century. The fond Boer War portrayals in *Punch* magazine of the mother lion being aided by her vigorous and growing cubs was not merely a journalistic fancy about the role of the Dominions. Sir John Seeley, in his highly influential book *The Expansion of England*, had argued in 1883 for a fusion of the self-governing white colonies with the motherland to produce a "Greater Britain" that would be able to maintain itself against Russia and the United States in the first rank of the powers.[12] By 1902, a more worried Oppenheim was writing that "Historically, the doom of Great Britain would seem to be certain but for the new factor introduced by the existence of powerful and patriotic colonies."[13] An imperial battlefleet, based perhaps on Gibraltar, with warships paid for by all self-governing parts of the Empire, beckoned as an ideal scheme to help ease Britain's global problems. It certainly seemed attractive to a worried British Admiralty, which at the 1902 Colonial Conference pointed out that whereas the UK spent fifteen shillings and one penny per head of its population on naval expenditure, New South Wales spent eightpence-halfpenny, New Zealand sixpence-halfpenny, and Canada nil.[14] Yet was not the safety of the sea lanes from Sydney and Halifax to London and Liverpool of equal concern to the inhabitants of both the first-named cities and the last?

Although Canadian imperialists, Round Table members, and the Canadian Navy League echoed these British hopes, it hardly needs to be said that there was considerable objection to contributing subsidies to an imperial fleet or to establishing a large Canadian navy. Whereas a Dominion such as New Zealand was becoming increasingly aware of its total dependence upon the workings of British sea power and was thus more willing to comply with London's wishes, Canada's own fate was inextricably bound up with that of its powerful neighbour to the south. Either the United States was deemed to be hostile, in which case the chief Canadian concern was the defence of its lengthy, open frontier, and its naval requirements could be left to the British Admiralty; or the United States was friendly, in which case it was difficult to see a serious strategic threat to Canadian soil. Well before the famous remark of 1924, many Canadians felt that they were living in a "fireproof house, far from flammable materials." Furthermore, in an age when Canada's own national identity was being stressed, all talk of imperial naval contributions and co-operation seemed to imply more rather than less dependence upon Whitehall and Westminster, which in turn provoked the deep suspicions of French Canadians and isolationists. Finally, there was the argument, neatly offered by Laurier, that Canada *was* contributing to the Empire's strength by concentrating its resources upon developing the Canadian Pacific Railway.[15]

If the latter arguments seemed very self-serving, they had a validity in the larger context of defending British naval mastery (which we shall examine in a short while). At the time, however, it was the more immediate needs of ships and men which were being asked for and which were apparently disregarded by Canada's politicians. Yet within another few years, the further erosion of Britain's naval supremacy seemed to have reached crisis levels. Despite the successful conclusion of an alliance with Japan (1902), a settlement of many outstanding difficulties with the United States in the western hemisphere (c. 1901–3), and a colonial entente with France (1904), the British found that the rising threat from the German High Seas Fleet across the North Sea was forcing drastic changes in their naval policies. More and more battleships had to be relocated into the North Sea, leaving only small squadrons to operate east of Suez and in southern Atlantic waters. The Pacific Station was abandoned. Overseas bases for the Royal Navy (including Esquimalt, Halifax, and Bermuda) were downgraded and their establishments reduced or withdrawn altogether. Under Admiral Sir John Fisher's dynamic (and somewhat frenzied) reforms, 154 smaller and older warships were struck off the effective list in order to employ their crews in the Home Fleet's new squadrons. Yet even the build-up of the latter force did not bring security to British minds. By 1908–9 a full-scale "naval scare" had arisen in the light of the German battlefleet's increased size and future building capacities, and the Asquith government's decision to lay down eight Dreadnought-type battleships in one fiscal year was felt to bring only temporary relief.[16] But if Britain's own security was at risk, were not the Dominions also endangered? This, at least, was the message Whitehall sought to get across, it being perhaps best expressed in Sir Edward Grey's confidential statement to members of the Imperial Conference of 1911: "if control of the sea was lost, it would not only be the end of the British Empire as far as we are concerned, but all the Dominions would be separated from us, never to be rejoined; because the control of the seas, once having passed to a great European power, would never be allowed to return again; and not only would the Dominions be parted from us, but they would also be separated entirely from one another."[17]

Even before that time, some Canadian steps had been taken away from the abstentionist defence policy of earlier years. While always opposing moves towards any political-constitutional centralization, Canada was willing to agree to military staff co-ordination and training, integrated weapons procurement, and other practical measures. The Canadian government had acquired, *nolens volens*, the bases at Halifax and Esquimalt in 1905; five years later, with the actual formation of the Royal Canadian Navy, there at last existed a Canadian organization to administer its own major bases.[18] The very creation of the RCN itself reflected the decision of the Laurier government, urged on by imperialist opinion, to render support to Britain during the Anglo-German naval race, not by offering subsidies but by the establishment of a home-based navy which would provide local maritime defence and work "in close relation to the imperial navy."[19] It is worth noting that the decision was in line with the steps already taken by the Australian government, which had long paid a naval subsidy to Britain but in 1909 created its own navy, with local defence responsibilities.[20] The replacement of British overseas squadrons by Dominion navies was a global trend, symptomatic in many ways of the ending of the Pax Britannica. As Fisher enthusiastically put it to a confidant, "We manage the job in Europe. They'll manage it against the Yankees, Japs, and Chinese, as occasion requires out there."[21]

But this fond hope was not to be, at least in the Canadian case. Quite apart from the fact that the "Yankee" fleet was massively larger than anything Canada could produce and the even more telling fact that it was not envisaged as a threat to Canadian interests, the good intentions of building up a medium-sized Canadian navy were ruined by the political controversy surrounding the Borden government's offer of 35 million dollars to enable the British to construct three new Dreadnoughts. Instead of providing reinforcement to the sagging British naval mastery, the Borden gesture led to defeat in the senate, an opening up of all the traditional French-Canadian and isolationist suspicions about closer ties with Britain, and a paralysis in Canadian naval development.[22] When war in Europe did break out in 1914, the RCN possessed a mere two cruisers, transferred from and largely crewed by the Royal Navy. By contrast, the Royal Australian Navy was a quite significant force, with one battlecruiser, four cruisers, and three destroyers, which could both provide local maritime defence and contribute to the protection of imperial sea-lanes.

It was no doubt in consequence of this sorry tale that the author of the chapter "Canada in the World War, 1914–1918" in the relevant volume of *The Cambridge History of the British Empire* was content to note "Canada's own naval contribution to the World War was so small ... that no Canadian naval history need be recorded here."[23] This is a true enough summary, if one's measure of naval history is the classical one of fleet actions: apart from the alarm caused on the west coast early in the war that Graf Spee's squadron might raid Canadian waters, there was no other prospect of the country's meagre naval forces being engaged in, or being able to influence, the course of the *surface* war. The reason for this, however, was not simply the state of the RCN at the outset of the war. It also lay in the fact that, numerically and geographically, the Allied fleets held the upper hand. Much as the British had worried about the size of the High Seas Fleet before 1914, their own Grand Fleet had remained larger, and its numerical and firepower advantage widened during the conflict. Moreover, although unable itself to bring the German navy to a really decisive fleet battle, the Royal Navy was able to retain command of the sea simply by foreclosing the exits from the North Sea; this not only prevented German egress to the Atlantic but also cut off the supply of overseas materials which might contribute to the German war effort. In the Mediterranean, the British, French, and (later) Italian navies made any aggressive move by the Austro-Hungarian fleet suicidal. In the Pacific, the Japanese navy was unchallenged. British, Australian, and Japanese warships patrolled the sea lanes of the South Atlantic and Indian oceans. When the powerful United States Navy entered the war in 1917, the imbalance between the surface fleets of the two sides became even more marked.[24] In these circumstances, the addition of a squadron of Canadian cruisers—or even battleships—would not have been terribly significant strategically, even though it would have been of immense importance to the fledgling RCN.

But the maintenance of "naval mastery" was not, nor had it ever been, something which concerned fleets and fleet actions alone. Historically, Britain's own maritime and imperial supremacy had depended not merely upon the possession of a powerful navy—although that was a necessary prerequisite—but also upon a flourishing productive base and adequate finances to sustain a long, dawn-out conflict. Also vital, indirectly, was its dependence upon the preservation of the European *military* balance of power, to ensure that no single state dominated that continent and was then able to turn its massive resources against the island-state.[25] If the German Army were checked in Europe, and the Allies were able to meet the grinding costs of the 1914–18 war, then—given the inferiority of the High Seas Fleet—those achievements would ensure final victory. If the German army was triumphant on land, or if the Allied campaigns collapsed for want of men, munitions, and money, even their existing maritime advantage might not prevent disaster.

In this grand-strategical sense, therefore, the concentration of Canadian resources upon (a) supplying an army to fight alongside the British and French in western Europe and (b) mobilizing industry, raw materials, and finance to sustain the unprecedented "total war" of

1914–18 were both perfectly logical. The sheer numbers of men were impressive: "Canada recruited 628,964 soldiers, of whom 458,218 served overseas and 56,639 lost their lives";[26] but perhaps even more outstanding was the quality of the troops which fought at Vimy Ridge and in the great August 1918 breakthroughs. The country offered what the British and Allied commanders had most need of: high-class fighting units to take on the formidable Germany army in the field. In the same way, the Canadian decision to pay for its own share of the campaigning (rather than rely upon imperial subsidies), and to manufacture for the common war effort, were precisely what the British Empire required. Already by the beginning of 1916, "250 factories were executing war orders, which now reached $500,000,000,"[27] and these were swiftly eclipsed by the later war efforts. By 1917 and 1918, Canadian factories were producing 30 per cent of the ammunition used on the western front, not to mention 3000 aircraft. Financially, the floating of war loans in Canada to the total of approximately $2,200,000,000 was a staggering indication of how the country's wealth could be mobilized for the overall conflict.[28]

In a smaller way, but more directly related to matters naval, Canada contributed to the rapid expansion of Allied small escort vessels when the seriousness of the German U-boat menace was finally realized. This too was a reminder that naval mastery might not be preserved by battlefleet actions alone, and that auxiliary fleets, minesweepers, trawlers, corvettes, and (as the war progressed) aircraft and submarines were also important. If the industrial facilities did not exist for the construction of these craft, then the parts were ordered in the United States and assembled in Canada. By this means, the Canadians not only assisted the general naval predominance of the Allies— assembling, for example, twenty submarines for the Royal Navy and eight for the Italian Navy—but also responded to the Admiralty's urgent requests to create a flotilla in North American waters which would counter the U-boat menace and complement the Royal Navy's squadrons on the other side of the Atlantic. By the end of the war, this Canadian-based force consisted of over a hundred vessels, chiefly trawlers and drifters to be sure (and only twenty-five of them actually Canadian), but a significant forerunner to the RCN's contribution in the Second World War.[29]

Since these supports to the preservation of naval mastery were far less visible, and seemed far less important, than the battles at Ypres and Cambrai, it was perhaps scarcely surprising that the RCN suffered considerably during the post-1919 retrenchment. Indeed, such was the desire, common among the western democracies, to reduce defence expenditures once the war was over, that some observers thought the RCN was lucky not to have been scrapped altogether! In the event, the Conservative administration's decision to maintain a modest fleet of one cruiser, two destroyers, and two submarines was abruptly changed when Mackenzie King's Liberal party came into office late in 1921. Its original intention was to pay off all five warships, arguing that this "would be more in keeping with the protection of our coasts than it would be in harmony with high-seas fighting, because the fleet as now constituted is for action on the sea, and not for the protection of our harbours and coasts as we understand that protection."[30] This philosophy was a deliberate retreat to a merely coastal-defence role. In the event, one destroyer was kept in commission on each coast but was used for training reservists. The naval budget hovered around 2 million dollars per annum and then slowly declined throughout the 1920s; all pre-war and wartime thoughts of producing a decent-sized service withered away.

But this decline, however painful to the RCN itself, again needs to be placed in context. Although the First World War had caused a diminution in Britain's naval capacity, and a corresponding rise in that of the United States, the two countries with which Canada enjoyed a special relationship had settled their maritime differences at the Washington Conference of 1921–2 and possessed equally strong fleets. By contrast, the High Seas Fleet was at the bottom of Scapa Flow, and the German submarine services had been abolished. France was not a threat, and Italy had not the strength to be a danger. The enigmatic Soviet republic paid little attention to sea power, instead concentrating upon "socialism in one country." The only possible danger lay in the Japanese navy, but that seemed much less worrying after the Washington Conference, and it was difficult to envisage the political and strategical circumstances in which Tokyo would give priority to operations against Canada before first grappling with the American or British fleets. Given the general framework of international relations after 1921, and the extent of the naval mastery which was now shared by the Anglo-American navies, a somewhat larger RCN would not have made much difference.[31]

Thus, although the British Admiralty expressed its "great disappointment at Canada's decision to abolish her seagoing squadron," since the reserve basis which remained "can be of no real assistance in the naval defence of the Empire,"[32] this was an altogether less serious matter than the signs of political isolationism and near-neutralism which permeated Ottawa and Quebec in the 1920s and 1930s. Based in good part upon a natural recoil from the bloodbath of Flanders fields, and mingling with the equally natural drive of the white Dominions (not just Canada alone) for a redefinition of imperial ties to

Britain so that the political autonomy of the member-states of the Commonwealth would be fully recognized, this emphasis upon separate Canadian policies in the Mackenzie King era also brought with it negative undertones. There was a general dismissal of the "Old World" as feckless, irresponsible, and belligerent compared with the higher moral qualities of Canadians and Americans, as well as an exaggerated suspicion that each and every proposal emanating from Whitehall was devised to entangle Canada in some distant quarrel and compromise its freedom of action, and a desire to reduce the consultative and co-operative elements in imperial defence so that anything more than cosmetic proclamations became impossible.[33] One does not have to subscribe to Correlli Barnett's powerful and extremely hostile portrayal of King (and especially of Skelton) to agree that the constant Canadian stress upon separate foreign policies, its avoidance of any commitments either to the League of Nations or the imperial defence, its numerous signals of discontent, from refusing to participate in the Locarno Treaty in the 1920s to hinting that Canada might remain neutral in the event of a war fought over central Europe in the 1930s, unhinged even the modest proposals for international co-operation in this period.[34] While such Canadian (and South African, and Irish Free State) postures were merely unsettling to the British in the relatively untroubled decade which followed 1921, they were strategically alarming during the international crises of the period 1931–9.

By the 1930s, the margins of safety for the democracies had been reduced considerably. With Japan seeking to alter the status quo in the Far East and Pacific, with an unpredictable Mussolini keen to improve his position in the Mediterranean and North Africa, and with Hitler demanding changes in central Europe—and all three powers arming as fast as their economies would allow—the foreign scene was much more threatening than it had been for twenty years. Furthermore, this situation was worsened by the abstention of Russia as a factor in the European balance (compared with pre-1914), by the economic weakness and political paralysis which affected France by the mid-1930s, and perhaps especially by the isolationist stance of the United States.[35] All these considerations could be seized upon by British politicians, themselves eager to avoid foreign entanglements and to appease the revisionist states. To that extent, the introspective and discouraging tone of Canada and some other Dominions toward defence co-operation and a co-ordinated foreign policy can be regarded merely as one additional reason for Whitehall to avoid getting into another large-scale war.[36]

But there was perhaps more to it than that. By the mid- to late-1930s Britain itself was no longer the power it had been in Laurier's time.

The costs of the First World War, together with the economic disaster of the Great Depression, had undermined much of the country's industrial base and reduced its financial credit. If, despite the best efforts of London's appeasers, a European struggle with countries such as Germany and Italy took place, Britain possessed far fewer resources to sustain such a conflict than it had had in 1914.[37] In such circumstances, the Canadian hints in 1937 and 1938 that it would not fight over, say, the integrity of Czechoslovakia were full of import, and not just to George VI, who worried that he might be declaring his belligerency as King of New Zealand and the United Kingdom at the same time as he was declaring his neutrality as King of Canada and South Africa! Possibly the most serious blow would relate to the question of gaining access to Canada's matériel and financial resources, now ever more significant given Britain's economic decline and all-important American neutrality legislation.[38] But there was also the question of acquiring Canadian troops, another critical factor given the inter-war decline of the British Army and the size of the *Wehrmacht*'s build-up.[39] Finally, and much more significantly than was the case in 1914, there was the question of Canadian naval assistance in the event of a renewed assault upon trans-Atlantic trade routes by German U-boats.

There is, fortunately, no real point in offering here a counter-factual analysis of "how would Britain have fared without Canadian participation in 1939?," for the simple reason that that participation occurred and was, by all accounts, overwhelmingly popular. It has been very plausibly argued, by Bothwell, Granatstein, Hillmer, Holland, and others, that despite Mackenzie King's insistence upon Canada's resolution of its own destinies, he and his government recognized an unwritten obligation—"a self-evident national duty"—to come to the aid of the mother country in the event of war.[40] What was more, even when Ottawa was warning of the need to settle central European issues by peaceful (that is, appeasing) means, it was also agreeing to certain measures of preparation for war which turned out to be extremely useful in the event. Alongside the repeated insistence upon Canadian autonomy, therefore, one ought to note the development by the mid- to late-1930s of such practical measures as the purchase of Royal Navy warships, the increases in the defence estimates, the agreement to use Canada as a "sanctuary" for British war production, and the air training programs. In sum, "the way was open for a more flexible, if more submerged, relationship. British officials gave up their nightmares of neutrality and succession when Mackenzie King felt compelled to make the occasional 'nationalist' statement, whilst Mackenzie King refused to be stampeded by isolationist pressure when it came to hard decisions."[41] While there is something in this sort of explanation, it does appear a sophisticated, retrospect view. What is much more probable is that King, despite his idealistic and religious tendencies, found it comfortable to run a Canadian version of what Chamberlain's advocates have termed a "twin-track" policy: hoping to settle things amicably on the one hand but preparing for the worst (by a post-1936 rearmament) on the other. In this view, Chamberlain's effort at Munich—showing that he, at least, was desperately anxious to avoid war—was vital in swinging both Dominion and American opinion in favour of Britain when Hitler launched his further aggressions in 1939.[42]

When the Second World War broke out, therefore, Canada was poised to play a far larger role than in 1914, partly because of its own growth and partly because the Allied camp consisted only of Great Britain and France. Within another year France itself had been eliminated and Italy added to the other side. In addition, the critical British need to maintain good relations with the United States also enhanced Canada's role, at least in 1939–41, when Mackenzie King's government could act as a channel between Whitehall and Washington over sensitive issues. More important still, Canada could resume its role as a munitions supplier and training base for the British Empire, although this again could only take place with the assistance of American technology, organizational expertise, and war-related materials. The decisions reached by the Joint Economic Committee and the later Joint War Production Committee to integrate Allied munitions productions so as to avoid overlap—meaning that Canada built aircraft but not aero-engines, mortars and scout-cars but not landing vessels—make it extremely difficult to disentangle the country's exact contribution to the total armaments output of the Allies. But what is clear is that this massive industrialization was good not only for Canada but also for the democracies' overall strategy; by 1945, Canada was the fourth largest munitions producer on the Allied side. Financially, too, its trade and balance of payments had flourished, which had allowed it to make its many loans and gifts to a near-bankrupt Britain in the critical months prior to the passing of the American lend-lease legislation.[43]

The second major Canadian contribution was not so much preserving as *recovering* the balance of power in Europe upon which so much of the western maritime predominance rested. Simply because of the German overrunning of France and much of western Europe, this task could only take place under circumstances altogether different from those of 1914–18. On the one hand, the sheer lack of trained and equipped British, Dominion, and imperial troops to take on the

Wehrmacht after 1940 meant that a large-scale campaign in western Europe had to be avoided for some time (and Dieppe showed, among other things, how difficult it was to penetrate German defences unless one did possess overwhelming force). On the other hand, by the time the actual campaign in northwestern Europe was under way, the British Empire had been joined by what were fast becoming the two military super-powers: the US and the USSR, the size of whose armies far eclipsed those of Canada and even Britain itself. (By 1944–5, the Americans had sixty-one divisions in the west, the British twelve, and the Canadians five; in the east, the Russians had around one hundred and seventy on the German front alone.) But whereas the Canadian military and aerial contribution looked small in terms of overall Allied numbers, it—together with those of the other Dominions and India— had been highly significant in producing more than double the number of divisions which the British Commonwealth could have raised had the troops come solely from the UK itself.[44] And numbers alone do not measure the quality of the Canadian troops, especially in the Italian campaign.[45]

But the most interesting Canadian development in the Second World War, from the perspective of western naval mastery in its purely maritime manifestations, was the rapid growth of the RCN and the plans which it developed for the post-war world. Given the general strategical context of the war against Germany—that is, a good British (and later, Anglo-American) superiority in surface fleets, a desperate need for soldiers, tanks, and aircraft to counter their German equivalents, and the absolute necessity of a flourishing productive base—it might well have been supposed that the Canadian navy's wartime role would have been kept as small as it had been in 1914–18, so that the nation's resources could be channelled into other areas. Two things, however, checked this relegation. The first was the seriousness of the threat posed by long-range U-boats, which demanded an all-out response on *both* sides of the Atlantic. The second was the evolution of the RCN's own ambitions to create a "big-ship" navy, with a role far exceeding that of a coastal defence force.

All this is not to imply a smooth and impressive transformation in the RCN's capacities during the war. It was, at the beginning, the smallest of the services, with a professional (that is non-reserve/militia) strength of 1800 men, compared with 4500 in the Army and 3100 in the Air Force),[46] and it possessed a mere thirteen ships: six destroyers, five minesweepers, and two others. Moreover, since the most pressing strategical need was to give support to the European "front," much of that force was soon despatched to Britain, somewhat in parallel to the transfer of the First Division and the recruitment of Canadian airmen into the RAF. However, when the Battle of Britain was over and the threat of a German invasion of Britain receded, the greatest challenge to the Allied cause in the west for the next few years was that posed by the U-boats. It therefore made sense for Canada to devote considerable resources to the development of its anti-submarine capabilities, especially in the northwest Atlantic. The Admiralty strongly encouraged that development. The compelling strategical logic of this concentration was steadily matched by the dozens and dozens of corvettes, trawlers, and minesweepers which the RCN operated out of Halifax and other ports, with the service eventually possessing a total of 375 armed ships by 1945.[47] But it was far less easy to secure naval command arrangements satisfactory for Canadian aspirations. It also took a long time to transform mere vessels and crews into *effective* U-boat-sinking and convoy warships. The first of these problems has been well covered recently;[48] in retrospect, one can regard the RCN's claims to operational control in the northwest Atlantic as being both a perfectly logical organizational step *and* as reflecting the Dominion's traditional concern to avoid being transformed from a sub-unit in the British imperial forces to an appendage of the American command system.

Given the "touch-and-go" position of the trans-Atlantic convoys in their struggle against Dönitz's wolf packs, the question of the RCN's anti-submarine capacities is a far more serious one for students of sea power. What is not required is to condemn the RCN with the scorn which McIntyre's *U-Boat Killer* did or simply to ignore the problem as the old official histories do.[49] Operationally, it now seems clear, the Admiralty planners were simply placing far too much weight upon the shoulders of the RCN escort groups, expecting them to take the convoys through the lines of German submarines without severe losses. The tremendous expansion of the service in the first three years of the war left it, inevitably, with large numbers of half-trained crews, who obviously had far less experience than the Royal Navy's professionals. But what was even more detrimental was the fact that the RCN's equipment was so old; none of its ships had the "Hedgehog" mortar by autumn 1942, and very few were fitted with High Frequency Direction Finding (HF/DF) or with modern radar. Most RCN vessels were small or slow, of the corvette type; and what few destroyers it possessed were never as powerful and speedy as the Royal Navy's front-line vessels. In such circumstances, the losses of convoys SC-107 and ONS-154 ought not to be seen as signs of a peculiarly Canadian incompetence at sea (especially since the C escort-groups usually contained a fair number of British vessels).[50] On the other hand, it was also sensible for the Admiralty to suggest that the Canadian escort groups be reassigned for a while for training or to the less demanding trans-Atlantic route to North Africa, even if this actually meant that the RCN played little part in the all-decisive convoy battles of March-April 1943 (just as it was also sensible, to employ a military analogy, for the British High Command in France in 1914–18 to put crack Australian and Canadian divisions along the most difficult parts of the Western Front at critical times in that struggle).

By mid-May 1943, the RCN escort groups were being reintegrated into the North Atlantic convoy runs once again; from then until the end of the war their role was unquestioned. More to the point, the existence of a small-ship, local-defence-plus-escort-duty navy was being increasingly regarded as inadequate by many leading Canadian officers, who argued for the necessity of creating an "offensive" fleet for the forward protection of "the oceans adjacent to North America," for the "maintenance of Imperial sea communications," and for a navy which reflected Canada's position "of some eminence" in the western world.[51] Carriers and cruisers were therefore a necessity, and they in turn would require screens of fleet destroyers. To be sure, there would still be a place for frigates and minesweepers in the RCN, but it is clear from even a cursory glance at the planners' projections of the future composition of the navy that the greater part of its personnel and expenditure would be allocated to a "blue water" fleet. Somewhat late in the day, Mahan was at last coming into his own in the Dominion of the North.

Two further remarks need to be made about this Canadian effort at a *Flottenpolitik*. The first is that, despite the occasional Royal Navy reservations about the operational capacities of the RCN, the Admiralty in London clearly encouraged these "big-ship" ideas. The nature of the informal RN-RCN deal is not clear, but the Admiralty most likely had been timing its requests for Canada to man Royal Navy vessels, and its offers later in the war to transfer Royal Navy carriers, to fit in with its sister service's own tactical manoeuvres in Ottawa. It is highly unlikely that the Admiralty planners knew of the extent to which the Second World War had devastated Britain's capacity to act as a great power in the future,[52] but they were certainly aware that when the war ended there would be a considerable reduction in the Royal Navy's complement; and the more warships that could be transferred to the Canadians, the Australians, and others rather than being scrapped would help to sustain western naval mastery in the future. Hence the First Sea Lord's effusive welcome to the RCN's becoming "a 'big ship' navy able to take an even greater part both now and after the war in maintaining the Naval tradition of the British Commonwealth."[53]

The second point is also obvious. When that cable of congratulations from Whitehall was read out to the Canadian war cabinet, the whole notion of a "blue water" navy was vigorously contested by Mackenzie King. His opposition not only anticipated the post-war efforts, which would be made on grounds of economy, to reduce the requests of the Canadian armed services but also reflected his own cultural dislike of the military per se and of all overseas entanglements.[54] In addition, it might be argued, it symbolized the ambivalent feelings which the Canadian political establishment, and certainly the Liberals, had had towards sea power and indeed towards all military power.[55] Either there would be (as King fondly hoped) no real threats to western security in the future, in which case all talk of an "offensive," "big-ship" fleet was superfluous, or there might well be a threat, but it was difficult to see why Canada should make a special effort in that area given the overwhelming strength of both the American and British navies. To be sure, Canadian naval planners were quite adept at justifying the fleet build-up in nationalistic terms—to avoid excessive dependence upon the Americans in the post-war world, for example—but this was going to be a difficult argument to sustain for long in the actual circumstances of the post-war world.

The story of Canada's contribution to the attempts to preserve western naval mastery in the post-1945 era is, therefore, one in which the elements of continuity are much more obvious to the detached observer than are the elements of change.[56] The first of these was the continued problem of defining and defending the role of the RCN itself, especially in an age when sudden thermonuclear war seemed the most alarming threat to national security and thus little else mattered. Yet the fact is that all conventional navies in the West faced the same intellectual problem (until the post-1960 expansion of the Soviet surface and submarine fleet provided a raison d'être). What is more to the point is that Canada's geopolitical position made it harder for the RCN to argue the case for a good-sized navy than did, say, Australia's position, which is at least one reason why Australia, with a lower per capita and total GNP and a considerably smaller population has consistently spent more on defence in general and on the naval service than Canada. And while it was true that the Royal Navy was steadily shrinking in the post-1945, and especially in the post-Korean War and post-Suez periods, its place was being taken over by the enormously powerful US Navy, which, it could be argued, took away any pressing need for Canada to step into the breach.

Second, if there were roles for Canada's armed forces in the general defence of the West, these seemed to lie in other fields: in the development of adequate air forces, both for the protection of the polar border (which, now for the first time, appeared as a vulnerable frontier) and in a more general sense, given the importance which all powers attached to command of the air. It comes as no surprise to learn that as early as 1948 the RCAF was allocated more than the army or the navy, and that it was expected to spend more than the other two services combined.[57] The other obvious area was in the field of both an aerial and a military contribution to the NATO forces in Europe, in line with what the United States and Britain were also doing. This was a massive departure from the traditional Canadian peacetime policy of avoiding any commitment to what Laurier and Mackenzie King had called the "vortex of European militarism." However, this plan was also within the logic of that other strand in Canadian security policy, of helping to preserve the European military equilibrium and thus the safety of the North Atlantic waters. Since most Western commentators were constantly preaching the lessons of the 1930s appeasement policies,[58] and since anxiety was expressed at the build-up of Soviet power in central Europe, the need to respond to that threat seemed incontestable. It left the RCN, however, as the "Cinderella service," in both strategical and financial terms, once its brief participation in the Korean War faded from public memory.[59]

One final, significant element was the resumption of the political tradition, seen most clearly in the Liberal party, of keeping defence expenditures to a minimum. This was not an especially Canadian phenomenon—it was evident in the British Labour party and in many political parties in other European democracies—but it seems to have had a particular strength in Canadian fiscal and political affairs and to have interacted with those home-grown assumptions about geopolitical security and isolation (or at least distance) from the "front line" which made similar sorts of reductions in defence expenditure much more difficult for, say, British or West German left-of-centre parties to push through. Given the alarming atmosphere in the early stages of the Cold War, and the NATO efforts to find some form of parity between its members' defence burdens, the relatively low level of the Canadian outgoings was already causing embarrassment to the government as early as 1950. As James Eayrs points out, the implausible efforts of Brooke Claxton to add civil aviation and even "some part of the cost of the RCMP" to the defence expenditure total to make it look respectable were only reminiscent of Laurier's argument that improvements in Canadian railways were an indirect contribution to the defence of the Empire. "For by such semantics of accounting every dollar spent by government could be presented as outlay upon national defence."[60]

Consequently, by the time of the Trudeau administration defence spending had become a low government priority indeed, and all comparative statistics covering the period from the 1960s to the early 1980s have revealed how low down the lists—in one of Gavin Kennedy's tables, forty-sixth among the nations—the Canadian position is when it comes to measuring the share of GNP and per capita income devoted to defence.[61] One need not agree with the tart views of the editor of *Jane's Fighting Ships* about "the failure of successive [Canadian] governments to understand or accept the basic principles of naval planning"[62]—for he is avowedly *parti pris*—to wonder about the political drives of a country which devotes a smaller percentage of its GNP to defence than every other member of NATO except Luxembourg.[63] Depending upon one's political proclivities, this can be seen as a measure of virtue or of malignant neglect. From the perspective of assessing the Canadian role in the evolution of naval mastery, it can only be seen as a cramping factor, not compensated for by a proportionately larger Canadian contribution towards security elsewhere.

In institutional and morale terms, the greatest blow dealt to the RCN undoubtedly came with the unification of the armed services under Hellyer in 1968. Of the effect upon the services' esprit de corps, and the diversion of energies from military preparedness to bureaucratic reorganization, there can be no doubt.[64] In the larger context in which this present essay moves, however, this does not seem as significant as the facts mentioned above and with which, by means of a brief recapitulation, the essay will conclude.

What has been argued above is that, with all due recognition to the importance of maritime operations themselves, "naval mastery" cannot be properly understood without reference to the geographical, economic-technical, and sociopolitical contexts within which navies must operate. In this respect, Canada provides a fascinating example of how one particular country has attempted to relate to maritime matters. Although its historical and geographical position made it a nation very much created by the application of sea power, its politico-cultural heritage in the larger worlds of the British Empire, the Monroe Doctrine, and the "western alliance" seemed to render it the least endangered of the democratic states from the late nineteenth century onwards. If and when it needed to partake in the defence of the West, there was a good case—in terms of grand strategy—for concentrating its resources upon munitions production and military endeavour. This was not fully true of the Second World War, where Canada was called upon to play a direct role in the preservation of Allied naval mastery. By extension, it is possible to argue that the Canadian contribution to NATO need not be judged by strictly maritime criteria, provided that the West's naval lead remains and provided also that the Canadian contribution to western defence is correspondingly large in non-naval areas. This latter provision, however, is unlikely to be fulfilled when the share of national income devoted to defence shows all the signs of the "fireproof houses" tradition. *Pas d'argent, pas de Suisses*—the old maxim of Renaissance monarchs—may be an awfully economic-determinist note on which to end this essay, but like many old sayings, there may be a lot of truth in it.

Chapter 2

STRATEGY AND MARITIME LAW: "FREE SEAS" AND THE CANADIAN NAVY

Barry D. Hunt

INTRODUCTION

Others papers in this collection raise a number of points that have particular bearing on strategy and maritime law. One concerns Paul Kennedy's emphasis on a wider or extended "Western" naval mastery that has replaced the Royal Navy's earlier monopoly and how Canada's forces have played their part in exercising that mastery. The elements of continuity in the processes by which the RCN has had its roles determined are striking indeed. And those who now might attempt to press the RCN's case, solely on the basis of hard-nosed strategic realism, will still have to come to grips with the political and emotional realities of Canadian nationalism that sometimes pull in contradictory directions. No less than the Imperial Defence enthusiasts of the late nineteenth century, or the proponents of a centralized Empire Fleet in the interwar period, so today SACLANT and NATO must somehow accommodate what Admiral Richmond in the 1930s derisively called the self-seeking "state patriotisms" of the various Dominions. All this may help explain why almost everything written by or about the RCN has been preoccupied with organizational and budget-sharing matters, and why more fundamental questions of policy and doctrine have been virtually ignored.

Another consideration, suggested by Donald Schurman's paper, has to do with the nature of established naval strategic thought and the fact that its applicability to Canada's and other lesser navies' cases is anything but direct or apparent. The work of the founding fathers in this field was after all characterized by their preoccupations with the exercise of maritime dominance. Their discussions of fleet actions, blockades, combined operations, trade warfare, and naval diplomacy revolved in their various ways around the central notion of an all-encompassing command of the seas that permitted almost anything to he who gained it and precious little to he who could not. Between the two world wars, this feeling that orthodox theory had been written exclusively for the Anglo-Saxon maritime giants prompted younger naval experts in Germany, Italy, and Russia to find alternatives that served their particular needs without necessarily having to face the major navies head on. Fortuitously, the Germans' decision to apply their variations on "tonnage warfare" in the Second World War proved to be the ultimate justification for the RCN's vastly increased role in the second Battle of the Atlantic. And it may be that ambiguities about the priority which the Soviet navy now assigns to anti-shipping functions lies at the heart of the RCN's present dilemma in making its largely single-scenario case stick.

One purpose of this paper is to suggest that recent developments in the field of international maritime law provide a similarly compelling reason—perhaps even a basis—for re-examining the fundamentals of Canada's naval position. Only indirectly will any attempt be made to trace the connections between strategic thought and the awesome technical details of the law of the sea as it has emerged from the efforts to create a new international regime for the oceans and the seabed. That connections do exist can be taken as a given. The evolution of the law of war has always reflected specific operational assumptions; conversely, strategy has been and will continue to be circumscribed by the law's progress.

Until comparatively recently, Canadians had little reason to question the strategic and legal underpinnings of their naval policy. As partners in the Western oceanic community, our acceptance of the major naval powers' traditional assumptions was automatic. Anglo-American variants of the Grotian doctrine of "Free Seas" were accepted, or ignored, as part of our general intellectual inheritance. They still are, one suspects, by most Canadian naval planners. With one brief exception, the Canadian senate's 1982–3 study of Maritime Command devoted no attention to this dimension. The omission would not be worth mentioning were it not for the fact that this acceptance, or indifference, no longer motivates those who make and execute Canada's foreign policy. Indeed, since the late 1960s, Canada's stands on international maritime law, particularly in the United Nations Conference on the Law of the Sea (UNCLOS) negotiations and related arms controls matters, entailed radical policy departures that have placed the country in the role of a leader and frequently aggressive champion of the so-called "coastal states." This loosely defined bloc of nations have, in common, important sea frontiers and interests though not extensive oceanic naval, commercial shipping, fishing, mining, or research capabilities. They are themselves vulnerable to the "blue-water" intrusions of the maritime powers (the US, USSR, Great Britain, and France). The underlying reasons for this dramatic departure in Canadian policy and its implications for defence have not been widely discussed except perhaps for the emotional outbursts that have followed the voyages of *Manhattan* and *Polar Sea*. Almost no public concern has surfaced about the possibility of serious dichotomies between our foreign policy and our defence policy and the compatibility of our positions in UNCLOS with our obligations within NATO. This is not to suggest that the shift to a coastal state stance was unjustified or imprudent but, rather, to question whether strategic and naval operational considerations were important determinants. In abetting and frequently leading the coastal state's expanding challenges to the established international regime based on "Freedom of the Seas," Canada could well find its longer term national security interests at serious risk.

These challenges to traditional assumptions result from a complex of factors that have altered the character of the international maritime environment itself.[1] Ocean use demands have been growing in degree and kind as all nations have increased their dependence on the seas for trade and shipping and for food, energy, and minerals. The appearance of newer navies—most obviously the Soviet but also a number of smaller ones deploying worrisome local denial capabilities—have contributed to a diffusion of seapower. These capabilities, tied in to the potentials for new conflicts over territorial demarcation disputes spawned by the UNCLOS agreements, have impinged on the access rights formerly enjoyed by the major navies. And the persistence of widespread technical, conceptual, and even moral uncertainties concerning the usefulness of military instruments in the nuclear age have further contributed to this erosion of naval self-confidence. Not surprisingly, the major naval powers frequently have found themselves in an uncomfortably defensive stance.[2] When the Reagan administration in the US, shortly after coming to office in 1981, gave notice of its intention to review UNCLOS III's achievements, it found itself out of step with the general world mood and uncharacteristically in step with the Soviet Union in propping up what many perceived as an outdated theology. Seen against a broader historical perspective of maritime law's evolution, however, the superficiality of such judgments should be evident and perhaps provide Canadians with cause to reconsider or update our own thinking.

STRATEGY AND LAW TO 1945

Prior to the end of the Second World War, the law and seapower relationship revolved more directly than is now the case around strategic considerations and involved the evolution of a customary framework that accommodated the naval powers' exercise of their visit, search, and seizure practices with the counter-claims of non-belligerent states to be left free to carry out their affairs unmolested. At the centre of this framework was the doctrine of "Freedom of the Seas" which Julian Corbett described as one of those "ringing phrases which haunts the ear and continues to confuse the judgment." Except for the very earliest stages of its naval history, Great Britain championed a particular variant of that doctrine: namely that of maritime or belligerent rights. As the leading naval power, Britain resisted international efforts to codify restrictions on blockade—preferring instead to preserve on the oceans "the law of the jungle," as it were, where the bigger cats generally prevail. The Grotian ideal of "free ships, free goods" was the preserve of the neutral powers. And the conflict of perspectives over Belligerent versus Neutral Rights provided the occasion for any number of armed clashes and potential clashes such as the various armed neutralities of the eighteenth century and the War of 1812. The most dramatic of these in recent history occurred during and after the First World War when Anglo-American differences on this question brought relations between the two powers to a state of open confrontation.[3]

American public criticisms of British trade control methods visibly angered British officials, many of whom resented the fact that while the Royal Navy carried the naval struggle against Germany, the United States—despite its righteous defence of international justice—appeared to be looking cynically towards its own place in the post-war order of things. The Admiralty could not ignore the fact that after the Americans did enter the war in April 1917, they applied their own controls as vigorously and extensively as the British and yet, by refusing to call themselves an Allied power, continued to deny any acquiescence in London's interpretations of Belligerent Rights. These differences survived the war to surface at the Paris Peace Talks where the "Freedom of the Seas" question—the second of Wilson's Fourteen Points—threatened to blow the talks apart. The issue was eventually side-stepped as a result of some hard bargaining on other unrelated issues and also the firm stand of the Admiralty in pointing out that no compromise was possible on this question without striking at the very heart of the naval strategic system.

The issue threatened to resurface in 1927 following the collapse of the Geneva Naval Conference when it seemed that further extensions of quantitative naval limitations were closed off. By then, the naval scene had altered dramatically as Anglo-American parity in capital ships became a reality after the Washington agreements of 1921–2. British experts worried less about the possibilities of a war against the US and more about the probability of a war in which the US—as a neutral—could challenge or force a blockade. Within Foreign Office circles, there was also a feeling that some easing up on Britain's position of Belligerent Rights might be justified, particularly if it could be linked to a wider accord. As Robert Craigie, head of the Foreign Office's American Department, suggested:

> to leave these problems of prize law in a fluid and indeterminate state is like leaving dynamite lying about loose in a ship which may at any moment encounter a terrific storm. As far as Anglo-American relations are concerned, it is tantamount to keeping in being the one question which may conceivably lead to an eventual explosion. By insisting on keeping our hand free now, the Admiralty would run the risk of seeing our activities unnecessarily circumscribed later by a United States determined to "go the limit" in protecting neutral rights.[4]

The result was the appointment of a special subcommittee of the Committee of Imperial Defence, chaired by Lord Salisbury, to conduct a thorough examination of the whole legal issue. It was a difficult task, made worse by the fact that the full impact of the Great War on conventions covering belligerent-neutral relations was anything but obvious. Indeed, the war had raised more questions than it had settled. In W.N. Medlicott's view, it "had created conditions for which the existing prize law was unprepared, and the point at issue between Great Britain and the neutrals was, or should have been, not whether the letter of the existing law was being observed, but whether the new practices demanded by the changed conditions of economic warfare were in accordance with the spirit of international laws."[5]

But consensus on that "letter" or "spirit" had never been achieved. The 1909 Declaration of London that many experts referred to as at least a reasonable statement of what "enlightened" jurists considered the spirit to be—or what the powers would tolerate—was never ratified. Moreover, many of the more effective control measures against which the neutrals protested were in fact extra-legal or "interferences by sovereign right," thus leaving many of their complaints devoid of legal foundation. Yet, as will be shown, the existence of that 1909 code did, from 1914 on, exert powerful psychological constraints on all the participants.

It was this psychological dimension that especially worried the RN's spokesmen on the Salisbury Committee, Maurice Hankey and Admiral Richmond. They sought to reassure their colleagues of the bases of British policy by refuting the American assumptions that somehow contraband and blockade violated the natural order of things. In Richmond's judgment, this simply did not square with historical realities:

> National advantage, not a philosophical attitude towards war or humanity, was ever the spring of their policy. As neutrals, or belligerents weak at sea, we see them advocate immunity to its utmost lengths. As belligerents allied to strong naval powers, they advocate the strongest measures against commerce ... Circumstances, not philosophy, have dictated the attitude of nations, and it is idle to cite humanitarian motives, or to quote imaginary "Rights of Man" as though some high moral purpose informed policy. It did not—insofar as immunity is a principle, it rests solely upon national advantage. It can find no support in any philosophy of war, in any natural rights or on any ethical basis. None of the claims will stand examination, nor the test of historical experience.[6]

Britain had always pursued her belligerent rights position not on the basis of any moral justification but as a matter of policy. And it seemed obvious that as the Americans themselves would come to grasp the implications of their own status as a leading naval power they would inevitably move closer and closer to British thinking, as indeed eventually happened.

The extent of the Americans' conversion was nowhere more dramatically illustrated than by their initial stance, in the opening phases of the Second World War, of "renunciatory" neutrality whose provisions of self-imposed isolation far exceeded the dictates of the existing law. After 1940, that position was quickly superseded by highly discriminatory policies and eventually by open disregard of neutral obligations. By then the doctrine of "Freedom of the Seas" had come to mean pretty much what it now does.

As much as it clearly suited British, and eventually American and other Allies', purposes to preserve the legal ambiguities as much as possible, this did not mean that such law as did exist was ignored or was without effect on events. Although by 1939 virtually none of the law's more contentious aspects had been settled, the legal system put into operation that September closely approximated that earlier one and was restricted to establishing general contraband controls and the negotiation of war trade agreements with adjacent European neutrals. More comprehensive measures, such as forcible rationing of materials, pre-emptions, and enemy export controls, were withheld for later Cabinet approvals. So were plans for even more drastic options, such as air attacks against industrial targets, until German activities justified their use on a reprisals basis. By 1940–1, Germany's military successes and its disregard of standards of right conduct showed that much of this preoccupation with neutrals' rights had been misplaced or was simply overtaken by events. Still, it should be emphasized that even Germany's disregard was never total, at least with respect to operations at sea. In both world wars, when the law was stretched by either side, invariably it was justified on some basis, such as reprisals or "novel circumstances." Not surprisingly, the fact that justifications were usually close to hand led many neutrals to regard them as prescriptions for a general lawlessness. This is an important point for, so long as powerful neutrals did continue to exist, none of the belligerents could afford openly to ignore or antagonize them. The law therefore acted as a powerful constraining factor. From his study of how the law exerted this inertial influence on all the belligerents' decision-making processes, D.P. O'Connell concluded that:

> What emerges from the study of these occasions when the rules of international law were deliberately ignored in the pursuit of strategic and tactical objectives is that the circumstances in which this neglect is expedient or even possible are restricted, and that they have never arisen immediately upon the outbreak of war, nor even in its early stages ... Before international law has been discounted there has always been a graduated escalation of the war, to the point where no important neutrals stand aloof from the conflict, and the military situation has become so desperate that the limitations of the conduct of operations have ceased to be of persuasive value or political importance.[7]

THE LAW AND NAVAL WAR SINCE 1945

The impact of the Second World War on the law of the sea or, rather, how much of the conventional wisdom survived the transition into the nuclear age, are even more difficult questions for us to assess than it was for Medlicott looking back on 1914–18. Again, the Second World War raised more questions. It also altered the language, if not the substance, of the discussion such that those concepts which did survive remain hidden in a semantic limbo that creates confusion as to which of them could be called again into service. Two of the law's more fundamental distinctions were badly bruised by the transition. Neutrality, and the neutrals, were amongst the war's more important victims. And the legal status of belligerency has been totally obscured (though not obliterated, as was the intent of the United Nations charter's articles 2(4) and 51 that outlawed the use of armed force except in "self-defence"). The blurring of these distinctions has not meant that recourse to military solutions has vanished, only that their justification in terms of "self-defence" has raised the premium on semantic dexterity. Naval forces have been employed in many situations since 1945, although the circumstances surrounding their use have been so varied as to make generalization about them nearly impossible. All have been characterized, however, by a noticeable reluctance—in some cases, an inability—to extend their applications and effects beyond contiguous waters. This is a radical difference from pre-1945 experience when the very essence of "blue-water" theory suggested that the defence of one's coast began on the enemy's. No doubt that law per se has been a less important factor in this than changing international political norms that virtually oblige all governments to account for their military actions before public opinion, at home and abroad. The limited naval capabilities of the combatants may also have been a factor, at least during the first postwar decades when US naval monopoly masked these potentials. More recent challenges to that monopoly have further inhibited the use and the self-confidence of Western navies; like its British predecessor, the Pax Americana was always something of an illusion which once challenged did present serious though not insurmountable constraints. In the few instances where events have threatened to spill over beyond the coastal waters of the contestants and possibly involve the ships and interests of third parties—notably the India-Pakistan war of 1971, the Bab el Mandeb Straits in 1973, the US mining of Haiphong and the as yet un-attributable mining of the Red Sea, and possibly also US proposals to "blockade" the China coast in 1950 at the outset of the Korean conflict—the time factor was probably critical. Had such situations extended for any length of time, the conventions covering belligerent-neutral rights might have been dusted off and given the fresh look they have not had since the Second World War. In this respect, it is useful to recall that the blockades of both world wars never conformed precisely to the then accepted conventions. They were new responses to new conditions that seriously stretched the old regime. The "totality" of both wars necessitated progressively unrestricted methods by both the German and American submarine offensives and, as well, by the British-Allied trade counter-offensive. Should any future war threaten to become total, the law will be the least of its victims. If, however, future conflicts are to remain something less, appeals to legitimacy will be central in determining what can be contemplated. Whether the naval powers will continue to be best served by a regime that is as open-ended as possible is no less pertinent a question than it was for the Salisbury committee in the late 1920s.

The 1982 Falklands war offers some interesting lessons in that regard for, although the United Nations' charter again failed to prevent conflict, there was widespread consensus that Argentina's actions could not be allowed to add to an already extended list of such violations without completely undermining the whole principle of article 2(4). And legitimacy was an important factor in both Argentina's and Britain's diplomatic offensives to secure world public opinion. Here the British clearly came out on top, though not without flutterings in some corners following the sinking of *Belgrano* and the landing of troops. And British meticulousness in applying the rules of conduct undoubtedly reinforced international condonement of her actions in, if not her claims to, the islands. Indeed, both sides' compliance with established legal conventions—the so-called *jus in bello*—was of a very high order.[8] Most interesting of these perhaps was Britain's use of the two hundred-mile maritime exclusion zone. As originally declared on 12 April 1982—five days after the severing of diplomatic relations—this zone did not fulfill traditional conditions for effective blockade nor was it intended that it should. It was little more than a formal warning to Argentine naval vessels that were, in any case, subject to attack anywhere. Nor did it apply to merchant or neutral vessels. Subsequent refinements and extensions by the British declarations—on 23 April to include all Argentine military vessels and aircraft and merchant and fishing vessels engaged in surveillance work; on 30 April to include "any ships and aircraft"—did give it the characteristics of a true war zone or blockade that incautious third parties challenged at their risk. The successful attack against *Belgrano* on 2 May—outside the exclusion zone—in no way invalidated the concept any more than had German high seas attacks beyond the declared British Isles war zone in the Second World War. The British extension of their war zone to twelve miles off the Argentine coast on 7 May did raise a protest from the USSR, not about the right of blockade per se, but about the extent of the high seas then barred to third parties. In the case of the Americans, once their diplomatic initiatives to forestall hostilities had failed, they made no attempt to resort even to such euphemisms as "non-belligerency" or "renunciatory neutrality," although some such was their status as they supplied Britain all the support they could short of direct operational involvement. Once again, the duration of hostilities was important. Had they lasted much longer, the precedents thereby established might well have helped to clarify how much of the conventional legal wisdom is now operative.

THE NEW OCEAN POLITICS

This relegation to limbo of the legal concepts of belligerency was in some measure an incidental byproduct of the post-war redirection of international concern away from efforts to codify rules covering use of the "Great Common" towards a redefinition of that Common itself. In this process, strategic considerations played second fiddle to the economic and social priorities of a changing international political arena characterized by East-West competition and a more generalized struggle between developed and undeveloped nations. The driving engine of these new ocean politics has been resources and obvious inequities in their distribution and management. The primary dividing line in their debate has been not belligerents versus neutrals but, rather, maritime versus coastal states. Yet, even these categories are oversimplified since states have frequently crossed that divide whenever the prospects for international solutions clashed with their own national concerns. Altruism and self-interest are still at odds, and this has led to some very complex issue-specific coalition politics. Their net result, however, has been a steady progression of assertions favouring the coastal states, at the expense of the high seas. Three UNCLOS conferences have attempted to regulate these latter-day Enclosure Acts applied to the last Great Common. And while anyone who attempts to trace their evolution in detail might be forgiven for feeling they have been going on forever—offering permanent employment for a whole generation of lawyers, diplomats and bureaucrats—they amount, in historical terms, to a short burst of intensive effort that has brought about an unprecedented range and rate of change.

Following nine years of preparatory work, UNCLOS I at Geneva in 1958 produced four conventions: on the High Seas, the Continental Shelf, Fishing and Conservation of the Living Resources of the High Seas, and the Territorial Sea and the Contiguous Zone. But while agreement was reached on coastal states' control over their continental shelf resources, none was possible regarding the limits of the Territorial Sea. That question also eluded UNCLOS II at Geneva in 1960 when, by a single vote, a US-Canada proposal for a six-mile territorial sea linked to another six-mile contiguous fishery protection zone failed. The limited number of treaty ratifications and growing incidences of unilateral claims—such as the two hundred-mile claims of several

South American countries, various fish wars, and resource disputes—prompted the leading maritime powers to contemplate another conference directed specifically at defining the breadth of territorial seas and rights of passage through straits effected. At that point too, Ambassador Arvid Pardo of Malta issued his call before the 1967 General Assembly for an international regime to govern the seabed beyond national jurisdictions as "the common heritage of mankind." These were the initiatives, followed by various ad hoc and preparatory committees, that led to UNCLOS III perambulating the world in almost constant session from 1974 until convening for signatures at Montego Bay in 1982.

The outcome was a comprehensive and complicated Convention running to over three hundred articles.[9] Because its underlying philosophy is based on the notion of equitability and not on the possession of influence or military power it represents a major victory for the developing nations. Agreement has finally been reached on various jurisdictional limits, though not on the basis of overall consensus since many of the industrialized and maritime nations have refused or delayed their signatures. The Convention provides for a twelve-mile territorial sea and an exclusive economic zone (EEZ) up to two hundred miles, as well as certain exploration and exploitation rights in continental margins beyond that limit. Within its territorial seas, the coastal state will exercise complete sovereignty; within the EEZ sovereign rights apply only to resources and measures to protect the maritime environment. Outside states will still enjoy within the territorial sea the right of innocent passage that cannot be permanently suspended. In the EEZ, outside states will have freedom of navigation and overflight everywhere. On what is left of the high seas, full freedoms of navigation, overflights, fishing, and so on, survive. It might be noted here that coastal state rights within the EEZ are held to be *sui generis*; that is, rights over resources will exist only as defined in the Convention. Previously, rights were held to be by exception to the normal freedom of the high seas and legal presumption normally favoured such freedom. Now the opposite will pertain, and the predomination of the freedom of high seas in this respect is lost—a worrisome feature as traditional rights of navigation within the two hundred miles (formerly high seas) will likely be threatened by future extensions. International straits through which a high seas route no longer exists are protected by a regime of "Transit Passage" that is more liberal than conventional innocent passage because it cannot be suspended and does not permit overflight and the submerged transit of submarines.

The specific issue which has caused the US, Britain, and others to withhold their signatures is contained in Parts XI and XIV relating to the creation of an International Seabed Authority (ISA). On this, the Reagan administration has been much less circumspect than some others in objecting to the provisions for licensing, concession sharing, technology transfers, profit distribution, price regulation, and, above all, domination in the control machinery by Third World interests as a result of non-discriminatory voting rights.[10] Faced with accepting or rejecting the entire Convention as a package, the president's decision to concentrate on these ISA aspects presented some tricky problems. But by basing his arguments on the notion of a conflict between a free market economy and the principles of American entrepreneurship as against the protectionist approach of the Convention's "common heritage" arguments, Mr Reagan no doubt reassured his own domestic constituents. No less important however, was the fact that dissatisfaction with the convention's security aspects did not have to be admitted publicly, though it is clear from the work of his transition teams and their activities before various congressional and senate committees that security concerns were and are very real.[11] This decision not to broach openly the security ramifications, or to circumvent them deliberately, was always present in the UNCLOS III negotiations, and the maritime powers' toleration of the final transit and access provisions always represented a minimalist compromise position only.

Whatever the possibilities for major changes in the current positions of the maritime powers, the Convention's very existence—ratified or not—will exert a profound psychological impact, much as the 1909 London Declaration did. As Barry Buzan noted in 1978, UNCLOS III has "established a new framework for the law of the sea, regardless of whether any new convention comes into force."[12] The phenomenon, described by various experts as "propertization," "territorialization," or "creeping jurisdiction" is now an established fact, although the limits to which it eventually may be extended remains an open question. What is clear is that the principle once admitted has no inherent logical limit. As Ken Booth has suggested:

> The future extension of zones may be a distant event: a more immediate possibility is an intensification of national regulation within the existing EEZs. The "natural" tendency will be for governments—for no other ulterior motive than that of governing efficiently—to push out the regulations of the territorial sea into the EEZ. The naval powers can be expected to try and hold out against this. If they think such a possibility is illegitimate and un-

acceptable, it is salutary for them to be reminded that it is only a very short time since westerns' opinion scoffed at the "bizarre" Latin American claims for jurisdiction out to two hundred miles.[13]

Whether this portends a hopeful or a worrisome future depends very much on where the viewer stands as a proponent of coastal or maritime navalism and on his faith in the future of the United Nations or any international regulatory regime. In this, as with other aspects of internationalist activity such as arms control and disarmament, idealism and realism are ever at odds.

THE CANADIAN DILEMMA

At first glance, Canada's visible leadership role in the UNCLOS negotiations might suggest a clear commitment to internationalism. Her contribution has been cloaked in the garb of the selfless, helpful fixer long associated with her role in the Commonwealth and the United Nations, and in arms controls and peacekeeping. The energy, talent, and indeed the size of our UNCLOS delegations, and our chairmanship of various key committees, have been a source of justified pride, and especially so for more ardent nationalists whenever those delegates found themselves taking stands independent from those of their American and British counterparts. That aside, however, Canada's positions as a leading spokesman for the coastal states bloc, frequently at the expense of the maritime powers' and, as well, Third World interests, have manifested a brand of ungenerous chauvinism unmatched since the days of Mackenzie King. Our leads on behalf of the two-hundred-mile economic zone and claims to the continental shelf beyond (on the east coast extending for four hundred miles) might well be regarded as Peyton Lyon and Brian Tomlin suggest as "the greatest territorial grab in history, and Canada has led the pack."[14]

This mentality has been especially evident over the question of international straits. As much as any, this issue has openly ranged our interests as a member of the western economic community and of NATO squarely against our concerns as a northern Arctic power. And the North West Passage, although it is only one of our coastal waterways—none of which are admitted to be international[15]—has played the central role in determining our policy in other areas. Prior to 1969, Canadian arguments on straits conformed to conventional wisdom concerning freedom of the seas. At the 1958 and 1960 Geneva sessions our representatives did push for extended coastal authority beyond the then three-mile territorial sea limit for fishery purposes. Otherwise, they held the line with the maritime powers in seeking the narrowest limit definitions possible.[16] When, in 1963, the Pearson government proposed to apply straight baseline demarcations around the Arctic archipelago—thereby enclosing the Northwest Passage—the Americans and British pointed to the precedents that would be established for other archipelagic states in the Pacific and the consequent threat there to western naval access. These same arguments forestalled the government's plans to apply straight baselines for fishery purposes on the Atlantic and Pacific coasts in 1966. Inconveniently, they were no less valid when the Trudeau government came to face the nationalist outbursts occasioned by the voyages of *Manhattan* in 1969 and 1970 and the need to find acceptable alternative arguments. Circumventing expert legal advice, the government determined to abandon convention and to establish its claims unilaterally by declaring its one-hundred-mile Arctic pollution control zone.[17]

This unusual device served the purposes of at least temporarily silencing domestic criticisms and bidding for time. Yet the fact that Canada's so-called "Arctic exception" arguments did gain some acceptance in later UNCLOS talks and achieve at least tacit acceptance by the US should not divert attention from the reality that the legal basis of these claims was never clearly stated. And serious doubts that they ever can be clarified continued to underpin our reluctance unilaterally to declare sovereignty. The Arctic Waters Pollution legislation of 1971 was therefore embraced as an indirect method of asserting de facto limited jurisdiction while minimizing international opposition.[18] Concurrently with this legislation, the government also amended its position—established since 1929—of accepting the compulsory jurisdiction of the International Court of Justice. Now disputes arising from this legislation were to be specifically excluded. This was a departure which, though never publicly highlighted, spoke volumes about the extent of those doubts.

These examples are cited not to dispute the existence of genuine Canadian interests in these areas or to argue that in seeking to protect them enlightened national self-interest should not be a primary consideration. Policy and strategy planning are after all inherently ethnocentric pursuits. What is open to doubt is whether by its coastal state stance Canada has abetted and exploited international legal progress at the expense of even greater national interests—international stability and war avoidance—that did underpin the country's pre-1969 foreign policy. It may be, in view of the external forces associated with the new ocean politics, that the time has come to abandon the legal and strategic doctrines associated with "Free Seas." Rather than working to slow down the processes of "Enclosure," Canada would be best served by policies that put it well out on the leading edges of reform. Such reasoning should not be accepted, however, without conscious recognition of its implications for membership in the Western alliance.

The virtual absence of informed public debate, of sustained discussion in parliament or its committees, or of extensive contributions from concerned shipping, mining or other interest groups provides little reassurance in this regard. Even where differences between government departments have emerged, as in the Interdepartmental Committee on the Law of the Sea, the external observer has no basis for assessing how they were resolved. No less difficult to discern is the extent to which defence was ever a priority consideration. Circumstantial indications suggest it was not. Department of National Defence representation on Canada's large UNCLOS delegation— usually consisting of one officer—was proportionately smaller than any of the other Western or Soviet delegations. And without access to internal DND studies or position papers, one cannot assess their quality or impact. What does seem clear is that the bases of Canadian policy have never been clearly enunciated. And until they are—in the official, if not the public mind—balanced approaches aimed at either preserving or removing existing legal ambiguities are not possible. Neither can there be much hope of a settled naval policy or of operational and building doctrines to give it substance. The present government's announcement on 10 September 1985 of its intention to press ahead with straight baseline demarcations, to increase military surveillance flights, to proceed with construction of a *Polar* Class 8 icebreaker, and to take its chances with the world court may have smoothed a lot of feathers that were badly ruffled by that summer's *Polar Sea* incursion. And it may be that the symbolism of owning the world's most advanced icebreaker will be no less important than that of maintaining an understrength brigade on the central European front. The value of bluff in either case should not be underrated, provided one understands just who is being deceived.

Chapter 3

HISTORICAL STRATEGY AND ITS USES IN LARGE AND SMALL NAVIES

Donald M. Schurman

GENERAL IMPLICATIONS

This is not a modern paper on strategic studies. For the modern era (since the Second World War), that would require a good deal of attention to technical detail, with some of which I am not particularly familiar. But it is in my province to ask what relevance history, and more particularly strategy based on history, has for naval policy planners and statesmen who are concerned about the formulation of such policy. It is also within my province as a naval historiographer to enquire whether that theory based on history applies differently to larger or classical navies than it does to smaller navies. First I will discuss some general implications of traditional or historical strategy. Then I will consider the application and utility of historical strategy to modern smaller navies. Since this conference is riddled with experts, past and present, on the Canadian navy (if it may be called such) and its history, I will not venture into that area. As befits a general keynote paper the approach adopted is exploratory and the conclusions often more implicit than stated.

The tools for examination of the general implications of historical strategy come from two sources. The first is the teaching of naval history to graduate students. Most of the historians who attempt it are faced with a choice of teaching history from which some strategic or patterned sense can be deduced, or of teaching strategy by using the works of the classical naval strategists, where history is ransacked for examples of their wisdom, or error, according to the particular bias of the instructor. Few historians escape this dilemma, and since easing the load of preparing lectures and seminars leads naturally to selecting material used by a Mahan, Corbett, Richmond, Brodie, or Ropp,[1] we very often approach even the writing of history by peeping through a "strategic principles" keyhole. Certainly I plead guilty, notwithstanding that my students are constantly warned to regard "principles" of naval policy with extreme suspicion. The late great maritime historian R.C. Anderson,[2] whom Julian Corbett proposed for membership at the Athenaeum Club in 1913, refused to talk to me about Corbett for my book because "he [Corbett] was trained as a lawyer and therefore all his historical conclusions were predetermined,—in the lawyer fashion."[3] Thus Corbett was passed off as a useless guide. Looking back, I can only say that the intelligent sceptic is always to be preferred to the idolater, even if he is not always easy to take, and Anderson had a point.

Anyhow, for the naval historian, unless he is fortunate enough to have an undergraduate course in the subject where he can roam untrammeled by the constraints involved in teaching footnote-hunters, naval history is inextricably bound up with the mixture of history and its handmaiden strategy. It may well be, as Elias Canetti is fond of saying (as was Karl Popper),[4] that the most culpable men in the world are historians, since they usually gravitate with characteristic mindlessness to either woods without trees or trees without woods, mainly because they unthinkingly accept the power processes of the times they portray, and pass on the resulting foolishness to posterity (us!).[5] But naval history, if it is a discipline at all, perambulates across the centuries with great self-confidence, in search of acceptable pedagogical lessons. This is a dangerous past-time in this present age where no historian can keep up with the general literature for a ten year period of history, much less a thousand years. One is always blundering into some inconvenient expert, hitherto unknown. It is, therefore, not surprising that we look for methodological pegs on which to hang our material; nor is it surprising that the pegs we have usually used have been the great naval historian/strategists of the past. We all still use them.

So the second tool is the use of classic naval historians. The great naval historians were and are worth the trouble. It does not take much reading to appreciate that naval historians, after we get past such mindless recorders as Campbell[6] and William James,[7] looked, as did all other historians of consequence in their time and since, for an ideological measuring scale that would give their work shape and point. Nobody writes in a vacuum. Mahan wrote about England to educate the Americans on what it took to be the top naval nation. Corbett used naval history to show how the subtle blending of naval purposes with state policy, involving co-operation with the soldiers, had produced what Gerald Graham has called "Naval Supremacy."[8] This naval supremacy built up through trial and error from Elizabethan times onward created an expertise easily recognizable in the age of Nelson. Its resulting reflexes were still in place as late as 1939–45.

Now these pioneers were using history: for propaganda purposes in the case of Mahan, and to help British senior naval officers understand the policy relationships that sent them to sea in the case of Corbett. Mahan was successful. He inculcated in several generations of naval officers the congenial idea that it was vital to be the top naval nation.[9] He bored them with his history, but they heard his assertions: so much so that the First World War was only a passing interlude for the US Navy (USN) on its way to being top navy. The British, not the Germans, were their real preoccupation. They were bent on displacing the Royal Navy as the top navy. Mahan's history was inorganic, that is to say he allowed his naval wars to take place against a fixed scenario. It did not change in response to events. He was mistaken in his view that naval power was the main ingredient in world dominance,[10] and his case studies have now been mostly exploded. His ignorance of the real importance of land power lies exposed, as it has done since Sir Halford Mackinder demonstrated the fallacy of thinking that sea power could ultimately dominate land decisions.[11] He was an interesting relic. He was a good historian of his type and time. Nevertheless, he spoke the language of power, and the dedicated naval professionals of the great land power to our south still imbibe his milk. Everybody, it seems, must make either reference or obeisance to Mahan, before going on to talk of other naval strategic historical *or* strategic concerns. I have just done so in this paragraph!

Corbett was not much use as a naval prescription chemist for any navy except the British. He was concerned to show them the historical reasons for actions that often seemed almost axiomatic to them. His most frequently quoted book is *Some Principles of Maritime Strategy*.[12] It is not a universal textbook aimed at the world outside Britain. Actually, his best strategic books were his historical ones, especially *Drake and the Tudor Navy*[13] and *The Successors of Drake*.[14] Both were finished by 1900, and both were written to show that without a co-ordinated state policy, and without army-navy co-operation, the navy was as useless as the proverbial bull's mammary glands. The "strategy" book was written because senior naval officers could not wade through his historical books.[15] He had to teach these braided technocrats at the war college, so he compiled his "principles" to meet the need. (Actually, at Newport, Mahan had faced *that* problem also.)[16] There were many intelligent naval officers, of course, and some of Corbett's ideas had filtered into naval planning by the First World War.

But as universal strategic pundits, neither Mahan nor Corbett appear terribly impressive (as opposed to popular) in retrospect. Mahan was a successful propagandist and Corbett was a successful historian's historian. Fighting admirals had little regard for Mahan. Admiral Erben kept a canary in USS *Chicago* to "drown the scratching of that damned everlasting pen next door" (Mahan writing his books in his cabin).[17] In 1908 the British Admiral H. (Tug) Wilson was asked to elucidate and distribute the country's naval war plans to the fleet commanders. He wrote to them that these plans were all-important, except for the introduction, which was all historical, not written by a naval officer, and therefore worthless.[18] This judgment referred to Corbett's introduction which Admiral Sir John Fisher labelled "immortal," stating "it's going to live!!"[19] This is not an historian's complaint that his own or his fellow practitioners' advice is ignored by the practical men of power; it is merely a statement that, quite apart from Wilson's judgment, the navy's decision makers were 99 per cent dominated by the material characteristics of the iron and steel vessels they commanded. It is not just in the last forty years that technical constraints have played the largest role in determining policy.[20]

As far as naval history or strategy is concerned if Margaret Sprout's chapter had not appeared in Edward Meade Earle's *Makers of Modern Strategy*[21] it is likely that Mahan would now be as dead as the dodo. But this brilliant essay dusted off the old fossil and placed him front and centre to accompany the USN into battle once more. It really said nothing new about Mahan but succeeded in making him appear relevant to the new war.[22] Corbett's detailed ideas about war policy, historically developed, had penetrated many British brains by 1939. With modifications, the Royal Navy used ideas that he had originally generated with some, and it could be argued brilliant, effect. After all he had constantly reiterated the connection between foreign policy and naval policy and the need for co-operation between the services.[23] Stephen Roskill was aware of all this when he wrote it up after the war.[24] Interestingly enough, Roskill's own book on strategy is, in my opinion, his least successful or relevant.[25] Both Mahan and Corbett, of course, were and still are useful in teaching naval officers (and others) to understand their own past and helping them to appreciate real alternatives when they perceive them. In England, between the wars, Admiral Sir Herbert Richmond[26] strove for the same effects, and he was extremely relevant for contemporaries. Like Captain Liddell-Hart he was relegated to outer space by Churchill. This is nothing new. In the United States, after the war, Admiral Morison,[27] Bernard Brodie, and Theodore Ropp exerted influence, but although they were all, in my opinion, more intelligent than Mahan, they never came close to dethroning him. Recently John B. Hattendorf[28] has dusted off

Stephen B. Luce,[29] who was easily more intelligent than Mahan, but Luce will be lucky to effect a lodgement in the outer works much less take the citadel of Totem Worship Castle.

Considering who gets the palm, and for what reasons, it is not surprising that historians sometimes get a bad name. We are often supposed to believe all the nonsense that is handed down from the past no matter how inane. It is seldom that we go to a conference without hearing someone attack the "strategic ideas" of some defunct historian, *but no one is interested in a critical examination of the historical studies on which those ideas are based.* That may even happen here.

It is important for planners to be able to evaluate strategy through a knowledge of history. I would like to pose the following question. Aside from "common sense," if a student in a staff college, or even a politician, is asked to evaluate the strategic ideas of an historian, or to distinguish between the strategic ideas of two historians, how does he do it? *How is it to be done by one who does not know any history?* No one would listen to a person who had no mathematics or physics but was attempting to distinguish between two theories of communications, involving, ultimately, considerable investment in a particular system. Would they?

Whether we like it or not, the great strategists of the past, most of whom were historically trained, are still in place to influence planning, both military and naval. I think what I have said will indicate that I do not necessarily think that such dominance is "a good thing." However, it does seem to be unavoidable. This result stems not so much from their theories, based on history, being redundant (and some of them are), as from the fact that they are often served up as axioms to be accepted rather than as problems to be worked through. However, intelligent naval historians of the past were working through real alternatives when studying state naval policy as history. The process of studying the shifts and changes of policy from year to year, and even from day to day, gave them an eye for norms and exceptions that were often translated into strategic rules. To understand these things, and to treat the axioms or rules with the respect and suspicion that, paradoxically, they demand, requires knowledge of the historical process and some experience of that method. It is the process that historians must defend, and those who have gone through it have something to offer to defence planners.

Of course it is lunatic to try and compare a nuclear missile with a smooth bore gun projectile, although some military historians believe that old weapons are reincarnated in different earthly shapes and forms. Maybe this is so. However, I am not prepared to defend interesting similarities as if they were clones. Nor does history, in general, "repeat itself." What does happen is that, over time, similar situations do arise, situations involving choice. A person trained to see how the best minds in previous generations dealt with such choices is in a pretty good position to spot alternatives and choices today. Strange as it may seem, it is still possible for a Nelson to appear more intelligent than a modern admiral—and I am not referring to his canned maxims, put together and dished out by lesser minds in the service. It is never the masters we must fear, but their damned disciples! History as process is of value to every service officer who has the intelligence to come to grips with it. I am reliably informed that now, in the United States, the army and air force, and to a lesser extent the navy, are moving strongly in this historically conscious direction.

Bringing up such a colossus as the United States leads to the question of what use all this is for smaller countries which may wish to determine general naval policies but seldom can. Of how much value is all this Great Power-oriented history to them? Canada comes quickly to mind. Do we have countries to whom we can compare ourselves? Some seem to me to be worthy of our attention.

THE APPLICATION OF HISTORICAL STRATEGY

Smaller countries—Norway, Sweden, The Netherlands, and Singapore—were chosen for reasons of accessibility to the writer in a short time constraint. The material is based on conversations and correspondence with members of the naval forces or educational establishments of those countries over the years, upon personal observation while visiting them, and upon published works that have emanated therefrom. In order not to embarrass my correspondents, I put it forward as a personal appreciation, which, of course, it is. In the case of Canada, I teach at the largest of the Services Colleges, and have lectured at the Toronto Staff College since 1959, where I have had the opportunity of looking at the course guides for that period. In the case of Norway, I have obtained somewhat detailed descriptions of the naval history and strategy courses in the various service establishments as they exist now. I have also taught and worked in Singapore.

Singapore

Singapore is a small country. It has a population of under 3 million, an integrated service structure not unlike that of Canada, and a sea-defence problem that is obvious. There is a national service system in place. This city-state is not a formal adherent of the large east-west alliance systems and has in the past looked to Switzerland, Finland, and especially Israel for role models. The navy is a part of a small integrated force that has limited strike possibilities, but whose main purpose is to ensure some measure of security for the country, caught as it is between 150 million Indonesians to the south and 13½ million Malaysians to the north. Its large, ethnically Chinese population makes it sensitive to movements that involve the Chinese "diaspora" and indeed to any population shift that radically threatens the balance of its multicultural society. It is not surprising that the largest role taken on by the naval forces over the last ten years has been the shielding of Singapore from the thousands of "boat people" who left Vietnam.

Some of the officers of the select small Singaporean naval force are educated at the National University of Singapore. There, those who have proceeded through the history pattern are exposed to classical naval and military strategy purveyed through the medium of history, and such officers are provided with a sound grounding in military history. Relevance is a key objective of these studies, but they are far-ranging.

Having said that, it must be noted that apart from campaign studies, of which their own history provides good examples from the Second World War, strategy and training are dominated by tactical and technical realities. Furthermore, the amount of time that can be given to strategic studies in the wider sense is rigidly restricted by an iron timetable geared to the sea-time requirements of active service.

What kind of naval strategic training do they get? In the university courses they are given Mahan, Corbett, and Brodie. The staff colleges, in such time as is available, generally use Mahan as a basic. This is because Mahan is still respected in Britain and Australia, but more important, he is revered in the United States and is even quoted upon occasion by the Russians. In brief, Mahan impresses by reputation and hence is the most popular. Popularity counts, for naval officers. Mahan's work was then, and still is, a bestseller; also, for those composing staff college reports, there is more stuff with which to pad footnotes. This comment applies not only to Singapore!

At the same time it is quite clear to every course planner in Singapore that the financial, economic, or manpower strength to implement any part of a Mahanian strategy does not exist in Singapore. No doubt, the naval advisors to the government are faced with the same ambiguity. At the very most, Mahan might seem to provide evidence for what possible opponents of Singapore might do, and the Singaporeans are not behind hand at reading the pattern of power politics.

Singapore is interesting. Superficially one might think that it is merely a willing ally of the United States. On the other hand a deeper look shows it to have for its closest associates the other members of ASEAN, and yet these are the people whom the Singapore Armed Forces might have to defend against. The global struggle is not lost on the Singaporeans, but they are not dominated by it. There is more than one way of looking at the national interest. They must have flexible approaches. Canadians should know that *the size of the Singaporean Armed Forces is about the numerical size of the Canadian Armed Forces.*

The Netherlands

The Netherlands is a traditional seapower with a strong and vibrant naval historical tradition. It has a population of almost 14 million. Its littoral is not vast but, like that of Singapore, it is extremely lively. However, the Dutch have always considered their own experience of sea defence at home, and in the East Indies, the main basis for strategic analysis, and this attitude has grown stronger in the twentieth century. They have proceeded with little or no reference to the historical experiences of other navies, and they have usually preferred to go it alone. However, when forced to co-operate with other navies they have tended to restrict themselves to a clear, technically defined role. The experiences of occupation and loss of empire have generated caution.

With regard to history, the Dutch Naval Academy gives attention to a distinguished national past at sea. At the advanced institution (koninklijk institute voor de marine), the Royal Institute for the navy, strategic and historical material is covered. However, this seems to have a minimal influence on naval planning. Since the early 1950s The Netherlands has accepted a "single scenario" for defence against Soviet attack on the central front in Europe, and a part in the sea battle line set up to secure NATO Atlantic support movements. A strong anti-submarine role was accepted, and the Dutch navy became remarkably proficient in that capacity. This, perhaps, has been at the expense of any flexibility and strategic insight that might enable planners even to contemplate the relevance of other scenarios. This singleness of purpose could have the effect of making the navy politically vulnerable in a rapidly changing strategic and technical environment.

It is not surprising that military and naval history are not generally considered a relevant field of study for top members of the Dutch naval hierarchy, although no doubt some of them might deny this.

Norway

Norway is another NATO adherent. The country has a population of about 4 million, a long littoral, and, like Singapore, compulsory national service. Naval history is taught in the Naval Academy by a trained naval historian. There, the cadets receive 146 hours of historical training in the third and fourth years. About one-quarter of this time is devoted to Scandinavian sea-history before 1905, and Norwegian sailors, reasonably enough, get most attention. Much of the remaining time is divided between the Norwegian experience in the First and Second World Wars (one as a neutral, and the other as a combatant). Neutrality, with its advantages and pitfalls, is examined. Some time is given to the American, British, and German sea experience in the two wars. One professor at the Naval Academy also lectures at the Norwegian Naval Staff College. Here he covers, in the limited time available, historical strategy.

In the Defence College, where officers of the rank of Lt Colonel and above forgather, there is *no* study of history or strategy from an historical viewpoint. The conclusion must be that, as in the case of The Netherlands, junior officers are given a national historical background at the Naval Academy, and that this approach is followed up in more than a merely token way at the Staff College, but it is not emphasized. However, it also seems clear that senior officers are not "tasked" with such relics from the past. This, no doubt, is as they want it, since "policy" is not related to history but to present circumstances and to current tactical and technical commitments. This means that it is not possible even to contemplate flexible strategic change based on a knowledge of historical constraints and opportunities. At the National Defence college only history since 1945 is used, and even that is tilted towards the present. Thus there is no basis for the rational measurement of other possibilities, except for the one that happens to exist as a result of the "threat."

Sweden

Sweden, with a population of 8¼ million, and with a littoral almost completely confined to the Baltic Sea, is a neutral state and, like Singapore and Norway, has national service. Swedish naval personnel receive, like the Norwegians, training in traditional history at the junior level. Their present strategic stance depends in no way upon the doctrines of great strategic thinkers, nor does it depend on an understanding of the history of the larger maritime command powers that spawned them. Despite the fact that Sweden is outside NATO, its naval policy, like that of Norway and The Netherlands, is based on tactical and technical constraints. It is certainly not based on historical or maritime appreciations of the place and use of seapower. Whether Sweden likes it or not, the country is dominated by perceptions of what will happen if the Soviet "threat" materializes. Much flexibility is not possible under these circumstances.

Canada

Canada, too, with a vast littoral and a somewhat larger population than the examples given, is dominated by the "threat" argument and the consequent alliance pattern. It does differ in that it has borders (according to some definitions) with both the Soviet Union and the United States: it sits in the jaws of a nutcracker position, like Singapore. It is also different in that its sea traditions have been inherited from Great Powers, principally Britain, and have recently been influenced by another, the United States. In the course of the twentieth century, the country has merely exchanged one naval-protector ally for another, moving, congenially enough, from one imperial orbit to another.

Canada provides her sea-element officer trainees, at least those who attend service colleges, with broad seapower history and strategic appreciations. Those who go on to university postgraduate study, either at one of the services colleges or at a civilian university, may add to that base in some depth, although it would be wrong to think that postgraduate postings for such study are high on the general priority list amongst service career planners.

Very few naval officers attended the RCAF Staff College in Toronto. When it became tri-service there was a long period when the naval portion of the course was peripheral. However, with the formation of the separate service course patterns in the mid-1970s, more emphasis was given to problems of seapower. Lectures were given, with reading list support and discussion periods, to introduce this educationally highly diverse audience to the connection between strategy and history and the relation of both to modern problems. Recently, the curriculum has been revamped. It is now highly American-oriented, and Mahan gets more attention, although he does not entirely dominate the stage. The student problem there is the same as student problems at all staff colleges: how can one induce students to do the detailed reading that any realistic appraisal of sea strategy must involve? The library is not overburdened with demands from students for more American-oriented reading lists and books, but certainly some do develop an appetite for historical examples. Students are not overly impressed with course material that carries the stamp "Made in Great Britain" or "Made in the US." They are not bored with Canadian sea history, and it is high time that a textbook is written to fill the need. They are not bored with extra-Canadian history per se, but they *are* bored with canned imports from British or American staff colleges. I am quite certain, from the experience of fielding questions at the staff colleges for over twenty-five years, that it is at the connecting point between modern national policy lectures (often presented so well by our political science brethren), and the general history of seapower, that staff college students come up against a missing link. This is because, without some historical training, the connection between the constraints of modern policy and commitments and the past historical tradition is not always easy to grasp. An appreciation of that no man's land could make it possible for them, in later years, to think in terms of alternatives without constantly feeling that they are doing something disloyal if they should cast their minds in unorthodox directions.

It seems to me important that Canadian naval officers should have a background of both Canadian and foreign naval strategy based on historical considerations as part and parcel of their experience, in the same way that soldiers are automatically indoctrinated with the work of Stanley[30] and Stacey,[31] and now, one hopes, Desmond Morton. In 1956 George Stanley decreed that naval history should be taught at the Royal Military College at Kingston. I taught it. At the beginning, it looked like an oddity. It has since become a subject of intrinsic importance. Now, with the additional work of Dr B.D. Hunt,[32] RMC has a very strong naval history program. At RMC and at Royal Roads moves have been made towards filling the Canadian content gap.[33] It remains for a Canadian naval historian to make a stronger junction with our own and foreign traditions. We already get plenty of input from the British and Americans and their pundits. It would be unwise to downgrade this knowledge, on which our present alliance functions. But we *can* learn from others whose policy choices are also happily or unhappily circumscribed, either by political viewpoint or merely by hard circumstances. To this end I have, at RMC, encouraged contacts between Canadian military and naval historians and military and naval historians from "smaller countries" where we have much to teach each other. The connections are even yet only tentative. Living where we do, we have few real defence options. It is wise, in my view, that we should make the most of what we have.

The foregoing general and specific considerations give rise to a few reflections. Each country does, of course, have a unique defence situation; nevertheless, aspects of every unique situation are common to other countries. Furthermore, these common aspects are more numerous between us and "small navy" countries than they are between us and the great naval powers, or even between the intermediate naval powers and ourselves.[34] We are not the only country to wrestle with the fact that a role involving a "single scenario" often leads to a cul-de-sac in the strategic appreciation process. "Do we want to get out of the bag?" or "Can we get out of the bag?" or even "Could we stick an arm out of the bag?" are questions that other nations face; they are not peculiarly or particularly Canadian.

On the historical/strategic level, it should be clear that canned strategy based on the history of the age of sail is no one's panacea. However, it is useful since it builds flexible habits of mind. The classical theories behind top navies are well worth study, but, except in an alliance context, they do not correspond to the realities of our situation, *or to any alternative that we, as a small naval power, might choose.*

The French thought themselves into an alternative strategy in 1692, and this *guerre de course* strategy brought on the collapse of the Bank of England in 1695![35] The same nation devised the *jeune école* strategy of 1885, another attempt at maximum effect for minimum expenditure. The Germans devised a "risk" fleet strategy and later a trade interdiction strategy based on the submarine. Whatever we may think of the former, the latter came close to success in two world wars. To repeat: it is wise to have alternatives and to be in a position to make the most of what we have. Only flexibility of thought can generate such effects. Naval history has something to teach Canadian naval planners in that respect, if they know some history as opposed to attempting to commandeer it in a crisis, or, as the Elizabethans used to say "when need is."

Chapter 4

MARCOM EDUCATION: IS IT A BREAK WITH TRADITION?

Richard A. Preston

ROYAL NAVY TRADITION

For most of its first forty years the Royal Canadian Navy depended heavily on Britain for the education and training of its officers. That exerted a powerful influence on the establishment of British naval traditions in Canada. By examining the development of naval training and education in the Royal Navy and then in the post-war RCN and MARCOM (the present Maritime Command of the unified Canadian Forces) this essay examines whether the Canadian navy has now departed significantly from Royal Navy traditions.

Our first step must be to establish what British naval tradition was and whence it was derived. Civilians find some naval traditions curiously incomprehensible, inexplicable, anachronistic, or irrational. Take for instance the sailor's collar, designed to protect his uniform from tarry pigtails, and bell-bottomed trousers, easy to roll up when scrubbing the decks. Both have long been quite non-functional, yet they have often been defended as essential parts of an all-important tradition. They were indeed a small part of those traditions that, taken as a whole, were a vital source of inspiration for the Royal Navy.

The influence of RN tradition is often emotional rather than intellectual, but it is soundly based on historical precedent. Some elements date back to the founding of the navy by Henry VIII in the sixteenth century and to the subsequent exploits of the Elizabethan sea-dogs. However, the latter were merely practical seamen with a corsair's fighting expertise, willing when called upon to serve the great Queen Bess. They were not the prototypes of later career naval officers. The Royal Navy therefore draws its inspiration from the eighteenth century, from the sailors of that day who made Britain preeminent on the oceans for over a century: Anson and Middleton the administrators, St Vincent, who devised the technique of naval blockade, and Richard Howe and Jervis who, among others, won great victories. The greatest hero of all was, of course, Nelson, around whom there grew an elaborate mythology,

Nelsonian leadership mythology tells us something about the nature of RN tradition. He is usually remembered most for his tactical genius, sometimes called "the Nelson touch," which stressed dash and aggressiveness. But what was probably Nelson's most valuable contribution to the defeat of Napoleon was strategic: his rigorous enforcement of blockade in all weathers. Stress on staying at sea did indeed become a vital part of RN tradition, but it was not as specifically associated with Nelson as was his penchant for close bombardment. Naval tradition, in other words, does not require strict historical accuracy to be effective.

The Nelsonian tradition is a supreme example of the influence of heroes and leadership. The nature of service at sea requires effective leadership in a unique form of unchallenged command. Nelson's successes arose primarily from his charisma as a great leader. The United States Navy utilizes this leadership aspect of tradition by slogans: Lawrence's "Don't give up the ship," Perry's "We have met the enemy and they are ours," and Farragut's "Damn the torpedoes. Full speed ahead." Although these are American examples, some of them from wars against the Royal Navy, this kind of inspiration seems to be universal. Indeed, there is something peculiar about the men who go down to the sea in ships that sets them apart and makes them accept, and respond to, a leadership mythology that transcends national barriers. Nelson is almost as much a source of inspiration in the USN as in the RN, even though he made his great reputation after the American Declaration of Independence. Stories of leadership at sea thus appear to be a universal stimulant of morale.

Although the sea was not a part of Canadian life, as it was of life in Britain, Canada inherited a traditional mythology and mystique directly from Britain, the mother country of many Canadians.[1] Those Canadians who felt the pull of the sea and embarked on a naval career or on temporary war service at one time felt themselves to be a part of the Royal Navy. They therefore adopted the RN's morale-building traditions.

In 1935 a popularly written yet thoughtful study of the Royal Navy in the twentieth century with a rather misleading title, *No More Heroes* (which was read in manuscript and apparently endorsed by a former First Sea Lord, Admiral Sir Charles Madden) appraised the value of

RN tradition. Its author, Charles Owen, a former naval officer, said that the navy as a whole, and its colleges at Dartmouth and Manadon in particular, still preserved the best elements of the old tradition. He summed up their influence as the production of "a confident corps of officers conditioned to keep their head[s] under fire, not to flinch in adversity, and to win the war if not the battle." Owen also noted that at Dartmouth "the old pride of service, the tradition of excellence, the fastidious approach to training seemed unimpaired," and that "morale was high."[2] These qualities came to the RCN along with RN techniques of administration and operation developed over more than two centuries.

However, in addition to this technique and mythology of leadership and operations, the RN tradition included certain other specific features that were also influential. In my opinion three were basic: recruitment of officers at an early age, selection of officers from an elite social group, and insistence on sea service. These were as important in their way in RN appointment, education, and training as was indoctrination in hero worship, leadership, and service; and they appeared to contribute much to morale and so to victory.

These three elements of the RN tradition, which were closely related, were present from the beginning, though they were modified somewhat with the passage of time. In the seventeenth century Samuel Pepys, the diarist and great naval administrator, had formalized the practice of appointing midshipmen for early sea service because he believed that "no degree of land education in use anywhere in England, whether of the liberal or science sorts, qualifies a man for sea employment or gives him any considerable help towards it."[3] Pepys's midshipmen, modelled on the so-called "captain's servants" appointed before his time by senior officers to serve a kind of apprenticeship, were young aristocrats or young gentlemen. Pepys's were to be in their early teens. His contribution was to bring these boys under Admiralty control.

It was soon realized that if gentlemen officers were to exercise effective command of the less well-born ships' masters who handled the ship and the crew, they must be able to navigate. They must therefore study mathematics. So in 1729 the Admiralty established the Royal Naval Academy at Portsmouth. Under various names this institution lasted until 1837. During most of that century, however, only about one-fifth of potential officers entered the navy through the academy. The remainder were still appointed by individual sponsors. Then in 1837, when the Royal Naval Academy was abolished, it was ruled that in future all officer candidates must take an academic entrance examination; from that time until 1857 all were sent to begin their naval careers at sea as midshipmen on a warship.

The entrance examination was, however, a farce, and sea service proved to be unsuitable for the academic side of training. Civilian schoolmasters had been appointed to warships at least since 1702. At first they had only taught boys on the lower deck, but ships' officers, often themselves uneducated, gave the "schoolie" little leeway to do his work. In an attempt to remedy this in 1836, the civilian schoolmasters had been made wardroom warrant officers, and in 1840 their position became "naval instructor and schoolmaster." As naval instructors they also became responsible for officer education. Eventually in 1861 they were commissioned, but they still remained low in the chain of the ships' command. Michael Lewis says, "We are bound to suspect that the schoolmaster often fought a losing battle with the executive officer for the presence of his scholars in the place of teaching." Education at sea thus took a distinctly secondary place to running the ship.

In 1857 the Admiralty tried to get the best of both shore and sea training by transferring cadet education to moored hulks, a succession of which were named HMS *Britannia*.[4] Again it was a failure. The "training ships" were hybrids that never adequately fulfilled the purpose of either training or education. Furthermore, by 1857 steam propulsion was about to change the nature of the officer's job. Accelerated technological progress necessitated that the officer have more education.

On the other hand, early sea service was still seen to be desirable. But Julian Corbett, the influential naval historian of the early twentieth century, while agreeing with Pepys's dictum that no training in authority and responsibility could equal that to be acquired on a big sailing vessel where a young officer was "constantly exposed to the necessity of accurate watchfulness, precise action, and quick decision," added, "you can't train except at sea ... at sea you can't teach." He argued that the battleships and cruisers on which midshipmen served after leaving their training ship could not provide the same opportunities as had the sailing ship "for the youngsters to feel the spur of authority and the sting of responsibility." Potential officers, he believed, must first be educated.[5] Yet tradition was so strong that, in addition to Corbett's eloquent persuasiveness, it took the forceful personality of First Sea Lord "Jacky" Fisher and the political clout of First Lord Selborne to overcome those who argued for the continuation of the old training ships. So in 1904 it was decided that the naval educational process would be brought ashore and set up in the Royal Naval College at Dartmouth to precede midshipman-service at sea.

Tradition still endured. The college's proximity to the sea was regarded as essential to its purpose, the college was named HMS *Britan-*

nia, and until 1916 the last old hulk of that name served as Dartmouth College's administration depot ship. The college had a quarterdeck and also used other ships' nomenclatures and procedures. Cruises were an important part of its training, and sailing vessels were attached. Indeed sailing was still considered so important that in 1922–3 the Admiralty actually approved the reintroduction of universal sail-training for cadets, a decision which was enthusiastically supported in parliament and the press. This move backwards failed to come about only because of the cost.[6]

Apprentice-type sea-time for midshipmen still remained. After cadets graduated from Osborne and Dartmouth, which they attended when aged 13 to 18 (the years in which British upper-class boys were at a "public," that is a private, boarding school), they went to sea for two years with the fleet as midshipmen before returning to take a sub-lieutenant's course at Greenwich. Then in 1913, because Dartmouth was not producing enough midshipmen, a "Special Entry" at age 18 was introduced to channel public-school boys directly into the navy as midshipmen. Although some naval officers claimed that Osborne-Dartmouth middies helped the "pub" snotties learn the ropes, and that they had better careers in the navy,[7] the academic quality of the public-school products was in fact higher, and their lack of initial naval training probably did not make much difference to their professionalism and careers.

Britannia had stressed indoctrination, and Dartmouth was designed to follow the same line.[8] The civilian masters at Dartmouth were described as "devoted men who had a difficult time." They were always "with, but after" the naval officers on the staff. The consequence was recalled by Captain E.S. Brand, RN, a Dartmouth graduate who became Director of Marine Operations for the Canadian Coast Guard. "Unhappily in spite of all their efforts we were not educated. This was clearly brought home to me when I was serving in *Cumberland*, and later in *Thunderer*, dealing with Public School cadets whose outlook and knowledge were much broader than my own." Brand, unintentionally, also cast doubt on the quality of character training at Dartmouth. Talking about the daily practice of solemnly recording in "Logs" what each cadet had done in recreation each day, he said, "this system could be justified by the excellent training in telling a lie with a straight face which it provided. Very useful in life." The official historian of the college quoted Brand without comment.[9] In 1910 a retired officer said that Dartmouth cadet life was an ideal existence, with interesting work, but no "strenuous mental challenge."[10]

Although a parliamentary commission in 1913 had declared that the Dartmouth masters were better than those at the average public school, and that consequently the cadets received a better liberal education,[11] a novel published in 1919 by a Dartmouth graduate caused a sensation when it showed that this was misleading. It revealed that the system of training midshipmen did nothing to occupy their minds.[12] Twenty years later retired Admiral K.G.B. Dewar said that the training of British naval officers was "purely technical, tempered by a pathetic faith in mathematics as an instrument of culture." It "crammed with facts instead of equipping with faculties." The American specialist on British naval history, Arthur Marder, who quoted Dewar's statement, added that RN officers continued to think that dash and gallantry would get them through.[13]

The sub-lieutenant's course at Greenwich, taken after two years at sea, was, it is true, intended to make men think and so contained a great deal on the humanities and international affairs, but Commander J.M. Kenworthy (later Lord Strabolgi), sailor, politician, and journalist, showed that few on the course took it seriously. "The mentality of most of us was utterly irresponsible. We were keen on our profession but we meant to have a good time while we were ashore."[14]

Furthermore, tying entry to *Britannia* and to Dartmouth (and also the Special Entry) to the public-school age groups had perpetuated recruitment of officers from the upper classes. In 1931 a Labour member of parliament asked in the House of Commons which schools could nominate for cadetships. He was told that nomination played no part. Any boy from any school could apply.[15] What he was not told was that announcement of the entrance examinations was sent only to the public schools.[16] In the common examination administered for the army, air force, navy, and Royal Marines after 1925, the War Office frequently asked that the need to pass the army entrance examination, taken one year after school certificate, that is at seventeen, should be overlooked if a candidate had qualified on the interview. It also accepted nominations of failures whose age would not permit another chance to write that examination.

These practices eased the way to army commissions for some public-school boys who were inferior intellectually. The navy, it is true, struck out many more candidates than the army, especially paymasters,[17] but service in the RN as officers was notoriously even more restricted to men of birth and wealth than was service in the other arms: only the cavalry and household regiments were more exclusive. As late as 1942 Lord Chatfield, former First Sea Lord, and Minister for Coordination of Defence in the War Cabinet, claimed that entry to the navy was "very open": "As long as a lad can speak the English language and is likely to be a leader, as opposed to a mere brainy lad, he has a proper chance of being selected to go to Dartmouth."[18] However, "speaking English" in interviews could mean having a proper accent, the hallmark of class distinction. An American historian has suggested that this belief that boys from the upper classes made the best officers was also prevalent in the US Navy.[19]

Such class consciousness, which the RN to some extent handed on to the RCN, was associated with what Janowitz called the heroic tradition, but RN training was also technological and administrative, something like Janowitz's managerial element. However, it left intellectual development to the individual. Fortunately for the navy, the lofty isolation of the captain, and even of junior officers, aboard a ship at sea over long periods did provide opportunity for those who were intellectually inclined to develop their minds by reading. Among average RN officers, on the other hand, academic quality was, not surprisingly, quite low. Michael Lewis has told us that in the early twentieth century, when the RCN was born, interference by the captain and the "Number One," calling for midshipmen to perform practical tasks, was still a powerful impediment to RN education.[20]

Even as late as 1975, long after entry had been broadened beyond the public schools, Charles Owen, whose appreciation of the value of the RN tradition was quoted above, criticized the continuation of a limited perspective. "When the Admiralty Interview Board vets officer candidates, the author was told, its members look no further than what Dartmouth is likely to find acceptable; and at Dartmouth, in the case of the executive product, it is thought more realistic to turn out potentially sound officers of the watch than to worry too much whether the output includes material of admiral calibre."[21]

The RN's transference of this training and education system to the pre-Second World War RCN through Canadian officer-production, both in the significantly named but short-lived Royal Naval College of Canada and by the training of Canadians in British naval establishments, is covered effectively in articles in *The RCN in Retrospect* by Rear-Admirals P.W. Brock and Richard Leir.[22] They show that young Canadians accepted the RN tradition in a general way but were aware of its weaknesses and, even more, of its inconsistencies for Canada.

After the Second World War the Royal Navy soon eliminated entry at age thirteen, increased academic requirements for entrance, and opened the way for secondary school boys to apply for commissions; many now enter Dartmouth with a university degree or take one afterwards. The public-school accent is no longer universal in the wardroom. But a visit to Manadon in 1987 revealed that, although the public-school output is only a miniscule part of British school-leavers, about 50 per cent of the officers there still come from that traditional source. The widening input came after Canada had cut the painter.

68   THE RCN IN TRANSITION

The RN's early influence on the RCN thus derived, for good or bad, from the old Royal Navy. It incorporated the all-important RN tradition, including its mystique, along with a penchant for some practices in selection and education at an early age that were of doubtful suitability for Canada, and also along with the RN's heavy emphasis on indoctrination and training at the cost of advanced education.

ROYAL ROADS AND THE RCN-RCAF COLLEGE

To meet the need for the great expansion of the RCN during the Second World War, many duration-only officers had to be produced quickly in Canada. For this, the RCN professionals, along with British officers borrowed from the Royal Navy, proved an invaluable source of RN expertise and motivation. But in 1940, painfully aware of the disadvantages it suffered through having not had a system of producing regular officers in Canada, the RCN planned to reopen its own college. Set up on the Dunsmuir estate near Victoria in 1942, Royal Roads was intended to give a two-year course based on junior matriculation until the war ended. Thereafter it was to be three years, followed by sea service with the Royal Navy for two more years, and then the sub-lieutenants' course at Greenwich. In 1942 Royal Roads was planned as a junior college that provided a general education in the sciences, humanities, and technical naval subjects. It adopted the US Naval Academy's recitation system with small classes and, like Annapolis, emphasized conversational methods for learning foreign languages; in most other respects, however, it was modelled on Dartmouth. It charged fees, and its sports included British rugby and soccer. It emphasized mathematics and science for entry, but at an age younger than that at which French Canadians usually graduated from Quebec classical colleges. It therefore catered solely to upper middle-class Anglophones,[23] a Canadian version of the public-school boys who found their way to the Quarter Deck in the old RN.

Evidence of the extent to which Royal Roads deliberately borrowed from British RN tradition is shown by the introduction, or reintroduction, of corporal punishment. Rear-Admiral Brock has stated that at the old RNCC in 1910–22 there was nothing like the physical hazing known at RMC as "recruiting," or like its equivalent in the Royal Navy, which had occasionally led to a court-martial for the sub-lieutenant of the gunroom.[24] However, Captain J.M. Grant, the first Royal Roads commandant, told the official historian of the RCN in 1945 that his internal system of discipline was modelled on Dartmouth, probably meaning his own experience as a cadet there. At Royal Roads in 1942, according to the official history, "cadet captains [were] appointed to take charge of their fellows, and punishment by caning [was to be] administered for serious misdemeanours."[25] Flogging had, of course, ended in the Royal Navy in the mid-nineteenth century, but beatings continued officially for midshipmen and cadets until the 1930s, when they were supplemented by surreptitious canings by cadet captains, a practice to which the authorities apparently turned a blind eye.[26] I have no information about the exercise of this outmoded practice at Royal Roads during or immediately after the war, but the implications are obvious.

By 1945, however, it was apparently realized that for various reasons Royal Roads would not be entirely satisfactory as the sole source of officers for a Canadian navy. In that year twenty-five cadets were posted to the cruiser HMCS *Uganda* for a year. Although these were not as carefully screened as the Special (public school) Entry of the Royal Navy, their educational qualifications had to be quite high. Those who proved themselves during their year at sea would be promoted midshipman. This short-lived experiment seems to have been an attempt to select young Canadians as RCN officers on the basis of individual merit rather than on the traditional British basis of class and wealth. During their year's apprenticeship they would gain personal experience of the ratings on the Canadian lower deck in the same way as British midshipmen had done in the Royal Navy.[27]

When war with Japan ended and Canada began to cut its military forces drastically, Royal Roads was at risk under a severely limited defence budget. The RCAF also wanted a college, but realized that it would not get one of its own, so both services decided to join forces at Royal Roads. In the RCAF, although it was believed that air crew for modern planes should start to fly as young as possible, it was also felt that aircrew recruits must have academic qualifications at least as high as senior matriculation. The air force therefore insisted on senior matriculation for entry to the combined RCN-RCAF college that opened at Royal Roads in 1947.[28] This meant a further step away from the traditional "catch'em young" philosophy of the Royal Navy. For the first time, Canada was coming to terms with the idea of a university-level education for naval officers.

When Defence Minister Brooke Claxton approved the reopening of the Royal Military College in 1948, it was a four-year, university-level, tri-service services college associated with Royal Roads. After two years at Royal Roads, Air Force cadets were to proceed to Kingston to complete their four-year course. In accordance with RN practice, naval cadets in both colleges were to go to Britain, either to serve as midshipmen in the fleet for two years or to study at the Royal Naval Engineering College at Keyham. After two years afloat the "seamen" midshipmen, now lieutenants, were to attend the Royal Naval College at Greenwich for the six-month course followed by nine months of technical courses in the United Kingdom. Thus early sea service and the connection with the Royal Navy were both maintained.

The refusals of some ratings on two destroyers and on the carrier HMCS *Magnificent* to respond to orders for duty (which were carefully described as "incidents" in order to avoid the much more serious implications of the word "mutiny") suggested to the commissioners who investigated them that sometimes, and in some respects, the inheritance of these British naval traditions in the education of officers had not served well in a Canadian environment. The *Mainguy Report* commented on an "artificial distance" between officers and men that had been inherited from the RN with the senior service ethic. It said that this was foreign to Canadian usage and custom. Commissioner Louis Audette, in his article on the lower deck, did not blame Royal Naval tradition itself but held that the "artificiality of the superiority arose exclusively from its importation." The Mainguy Commission of Enquiry believed that RCN ratings were "more Canadian than RCN officers and that they therefore resented the officers' adoption of some aspects of British social traditions."[29]

The commissioners concluded their report by saying "we have also sought to interpret the wishes of the great majority of men by stressing the need to 'Canadianize' our navy. In so doing, we wish to record that, in common with most thoughtful Canadians, we have an abiding admiration and respect for the grand traditions and institutions of the Royal Navy and for their continuing beneficent and steadying force wherever British and Canadian ships may sail. We hope that all that is good in these shared traditions will remain with us and that only what is inefficient and inconsistent with our national need, character, dignity, and special conditions will disappear from the navy of Canada."[30]

The "incidents" on *Magnificent* and the findings of the Mainguy Commission were responsible for changing the pattern of Canadian naval education. From 1951, naval cadets, like their fellow cadets in the army and the air force, were to get their full education and a gradually increasing amount of training under Canadian auspices. Engineer officers were to complete a degree course either at a Canadian university or at RMC with an extra year at a university. Executive branch officers were to be assigned as midshipmen on Canadian ships.

THE CANADIAN SERVICES COLLEGES

Two Canadian innovations exerted a significant influence on the manner in which Canada assumed responsibility in 1951 for educating and training its own naval officers. First, it had been firmly established in 1948 that cadet education in Canada would be tri-service, something that was bound to dilute the naval environment in which training and education took place. Second, the introduction in 1951 of the Regular Officer Training Plan (ROTP) permitted entry on an equal basis through both the Canadian Services Colleges and the universities. This led to an almost complete elimination of the traditional practice of RMC only producing reserve officers (and also through the University Naval Training Division [UNTD], the army's Officer Training Corps [OTC], and the air force's University Reserve Training Programme [URTP]), on the assumption that some would go regular. Complete restriction of officer education in the services colleges to future regulars continued to be a matter of debate for some time and was eventually slightly qualified, but ROTP conditioned Canadian military and naval education profoundly. Both innovations weakened those ancient traditions—induction as young as possible, early sea service, and selection from an elite group—that the RCN had inherited from the Royal Navy.

It is important at this point to stress that the Canadian officer class had never been as narrowly exclusive as that in Britain, and that input into RMC from private residential schools had steadily fallen since the First World War. Although it actually picked up a little in 1948, under ROTP it soon fell to a quite small percentage.[31] It is also important to note that in the RN itself traditions had already been altered through the centuries by the need for more general and technical education, and soon these were to be altered even more. In Canada the process was accelerated to meet Canadian needs.

This brings us to a third, little-known innovation that affected Canadian officer production. Until the Second World War a "professional officer" meant one with technical qualifications and functions, especially in the army but also in the navy. The "professionals" were the engineers or others who required special technological education. The emergence of a new understanding of the meaning of the word "professional" to apply to all permanent force officers is usually assumed to have come from the important work of the American sociologist Morris Janowitz. His seminal book is entitled *The Professional Soldier*. Samuel Huntington and Morris Janowitz did not produce their volumes, both of which defined military professionalism, until 1957 and 1960 respectively.

Over a decade earlier than that, British naval historian Michael Lewis, dealing with the history of Royal Navy officers, had already indicated that all naval officers, however employed, were "professional men" like those in medicine, law, and the church. Lewis had demonstrated that in the course of centuries, but more especially after the appearance of powered warships and technically advanced armaments, naval officers had come to need more than just skills in ship-handling and ship-fighting and a little mathematics for navigation. The concept that a naval career was a profession in that wider sense meant that preparation for it could not be based on craft skills acquired by rote training but must include intellectual understanding developed by academic education. Royal Navy training had therefore increasingly involved general, as well as technical, education.[32] It was this need for general and technical education that had already caused the raising of the age of first induction into a naval career and the postponement of the commencement of sea service. It had also challenged reliance on an apprenticeship—sending young boys to sea as midshipmen—as the sole method of producing naval officers.

What was still left unsettled when Canada took over full control of its naval education program was what the most suitable kind of academic education to prepare for the modern naval profession should be, how and when the particular skills that were still needed by a naval officer could be imparted, how far the naval profession was distinct from a military profession in the broader comprehensive sense of the term "military," and whether there should be something in RCN education that was peculiarly Canadian. The quest for a solution to these problems runs like a multi-strand thread through the history of naval education in Canada after 1951.

Rather than duplicate the US Navy's four years of common basic training for all naval officers, Canada had adopted the Royal Navy's system of educating executive and engineer officers separately after a short preliminary common course. The RN system permitted earlier sea service for potential executive officers. The RCN had established Royal Roads in 1942 on the Dartmouth model to provide a short preliminary common course for the career professionals of both types that it expected to need for a larger navy after the war. Then in 1947 the raising of the academic requirement for entry to Royal Roads from junior to senior matriculation at RCAF insistence seemed likely to cut down the number of potential applicants. As the navy was smaller, this did not at first seem to threaten it with a shortage of permanent officers as much as it did the army.

However, the RCN accepted ROTP in 1951, not only to help it keep its college but also because it might also help to guarantee a reliable supply of officers, especially engineers. The Royal Military College commandant and his staff argued against the proposed introduction of ROTP and for the retention of the reserve entry (RE), saying that ROTP would lower standards. The Canadian Services Colleges Committee rejected that opinion. Lt-Commander J.C. Mark of the Director of Naval Education's staff, who chaired the committee, went on to suggest lower fees, more scholarships for reserve entry, and rigorous academic selection of those RE cadets who would simultaneously be admitted.[33] Then, when General Guy Simonds, Chief of the General Staff (CGS), proposed to try to solve the army's serious officer manpower problems by reducing the Canadian Services Colleges entirely to a two-year course starting with junior matriculation, the navy concurred. This was just what it had established at Royal Roads in 1942, though without the ROTP assistance and obligation. The navy now linked Simonds's proposal with its plan to send its engineer officers to a Canadian university after two years in a CSC, instead of to the RN College at Keyham, England. It wanted its deck officers to go straight to sea. This linkage did not come to anything, however, because Simonds's proposal was unsuccessful.

When ROTP became the exclusive means of entry to the CSC and university cadetships, the navy now argued for a partial reintroduction of reserve entry by saying that in the past it had secured better quality officers from reserve graduates who opted to go regular than from those it now got from the ROTP cadets at the bottom of the class, who would be the ones displaced by addition of RE recruits. The army and the air force representatives retorted that figures derived from the past no longer applied because young men whose parents could afford the cost of reserve entry but who had already made up their minds to go regular would have already signed up for ROTP when they entered the CSC's.[34] Nevertheless, the navy was still anxious to tap a younger entry group from the traditional social classes in the old style. On one occasion it suggested that a two-year course could bring junior matriculants up to the senior level.[35] The new CSC, Collège Militaire Royal (CMR), was doing the same thing in one year, not two, but the navy obviously assumed that such a two-year course would have a larger content of practical naval training along with a lower academic level. It was striving for at least a partial return to the old RN system. The four-year academic course in an almost exclusive Regular Officer Training Plan survived these and other assaults, though only because of Defence Minister Claxton's belief in the tri-service system that he had created, and because the RCAF was adamant that it must have a four-year course for all its career officers.

Meanwhile the RCN's efforts to train its executive officers as midshipmen on Canadian ships, begun in 1951 after the *Mainguy Report* ended the practice of sending them to the Royal Navy, had been found wanting. Canada's fleet was too small and its carriers and cruisers were unable to reproduce the midshipmen-training experience that the

RN's battleships and heavy cruisers provided. An ad hoc committee chaired by Admiral E.P. Tisdall was set up to recommend changes in personnel structure to suit Canadian conditions and was instructed to include officer education and training in its purview.

Tisdall reported in 1957. Reflecting the conclusions of the Mainguy Commission, he explained that, until its huge expansion during the Second World War, the RCN had followed the political thinking of the period and so was modelled on the Royal Navy. Since 1939 it had been passing through a transitional period of technological change, expansion of personnel, decrease of personal organization, lessening of Royal Navy influence, and rapid industrialization in Canada. His committee believed that the majority of future Canadian naval officers would be general duty officers whose early training must provide the necessary foundation for later higher command. Tisdall affirmed that he and his colleagues still believed that the best way to train naval officers was in a naval environment, but they accepted that tri-service education was here to stay. He revealed that the Navy Board had approved a proposal that future executive officers should take the four-year CSC course. Tisdall believed that 50 per cent of these general duty officers should come from the services colleges.

Tisdall thus departed from the point of view expressed by Canadian naval officers who had previously addressed this problem. He declared that the present standard of senior matriculation for entry to RMC and the four-year academic course should apply for the navy. He suggested that "during the first two years, all cadets would take the same courses. In the third and fourth years cadets would be permitted selection of subjects on their ability, aptitudes, and desires." He went on to say, "it is essential that the bias of these courses should be towards liberal engineering and that they achieve degree level at the end of four years," and he added, "we are of the opinion that a fundamental knowledge of the sciences and humanities is an essential requirement for command of a modern ship so that ships, weapons, equipment and men may be maintained and used intelligently within the full level of their capabilities."[36] This was a dramatic rejection of the navy's belief in early apprentice-type training and a marked departure from old RN traditions.

The Tisdall Committee also said that some of the naval graduates destined to be engineers should take further "postgraduate training" to obtain the degree of Bachelor of Engineering in one year. Apparently what was meant by this was an honours Bachelor's level of science degree to be obtained in a fifth year. Tisdall had been told that with RMC's existing facilities that college could provide the extra year. He went on, "thence these officers should proceed to a recognized university or technical institute for further postgraduate training in their respective fields to the level of master."[37] The Tisdall Committee thus endorsed a further revolutionary change in Canadian naval education, that in addition to a four-year general academic course for all naval engineer officers there should be an honours degree that could be obtained at RMC in an extra fifth year, and that a significant number of naval engineers should then be sent to university graduate schools.

In 1957 the Department of National Defence set up another committee to report on the Regular Officer Training Plan. Although not a naval committee it was, of course, to include the production of naval officers in its scope. Its chairman, Captain W. Landymore, RCN, a naval officer, was an RMC "ex-cadet," but the other members had had no connection with that college. Landymore suspected that the chairman of the Chiefs of Staff Committee, Lieutenant-General Charles Foulkes, who had struck it, expected it to find that the CSC's were a more expensive method of producing officers than the university ROTP and should therefore be closed. Instead the committee found that, when all costs to the public through federal and provincial charges were taken into consideration, the cost of the university ROTP was about the same as that of RMC and only slightly less expensive than Royal Roads and CMR. It therefore assumed that the services colleges would continue. Because attrition was much higher in senior matriculation year, it recommended against extending entry with junior matriculation, except in the special case of Collège Militaire Royal in the province of Quebec. It also ruled against reintroduction of reserve entry. Finally, in order to attract more applicants, Landymore suggested that RMC should have the power to grant degrees. With regard to administration of the colleges, Landymore proposed that a director of the Regular Officer Training Plan should be appointed to correlate the activities of the three services colleges and of the ROTP units in the universities.[38]

In July 1957, Dr Percy Lowe, head of the RMC mathematics department and a wartime director of naval education, suggested in the RMC Faculty Council that a pass science degree taken in four years would serve the RCN's needs.[39] But when the Personnel Members Committee approved a degree for RMC, it made no provision for a fifth year needed to bring selected cadets up to the honours level required for entry to graduate school without prerequisites.[40] RMC was therefore now constrained to plan for an honours degree to be taken in four years instead of five.[41] The establishment of an honours degree within the four-year period necessitated a readjustment of courses and the use of a spring term after the annual examinations, a device that had already been adopted for certain engineering specialties.

The CSC advisory board discussed the *Landymore Report* in December 1958. It found that the Canadian Armed Forces were not attracting enough successful matriculants sufficiently motivated for service careers and that there was considerable evidence that cadets now had a "degree-motivation" rather than a "service-motivation." The commandant of Royal Roads, Colonel P.S. Cooper, responded that the reason for this lay in the home and society generally, and that the emphasis should be on motivating young men after they were admitted to the ROTP program.[42]

Peter Newman, in his book *The True North*, has suggested one reason for this problem. He said that "sometime during the sixties, the country's social establishment ... deserted Royal Roads and Royal Military College for university-level education."[43] Actually, as shown above, he got the timing wrong. The traditional source of supply of officers from upper middle-class families had begun to dry up long before the 1960s. Furthermore, the CSC's now gave a "university-level" education. So Newman is also wrong in suggesting that explanation for a decline in middle-class interest in a military career was their desire for a more academic education. It seems clear that the root cause was that exclusive social privilege in an officer corps no longer induced enough young men of the country's upper-class establishment to meet Canada's need for officers for its larger navy. As Landymore had discerned, a reduction of the entry level and of academic standards in order to admit more reserve entry recruits on the old system would not have solved the manpower problem. It was now necessary to attract recruits from the Canadian population as a whole with a free university education and to indoctrinate them to accept those military and naval responsibilities that had once been associated with class privilege.

Indoctrination towards a particular service was inevitably weaker in a tri-service college system than in a one-service college. Although Royal Roads preserved more of the traditional activities and environments of a naval college, naval innovations at RMC, such as the use of the bosun's call, were mere tokenism. However, the presence of naval staff officers at RMC and the introduction of courses with some naval content did provide some "naval environment." More important still was the appointment of naval instructors in academic departments, temporarily at first, and later on a quota system. Finally there was the influence of two naval commandants, Commodores D.W. Piers and W.P. Hayes, when, in due course, the navy took its turn commanding the college. Piers drew attention to the time a century ago when a commodore's broad pendant had last flown on Point Frederick when it was an RN dockyard.[44] Hayes looked to the present and future. More open to change than naval officers are usually assumed to be, he started to bring alterations in cadet life, such as the elimination of unenforceable regulations, to accommodate the college to modern youth lifestyles. In the words of a later director of cadets, such regulations were a "negation of basic integrity." These reforms, although criticized by some traditionalists as harmful "liberalization" of basic discipline and the abandonment of tradition, were introduced deliberately as constructive steps toward improving the quality of the input into the services.[45]

But motivation for the naval service, rather than simply for a military rather than civilian career, inevitably depended even more on the period of summer professional training with the navy than on the winter educational program. The Tisdall Committee accepted the fact that tri-service education prevented training "from the start in a naval environment, teaching ... what experienced seamen consider to be right," but it held that "during the summer months, professional naval training [should be] properly integrated with their educational training ... carried out at the coasts, leading at the end of the 4th period to the completion of what is now known as 'courses for the rank of lieutenant'." It added that the present syllabi would have to be modified to include the aspects required to meet this principle.[46]

So summer training had to do more than provide professional expertise. It had to motivate. It had not always done that very well. In the early years of the tri-service system there had been complaints from naval cadets that, although they enjoyed the long cruises, they had been put to chipping old paint from ships' rails, and their summer academic courses were below the standard of those they had already taken during the winter. However, there was improvement over time. In the summer of 1962, two RMC cadets trained with the US Navy. They reported that although they gained valuable experience with equipment in the American ships, their training there was not as thorough as it was in the RCN.[47]

The CSC system and ROTP had been established to produce career officers for all three services. In addition to attrition during college years, many junior officers were exercising their option of withdrawal after the completion of their obligatory term of service after graduation. The navy was especially affected. Critics blamed attrition before graduation on courses that had, in their opinion, too much academic content and too high standards, but one answer to this was that academic attrition in the universities was just as high. Critics of excessive exercise of the withdrawal option said it was owing to both the recruitment of too many whose initial interest was academic rather than military and the colleges' failure to win these students over to service careers. Exercise of the option of withdrawal was, in fact, also probably dependent in part on conditions in the service itself. For example, an army study had documented charges that there were senior officers with undesirable attitudes;[48] there may have been counterparts in the navy. There were undoubtedly also some young officers who were irretrievably unsuitable for a career that required a certain degree of dedication and sacrifice.

A 1961 survey showed that the loss was highest among naval engineers. Forty-four per cent did not stay for life-long careers, many of them no doubt attracted by high rewards in industry. But if the Canadian Military Colleges (CMC's; their designation was now changed) had been less successful in motivation than they had hoped, they could find some comfort in the fact that the percentage of naval engineers from universities who withdrew was 75 per cent.[49] This showed that they had not been out of line in opposing total reliance on the universities rather than the military colleges.

There is no simple yardstick to measure precisely the contribution of the tri-service officer-production system to the single-service RCN from 1948 to the mid-1960s. Lieutenant-Colonel D.J. Goodspeed's *The Armed Forces of Canada, 1867–1967*, published as a centennial volume, implies that its general effect was good.[50] In that period the RCN expanded from less than 7000 officers and men to over 20,000. On its fiftieth birthday in 1960 it was a "fairly substantial force" of sixty-two ships. Plagued in the early years by a shortage of trained specialist personnel, it had developed an elaborate training program while at the same time undertaking operational duties during the Korean War and in connection with NATO and United Nations responsibilities. Along with the other two services it now drew recruits from all walks of Canadian life and all provinces. Its tradition, modified from British precedents by Canadian history and experience, was now influenced by the United States as well, especially in matters of technology. It had developed a fleet of twenty-one escorts with sophisticated anti-submarine capability that was Canadian in design and superior to that in other navies. When the new Canadian flag was hoisted on 15 February 1965 the RCN was already distinctively Canadian, largely because of its education and training.

However, the RCN had lost neither its sentimental connection with the Royal Navy nor its naval distinctiveness. General Jean Allard, the second chief of the defence staff under unification, says that when Paul Hellyer arranged to substitute a new flag to replace the white ensign, instead of the white anchor on a blue background which Allard was expecting, the minister personally unwrapped an ensign with a blue anchor on a white background, like the RN's white ensign; he did so *"sans consultation."*[51] One suspects that some senior naval officer had persuaded him to alter Allard's intention, a sign of MARCOM's independence of spirit and fondness for British tradition.

UNIFICATION

During the integration and unification of the Canadian Forces in the 1960s, popular rhetoric revolved around the theme that a decline in morale was likely to come from the loss of traditional ranks and uniforms. Only to a lesser extent were critics concerned with the suitability of a unified organization, supply, and strategy for conducting operations in each of three separate physical environments. Alarming charges in the media in that latter respect were extravagant. The public had to be reassured that in the unified forces pilots would not command ships and sailors would not repair aircraft.[52] Nevertheless there did seem to be a danger that abolition of the RCN would weaken the traditional bases of naval education and so of morale.

As a protective measure, Maritime Command (MARCOM) was in fact largely synonymous with the former RCN. Most former naval personnel were reclassified as Maritime Surface and Subsurface (MARS) and Maritime Engineering (MARE). Exceptions existed in those branches and trades that could be used in all three former services, such as in communications systems and for chaplains. Furthermore, by the late 1970s, when the shock of unification had died down, MARCOM officers were again talking informally about "naval education" within the context of their current organization. A change in name may have had less effect than many critics had feared.

All the same, at the time of amalgamation, significant differences between the structure of education and the training systems in the three services presented problems. During the preliminary integration period, 1964–7, Allard, who as director of operational preparation introduced the new system, perceived this. Army training was primarily a regimental responsibility conforming to standards laid down by the General Staff. Allard argued that for the navy and the air force war was first and foremost an "affair of the machine." He noted that, as a result, training was carried out in those services by the personnel branch. Hellyer, the minister, favoured the navy-air force system for the combined forces, but Allard saw this as a threat to the army's regimental system and spirit. He feared that his beloved "Van Doos" would be lost in a multi-environment force like the US Marines. This would have eliminated one of the few evidences of a French-Canadian presence.[53] He claims that he appealed to Rear-Admiral Landymore to co-operate with him in preventing those aspects of unification that would also threaten the traditions of the RCN. But Landymore (who does not remember the appeal) was opposed to any degree of unification because it appeared to him to threaten naval morale and efficiency. A little later he resigned his commission.[54]

The tri-service system, of course, had long separated academic development in the winter from military classification training in the summer, leaving the latter entirely to each service. A Chief-of-Personnel-Development study was to claim in 1976 that this separation was in line with developments elsewhere, such as Australia and the United States. According to the study, this division also conformed to a principle laid down by the USN Chief of Naval Operations who said, "academic and professional development shall be measured and published independently. Final class standing [at Annapolis] shall be based on a weighted average of the two which allocated the principal emphasis on academic performance."[55] But this assertion overstates the trend elsewhere at the time. In neither Australia nor the United States was the separation of the two elements in officer preparation, education, and naval training as wide apart as it was under the tri-service system in Canada. Under unification Canadian naval cadets, as we have seen, continued their academic education collectively with the other arms, leaving their professional naval training, as before, to MARCOM. Naval morale, rather than expertise, was now at risk.

It is difficult to measure the effect on naval cadet morale, commitment, and training of the acrimonious debates over unification and the subsequent loss of senior RCN officers. General Allard claims that the navy's petty officers informed him confidentially that they were not in agreement with the admirals and senior officers about unification and that they were glad to change out of the traditional uniform, which had often meant they were identified as part of the British navy.[56] On the other hand, navy blue had identified them as sailors, and many ratings wanted to keep that, even if only to impress the girls in Halifax. Cadets on summer training may thus have been subject to conflicting influences, but their morale may not have suffered as seriously as senior officers believed, because many of them had not been accustomed to wearing navy blue.

What was probably more significant in the long run was something quite different. Unification led to an intensified search for both a military professionalism in the broader meaning of the term "military" and a Canadian doctrine on which professionalism in the Canadian Forces could be built. This general quest may have served to divert some attention from traditional naval training.

The need for a definition of military professionalism was not new. When Michael Lewis indicated the way in which Royal Navy officers had become professionals as a result of a growing need for both technical and general education, he had not found it necessary to spell out that this included responsibility, service, and a corporate spirit. Huntington and Janowitz were to examine these points later, but these things were taken for granted in the Royal Navy before 1939. This assumption had also prevailed in Canada's small pre-war regular forces. But when larger post-war forces required a larger supply of officers, the Department of National Defence (DND) and each of the three separate services, borrowing from American sociological theory, began to look for evidence of responsibility and the corporate spirit as the essential elements in military professionalism for the larger numbers now being commissioned in all three services. What had formerly been taken for granted must now be stimulated by deliberate indoctrination.

The most convenient, though perhaps not necessarily the most accurate, yardstick for measurement of indoctrination was the extent of individual commitment to a service career. Lack of commitment found among service officers or ROTP cadets was contrasted with the high degree of commitment allegedly displayed by pre-war regulars, militia officers, and wartime volunteers, even though the professional expertise of the latter two groups was often far below what was expected of a career professional. Commitment, rather than competence, thus tended to become the hallmark of professionalism.

When General Allard became Chief of the Defence Staff, he established the Officer Development Board (ODB) to seek a Canadian professional doctrine that would apply to all officers of the three former separate services. The first member of ODB was Major-General Bernard J. Guimond, chief of staff in the division of Francophone instruction. Allard made him vice-chairman and appointed Major-General Roger Rowley chairman. According to Allard, Guimond had already decided that the ODB investigation should include pre-commissioning education in the Canadian Military Colleges.[57] Consequently, the ODB study was directly concerned with cadet education and training. After a thorough study of the military ethic and a military philosophy, Rowley recommended that all post-commissioning and cadet education be centralized in one place. He preferred Ottawa-Hull as the site because it was a bilingual community and was the location of the federal bureaucracy, National Defence Headquarters, and the National Archives.[58] ODB also stated that in the future naval officers would need to become expert in many new tasks over and above the present demands of ASW and fleet defence. "Most of these will be directly related to naval support for land forces which is essential to the concepts of mobility which the future will demand."[59] This must have seemed to sailors to imply some reduction in the independent strategic role of the naval forces, thus threatening their autonomy and morale.

The ODB's recommendations were shelved, partly because they seemed to reflect Pearsonian internationalism rather than Prime Minister Pierre Trudeau's Canadianism, and because they had not taken cost into consideration. A shorter follow-up study produced another report which began with the premise that, in order to lay down a doctrine common to all Canadian military professionals, it was first necessary to define the Canadian identity that the professionals served.[60] Following General Allard's lead, ODB had in fact already stressed a need for bilingualism and for more equable regional representation in the forces.[61] These objectives, conforming with Trudeau's approach to Canadianism, led to measures for applying to the Canadian forces the principles of bilingualism, as set out by the Bilingual and Bicultural Commission and adopted as government policy. The cadet colleges, like the forces as a whole, therefore must now bring in more French-Canadian recruits and at the same time add more second language training (SLT). Obviously, adding courses taught in French for French-Canadian recruits and finding time for instruction in French for Anglophones imposed a heavy strain on the RMC budget and timetable. To provide functional bilingualism, SLT would involve at least five hours a week, which had to be taken from either the academic or the military program.

Faculty members feared that a reduction in the academic program would endanger university accreditation for the RMC degree. So academics at RMC held that SLT was part of military training. On the other hand, the military (including naval) staff saw bilingualism as a further threat to the development of professionalism in the forces, about which they were already seriously concerned. A compromise was reached: class periods changed from fifty to forty-five minutes. The loss of class time was recovered by extending the teaching period within the academic year, and by cutting out one summer of military training but adding to the number of summer training periods a preliminary basic training camp.[62]

SLT brought heavy increases in cost, both for instruction and for construction of new buildings. Although new science buildings needed at RMC had been approved only belatedly, construction of a building for SLT came easily and quickly. James Richardson, minister of national defence, who informed the generals in National Defence Headquarters that his colleagues in the cabinet frequently questioned the high cost of the military college system as a whole, called for a "rationalization study" to justify claims that military colleges were the best method of producing officers.

The study, chaired by the chief of personnel development (CPD), Major-General J.J. Paradis, found it impossible to draw hard and fast conclusions from comparative cost analyses. However, it did conclude that "all factors taken into consideration, CMR's academic, administration, and support costs compare favourably with those of a given [Quebec] civilian university of comparable size and enrollment, giving credence to the tentative conclusion that CMC costs in these categories may compare favourably also." Thus the continuation of the CMC system for producing Canadian officers, including MARCOM officers, was endorsed.[63]

Meanwhile, classification training on the former naval lines had continued during the summers. It is difficult to determine how far the diversion of attention to military professionalism, the creation of a distinctive Canadian military professionalism, and measures to promote anglophone bilingualism and also bring in more French Canadians had all distracted from the quality of the naval training that had traditionally produced dedication to a naval career. The CPD study group turned to an attempt to evaluate the academic courses in the CMC's themselves on the basis of information obtained from a "select group of 'experts' who individually or collectively are in the position to speak for their branches or classifications," a rather questionable foundation since it would frequently have too narrow a perspective. On that basis it proposed to "recommend changes in programmes or organization necessary to enable the Military Colleges to graduate officers who will more effectively satisfy the long-term professional requirements of the officer corps."[64]

In response to this proposal, some branch leaders from MARCOM and other commands urged changes to make the CMC curriculum conform more to what they thought that professionalism required. The study group then came to the general conclusion that improvements might be achieved by reducing the number of academic courses of study, the number of lectures, and the amount of classroom time during the academic year. It also believed that the military development side of the colleges needed attention and it recommended more emphasis on classification service orientation during the winter terms. The findings of the study group thus show that, in addition to cabinet complaints about the high cost of the CMC's, some members of the Canadian forces believed that the colleges were not effectively performing their task of producing officers because they were "too academic" and "not sufficiently military." The group proposed that a second task force, including representatives from the three colleges and outside members, should be set up to make specific recommendations for a revised program.[65]

Other complaints that some graduates of the Canadian military colleges lacked motivation, and therefore professional spirit, came to National Defence Headquarters. Colonel W.G. Svab, commander of the No. 202 Workshop Depot in Montreal, reported on two officers who were "completely disgusted with the military life" and unable to accept that "they could be called upon to manage violence." He said that they had informed him that they had these anti-military feelings since their second year in a military college. He wondered why their attitudes had not been noted there. These two ex-cadets said that they had entered the ROTP scheme at sixteen to get an education and that no one had instructed them on the facts of a military career. They found mess life an anathema. Svab suggested that the military colleges should reorient their curriculum towards developing military officers rather than naval engineers.[66]

Similar complaints were also made with regard to lack of naval professionalism. Vice-Admiral D.S. Boyle, commander of MARCOM, complained about junior officer training and motivation in the Naval Operations Branch. He said that for years there had been difficulty in retaining young officers to serve at sea, with resultant high wastage. Numerous changes had been made since the time of the *Tisdall Report*, but the losses continued. He said that professional sailors were concerned because wastage rates were high and professional capability had dwindled. "It is apparent to those who know anything about producing a professional for service at sea that we are not on the right track." One of his squadron commanders had sent him a report that showed how the experience level was going down. "A continuation of such a trend, when ships' systems and tactics are increasingly complicated, provides warning of possible trouble ahead."

Boyle specifically complained that MARCOM was now required to add Officer Professional Development Courses of a general military nature to meet the ODB's professional criteria in the very years when they would like to be developing a professional sea-going officer. He proposed to establish a study team from MARCOM to review the problem, but he said it would not examine the ROTP or other early Canadian Forces training without concurrence and involvement from National Defence Headquarters. He asked for approval for the posting of an officer to head the study.[67]

Replying to the first of these letters of complaint, Brigadier-General J.E. Vance, DGRET, suggested that precipitate action on the basis of specific examples of lack of motivation should be avoided, but that one possible way of reversing the situation might be to tailor the CMC courses more closely to military needs.[68] It may be assumed that he used the word "military" in its broader sense.

In November 1976 the Assistant Deputy Minister (Personnel) set up two task forces to investigate professional military and academic development in the colleges. The latter, chaired by Dr A.C. Leonard, dean of engineering at RMC, made several radical proposals to tailor the CMCs' academic curriculum to what it assumed were the Canadian forces' needs. These changes included the dropping of honours in French, English, history, and chemical engineering.[69] The Military Task Force, chaired by Colonel J.D. Young, Director of Professional Education and Development, said that military leadership and indoctrination had been under-recognized at the CMC's in the past, but it made no specific suggestions for changing the current military leadership and management courses. Instead, moving into the field of the academic task force, it outlined what it called a military core of humanities and science courses that should be included in all officer-cadet programs.[70]

Both task forces were severely criticized by the RMC faculty for inadequate representation of academic experience and opinion and for presuming to make radical proposals for academic revision on the basis of only a brief cursory study. In the following year, however, an RMC committee revised some of the academic courses to relate them more clearly to military, including naval, interests.

MARCOM had submitted a specific proposal related to naval education to the CPD Rationalization Study. A Maritime Officer Production Study (MOPS) had suggested the introduction of a split-degree program whereby MARS cadets would go to sea for five years after their second year in a CMC. Thereafter, if they wished, they could return to complete a degree. The branch advisor of MARS had asked that "this question be examined in depth and a formal reply given." The academic task force therefore consulted CMC faculties and staffs. Royal Roads respondents were favourably disposed but feared that it might divert some MARCOM cadets to other classifications. They recommended a trial period. CMR members were in favour if the interval at sea was to be no more than two years. RMC faculty, having experienced good results from a large number of officers who had studied at RMC as UTPO's or as postgraduate students, were also inclined to approve the proposal, though with some qualifications. The task force concluded, however, that there could be unforeseen consequences. It therefore only recommended that the question be studied by the Director-General of Recruiting, Education, and Training.[71]

In 1978 the split-degree proposal came before the CMCs' advisory board, but once again it failed to win approval. There was some degree of consensus on the board that classroom instruction was not the best way to produce military leaders, but the board was swayed by the fact that the various proposals for a two-year or a five-year intermediary service at sea had not been bridged by compromise. It is noticeable, however, that the Directorate of Professional Education and Development had given the split-degree proposal a low priority on the board's agenda.[72] It seems clear that a return to earlier sea service had become, or perhaps had been from the beginning, a dead issue for the decision-makers in Ottawa.

Apparently that was not the case outside departmental circles. Many former members of the RCN continued to believe that postponement of sea service seriously impeded professional naval development. Their concerns were echoed in 1979 by the commandant of the Naval Officer Training Centre (NOTC) at Esquimalt, who alarmed members of the CMCS' advisory board by talking of the poor indoctrination of cadets and about their many requests for reclassification. Some members of the board therefore revived the split-degree proposal. Various members suggested ways in which it might be achieved, for instance by deferring Second Language Training, or by giving language training at sea. However, two former Royal Roads cadets on the board voiced an opinion that others had expressed earlier. They argued that the root of the problem was that NOTC cadets were unhappy with the navy's approach to training, saying that it was "too traditional." They declared that times have changed, and "so should the navy."[73] MARCOM's problem was thus described not merely as a question of earlier or later sea service but also in terms of whether its approach to training served modern needs.

For naval engineers a four-year CMC course was considered essential to adequately verse them in the fundamentals of new technology. Proposals from some branch leaders that the CMC course should be redesigned to meet the immediate practical needs of junior officers were rejected because in these days of accelerated change such practical expertise would be useful only briefly. RMC courses were therefore, and still are, fundamental and theoretical, rather than narrowly practical, so that graduates may keep themselves abreast of technological change for a longer time. RMC is now producing about 97 per cent of MARCOM's fully qualified naval engineers. The course that is most popular with MARE cadets is honours electrical engineering. But because this production of engineers is not enough for MARCOM's total needs, the college has also introduced other means to enable serving officers and ratings to upgrade their academic qualifications. Meanwhile, on the principle that professionals who are actively engaged in research are the best means of stimulating advanced study, RMC professors are expected to conduct research. The science and engineering faculties now receive nearly two million dollars annually in DND/CRAD (Chief of Research and Development) grants, or by DND agency contracts, and at least half of this research has direct or indirect naval application.

The shortfall in the production of MARE officers was, however, still being made worse by attrition. From 1978 to 1983 about 11 per cent of cadets left after basic training. While some officers believed that the solution to this and later attrition was a return to basic officer training in "the old navy way," MARE attrition at that level was in fact only slightly higher than that of other branches in the Canadian Forces. Later major losses were 7 per cent when young lieutenants completed their first period of engagement and then another 7 per cent when older lieutenants at the end of the next period of service could retire without pension loss. By 1983 posting vacancies in the branch had grown to over one hundred.

A MARE study in that year, followed by professional development seminars in 1984, analysed MARE's structure, training, and development. The MARE classification had been divided into four subclassifications: marine systems, combat systems, naval construction, and naval architecture. For these subclassifications, academic requirements and subsequent training varied. The study concluded that what was needed was not merely to attempt to reduce attrition, but also a means to secure an increase in the input of officer candidates. The result has been that technologists without a university degree are eligible for some classifications. The early portion of all MARE training is done in common with MARS officers. Later periods meet special needs.

In 1983 the maritime engineering recruiting quota for ROTP approximately doubled to 172. With the expected rate of attrition, this would produce about 100 qualified engineers. In 1984 the recruiters succeeded in enrolling 168. Although this increase was no doubt partly owing to the current economic depression, it seemed a good augury for the future.[74]

The shortfall in production of MARCOM officers through ROTP in the CMC's, had necessarily led to a greater reliance on other schemes for producing officers, namely direct entry, subsidized university education for serving officers, commissioning from the ranks, and the Officer Candidate Training Plan. The latter was a revitalization of the old HMCS *Venture* scheme of producing officers whose minimum qualification could be as low as an Advanced Level [Ontario] Grade Thirteen. The Naval Officers Training Course of 54 weeks was, and still is, all that is required to qualify for a commission. It is to some extent equivalent to the summer training programme for ROTP cadets. About three-quarters of the annual entry to commissioned ranks, especially to the MARS classification, comes from these alternative programs, mainly through the Officer Candidate Training Plan. Consequently, this measure to offset the shortfall has resulted in a substantial return to earlier sea training. To avoid the growth of a caste system within the command, pitting graduate officers against others, a Regular Officers Career Development Plan was authorized by parliament on 20 December 1975; it provides a three-tier system by which all MARCOM officers move from short service engagements or obligatory service to intermediate engagements and then to indefinite service. Each step is to be made at stated minimal intervals, with the retirement of those who fail to qualify within a set time. It may be, however, that while this gives the officer corps a single face as a "band of brothers," it will cause dissatisfaction among graduates when their training programs have to be geared to a lower academic level of achievement. Finally, as MARS officers are more likely to be drawn from the entrants with lower entering academic records and, as in all military forces, preference for command tends to go to combat officers, some navy chiefs may be drawn from entrants who originally had a lower academic and intellectual basis on which to build.

Thus, MARCOM education and training differs in certain respects from what was established at Royal Roads in 1942 on what was then assumed to be an RN model. Youthful entry and early sea service have had to give way before the need for a basic preparation to cope with advanced technology. Shortfall in recruiting has, moreover, meant that MARCOM's switch to a level that the US Navy has long maintained for all its officers—a preliminary standard of four years of college education before the beginning of sea service—does not apply in MARCOM across the board and not even for all MARE officers. On the other hand, selection from an elite social group has effectively been replaced in Canada by recruitment from the nation as a whole.

The mythology of Royal Navy tradition that recalls past glories and leaderships, which tends to have a universal impact for all sailors, is no longer the sole source of Canadian naval morale. Service for Canada is an additional source of inspiration reinforced by the navy being made typically Canadian. Furthermore, as it must now draw equally on the population as a whole, MARCOM includes both founding races. Second Language Training is one means to achieve this end by recruiting French-Canadians who previously formed only an insignificant part of the fleet's manpower. It is also required for anglophones, partly because francophones suffered from a handicap in competition for promotion as they had to acquire a second language. Second Language Training for anglophones therefore not merely makes for better communications within the forces but also removes the disadvantage formerly suffered by French Canadians. Originally introduced by offering incentives, SLT is now being made obligatory by penalties in relation to entry and promotion. An SLT qualification is to be required of all combat officers. In MARCOM efforts are being made to incorporate it into the training program. Those Canadian officers who are concerned about the decline of professionalism will undoubtedly see this as a further drain on professional military training. For some other Canadians it appears to be essential if the forces are to be truly Canadian.

There are still some deep-seated causes of dissatisfaction. Foremost among them are the continued influence of prevailing youth cultures and the apparent inability of some traditional naval training to adjust, both of which threaten morale. Another is that Canada does not pay its full share of Alliance costs, and MARCOM ships were for too long allowed to run down, so that they were often unavailable for sea service and training. An important source of professional pride had been somewhat undermined. Present plans to re-equip with new ships may therefore be at least as important in restoring naval morale as the elimination of certain aspects of unification, for instance by restoring uniforms in traditional colours, a measure announced in 1985.

The effect of these measures remains to be seen. Those senior officers ultimately responsible for MARCOM's development apparently believe that what is good in the inspirational traditions of sea service and leadership, the traditions that the Royal Canadian Navy inherited from the Royal Navy, will not be lacking in Canada. The essence of what the RCN originally drew from the Royal Navy—its professionalism—is to be adapted to rapid social and technological change and to Canadian needs by the complete Canadianization of naval education and training. The Canadian navy has undoubtedly departed from some RN traditions, but it is an amicable, and by no means damaging, separation.

Chapter 5

THE END OF PAX BRITANNICA AND THE ORIGINS OF THE ROYAL CANADIAN NAVY: SHIFTING STRATEGIC DEMANDS OF AN EMPIRE AT SEA

Barry Morton Gough

In the same critical year that the Royal Canadian Navy came into existence, 1910, its mother service, the Royal Navy still possessed an uncontested preponderance at sea. Great Britain and the Empire held the trident of the seas. That strangely curious interlude in world affairs known as the Pax Britannica was drawing to a close. On nearly every sea and ocean Britain possessed coaling stations and bases, the anchors of empire so to speak. On nearly every coastline she boasted cruisers or gunboats enforcing her mandate of the freedom of the seas. And even if those overseas fleets had been reduced rather savagely in the course of the previous few years, reorganized cruiser squadrons still showed the pirates, the slave traders, and Britain's testy rivals that the United Kingdom and the British Empire intended to keep the peace of the seas. Although in the corridors of power in Westminster and Whitehall politicians, strategists, and bureaucrats might sternly debate the question of future British naval and military obligations in future wars, there was never any discussion of yielding to a foreign power the sceptre of the seas.

Why, if Britain remained paramount at sea, did Canada create a separate naval organization? The answer to that is complex and is in keeping with the responsive characteristics of Canadian naval traditions. Here I should like to explore the dimensions of this topic, review the historical studies that have centered on the theme, re-examine the immediate causes in international affairs that induced a Canadian response, and make a distinct appeal that we not only see Canadian naval origins as a search for autonomy in relation to Great Britain and the British Empire but that we also regard them as an acceptance of new obligations in international affairs.

The creation of a Canadian Naval Service, the immediate forerunner of the Royal Canadian Navy, constituted a significant step in Canada's search for Dominion status. Yet it was not so much an act of independence as one of co-operation with the Admiralty on terms agreeable to Canada. Put differently, the continuities of Anglo-Canadian naval policy, not the seemingly apparent departures in control from London to Ottawa merit our appreciation. Canada's new authority for a naval service was a logical outgrowth of the imperial-colonial relationship, one which had a parallel in the quest for self-government and for control of the Canadian Militia. The foreign policy of the Empire being indivisible, the question was not whether Canada would fight against an enemy but to what degree and under whose control should that contribution in men, guns, and butter be made. Thus in 1902 when the Rt Hon. Joseph Chamberlain, MP, secretary of state for the colonies, cried "the weary Titan staggers under the too vast orb of its fate" and asked the colonies to shoulder their share of the burden, Canada's answer, given by the prime minister, Sir Wilfrid Laurier, was bluntly "If you want our aid, call us to your councils."[1] And there is some evidence to suggest that Laurier was sufficiently devious to avoid accepting any invitations that might come his way.

INTERNATIONAL NAVAL RIVALRY, 1860–1910

Since 1815 the influence of British naval might had been well nigh ubiquitous on all the major seas and their annexes. In the age of Pax Britannica the Royal Navy had been employed on countless warlike duties, and it can be argued with good reason that the Pax was not as peaceful as we have been led to believe.[2] In keeping "a security for such as pass on the seas upon their lawful occasions," the Royal Navy supplied an enduring contribution to the humanitarian needs of the world.[3] Whether the objects were putting down pirates or freeing slaves, surveying the seas or keeping ocean lanes open for trade, the navy provided the trusted weapon of government, serving especially Foreign Office and Colonial Office needs of an ever-expanding trading network, a burgeoning merchant marine, and a multiplying number of colonial settlements and entrepôts overseas. These obligations meant keeping a gunboat navy on "foreign" stations "showing the flag." Everywhere the white ensign appeared there was armed force to maintain free trade, open trade links, and secure British national advantages. In consequence, the British Empire owed its existence and continued good health to the security of the seas.

"The trident of Neptune is the sceptre of the world," said the French in shocked awe in 1815.[4] That was doubtless true. Britannia held the trident, could rule the waves, and where necessary, could waive the rules. With fleets and bases in both home waters and vitally important distant seas, Britain's influence remained profound in 1910.

Nonetheless during that long century new rivals had been presenting themselves. New powers had emerged in the struggle for overseas colonies and markets. Rivals to Britain's empire had acquired bases of repair and supply, beachheads of trade and commerce, railways and entrances to interoceanic canals. Britain's once comfortable lead in bases—Viscount Castlereagh's 1816 keys to security of trade and military protection—was shrinking fast.[5] And in guns and gunnery at sea not always did Britain's position rank first. The eighty-ton guns of Her Majesty's newest battle ships were "portentious weapons," murmured Prime Minister Gladstone, who added thoughtfully, "I really wonder the human mind can bear such a responsibility!"[6] But bear it the mind did, and this was largely because foreign rivals forced upon an essentially conservative Admiralty Board the necessity of change. Take for instance armament. French gunnery and shells of the 1860s brought their Lordships at the Admiralty to rapt attention. In fighting ships alone, despite continental rivalry, Britain's lead had been maintained from the 1870s onwards. Under terms of the famous Naval Defence Act of 1889, the navy was made theoretically superior to the combination of the fleets of any two European powers.[7] Nonetheless, British naval primacy was facing serious contenders. British power was declining relative to other powers. "Will the Empire which is celebrating one century of Trafalgar survive for the next?" asked J.L. Garvin, later the editor of *The Observer*.[8] And each year naval estimates increased or were more specifically directed to the means of fighting a real war, not another repetitious, minor gunboat action.

But who would be the enemy? As late as the year 1902—cabinet memoranda and the informed periodicals of the day duly attest to this—British strategists were by no means sure which nation would pose the major threat. From time to time France and Russia were mooted as near and present dangers. However, France's weakness at sea relative to Great Britain revealed itself in 1898 during the Fashoda crisis and manifested itself again during the 1900 invasion scare in the United Kingdom. It was even more pronounced by 1902 because France built small battleships and inadequate armed cruisers, while Britain, Germany, Austro-Hungary, and Italy were building large battleships—Dreadnoughts. By 1904 France had entered an *entente cordiale* with Britain and the two ancient rivals settled their overseas differences. Russia, France's ally since 1894, posed a naval threat to Britain in the eastern Mediterranean. But that navy's loss to the Imperial Japanese Navy at the Battle of Tsushima Straits momentarily removed Tsarist Russia as a naval power, and in 1907 Russia and Britain became treaty signatories. In 1902 Japan became a treaty ally; in 1907 that country assumed naval paramouncy in Eastern seas, with British concurrence. Leaving aside Italy and the Austro-Hungarian Empire, that meant that Imperial Germany remained the most likely contestant to British authority at sea.

In fact, not until 1902 did the Admiralty identify Imperial Germany as the most likely opponent.[9] During these early years of the century, British maritime strategy gradually shifted toward preparing for a war against Germany. That involved a concentration of naval strength in what would be the decisive theatre, in northern waters. This modification, Admiral of the Fleet Sir John Fisher liked to point out, was "so unostentatiously carried out that it was only Admiral Mahan's article in *The Scientific American* that drew attention to the fact, when he said that 88 per cent of England's guns were pointed at Germany."[10]

The *Dreadnought* scare of 1909—when Germany's shipbuilding program seemed to threaten British pre-eminence in the number of battleships and other classes of vessels—led to wide-ranging public discussion, heated parliamentary debate, an enhanced construction program, and, of particular interest here, a new need, perhaps never before manifested, with regard to maritime strategic requirements. The key question remained: How could Germany be contained at sea by Britain and the Empire? To this Canadians had their own answer.

CANADA AND THE ROYAL NAVY

At this juxtaposition of world events and new strategic realities a distinct Canadian naval organization came into being. The historian, bewildered by the rhetoric of the Canadian autonomists, can point to a specific act of parliament, which received formal assent on 4 May 1910, establishing a Department of Naval Service and putting in place particulars of organization, training, and regulations. Under this statute, "naval forces" were defined as "those naval forces organized for the defence and protection of the Canadian coasts and trade, or engaged as the Governor in Council may from time to time direct."[11] The historian can also find that the Royal Canadian Navy had its precursors in coastal defence forces, in colonial gunboats, in coast guard vessels, and in fisheries protection vessels. Moreover in the history of provincial marines, naval militias, and naval leagues the historian can discern certain Canadian enthusiasm for a distinctly Canadian naval service. Besides, the country's shipbuilding heritage had given the world one-quarter of its wooden sailing ships of the late nineteenth century. In all these ways and others as well it seems logical that the Dominion came naturally into possession of a naval organization.

In recent years when the writing of Canadian navy history has truly come into its own, and even the high art of Canadian naval historiography has been born, discussion about the origins of the RCN continues.[12] The practitioners of this branch of scholarship have gone beyond merely political and constitutional aspects of Canada's naval service. Rear-Admiral Nigel D. Brodeur and Richard Howard Gimblett have argued, though in different ways, that the roots of the Canadian naval force lie deeply in the Fisheries Protection Service, which in 1892 possessed a form of naval status.[13] A comprehensive view by Thomas R. Melville explores in great detail the intergovernmental relations of Britain, Canada, and other dominions, explaining Canada's naval origins in relation to Canadian pressures and imperial defence.[14] We can also find in the political history of Canada and in various studies of Imperial defence how the Naval Service Act met both the country's needs and the Empire's expectations.[15] Generally speaking, in these inquiries into the hows and whys of Canadian naval origins the shifting international maritime and strategic dimensions are frequently forgotten. The great world affairs of that age are sometimes neglected altogether by that abiding Canadian preoccupation "Who's in charge?"

In terms of shifting maritime strategic needs, Canada's act of naval independence in 1910 was a logical extension of international realities and imperial needs in the western hemisphere and the Pacific Ocean. Japan had secured dominance in the western Pacific at Tsushima and was an ally of Britain and the Empire. Correspondingly, the United States possessed naval dominance in the eastern Pacific, the Caribbean, and the western Atlantic. Given a state of Anglo-American peace, Canada's defence needs against invasion lay in the Monroe Doctrine and a secure America: that is, a Canada defended by the predominant land power and sea defence capabilities of the United States Navy. Prime Minister Laurier was prepared to acknowledge this Anglo-American Pax as early as 1902, though to this day the thought that at the height of its prowess the British Empire in North America was being sustained by United States military and naval might does not sit easily with the Maple Leaf patriot. And in 1910 that explains why the Canadian naval service took so many pains to be non-American in its organization and to be ready to serve as an integrated imperial force in time of national and imperial emergency.[16] That the Canadian navy had its roots in American security is paradoxical but true.

In the murky background of all this Canadian zeal for self-control lies the distant figure of Sir John Arbuthnot Fisher, later first Baron Fisher of Kilverstone. He unwittingly did the Canadian nationalists a great act of good. Sir John, who became First Sea Lord of the Admiralty on Trafalgar Day 1904, had been commander-in-chief on the Royal Navy's North American and West Indies station for eighteen months beginning August 1897. In his usual tours of duty in and out of Halifax, Fisher obtained a warm appreciation of American enthusiasm for naval power. When he was based at Bermuda or visited United States ports-of-call he enriched his friendships with American naval officers, most notably Rear Admiral William Thomas Sampson during the Spanish-American War, and acquired a healthy respect for American naval capabilities and western hemispheric realities. A British war against the United States lay beyond Fisher's comprehension. Thus he readily accepted the Americas as the zone of United States' dominance.

By contrast, Fisher tended to see Canadians as colonial laggards, more often than not willing to let the British do the work and pay the bill. "He says he knows the Canadians," wrote Captain Edmond Slade, RN, of Fisher in his diary, "and that they are an unpatriotic grasping people who only stick to us for the good that they can get out of us, and that we ought to do nothing whatsoever for them."[17] What Fisher thought best, and he preached this doctrine when he went to the Admiralty in 1902, was to withdraw the main British fighting units from the North American and West Indies and Pacific Stations and to leave the Canadians to get along more agreeably with their American neighbours.

The Lords Commissioners of the Admiralty did not, on face value at least, see things Fisher's way. Or if they did they could not say so publicly. They continued to preach the unity of the Empire and of the fleet: "One life, one flag, one fleet, one throne, Britons hold your own!" They discussed the idea of the unity of the fleet at colonial, imperial, and naval defence meetings in 1902, 1907, and 1909. They argued for financial contributions to ease the capital costs of new units for the fleet. They argued that this would best benefit all constituent parts of the Empire. Anxious strategic reports emanating from the Admiralty, sometimes on the basis of secret intelligence gathered by plainclothes naval officers who had examined American capabilities, indicated the difficulty if not the impossibility of defending Canada against American invasion.[18] But at the highest political level in Britain such views were unacceptable and not fit for public consumption.

Let us trace a specific example of this through the documents. In late August 1904 Fisher, then Second Sea Lord but in his additional capacity as first and principal naval ADC to the King, wrote to Lord Knollys, the private secretary to Edward VII, to advise His Majesty on the state of international relations and the condition of the navy. "I think the King ought to know what is going on," he advised in his characteristically trenchant prose, "and so I venture to send the very rough notes from which I lectured to [Prime Minister Arthur] Balfour. *Vast changes are indispensable for fighting efficiency and for instant readiness for war. We have neither at present*! We have got to be ruthless, relentless, and remorseless in our reforms! Otherwise, we may as well pack up and hand all over to the Germans. France is the *one* country we have got to be friends with! I put the United States out of the question, as we ought to clear out from that Hemisphere altogether!"[19] In his view the British fleet was obliged to prepare for a major war, not for another gunboat engagement. He remained worried that some future West Indian or Central American obligation would deflect the Royal Navy away from its main strategical assignment. The Committee of Imperial Defence was of a similar mind but fell just short of Fisher's view when it said in 1904 that Canada could not be defended against a United States attack and thus that only a small garrison ought to be maintained at Halifax.[20] The War Office was seeking economy, too, and in an age of a thorough discussion of how to match resources with requirements the British garrison kept at Halifax was one obligation which London sought to pass to the Dominion as expeditiously as possible.

In December 1904, as well, Fisher's scheme to reorganize oversea squadrons was effected. Behind this reform, as others, lay the Fisher motto: "The fighting efficiency of the fleet and its instant readiness for war." To Fisher, "strategical ('and not sentimental') requirements had to be met."[21] It reflected the revolution in Admiralty strategic thought that recognized the most likely danger to be Germany. It announced the end of the gunboat navy. It foreshadowed the end of the Pax Britannica. For all intents and purposes the North American and West Indies Station was disbanded. Halifax became a backwater of Admiralty strategy. The great "Warden of the North" was not included in Fisher's five strategic keys that belonged to England and locked up the world to British naval supremacy: the others were Singapore, the Cape of Good Hope, Alexandria, Gibraltar, and Dover. With the Admiralty having all but abandoned the century-long tradition of keeping a fleet in the western Atlantic for securing British interests, the question of land defences of Canada now assumed a greater importance. Canada's defence needs after 1905 were of continuing concern to British strategists.[22] But in sum what Fisher's reorganization meant was that Britain acknowledged that she could not be supreme everywhere on the seas that she might wish to be. Concentration of force, not dispersal, was what was now needed to secure national ends. If that meant abandoning Canada to American annexation, Fisher and the Admiralty noted in their private documents, so be it.

These views of Fisher and some of his colleagues were not for public consumption. The First Lord of the Admiralty, the Earl of Selborne, who drafted the key memoranda on imperial naval defence for this era, possessed a diplomatic tact not found in Fisher. He was profoundly shocked by Fisher's "violent hostility to Canada."[23] Fisher's view that Britain should not spend one pound for the defence of the Dominion did not strike Selborne or many of his political colleagues as a wholesome means of maintaining and enhancing intragovernmental defence co-operation. In consequence, Selborne anxiously promoted the opinion that Fisher's views were his own, not those of the Admiralty.[24] He also argued that abandoning Canada would be a dishonourable and unnecessary act, one likely to split the Empire without any possibility of reunion.

Thus if Fisher advanced the cause of Britain's hasty strategic withdrawal from the western hemisphere, the Admiralty would be successful in their policies in only two ways: firstly, the withdrawal of the North American and West Indies fleet; and secondly, the transfer of Halifax from British to Canadian hands and the closing of the Jamaica dockyard. The War Office, more cautious than the Admiralty, was less anxious for an immediate withdrawal of British troops from Halifax. Fisher acquiesced to the idea. Keeping a few redcoats in Halifax, he wrote (employing the adage of Lord St Vincent), would afford a "comforting spectacle to the old women of both sexes in Halifax."[25] Fisher did not get his way in the case of the West Indian base St Lucia, which was maintained as a place of supply. Nor did he succeed with Bermuda, which was maintained (though on a reduced scale) and used increasingly by the United States Navy. Ascension, too, was reduced. Antigua had already been abandoned as a base.

Fisher's so-called reforms of fleets and bases signalled the end of the Royal Navy's obligations for the specific coastal defence of Canada. They also relinquished Britain's traditional command of the Caribbean to the United States. The withdrawal of forces generated apprehension in Canada. As Governor General Lord Minto complained in 1906, older Canadians bitterly resented these "withdrawals of the flag" for they largely "removed the possibility of the appeal so often made to the flag in the case of some trading schooner that had got into difficulty ... In considering imperial defence in an Empire such as ours one must not be guided alone by purely practical considerations but must take human influences into account."[26] But at this time, more frequently than otherwise, sentimentality was not the driving engine of defence planning.

From the Canadian perspective, Fisher's changes marked the need for a national commitment to sea security. They brought into Canadian possession two great bases: one lying athwart the major sea lanes of the North Atlantic, the other situated adjacent to the great circle route of trans-Pacific commerce. As well, Fisher's reforms, endorsed by the War Office, the Committee of Imperial Defence, and the cabinet, led Canada to secure even more than before the garrison and artillery needs of these bases. These bases and garrisons were forerunners to the organization of a naval service which was in itself a preliminary to a Canadian fighting capability at sea.

Fisher alone cannot be blamed or credited with these profound changes. He stands at the centre and around him move the events: the shifts of international relations, the changes of strategy, the revolutions in material. He had his *confrères*. Look, for example, at the activities of Richard Burdon Haldane, MP, secretary of state for war. For a start he disbanded two guards and eight line battalions of infantry and one out of eleven native regiments used for colonial duty. He also closed the garrison at St Helena, reduced the establishments at Gibraltar, Malta, and Ceylon, "and made the defence of Halifax and Esquimalt an exclusively Canadian concern."[27] By the time Haldane completed his work at home he had remodelled the regular army, restructured the reserve forces into the territorial army, and put in place an expeditionary force to fight a continental war in Europe. In other words, the army had its Fisher too, and one who was acutely aware of how shifting forces of international affairs affected British policy: "The days when splendid isolation was possible were gone," Lord Haldane wrote in reflection. "Our sea-power, even as an instrument of self defence, was in danger of becoming inadequate in the absence of friendships which would ensure that other navies would remain neutral, if they did not actively co-operate with ours."[28] In short, only in alliances—with Japan, France, Russia, and perhaps even the United States—could ultimate naval preponderance of the British Empire be secured.

BRITAIN AND THE COLONIAL NAVIES

The search for friends and allies actually began at home, within the Empire.[29] No matter how passionately the Colonial Secretary, Chamberlain, might appeal for colonial contributions to imperial defence, no matter how strongly the self-governing colonies might resist London's demands and cry for a voice in councils, the Admiralty was moving toward an increased centralization and organization of naval administration and fighting strength. Colonial naval forces—as authorized by the Colonial Naval Defence Act of 1865—were now being discouraged, eventually to be replaced by the concept of the unitary fleet. In 1902, for instance, the Admiralty policy as presented at the Colonial Conference stated explicitly that any auxiliary squadron, (meaning the New Zealand and Australian subsidized squadron) was to be under Admiralty control in time of peace or war—a departure from the 1865 statute which gave Admiralty control only in an emergency. The intent was to make possible, when necessary, a combination of all units in East Indian, Australian, and Chinese waters.

Even more generally the 1902 Admiralty memorandum strongly criticized the folly of maintaining local navies or of keeping units on a particular coastline. The Admiralty emphasized control of communications. As the memo indicated, "the importance which attaches to the command of the sea lies in the control which it gives over sea communications." The advantages of gaining command of the sea were equally illustrated by historical example. To cite one case, "the fall of Quebec and the conquest of French Canada was mainly due to the fact that our superior sea-power closed the Gulf of St Lawrence to the French and opened it to us. In any similar struggle in the future, this route will be as vital as in the past." The Admiralty also laid stress on the importance of the great battle for supremacy, because the great development of French, German, American, and Russian navies (Japan is not mentioned) required a British concentration for the decisive encounter. The enemy would likely threaten detached squadrons and prey on trade, and this would require detachments from the concentrated force. To do this effectively, control of communications remained vital. "The immense importance of the principle of concentration and the facility with which ships and squadrons can be moved from one part of the world to another—it is more easy to move a fleet from Spithead to the Cape or Halifax than it is to move a large army, with its equipment, from Cape Town to Pretoria—points to the necessity of a single navy under one control, by which alone concentrated action between the parts can be assured." The navy, the memorandum concluded, would take the offensive against enemy force, and the navy would have to be prepared to meet the strength and composition of the hostile forces.[30]

As has been suggested, the strategic principles employed in this celebrated document represent the rise of "blue water" thinking.[31] The Admiralty wanted flexibility coupled with control, and that meant possessing sufficient power to conduct a vigorous offensive against outlying hostile squadrons without unduly weakening forces concentrated for the anticipated decisive battle. Professor Gerald Graham, in assessing this stage of Admiralty thinking, indicates that even in 1902 their Lordships were maintaining a traditional role in both hemispheres. "Without aggressively straining for dominion, Britain's unique predominance as mistress of the seas remained intact."[32] This was undoubtedly so. Yet as Professor Donald Gordon has stated, there was no universal colonial acceptance of the concept of communications control. Canada and especially Australia fumed about being dictated to by an insensitive mother.[33] "The establishment of special forces," complained an Australian-Canadian memorandum, "set apart for general imperial service, and practically under the absolute control of the imperial government, was objectionable in principle, as derogating from the powers of self-government enjoyed by them, and would be calculated to impede the general improvement in training and organization of their defence forces."[34]

Despite these appeals, one cardinal principle of action was emerging: Admiralty initiative. Concentration of the navy and one fleet by control of communications became strategic bywords. The principle cut right across touchy colonial desires for a share in policymaking. Therein was presented a problem which Winston Churchill as First Lord of the Admiralty in 1911 scarcely understood and neglected to his peril.

The Fisher reforms and Canada's own creation of a naval organization made a co-ordinated imperial foreign policy even more vital. Australia had a navy, and New Zealand, Natal, and other possessions were making specific financial contributions to the fleet. Thus, as Secretary of State for Foreign Affairs Sir Edward Grey explained, British sea dominance would have to be effected through imperial organization. Under a separate 1911 conference on strategy held by the Committee of Imperial Defence, the needs of the Admiralty for control and efficiency of an imperial navy had to be reconciled with the requirements of Canada and Australia for financial and administrative autonomy. By agreement, the Royal Canadian and Royal Australian navies were to have training and discipline similar to that of the Royal Navy. In time of peace they were under Dominion control in Dominion waters and under Admiralty control outside those waters. In time of war they were to come under Admiralty control if and when so placed by the Dominions.[35] This was a triumph for dominion autonomy, but it did little to give credence to the idea, now mythical, of "imperial defence."

THE END OF PAX BRITANNICA

On reflection, the end of Pax Britannica and the origins of the Royal Canadian Navy have their roots in the same problem: How could the sea supremacy of the British Empire be maintained in the face of new strategic realities? In 1889, Lord Dunraven, the First Lord of the Admiralty, defended the "two-power standard" and identified the key requirements of naval paramouncy for Britain: "the defence of the Empire, the safeguarding of the trade of the national and imperial commerce, are really the foreign policies of this country."[36] As with Dunraven, so with Castlereagh three generations before. Imperial defence was vital, said the British; indeed it was inseparable from national defence. The same held true in 1910. The Dominions for all their desire for autonomy were part and parcel of the whole reorganization of the naval and military services in the years which closed that era when Britain alone was perceived as being mistress of the seas.

The changing nature of international affairs compelled a Canadian response. The United States, emerging as the predominant power in the Americas and adjacent seas, freed Britain from obligations there and allowed Britain to bequeath to Canada two bases as well as obligations for local sea and shore defence. At the same time, the rise of German naval power initiated another Canadian response. Given the inseparability of Canada from the Empire and the indivisibility of foreign policy, the question emerged, "How could the Canadian naval service best serve the defence of Empire as well as that of the Dominion?" The interminable differences of opinion among various representatives at the imperial and naval conferences, especially in 1902, 1907, 1909, and 1911, were not about loyalty or ultimate purpose. They were really about technique: that is, who would control what in what circumstances. The resulting changes in the world's balance of power, especially the enhanced status of the United States, Japan, and Germany and the reduced influence of France and Russia, and the technological revolution that fueled these rivalries, meant that Britain and in consequence Canada were obliged to face these new realities. Thereby was the Canadian Naval Service born.

But to repeat: the new carried within it the old. The continuity of traditions, the integration of training and weapons, the forged link in time of war in 1914 all were an extension of ancient techniques under control of new masters on both sides of the Atlantic. Besides the reality there remains the image, and perhaps in the end it is the image that burns most brightly on the mind. The Canadian Naval Service was born in the same tradition of "Look to your moat" and of "Keeping the policy of the seas." It carries, too, the heroes of the mother navy's past and even the names of some of its ships. Thus it was not without accident at the critical moment, so long anticipated, when HMCS *Rainbow* put to sea from Esquimalt on 3 August 1914 to protect trade and if necessary inflict a blow on Admiral Graf von Spee's cruisers that she carried this celebrated charge sent her from Ottawa: "Remember Nelson and the British Navy. All Canada is watching."

As in 1910 so too in future years, in war and in peace, even to the present. The near half-century of conflict which ended in 1945 and the near half-century since 1945 of nuclear peace (that now can be seen as so different from its predecessor) have been characterized, as far as Canadian foreign policy and naval and military commitment are concerned, by four constants: the dictates of geography; the state of international relations; the actions of allies; and the reactive or responsive posture of the nation itself. Canada, by its northern location inseparable from the main currents of international events, has responded to the shifts in the international balance of power and to new strategic realities, has worked in conjunction with its principal allies, most notably Great Britain but also the United States and more recently member states of the North Atlantic Treaty Organization, and has, at bottom, developed policies to fit its own needs.

Only in 1914, by the King's declaration of war on Canada's and the British Empire's enemies, did Canada find itself at war without making an independent decision on the matter. Even then, it must be quickly added, such declaration was a constitutional obligation of fact, the Crown being as of yet indivisible and the technical characteristics of Dominion status not yet defined. All the same, the degree of Canada's commitment in men, material, and finance remained the nation's question alone. Today as yesterday that fundamental premise remains inviolate. The Pax Americana may have replaced the Pax Britannica in some of its particularities; the world's democratic leadership may have shifted westwards across the Atlantic from Westminster to Washington, and Canada's position as principal trading partner to the world's ranking western power may now be even more prominent than it was in the heyday of the British Empire. But, all these matters aside, the choice is Canada's to make as to its material contribution to its own defence; as Canada's history amply demonstrates, the nation's sea security ranks as a pre-eminent need.

Chapter 6

HARD LUCK FLOTILLA:
THE RCN's ATLANTIC COAST PATROL, 1914–18

Roger Sarty

In 1918 the Royal Canadian Navy—a tiny service that had nearly been scuttled by political controversy—suddenly had to protect Canada's waters against raids by three large U-boats. The events of these difficult months have been virtually forgotten. Most strikingly, they are not mentioned in the official history of the naval service.[1] It was an experience that senior Canadian sailors preferred not to dwell on, for although the hastily assembled flotilla kept losses of merchant vessels to a minimum, individual officers and ships performed very poorly at critical junctures. Much of the fault lay with the virtual absence of thoroughly trained seagoing personnel, suitable vessels, and shore bases to support them. Yet for nearly a decade before the outbreak of war, British and Canadian officers had pressed the Canadian government to establish an appropriate naval organization on the east coast, and that made the legacy more bitter still. Paradoxically, in 1917–18, when Sir Robert Borden was asserting national control over the Canadian army fighting in Europe, the defence of the Dominion's home waters depended upon the meagre resources Great Britain and the United States chose to provide.

Prior to the First World War no one, aside from a few imaginative individuals like H.G. Wells and Admiral Sir John Fisher, anticipated that submarines would prove to be a decisive weapon against merchant shipping. The British Admiralty's great fear was that fast enemy cruisers or armed merchant ships would evade the Royal Navy's squadrons to strike at the Empire's trade and ports, much as Confederate warships like the CSS *Alabama* had done in the face of overwhelming United States naval superiority during the American Civil War. It was against this threat that Great Britain repeatedly advised Canada to develop naval defences, but these would have been equally effective against the u-boats that arrived off Nova Scotia in 1918.²

Britain threw the whole of the responsibility for local Canadian naval defence onto the Dominion government in 1904–6 with the closure of the dockyards at Halifax and Esquimalt, the withdrawal of the army garrisons from these fortified ports, and the reduction of the North America and West Indies squadron to a single cruiser at Bermuda. The government of Sir Wilfrid Laurier immediately provided Canadian troops for the fortresses, but both British services advised this was not enough. Modern torpedo craft—torpedo boats, destroyers (in effect, large torpedo boats), and submarines—were now an indispensible adjunct to fortifications on shore. These relatively economical vessels would at least provide an early warning of an attack, and they might effectively counter raids on shipping or coastlines a hundred miles or more beyond the range of coast artillery.³

The Laurier government would have been content to organize such a coast defence flotilla when it founded the naval service in 1910. Under pressure from the Admiralty, which also wanted support on the critical north Atlantic shipping routes, the Canadians agreed to do considerably more. The 1910 program included not only six large destroyers but also four light cruisers for trade defence on the high seas.⁴ Robert Borden's cancellation of this program when his Conservative government came to power in 1911, and his attempts to provide more direct support for the Royal Navy in the form of financial grants for the construction of dreadnoughts, are famous events in Canadian political history. Less well known is that in 1912 the Admiralty advised that Canada should also carry on with a version of the Laurier fleet for trade and coast defence. Forces required for the local protection of the Halifax approaches and the Gulf of St Lawrence included a small cruiser, eighteen torpedo boats, and a dozen submarines. In June 1914 the prime minister responded to efforts by the Admiralty and the Canadian naval staff to revive these proposals with a note that he would not have time to look at the papers for a few weeks. By then it was too late.⁵

When war broke out, the RCN was incapable of undertaking a seagoing role. The total strength of the service was only 350 regular personnel and the 250 minimally trained members of the Royal Naval Canadian Volunteer Reserve. Resources on the east coast amounted to the old cruiser, *Niobe*, for which an adequate crew could not be mustered, and the small, outdated, and poorly maintained dockyard at Halifax. The Canadian government placed *Niobe* under British control; the Royal Navy completed the crew and she put to sea with the North America and West Indies squadron, now expanded to about a dozen cruisers. With a handful of small vessels borrowed from other government departments or chartered from commercial firms, the RCN was only able to examine merchant ships entering Halifax, sweep the harbour's immediate approaches for mines that might have been dropped by German raiders, and mount the occasional lookout patrol along the Nova Scotia coast. Even these services could not be properly carried out.[6]

In November 1914, at the urging of the Canadian naval staff and the British commander-in-chief of the North America and West Indies Station, Borden began to press the Admiralty for destroyers and submarines. He wanted to build the warships in Canada and borrow others from the Royal Navy in the meantime. The success of U-boats against merchant shipping during the first half of 1915, and persistent intelligence from German circles in the United States that the campaign would soon extend across the Atlantic, seemed to strengthen Borden's case. These would be excellent anti-submarine vessels; the commander-in-chief warned that his unmanoeuvrable cruisers could only run for cover in the face of U-boat attacks.[7]

The Admiralty held to the opinion Winston Churchill, the First Lord, had given in October 1914: Canada should restrict her effort to the raising of land forces.[8] No torpedo craft could be spared from European waters, and production in Canada was not practicable because armament, specialized equipment, and skilled manpower would have to be obtained in the United Kingdom, thereby disrupting British shipbuilding. In any case, the U-boat threat to Canada was potential rather than actual; the only immediate requirement was for coastal patrols to ensure that German agents or sympathizers did not establish fuel caches in isolated areas to support long-range submarine operations. During the summer of 1915 the RCN accordingly established the Gulf of St Lawrence patrol, which normally included seven ships that had been obtained by purchasing private yachts in the United States and borrowing additional vessels from other departments. Operating from an improvised base at Sydney during the navigation season, the force returned to Halifax during the winter months.[9]

It seemed that the RCN's major contribution would be the supply of personnel to the British service. In 1916 the overseas division of the Royal Naval Canadian Volunteer Reserve (RNCVR) was organized; by the spring of the following year nearly twelve hundred recruits, most of them with seafaring backgrounds, had been sent to the United Kingdom. By that time, too, some forty-seven RCN officers were serving with the Royal Navy, including the best of the young officers in the service.[10]

Events in late 1916 and early 1917 thrust much larger responsibilities on the RCN. Germany commenced a renewed U-boat offensive to cut the Atlantic shipping lanes that sustained the Allied war effort with men and material; intensified with the declaration of "unrestricted submarine warfare" on 31 January 1917, the campaign nearly succeeded. Visits to the United States by the merchant submarine *Deutschland* in July and November 1916 proclaimed the transatlantic capability of the U-boat arm. More disturbing were the exploits of the fighting boat U-53 which on 7 October 1916 appeared at Newport, Rhode Island, cast off without refuelling, and sank five Allied merchant ships off Nantucket the next day. In November the Admiralty informed the Canadian government that its flotilla of twelve vessels should be tripled in size, but the only assistance the Royal Navy could offer would be the services of an experienced officer to organize and command the expanded patrol. During the 1917 shipping season, purchases of civilian vessels and further transfers of other Canadian government ships increased the strength of the patrols to about twenty-two vessels. Early in February the government had also placed orders with Polsons in Toronto and Canadian Vickers in Montreal for the construction of twelve trawlers.[11]

Much larger shipbuilding orders came from the Admiralty that same month. Possibly influenced by bitter Canadian remonstrances that the Dominion was being asked to increase its anti-submarine effort after Great Britain had drained the country of suitable ships and men and refused to sanction warship construction in Canadian yards, the Admiralty asked Ottawa to place contracts for thirty-six steel trawlers and one hundred wooden drifters. Orders were accordingly given to shipyards on the St Lawrence and Great Lakes. Although the vessels were being built at British expense, the Admiralty suggested rather obliquely that they would be used on Canada's Atlantic coast. Confusion in Ottawa about this bred a good deal of correspondence and discussion in which the Admiralty left open the possibility that the vessels might have to be used elsewhere. This was reasonable in view of the gravity of the crisis the Royal Navy faced in European waters, but it created serious difficulties for the RCN in planning for the expansion of Canadian patrols. In July 1917, the Admiralty asked Ottawa to place orders for a further twenty-four trawlers. Unlike the twelve Canadian trawlers, which were named for battles of the war (*Arras, Arleux*, and so forth), the vessels building on imperial account were merely numbered: 1-60 in the case of the trawlers, and 1-100 for the drifters.[12]

Although a large number of anti-submarine vessels were now building in Canadian yards, these were modest craft. The trawlers measured about 130 feet in length and displaced 130–40 tons; they mounted a single 12-pounder gun and could make a speed of 10 knots. The wooden drifters were only 84 feet in length, carried a 6-pounder, and could move at no more than 9 knots. In fact, the most capable of the Canadian vessels were seven "auxiliary patrol ships" (*Canada, Cartier, Acadia, Hochelaga, Lady Evelyn, Margaret,* and *Stadacona*) acquired in 1915 and 1917 from other government departments and through the purchase of yachts in the United States. Good sea boats, each of these vessels displaced from 700 to 1050 tons, measured 170 to 210 feet in length, and could make from 11 to 16 knots. All ultimately carried at least two 12-pounder guns; four of the vessels mounted a single 4-inch, albeit not of the latest and most powerful type. Normally operating out of Sydney in the Gulf and in the waters to the south of Newfoundland, they formed the backbone of the Canadian patrols until the end of the war.[13]

While the Canadian government struggled to expand the Atlantic coast patrols, the U-boat crisis of 1917 was reshaping naval operations in North American waters. On 6 April the United States declared war on Germany as a direct result of U-boat attacks on American shipping. Having no idea of how close the U-boats were to winning the battle on the shipping lanes, the United States Navy had made no special effort to expand its anti-submarine forces. On learning from the Admiralty of the desperate state of affairs in European waters, the American navy department began to send overseas every suitable vessel that could be spared. Thus, although the Canadian government hoped that the Americans could offer substantial assistance in patrolling off the southern tip of Nova Scotia and in the Bay of Fundy, the navy department was only willing to undertake occasional visits with larger ships to the deep waters off the Bay of Fundy.[14]

So severe were Allied shipping losses at the time of the American entry into the war that the Admiralty soon decided to sail merchantmen in defended convoys. This ancient method was thought to have been impracticable or even suicidal with modern steamships, but it proved to be the key to victory. Transatlantic convoys began to sail from Hampton Roads, Virginia, New York City, and Sydney, Nova Scotia, in July 1917. As the system developed, the Sydney convoys, known as the HS series, were reserved for slow cargo carrying vessels from Canadian and American ports. In September the HX series of fast troopships and merchantmen started to sail from Halifax. A reorganization of the convoy system in March 1918 transferred the HX series to New York and instituted the HC series for troopships and cargo vessels of medium speed (11 ½ knots) from Halifax. Meanwhile, with the freeze-up of the St Lawrence in December 1917, the HS series had assembled at Halifax until navigation opened again at Sydney in

July 1918. British and American cruisers escorted the convoys through their entire passage to guard against the ever-present danger of German surface warships breaking out of the North Sea; antisubmarine vessels joined as the convoys approached the zone of intense u-boat operations off Britain and the west coast of France.[15]

Successful as the convoy system proved to be, it did inject yet another naval authority into the already confused organization on the Canadian east coast. Rear-Admiral B.M. Chambers, RN, and his staff arrived at Sydney in August 1917 to organize the Canadian convoys; Chambers reported directly to the Admiralty. Control of all other shipping that sailed from Canadian ports was, however, under Canadian naval staffs at Montreal, Quebec, Saint John, New Brunswick, Sydney, and Halifax, all of whom reported to naval headquarters in Ottawa. In charge of both the establishments at Halifax and the local naval defences of the port to a distance of about ten miles from the harbour mouth was the superintendent of HMC Dockyard, who also reported to naval headquarters. From December 1917 the appointment was held by Vice-Admiral W.O. Story, RN (ret'd), an employee of the Canadian government. The patrols organization based at Sydney was another separate command, directly under naval headquarters; the division of responsibility between the patrols and Admiral Story for the seaward defence of Halifax became a source of continuing controversy as the Canadian flotilla began to expand in 1917.

Co-ordination of the many authorities at convoy ports in both Canada and the United States fell to the commander-in-chief North America and West Indies, Vice-Admiral M.E. Browning, who was succeeded by Vice-Admiral W.L. Grant in February 1918. It was an enormous task and an extremely frustrating one because the commander-in-chief's power of command was restricted to British warships operating in the western Atlantic and the Royal Navy's base at Bermuda. Although Browning and Grant were normally at Washington liaising with the navy department, they both visited Halifax and Ottawa regularly. On many of the most important questions they, rather than Admiral C.E. Kingsmill, director of the Canadian naval service, acted as the senior naval advisors to the Canadian government.[16]

Much less successful was the officer sent out by the Admiralty in March 1917 to command and reorganize the Canadian patrols. Earlier in the war Vice-Admiral Sir Charles H. Coke had flown his flag at Queenstown on the coast of southern Ireland; he appears to have been remembered primarily for the fact that *Lusitania* was lost within his command. Having accepted the rank of commodore second class for the Canadian appointment, he nevertheless behaved as if he were the senior admiral of the RCN, interfering in a wide range of matters outside of his mandate and giving little attention to the questions he had been hired to tackle. In June the Admiralty agreed to recall Coke, observing that "his advancing age has seriously told on him."[17]

The commodore's departure did not immediately improve understanding between London and Ottawa. In July, naval headquarters concurred in the selection of Captain J.O. Hatcher, RN, as Coke's successor, and at the end of the month the Admiralty appointed him "Captain in charge of Patrols." In an obscurely phrased cable, however, Kingsmill had left open the question of whether Hatcher would actually command or merely assist with the organization of the patrol. While Hatcher was on passage, naval headquarters appointed Captain Walter Hose, RCN, to the patrols command. Greeted with this development on his arrival, the British officer nevertheless agreed to serve as an advisor, and he set to work on a plan for the employment of the trawlers and drifters building on imperial account.[18]

In September the Admiralty threw a spanner into the works, announcing that the first sixteen trawlers and fifty drifters completed would be employed overseas. Hose, who misunderstood the function of drifters, believed that the remaining fifty vessels of that type would be too few in number to do anything useful and should be offered to the Admiralty in return for some additional trawlers. Hatcher and the commander-in-chief disagreed, but Kingsmill supported Hose. Whatever the merits of the technical argument, Kingsmill realized that planning was futile until the Admiralty made a firm allocation of vessels. In November the Department of the Naval Service asked the Admiralty for a statement of the specific threat to Canadian waters and for "some definite scheme" of defence.[19]

The Admiralty responded on 3 January 1918 with a paper that became the blueprint for the development of the Atlantic coast patrols until the end of the war. "It is considered very probable," their Lordships wrote, "that an attack by one of the new submarine cruisers may be expected at any time after March ... Whether in the future more than one submarine or not operates on the Canadian coast at a time, the measures necessary to protect shipping will be the same, based on the assumption that at any moment one submarine may be in a position to attack every outgoing convoy." Because mines were an uneconomic load for submarines crossing the Atlantic, the most likely form of attack would be by torpedoes and deck guns. Minelaying by surface raiders was only a "possibility," although one that had to be guarded against.[20]

This appreciation was the basis for a fundamental recasting of the operations of the Atlantic patrols. Both the Hatcher and Hose schemes had merely strengthened the forces allocated to the flotilla's existing tasks: protection of the approaches to Sydney and Halifax, and the maintenance of a watch along the shores of the Maritimes and Gulf of St Lawrence. Intensified coastal patrols would not be useful, the Admiralty advised. Additional ships should instead be concentrated at Halifax and Sydney where their principal role would be to screen convoys as they formed up and provide an anti-submarine escort during the first hours of passage. As well, separate escort forces would be required to provide two anti-submarine vessels for the protection of each convoy out to a distance of two to three hundred miles. Finally, the St Lawrence patrol should be strengthened so that it could also serve as a mobile striking force, "available to be sent anywhere." In February, Hose drafted a detailed scheme that, closely following the Admiralty's paper, allocated thirty-three vessels to Halifax for escort and local defence duties, forty-six to Sydney for the same tasks, and thirty-one to the St Lawrence force, also based on Sydney. The Admiralty and the Canadian government readily approved these proposals.[21]

The appeal to London had had the desired result of bringing a more generous and well-considered allocation of resources to the Canadian patrols. The Admiralty was now willing to turn over all thirty-six of the first batch of trawlers building in Canada on imperial account and thirty-six of the drifters. Before the close of navigation on the St Lawrence at the end of 1917, the first three Admiralty trawlers and thirty-eight drifters had arrived at Halifax. Fifteen drifters departed for imperial service, but the other vessels joined the Canadian patrol.[22]

Manpower inevitably created difficulties. Early in 1918 it was estimated that about 2300 personnel would be needed for the ships and bases of the expanded flotilla; slightly over 1500 were then available. Arrangements by the Admiralty to man the imperial trawlers and drifters slated for Canadian service provided essential reinforcements. At least 230 and perhaps as many as 330 ratings from the Newfoundland Royal Naval Reserve ultimately served in the vessels, as did some 200 members of the RNCVR's Overseas Division who were returned from the United Kingdom. That still left a substantial shortage, especially for billets that demanded experience and extensive training. The Admiralty admitted a moral responsibility to give further help but could spare only a limited number of officers and technical ratings. In February 1918, for example, the Canadians asked for 25 skippers to command patrol vessels and 100 engine specialists; the British could offer only four of the former and 28 of the latter. There was no alternative but to place unqualified personnel in key positions and rush recent recruits into service.[23]

Obtaining the faster and more heavily armed warships needed to protect shipping and chase down U-boats beyond the reach of the local defence flotillas at Halifax and Sydney was an insuperable problem. The Admiralty's scheme included six sloops or destroyers and six "fast trawlers" (probably "P-boats" with a speed of 20 knots and modern 4-inch guns) to form the bulk of the long-range escort forces and the striking group of the St Lawrence patrol. In March word came from London that fast trawlers could not be provided for "some months" owing to delays in the construction program and that no destroyers could be spared; Canada should, therefore, appeal to the United States Navy for assistance. The commander-in-chief was in a difficult position: for the past year the British government had been minimizing the threat to the western Atlantic while urging the United States to send its best anti-submarine vessels overseas. On pointing this out to the Admiralty, he received the distinctly unhelpful reply that "there is no intention to propose any alteration in policy." Admiral Grant responded that he could not but "concur in the view generally expressed this side that we are very open to a sudden attack and sinkings possibly of large troop transports and am afraid that this would very probably cause great popular commotion in Canada and the United States."[24] Captain Hose was more blunt. Without the destroyers or fast trawlers there would be "not one gun" in his force "which would be able to get within range of a U-cruiser before the patrol vessel would, in all probability, be sunk."[25]

Plans for the RCN's submarines, CC-1 and CC-2, to reinforce the east coast patrols came to naught. The British Columbia government had purchased these American H class boats from their Seattle builders at the outbreak of war and turned them over to the navy for operations from Esquimalt. In the spring of 1917 the Canadian government complied with the Admiralty's request that the vessels go overseas where they would be much more useful than in British Columbia. The submarines arrived at Halifax with their tender, HMCS *Shearwater*, in the fall of 1917 after a harrowing trip by way of the Panama Canal during which their machinery repeatedly broke down. Once the vessels were refitted, the Admiralty now suggested, they should remain on the Canadian coast because of the growing danger of transatlantic U-boat raids. Poorly equipped and swamped with work, the ship repair facilities at Halifax were unable to make the boats fully operational, however. Their principal employment was for anti-submarine exercises with patrol vessels on the Bras d'Or Lakes beginning in August 1918.[26]

Air patrols were another method of dealing with U-boats. Although effective aerial anti-submarine weapons had not yet been developed, aircraft had afforded nearly perfect protection to convoys they accompanied as escorts. U-boats inevitably submerged in the presence of aircraft, whose crews might score a lucky bomb hit or would most certainly summon anti-submarine warships. Unable to move at a speed of more than a few knots while submerged, the U-boat soon lost contact with the shipping it was pursuing and had no opportunity to attack. On 7 March 1918 the Admiralty urged the Canadian government to organize an air service on the Atlantic coast as soon as possible but could offer no equipment of any type.[27]

With Canadian complaints about the lack of British help ringing in his ears, Admiral Grant appealed to the United States Navy in mid-April. Destroyers could not be spared but the Americans were prepared to send six submarine chasers and two torpedo boats, all fully manned, for operations under Canadian control. Grant also arranged meetings between American, British, and Canadian officers at Washington on 20 April and Boston on 23 April 1918 to secure further help for the RCN. Rear Admiral Spencer S. Wood, commandant of the First Naval District at Boston, agreed that his forces would assume full responsibility for both sea and coastal patrols as far as the 65th meridian (Lockeport, Nova Scotia), including the mouth of the Bay of Fundy. The Americans would also supply aircraft and personnel for Halifax and Sydney, while the Canadian Naval Air Service organized. Captain Hose brightened, believing that the aircraft would provide the offensive power his little ships lacked, but it soon emerged that the USN could not make good on the offer until mid-August.[28]

The eight American vessels arrived at Halifax during the latter part of May. Although the two old torpedo boats, *Tingey* and *DeLong*, were suitable only for patrols close to port, the submarine chasers proved extremely useful. Their 110-foot long wooden hulls carried powerful engines that delivered an impressive speed of 16 knots. For that reason, they were employed as the long-range escort force; three of the vessels moved to Sydney when the HS series began to sail from that port again at the beginning of July. Their armament, however, was light, including six depth charges and only a single 6-pounder gun.[29]

During May as well, the delivery of additional drifters and trawlers began as the ice cleared from the St Lawrence. By the end of July the last of the thirty-six drifters from imperial contracts and all but three of the forty-eight trawlers from Canadian and imperial orders had arrived on the east coast. About sixty vessels were based at Sydney, including those allocated to the St Lawrence patrol, and forty at Halifax. But grand totals can be deceptive. Most of the trawlers and drifters had only recently been commissioned, and their machinery needed a good deal of "shaking down" before it could be depended upon. Hasty construction under wartime conditions had also taken a toll; five of the named trawlers, for example, experienced such chronic engine trouble they were seldom sent on patrol. The Admiralty, moreover, had not yet delivered guns to arm several of the trawlers. Most seriously, ships' companies throughout the flotilla included a large proportion of personnel with little training.[30]

Progress was being made, however, in the fitting of depth charges and hydrophones. In February, one hundred and forty depth charges had been on hand, and a further seven hundred were ordered. These were issued on a scale of six per auxiliary patrol ship and five for each trawler and drifter. It appears that additional charges were carried as they became available; in mid-June, for example, *Trawler 30* stowed a total of ten, while a later report shows that *Cartier* had eight. In early 1918 there had been twenty-seven non-directional "general service hydrophones" available on the east coast, and orders had been placed in England for the more capable Mark II directional hydrophones. In mid-August, the latter equipment had already been installed on five vessels and was being fitted in at least three others.[31]

Slight as was the material help available from the United Kingdom, the Admiralty was able to give full and timely intelligence about transatlantic U-boat operations through the interception and decryption of German wireless traffic. The information was supplied to the United States Navy through Rear Admiral W.S. Sims, commander of American naval forces in Europe, and by cable to the commander-in-chief North America and West Indies who passed it by telegraph to Canadian authorities.

On 3 and 16 May 1918 the first intelligence reached the Canadian service: a U-boat had sailed from Germany about 19 April to strike at shipping off United States ports and could be expected at any time after 20 May. The boat was a converted mercantile submarine of the *Deutschland* class: the new long-range types of which the Admiralty had warned the Canadian government in January were still incomplete. Earlier operations by *Deutschland*s showed that because their lightly built hulls were more vulnerable to depth charges than those of fighting boats, they were less likely to make submerged attacks or strike at convoys. However, the converted merchantman had a formidable gun armament, including two 5.9-inch, for surface operations, and carried about 40 mines.[32]

The campaign in the western Atlantic opened, as the Admiralty had warned, on 25 May when U-151 attacked three American schooners south of the Delaware River. By 23 June, when the submarine was homebound, she had destroyed twenty-two vessels of some 52,000 tons off the central Atlantic states. This cruise set the pattern for U-boat operations in North American waters during the rest of the 1918 season. The boat made no attacks on escorted shipping and reserved her torpedoes for submerged attacks on large steamers that carried defensive armament. Otherwise the submariners sank their victims with gunfire, or boarded vessels and placed time-fused charges. Perhaps the most notable victory, however, was the destruction of the tanker *Herbert L. Pratt* which on 3 June ran into a minefield the submarine had laid off the mouth of Delaware Bay.[33]

By the end of June the Admiralty knew that another converted mercantile submarine, U-156, was on her way to North American waters. Within a week German wireless traffic revealed that the recently completed "cruiser" U-140 was following her.[34] Precisely where the boats would operate was not yet clear, but the Admiralty asked Admiral Grant what could be done if the Halifax approaches came under attack. Grant replied that although the First US Naval District was prepared to reinforce the Canadian patrols, the force would still be too weak to prevent a U-boat from operating close to the port or to provide convoys with long-range anti-submarine escorts. Ships en route to Halifax for convoy should be redirected to New York, New England ports, and Sydney. This proposal was related to a larger scheme for diverting shipping from threatened ports, but Grant was particularly worried about Halifax. The lightness of the forces there created special dangers because the troopships that sailed from the port were desirable targets, and the great width of the continental shelf off that part of Nova Scotia made it possible for the enemy to plant mines up to 130 miles from the harbour mouth.[35]

As Grant considered the Halifax problem, U-156 was approaching American waters. On 7–8 July she destroyed two large sailing vessels some four hundred miles southeast of Sable Island. Running in along 40 degrees latitude, U-156 then laid mines near the Fire Island light vessel. During the late morning of 19 July the 13,000 ton cruiser USS *San Diego* struck one of the mines and sank in twenty minutes with the loss of six of her crew. Two days later, the submarine came out of a fog bank within sight of vacationers on the beaches of southeastern Cape Cod and bombarded a tug and four barges under tow.

The first warning that U-boats would soon strike further north appears to have reached Canadian naval authorities on 26 July. Instructions for U-156 to operate in the Gulf of Maine had been decrypted at the Admiralty, but the news was not timely: on 27 July headquarters learned that the boat had already sunk an American schooner there five days before. The Admiralty also passed word that another U-boat had been assigned to the Gulf of Maine. This was derived from the earliest intelligence that yet a third submarine, the large purpose-built minelayer U-117, had been assigned to North American waters; U-140 was at the time approaching the central Atlantic states, the area to which she confined her operations. On 2 August, the Canadian shipping control and intelligence staff at Halifax broadcast a warning to all vessels that U-boats might be encountered anywhere between the latitudes of Cape Hatteras and Halifax.[36]

The danger to Canadian waters materialized quickly. After sunrise on 3 August the crew of the four-master schooner *Dornfontein* came ashore in lifeboats at Gannet Rock at the mouth of the Bay of Fundy, with the news their ship had been set afire by U-156 the day before. The trawler *Festubert*, then at St John, proceeded to search the area but found no trace of the submarine.[37] By that time U-156 was east of Seal Island, off the southern tip of Nova Scotia, where she set charges in four small American fishing schooners. The next day, the submarine destroyed the Canadian schooner *Nelson A.* twenty-five miles off Shelburne and, on the morning of 5 August, bombed the schooners *Agnes B. Holland* and *Gladys M. Hollett* near the Lahave Banks. Like the *Dornfontein*, none of these vessels was equipped with wireless, so word of the sinkings did not reach Halifax until the crews rowed to shore and notified authorities, at least twelve hours after the event.[38]

While U-156 advanced along the south shore of Nova Scotia, the flotilla at Halifax was hard pressed to carry out its basic mission of convoy escort and patrol in the harbour approaches. Engine defects had laid up five vessels in addition to those undergoing longterm refits and routine maintenance, while guns had not yet arrived to arm two of the recently delivered trawlers. When convoy HC-12 sailed in the early afternoon of 4 August, therefore, the warships available for service were fully occupied in providing the routine protection laid down in standing orders; under the charge of the flotilla were seventeen merchantmen laden with cargo and over 12,500 Canadian and American troops.[39]

In the morning the minesweeping division had swept to about fifty miles beyond the harbour mouth. Following were the three American submarine chasers who preceded the convoy by two hours to make an anti-submarine patrol. Sailing with the convoy was the "forming up escort and outer patrol force," which was organized in three divisions, each including one trawler and two drifters (there was probably a second trawler in one division). As the submarine chasers took over the van outside the harbour, the trawlers and drifters did their best to remain in company until dusk, but they must have fallen back as their patrol speed was only eight knots. One division then returned to port, while the others cruised in the outer patrol areas, one toward Shelburne and the other toward Sable Island.

Next morning, shortly after sunrise on 5 August, the British tanker *Luz Blanca* left port bound for Mexico. Her master had ignored instructions from the shipping control staff to wait until dusk and to zig zag. At 1140 local time, when the ship was about thirty-five miles south of the Sambro light vessel, a heavy explosion shook the after section. One tank flooded, but she was still able to make way and turned for port. Twenty minutes later U-156 broke the surface but then apparently dived. At 1400 the submarine reappeared and opened gunfire at a range of approximately four miles. The ship's RNR gun crew gamely returned fire, even though the torpedo hit had damaged the training gear on their 12-pounder. During the gun battle, which lasted for a full hour, the tanker sustained at least two serious hits, one of which wrecked the lower bridge, killing two crew members; the other stopped her screw and settled the issue. At about 1500 the crew took to the boats while U-156 continued to shell the hulk, which soon burst into flames. The ship was then seventeen miles south of the Sambro light vessel.[40]

Word of the attack was first received at HMC Dockyard shortly before 1345. (*Luz Blanca*'s wireless had been damaged in the torpedo explosion; the message presumably came from the American steamer *F.Q. Barstow* which was within visual distance of the attack.) Commander P.F. Newcombe, RN, who commanded the patrol depot at Halifax and, under Hose's direction, exercised operational control over the outer patrol and escort vessels, had the information broadcast to the trawler-drifter division still at sea, USS *Tingey*, then on the inner patrol, and the submarine chasers who were returning from HC-12 (one of these, SC-247, was short of fuel and had returned to port). *Tingey* was closest to the scene but did not receive the wireless broadcasts until 1630 (wireless procedures throughout the flotilla showed up badly that day). The trawler-drifter division, on the other hand, responded promptly to the first signals. These vessels should have arrived while U-156 was still on the surface, but they did not find anything in the hazy, thick weather. Newcombe subsequently blamed the division's senior officer for the failure. Thus it was the submarine chasers which were first on the scene, apparently at about 1700. They picked up two boatloads of survivors and made a hydrophone search for U-156 without result. Meanwhile, Newcombe hustled SC-247 and the remaining two trawler-drifter divisions back out to sea; he also pulled the trawler *St Eloi* out of dockyard hands and despatched her. At 2000 these vessels began to scour the vicinity of the attack. By the next morning (6 August 1918) the Halifax ships were making a general search of the Nova Scotia coast in co-operation with two trawler-drifter divisions from Sydney.

Admiral Kingsmill, in Ottawa, soon intervened. A report from Sydney on the sixth revealed that five of the auxiliary patrol ships were engaged in "domestic" tasks, assisting in the removal of cargo from a wrecked merchant ship, carrying coal and supplies to isolated light houses, and inspecting life-saving stations. Naval headquarters instructed Hose to recall the vessels for anti-submarine duty and asked what special orders he had given on learning of U-156's thrust into Canadian waters. None, came the answer from Sydney, because the standard patrols had been organized expressly to meet this contingency. Kingsmill's reaction has not come to light, but he was obviously unhappy, having already delivered an admonition about the necessity of deploying every vessel possible in an emergency. At the end of the month, headquarters handed virtually complete operational control of the Halifax outer patrol and escort flotilla over to Vice-Admiral Story, superintendent of the dockyard; Commander Newcombe, Hose's subordinate, was now responsible only for training and discipline. This was an attempt to clear up longstanding difficulties created by the muddled lines of authority at Halifax, but the events on 5 August undoubtedly contributed to the outcome.[41]

U-156's appearance had the greatest impact on the convoy system. Control over shipping on the coastal routes between Newfoundland, Nova Scotia, the Bay of Fundy, and the Gulf of Maine was greatly tightened; merchant vessels were often gathered into small convoys at Halifax, Sydney, and St John's under the escort of whatever warships were at hand. Certainly this system was neither rigorously organized nor complete, for the meagre strength of the flotilla made it impossible to maintain a regular schedule of sailings. The surviving logs of the auxiliary patrol ships and trawlers leave no doubt, however, that escort of coastal shipping was a major commitment for the vessels from August 1918 until the end of the war.[42]

Still more important were changes in the transatlantic convoys. Within hours of the attack on *Luz Blanca*, Admiral Grant began to make the diversions he had suggested the previous month. Ships from the St Lawrence for HC-13, the next medium convoy to sail, would assemble at Sydney rather than Halifax, while those from American ports would gather at New York. The two sections would then rendezvous at sea, clear of the danger area. Hose scrambled to provide what little protection he could for the ships coming down from Montreal, and the Sydney section sailed on 14 August, only two days later than the normal eight-day cycle. Meanwhile, on 8 August, the Admiralty informed naval headquarters that in future all ships for HC convoys would assemble at Quebec City. Wireless intelligence received that same day that another converted mercantile submarine would soon sail to mine the approaches to Halifax and St John's in mid-September possibly influenced the decision. By 10 August, the Admiralty was also aware that the minelayer U-117 would strike off Halifax and Cape Race after her initial operations in American waters.[43]

Estimates that U-156 was still lurking in the Halifax approaches were wrong. Actually, the U-boat had immediately headed to the southwest and sank the Swedish steamer *Sydland* about 180 miles off Cape Cod on 8 August. British submarine trackers did not correct their appreciation, believing the culprit to be U-117, expected to arrive at this time. U-117 had indeed turned up on schedule, and ran amok among the Georges Bank fishing fleet, about 100 miles from Cape Cod, on 10 August before continuing on to the southwest. Meanwhile U-156 sank two more steamers in American waters before heading back toward Nova Scotia on the homeward leg of her voyage.

Although not as successful as her first sojourn in Canadian waters, U-156's second appearance caused at least as great a stir. During the early hours of 21 August the crew of the steam trawler *Triumph* landed in boats at Canso and told a startling story: the previous day their ship had been overtaken by a U-boat whose commander had put a crew, two light guns, wireless equipment, and a supply of bombs aboard the Canadian vessel. Hose despatched three auxiliary patrol ships, two trawlers, and three American submarine chasers from Halifax to search the fishing banks off Canso and warn the fishing fleet there. Submarine chasers and trawlers from Sydney joined the hunt later in the day. Word soon came from the commander-in-chief that an American destroyer and eighteen submarine chasers, promised as reinforcements for Halifax after the sinking of *Luz Blanca*, were on their way and would search east of Nova Scotia during the passage. In addition, the USN despatched two patrol vessels to the Grand Banks.[44]

Triumph had set to work as soon as her new crew ran up the German naval ensign. The trawler and the submarine sank five schooners on 20 August and two on 21 August. Nothing more was heard from the raiders for three days; *Triumph*'s coal would have been exhausted in that period and evidence suggests the Germans scuttled her. In the early hours of 25 August U-156 reappeared off the Newfoundland coast, about seventy miles west of St Pierre where she sank the small British steamer *Erik*. Later that morning the U-boat fell in with a group of four fishing schooners about forty-five miles southwest of St Pierre and proceeded to sink the vessels with charges.

At about 1345, when U-156 was finishing off the last of the schooners, a Canadian patrol arrived from the northwest. *Trawler 22*, *Cartier*, *Hochelaga*, and *Trawler 32* were proceeding line abreast at intervals of three to four miles, on a southerly course. *Hochelaga*'s crew sighted two schooners at a distance of six miles, and the ship altered to an intercepting easterly course, intending to warn the fishermen about the U-boat threat. *Trawler 32* followed, but the other vessels continued on the original line of advance. At approximately 1400, when the distance was about four miles, *Hochelaga*'s crew saw a U-boat near the schooners—one of which instantly disappeared. The patrol vessel's commanding officer then altered course away from the submarine and back towards *Cartier* and *Trawler 22*, ordering *Trawler 32* to follow.

> On seeing *Hochelaga* make this last alteration in course and hoist a flag, Lieutenant McGuirk in *Cartier* altered course to North 25° East (Magnetic) to meet her. The time during which *Hochelaga* was steering towards *Cartier* was approximately seven or eight minutes. At the expiration of this period, when the vessels were about a mile apart, *Cartier* signalled to *Hochelaga* "What is your signal and what have you seen?" *Hochelaga* replied "Submarine bearing East," *Cartier* then altered course to the East, *Hochelaga* and Trawler No. 32 altering to the same course and coming up *Hochelaga* on *Cartier*'s port quarter, and Trawler 32 on *Hochelaga*'s port quarter. *Cartier* then signalled to *Hochelaga* to increase to full speed. Shortly after *Hochelaga* signaled to *Cartier* "Do you see reinforcements astern, don't you think it better to wait for them?" *Cartier* replied "Negative."
>
> The Submarine had by this time submerged while the schooner which had been seen from *Hochelaga* to disappear had capsized [sic] and could be seen on her side. *Cartier*, *Hochelaga* and Trawler No. 32 came up to her and cruised round; some empty dories were seen, but no signs of the submarine.[45]

Hochelaga's captain had had a failure of nerve. Instructions issued by Admiral Kingsmill to the east coast patrol a few weeks before had stressed that although the U-boats had a great advantage over the ships of the Canadian flotilla in gun power, the submariners, unwilling to risk even slight damage at such a great distance from home, were unlikely to stand and fight. Patrol vessels should therefore not hesitate to attack, especially if additional ships were within supporting distance. The U-boat would probably dive, thereby enabling the surface vessels to conduct a hunt with hydrophones and depth charges. If the Canadian ships inflicted any damage with their guns or underwater weapons, it would greatly reduce the submarine's chances of returning to base through the Royal Navy's defences in the North Sea and English Channel. There could be no excuse for *Hochelaga*'s captain. He had been on active service with the navy since September 1914, received a commission in the RNCVR in June 1915, and held ship commands since January 1917. A court martial at Halifax on 5 October 1918 found that he "did not, from negligence or other default, on sight of the enemy which it was his duty to engage use his utmost exertion to bring his ship into action." He was immediately dismissed from the service.[46]

As it happened, U-156's good fortune had also run out. After the encounter with *Hochelaga* the boat was able to destroy only one small schooner before shaping course for home on 30 August. On about 25 September U-156 was sunk in the Anglo-American minefields between Scotland and Norway; she was the only raider that failed to return from North American waters.

During the last week of August, U-117 had also come up from American waters as the Admiralty had warned. Between 24 and 30 August she sank four schooners and a steamer, the first of them south of Sable Island and the last about 150 miles southeast of St John's, as she headed for Germany. Because U-117 operated further off the coast than U-156, the shipwrecked crews were not able to reach shore and give word of the sinkings until twenty-four hours after the event. Some precautions had already been taken, however. In response to the intelligence received on 10 August that the submarine might lay mines in the vicinity of Cape Race, the RCN had despatched two trawlers equipped with sweeps to St John's, while the auxiliary patrol ships and trawlers escorting shipping to that port and patrolling the fishing banks also kept a watch on the area.[47]

Additional resources had become available during August to assist the Canadian flotilla in meeting its expanded commitments. With the delivery of 12-pounder guns early in the month, it was possible to arm seven trawlers that had recently arrived at Sydney and Halifax; no guns were available, however, for two of the last three Admiralty trawlers nearing completion at Great Lakes shipyards. Although the American destroyer and eighteen submarine chasers that patrolled off Nova Scotia on 22–24 August soon departed for operations in the United States sector west of 65° W, on 24 August the USS *Yorktown*, an old gunboat of 1710 tons with 5-inch guns, arrived at Halifax and appears to have remained on station there until at least the latter part of September. More important was the arrival on 19 August of a United States Navy air detachment at the seaplane station the Canadian government was building at Bakers Point near Dartmouth. Hastily assembling four Curtis HS2L flying boats, the American aviators made their first flights on 25 August. By the last week in September a similar detachment was ready for operations from North Sydney. The seaplanes provided cover for convoys at distances of up to eighty miles from port and performed coastal searches, supplying much-needed support for the outer patrol and escort divisions at Halifax and Sydney.[48]

An increment in the strength of the anti-submarine forces on the Canadian Atlantic coast was more than overbalanced by the RCN's responsibility for the defence of HC convoys from the new assembly port of Quebec. The route from that city to the open ocean, either through the Cabot Strait or the Strait of Belle Isle, was some six hundred miles long, and convoys had to be protected over the whole of it. U-boats could readily evade hunting forces in the deep channels and broad waters of the gulf but could easily locate and attack shipping confined to restricted routes by the Magdalenes, Anticosti Island, and the mouth of the St Lawrence River. Naval headquarters explained these difficulties to the commander-in-chief at the end of August, but he responded that "the Admiralty would not hear of any alteration." Admiral Grant did arrange for the release to the RCN of fifteen additional drifters and five trawlers from the second batch of twenty-four building in Canada on imperial account. Because of delays in construction only two of the new trawlers ultimately joined the Canadian flotillas, but during September eighteen drifters took up station. The bulk went to form patrols at Gaspé and the Strait of Belle Isle (a trawler from the St Lawrence patrol supported each of these forces), two operated from Rimouski, Quebec, and two reinforced the trawler-sweepers at St John's.[49]

Because Halifax was now being used primarily to escort coastwise shipping, Admiral Grant hoped that much of the force there could be sent to the St Lawrence. The Canadians were understandably reluctant to make substantial cuts at their main naval base. In the end, only three auxiliary patrol ships that had operated from Halifax in the wake of U-156's first visit, three or four trawlers, and a few drifters moved to Sydney.[50]

HC-16, the first convoy to assemble at Quebec, sailed on 3 September. From that time the auxiliary patrol ships assumed a greatly increased importance as the only vessels in the Canadian patrols with the speed and endurance necessary to escort the medium convoys through the gulf. When the convoys went by way of the Cabot Strait, as did HC-16, the American submarine chasers based at Sydney reinforced the escort, while trawlers and drifters of the Sydney flotilla mounted extra patrols in the strait and its approaches.[51]

The last submarine to operate in Canadian waters was the *Deutschland* herself, renamed U-155 after conversion into a long-range raider. As already noted, German signals decrypted in early August had revealed her mission and sailing date. When on 13 September the boat made an unsuccessful torpedo and gun attack on the British steamer *Newby Hall* about one hundred miles southeast of Sable Island, the Admiralty immediately warned the naval authorities on the Canadian east coast to expect both minelaying off St John's and Halifax and attacks on shipping on the routes between those ports. Four days later U-155 slipped in off Halifax to lay eight mines close to the Sambro light vessel and another six approximately ten miles southeast of Peggy's Cove. One mine that immediately broke away from its moorings was discovered floating and was destroyed with gunfire by the patrol vessel *Grilse* on 18 September. None of the others was swept up before the end of the war. They had been laid in fields that were clear of the war channels into Halifax where the minesweeping flotilla performed daily searches. Although this also meant that mines did no damage, the patrol vessels which used Sambro light vessel as a rendezvous were lucky to escape unharmed.[52]

Lingering in Canadian waters for at least a week after laying the mines, U-155 was rewarded only with the destruction of a single fishing trawler south of Sable Island. Once again Canadian warships patrolled the banks and warned fishermen, but this effort was not allowed to interfere with the protection of ocean convoys and the sailing of convoys on the coastal routes. As a further precaution the medium convoys from Quebec were now routed through the Strait of Belle Isle; plans had been made for a similar diversion of the Sydney convoys, but these were never carried out.[53]

Despite U-155's failure to inflict significant damage, the senior officers of the RCN and their political masters were profoundly unhappy about the course of events in 1918 and even more worried about what would happen in 1919. U-boats of the powerful new cruiser class would undoubtedly turn up, operating with the benefit of complete intelligence about the shipping and defences in Canadian waters. In September, C.C. Ballantyne, minister of the naval service, had written personally to Admiral Lord Wemyss, First Sea Lord at the Admiralty, to ask once again if Great Britain could supply equipment and armament for the construction of destroyers in Canada. Ballantyne was also dissatisfied with the performance of naval headquarters during the crises of August and believed a fundamental shake up was necessary.[54]

At the end of September, Hose reported that the shortage of personnel was having such a grievous effect on the efficiency of the patrols that the system of manning and training would have to be entirely revamped for 1919. The requirements for manpower laid down in early 1918 had been for the bare minimum actually needed to serve in the ships and shore establishments. In fact a "considerable reserve" of both officers and ratings was essential to cover temporary vacancies and allow systematic training. At the best of times the crews of the patrols spent only eight days out of twenty in port, and however energetically the instructional staffs worked, "it will be realized that it is impossible to fit in Hydrophone, Signal, Minesweeping, Depth Charges, and Gunnery Instruction, clean and refit, coal and store the ships, and also provide working parties." The result was that, although the officers and ratings of most crews were experienced seamen, they were "untrained, not only in the technical knowledge required to handle the weapons and offensive appliances on board the ships, but also in service discipline."[55]

The dearth of qualified personnel also placed an enormous burden on the handful of professional officers who commanded the shore establishments. Subordinates could not carry out even the most routine tasks without close supervision. Kingsmill was deeply worried during August and September that the health of some of the key officers might collapse under the strain. Certainly they were so overwhelmed by administrative duties that it was impossible for them to maintain a firm grasp of developments at sea.[56]

Senior officers, too, often worked at cross purposes. As the war ended, Admirals Story and Hose were again arguing over who controlled which parts of the Halifax flotilla. This was symptomatic of organizational difficulties that bedevilled the whole of the British and Canadian organization for the control and defence of shipping that had grown up in North America under the sporadic guidance of a remote and distracted Admiralty.

Most galling for the RCN was the lack of suitable ships. Hose vented his frustration at the end of October 1918 with a far-fetched scheme for the following summer. Observing that the existing ships of the patrols were "powerless to prevent the enemy from acting when and where he pleases against the shipping off Canadian Coasts," he advised that thirty-three destroyers and four submarines comprised the "minimum defence force required." Commander J.P. Gibbs, RN, director of operations at headquarters, observed that this was "quite outside the realm of practical politics," but he did believe that Canada should construct six large destroyers and eight submarines in her own yards. In any case, Gibbs warned, it would be "useless to build good ships ... if there was not a thoroughly efficient Dockyard to keep them in repair." The existing facilities at Halifax had failed to keep pace with the maintenance requirements of the existing flotilla, technically unsophisticated as those vessels were. It was scarcely worth refurbishing the damaged and decrepit buildings at the dockyard; an entirely new complex should be constructed. Kingsmill forwarded

Gibbs's paper to the minister, with a sharp reminder that the Laurier program projected in 1909–10 would have provided much of what was now needed. In fact, Ballantyne received a note from the British First Sea Lord at this same time that once more discouraged the construction of destroyers in Canada but that did promise that the United States would supply six of the warships early in the new year. All of this correspondence became irrelevant the moment it was completed; on 5 November Ballantyne called a halt to planning for 1919 in view of Germany's impending collapse.[57]

The encounter with the U-boats in 1918 contributed nothing to the fighting tradition that a young service, buffeted by political controversy and nearly bereft of public support, desperately needed. On the two occasions when Canadian warships were in a position to strike back at the enemy, their officers had fumbled badly. Gilbert and Sullivan might have written the script. The U-boats faced such slight danger of retribution that, in contrast to the deadly battle being waged in the eastern Atlantic, they were able to conduct freewheeling operations with not a little flair, rather like good-natured pirates. In most cases the submarines could make surface attacks and take full precautions for the safety of ships' crews. When it emerged that the steamer *Erik* lacked sufficient boats for the crew, U-156 took them on board, while searching for another victim with a surplus of boats. But the schooner *Willie G.*, the submarine's next target, was short of dories, so U-156 spared her and put *Erik*'s crew on board. Earlier in August, a German-speaking member of *Dornfontein*'s crew had had a chance to chat with one of the submariners; the latter produced a photograph of himself, with the address of his mother in Hamburg on the back, and asked the Canadian seaman to mail it if he heard that U-156 had been sunk. Although the American and Canadian press in reporting the U-boat attacks emphasized Hun brutality, such vignettes as these led some newspapers to refute a growing sentiment that the U-boat crews were actually gentlemen, forced by difficult circumstances to do a nasty job. The German officers had been hoping for such an effect. They explained to many of the seamen they cast adrift that the object of the attacks was not to inflict death and injury but to sink ships as a warning to President Wilson (they never mentioned Sir Robert Borden) of the futility of continuing the war.[58]

Yet the Germans had expended a good deal of effort in Canadian waters for very meagre returns. Only two substantial vessels—*Luz Blanca* of 4868 tons, and the steamer *Bergsdalen* of 2500 tons—had been destroyed, the latter by U-117 in a torpedo attack on 27 August. The fishing vessels of 250 tons or less that accounted for the bulk of the submariners' victories were attacked largely because the U-boats could not find more worthwhile targets. U-156 reported by wireless that although there was plenty of shipping between New York and Halifax, little could be found to the north of the latter port; the captain of U-117 was reduced to asking the masters of ships he sank where the steamer routes were located and showed his exasperation by threatening to take one of them prisoner if he did not co-operate. Here lay the great achievement of the Canadian flotilla. During late August more than a dozen steamers had travelled between Sydney and St John's through the waters patrolled by U-156 and U-117, but they had sailed in groups under the protection of trawlers and auxiliary patrol ships; as a recent author put it, the great virtue of convoy was that "the ocean suddenly seemed to the U-boats to be devoid of shipping."[59]

The ultimate object of the Royal Navy's operations during the First World War was to ensure the "safe and timely" arrival of the merchant shipping upon which Britain's survival depended. All-out efforts to hunt down and destroy U-boats failed to reduce their numbers; in the end, convoy proved to be the only way to secure the Atlantic sea lanes. The Canadian patrols made a small but significant contribution to the success of the convoy system. That contribution must be measured not only by the number of merchantmen that sailed safely and on schedule but also by the fact that Great Britain did not have to divert one major anti-submarine warship from the critical battle in the eastern Atlantic to protect the coastal waters of Canada and Newfoundland.

Chapter 7

INSHORE ASW IN THE SECOND WORLD WAR: THE U-BOAT EXPERIENCE

Michael L. Hadley

The German experience of anti-submarine warfare (ASW) in Canadian waters presents a "periscope view" unflattering to the Royal Canadian Navy.[1] It reveals Canadians as weak and inexperienced, operating in a "no-man's-land between Empire and USA."[2] The verdict could not have been otherwise. Indeed German submariners would now argue that the topic of inshore ASW is rather curious: there simply was not any ASW, or at least nothing particularly worrisome that one might care to discuss. As we know, Canada's commitment to playing as large a role as possible in alliance warfare, and as a consequence to the protection of convoys on the high seas, left limited resources for home defence. Admittedly, early defence scenarios had anticipated an inshore threat. But many of the vessels designed and rapidly built to counter it were siphoned off to serve as the "Far Distant Ships."[3] This created a "defence gap" that actually invited the U-boats' "Happy Time" off the Atlantic coast in 1942. Admiral Karl Dönitz saw in the North American coast a chance "to strike a real blow in waters in which anti-submarine defences were still weak."[4] The eastern seaboard thus "provided commanders with areas which [were] not hemmed in by defences and which offer[ed] better chances of success."[5] Canadians, as Germans later realized, eventually came to grips with the threat; their performance curves crossed in 1943, the turning point of the Battle of the Atlantic. At the outset, however, rapid expansion of the Canadian fleet, inadequate training, and outdated equipment led to an unstable mix, often resulting in a poor performance.[6] These facts refute the myth that Canada's burgeoning production of hulls brought with it the concomitant skills, technology, and experience to make an effective naval force. If the Canadians' radar and primitive sonar (then called asdic) hampered anti-submarine warfare, then geographic and hydrographic conditions exacerbated it even further. These the Germans regarded rather as a two-edged sword.

The advance of German submarines into Canadian waters was in every case a voyage of exploration. German naval headquarters do not appear to have drawn many navigational conclusions from the brief operations of U-117 off Halifax in 1918, nor did they publish their navigational atlases for the use of submarines in the Canadian zone until late 1942. Not until one year later did they publish the navigational *Sailing Directions* for the St Lawrence.[7] By this time the major U-boat sorties had already taken place, or else were so far advanced that the hydrographic office was of little help. In any event, Admiral Eberhard Godt, former Chief of Staff, Operations, to Karl Dönitz, frankly discounts the value of these well-documented navigational publications. Not only did they lay special emphasis on sub-surface characteristics of the Bay of Fundy—which was never a real interest of the German Navy—but to his mind were put together by "back-room headquarters boys" with little operational experience.[8]

Thus it was that the U-boats' experience of Canadian ASW was as much an initiation into the natural phenomenon of inshore undersea warfare as it was a confrontation with Canadian technology and tactics. It is perhaps noteworthy that German submariners were virtually unaware of any specifically "Canadian" fleet: their opponents were with slight exception deemed to be either "English" or American. Even as late as January 1945, U-1232 stood off the Sambro lightship in the Halifax Approaches in order to "teach the Yankees a lesson."[9] The Commander U-boats (BdU) accumulated reports in order to flesh out the profile of Canadian forces but, with the exception of a 1943 update of the coast of Nova Scotia, seems never to have provided current cumulative information on Canadian waters. Thus despite the sorties of seven U-boats into the St Lawrence in 1942, their successors of 1944 did not anticipate the conditions they actually found.

The Canadian zone, which U-boats now explored for the first time since 1918, comprised thousands of square miles of open ocean in which the submarine could choose its initiatives;[10] over 18,000 miles of coastline in the St Lawrence and maritime region alone offered potential seclusion. Germans discovered that hydrographic anomalies—particularly those on the Newfoundland Bank, Sable Island Bank, the St Lawrence River, and along the Nova Scotia coast—favoured the U-boat as well. As a counter to these natural barriers, a variety of inter-related technologies and techniques criss-crossed the battle zone. These ranged from the ocean-wide U-boat tracking systems provided by combinations of "Huff-Duff" (HF/DF) and Operational Intelligence, to close-range tactical sensors: hydrophones to within 20 miles, radar and radar detectors (GSR) from 3 to 16 miles, and asdic (sonar) from 1200 to 1500 metres.[11] U-boats sometimes guided themselves onto targets by monitoring the 600 m emergency broadcast band.

If Canada's lack of preparation for anti-submarine warfare in these unforgiving waters was indefensible, her territory was under the circumstances quite undefendable. It is therefore striking that German submariners did not wrest greater success from the tactical advantage that lay firmly in their hands. As it turned out, equipment failure was a root cause: about half their torpedoes were duds, and mines broke loose from their moorings and betrayed the fields of Halifax and St John's. This was a major source of a U-boat crew's frustration and anger: to have crossed the Atlantic under duress into unknown waters only to find one's armament inadequate for the task. Torpedoes spun in the tubes, became surface runners, and sometimes even bounced off the hulls of intended victims. Commander U-boats (BdU) responded in most cases by urging his crews to pay more attention to detail and to unceasing drill at sea.

The German submarine of the Second World War, we might be reminded, was essentially a submersible torpedo boat.[12] It operated primarily as a surface vessel. The Canadian operations of U-111 and U-123 in May-July 1941, for example, ran only 3 per cent submerged. That of U-69 in September–October 1942 ran 10 per cent submerged. Even as late as spring 1944, U-548 (which sank HMCS *Valleyfield*) ran only 40 per cent submerged.[13] The low silhouette of the surfaced submarine, and its speed of fifteen knots on diesel power, facilitated penetration of the opponent's defences. Designed for a maximum depth of 100 metres at up to seven and one-half knots for limited periods, it would cruise submerged at sixty metres; in emergencies it actually exceeded three times its "safe" depth. Equipped with a multiple hydrophone array forward, 3.7 cm and 2 cm guns, fourteen torpedoes, and, in the course of time, a series of relatively successful GSR radars or radar detectors, it is considered by many to have been the best integrated maritime combat system of the day.[14] The introduction of the schnorkel or "Snort" in 1943–4 in response to growing allied air superiority permitted longer periods submerged. Thus U-boats rarely surfaced in the St Lawrence during the summer of 1944. By the same token, however, low submerged speeds prevented U-boats from overtaking targets or from gaining optimum tactical position. As it turned out, the U-boat retained tactical advantage even when the Allies' operational intelligence knew of its general presence.

The Germans felt their tactical advantage strongly. For as Canada's

Director of Operations Division advised the Chief of Naval Staff in Ottawa in November 1944: "The Schnorkel [had] reduced the possibility of sighting to a minimum, and the only way in which the positioning of a U-boat was likely to be fixed [was] by offensive action on its part."[15] Had German *B-Dienst* decryption services intercepted Allied TAS (Torpedo-Anti-submarine) messages, submariners would have found the explanation for the closer screens by which the Allies responded. As one such message explained: "the introduction of the Schnorkel renders air reconnaissance and distance screens of little use for detection."[16] By way of amplification it continued: "Maximum Asdic protection is provided by forming an Asdic screen two miles ahead when the convoy is formed on a broad front and maintaining escorts both ahead and along the flanks when the convoy is formed on a narrow front." This, as will be seen, may account for the closer screens which U-boats encountered in inshore waters when preparing their close range attacks. Not until April 1945 did the complete submersible (Type XXI) enter service. Capable of operating submerged for extended periods without projecting any special breathing/exhaust gear above the surface, it could evade radar and visual detection completely. It became operational too late to influence the course of the war.

The question of Allied screens necessarily influenced the German submariner's tactical thinking. Indeed the shift to close screens alluded to above was somewhat of a surprise. For two years earlier, in 1942, the distance screens of ocean convoys had proven exceptionally exasperating. The war diary of U-533, for example, documents their effect upon the attackers of convoy ON-115.[17] Its commanding officer complained that distance screens frustrated attempts at gaining a good sighting of the convoy even in good visibility. The screens also exacerbated the U-boat's problem of maintaining contact and gaining advance firing position: once detected by escorts and pressed under, the U-boat lost all chance of observing the convoy's course changes for many hours. Daylight submerged attacks, the German commander noted, were impossible without "absolutely clear advance position at the extreme edge of visibility, with reference to distance screens." Distance screens almost completely precluded observations of the convoy's evening diversionary change of course. Since a U-boat could penetrate a distance screen only in darkness, the Germans remained for two to three hours completely dependent upon the escorts' behaviour. But even once having broken through the screen, Germans faced a further problem: finding the convoy was now "almost exclusively a matter of luck and [the U-boat captain's] instincts." In the case of convoy ON-115, once U-boats had gotten right inside where "earlier a U-boat was disturbed least of all" they faced a new challenge: "corvettes and destroyers [and] starshell" spoiled the chase.

Admiral Karl Dönitz's strategic aims in the North American war zone were twofold: tie down as many Allied defence forces as possible and, initially at least, sink as many independent vessels as possible so that convoys could not be formed. Significantly, wolf packs played virtually no role in this zone; it was the hunting ground of the solo sortie. Such independence offered special opportunities to aggressive U-boat commanders in the "Battle of the St Lawrence" of 1942; it restricted their more solicitous successors two years later in 1944. Had these later boats been more aggressive and not feared the Canadian direction-finding system, they would have been more successful. Indeed had they communicated with one another by radio as their predecessors had done, they would doubtless have picked off a considerable tonnage of the coastal trade even in the 1944 shipping season when the gulf was officially closed to overseas traffic. Significantly, the then current captain's manual *Handbuch für U-Bootskommandanten* insisted on the principle that each submarine was a loner even when operating in packs.[18] To be sure, whether situated in Berlin or Kerneval, BdU retained overriding authority and caused a striking amount of often routine and unnecessary message traffic by broadcasting his characteristic "whip-crack" signals: he assigned tasks, directed scenarios, formed and dissolved groups, called for weather reports, and upbraided the recalcitrant. (Most of these, by the way, were read by Commander Rodger Winn, RN, in operational intelligence in London, who communicated it to naval service headquarters in Ottawa.) Yet Dönitz also recognized the principle that the on-site commander was the best judge of his own circumstances. BdU in fact granted his commanders far greater freedom and latitude than the Allies often realized. Thus, for example, the first foray deep into Canadian territorial waters in the Gulf of St Lawrence in May 1942 was not the direct decision of German naval headquarters, but an initiative left to the independent judgment of a submarine commander.

U-boats undertook a number of major operations in Canadian waters in pursuit of Dönitz's policies. They successfully pursued their tonnage war by attacking the eastern seaboard from St John's to Charleston, NC, in Operation *Paukenschlag* from January to April 1942; their penetration of the St Lawrence River and Gulf via both Cabot Strait and the Strait of Belle Isle from May to October 1942 caused what has been called the "Battle of the St Lawrence." They successfully attacked the Wabana anchorage in Conception Bay, Newfoundland, in both 1942 and 1944 and sank ships at the loading docks of Bell Island. U-boats landed spies in Saint John, New Brunswick, and in New Carlisle, Quebec, and in 1943 established an automatic weather station in St Martin's Bay, Labrador, that was not discovered and identified as German until 1981.[19] They undertook two navigationally successful clandestine operations to embark German prisoners of war from Pointe de Maisonette in the Baie des Chaleurs, and from North Point, Prince Edward Island—in the latter case by navigating under the ice in a pre-schnorkel boat. They laid mines off St John's and Halifax. The amount of shipping sunk is a matter of record. Besides the heavy toll of merchantmen, Canada lost vital warships: HMCS *Raccoon, Charlottetown,* and *Magog* in the St Lawrence; HMCS *Valleyfield* on the Newfoundland Bank; and HMCS *Clayoquot* and *Esquimalt* in the Halifax Approaches.[20] Throughout the war, U-boat commanders faced the notorious difficulty of correctly assessing the class and tonnage of ships they sighted or attacked. Fairmiles became "corvettes," Bangors became "destroyers," merchant tonnage could vary as much as 25 to 30 per cent. This seems not to have been a case of wishful exaggeration, even though German naval headquarters had issued manuals on the subject of identification and tonnage estimation in 1939 and 1943.[21] Incorrect estimations of success exacerbated the problems of the German naval staff in evaluating its own tactical and strategic position.

Dönitz and his commanders knew, of course, that well-placed submarines could inflict damage beyond the obvious effect of lost tonnage. Even largely unsuccessful attacks could trigger reactions with far-reaching political, logistic, and psychological ramifications. German intelligence and propaganda exploited these situations, and broadcast in many languages their "news" of successes. These official military broadcasts (*Wehrmachtsberichte*) were an immediate morale-booster for the U-boat crews. They looked forward to the broadcasts and were of course delighted when the exploits of their own U-boat were extolled. A salient case is that of the St Lawrence operations of 1942. These had a noticeable impact upon Canadian public opinion, embittered federal-provincial relations, and eventually forced the Canadian government to close the gulf and river to Allied shipping. German submariners watched with interest. In the light of German monitoring of radio and press, and the German coverage of the St Lawrence situation, it is difficult to understand why BdU sent his U-boats into the zone two years later when closure was obviously public knowledge.

The "peacetime conditions" in Canadian inshore waters, to borrow a recurrent notation from U-boat war diaries and message logs, elicited the incredulity and sometimes even scornful criticism of U-boat commanders. The whole area seemed out of joint with the times. Accustomed to the blackout and the wartime illumination measure

(*Kriegsbefeuerungsmassnahme*) governing lights and beacons in the hazardous waters of the European war zone, they now enjoyed the full range of navigational aids. Indeed Canadian authorities remained convinced throughout the war of the necessity of maintaining full navigational facilities at all times except in utmost and immediate danger to shipping by enemy forces. The decision had not been taken lightly, and it seems justified under the circumstances.[22] If Germans found the waters peaceful, they found the defense forces both scarce and inadequate. Canada's desperate lack of escort and patrol vessels for home defence, and her apparent inability to grasp the dynamics of battle, led Germans to disparage her strategy. They held an equally jaundiced view of Canadian tactics; surface escorts, they observed, tended to break off firm sonar (asdic) contact instead of hunting to exhaustion or destruction.[23] The record is clear, however, that the combination of limited Canadian resources and a necessarily confining Allied escort doctrine precluded extended aggressive initiatives by the RCN.[24] Quite simply, having succeeded in pressing the U-boat down, escorts had to stick with the convoy.

A clear measure of the U-boat's tactical advantage may be seen by both its ease of access to Canadian waters and its almost complete immunity from Canadian forces. The record is clear that inshore navigation—despite the U-boats' often woefully inadequate navigation packs[25]—presented no real problems. Penetration of such waters as the Strait of Belle Isle, Wabana Anchorage, the St Lawrence River system as far inland as Rimouski, the Bay of Fundy—even navigation under the ice of Cabot Strait and a variety of clandestine operations—were relatively simple exercises. The ultimate failure of these clandestine operations cannot be blamed on the submarine as a covert combat system. Extraneous circumstances had foiled the ventures. The submariners quite correctly felt this most harshly. The U-boat's relative immunity from Canadian forces is equally clearly documented. Indeed, U-boat losses in Canadian waters were light. Significantly, none fell victim to the RCN. Of the nine U-boats sunk, four were lost to the United States Navy, two to US naval air, two to merchantmen, and one to the RCAF.[26] The effectiveness of inshore ASW should of course not be measured solely by numbers of U-boats sunk, but by the numbers pressed down and therefore held out of combat. This was a major feature of the German experience. German war diaries document repeated frustrations at the U-boat's inability to lock onto targets and pursue its quarry. Yet here again, major credit did not fall to the RCN but to the RCAF. The testimony of Paul Hartwig (U-517) for the period September to October 1942 in the St Lawrence is especially telling. He still recalls the stress that RCAF surveillance, "scare charges," and attacks caused his watch officers. Planes would unexpectedly swoop down on them, buzz them, drop out of a cloud, or skim low over the water out of the sun and drop bombs. Even when the attacks were inaccurate, the bombs made "one hell of a ruckus."[27] All his officers had been badly shaken by such attacks and consequently preferred to stand their watch submerged.

Germans would argue that electronic warfare (EW) ultimately proved a more effective defence barrier than depth charges and guns. Initially, however, bad weather formed Canada's first line of defence; from 1942 onwards, radar formed the second. Storms battered surfaced U-boats, severely hampering their radius of action. Gales reduced their speed and frustrated their attempts at gaining advance firing position ahead of oncoming targets. In fog, they ran blind and could not locate targets. Periscopes and deck guns froze and could only be thawed by submerging. Though radar rarely led Canadians to successful anti-submarine attacks[28] in the early years of the war, it emerged in 1942 as a tactically effective form of defence: Germans found themselves thwarted by it. By activating the Germans' search radar (GSR) or radar detectors, it too pressed the U-boat under and kept its crew in a state of misapprehension.

By 1942 the Germans' "FuMB" (GSR) passive warning devices could only detect the general bearing of foreign radar emissions—not yet the range.[29] Trials had begun in August 1942 with this "Metox" VHF heterodyne receiver for airborne ASV (air-to-surface-vessel) radar in the 1.5 metre range. Called the "Southern Cross" (or "Biscay Cross"), it was a primitive device that had to be dismantled before every diving manoeuvre. By June 1943 the "Naxos" (FuMB 7) detecting receiver was derived after analysis of the captured 9 cm "Rotterdam-Gerät." August 1943 saw the "Wanze" (W-Anz-g 2) automatic frequency scanner covering frequency ranges 150–200 cm. This had a "Borkum" back-up receiver in the 70–350 cm range. December 1943 saw experimental installation of "Hohentwiel" (FuMO) for both reception and ranging. The 1944 version, retaining the oscilloscope display of its predecessors, could detect a submarine at 5.5 kilometres and a 6000-ton merchant ship at 15 kilometres. May–June 1944 saw the "Tunis" (FuMB 26) 9 cm detector (the "Fliege") and a horn radiator ("Mücke") for the American 3 cm radar. On tests, the "Tunis" picked up aircraft from 300–1000 metres altitude at ranges from 40–80 kilometres. For the principal sorties against Canada, however, German U-boats carried the more primitive devices.

Even when not entirely convinced in the early days that they had been detected by radar—and in any event unable to gauge the range—Germans had little choice but to submerge. They returned to periscope depth once danger was deemed to have passed. It seems, therefore, that the combination of the RCAF microwave system in the St Lawrence gulf,[30] the airborne ASV metric and later centimetric radars—and to some extent the shipborne versions (SW1C, SW2C, RX/C, 286, 271)—triggered what the war diary of U-132 quite typically described in 1942 as its irritating and unproductive "dolphin-like" tour of the Canadian zone. It eventually forced the U-boat to withdraw altogether.

There were notable exceptions, however. U-69 sustained the steady maximum-amplitude squeal of its GSR during its three-hour approach to Quebec-Labrador convoy NL-9.[31] Despite the obvious conclusions that Canadians had caught the final critical phase of the attack, U-69 sank the ss *Carolus* off Pointe Mitis light; this was the deepest point inside the St Lawrence that a U-boat had yet reached. Ironically, the GSR warning had ceased on the final leg. This sudden break in what must have been the Canadians' firm radar contact hints at technical inexperience in the screen; but in all likelihood it was the result of the notoriously unreliable SW1C or SW2C fitted in Canadian escorts. As far as U-69 was concerned, the Canadian "radar operator was having a gorgeous snooze."[32] U-541 undertook a similar manoeuvre in the St Lawrence in 1944, but almost lost out to a bold response by HMCS *Norsyd*. Unfortunately for *Norsyd*, the range was too close to bring the powerful hedgehog ahead-throwing weapon to bear. From 1942 onwards, the mere presence of radar-equipped RCAF patrols caused what German intruders described as conditions "exactly like those in the Biscay." Indeed, U-802 discovered in August 1944 that the concentrated air surveillance south of Newfoundland meant that "pure Biscay conditions" prevailed here as well. The Germans were of course unaware in 1942 that the ASV of the time was virtually useless for detecting U-boats in the gulf;[33] indeed it did not begin to play a large part in mid-ocean operations until later that year. Nonetheless, it exerted a pressure which Germans alone could feel throughout the war. In effect, then, the mere presence of air cover denied U-boats freedom to move at will on the surface.

Submerged operations, with consequent reduction in speed and range, exposed U-boats to local anomalies in the frequently poor echo ranging conditions of the Canadian zone. At periscope depth they depended for target acquisition on optical sightings and hydrophone detection. Below that depth, of course, they derived target data from hydrophones alone. Here they encountered problems peculiar to shallow water (under 100 fathoms) which did not obtain in the deep water of the Atlantic convoy battles: radical fluctuations in underwater sound propagation and transmission. U-boats reported, in the words of U-132, that hydrophone conditions in the St Lawrence were "very bad and frequently deceptive" owing to "water layering." On two occasions on the Newfoundland Bank, for example, escorts with small convoys approached undetected to within 800 metres and actually overran the U-boats. But echo-ranging anomalies in shallow water, the Germans quickly discovered, also worked to the U-boat's advantage. U-43, for example, drew special comfort from the fact that "the considerable water-layering exerted a favourable effect on the U-boat for depth-keeping as well as [against the enemy's] sonar and hydrophone operations."[34] Once apprised of the situation, Admiral Dönitz forewarned his commanders of the tactical opportunities which these "unfavourable asdic conditions" provided.[35] Germans recognized that false echoes from seabed anomalies (reefs, wrecks, ridges), loud and troublesome reverberation, wide variation in ranging even over short transit distance and time all helped U-boats evade detection. Many knew they had actually been caught by sonar (asdic). The infrequent attacks following such detection confirmed their grasp of the Canadians' predicament. Where sonar had actually struck the target's reflecting surface—and technically speaking had detected the submarine—local anomalies (and perhaps the operator's inexperience) had prevented identification.[36] From the earliest days, therefore, U-boats chose areas of operation where the influence of anomalies was likely to be greatest. In this light U-boats escaped to the shallows after executing a torpedo attack—and not to the depths as the Canadian defenders expected. The bottoming technique—lying on the bottom with machinery switched off when being hunted or harrassed—proved particularly successful in coastal waters, the Strait of Belle Isle (U-111), Sable Island Bank (U-132), and in the Halifax Approaches (U-806 and U-1232). The Allies had not yet developed the system of attacking a submerged submarine after location by echo sounder.[37]

Significantly, Germans found that the thermal and saline layerings which sheltered U-boats from sonar (asdic) probes offered another tactical advantage. In the St Lawrence in particular they provided a solid shelf on which the U-boats could rest silently with engines stopped at what submariners called "lurking stations." Here it was not even necessary to operate the automatic trim damper or hovering gear. According to the record of U-541 in the Gulf of St Lawrence in 1944, for example, the water layers bore the vessel evenly, concealed it, and made the crew feel "as secure as in the bosom of Abraham."[38] At this period U-802 recorded lying suspended in the St Lawrence mouth with engines stopped and a clear periscope view of the tactical zone without betraying its presence to Allied hydrophones. At other times, however, the same anomalies proved worrisome: "the shifting water layers," in the typical words of one war diary, sometimes thwarted an otherwise routine dive or caused a sudden buoyancy. Paul Hartwig (U-517) frequently "damned the layers," his war diary reveals; they frustrated the smooth execution of otherwise swift and calculated diving manoeuvres.

German successes derived as much from random searches as from effective advance positioning. Whereas the former depended upon the unexpected and fortuitous approach of a victim (ss *Caribou*, HMCS *Charlottetown*, and *Shawinigan*), the latter depended upon astute assessment of the tactical situation (loss of HMCS *Clayoquot* and *Esquimalt*, and the attack of U-1232 on Boston-Halifax convoy BX-141). Sound intelligence and deduction played varying roles in both of these situations. It is significant that while *B-Dienst* decryption of Allied signals frequently kept German commanders apprised of potential tactical situations and possible targets, it never really led directly to any successful actions. Unescorted merchant vessels, of which there were many even as late as 1942, were relatively easy prey once they had come within torpedo range. Obviously, the German encounter, either with independently routed vessels or with "rompers" and "stragglers" from convoys, confronted them only with very basic ASW: the victim's defensive zig-zags, radical course changes, and in isolated cases, effective use of deck guns. The spirited fight of the ss *Bayou Chico*, a straggler some six miles astern of her outbound overseas convoy HX-181 on the Sable Island Bank, is a good example. She took aggressive action against the attacking U-754, purposefully closed the range, and bombarded the enemy with what the German submariners recorded as indeed well-placed shells. The freighter's protracted evasive action prevented U-754 from getting into firing position. Her emergency call (which the U-boat monitored) summoned a Bolingbroke from Sydney's 119 Bomber Squadron. In the words of U-754's war diary, the bomber forced the U-boat to crash dive under the "well-placed bombs" of two attacks.

Whatever the target, whether single ships or convoys, U-boats preferred to effect torpedo attacks at close range: anywhere from 400 to 1200 metres. German torpedo tactics reveal the close-quarters problems of Canadian ASW screens and tactical doctrine. We see this in three actual models: the single-ship convoy with single escort; the single-ship convoy with two-ship escort; and the multiple-ship convoy with multiple screen. Germans found none of them difficult. For once within the required close range, perspectives changed rapidly and the gaps in the screen opened fast.

When firing the straight-running contact torpedo, Germans were of course largely confined to a firing angle of 90° to the target's course. With the introduction of the FAT and LUT angular search torpedoes in 1942 (known to Allied forces as the "Curly" because of their serpentine course pattern), target inclination was no longer a limiting factor. The torpedo could be set with normal gyro angling to run straight for a specified range before commencing its angular search. This consisted of a series of pre-set "short legs" or "long legs" until the torpedo either hit a target or expired and self-scuttled. Clearly, a number of these twisting about inside a convoy created chaos. The year 1943 saw a radical and even deadlier innovation: the T-5 acoustic "Zaunkönig" torpedo, known in Allied circles as "Taffy" or GNAT.[39] Equally independent of target inclination, this electric trackless torpedo could be aimed by hydrophone and fired while the U-boat was completely submerged. It ran straight until its acoustic head locked onto a sound source and homed onto the target. It is tactically significant that even after a periscope-depth shot a U-boat had to dive quickly to 50 metres in order to escape its own acoustic torpedo. In a sense, this rendered the submarine temporarily *hors de combat*. The impact of the "Zaunkönig" was unprecedented in torpedo warfare. A single shot, for example, sheered sixty feet off the stern of the frigate HMCS *Magog*; blasted the whole stern of the Bangor HMCS *Clayoquot* into the vertical; and disintegrated the corvette HMCS *Shawinigan*.[40]

The night surface attack of U-69 against the Newfoundland ferry SS *Caribou* on 13 October 1942 in Cabot Strait was one of those fortuitous events which swift action turned to tactical success. The *Caribou* was being screened from astern by the Bangor HMCS *Grandmère* in accordance with the Western Approaches Convoy Instructions' diagram for a single-ship escort. Every tactical advantage rested with U-69, whose low-lying hull lay obscured from view as it chose both the time and place of attack. The German commander knew that as the minesweeper HMCS *Grandmère*—which he identified as a "two-stack destroyer"—was escorting from astern, her hydrophones would not have distinguished the U-boat's propeller noise from that of *Caribou*. Under ideal conditions, *Grandmère*'s maximum sonar range lay between 1100 and 1400 metres; but the U-boat commander heard no sonar. He did not realize that *Grandmère* was without radar. In short, *Caribou* sank in four minutes with a single shot. HMCS *Grandmère* searched unsuccessfully for U-69 for over two hours before returning for survivors of the sinking. Subsequent Allied analysis of U-69's attack urged the doubtless correct view that a single ship would afford more effective protection zig-zagging 1850–2800 metres ahead or else— subject of course to the relative speeds of convoy and escort—circling the merchant ship at 15 knots at a range of 2800 metres.[41] Significantly, however, U-69 had fired from a range of 650 metres. Paul Hartwig's U-517 struck the 5649-ton SS *Chatham* in the Strait of Belle Isle under similar circumstances. She was a single-ship convoy of American troops escorted by USCG *Mojave* enroute from Sydney to Greenland. An American critic has observed that Greenland convoys "were given the slowest and worst equipped escorts, under Coast Guard officers and crews who had been given slight training in escort duty or anti-submarine work."[42] Hartwig would have agreed.

Three years later, in January 1945, single escorts screened convoys from the van. This was the scene when U-1232 sighted Sydney-Halifax convoy SH-194; it consisted of three ships in line abreast, led by the Bangor minesweeper HMCS *Kentville* and covered by an RCAF aircraft. U-1232 positioned itself in advance of the oncoming convoy "just as taught in submarine training school" as its war diary notes, and let the escort pass before attacking. Two T-39 torpedoes, the first at a long range of 2200 metres and the second from 1200, sank two ships. *Kentville* suspected a GNAT acoustic attack and deployed her CAT gear. This was a Canadian designed drogue similar to, but lighter than, the British "Foxer."[43] It consisted of a metal rig in the shape of a large crossbow towed by any escort fearing attacks from an acoustic torpedo. Towing it through the water caused the two crossbars to vibrate or "chatter" violently. This produced a shrill tone that drowned out the lower-frequency noises of the ship's engines and screws, thus decoying the German torpedo. It had a major disadvantage: the screeching noise prevented effective use of sonar and hydrophone. Thus *Kentville* was protected, but powerless. Ironically, the CAT played an offensive role of which Canadians were unaware; it was a psychological weapon. German war diaries and recollections document the impact on submarine crews of these "screeching circular saws" whose "screaming sustained tone" gave the impression of a U-boat being sawed in half. Even once the sound source had been identified in 1944, it thwarted many a crew. Werner Hirschmann, engineer officer aboard U-190, described in his personal diary after surrendering in May 1945 his first glimpse of the CAT aboard HMCS *Prestonian*: "We watch a strange looking piece of equipment being lowered over the stern. We assume it is the infamous 'circular power saw' which made life hell for us for so many weeks. (Even now a similar noise strikes a raw nerve, even if it's only the humming of a fly.) Too obnoxious are the memories of that devil's instrument."[44]

Detailed examination of the variables in the multiship convoy with multiple screen in inshore waters provides no new or startling twists in the German perception of the ASW problem. But it does provide cogent documentation of the quandary which escorts faced when caught between their responsibilities of assuring the safe and timely arrival of a convoy and the opportunity of making a kill. In a night surface attack against Quebec-Sydney convoy QS-15, for example, U-132 sank three ships (*Hainault, Anastasios Pateras, Dinaric*). The Bangor HMCS *Drummondville* illuminated it with starshell, attempted to ram during the enforced emergency dive, and bracketed U-132 with what the U-boat's war diary described as "three well-placed depth charges." Revealing what Germans regarded as the typical Canadian lack of tenacity, *Drummondville* broke off an engagement which with firmer resolve—and without her primary responsibility of protecting a convoy—might have led to a kill. The damaged U-132 had difficulties in depth-keeping. Surprisingly, the Assessment Committee, which later gathered more of the facts than *Drummondville* had—and had of course much more time to ponder them at ease—concluded that there was insufficient evidence of the presence of a U-boat at the spot where *Drummondville* had attacked.

The commanding officer of HMCS *Skeena* had experienced a similar situation when escorting convoy SC-42. He recently recalled how much more successful his encounter might have been if, like Admirals Horton and Dönitz, he had first served in submarines.[45] He had needed the submariner's grasp of battle, and the "periscope view" of Allied tactics. If the surface commander had shared the submariner's perspective on underwater warfare, the argument ran, he would have made more effective decisions once he had actually engaged the enemy. In such close-quarters situations, the escort commander's understanding of the U-boats' turning circles, deep-diving techniques, manoeuverability, and torpedo range would have been crucial. He would also have known just how much punishment a U-boat could take. In the event, the Canadian navy of the Second World War seems always to have been short of "tame" submarines against which to hone its anti-submarine skills; more particularly, there were none in which to initiate surface sailors into the submariner's combat world. As circumstances had it, the "wild" submarines of the enemy revealed their secrets all too gradually. It is none the less striking just how accurate was the cumulative data amassed by naval intelligence through the interrogation of U-boat survivors. German experts would have quibbled over details of the technical assessment, but the general appreciation was surprisingly sound. It was supported by analyses of RCN Operational Research.[46]

Prior to the cumulative intelligence assessment of 1944, however, U-boat tactics left ample room for Allied doubt. Thus once having left the St Lawrence, U-132 effected a daylight attack at periscope-depth against inbound overseas convoy ON-113. Shallow water anomalies on the Sable Island Bank enabled it to penetrate the screen and sink the 6734-ton *Pacific Pioneer* from 800 metres. Even a well-equipped destroyer in the St Lawrence proved ineffective. Hartwig's U-517 penetrated the five-ship screen of the twenty-one-ship Sydney-Quebec convoy SQ-36 despite HMS *Salisbury*'s passing it to within 150 metres. Forced to crash dive after sinking the *Saturnus* and *Inger Elisabeth*, Hartwig self-assuredly sensed the escort break off the attack. He heard no hint of sonar.

The special operations of U-536 in the confining waters of the Baie des Chaleurs in September 1943 provide a salient case in point. The Germans had arranged to penetrate the bay in order to pick up escaped prisoners of war. Canadians, on the basis of intelligence sources, had laid a trap by allowing it to penetrate the bay and approach the shores of Pointe de Maisonette. Despite its initial detection by radar, the U-boat ultimately escaped submerged by eluding a coordinated cordon of ships ready to pounce. The net consisted of no less than one destroyer, four corvettes, and five Bangor minesweepers. It even proved possible for U-boats to elude the anti-submarine search tactic known as "Operation Observant." Here a task force would establish a perimeter search around the last known position ("datum") of an enemy submarine, gradually narrowing the area of search by rigorous application of hydrophone and sonar (asdic) doctrine. The "Observant" patrols would advance the search area along the U-boat's presumed escape course. In one case in the notoriously difficult waters off Halifax, the cool and astute commander of U-806 eluded an "Observant" consisting of twenty-one ships. He correctly construed the circular search patterns around his initial firing position by extrapolating inferences from asdic sources and his own hydrophones. He grasped the Canadians' principle of expanding the radii of the circles according to his own estimated direction and speed of advance. Creeping attacks, as will be seen, deprived the U-boat of the very kind of sound-ranging data which enabled U-806 to effect its escape.

In general, Germans liked to choose choke-points for attacks. Sometimes this was fruitless, as when U-802 and U-541 lurked for days in the mouth of the St Lawrence. Curiously, it was not until January 1945 that a U-boat chose the obvious choke-point in the Halifax Approaches: U-1232 chose for its attack on Boston-Halifax convoy BX-141 the very point where the eight-column twenty-ship convoy with four escorts was manoeuvering into single line to enter Halifax harbour. Commander, U-boats (BdU), had for some time been urging his commanders "to get in there"; Ackermann (U-1221) had been scolded by Admiral Dönitz for merely having reported the good pickings that might be had, but himself doing nothing about it. The solicitous Lessing (U-1231) had lain many miles off Sheet Harbour, Nova Scotia, on 23 December 1944 and complained in his log of "feeling like a moored mine, waiting" for something to run into it. Hornbostel (U-806) had touched the nerve by sinking HMCS *Clayoquot* on Christmas Eve 1944 off the Sambro lightship. Dobratz (U-1232) alone had concluded correctly: merchant masters would be concentrating on manoeuvering in close quarters; few, if any, would be primarily preoccupied with thoughts of a submarine attack.

Against these sobering scenarios of U-boat tactical advantage one must place the effectiveness of the Allied creeping attack which two U-boats underwent after completing their Canadian operations.[47] This was a slow attack against a deep target; it had the advantage of maintaining constant sonar (asdic) contact with the U-boat without betraying the exact position or even the presence of the actual attacker. It was a type of leapfrog played by two attacking vessels. The attacking ship would maintain sonar contact with the target while the directed ship took station astern with the sonar switched off. This deprived the U-boat of the opportunity of assessing the attacker's range. Once steadied up on the same course as the submarine, the directing ship conned its partner onto the target in order to execute the attack. The records and accounts of survivors of this anti-submarine tactic attest to its effectiveness. Significantly, the successful attacks against U-845 and U-536 were carried out by experienced, trained, and well-equipped Canadian warships in the North Atlantic; equally important, they were encumbered neither by inshore hydrographic anomalies nor by responsibility for a convoy. Their success validated the concept of the Support Group.

By this time anti-submarine countermeasures were enhanced by a telling expertise in radio direction-finding. Thus when U-541 finally broke radio silence on the Newfoundland Bank on departing its 1944 patrol of the St Lawrence it was subjected to a rapid attack. As its commanding officer recently recalled: "From my perspective the Canadian defences had reacted and operated magnificently. Swift detection of our radio transmission, good evaluation with precise position, good attack by aircraft with sparing and rational use of radar. If we had dived but a few seconds later, the bombs would possibly have hit us at the beginning of the diving manoeuvre."[48]

By now the "Happy Time" of the submarines was long since past, and what they called their "Sour-Pickle Time" (*Saure-Gurken-Zeit*) had begun. The shift derived as much from the Canadians' increasing professionalism and improved equipment in ASW as from the Germans' serious problems both with fleet sustainability and support, and with lack of well-trained crews. "Professional pride played an enormous role in [the German submariner's] determination to keep on going, regardless of the costs," a senior survivor of U-190 recently recalled.[49] The same held true for the Royal Canadian Navy. Technological and tactical developments were of course crucial in making ASW effective. But as Germans readily recognized, what ultimately mattered was the ability of seamen under pressure of combat to grapple successfully with conflicting priorities at the cutting edge of the decision-making process. Here in the *Entscheidungsvorfeld*, as Germans call this leadership predicament, ASW was subject to all the human foibles. It was here that Germans recognized their special rapport with the adversary. Commenting on James Lamb's *The Corvette Navy*,[50] and laying past politics and enmities aside, a German survivor of Canadian inshore warfare observed:

> Were it not for the difference in nationality, Lamb could be considered a capable interpreter of the scenario, the feelings and the moods of our own Navy ... the foul-ups, the frustrations, the elations and the reasons for being out there were very much like the ones we went through. It only confirms our feeling we had all through the war, that there was a far higher degree of affinity between us and the allied naval forces than could ever exist between us and the German Army or Air Force.[51]

Such words of reconciliation mask the real bitterness of the war which many veterans quite understandably cannot forget. But at a time when Canada's navy is looking for new directions, the timely words of a former opponent remind us of the kinship of those who follow the profession of the sea.

Chapter 8

INSHORE ASW: THE CANADIAN EXPERIENCE IN HOME WATERS

Marc Milner

No other Second World War operations gave the Royal Canadian Navy more difficulty than anti-submarine warfare (ASW) in the Northwest Atlantic.[1] Despite the establishment of a good defensive system by the spring of 1942, losses to shipping in the region in that year were high and without compensating U-boat kills. Similarly, later in the war when the Allies sank U-boats in large numbers, the RCN was unable to locate and destroy submarines in the Canadian zone, despite precise intelligence and increasingly more effective support from the Royal Canadian Air Force. The overriding reason for the failure of ASW—as distinct from anti-submarine (AS) escort—lay in the navy's willingness to concentrate on operations in areas of greater strategic importance. Not surprisingly then, it was the struggle to understand and master the coastal environment itself, prompted by the ASW stalemate and changing German tactics by 1944, which proved most crucial to the development of the post-war RCN.

Like its larger counterparts, the RCN perceived the submarine as an inshore threat on the eve of the Second World War. The experience of U-cruisers off Halifax and the Cabot Strait during the First World War confirmed for the Canadians the British-held belief that submarines were a threat in harbour approaches and in the focal points of trade. The institution of escorted mercantile convoys in 1917 had swept the high seas of easy targets and robbed U-boats of their preferred tactic of surface gunnery actions against solitary merchantmen. In the last eighteen months of the war unescorted targets were easier to find inshore, but the presence of constant patrols forced submarines to operate submerged for most of the time. Limited tactical mobility in turn necessitated that submarines operate in heavy traffic areas.[2]

Although some Germans, among them one named Karl Dönitz, were on the verge of breaking out of this restrictive strategy in 1918, time was against them. Where ASW stood at the armistice—submarines waiting in the focal areas of mercantile shipping, yet held in check by massive naval and air power—was also where ASW stood twenty-one years later.[3] In the strictest sense, ASW in 1939 was by definition inshore. Certainly this was true in the Canadian case, where defence against the submarine was confined to the approaches to Canada's major defended ports. In these waters convoys could expect an AS escort, supported by air patrols and the port's roving AS forces. The problem offshore was, for the moment at least, one of the defence against conventional warships and armed raiders. There was even some doubt within the RN if "asdic," as the early sonars were called, would work effectively in deep water, and apparently all interwar AS exercises were conducted inside the 100 fathom line.[4] Faith in asdic's ability to locate a target (and in the ability of weapons to destroy it) was unaffected by considerations of water and bottom conditions, although these were under investigation by the academic community.[5]

Not surprisingly, then, when war broke out in 1939 the RCN and the RCAF began to escort convoys in the approaches to Halifax harbour in a way reminiscent of 1917–18. In the event, it was not until the last year of the war that U-boats posed a serious threat in those waters, and in the meantime submarine warfare passed through a complete cycle of development, propelled by two factors: bold and innovative U-boat tactics and Allied maritime airpower.

Aggressive use of submarines, even in the presence of naval and air forces, and typically on the surface in all but moments of extreme danger, were the hallmarks of Germany's U-boat campaign until December 1943. But it was airpower more than anything else which shaped submarine tactics, by defining areas where submarines could and could not operate with impunity. When beyond the range of effective airpower the Germans used a free-wheeling strategy of massed surface attacks against escorted convoys: the famous wolf packs. When operating within range of effective airpower, submarines had to resort to solitary patrols in assigned areas. For our purposes then, airpower broadly defines the difference between inshore and oceanic ASW up to the end of 1943. The range of effective airpower in this period also happened to encompass the area known as the Canadian Coastal Zone, later referred to as the Canadian Northwest Atlantic, a theatre of war commanded by Rear-Admiral L.W. Murray, RCN. After 1943 airpower reigned supreme over the North Atlantic, and the distinction between inshore and offshore ASW would lie at the 100 fathom line.

In the early years the *effectiveness* of airpower was the crucial factor, and it was here that the Canadian inshore experience recorded its first important distinction from the British. The effectiveness of the RAF's Coastal Command drove U-boats further to seaward through 1940 and early 1941, establishing an area within 600 miles of British and Icelandic bases wherein it was largely impossible for Germans to conduct pack operations. Canadians hoped for similar success but failed because of local weather conditions. When, in October 1941, approximately twenty U-boats moved into Newfoundland waters to attack convoys, the Digbys and Catalinas of the RCAF's No. 1 Group had little luck in finding the packs or in checking their offensive. Convoy SC-52 was actually driven back by U-boat attacks 150 miles from the Newfoundland coast, partly because poor flying conditions forestalled air support for the escort.

Prevailing westerly winds and dearth of alternate fields limited seaward flying from Newfoundland to about four hundred miles with Catalina and Digby aircraft: barely two-thirds of the performance obtained by Coastal Command with similar aircraft. Persistent fog and generally poor conditions allowed U-boat packs to operate well inside the theoretical effective range of No. 1 Group's aircraft. Throughout 1942 and early 1943 the Canadians tried, despite conditions, to reduce the level of pack operations under their noses, but without much success. It was only in 1943, with the help of modern 10 cm radar in naval escorts and the general defeat of the U-boat packs further to seaward— with assistance from new very long-range RCAF Liberators operating from Gander—that the fog-shrouded waters of the Grand Banks were swept of wolf packs.[6]

Even so, local conditions off Newfoundland mitigated against effective ASW and surveillance. Aircrew could never be sure whether the blip on the radar screen was an enemy submarine or a towering iceberg. In darkness or heavy fog only the foolhardy would sweep in at wave top to classify the contact. Naval escorts too faced rather unique problems as a result of icebergs. During the battle for ONS-5 in May 1943, HMS *Pelican* twice set ramming course and speed for a target she had classified as a U-boat by hydrophone and had verified with her radar. *Pelican*'s captain decided at the last moment it was not a U-boat at all, and close inspection revealed the contact to be a small iceberg, growling and hissing like a moving U-boat as it rode on the waves.[7]

Although the Germans sank four ships in two daring attacks on Wabana anchorage in 1942, action in waters to the north and east of Newfoundland tended to focus on ensuring that eastbound trans-Atlantic convoys cleared the focal area off Cape Race without interception, or that the battles around westbound convoys were brought to a swift end. In these operations RCAF aircraft sank two submarines in the fall of 1942.[8] But this area was essentially one where solitary u-boat operations blended with and supported those of packs patrolling the air gap. The real focus of inshore operations was in the Gulf of St Lawrence and around Nova Scotia. There the RCN anticipated, and experienced, a major German inshore campaign.

By early 1941 defensive arrangements in the approaches to Halifax and Sydney were operating well enough. Convoys received inshore AS screens until handed over to the deep ocean escort of armed merchant cruisers. "Strike forces," consisting of groups of two corvettes, were planned to meet enemy incursions into coastal waters. Their task was to seek and destroy.[9] The gulf was also to be protected by "hunting and striking forces (which would co-operate with Air Forces) disposed at strategic points in the area." In theory these forces would swarm to a sighting and kill the intruder, while merchant shipping was routed clear of the area.

The Canadian penchant for strike forces and offensive operations was overwhelmed by a need simply to protect shipping. When the first u-boats moved west of Cape Race in January 1942, they found shipping off Newfoundland and Nova Scotia moving in escorted convoys, well routed by competent shore staffs.[10] This defensive system was extended until all available RCN forces were absorbed. On 1 May even Bangor minesweepers and motor launches were pressed into escort duties.[11] Although by all accounts the standards of efficiency among these ships was lamentable, their presence was enough to encourage the Germans to seek easier targets in American waters or to limit attacks to independently routed ships. By September the duties of the Halifax-based Western Local Escort Force (WLEF) were extended to New York and pushed to the edge of the Grand Banks, a distance of 1200 miles: fully one third of the transatlantic route. Despite this tremendous responsibility, apparently only one ship was lost from convoys off Nova Scotia in 1942.[12] This success was owing in no small way to the fact that effective airpower spared WLEF convoys the danger of u-boat pack attacks, while routing followed a corridor wide enough to make an individual submariner's search problem extremely difficult.

The development of successful ocean convoy routes off the coast was dependent upon using all available escorts. When the gulf opened for navigation in the spring of 1942, the navy had no ships to implement its elaborate offensive plans. The business of search and destroy therefore fell to the RCAF, while the RCN assumed close escort duties around Quebec to Sydney convoys.[13] The confines of the gulf meant that there was little scope for successful evasive routing, particularly between the convoy assembly area at Father Point and Cap Gaspé: "the slot." At a time when the key to defence of convoys was evasion, this was a serious problem. One scheme to overcome the slot was to sail convoys to clear the area in daylight, but in practice timing was never that good.[14] The first attack, by U-132 on QS-15, occurred in the middle of the slot on a bright moonlit night on 16 July. Three ships were lost. Attacks in September on QS-33 and SQ-36 occurred at the choke points at either end, off Cap Chat and Cap Gaspé, and three of the four were either at night or in difficult visibility. Only the last attack, by U-165 on SQ-36 off Cap Chat, took place in broad daylight.[15]

The battles for QS-33 and SQ-36 were both ding-dong affairs: classic inshore confrontations. U-517 held a position off Cap Gaspé in the convoy lanes, while U-165 held a similar position well inside the river off Cap Chat. It was the convoys which came to them. The only truly effective Canadian response was to suppress the U-boats with airpower. Hartwig's U-517 was particularly heavily attacked during September as he patrolled off Anticosti and Gaspé. In this instance his nemesis was 113 Squadron, Hudsons operating from Chatham, New Brunswick, under Squadron Leader N.E. Small, one of the brightest and most innovative maritime airmen in RCAF history. In the summer of 1942, Small's was the only squadron of Eastern Air Command to adopt new Coastal Command tactics, including higher patrol altitudes and white camouflage. His innovative tactics had already accounted for U-753 off Nova Scotia in July. As a result, all the attacks on U-517 and U-165 by aircraft in September 1942 were made by 113 Squadron, including four on Hartwig in three days. Luckily for the Germans, Small was one of a kind.[16]

Although it was airpower that checked the German offensive in the gulf in 1942, it alone could not stop an aggressive submariner from pursuing his task—as Hartwig demonstrated. There was little merit in forcing a submarine down where it would be overrun by the targets it sought. It now fell to naval forces to develop countermeasures. The RCN made sure that at least a few gulf escorts had modern type 271 radar and increased the strike capability by adding two destroyers to the force. However, the size of escort groups remained too small and, with little likelihood of an increase, it was decided to close the gulf. The gulf in late 1942 gave the RCN its first, albeit unsuspecting, glimpse of what 1944–5 held in store.

Heavy losses in the St Lawrence—twenty-two ships in 1942— compared unfavourably with the negligible losses to the main convoys off Nova Scotia, but the RCN understood the reasons well enough. In an area where the enemy could be neither avoided nor entirely suppressed, good ASW by naval forces was imperative. Assessments in early 1943 concluded that in only about half of the contacts with U-boats had escorts taken "adequate and co-ordinated offensive action during or after the action." And in the case of the gulf in particular, "the absence of an adequately co-ordinated escort group organization was ... the most important factor contributing to our lack of success against the U-boat in the areas."[17] It was also well known that local asdic conditions in the Canadian zone were notoriously bad.

For a number of reasons then, the Canadian Coastal Zone had one of the worst ASW records of any theatre of war by 1943. While the world average of U-boats sunk versus merchant ships lost was one to ten, Canadian researchers concluded that no less than 112 ships had been lost in the Northwest Atlantic during 1942 (mostly independently routed) in exchange for the lone kill by 113 Squadron. It was believed that the Germans were well aware of this poor record and would exploit it with a massive campaign in 1943. To meet this the Canadians evolved a three-phased offensive in 1943,[18] although only one phase was to have any impact on German operations in that year.[19]

The first aspect of the 1943 offensive was the alteration of WLEF's tactical doctrine. At the end of March, Captain (D), Halifax, Captain J.D. Prentice issued the first part of "Hints on Escort Work," which were intended to provide escort captains with guidance in WLEF's unique operating conditions and encourage an aggressive response to U-boat contacts.[20] Prentice admonished his officers always to "think in terms of destruction of submarines" and to conduct their operations on the basis of what "will give you the greatest chance of a kill ... rather than in terms of safety of the convoy." "History has shown," Prentice went on, "that the only sure way of achieving this objective (safe and timely arrival) is to ensure destruction of any enemy forces which approach." Although Prentice's zeal led him to warn of the potential danger from pack attacks (a possibility discounted by senior officers) if such a doctrine was adopted, he did advance innovative tactics for mixed-vessel WLEF groups faced with the threat of a lone attacker. Bangor minesweepers, for example, carried better asdics than contemporary corvettes in 1943, and Prentice assigned them the primary AS hunting role around a stricken vessel. Destroyers, with their better radar, were charged with surface sweeps, while the corvettes undertook rescue and salvage work. Even the positioning of Bangors in the screen was intended to place them upwind of the convoys to enhance their chances of an asdic contact in the downwind sweep following an attack.[21]

Fortunately, WLEF's aggressive new posture was untried. So too was the offensive in the Gulf of St Lawrence. This elaborate plan called for large forces and, like Prentice's schemes, was based on Bangors, possibly for the same reasons. Close escort work fell to six coal-fired AS trawlers of the RN, supported by no less than four other formations: six Bangors of Sydney Force, four corvettes of Quebec Force, six Bangors of Gulf Support Force, and four flotillas of motor launches (ML's) acting in the dubious capacity of Gulf Strike Force. Theoretically, the latter were reaction forces, poised to respond to any sighting, while Quebec, Sydney, and Gulf Support Forces all had more or less roving commissions. The Bangors of Gulf Support Force, in particular, were tasked "to take offensive action against U-Boats and to support striking group."[22] Significantly, all of the Bangors committed to the plan were short ranged and therefore logical choices for gulf operations.[23] However, the mix of forces in the scheme is an interesting one. As mentioned, the Bangors then had better asdics than Corvettes and it was these ships which were designated to form support forces and to carry the war to the enemy, not the four corvettes of Quebec Force. The latter, however, were fitted with modern type 271 AS radar: essential for an effective surface screen at night. The four flotillas of ML's and the AS trawlers made up numbers lacking in 1942.

Although two U-boats penetrated the gulf in 1943, the anticipated German offensive never developed there either. The RCN kept busy, nonetheless. The Bangors conducted an enthusiastic but entirely unscientific survey of asdic conditions in the gulf during the shipping season, resulting in a report from the Gaspé AS officer in November. Perhaps the only significant finding of the survey was the fact that of all the gulf areas, it was that between Cap Gaspé and Anticosti which gave asdic operators the most trouble—the area where Hartwig had hunted so successfully the previous year.[24]

In fact, the success of the German campaign in 1942 led the navy, which did not have its own research and development establishment, to ask the National Research Council for help in undertaking oceanographic surveys off the east coast. The NRC responded by sending a representative from its Acoustics Division to the Woods Hole Oceanographic Institute in Massachusetts to study the new science of "bathythermography," or BT: the variation in water temperature by depth and its impact on sound propagation.[25] It also led the director of AS, Commander A.R. Pressy, to ask in December 1942 for an oceanographic research vessel at Halifax. It was not until the end of 1943 that a suitable vessel was found. The Royal Society's schooner *Culver*, which had laid inactive in Bermuda since 1939, was not acquired until April 1944, fully a year and a half after the need had been articulated. After some work *Culver* sailed through a hurricane to Halifax in July, where further surveys found her unseaworthy. Costs of additions for oceanographic work would then have to be spent once the vessel was made sound. In September, not wanting to spend more good money after bad, the RCN declared *Culver* surplus to its needs, but the Royal Society refused to take her back. In the end, the navy and the Royal Society settled on a cash payment in October 1946 and *Culver* was scrapped. As a result, no suitable oceanographic vessel was found for the east coast before the war ended (*Ekholi* served on the west coast from 1944).[26]

While the search for a suitable oceanographic vessel got underway at a remarkably leisurely pace, a BT survey of Canadian inshore waters was conducted in 1943 from warships, the first such study on behalf of the RCN, and a BT officer was appointed at NSHQ.[27] In this respect the USN was well ahead. The Americans had discovered the problem of temperature gradients before the war, and on the basis of their work a scientist from Woods Hole had invented the bathythermograph. By 1942 the Americans were issuing charts of asdic conditions for the North Atlantic, including the Canadian zone, with details of temperature gradients and likely assured asdic ranges. In July 1943 each USN escort group was ordered to have two of its ships fitted with BT equipment, and by 1944—if not sooner—USN ships were taking BT readings once every watch. Although the 1942 BT charts obtained by the RCN were of questionable value, their marginal notes do explain sonar concepts which dominated post-war ASW.[28] At this point it is sufficient to note that the German inshore campaign of 1942 forced the RCN to take a more scientific approach to the problems of ASW. The resulting BT surveys by the NRC in 1943 formed the groundwork for the navy's developing understanding of the physical properties of coastal waters.

However, through 1943 and early 1944 the Canadians were absorbed by the third phase of the 1943 offensive: taking the war to the enemy. In the first months of 1943 the Germans themselves had been busy trying to win the battle in the mid-Atlantic, and for the balance of 1943 they struggled to overcome the devastating effects of losing that battle in the spring. Throughout the year they had to contend with the punishing offensive launched against them in the eastern Atlantic by air and naval forces, and by late 1943 German efforts were directed at trying to regain lost surface mobility. This attempt was frustrated by increasingly more sophisticated Allied use of forces, directed by accurate intelligence and the benefits of operational research.

The third phase of the 1943 Canadian offensive was part of that trend. In February 1943 the concept of hunts-to-exhaustion was first advanced in Canadian circles. The theory was simple enough. A diesel-electric U-boat could only operate submerged for a maximum of forty-eight hours, and its limited underwater speed of about two knots would keep it within a hundred miles of its last sighting. By conducting an expanding search over the area with aircraft and warships, and sweeping with radar and asdic, searching forces were almost assured of a second sighting and a second crack at the U-boat. At worst a second sighting would produce yet another cycle of sweeps on an already exhausted U-boat. In Canadian use these expanding searches were code named "Salmons."[29] A contact was, of course, essential to the ordering of a Salmon operation, although this need not have been a sighting or even a "flaming datum." In July 1943, to enhance the chances of contacts, the Canadians introduced daily estimates of U-boat positions based on all available intelligence. These "Otter" signals covered U-boat approach routes and patrol areas, generally well known either by Ultra or by DF fixes, allowing forces to concentrate their searches where a contact was likely.

Salmons, sweeps in Otter areas, and similar tactics in the eastern Atlantic forced a change of U-boat tactics before Canadians could master the intricacies of combined area searches.[30] The RCAF began to patrol Otter areas in July, but it was not until October 1943 that the first Salmon was ordered against U-537. It failed because the sighting aircraft left the scene following U-537's crash dive, and bad weather obscured the search area. Two subsequent Salmons directed at U-537 also failed, although the submarine was suppressed. What were to become persistent problems with naval forces in area searches were demonstrated at the end of the year, when U-543 was located off Flemish Cap. While the air force failed to cover the area properly, the new frigate group conducting the search failed dismally. It managed to find U-543 but suffered two attacks from the bold submariner and nearly lost *Swansea* to an acoustic torpedo. Later searches for U-845, U-539, U-802 (which sank *Watuka* off Halifax), U-580, U-856, U-548 (which sank the frigate *Valleyfield* off Newfoundland as she sailed blithely through an Otter area), U-1222, U-107, and U-233 between January and May 1944 all failed, although U-856, U-580, and U-233 were subsequently sunk by USN forces (the last in an Otter area).[31] Apart from an almost total failure of naval and air forces to coordinate efforts, the biggest problem with these unsuccessful Salmons was the RCN itself. As Commodore H.E. Reid, RCN, Flag Officer, Newfoundland, observed in March 1944, "Recent unsuccessful hunts off Halifax and Newfoundland, where a U-boat was known to be present, by motley assortments of ships in various states of efficiency and training, lends emphasis to the fact that none but a highly trained, thoroughly co-ordinated and ably led team can hope to destroy U-boats at this stage of the campaign."[32]

It was perhaps unfortunate that the Germans did not, in 1943, put the Canadian three-phased offensive fully to the test. This was the only time during the entire war that the RCN's forces in the Northwest Atlantic were numerous enough to permit a flexible and aggressive response to any incursion. By the time Commodore Reid pencilled his lament for the state of ships and groups in home waters, the RCN had already begun to concentrate its effort in the eastern Atlantic. There Canadian warships sank ten U-boats between June 1944 and the German capitulation, earning a commendable reputation for excellence. But not so those fated to make do in the Canadian zone: it simply was not crucial to the outcome of the war. Although encompassing an area half that of the British theatre, where about twenty support groups operated, the Canadian zone seldom had more than two such groups.[33]

Finally, by December 1943 the press of Allied airpower forced German submarines to operate primarily submerged.[34] To this development were added three others. In early 1944, U-boat commanders ceased frequent HF transmissions and began to patrol silently, virtually eliminating DF fixes as a source for Otter areas.[35] By the spring they were also operating with schnorkels, a device which allowed U-boats to operate for days on end without surfacing. In May the *RCN-RCAF Monthly Review* noted that the schnorkel was "of particular value in areas like the Bay of Biscay and the coastal waters of North America."[36] Much of the Allies' effort thereafter was devoted to finding ways of locating schnorkels, but the task was a daunting one. Even modern airborne radars could cover only one-tenth of the area previously swept for surfaced U-boats in calm seas, and one-fiftieth in moderate conditions.[37] In the last year of the war, aircraft reverted to a more sophisticated version of the old scarecrow role, keeping U-boats down. It now fell to navies to develop effective ways to deal with a sub-surface problem—again. As a final point, the fall of French bases and the limiting effect of schnorkel operations restricted U-boats to theatres easily reached from Norway. The Germans therefore concentrated much of their effort around Britain, but Canadian waters were about the only other major theatre within range.[38]

Until the inshore schnorkel campaign off Britain developed in mid-1944, no major changes in German tactics were anticipated. In February the British observed a general reluctance on the part of German submariners to remain inshore at all, preferring to linger where there was searoom.[39] It was not until later in the year that they overcame this reluctance, partly as a result of the success of schnorkel. In the meantime, the RCN pressed on with its work on inshore operating conditions, including a renewed effort on bathythermography. Not everyone was enthusiastic about the potential of the new science. The AS Staff Officer at Halifax, Commander P.M. Bliss, RN, responded to the prospects of another BT survey in 1944 in definitely negative tones.

"It appears to me," Bliss wrote in December 1943, "that no practical results are at present being aimed at and, in addition, I am extremely doubtful if any practical results can ever be achieved."[40]

As Bliss explained, it was already known that asdic conditions inside one hundred fathoms were dreadful in all but a few months of spring and fall: serving officers would simply have to make do. Fortunately, more enlightened approaches to mastering the inshore U-boat prevailed. By the end of 1943 the boffins at NRC were throroughly involved in the problems of underwater acoustics. They were well aware, as J.P. Tully reported in January 1944 after attending an oceanographic conference with USN scientists in San Diego, that the Americans were using BT "for immediate tactical purposes." In addition, the USN employed it to develop "tactics and strategy resulting from a knowledge of the sound beam patterns and ranges" which BT provided. Significantly, Tully warned that American efforts, which were directed at compiling deep ocean asdic range "prediction charts," were not directly "applicable to the coastal areas where bottom effects and fresh water run off exert considerable influence."[41]

The importance of sorting out the inshore problem was therefore evident to NRC by early 1944 and was the subject of a special San Diego conference also attended by Tully in April. The Acoustics Division followed through in May 1944 with the establishment of the Atlantic Oceanographic Research Group at St Andrews, New Brunswick, specifically to study inshore conditions. By August the NRC's first tentative report, "Asdic Ranging Conditions in the Halifax Approaches," appeared. It concluded that BT would be of help in inshore ASW.[42]

The first RCN operational use of bathythermography, under trial, occurred in September and October 1944, when a wave of U-boats penetrated the Canadian zone, attacking in the gulf for the first time in two years.[43] Attempts to stop their advance with barrier patrols across the Cabot Strait and heavy air searches in Otter areas all failed, although U-802, U-541, U-1223 and U-1228 were all suppressed. U-802 reported, "it strikes me odd that the aircraft are always flying back and forth over the area on a north-south course, while I have been standing to and off land on north-south courses for the last 7 days."[44] One steamship and the corvette *Shawinigan* were sunk and the frigate *Magog* and one steamer damaged.

As in 1942, it was aircraft that checked the campaign in the gulf. Rear-Admiral L.W. Murray, commander-in-chief, Canadian Northwest Atlantic, sent in a scratch team from his two frigate groups, EG-16 and EG-25, to locate and destroy the submarines. Not surprisingly, it posed little threat to the U-boats, and its innovative use of daily BT readings to establish assured asdic ranges failed to produce results.

The support group also did not understand how to conduct itself when working with aircraft using sonobuoys, and Captain (D) Halifax found that there was a general failure to maintain good plots of searches.[45]

In the aftermath of the 1944 gulf campaign there were some noteworthy developments. Lieutenant R.A. Nairn, the AS officer of the frigate *Springhill* who had been responsible for the daily BT work, was posted to Murray's staff for BT duties.[46] Nairn's comment that his attempt to foster BT use was hampered by the lack of suitable pamphlets and books was acted upon, and the first RCN BT handbook appeared in November. The navy also authorized the equipping of all senior officers' ships with two deep and one shallow BT sets, and instructed the daily recording of BT conditions (in contrast to the USN's practice of once each watch), for forwarding to St Andrews for evaluation. As a final point, the "highest priority" was given to the fitting of the new "Q" depth determination attachment to the asdics of EG-16 and EG-27.[47]

While scientific means of locating inshore U-boats were getting underway, tactics for dealing with them were under constant development. As the problem of schnorkelling submarines was being tackled it was determined in August, through experience in British waters, that U-boats were now bottoming when in danger of counterattack.[48] A method of classifying bottom contacts using echo sounding was tested by the RCN's EG-11 (Captain J.D. Prentice, RCN) in the English Channel under CinC, Western Approaches direction; although time consuming, it was found to work.[49] While this would allow classification of a specific target, the U-boat still had to be kept down, and the Admiralty advocated a saturation area search. Filling the water with active asdic noises would encourage the U-boat to remain on the bottom and exhaust itself or to try to creep away, in which case it could be located by the searching vessels. Whatever the tactics, stress was always placed on ensuring that highly trained men and ships were employed.[50]

Saturation tactics and echo sounding classification of bottomed targets were used in EG-27's unsuccessful attempts to locate U-1232, after her sinking of three ships from BX-141 off Chebucto Head on 14 January 1945. RCN warships filled the water with sound, including streaming anti-acoustic torpedo gear: a standard procedure when faced with an attack. Many non-sub contacts, such as Sambro Bank, were attacked, but asdic conditions on the whole were remarkably bad. At one point escorts passing close to the wreck of ss *British Freedom*, lying upended with her stern on the bottom and her bows pointing skyward in the crisp winter air, could not even get an asdic contact on the submerged part of the hull.[51]

The search for U-1232, which lasted from 14 to 21 January 1945, demonstrated typical Canadian zeal, but it failed for reasons well beyond the control of ships' captains. Captain (D) Halifax, the officer responsible for the efficiency of all destroyers and other escorts operating from this base, lamented repeatedly throughout late 1944 and early 1945, that haste to commission new ships kept operational escorts from training, with discouraging effects at sea.[52] The search for U-1232 was also complicated by Murray's tinkering in operations which came within the purview of the commander of the port, Commander G.P.B. Ashe, whose operational control extended for a twenty-five-mile radius off Chebucto Head and included the Local Defence Forces. In the aftermath of the search Ashe complained that Murray's failure to keep him informed of events and to repeat pertinent signals, and the incompatibility of procedures between Murray's ships and the local defence force, all contributed to confusion and several collisions. What Murray thought of Ashe's complaints remains a mystery.[53]

It was assumed that U-1232 was able to make good her escape because of poor asdic and weather conditions. It remains to be seen if that was true or if the real problem was more fundamental. Ashe at least felt that the search was poorly handled, and one can question the applicability of saturation tactics. The NRC's report on bottom conditions off Halifax, issued in November 1944, observed that the area for twenty-five miles offshore contained many outcrops which were a source of false echoes and loud reverberations. "A rough area is present in the Halifax close approaches," the report concluded, "favouring listening as a method of detection over echo ranging." This report, and one on refraction errors in asdic ranges off Canada's east coast, were not passed to Murray until mid-March 1945.[54] The director of operations at NSHQ, Captain D.K. Laidlaw, RCN, felt it unlikely that the navy would have any luck at all in finding bottomed targets off the Canadian coast.[55] His sentiment was in some way shared by Captain Prentice, who found asdic conditions off Canada much worse than those he had experienced off the UK.[56]

Although bathythermography had been used in the Gulf through the fall and by EG-27 in its search for U-1232, the science of oceanography had yet to make an impact on RCN operations. Captain D.L. Raymond, RN, director of warfare and training at NSHQ, observed at the end of January 1945 that BT "has not been used extensively for determining the distance apart of searching vessels, since it is a new gear, and there is not as yet enough data on its performance to prove its value."[57] The Americans were making use of BT to establish assured ranges and thereby to space ships in searches, and their kill rate offshore was impressive to say the least. The RCN, reflecting a conservatism evident among scientists, considered this American experience too narrowly confined to deep sea conditions. Canadian caution was confirmed during the hunt for U-1232, when RCN and USN officers met to discuss ASW problems in the approaches to Halifax. In his report to the CinC, US Fleet, the commander of task group 22.9 warned that USN hunter killer search and attack procedures were not applicable to shallow water with irregular bottoms, and that the USN would have to do some homework if it planned to meet an inshore challenge.[58]

For the moment at least Canadians assumed that the "assured" range off Halifax in winter was zero, and that it was better to keep ships at the theoretical maximum range and at least sweep over the U-boat.[59] Scientists and sailors alike were also beginning to understand that local conditions were indeed unique. In summer a pronounced negative temperature gradient (decreasing temperature with depth) was present, with a warm surface layer which trapped sound waves in a narrow channel, and a sharp negative thermocline below which sound was bent, or refracted, sharply towards the bottom. The result was occasionally long ranges on targets near the surface, but very short assured ranges below about 30–60 feet. For brief periods in the spring or fall Canadian waters were "isothermal," that is largely uniform in temperature as depth increased. These conditions produced good ranges with little refraction error: a phenomenon noticed long before scientists explained it. Arctic air masses moving across Canada and out over the coastal waters in the winter produced a slight positive temperature gradient: a warming of the water with increased depth. In this case the asdic sound was refracted upwards by the warmer sub-surface temperatures, limiting asdic penetration to about 200 feet. This phenomenon was first observed in February 1944, in the searches for U-539 and U-854. To overcome it the RCN had to rely on asdics with Q attachments, which could direct the sound beam downwards, or adapters attached to the existing hull-mounted asdics to depress the transducer 6° from the horizontal. To date there is no evidence of success in the Canadian zone with either procedure.[60] As a final point, it should be remembered that winter weather off Canada was, and is, extreme. For this reason priority in arcticization of escorts was given to those based in Halifax.[61] No support group serving in British waters had to contend with the numbing cold which faced Murray's ships.

Quite apart from the difficult water and weather conditions, the RCN was up against a tougher, more aggressive enemy by late 1944. The Germans' reluctance to operate inshore had given way to a willingness to press well in and attack in the presence of escorts. U-806's sinking of *Clayoquot* and the steamer *Samtucky* in December, and U-1232's attack on SH-194 off Egg Island and BX-141 in the approaches to Halifax in January, all pointed to the need for more and better trained escort groups and the development of better ways to detect submarines inshore. Various means were under consideration by several committees, including pre-laid sonobuoy fields, deep mine fields, sonobuoy barriers in the entrances to the gulf, magnetic anomaly detectors, blimps, and even acoustic torpedoes sown as smart mines. None of these ideas were acted upon for a variety of reasons.[62]

Worse still, the RCN continued to send trained support groups overseas. EG-16 was transferred to Britain in March and its place taken by EG-28, the RCN's seventh frigate group. Like Murray's other support group, EG-27, its task was to shepherd convoys in and out of the entrance to the harbour and to be on hand for searches. In a pinch, the Canadians also relied on American Hunter Killer Groups, such as Task Group (TG) 22.9 which participated in the hunt for U-1232.

The constant movement of ships and the danger of enemy action kept both support groups busy, with a noticeable impact on efficiency. In Halifax, Captain W.L. Puxley, RN, complained to Murray at the end of March 1945 that his support groups desperately needed training. From "one work up period to the next," Puxley wrote, "no opportunity has occurred to exercise with a submarine."[63] In particular, he wanted to sink a derelict submarine as a target and, in any event, to obtain practice time on a bottomed submarine as soon as possible. So too did the senior officer of EG-28, Lieutenant-Commander J.E. Mitchell, RCNVR. On 11 April, Mitchell complained to Puxley that his group had had only two days training since its formation in February and that some ships had never trained together. Specifically, Mitchell wanted exercises with one of the tame submarines employed by HMCS *Cornwallis* to train asdic ratings. Ironically, five days later EG-28 was tasked to find U-190 just after she sank HMCS *Esquimalt* five miles off Chebucto Head. The day after the search began Puxley informed Mitchell that he would arrange training at Cornwallis right away. In the meantime, U-190 remained submerged; the hunt, with assistance from the USN's TG-22.10, found nothing. U-190 later surrendered to RCN forces in the mid-Atlantic on her way home.[64]

EG-28's pathetic plea for training on the eve of the hunt for U-190, and the persistent complaints of Captain (D), point to the key weakness in ASW in the Canadian zone. Operational researchers later tackled the thorny question of why hunts in British waters produced so many U-boat kills, while those in Canadian waters offered none. One of the important differences was that the overwhelming majority of hunts off Britain were conducted by well-trained support groups. Moreover, British-based groups were numerous enough to reduce the time between first contact and the start of a search to about half that in Canadian waters. Support groups featured in less than half of the RCN's searches organized off Canada, and there was a tendency for the group to consist of the first escorts away from the jetty. Allowing for differences in the types of ships available, and the more difficult water and weather conditions, operations in British waters were found to be twice as effective as those in the Canadian zone. As the researchers concluded, "lack of experience and adequate training," poor co-ordination between searching forces and between ships and shore, and the small number of support groups available all led to a nil score for Canadian-based escorts. Were it not for these factors, the RCN would have sunk at least one U-boat in home waters during the last year of the war.[65]

It is perhaps sufficient commentary on the efficacy of the RCN to note that no U-boat was sunk by a Canadian warship west of 50° and north of the Caribbean. U-boats destroyed in the northwest Atlantic fall into two broad categories: those sunk by aircraft in 1942 when the Germans operated boldly on the surface, and those sunk by the USN at the extreme limits of the Canadian zone late in the war (in addition, HM Trawler *Le Tiger* sank U-215 on Georges Bank in 1942). Both of these concentrations of sinkings represent distinct phases of the war at sea. The earlier period was one in which U-boats operated largely on the surface and could be countered by escorted convoys and airpower. Pursuit of underwater contacts at length was seldom possible and in the event were unsophisticated by later standards. The success of airpower in sinking U-boats was attributable entirely to catching submarines by surprise on the surface.

The later period was characterized by the German's adoption of fully submerged tactics, which required a high degree of training and skill to overcome. These qualities were demonstrated by RCN support groups operating in British waters and by those of the USN in the western Atlantic, but not by the forces under Murray's command. The failure of inshore ASW—as distinct from AS escort—in Canadian waters was, therefore, largely the result of concentration on other tasks: defence of shipping in 1942, and the offensive against U-boats in the British waters in 1944–5. Just how successful, how well trained, and how proficient RCN groups overseas really were remains to be determined. For now, at least, it appears that their achievement, coupled with the home establishment's struggle to master the environment itself, produced a world leader in ASW in the post-war years.

Chapter 9

CANADA AND THE WOLF PACKS, SEPTEMBER 1943

Jürgen Rohwer and *W.A.B. Douglas*

On 22 November 1942, the British Government Code and Cypher School at Bletchley Park received from the Operational Intelligence Center at the Admiralty an observation that the U-boat campaign was "the one campaign which Bletchley Park are not at present influencing to any marked extent—and it is the only one in which the war can be lost unless BP *do* help."[1] The codebreakers responded with their dramatically successful penetration of the Triton code on 13 December 1942, but in February 1943 the German xB-Dienst decrypted so many Allied routing signals and Admiralty U-boat situation reports that the number of convoys intercepted rose critically. Furthermore, on 10 March the Germans changed their weather code book, by which (together with a short signal code book captured in U-559), Bletchley Park had broken into the Triton settings of the four-rotor cypher machine "M4."[2]

When the key word ordering this change was intercepted on 8 March, the Admiralty's director of naval intelligence warned "that the Submarine Tracking Room will be 'blinded' in regard to U-boat movements for some considerable period, perhaps extending to months."[3] Disaster was at hand, because between 6 and 20 March U-boats sank 41 out of 202 ships in four eastbound convoys. British, American, and Canadian delegations to the Atlantic Convoy Conference of early March were still trying to sort out a very imperfect system of convoy defence, amid considerable bureaucratic infighting. German overconfidence—the *Kriegsmarine* failed to change the short-signal code book, so that Bletchley Park was able to crack Triton again in only nine days by using "bombes" (primitive computers) to analyze the massive signal traffic generated by the battles for HX-229 and SC-122—saved the day for the Allies.[4]

The first five "support groups"—formations free to turn their attention to convoys under immediate threat rather than being tied to a single convoy, including one with a USN escort carrier—came into operation in the following weeks. With the help of a limited number of very-long-range (VLR) Liberators based on Iceland and Northern Ireland, the new forces, meagre though they were, fought off U-boats that were still achieving a 60 per cent interception rate, decisively reduced the number of sinkings, and sank so many submarines that on 24 May 1943, Commander, U-boats, had to break off wolf pack operations on the northern convoy routes.[5]

Grand Admiral Dönitz conceded he had lost a battle, but not the tonnage war he was waging against Allied shipping. "We have succumbed to a technical problem," he said, "but we shall find a solution."[6] Increased air cover and a "locating device" used by surface vessels had to be overcome. If the locating device turned out to be the new 9.7 cm radar, or even if it was radiation from the "Metox" radar search receiver carried in U-boats, a new passive search receiver on the 9.7 cm band, "Hagenuk Wanz," as well as another new search receiver, "Naxos," would neutralize shipborne radar. To fight off attacking aircraft, each U-boat received one quadruple and two twin 20 mm mountings. The improved acoustic homing torpedo "Zaunkönig" would be an effective counter to attacking escort vessels. Dönitz looked forward confidently to resuming the offensive in late summer.

His strategic appreciation, like his tactical plan, was flawed by wrong assumptions. According to his figures, Allied shipping had lost 30 (as opposed to 21.5) million gross registered tons and built only 15.5 (as opposed to 16.5) million, and he thought immense leeway had to be made up before large-scale amphibious operations could take place against Fortress Europe. Any reasonable success, he concluded, would significantly delay Allied invasion, besides tying down the naval and air forces which otherwise could be used in offensive operations against Germany.[7]

So Dönitz gathered strength for the renewed battle on the northern routes and, having failed to identify the real source of danger, the penetration of his cyphers, turned attention to the central Atlantic, to concentrate on convoys from the United States bound for the Mediterranean, beyond the range of land-based air cover that was now beginning to close the "Greenland Air Gap." Since Enigma intercepts permitted effective re-routing of convoys on southern routes, and led to devastating attacks on U-boats and their supply vessels, Dönitz suffered further defeat. Moreover, allied air and naval operations in the Bay of Biscay, with the help of centimetric airborne radar and new search tactics, increased Allied sighting and sinking rates.[8]

Early in June, U-boats began transiting the bay in groups of two to five boats to provide mutual support against air attack, while Ju-88C long-range fighters tried to provide air cover. British Beaufighters and Mosquitoes outperformed the German aircraft, however, and with operations "Musketry" and "Seaslug," constant search by RAF Coastal Comand ensured quick air support to any unit reporting a U-boat group. When German "Narvik" destroyers and "Fleet" torpedo boats went out to support damaged U-boats and to escort U-tankers, British cruisers and fleet destroyers provided added strength to naval support groups. By 2 August, aircraft had sunk eighteen U-boats; ships had sunk three. Eleven U-boats had to return to harbour with damages. Against this, eight aircraft were shot down by flak and six by fighters, an exchange rate that forced Dönitz to abandon group sailings and postpone further departures from French ports until U-boats got their new "Hagenuk Wanz" search receivers.[9]

In August, U-boats had more success, returning to their French bases by running close to the Spanish coast along the "Piening Way" (named after the captain of U-155 who found out how to confuse British radar with echoes of the hills on the coast).[10] He-177's and long-range fighters destroyed seventeen ASW aircraft and six fighters in three weeks. FW-200's were also attacking convoys on the UK-Gibraltar route, forcing the reallocation of ships and aircraft to convoy escort farther out to sea. Operation Percussion, a combined sea and air effort to close the Piening Way was countered by Luftwaffe Hs-293 glider bomb attacks. On 25 August, fourteen long-range Do-217 bombers attacked the 40th Escort group off Cape Ortegal, and on 28 August, eighteen Do-217's attacked the First Support Group, destroying the sloop *Egret* and hitting the Canadian destroyer *Athabaskan*. It was a timely success for Dönitz, who on 23 August began to assemble his forces for the return to the northern convoy routes.[11]

He was of course at a severe disadvantage, since the Operational Intelligence Centre in the Admiralty and OP-20G in Washington read the orders he sent to U-boats at sea. The only thing working in his favour was delays in decryption, which ran from several hours at the height of a convoy battle to as much as eleven days in the preparatory stages. He had tried to deceive Allied naval authorities about the disposition of U-boats during the summer, but the submarines sent to simulate large groups, by transmitting radio messages from various positions on different frequencies, simply exposed themselves to detection and attack.[12] Moreover, Commander Rodger Winn, officer in charge of the British Submarine Tracking room, had produced a reference to a British sighting report in an Enigma intercept, which persuaded the Admiralty to change Naval Cypher No. 3, on 10 June, to the new Cypher No. 5. When the xB-Dienst started decrypting signals again, some weeks later, the process proved to be too slow for operational purposes and only provided information about straggler routes and changes in ship destinations.[13]

In the meantime, Allied naval commanders were enjoying the fruits of improved organization, a disposition of forces arranged at the March convoy conference. Now that the danger of wolf pack attacks was removed, the northern convoys could be sailed along the shortest great circle routes, shortening the rhythm of the fast HX/ON convoys from 7 ½ to 6 ½ days, and of slow SC/ONS convoys from 13 to 11 days, the average size of convoy being seventy-two ships in twelve columns of six. On these northern routes, four British and five Canadian escort groups comprising twenty-four destroyers, five frigates, and fifty-four corvettes, including five Norwegian and four French-manned vessels, had only 65 per cent, or a total of fifty-four ships, ready for sea. Partly this reflected inadequate maintenance and harsh conditions of service in the North Atlantic.[14]

Elsewhere, the convoy routes between the UK and Gibraltar or Sierra Leone (OG/XK, OS/SL, MKS/KMS, MKP/KMF), and between the United States and the Mediterranean (UGS/GUS), also adapted their rhythms to new circumstances. Nine British escort and support groups, consisting of seventy-three ships, of which fifty-four or 73 per cent, were available, protected convoys on the UK-Gibraltar-Freetown run; six American escort groups of the US Tenth Fleet, for which fifty-five ships (including five Coast Guard cutters) were available, looked after the US-Gibraltar run. The USN also provided two task forces of one battleship and fourteen to fifteen destroyers each for fast troop convoys to Gibraltar or the UK (UGF/GUF, UT/TU), and a task group of six destroyers for tanker convoys (CU/UC) between the Caribbean and the UK. Providing additional punch were six American "hunter killer" groups, one allocated to the northern routes, the rest to the central Atlantic area, with one escort carrier and three four-stacker destroyers each. Three British and one Canadian support groups, comprising eleven sloops with anti-aircraft armament, eight frigates, and six corvettes, operated in the Bay of Biscay.[15]

Allied ASW air forces at this period tended to be concentrated in the Bay of Biscay and central Atlantic. On 23 August, of the 169 VLR and long range British and American aircraft available to Coastal Command for the Bay offensive, 90 were operational. Of the 84 British and Canadian aircraft available to Coastal Command in Northern Ireland and Scotland, only 29 were operational. Another 29, of the 47 American and British aircraft based on Iceland, were also serviceable for flying on the northern routes. Eastern Air Command, RCAF, had 15 of its 27 Cansos and VLR Liberators based on Newfoundland (where the only RCAF airfields within range of mid-ocean operations were situated) in serviceable condition. Since July these forces had provided continual air cover across the North Atlantic.[16]

Allied commanders were expecting a renewal of U-boat operations in the region. Rodger Winn offered an appreciation on 30 July which was the basis of measures taken in September:

> It is common knowledge both to ourselves and the enemy that the only vital issue in the U-boat war is whether or not we are able to bring to England such supplies of food, oil and raw material and other necessaries, as will enable us, (a) to survive and (b) to mount a military offensive adequate to crush enemy land resistance. Knowing that this is so, the enemy in withdrawing from the North Atlantic must have intended an ultimate return to this area, so soon as he might be able, by conceiving new measures and devising new techniques, to resist the offensive which we might be able to bring to bear upon him there ... but it might be the last dying struggle of a caged tiger for the enemy to send back in September or October into the North Western Approaches his main U-boat forces, unless in the meantime, he acquires by sheer luck, or the brilliance of some unknown inventor, the antidote and the panacea to all those well proven weapons which our armoury contains ... Even if heavy losses of merchant shipping and escort forces on the North Atlantic convoy routes were to be suffered ... no fear need be felt as to the ultimate outcome.[17]

This assessment took no account of the Zaunkönig acoustic homing torpedo or the new fast diesel U-boat types XXI and XXIII, nor of the Walter types XVII or XVIII which were in the offing. Winn's confidence was justified, all the same, because except for the torpedo, which was known to be under development, Dönitz could not yet call on the belated additions to his submarine fleet. A year later, Admiralty intelligence reports would be much less sanguine, but by the same token, German sailors would by then no longer be in a position to exploit their new assets.[18]

The necessary strategic and tactical moves by the protagonists, in the next phase of operations, were governed by the constantly changing disposition of ships and aircraft[19] between 23 August and 19 September, when U-270 would make the first sighting report of ONS-18. As U-645 and U-305, the first of the boats to sail for the new wolf pack offensive, safely negotiated the Bay of Biscay, the slow convoy ONS-16, escorted by the Canadian group C-3, and the fast convoy ON-198, escorted by C-1, were westbound and the fast convoy HX-252 with C-1 was eastbound, in the mid-ocean area. On the UK-Gibraltar route were MKS 21, northbound with the British escort group B-4, and a combined southbound convoy, KMS-24/OG-92, escorted by B-1. U-523 stumbled into this force with fatal consequences when HMS *Wanderer* and *Wallflower* detected and sank the submarine with depth charges. A few U-boats were transiting the Piening Way; one of them, U-134, fell victim to a Leigh Light, a Wellington of 179 Squadron RAF, fitted with the Leigh Light for illumination of surface targets and based on Gibraltar.

Sea and air forces associated with Operation Percussion swamped the area off Cape Ortegal and Finisterre; the mine-layer U-214, bound for Panama, and the anti-aircraft submarine, U-621, off to support other U-boats to the west, managed to avoid detection. The encounters of 25 and 28 August, resulting in the sinking of *Egret* and damage to *Athabaskan*, further improved U-boat chances. The cruiser HMS *Bermuda*, charged with opposing German destroyers, was too far off to be involved, while the support groups moved west, leaving the Piening Way uncovered. The next pair of North Atlantic U-boats, U-260 and 338, had no difficulty transiting the Percussion area. And it was at this time that the big Japanese submarine I-8 evaded detection on its way into Brest.

By 27 August, SC-140, escorted by C-2 and HX-253, escorted by B-3, were approaching the mid-ocean area from the west, while ON-199, with C-5, was emerging from the Irish Sea. U-229 and U-386 managed to get out between 29 and 31 August, at which point OS-54/KMS-25, with Escort Group 39, had begun its southerly passage to Gibraltar and MKS-22/SL-135, with EG-37, had reached a point off Biscay on the way north. On 29 August, HMS *Stonecrop* of the outer screen of this convoy detected U-634 and, in company with the experienced sloop *Stork*, carried out a 15-hour hunt that ended in destruction of the U-boat.

Sheffield, at this time, was on her way to relieve *Bermuda*, both ships giving a wide berth to the Biscay bases in case of glider bomb attacks. U-229 and U-386 managed to pass through the danger area without incident, and since six boats slated for operations on the northern routes were now safely at sea, Commander, U-boats, ordered them to head for Quadrant BD 60 (a reference on the German Naval Grid about 400 nautical miles north of the Azores) on 30 August. There was considerable activity in the region: three type IX boats bound for distant operations were transiting the area, and were replenished by U-460; the 5th Support Group intercepted and damaged U-760, which limped into El Ferrol to be interned by the Spanish; U-214 and U-621 rendezvoused to transfer a cathode ray tube; U-386 was attacked by an aircraft but received no damage, and convoy UT-1 entered the region from the southwest. Nothing happened, however, to affect the pending operation in the North Atlantic. By 5 September, the shipping situation in the mid-ocean area was developing along the lines anticipated by Dönitz: ONS-17 with B-6 and ON-200 with B-7 westbound, HX-254 with C-4 and CU-4 with task group 21.6 eastbound. Over the next five days convoys kept up their rhythm and four more boats—U-731, U-341, U-758 and U-584—reached the area, about eight hundred nautical miles southwest of Ireland, where they were to be replenished by U-460.

On 10 September, Commander, U-boats, ordered the next ten boats, U-402, U-641, U-448, U-952, U-666, U-387, U-270, U-413, U-603 and U-377, to head for reference points where they could expect to intercept convoys about 20 September. The next day he ordered three boats from Norway (and therefore not fitted with Zaunkönig torpedoes), U-238, U-422 and U-275, to a heading point further north than the others. On 15 September he ordered the boats into a patrol line, giving the end positions as reference points, as follows: "On 20 September 2000 hrs U-275, U-422, U-341, U-260, U-386, U-731, U-238, U-305, U-270, U-645, U-402, U-584, U-229, U-666, U-641, U-952, U-378, U-758, U-377 and U-603 form Group 'Leuthen,' distance between the boats seventeen miles."[20] Because the xB-Dienst had not been able to reconstruct the new convoy rhythm correctly, although this line covered the routes for convoys ONS-18 and ON-202, the plans for interception miscalculated the time at which they would pass through these areas. It will be noted, too, that U-413 and U-448 were still too far away to join Group "Leuthen."

Allied intelligence allowed naval authorities to follow Dönitz's moves after the fact but not to frustrate them. On 4 and 5 September, for instance, Commander, U-boats, ordered three TIX boats, U-515, U-536, and U-170, to rendezvous in square CE 40 for replenishment. On 7 September he cancelled heading points given to U-460 and the type IX boat U-536, then ordered U-460 to replenish the five boats U-645, U-305, U-260, U-338 and U-386 in square BD 9146 on 10 September. On completion the combat boats were to return to their waiting areas while the type IX's U-669, U-536, and U-170 (U-515 having been damaged by depth charge attack from the escort of MKF-22) were to steer for BD 87 for their own replenishment. The first part of the message of 7 September was decrypted during the night of the 13th, and the second part 28 hours later. Because the grid squares were super-encyphered there was some difficulty identifying their location. As soon as the second replenishment area was established by the Submarine Tracking Room, however, the Admiralty ordered US Task Group 21.12, the carrier USS *Bogue*, and three destroyers (closest of the five US carrier task groups then at sea) to the position. The ships arrived on 17 September, by which time U-460 had replenished the two surviving boats (a Wellington of 407 Squadron RCAF having sunk U-669), so *Bogue* and her consorts headed for the waiting area to the north. Again, they were too late, because the U-boats of Group "Leuthen" had already started for the patrol line.[21]

That episode illustrates the importance of the time factor. Carrier groups 21.11 with *Santee* and 21.15 with *Card* had been in easy range of the replenishment area between 7 and 9 September, when Allied U-boat estimates showed much more concern for submarines off Newfoundland and Nova Scotia, or en route to the Caribbean and West Africa, than to the west of Ireland. So convoys continued to sail their planned routes, ON-200, ONS-17 and ON-201 westbound, HX-255 and SC-140 eastbound, OG-93/KMS-26 and XK-11 northbound, GUS-14 and GUF-10 westbound from the Mediterranean, the tanker convoy TO-8 going south west to the Caribbean, and the eastbound UGS-16 to the Straits of Gibraltar, followed by UGS-17.

Just before 6 AM on 14 September, Bletchley Park decrypted the second part of the signal that sent U-645, U-305, U-260, and U-338 to their waiting areas and allocated a waiting position to U-386.[22] Adding to the significance of this new information was a series of messages which had been coming in for the past few days, from Dönitz to his U-boat commanders, about their passage through Biscay, the use of "Aphrodite" radar-deception balloons, the "Hagenuk" search receiver, and the code-word "Zaunkönig."[23] These messages were simply repeating information the addressees already had; they were designed to keep the U-boat commanders up to the mark, but it is more likely that, super encyphered as they were in "Offizier" cypher, although this meant they took longer to decrypt, they also drew Rodger Winn's attention to the operation. Something out of the ordinary was in the wind, just as he had anticipated would happen at about this time.

For the moment all that the Admiralty could do was wait for the next move. HX-256, eastbound with its sixty-one merchantmen, escorted by C-5 under the command of Commander H.F. Pullen, crossed the mid-ocean area between 14 and 23 September north of the great circle route. The slow convoy ONS-18, with twenty-seven ships in eight columns, and the merchant aircraft carrier *Empire MacAlpine* with eight Swordfish aircraft, escorted by B-3 under Commander Martin B. Evans, RN, emerged from the northern channel on 14 September. Two days later the fast convoy ON-202, forty ships in ten columns escorted by C-2 under Commander P.W. Burnett, started west. The two convoys were to follow parallel courses.

On 17 September, "Leuthen" boats, as they approached the route ordered for HX-256, passed near *Mauretania, Queen Elizabeth*, and the convoy UC-4, without sighting them. It so happened that the Canadian support group EG-9, under Commander C.E. Bridgman, RNR, sailed from Plymouth at this time to relieve Commander F.H. "Johnny" Walker's British 2nd support group in the Bay. The groups had been given a rendezvous further west than normal in order to be closer to the U-boat waiting area discovered from the decrypts of 13 and 14 September. Then, on the morning of 18 September, the Operational Intelligence Centre became aware of "Leuthen's" patrol line. Assuming the worst possible case, the Admiralty placed the reference points farther west than they should have been, which seemed to place HX-256 in immediate danger, so EG-9 received orders to join that convoy at best speed. At the same time, ONS-18 and ON-202 received diversions that, because the estimates were wrong on both sides, came too late and would prove to be too short legged.

On 19 September, some precise intelligence started to come in. Liberator A/10 of 10 (BR) Squadron, RCAF, providing coverage to ONS-18 on a flight from Reykjavik to Gander, destroyed U-341 about 160 miles west of the convoy. In addition to this, escorting vessels began to get HF/DF bearings.[24] On the evening of 18 September the decrypt of a signal sent on the 16th showed that the boats were only to attack westbound convoys, expected on 21 and 23 September respectively. Finally, on the evening of 19 September and the morning of the 20th, a series of admonition signals which had been sent in "Offizier" cypher were decrypted. They gave the game away.

> Directives for the first convoy operation:
> (1) On passage:
> At all costs remain unseen both during the passage ... and when in the line. Nevertheless utilize any favourable attacking opportunities. Picking up the convoy: defence and successful operation depend on surprising the enemy. During the present Mediterranean offensive, convoys in the Atlantic are perhaps weakly escorted. The Morocco operations are a precedent for this.
> (2) During operation:
> First essential is to act all alike in the various stages as set out in "Gedanken über Geleitzkampf" ["ideas on fighting convoys"]. At the outset endeavour to make full use of the surprise blow. Go over to the open offensive only on receipt of the short signal.[25]

Four hours after this another signal spoke of "a particularly long approach passage for which large scale preparations were necessary"; then came the second part of the first signal:

> The decimation of the escort must be the first objective. The destruction of a few destroyers will have considerable moral effect upon the enemy and will greatly facilitate the attack on ships of the convoy in addition. When engaged in getting ahead of the convoy on the surface, do not form any group that consists of more than two boats. Your aim must be to spread yourselves evenly round the convoy in order to split up the defence.
> (3) I expect of all commanding officers that each chance of a shot at a destroyer will be utilized. From now on, the U-boat is the attacker—fire first and then submerge.[26]
> sgd. Commander-in-chief

The preliminaries were over. U-402 had sighted ONS 18 shortly before midnight on 19 September, and at 0406 U-270 sent his enemy report:

> beta/beta: Convoy square 1944 AL, 270 degrees. Otto. [U-270][27]
> Commander, U-boats answered:
> Leuthen at'em. [An Leuthen ran]. Otto report contact. Manseck [U-758] report weather at once.[28]

Over the next three days there were to be seven direct confrontations between the boats of Group "Leuthen" and the two convoys they were attacking. Allied naval authorities ashore knew roughly what to expect. They had read Dönitz's instructions to his "Zaunkönig" boats to "use weapons as often as possible .... [to] stay at periscope depth if enemy comes towards you" because they "would have plenty of time to go deep."[29] There was a healthy respect for allied air superiority— "even in mid-Atlantic only the most essential men should be on the bridge ... No strength through joy parties"—but clearly, from the signal decrypted that day, the submariners were expected to take the offensive.

The escorts to be involved in this battle had worked together in their respective groups before: a proven necessity. Commander Burnett of C-2, with ON-202, was in the destroyer HMCS *Gatineau* (with Lieutenant Ernest M. Chadwick, RCN); his group also included the destroyer HMS *Icarus*, the corvettes HMCS *Drumheller* (Lieutenant-Commander A.H.G. Storrs, RCNR) and *Kamloops* (Lieutenant Donald M. Stewart, RCNVR), and HMS *Polyanthus*. Commander Evans of B-3, with ONS-18, sailed in the destroyer HMS *Keppel*, with the frigate HMS *Lagan*, the British corvettes HMS *O'rchis* and *Narcissus*, and the free French-manned corvettes FFS *Lobelia Renoncule* and *Roselys*. Commander Bridman of EG-9 sailed in the frigate HMS *Itchen* and had under his command the Canadian destroyer HMCS *St Croix* (An old American fourstacker acquired in the 1940 destroyers-for-bases deal, commanded by Lieutenant Commander A.H. Dobson, RCN) and the Canadian corvettes HMCS *Chambly* (Lieutenant A.F., "Tony" Pickard, RCNR), *Sackville* (Lieutenant Angus H. Rankin, RCNR) and *Morden* (Lieutenant E.C. Smith, RCNVR). None of the information recently picked up ashore was available in these ships, but their officers were generally well briefed, and the ships' companies had extensive experience in assessing the capabilities of their enemy.[30]

All boats in "Leuthen" were Type VIIC's. Displacing 760 tons, they were capable of 17 knots maximum on the surface (about the same speed as a frigate and faster than a corvette), 7.6 knots submerged. They were fitted with one stern and four bow tubes, and fourteen torpedoes each. It will be recalled that four Zaunkönig's were to be found in all but four of the boats; each boat also had at least four FAT 3 pattern running torpedoes. They all had the enhanced anti-aircraft armament ordered for transiting the bay; none had radar. The Hagenuk Wanz picked up aircraft radar, but during this operation there is no evidence they could pick up ship-borne type 271 centimetric radar, which was to give the escorts an enormous advantage. Sometimes, of course, radar broke down, and that evened things up. The *Gruppen-Horch-Gerät* (group listening apparatus), a hydrophone array that could hear a single ship at a distance of up to 20 kilometres and convoys up to 100 kilometres, gave the U-boats perhaps their most important source of intelligence.[31]

It was at 0050 Greenwich Mean Time that Oberleutnant Paul Otto made out several shadowy shapes to the north of his position. At 0155, when he first began to transmit his "beta-beta" report (called a "B-bar" report by Allied intelligence), his transmission was immediately picked up by Commander Burnett's High Frequency Direction Finding (HF/DF) organization in C-2. The rescue vessel *Rathlin* at the rear of the fourth column obtained a first-class bearing, 210° true. Burnett delayed some time before acting on this, no doubt to see whether other bearings would reveal more boats in the vicinity. (U-238, approaching from the south, might have made a sighting report if he had not intercepted U-270's signal.) At 0225 Burnett sent *Lagan* off to investigate; at 0244 the vessel obtained radar contact and *Gatineau* set off to assist in the hunt. At 0259 U-270 fired a "Zaunkönig" (called T5 in the firing reports) and from a range of 3000 metres destroyed *Lagan*'s stern with a direct hit at 0303. It was a spectacular start for Dönitz's new offensive.[32]

Gatineau responded with an accurate ten-charge pattern that temporarily disabled U-270, and Otto withdrew to the south. Perhaps unfortunately for the convoy, in the light of later developments, U-238 had failed to observe this little battle. Kapitänleutnant Horst Hepp had been busy shadowing the convoy, which he detected at 0255 after following up the original "B-bar" report. Thus he was not diverted from his objective when *Gatineau* carried out several more attacks on U-270, all less effective than the first, between 0310 and 0345. During this period the rescue trawler *Lancer* made her way to the scene, and the tug *Destiny* attempted to close *Lagan* amid a confusing welter of contradictory orders, while *Gatineau* screened the damaged frigate prior to her departure under tow.[33]

U-238 established firm contact with the convoy at 0245 then kept strict radio silence and avoided detection. At 0356, however, the U-boat came too close to *Polyanthus*; the corvette acquired radar contact and attacked, forcing the boat out of contact, but Kapitänleutnant Horst Hepp was not to be denied for long. By 0530, as *Gatineau* was coming up from astern to resume station, the U-boat had manoeuvered into a position from which Hepp could not only shadow but also attack from the ideal vantage point. By 0645, about fifteen minutes after daybreak, Hepp had submerged in the path of the approaching ships. The leading vessels of the screen, *Polyanthus* and *Kamloops*, steamed over the U-boat without obtaining contact, and this brought on the second confrontation. At 0732, from a range of less than 1000 metres, the submarine fired T3 torpedoes at the *Frederick Douglas* and *Theodore Dwight Weld*, the leading ships of the port wing and inner columns. Hepp saw both ships fatally hit within 25 seconds, the latter sinking immediately and the former remaining afloat with a pronounced list, before diving to 160 metres to pass under the convoy.[34]

Two other boats were approaching from the north. At 0704 U-731 sighted the mastheads and smoke of the convoy at a distance of about nine miles, and at 0720 U-338 sent in a sighting report. Evidently C-2's HF/DF guards missed this signal, because Burnett did not react to it in any way. In any case, he had his hands full with U-238. At 0800, after conducting the standard daytime search in such circumstances, Operation Artichoke, and dropping three patterns of depth charges on a contact (probably "non-sub," as no attacks appear in Hepp's KTB at this time), *Gatineau* returned to her position on the screen. *Polyanthus* stayed behind to protect *Rathlin* while the rescue vessel picked up survivors. *Polyanthus*' subsequent attacks at 0824, 0932, 1005, and 1025 were duly recorded by U-238.[35]

The convoy had already begun to leave behind a trail of destruction, and only two U-boats had so far made firm contact. Burnett therefore proposed to Commander Evans, commanding group B-3, that EG-9 be used to reinforce his sparse screen as well as that of ONS-18. Evans agreed instantly; the commander-in-chief Western Approaches, Admiral Sir Max Horton, RN, went still further and ordered the two convoys to join. This was a classic example of seamen applying well-established naval doctrine, in this case the so called N^2 law, by which the ratio of attacking opportunities was bound to decrease with a larger number of ships and escorts, with minimum fuss or delay. Evans, in his report of proceedings—an elegantly written document—recorded his reception of the order: "From all indications of D/F bearings and surface sightings ON 202 ... was the centre of attraction around which the beasts of prey were gathering. I felt rather a brute in leading my poor little ONS-18 into the turmoil, although our delight at a chance of activity—with a handsome escort—after months of dreary ocean plodding were only tempered by regret at the absence of my (late) Polish destroyers."[36]

Of course, the business of joining up two good-sized convoys in mid-ocean was incredibly complicated. Horton had to have supreme confidence in the ability of the men who had to carry it out. Perhaps it occurred to him also that the manoeuvre would confuse German intelligence, ashore and afloat, as much as it might the ships and escorts involved. Otherwise, two convoys in a state of confusion could have been easy meat, with the pack in full cry, eager for blood. Horton knew as well that under daylight conditions he could depend on aircraft to keep the U-boats at bay for a time. VLR Liberators from 120 Squadron, RAF, based at Reykjavik, did not disappoint such expectations. At about 0945, Liberator F-120, flying a close escort patrol, sighted U-386 about twenty miles north of ONS-18, and X-120, en route to join ON-202, sighted U-731 fifteen miles north of that convoy. Both aircraft attacked unsuccessfully, but the latter homed HMS *Icarus* on to U-731 before starting a close escort patrol for the convoy at 1035.[37]

Broken clouds and visibility at sea level of about seven miles gave aircraft a distinct advantage. While *Icarus* kept U-731 firmly out of the way, the Liberators provided a good screen for the remaining ships. Murphy's law came into effect at this point, when a corrupt group in the coded message from commander-in-chief Western Approaches resulted in ON-202 turning to the south at 1300 instead of maintaining the steady course and speed of 287°, 9 knots, by which both ONS-18 and EG-9 were calculating an interception in the early afternoon. ONS-18 at the same time altered to the northeast—a radical alteration that can only have been accomplished by all the ships in convoy turning together—thus gradually opening up rather than closing the distance between the two convoys.[38]

The escort commanders compounded the problem by turning both convoys towards enemy submarines: ON-202 in the direction of U-338 and one other U-boat; ONS-18 into the path of U-386. This became evident when at 1405 Liberator X-120 sighted two U-boats about six miles on the port beam of ON-202, and Liberator F-120, a few minutes later, sighted U-386 twenty miles on the starboard bow of ONS-18. Effective co-operation between sea and air escorts enabled X-120—which had expended all its depth charges and homing torpedoes in the earlier attack on U-731 and now had to be content with pouring machine-gun fire onto the target—to home *Drumheller* on to the scene. The corvette sighted and attacked U-338, but the other U-boat escaped on the surface, undetected by any escort vessel. To the north F-120, similarly deprived of weapons, dropped two marine markers on the position where U-386 had dived.[39]

The U-boat commanders now had little idea of the position, course, and speed of the convoy they were trying to locate. Commander Evans's view, from the bridge of HMS *Keppel*, was that "the two convoys gyrated majestically around the ocean, never appearing to get much closer, and watched appreciatively by a growing swarm of U-boats." Oberleutnant zur See Fritz Albrecht, in the control room of U-386, saw things rather differently. He had been congratulating himself, at daybreak, that his location about twenty miles northwest of the convoy placed him in a "good forward position": all he had to do was make sure he kept well ahead of the convoy screen. F-120's unsuccessful attack earlier in the day had done nothing to discourage that idea. The sighting to the westward, at 1510, of a destroyer and a frigate (evidently *St Croix* and *Itchen* joining ONS-18), startled him; evidently, he thought, he would have to do battle with the convoy screen. The fact that there were two convoys nearby, steering almost opposite courses, never occurred to him.[40]

With the help of a newly joined Liberator, R-120, Evans located ON-202 early in the afternoon. At 1613 *Gatineau* sighted ONS-18 to the northwest, at the same time that Evans was formulating a plan to unite the two convoys while dealing with U-386. At 1629 *Keppel* got an asdic contact at 1200 yards (1100 metres), just as Albrecht was setting up an attack against the surface vessels. At 1635, according to the KTB of U-386, the sudden appearance of a V or W class destroyer at 400 metres, with rapidly changing bearings on the port quarter, prevented getting off a stern shot with one of his T5's. He saw *Keppel* turn towards him, black pendant streaming from the masthead and then dipped (lowered part way to indicate an attack in progress) just as he received the full impact of four heavy depth charge explosions. "Keine Schussmöglichkeit mehr"—"no more chance of a shot"—he conceded as he went deep to 160 metres. The next entry, not until 2245, is a survey of the damage caused by persistent attacks on the part of *Itchen*, *St Croix*, and *Narcissus*, which took over prosecution of the contact after Keppel rejoined the screen. With this third confrontation of the day, U-386 was out of the battle.[41]

Other U-boats were converging on the scene. As U-386 fell into its unintentional trap, U-260 and U-305 were approaching from the northeast, U-270 was catching up from the southeast, and U-952 was coming up from the south. Well astern of the others, U-645 came upon the wreck of the *Frederick Douglas* at 1800 and prepared to sink it with a *coup de grâce*. U-338, driven off by *Drumheller*, was pursuing on a course calculated to intercept the convoy after dark. From 1705 to 1905, U-305, which had sighted *Rathlin* and *Polyanthus* rejoining with survivors, manoeuvered to get ahead of the vessels for an attack.

Air cover greatly reduced the threat. At 1905, N-120, which had joined half an hour before and was flying a standard Cobra patrol (fifteen miles around the convoy in all directions), sighted, attacked, and destroyed U-338. Another aircraft, possibly R-120, appears to have sighted and attacked U-305; Lieutenant-Commander Dobson in *St Croix* decided to leave the pursuit of U-386 to his two consorts and cooperate with that aircraft. At 1933, U-305 came to periscope depth and sighted *St Croix* bows on. When the range closed to 1500 metres Kapitänleutnant Rudolf Bahr fired a T5, dove to 160 metres, and heard two loud explosions and a muffled echo, followed by a complete cessation of screw noises. It was the second successful use of a Zaunkönig torpedo.[42]

At 1940, U-952 sighted Liberator J-120 and remained on the surface to fight it out. *Narcissus*, recalled to the screen by Evans, obeyed new orders to help out the aircraft, which attacked unsuccessfully. With the torpedoing of *St Croix*—like *Lagan* crippled but still afloat—Evans despatched *Itchen* to the scene, detached *Polyanthus* from *Rathlin*, and ordered *Narcissus* to join the two escorts, while *Itchen* screened the Canadian destroyer. These dispositions served to reinforce an impression among the U-boat commanders that they were dealing with an advanced screen. The unintended deception transformed a series of separate actions into a single, prolonged fight between submarines and surface vessels. The fourth major confrontation of the battle, it allowed the main body of the combined convoy to steam southwest, getting further and further away from its greatest danger, while an assortment of escorts from C-2, B-3 and EG-9 assumed their screening positions, relatively uninterrupted by the enemy.[43]

At 2044, U-305 gave *St Croix* (lying with a heavy port list and her after mast hanging at a crazy angle towards the stern) the *coup de grâce* with a straight running torpedo. Three minutes later U-305 fired a T5 that exploded in the wake of *Itchen*, but the incident passed without much notice in the ensuing confusion. There was a pillar of flame as *St Croix* broke in two and sank with heavy loss of life; the melée of ships hunting the submarine, firing starshell in an effort to illuminate the scene, attracted other boats like moths to a candle. At 2100 U-270 decided to head for the starshell visible on his starboard bow; at 2141 U-260 sighted a searchlight to the east and at 2153 a thick cloud of smoke; at 2154 U-952 saw something like a red light in the same area, and at the same time U-641 decided to steer for the starshell. It was at this moment that U-260, having seen and been seen by one of the escorts emerging from the smoke, fired a T5 before diving to 170 metres and undergoing a depth charge attack. At 2230 U-952, which had been in contact for more than an hour, fired a T5 from the stern tube which destroyed *Polyanthus*, the most effective use of the Zaunkönig torpedo so far attempted. (U-229, which was sunk later in the battle, reported firing a T5 by signal earlier in the evening, and may have fired a second later on, but evidently missed the target both times.)[44]

During a lull in the action, *Itchen* picked up survivors for the second time. At 2316 Paul Otto in U-270 decided he had found the convoy again; at 2330 U-641 came upon *Itchen* and *Narcissus*, and both stopped and attacked. At 2349 U-270 fired at the same targets and continued to stalk them for three hours. At one point in this game he was illuminated by starshell "so well laid that they practically land on my stern, and burn underwater." He fired a T5 at 0235, went deep, endured some depth charge attacks, and finally resurfaced at 0430. Meanwhile, U-952 had surfaced at 0315 and U-305, steering southwest after sinking *St Croix*, surfaced at 0430, both to resume pursuit of the convoy. U-377, seeing the fireworks at 0015, submerged, heard weak hydrophone effect (HE) to the southwest, and followed it.[45]

U-378 was the only boat to gain a good tactical position that night, but *Sackville* picked up HF transmission at 0050 about eight miles ahead of the port column and put the boat down with three depth charge patterns, Lieutenant-Commander Rankin was no doubt unaware that U-378 had fired a T5 at him. At 0125 U-377 came up astern of the convoy, thought he had been seen in the moonlight, and fired a bow shot at a "destroyer"; at 0141. The U-boat underwent attack and did not surface until 0300, by which time all HE had disappeared. In the meantime Commander, U-boats (Befehlshaber der U-boote, or Bdu), drew the correct conclusion that U-270 and the other boats involved in the night's activities were too far to the east to threaten the convoy. His message to that effect was picked up by U-731, which consequently did not steer for the visible starshell but continued west, and by other boats in Group "Leuthen," which adjusted their courses accordingly.[46]

Before dawn on 21 September, a thick blanket of fog descended on the convoys, persisting until early afternoon, when it lifted for about an hour. The escort commander discovered to his surprise that ONS-18 was now disposed abeam of ON-202.

> Feeling rather provoked at the Commodore for not informing me of his intention to carry out this masterly manoeuvre [wrote Commander Evans], I started to write a peevish signal but fortunately had the sense to ask, before I sent it, if he knew of the situation. I found that he was under the impression that ONS-18 was astern of him, and that this most desirable change in the formation had been ordered by a higher authority.[47]

Vital air support was still provided. Even in the fog Swordfish from *Empire MacAlpine* flew off and performed hair-raising feats to land on the tiny flight deck in the murk. Liberators from Iceland, and on 22 September from Newfoundland, also flew close air patrols in the daylight hours; when they had to return to base Evans felt vulnerable and sent out the three survivors of EG-9, *Chambly*, *Sackville* and *Morden*, on stern sweeps.[48]

Until 1650 on 22 September, when the fog finally dispersed, a number of "brief encounters" took place. At 0410 on 21 September U-584 fired a T5 (said to be against *Chambly*, but the evidence is not clear); *Morden* attacked a contact about three miles ahead of the starboard wing column at 0455, and *Chambly* investigated a radar contact about ten miles astern at 1839.[49] U-952 sighted an escort vessel at 2320, and *Icarus* investigated a contact, possibly U-422, on the starboard beam at 2336. On 22 September *Chambly* attacked an unidentified U-boat, possibly U-238, five miles ahead of the starboard wing column; at 0154 *Renoncule* and *Roselys* attacked what was probably U-952 on the port quarter. At 0205 U-377, suddenly seeing a "destroyer" looming out of the fog, dove to 160 metres and at 0302, hearing HE all around, was presumably overrun by the convoy. At 0350 when he fired at a "steamer" and claimed to have sunk it, U-952 heard some torpedo explosions and "sinking sounds." At 0435 the AS trawler *Northern Foam* attacked U-305 astern of the convoy. At 0620 *Keppel* picked up the bearing of a high frequency transmission astern, carried out a "cataract"—a tactic designed to pounce on a target well astern when the U-boat least expected it—and in this instance managed to ram and sink U-229. At 1142 *Sackville* attacked U-377 ten miles astern, and at 1508 *Roselys* obtained a contact on the port beam which was later considered extremely dubious. Shortly after that, the visibility began to lift.[50]

Evans now found his ships spread out over an area of thirty square miles, with a gap of four miles between the two convoys. There was much confusion among both escorts and their charges about their relative positions and tasks, and in his efforts to regain firm control Evans admitted to a moment of weakness.

> At this time I received a report of a submarine 45 miles 250° from us ... [and] asked the Commodore to hold the southerly course until dark then turn to 260°, in order to side step the submarine. He agreed ... but then horrified me by asking me to pass a message to ONS-18 to form his convoy astern of ON-202. I immediately protested. The Commodore quite rightly pointed out that I was asking too much to expect a convoy of eighteen columns to carry out a 50° turn in the dark. Instead of cancelling my request to make the turn ... I made the very grave mistake of agreeing to the convoys being formed astern of each other ... influenced by the desire not to cause confusion by requiring an alteration of plans which had already been set going, and by the extreme difficulty of ... carrying out a discussion with two convoys who were still being controlled by their own Commodores and whose source of intercommunication was mainly provided by *Keppel* acting as messenger boy across the six or seven miles of water which separated them.[51]

"After living under a blanket for so long," added Evans, "it was very nice to come into the open air and find it filled with Liberators." At 1740 one of those Liberators, L-10 of 10(BR) Squadron RCAF, based on Gander, Newfoundland, attacked U-270 forty miles ahead of the convoy. The boat fought back with accurate flak. One round shot out an engine and another "parted the hair above the Navigator's left eye and came to rest, protruding half an inch out of the instruments in front of the Captain." Damaged, reaching the limit of prudent endurance, and unable to use a homing torpedo so long as U-270 remained on the surface, L-10 left for home. So did the submarine, which could no longer dive because of a break in the pressure hull.[52] At 1645 a second Liberator, X-10, found U-377 on radar, pressed home an attack with machine guns, and although failing to damage the boat wounded the commander so seriously he had to be carried below. U-377 withdrew for medical assistance. X-10 had in the meantime sighted U-402 about seven miles away and, having expended all main armament, traded gunfire until the submarine disappeared in a fog bank.[53]

At 1934 *Lobelia* attacked U-758 and drove the submarine away from the port quarter of the convoy with slight damage. Soon after two Swordfish from *Empire MacAlpine* attacked U-238, ten miles ahead of the convoy, but the slow old biplanes gave a wide berth to the U-boat flak; it was *Itchen* and *Narcissus* that eventually forced Hepp to withdraw and lose sight of the convoy.[54]

As night fell ten U-boats, undetected by aircraft, were still converging on the convoy. Thanks to the arrival of the frigate HMS *Towy*, delayed by repairs, Evans had since the afternoon of 21 September been able to place his HF/DF ships far enough apart, *Towy* being on the starboard wing of the screen, to obtain good cross bearings. From intercepted transmissions he anticipated attacks mainly from ahead or on the port side, with a less well-defined danger on the port bow. He had no knowledge of the threat from astern because U-boats in pursuit had made no sighting reports and did not give themselves away.[55]

At 2130 *Itchen* got a radar contact ahead of the convoy; ten minutes later N-10, attempting to join from ahead and experiencing radio problems, sighted the ships of the convoy and the wake of U-275 almost simultaneously in the growing darkness. Evans refused permission for the Liberator, which was not fitted with a Leigh Light, to drop flares: that would have disclosed the position of the convoy to every U-boat in visual range. Just before 2200 U-952 caught up from astern and fired a T5 at *Renoncule*, on the port quarter. Oberleutnant Oskar Curio mistakenly thought he had sunk the corvette, which got a radar contact at 2206; ten minutes after that *Northern Foam* sighted U-952. Both escorts attacked with depth charges and the U-boat started making water at the rate of four tons an hour. Curio nevertheless kept up his pursuit.[56]

At 2234 U-731 fired a T5 at the advanced screen, possibly at *Itchen*, dove to 170 metres, and did not surface until the convoy had passed. Just after this attack *Morden* and *Itchen* both opened fire at radar contacts. U-260, which partly penetrated the screen, may have been the target, although no mention of gunfire appears in the boat's KTB. Fifteen minutes later *Gatineau*, in the next line of screening vessels, also engaged a radar target. Once more U-260 noted destroyers very close, but not gunfire. The situation was, indeed, thoroughly confused. At 2359 *Itchen* opened fire at a U-boat almost at the moment that U-666 fired two T5s, one at *Itchen* and one at *Morden*. One of these torpedoes became the fifth Zaunkönig to function perfectly when *Itchen* blew up, taking with her, tragically, her own ship's company and the survivors of *St Croix* and *Polyanthus*. Three men lived, one from each of the three ships, because the Polish merchant ship *Waleha* courageously stopped to pluck them out of the water. Commander Evans in *Keppel* had no idea who had been hit—*Gatineau* thought it was the U-boat—until he later took a radio roll call and found *Itchen* missing. In the meantime *Chambly* got a radar contact, presumably U-584, which at 0007 fired a T5 at the corvette without success. This ended the fifth direct confrontation of the battle. The U-boats, with all the advantages of numbers and favourable positions, had not been able to get through the screen to the ships in convoy.[57]

U-238, U-305, and U-260 were now moving rapidly into attacking positions. On sighting the huge explosion at 2359, Hepp, in U-238, worked his way over to the starboard side, possibly being responsible for a radar contact made by *Gatineau* at 0105. Similarly U-260, coming up on the port quarter, may have been the radar contact reported by *Lobelia* at 0115. The shape of the convoy and the screening diagram now made the task of the U-boats easier than the broad front and shallow depth preferred by Evans. The convoy took much longer to pass a given point, with the sternmost vessels of ONS-18 six miles behind the leading ships in ON-202, and it made a much larger target for U-boats intercepting from astern or on the beam. There was, moreover, still a large gap between the convoys. With the best will in the world, no corvette, or even destroyer, could provide proper asdic and radar coverage on either flank of this large and misshapen formation.[58]

At 0200 U-238 brought on the sixth confrontation. Hepp watched several escorts on the outer screen carefully as he slipped unseen past them. When *Drumheller* obtained a contact, went to action stations, and fired starshell, Hepp took no notice; he coolly took up an attacking position 1000 metres on the starboard beam of ON-202 and fired three T3s. At almost the same moment U-260, on the port beam, saw and fired at *Chambly*. At the operational debriefing a few days later, Lieutenant A.F. Pickard recalled that he got radar contact at 4900 (about 4500 metres) yards and identified it as "submarine."

> Shortly after that [he stated] a ship was torpedoed. Pineapple dark was ordered. Convoy was illuminated by snowflake. There was a tremendous glare in the sky ... After chasing this fellow to a range of 1700 yards, went on starboard quarter. I was not illuminating. About two minutes after the contact failed: almost immediately an explosion astern shook the ship considerably. We went on and picked him up in the asdic at 1050 yards, went in to do an attack ... [before] the asdic went completely off.[59]

Chambly was lucky to escape destruction; the T5 seems to have exploded in her wake. She also gave effective protection to the port wing of the convoy. On the outer starboard column, by contrast, the second and third ships (*Skjelbred* and *Oregon Express*), and the fourth ship in the next column over (*Port Jemseg*), sank as a result of U-238's attack. When the boat broke off, 4000 metres from the nearest escort, Hepp recorded that it was suddenly illuminated by starshell. "[The destroyer] gave the impression," wrote Hepp, "of giving up the chase. [After some ranging shots] three salvoes landed. No result observed." Commander Evans said in his report of proceedings that "the attack by this submarine appears to have been delivered at long range, probably seven or eight thousand yards outside the screen." Had the starboard screen, especially *Drumheller* and *Icarus*, the closest escorts, maintained a sufficiently alert lookout, that should have been the case. U-238, however, had taken advantage of a lapse. That it happened during the middle watch, after three days and nights of exceptional vigilance, does not soften the consequences.[60]

U-952, U-305, U-758, and one other boat, possibly U-641, were still in a position to carry out further attacks. This led to the seventh and final confrontation. U-952 had surfaced at 0201, at 0329 intercepted U-238's shadowing report, and steered an intercepting course. U-758 had been in pursuit since just after midnight and made a similar alteration of course, west-north-west. U-305 and U-641, however, found themselves within hailing distance at 0041. They had seen starshell but refused to steer for it, believing it was another hunting group like that of 20 September; the "lesson" they had learned from that experience turned out to be a rather effective piece of disinformation. U-731 was steering for the HE to the southwest.[61]

The first to find the convoy was U-952. Curio noted in his KTB, at 0615: "At last, shadows to starboard ... Approximately ten shapes can be made out. Ahead and to starboard of the merchant ships ... disposed one ahead of another in column, the shape is that of a screening vessel ... Convoy is steering 220°."[62] He selected the two leading ships, firing a straight and pattern running torpedo at each. The first torpedo hit the leading ship in the first column of ONS-18 the American *Steel Voyager* (Curio was not aware of ON-202 several miles ahead); one dud torpedo hit the steamer *James Gordon Bennett*, and the other torpedoes appear to have missed. Curio watched until the closest escort, presumably *Renoncule*, was within 500 metres, then he dove and escaped unharmed. An entry in the KTB of 0652 notes that the whole horizon was lit up with starshell: "The screen," wrote Curio, "has woken up." Half an hour later he was forced to dive when the brightening sky placed him in silhouette, just as *Chambly* opened fire at a contact 5000 yards (about 4500 metres) on the port quarter.[63]

The battle had come to an end. U-758 did make contact at 0725, and about twenty minutes later fired at a steamer and its screening vessel (probably *Rathlin*, which had led a charmed life for several days, and *Renoncule*), but the attack failed. P-10 joining at daybreak attacked a U-boat, possibly U-641, about twenty miles astern. In his anxiety to join and report the submarine astern he overflew and failed to see U-305. Kapitänleutnant Bahr seems to have come across and shadowed *Rathlin* and *Renoncule* too and, although able to shadow them, could not get into a good attacking position. He gave up in mid-afternoon when he received Dönitz's signal to break off operations unless in position to attack.[64]

Aircraft sightings and attacks during 23 September probably prevented any other U-boats exploiting whatever advantage of position they had gained. P-10, on the way back to base, attacked U-422. It so happened that the deputy inspector general of the RCAF, Air Vice-Marshall A.E. Godfrey, was acting as waist gunner in the aircraft that day, and did "a very good job of shooting" according to the squadron's daily diary. Y-10, later in the afternoon, again attacked U-422 about 40 miles on the port bow of the convoy.[65]

Little time was wasted by either side in evaluating the battle. Soon after the escorts entered St John's, Newfoundland, their captains attended a "wash-up." Their reactions were perceptive, as should be expected of seamen who had spent at least two years engaging in more or less continuous anti-submarine warfare. It is interesting to note that U-boat captains, although in many respects obliged to assume more demanding technical responsibilities and take more independent decisions than commanders of surface vessels, failed to derive as much benefit from their experience.[66]

Commander Evans summed up the battle in his report of proceedings. As he rightly pointed out, only three U-boat attacks were made on the convoy. His estimate of how each attack occurred was close to the truth with the exception of U-238's unusual feat in the early hours of 23 September. He realized that U-boats were using acoustic torpedoes and had more anti-aircraft armament than before, and although not privy to the Enigma intercepts that had forewarned shore authorities, he deduced correctly that the only new tactic adopted by the submarines was to carry out carefully rehearsed attacks on the screening vessels themselves. "Whatever the danger," he wrote, "we shall only lose the initiative to the enemy—probably without saving ourselves—if we do not press home our attacks with the utmost vigour."[67]

Evans was not particularly impressed by the skill and motivation of U-boat commanders: "The statement in one of my signals that the enemy was showing greater determination in pressing home his attacks was due to the mistaken impression that a ship had been torpedoed at the same time as *Itchen* was sunk. I wish to withdraw that opinion entirely."[68] This suggests that Evans failed to appreciate to what extent the fortuitous diversion, created by encounters with U-386 and U-305 on 20 September, and itself a result of muddled Allied communications, followed by the protective shield of fog for such an extended period, saved the convoys from serious attack. U-boat commanders, without radar to help them, depending on their eyes and ears and unaware of the unusually strong screen, and harrassed (in two cases destroyed) by aircraft, did well to arrive in attacking positions at all. When they did, they concentrated first on the screening vessels. Horst Hepp in particular showed skill and enterprise in twice discovering and exploiting the weaknesses of the screen.

Surface vessels enjoyed the advantage of radar, but they sometimes squandered the advantage by inadequate maintenance of equipment. Lieutenant E.C. Smith of *Morden* admitted his asdic had only been working for twelve minutes during the entire passage. Radar constantly failed to detect U-boats well within radar range. A regular entry in the log of *Chambly*, every watch, read "armament inspected and correct."[69] Such attention to detail may help to explain that ship's effectiveness. Of even more importance, however, was the mental preparedness and motivation of ships' companies. In the dark and lonely hours of the middle watch on 23 September an apparent weakness in this respect manifested itself in the escorts of the starboard screen.

Aircraft, ultimately, spelled the difference. The "Greenland Air Gap" no longer existed. A battle on this scale and at this range from the nearest air bases, before about July 1943, might have been fought with the benefit of carrier-borne aircraft, but air cover from Newfoundland could not have been assured. Evans wondered at first if it was worth sending aircraft to fly over a fog-shrouded convoy, but he saw the value when visibility improved and he did not have hours to wait for Liberators to arrive on task. "On reaching St John's," he wrote, "I learnt that aircraft had been taking off in dense fog at very great risk. I can only say 'thank you', and assure them that their work is appreciated to the full, and their mere presence has an [invaluable] effect on the morale of both ships and escorts."[70]

Evans may not have realised how great a technological advantage he had with HF/DF. It, more than anything else, confounded the U-boat commanders. Some may have suspected, as Oberleutnant Otto Ites of U-94 had done in June 1942, that surface ships could home in on HF transmissions,[71] but German naval intelligence analysts, in spite of many clear givaways, never drew the conclusion that this was happening. If they had, they would have been able to exploit the situation deliberately by getting a warship to approach a U-boat head on, the ideal inclination for a Zaunkönig torpedo shot. As it was, HF/DF remained as much of a tactical advantage, as the ability to break Enigma was a strategic advantage, for the Allied navies.

The strategic consequences of the battle for ONS-18 and ON-202 were more readily appreciated by Allied than German naval authorities. Dönitz had to rely on radio reports from boats still at sea. They had reported twenty-four T5 attacks, claimed to have sunk twelve destroyers, and thought they had probably damaged three more. Other claims amounted to seven merchantmen for a total of 36,000 gross registered tons, as well as damage to three ships adding another 22,800 tons, against the loss of two (later found to be three) U-boats. This unqualified success appeared to have been achieved by no less than twelve of the twenty boats participating, in spite of the premature start to the operation. If the boats had reached their patrol line first they would have been able to co-operate, according to U-boat doctrine, against the attacks of aircraft. Furthermore, on two occasions, just as they thought they had weakened the screen by sinking first eight, then four, destroyers, fog descended to blind the U-boats. Even though Dönitz had warned the group that U-270 was attacking forces too far to the east, he evidently did not appreciate that this diversion had left the screen virtually intact.[72]

The relatively few reports about air attacks suggested to Dönitz that the Hagenuk search receiver and new anti-aircraft armament were working as planned. Ten U-boats, after all, kept in contact for more than three days and nights. It was time to exploit the victory. He ordered the eleven boats with enough fuel and torpedoes left over to form a new group, "Rossbach," to intercept the next westbound convoy, ON-203. The xB-Dienst had decrypted a four-day-old straggler's route for this convoy: not much, but enough to deduce the likely area for interception.[73]

In the Admiralty Rodger Winn had the benefit of all reports from Allied sea and air commands and was able to compare them with decrypted U-boat traffic, which was available within a few days. He thus became fully informed on Zaunkönig torpedoes, or GNATS, as they were christened by the Allies. Whether they hit, missed, went off prematurely, or exploded in the wake of a ship could easily be determined. Thus instead of the German assessment—thirteen sure an three probable hits out of twenty-four shots (a two-thirds success ratio)—the Submarine Tracking Room arrived at a total of two rather than ten hits by following shots, two by direct shots, and one *coup de grâce* against a merchant ship. Nine torpedoes, not three, as calculated by Commander, U-boats, exploded at the end of their run, four and not two exploded prematurely, and three in the wake of the target. Three were duds. The hit ratio of just under 25 per cent went down further still, as counter measures were applied in ensuing weeks, to less than 16.6 per cent.[74]

Coastal Command and the Admiralty responded to the new offensive by placing less emphasis on bay operations and returning a number of coastal command squadrons to 15 Group in Northern Ireland. A Canadian long range Canso squadron from Nova Scotia relieved the medium range Hudsons based on Iceland. Naval support groups cut short their operations in the bay to work with the northern convoys, and new groups came into being with the first two reconstructed Royal Navy escort carriers. Shorter delays in decryption meant more effective diversion of convoys and the timely despatch of forces to cover rerouted convoys.[75]

German allocation of U-boat patrol lines continued to depend on decryption of stragglers' routes, so that attempts by group Rossbach against convoys ON-203, ONS-19 and HX-258, between 28 September and 1 October, enjoyed no success. Between 3 and 5 October aircraft from Iceland sank three U-boats, damaged four more with the help of surface escorts, and prevented any kind of contact with convoys. Dönitz next redeployed Rossbach to intercept HX-259 and SC-143. On 7 and 8 October U-boats established contact with the escorts of SC-143 and carried out one successful attack against the Polish destroyer *Orkan*, but a strong air escort drove off the other boats and, in spite of heavy flak, sank three of them. A large German flying boat, the BV-222, for the first time used in reconnaissance of northern convoy routes, reported the convoy, but U-boats could only find and sink a straggler.[76]

From 15 to 18 October U-boats in the new group "Schlieffen," in operations against ON-206 and ONS-20, shot down two aircraft and sank one ship. Liberators in turn sank four U-boats, and ships sank two. From 23 October to 7 November Dönitz tried various stratagems to intercept ON-207, HX-262, SC-145, ON-208, HX-263, ONS-21 and HX-264. In the process, although none of the U-boats sighted a convoy, the support groups, which now included the escort carriers HMS *Tracker* and HMS *Fencer*, sank four more submarines. To the south an attempt at a short-lived attack by Group "Schill," with air reconnaissance support, against convoys on the Gibraltar route, resulted in the sinking of one merchant ship and the loss of more U-boats to aircraft, some of them from the newly established base on the Azores.[77]

Dönitz at last came to the painful realization that he was beaten. Continuous air cover for convoys, by land-based or carrier-borne aircraft using new location devices and more effective weapons, made interception of convoys and subsequent attacks virtually impossible with the available U-boat fleet. On 7 November he authorized orders for several hundred of the revolutionary new Type XXI U-boats, the first of them to be ready by the spring of 1944. The old Type VII and Type IX boats were to mount a campaign to deny the Allies the use of their ASW forces for offensive operations. They did divert large numbers of ships and aircraft, but not enough to prevent the Allied Operation *Overlord* in June 1944.[78]

Could the U-boats have prevented the invasion of Fortress Europe? Most historians answer this question in the negative by pointing to the spring of 1943, when the tide turned from the sinking of merchant ships to the destruction of U-boats. This study has shown that, thanks to the continued penetration of German cyphers and the steady growth of Allied naval and air capabilities in the summer of 1943, the initiative seized in May could be held long enough to seal the victory in September. Whether the true significance of the victory is fully apparent from these events, however, is another question.

To find the answer we really have to go back to the last six months of 1941, a period that tends to be overlooked because it was followed immediately by several months of disastrous shipping losses in the western Atlantic. By the most cautious estimate, the Submarine Tracking Room of the Admiralty, between June and December 1941, using Enigma decrypts, rerouted convoys around wolf packs so cleverly that between 1½ and 2 million gross registered tons of shipping (about three hundred ships) were saved from destruction.[79] It was an even more decisive contribution than the convoy battles or the Bay offensive of 1943, because without those three hundred ships (and possibly a hundred more that would have been lost if it had not been for the rerouting of early 1943), shipping and transportation problems would have forced the postponement of Overlord for months, perhaps even to the spring of 1945.

Nothing is certain in war. If the final outcome of the Battle of the Atlantic had never been in doubt, the importance of 1941 would have been clear to strategic planners of the day, and events might have unfolded in a different way. As it was, the final defeat of the wolf packs in 1943, necessary if the Allies were to take advantage of operational successes in late 1941, did not take place until Canadian naval and air forces had become full partners in the battle. Their contribution, accordingly, was decisive.

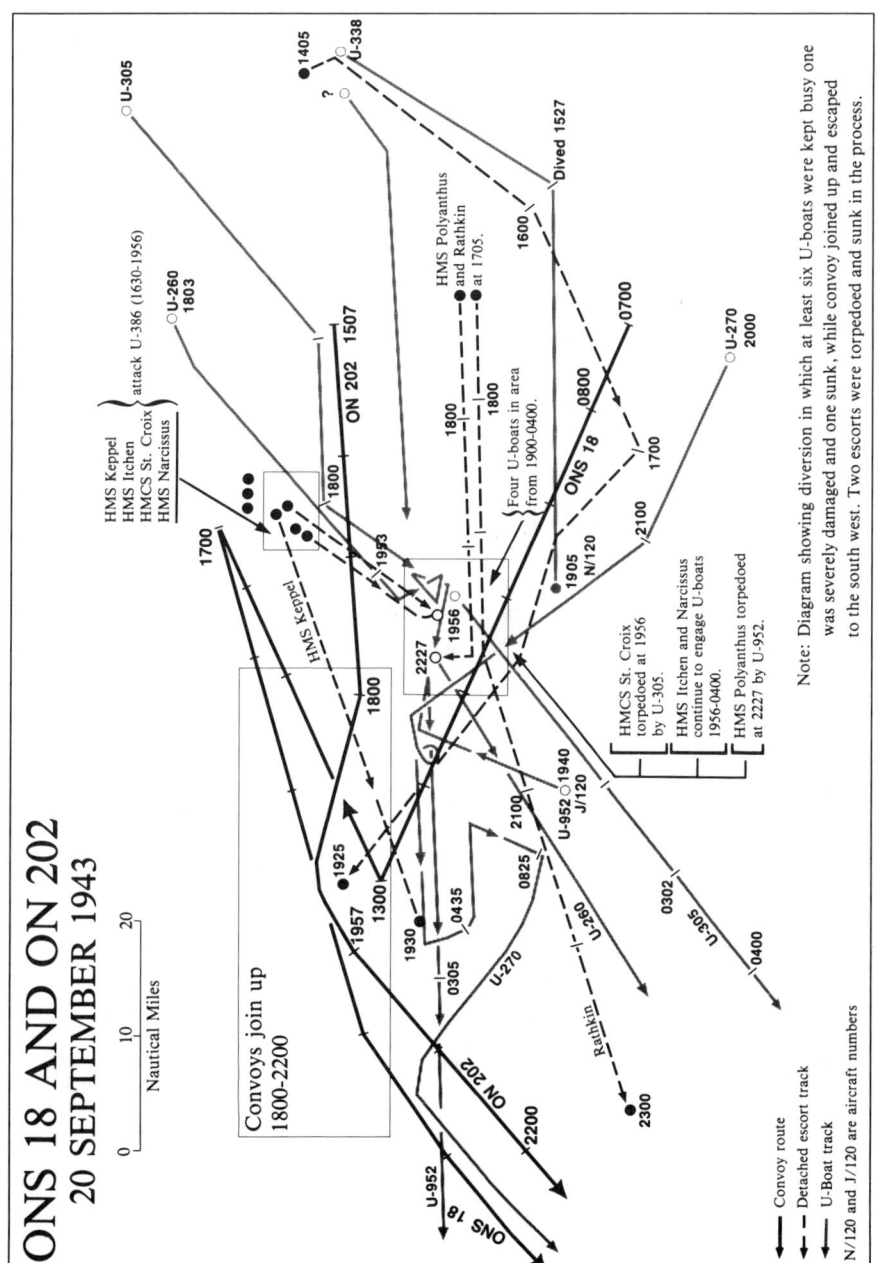

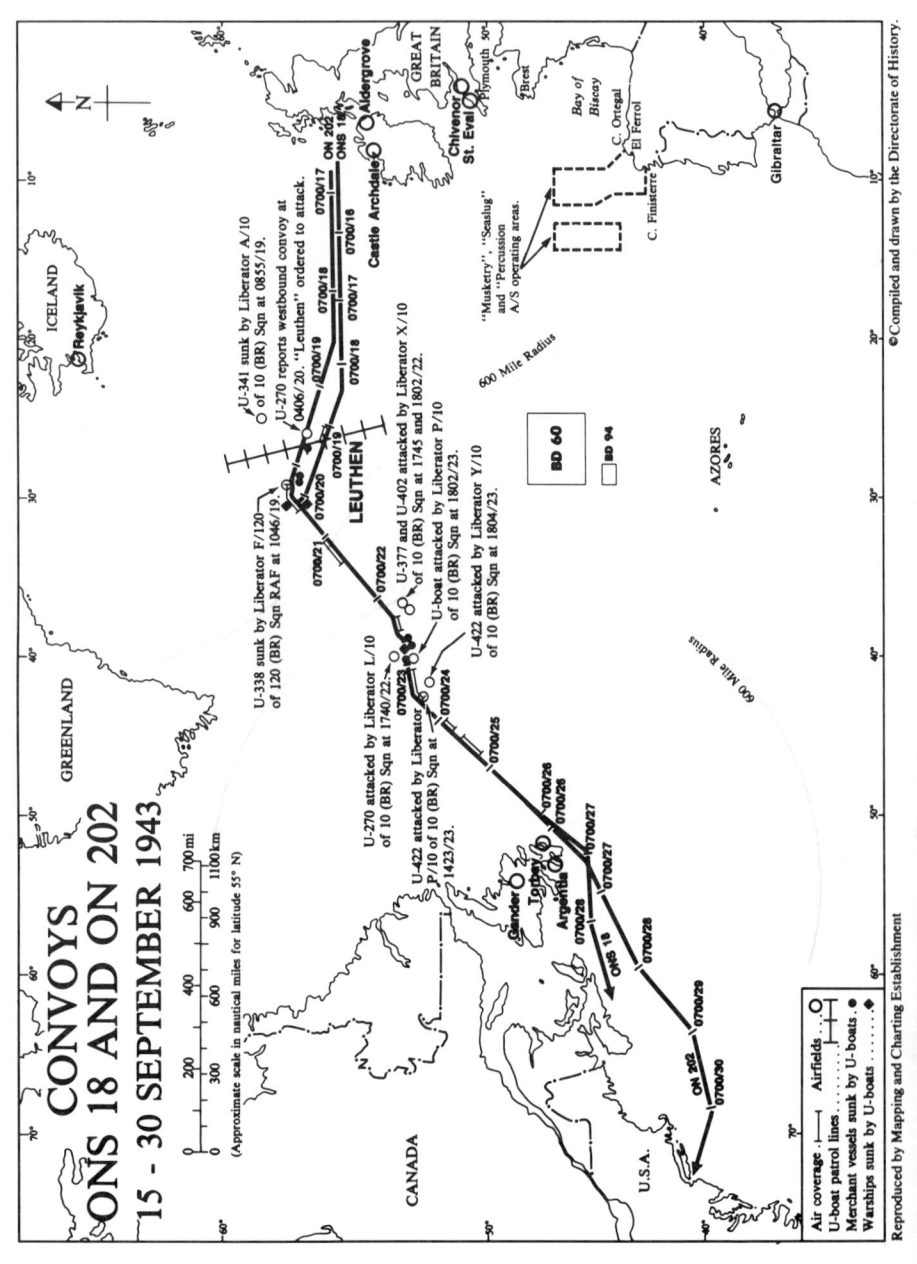

Chapter 10

THE "ST LAURENT" DECISION: GENESIS OF A CANADIAN FLEET

S. Mathwin Davis

SETTING THE SCENE

Introduction

This paper examines the decision processes by which the Royal Canadian Navy, from 1947 to 1953, moved toward anti-submarine warfare (ASW) with modern and sophisticated vessels in a post-war context. During the period concerned the Cold War had hardly started, the computer was far from an everyday tool of contemporary life, most of the doctrine on organization structure, decisionmaking, policy development, and so on had yet to be applied in the RCN and, from a technical viewpoint, there was nothing afloat to match the new destroyer escorts that the decision of those years would spawn.

The key elements of decisionmaking rested within a small circle. To be sure, it was ultimately necessary to involve the deputy minister's office, the Treasury Board, what was to become the Department of Defence Production, and in due course ministers of the Crown. Like ripples in a pond, the expanding convolutions gained momentum to overcome resistance. Our prime concern, however, is the stone that in this case fell into a very small pond, caused all the subsequent perturbations, confirmed the character of the Canadian navy for the next several decades, and provided a dominant influence that still governs naval affairs.

The Wartime Background

The wartime navy nurtured those who were subsequently to make the key decisions. Anyone aware of Canadian naval history must conclude that the country by 1945 had demonstrated an ability to build large numbers of simple warships. Equally clear was the nation's capability of producing the complex (for that period) electronic and other equipment developed under the pressure of war. Britain and the Royal Navy provided the designs and technical guidance, and the stress of wartime circumstances often put this arrangement to severe tests. Britain in this era had a strong and experienced engineering, manufacturing, and shipbuilding capability, which meant that first priority could be given to production of materiel, with the preparation of detailed drawings as a somewhat belated afterthought. Thus, lack of comprehensive guidance in Canada could easily result in a severe setback in production.

The lieutenants, lieutenant-commanders, commanders, and captains of the regular force who worked within this Anglo-Canadian relationship during the war were the principal decisionmakers after the war. There is for example a prescient photograph, taken in 1943 and published in James Boutilier's 1982 book *The RCN in Retrospect*, of three regular force commanding officers of RCN destroyers (Lieutenant-Commanders Hibbard, DeWolf, and Lay) who became flag officers in the late 1940s.[1] Remember that they and those like them had not only savoured a great Canadian success story—the expansion from a tiny nucleus in 1939 to the third largest navy in the world by 1945—but had also undergone their share of humiliations. Captain Donald Macintyre, RN, said of his Canadian allies that their ships "were units with which to make a show on the operations room maps and perhaps to give a semblance of security to convoys which would otherwise have gone unescorted, but they were little more."[2] Canadians resented such aspersions, but in their hearts regular officers knew there was some basis for the criticism.

Inevitably, RCN regular officers were products of the Royal Navy with whom they had trained and received their initial and moulding experience. No Canada badges marred (or enhanced) the Gieves uniforms[3] of those future admirals whose picture appeared in 1943, and the concept of workaday corvettes was as new to them as to the farm boys from Saskatchewan and the Eastern Townships who first took them to sea. It is important not to disparage this Admiralty imprint; even that hard-bitten corvette devotee who was so critical of the RCN officers, James Lamb, extolled the spectacle of RN ceremonial in HM ships at wartime Hvalfjord. "We were very proud," he wrote, "to be

... a Canadian branch of the Grey Funnel Line, a member of the White Ensign Club, and a sharer of all that marvelous mystique that went with it."[4] Of course Lamb's concept may not have been quite what the embryonic naval staff and naval board had in mind. At this point we cannot be privy to their thoughts, but we can take account of earlier Canadian naval policy proposals, and they suggest a fleet that was part of a centralized imperial navy, virtually at Admiralty disposal.

Even before the Naval Service Act of 1910, the Laurier government had contemplated building in Canada a fleet unit of cruisers, destroyers, and submarines using specifications, plans, and technical assistance from the Admiralty. Similarly, after the First World War, Admiral Jellicoe had recommended a comparable fleet unit, and even though what was acquired was a ridiculously truncated version that eventually shrank to almost nothing, Britain remained the source of equipment and doctrine alike. Without subjecting it to critical analysis, therefore, there is much to be said for Marc Milner's observation, in a survey of Canadian literature about the wartime navy, that "the war fought by the RCN between 1939 and 1945 was as much to anchor the navy permanently as to beat the Germans." Even though the concept of a navy that is "anchored permanently" is less than felicitous, it would be reasonable to conclude that the RCN was again contemplating its own fleet unit. In 1945, however, the connection with the Empire was far weaker than it had been before the war.

In 1940, 1941, and 1942 papers appeared at naval headquarters and elsewhere regarding the future peacetime navy. Captains F.L. Houghton, H.G. DeWolf, and W.B. Creery were involved, together with two RCNVR officers, Paymaster-Lieutenants J.S. Hodgson and G.F. Todd. The reservists, both with sound academic backgrounds, contributed their own ideas and gave substance to some of those of their chiefs. In 1943, the naval board instructed the plans division (DeWolf and Todd) to develop a series of papers about the continuing RCN. The result was an identification of international roles with allies and national tasks addressing the defence of North America. The naval plans division proposed a post-war fleet of four cruisers, two light fleet carriers, sixteen fleet destroyers, and other vessels. The naval staff, agreeing, was immediately seized with the need to obtain new ships during the war so that they would prove their effectiveness, win battle honours, and present the nation with a fleet in being when the war was over.

At the August 1943 Quebec Conference, the Royal Navy gave the RCN a helping hand by persuading Churchill to approach a reluctant Prime Minister Mackenzie King for the loan of Canadian naval manpower. Among other things, the RCN agreed to man two cruisers in

1944, and it appeared agreeable to the British that these vessels could be transferred to Canada when hostilities were over. Similarly, in October 1943 the Admiralty, with some RCN prompting, asked Canada to man two escort aircraft carriers. Thus, almost by the hand of providence (or at least a provident Admiralty) the RCN acquired the escort carriers *Puncher* and *Nabob* in mid-1944, the cruiser *Uganda* (later *Quebec*) in October 1944, and the cruiser *Minotaur* (later *Ontario*) in April 1945. Here, indeed, was the beginning of the "big-ship" navy to which permanent force officers had been motivated; at the Quebec Conference of August 1944 it was intimated that light fleet carriers could be made available to replace the escort carriers, initially on loan but to be bought or returned after the war.

In October 1944 the projected needs of a Pacific fleet unit, and the longer range requirements of a post-war navy, justified Angus L. Macdonald's ambitious plans, and the formal proposals by the Canadian Chiefs of Staff, for two carriers, four cruisers, eighteen destroyers, and 20,000 men. The fleet would serve national interests—no word of imperial responsibility is to be found in the six tasks given to the navy—but it was too much for the Cabinet War Committee. In September 1945, with Macdonald long gone (and on the outs with Prime Minister Mackenzie King), the committee briskly slashed the navy's demands, along with those of the other two services. On paper the RCN was left with about half the men it wanted and about half the ships. In fact, it would end up with even less. In January 1946, Mackenzie King opposed the acquisition of *Warrior* but agreed to accept one carrier if it could be used in the north. (Thus in 1948 the arcticized *Magnificent* would replace *Warrior*.) With its two cruisers, thirteen fleet destroyers, and about 7000 men, the type of task force sought in 1943 had finally begun to emerge. Ironically, this had come about largely with gifts from the RN, whose ties the RCN was seeking to loosen if not discard. The RCN could now face its future with the "big-ship" fleet that its senior officers—those at least who were shortly destined to fill the highest posts in the service—appeared to desire.

Deterioration set in quickly. As one-time naval officer John Harbron reflected in 1966, "Like a mighty wave, its foam laden crest broken on the beach, the Royal Canadian Navy in the fall and winter of 1945 was losing its strength."[5] When Rear-Admiral Harold Grant became Chief of the Naval Staff in September 1947, only eight ships were in active commission. Grant put a brave face on it. In a speech delivered shortly after he took office in September 1947, he defended the concept of a very few larger ships, noting their significance for training (in a wide range of equipment) as well as to provide seagoing experience for the more senior officers of all branches. At the same time he sounded a significant note, emphasizing the importance of the submarine and observing that the RCN was "actively engaged with the problem of anti-submarine warfare."[6]

Post-War Political Milieu

The intent of the immediate post-war years was to develop a defence organization that would facilitate the planning, equipping, and training of Canada's armed forces to meet any need that would arise. In 1947–8 this involved an expenditure of 240 million dollars (some 12 per cent of the federal budget), the navy's share being about one-fifth, or 47 million dollars, with an establishment of 7500 personnel. However, the general intransigence of the Soviet Union led to proposals—from Canada initially—for a security pact that would enhance the UN charter.[7] In March 1948, the British made proposals to extend the newly forming Western Union (Britain, France, Belgium, The Netherlands, Luxembourg) so that "all the countries directly threatened by a Soviet move on the Atlantic could participate: Norway, Denmark, Iceland, France, Portugal, Great Britain, the United States, Canada and Spain once it had a democratic regime."[8]

These proposals led to the prompt signing of the Brussels Pact; in the same month, discussions began in Washington relating to what would become NATO. Now, indeed, it became possible to sharpen the focus of Canadian defence policy against a perceived aggressor, with the objectives being identified as forces to defend against sudden direct attack; equipment, staffs, etc. for rapid expansion; and plans for joint defence with other nations to preserve peace or restrain aggression.[9]

Out of this came a clearer definition of the tasks for the navy: "At sea, our roles would largely consist of guarding the lines of communication as the RCN did so well during the last war. Canadian ships once again would be called upon to provide the vital protection for troops and supplies travelling the Northern seas our sailors knew so well."[10]

These were fine intentions, but with only fourteen fighting ships and twenty-two in reserve—few of them with significant anti-submarine capability—there was clearly a need for greater improvement than the minimal budget (about 280 million dollars in 1948–9) could provide. And, as we shall see, action did take place so that the White Paper of 1949 could state: "The main task of the navy would be, as in the last war, the protection of Canadian and allied shipping and Canadian Coastal waters. The navy is constructing ships for this purpose—minesweepers, an icebreaker and especially, fast escort vessels. A new type of escort ship designed especially for Canadian needs is under construction."[11]

Now, indeed, expenditure on defence began to rise significantly, as did the proportion of defence spending on equipment (from 12 per cent in 1948–9 to 24 per cent in 1949–50).

Thus, the era from 1946–9 began with an initial period lacking focus and precise objectives. The imperial connection was less relevant, but the association with the United States, in the Permanent Joint Board of Defence and the Military Co-operation Committee, had not produced specific tasks for the RCN. It was only with the impending obligations to NATO (and a greater concern for the Canadian north) that a renewed emphasis on the earlier role of anti-submarine defence provided the basis for a new thrust and approach, for which there would be major problems of re-equipping.

The Process of Decisionmaking

In basic terms, the decision process includes three main elements: finding occasions for making a decision; seeking possible courses of action; and choosing among courses of action.[12] Of these, the "finding occasions" aspect may arise as a fortuitous decision from outside or may be the result of a carefully engineered strategy or campaign to achieve a desired end. "Seeking possible courses of action," however, is much more a task for those directly involved. The selection may come from a fairly self-evident range of alternatives, or it may involve the development of innovative solutions to old or new problems. Once time and effort has been invested in this process, the final act of "choosing" may require little further activity. A good deal has been written about the demanding task of "seeking possible courses" and it is appropriate to our inquiry to identify some of the constraints that have been identified. These include: skills, habits, and reflexes that are more or less unconscious and determine an individual's performance; personal motivations, values, and loyalties; and limitations imposed by basic knowledge and information available.[13] And while a "rational" approach would demand an evaluation of *all* alternatives, time and available manpower usually involve: dividing major issues into manageable parts; finding a course of action that "satisfies"; limiting the range of search to well-understood alternatives; concentrating on short-run feedback; and taking note of what the organization can accomplish.

It has also been suggested that this intensely personal activity is subject, at the higher levels, to "extra-rational" (*not* irrational) processes that involve "intuitive judgement, holistic impressions derived from immersion in a situation and creative invention of new alternatives."[14]

An exciting illustration of these processes is given in Allison's classic study of the Cuban Missile Crisis.[15] Here, he suggests that, in government generally, decisions are made: by a conglomerate of semi-feudal loosely allied organizations each with a substantial life of its own; with results depending on the kind of output each can provide; having a tendency to use "standard operating procedures"; so that certain abilities/activities will have to be present before specific solutions can be proposed.

Thus, since decisions come about through people sharing and exercising power, much will depend on the capabilities and influence of those who propose, or oppose, the actions. And each of these bears the burden, or brings the contribution, of personal constraints, his own experiences and sensitivity, commitments to specific objectives, concern for personal standing, and obligations to particular groups.[16]

Our purpose, seeking to determine how the decision came about to depart from a small RCN carrier task force (not yet ASW-oriented) to a large modern ASW fleet calls for considerations of aspects that might be considered as political, military, and technical. Pending further review, it seems reasonable to suppose that the first of these will be—or will have the appearance of being—"rational." Thus it is likely that a case will be presented and its advantages outlined so that its acceptance will be a more or less foregone conclusion. It is probable, however, that this "decision" will be of a somewhat general and straightforward nature.

Our main interest lies in the work that may precede, and will certainly follow, this political "strategic" decision. This involves the choices—perhaps even *the* choice—that is presented for political approval and is adjusted or moulded so that, within the overall intent, various organizational or individual objectives can be enhanced or achieved. In this overall endeavour, certain significant aspirations can be noted: at the most senior levels, to maintain flexibility until all doubts are cleared; among peers, to get others committed to one's own view; and from below, to persuade those at the top to have confidence in what is being proposed.

To understand how these various tenets of decisionmaking (all too briefly outlined) apply in the present study, we must therefore embark in the first instance on a review of the individuals involved, with an interest and concern for their backgrounds, formative experiences, and possible ambitions, together with a consideration for the impact all this might have on their stance and input.

The Key Individuals Involved

In this study, as noted earlier, attention will be focused on the process within the RCN, generally leaving aside the demanding task of fighting the destroyer escort decision through the chiefs of staff, deputy minister, and government bureaucracy (see Appendix 1 re RCN hierarchy from 1947 to 1950).

Thus, as far as the RCN is concerned, the decisionmaking body of that era[17] was the Naval Board, including the Chief and Vice-Chief of the naval staff, Chief of Naval Personnel, Chief of Naval Technical Services (taking the place of the earlier Chief of Naval Administration and Supply) and the Assistant Chief of Naval Staff (ACNS)—later Assistant Chief of the Naval Staff (Plans) and (Air).[18] Essentially, therefore, the Naval Board included representatives of the interests of operations, people, and technology. For our purposes at present, it does not appear that Personnel had a significant involvement—their time would come later. While the Naval Board was the "deciding" entity it was not necessarily the "thinking" mechanism. Ideas and innovations would, quite appropriately, come from a lower level. Thus, on the fighting side, account must be taken of the participation of naval staff, under the ACNS (later ACNS(P)&(A)). While this had a number of branches reflecting various specialist interests, the Director of Naval Plans and Intelligence (DNPI), later Director of Naval Plans and Operations (DNPO) was clearly a force to be reckoned with, not only for his own contributions but also as a co-ordinating entity to bring together the interests and concerns of the other branches of naval staff.

These interests were similarly reflected on the technical side where, at that time, the ship itself—rather than the "integrated weapons system" of the future—was the paramount concern. Thus it devolved upon the Naval Constructor in Chief (NCC) to bring together—in a respectable vessel—the demanding and often divergent aspirations of operators and technical specialists.[19]

By the fall of 1947 the individuals filling the posts thus listed were nearly all in position—as indicated in Appendix 1—and most were to continue for the remainder of our period of interest. Their general characteristics and backgrounds (except for the NCC's) were remarkably similar. All, save Storrs and Brock, were "old RCN" born between 1897 and 1907 and graduates of the short-lived Royal Navy College of Canada. All had had frequent experience with the Royal Navy, and their wartime commands included destroyers, an RN cruiser, and an RCN escort carrier. Storrs (RCNR) and Brock (RCNVR) had both had experience with the Royal Navy and, during the Second World War, extensive smaller ship commands in ASW and minesweeping. The group as a whole, therefore, reflected the wartime RCN/RCNVR disparities—now brought into the fold together, albeit perhaps not wholly comfortably.[20]

The incoming NCC, Constructor Captain (later Commodore) R. Baker was, like his predecessor (Captain A.N. Harrison) on loan from the Admiralty's prestigious Royal Corps of Naval Constructors. He was an ebullient, dynamic individual and a brilliant designer. His earlier experience had been extensively with smaller warships and, during the war, largely devoted to the design and production of great numbers of new and novel landing craft. In this, he had visited the USN's Bureau of Ships for consultation in regard to their own huge building program of landing ships and craft.

To conclude, therefore, it would appear that the "old RCN" officers, now charged with making decisions, would have been less than true to their rigorous traditions and training if they had not continued to yearn for something approaching the "real" navy vessels in which they had been moulded. The "old reserve" officers, similarly, would have been less than true to *their* own experience of a very few years previously in the less elegant aspects of naval warfare—in minesweepers and escorts—if they had not sought some marked improvement from the somewhat primitive vessels in which *they* had fought during the Second World War. And, as we have seen, they were now in a position to introduce ideas and initiatives that would demonstrate to their RCN superiors that in spite of a non-traditional background they too had something significant to contribute.

And, for Baker, while far from the top in the hierarchy of the Royal Corps of Naval Constructors, there was the opportunity—even the obligation—in Canada to contribute to and implement major decisions regarding the shape of the future RCN.

THE APPROACH TO DECISION

Preliminaries

We have noted Admiral Grant's significant and prescient comment about anti-submarine warfare that was made towards the end of 1947, but the decision process begins somewhat before that. Thus, tripartite discussions in Washington during 1946 had led to an "Appreciation of World Strategical Situation,"[21] which identified the potential threat from Soviet submarines and noted the present lack of capability in the RCN to deal with the threat which would seem a matter "that should receive priority consideration." CNS, at the Chiefs of Staff Committee, was somewhat hesitant, noting that "by next year, a complete detailed plan would be available and the exact stages of implementation could be decided upon."[22] (See Appendix 2 for events in the decision process.)

This appears to demonstrate some hyperbole, for within naval staff the first recorded hint of change (so far as has been determined) in January 1947, came from the ex-RCNR commander A.H. Storrs, then serving as a assistant director of naval plans and intelligence (A/DNPI). Whether or not this paper[23] was inspired, it appears as the first introduction, in a written analysis, of the new realities and the way ahead: its simple purpose was "to review the future requirements of the RCN." It began with the observation that "Intelligence estimates indicate with some certainty that the optimum Naval potential of Russia lies in the field of the submarine weapon" and thus foresaw the future role of the RCN as being in the ASW field. In these circumstances it was noted that "the development of the submarine has made the bulk of present day surface escorts virtually obsolete. The escort of the future does not yet exist. It will be necessary, however, for it to have greater speed, better sea-keeping qualities and be of such construction as to promote rapid production in an emergency."

These perceptive observations introduced the concepts that would revolutionize the RCN and lead to major new construction programs. It was a bold initiative, well in advance of Western European Union, the Brussels Treaty, or NATO, and coming from an ex-Reserve Commander who "was inclined to walk carefully." Storrs's memo was forwarded by DNPI (Captain H.N. Lay) to DCNS as "Planning of Post War Navy"[24]—apparently, without significant impact. However, another naval staff division, the Directorate of Weapons and Tactics, reinforced these arguments (in July 1947), observing "if the only world power that ... could wage war with [the United States] insists on building a very strong submarine fleet, then we in turn must immediately commence the building or acquiring of an equally strong or stronger anti-submarine fleet."[25] The first hint of "things to come" was in October 1947 by reference[26] to plans to convert a destroyer to a convoy escort (AS) with: improved habitability, central cafeteria messing, and bunks. It seems clear then that Vice-Admiral Grant was being just a little premature in his speech of September 1947, but not unduly optimistic, by saying that the RCN was "actively engaged" in the problems of anti-submarine warfare.

Approaches to a Decision

The year 1948 saw a somewhat different but, as it would turn out, not irrelevant initiative for the RCN actively to "investigate the inclusion of one or more icebreakers in the fleet."[27] This was to involve the preparation of staff requirements based on the USN/USCG Wind Class: the vessel to be built in Canada from US plans. Significantly, this decision manifested a return to naval shipbuilding and, more to the point, demonstrated a changed approach with a leaning toward US concepts of ship construction and, particularly, toward US standards, especially in the complex areas of shipboard electrics and electronics. Further argument in support came, somewhat curiously, from a memo to the director of the naval air division from his deputy (Commander J.H. Arbick) suggesting that it was time for the RCN to decide on its future association and co-operation: with the RN, with the USN, or with both.[28] This evidently went forward, for some five weeks later there came a handwritten note from the VCNS (Rear Admiral Houghton):

> The D/DNAD may rest assured that the points he has set out in his paper are being given a great deal of thought and consideration.
> The problem is an extremely difficult one, and is not amenable to a clear cut decision, since it involves every single aspect of Naval Organisation.
> Thus, the search for a solution involves every one of us, and I should welcome further papers of a constructive nature to help us on our way.[29]

Initiation

All this led to the first stage of decision, with a letter from ACNS(P)&(A) to the USN seeking information on their intentions with regard to new construction and observing that "The Naval Staff has at present under consideration the question of the future construction of HMC Ships" and "exploring the possibilities of construction in Canada escort vessels of the USN type and fitted with machinery and equipment of USN design."[30] Here indeed was made evident a realignment worthy of Paul on the road to Damascus: an intent to follow the USN even to the extent of using USN plans and specifications.

From this groundswell of naval opinion came a measure of persuasion to politicians. Noting the long hiatus in naval construction, CNS advised the minister "if war broke out tomorrow, Canada's naval share of the Allied effort would be insignificant and it would be several years before she was able to effectively defend her own ports and coastlines [so that it was] . . . essential to make plans for the expansion of the necessary facilities in Canadian shipyards and industry."[31]

And thus the "end of the beginning" concluded with a naval staff paper, echoing Storrs's proposals of some sixteen months earlier and recommending

> that a building program be inaugurated in Canadian Shipyards at the earliest possible date. This program to include the laying down of four fast Ocean Escort Vessels and four of the smaller type vessels suitable for minesweeping and/or coastal a/s escort. This program should be commenced not later than the fiscal year 1949–50 and if possible a start made during the current fiscal year.[32]

Thus, as the discussions relating to NATO were beginning in Washington, Canada was taking the first steps to meet its naval obligations.

It is at this point—in what otherwise appears to have been a quiet summer—that we must take account of the arrival in July 1948 of Constructor Captain Baker, who appeared at a crucial moment in the decision process. While he was beginning to comprehend the Canadian scene, the approach to the minister now bore fruit, CNS noting to the chiefs of staff in September that the program for the next year contained proposals for naval shipbuilding.[33] When Cabinet Defence Committee met, a week later, the chiefs of staff rallied round with their view that "the likelihood of an accidental war was greater than at any time in the immediate past, and this situation was likely to obtain until the Western European powers had strengthened themselves militarily."[34] The idea of NATO solidarity was taking root, and the ministers agreed to examine the proposed programs in consultation with the treasury board, "it being understood ... that the Naval Program include provision for the initial construction of three large escort vessels."[35]

Implementation

Here then was the political decision, at least in a conceptual sense. Baker quite promptly brought the matter into sharp technical focus with a lengthy memorandum to naval staff.[36] From his own personal involvement he noted that, earlier in 1948, Admiralty had agreed to plan for a steam turbine driven AS frigate with machinery of 30,000 HP. The latter was only in the very early conceptual stages and the ship design could not be completed until machinery layout was available. Thus it was "unlikely that ships of [this] type will be ordered in the next year or two." Hence, in the long run, Canadian requirements might be met by building this new Admiralty design, which was essentially a destroyer. Baker then went on to suggest a new design, based generally on the Intermediate Class destroyer (of which Canada had some) but with a continuous forecastle giving much added space for "additional amenities, Operations Rooms, Communications Centres etc. required in modern designs." Here, in a sketch design that was presented, it was indicated that thinking was based on 34,000 SHP machinery being developed in the US for Brazilian destroyers.

This, then, was the genesis of a new idea, apparently based, as is so frequently the case, on modifications to an older concept. We might assume, however, that the innovative and brilliant Baker had some clear ideas of his own that were going to be introduced, for he went on to observe:

> This is really a proposal for a new design; in many ways more complicated than that of the Tribal Class Destroyers; hitherto the most ambitious naval shipbuilding project undertaken here. Whilst the experience of the Tribals would no doubt prove of very great value in the initiation of a new program we must remember that, for them, fully detailed drawings directly applicable to the ship were obtained from the UK whereas in this case all these drawings would need to be prepared in Canada with no direct outside help.

Here was an enunciation of the concept—and of the formidable problems it presented. Formidable problems indeed, for the constructor officers in naval headquarters at this time numbered just *six*, 50 per cent of them lieutenants.

It is pertinent to review Baker's subsequent recollections of these days.[37] While recognizing the earlier dependence on British designs and working drawings, his desire to embark on a new concept was helped by the inclination of naval staff to "Canadianize" their fleet and by the pressure for North American electrics and electronics. Thus he could assert, with the support of other technical departments, that the time had come for a change. In exchange, so to speak, for an enhanced naval constructor branch and for the development of a Naval Central Drawing Office to produce the working drawings, Baker now sought to please everyone, "usually a recipe for failure" as he observed. Thus there was to be British-designed (though Canadian-built) machinery for the UK-trained RCN naval engineers, US electrics/electronics for the electrical engineers, and a particular effort to meet the needs, as they *gradually* emerged, of the various naval staff divisions. In so doing, he maintained control over the design in order to introduce several of his own cherished concepts, including:

> the provision of ample extra space by the flush upper deck;
> well rounded deck edges and turtle back forecastle for good seakeeping;

smooth upper surfaces to facilitate de-icing;
special attention to stability in damaged condition;
good sea-keeping qualities;
construction on a "unit" principle;
much improved accommodation and habitability; and
an intent to produce a "different," that is, a Canadian vessel.

There was now an appreciable momentum as the focus turned from concepts to the actual design of the new vessels. A senior naval engineer was sent to Britain "to investigate the question of British propulsion machinery."[38] Toward the end of October[39] naval staff addressed the topic of "Construction of Escort Vessels in Canada." While there was a tentative set of staff requirements, there was (surprisingly) more concern with the need for rapid production, a topic urged by the recently appointed DNPO, Commander J.V. Brock. The latter urged the adoption of "US mass production methods," to which NCC, based on his wartime experience, noted that "US shipyards were very well organized during the war due to advanced planning and the availability of manpower which could not be duplicated in Canada even in wartime."

Nevertheless, the Naval Board supported the need for a special government study to review shipbuilding methods suitable for rapid expansion in an emergency.[40] It was clear by now—with the involvement of the Canadian Maritime commission and the Shipbuilding Committee of the Canadian Industrial Preparedness Association—that new naval construction was accepted as a reality, in spite of the absence of specific staff requirements or an approved sketch design. It is, therefore, not surprising that Baker felt it necessary in January 1949 to bring a measure of order by noting, with a certain irony, that "it is now understood that ships of this general type are included in the approved program and that it is the intention to start their construction as soon as possible."[41] He went on to observe that, while the British Y-100 machinery had been chosen and the main armament identified, "it will be noted that at the present time many of the items required to complete the design cannot yet be firmly fixed. Details of the design will undoubtedly remain under development for some considerable period."

However, a set of general particulars (such as dimensions and displacement) was offered, together with an outline sketch and reference to the various design innovations noted. Baker urged, in his memo to CNTS, that the Board should be made privy to these proposals. Indeed, the memo bears a handwritten note from CNTS: "Seen and approved by Board, subject to confirmation that complement figure of 250 refers to war complement." The Naval Board's approval, duly recorded, thus gave substance and credibility to the new design as a distinct entity: the St Laurent Class.[42]

Fulfilment

The real work of developing the design could now proceed, starting with a visit by NCC (with the director of weapons and tactics and a representative of the Engineer-in-Chief) to the UK to review the design, particularly the layout of the new Y-100 machinery. While this was, happily, somewhat shorter in length than had been contemplated, NCC had to report that "the boilers ... poked through the bottom" of the suggested hull form. This was somewhat disconcerting, but fortunately, Baker's colleagues in the Admiralty's Naval Construction Department were persuaded to redraw the hull shape so that the boilers could be adequately contained.[43]

While these excitements were afoot, the decision process returned to higher levels, with a submission to Cabinet from the Minister of National Defence noting that "it is essential to provide 10 additional vessels to meet, in part, the Royal Canadian Navy's share of the plan for the defence of Canada and that to do so, a shipbuilding program for the construction of ships designed to combat modern submarines, and of ships to deal with the modern undersea mines should be initiated."[44]

This all amounted to an intended expenditure of 33 million dollars; it would include three AS frigates (so called), four minesweepers and three gate vessels, generally reflecting Storrs's memo of some twenty-six months previous. Cabinet approved this "in principle" by the end of March, barely a week before the first meeting of the North Atlantic Council on 5 April.

Contractual arrangements now moved forward for the vessels and machinery, for the preparation of hull and electrical drawings, and for the model testing of the hull in Canada and in the UK. Thus at the end of May 1949, NCC produced the "final" sketch design with descriptive statement and outline plans. In seeking board approval, he somewhat optimistically exhorted all staff divisions to suggest recommended alterations so that these could be incorporated in the final design.[45] Even more optimistically, it was forecast that the design would be completed by the end of 1949 with the first ship ready in August 1952 or at the opening of navigation in 1953.

While the foregoing was a somewhat unorthodox approach to design development, it is interesting to compare Brock's account of the events occurring during his time as DNPO (from August 1948).[46] He recalls seeking guidance about new construction from ACNS (Captain Lay) who claimed that "he didn't know what was in CNS's mind" and simply suggested seeking two more Tribal Class destroyers in the hope of getting one. Brock, however, observes:

> I arranged with the Constructor in Chief of the Navy to tidy up the first conceptual plans of the new type of ship we two had been talking about, and together we prepared a brief outline description, quickly produced a few artist's sketches that looked handsome enough, although somewhat ahead of their time—with enclosed bridges and other modern improvements.

This proposal was produced just before a Board meeting with, it is reported, a proposal that seven ships be requested. Much furore ensued, since it was now too late to change the submission, which was "forcefully and skillfully" argued by CNS, winning the support of the Chiefs of Staff.

Brock's spirited account is probably no more the "whole truth"[47] than the more detailed—but clearly not wholly comprehensive—record that has been suggested here. However, Brock's concluding observation is certainly worthy of note: "At long last, we had broken free from the old ways and had started something new and exciting. In general, the navy was delighted, but there was a certain amount of resentment amongst some of my seniors over the fact that such an important development had evolved and was being brought to fruition in such a hasty and unilateral manner." Clearly—however it was accomplished—Brock, and Storrs before him, had as relative "outsiders" contributed significantly to change and innovation.

Consolidation

While the key aspects of major decisionmaking had now been accomplished, it is appropriate to conclude with some indication of the consolidation of these intentions. During June and July a flurry of contracts were issued to shipyards and machinery builders and for the creation of a naval central drawing office.[48] As well, after some months of deliberation[49] the "new Escort Vessels" were to be designated as DE's. However, in spite of these formal commitments to production, the staff requirements—that is, defining what was actually to be *created*—were still not complete and accepted. These, as "Proposed Final Staff Requirements" eventually came forward and were approved in September 1949.[50]

Since so much in the new design was innovation it seemed prudent to attempt some "real life" review of these proposals. Thus, during 1949–50, *Sioux* was converted, as nearly as possible, to the new habitability standards: bunks, cafeteria messing, modern galley facilities, more recreation space, and so on. And in 1950, *Algonquin* was converted as far as possible to the basic characteristics of the new AS escorts and could thus be considered a prototype.

The international situation now had its impact with the onset of the conflict in Korea. In July 1950, Cabinet Defence Committee agreed to accelerate the defence program, leading eventually to the ordering of a further four AS vessels—thus achieving Brock's proposal for seven. While this was an endeavour to meet a specific threat, it was clear in the presentation to Cabinet Defence Committee that there were broader issues.

> There can be no disguising the fact that the construction of a modern AS vessel is a very expensive proposition. However, the requirement both from the Canadian and NATO point of view is very urgent. In partly fulfilling this requirement the proposed program will give very substantial assistance to the Canadian Shipbuilding Industry.[51]

REVIEW AND ASSESSMENT

One of Allison's concerns about organizational decisionmaking was with respect to the inclination to be bound by "standard operating procedures." In the early post-war days, such a discipline for new warship design was not present in the RCN. The pre-war concept of everything being decided by the Board or by an "old-boy" senior officer caucus still appears to have been implicitly accepted. Into this tranquil pool of decision by intuitive inspiration were tossed not one, as we suggested initially, but three stones of concern or discontent. The ensuing intersecting pattern of relationships produced a somewhat confused surface which could be used to best opportunity by those suitably motivated. Thus there were varied patterns of concern or discontent:

> Politically:
> While NATO [in 1946] was still some way off, the need for an Atlantic alliance was seen as an opportunity for Canada to contribute and, possibly, be influential.
>
> As well, it was clear that naval construction was very desirable for shipbuilding and associated industries.
> Militarily:
> During 1946 it became accepted that the Soviet Union would be "the enemy" and that more emphasis, at least for the medium term, would have to be placed on ASW. However, something

better—clearly more effective—than wartime corvettes and frigates was required. And a larger fleet of smaller vessels would evidently give more scope for ship, squadron and possibly allied Commands.

It also appeared that the USN might be a better technical partner in naval construction than the Admiralty.

Technical:

Although naval engineers held to the traditions of their training and tended to prefer British machinery, electrical engineers saw US standards as the only solution. Naval constructors, not numerous enough to sway opinions, generally held to an Admiralty association.

In these circumstances, it developed that "finding occasion for a decision" was essentially a political task, illuminated by intelligence assessments and focused by Storrs into specific demands. The "possible course of action," primarily a military undertaking, proceeded slowly and without specific direction. Thus, for an appreciable period, the "possible courses" were limited simply to acquiring some more ships, perhaps of an American design. Several months were to elapse—long after political and contractual decisions were made—before the naval staff and board could say, with some precision, what they wanted these ships to *do*: that is, what armament, equipment, and so on they should have.

Choice, in the long run, came down to the "solution" that Baker could offer. As he was to note in subsequent writings, "staff say what sort of ships they want but must depend (appreciating it or not) on the shipbuilder and designer to indicate what sort of ship is possible." In this instance, with the brilliant input of Baker and the diligence of his miniscule staff, the solution was a radical new one. It might well have been otherwise. Indeed, innovation was helped since neither the British nor the Americans had, readily available,[52] the sort of design that the Canadians thought they wanted. In this case, "standard operating procedure" did not present an alternative solution.

One is struck by the way in which the process developed: not according to a preordained pattern but with political, military, and technical decisions moving in parallel. There is an exciting momentum to this, as with the ball being passed from one player to another as the team surges forward. It is, however, a less than wholly rational approach, where requirements are pondered and agreed upon, a design is developed, approval is obtained, and construction must proceed. Indeed, Baker must have felt this, for in the throes of all these endeavours he produced "Procedure to be adopted in the preparation of designs of

HMC Ships" (25 October 1949)[53] which was accepted by the Naval Board.

But, in the case of the St Laurents we are, possibly for the first and last time, dealing with a situation where there was scope for individual initiative. It was indeed the first time that the RCN had designed, from scratch, a major war vessel; it was the first time several officers in key roles could bring their individual capabilities into play. Among these were:

> Vice-Admiral Grant
> imperturbable warrior and effective advocate in DND and political circles;
> Commander Storrs
> intellectually aware of the developing strategic situation, experienced in command and articulate in presentation;
> Commander Brock
> suave and elegant as a newly accepted RCN officer, persuasive and tough in argument and—no doubt—not unconcerned about achievements that would establish his own position and reputation;
> Constructor Captain Baker
> brilliant designer, relishing the opportunity to give substance to his concepts, untrammeled by the constraints of the Royal Corps and diligent in gaining support while maintaining control of the concept;
> Rear-Admiral Knowlton
> as Chief of Naval Technical Services, providing a solid technical backing and undoubted RCN credibility to Baker's somewhat brash and ebullient presence.

It has been said that "failure is an orphan, success has many fathers"; in this context, the St Laurent Class was considered a success. As a response to a political concern relating to an emerging situation, the decision process was somewhat confused, with parallel and somewhat irrational approaches but with some eighteen months of exciting and sustained momentum. Storrs lit the spark, Brock kindled the flame, and Baker's enthusiasm (sustained by his hard-working staff) fuelled the conflagration.

With regard to the overall accuracy of this analysis, it is perhaps appropriate to quote from one of those involved. Writing in 1984, Rear-Admiral Brock observed:

> When trying to reconstruct and define historical events it should

be borne in mind that even the most accurate documented references alone are not enough. Minutes of important meetings very often fail to reflect what actually took place—sometimes deliberately. Furthermore, in a disciplined staff hierarchy such as exists in the services, one can never be sure whether the person signing the document wrote it himself, gave birth to the idea, developed the concept, or even understood the contents.[54]

He followed this somewhat daunting observation with the caveat that "the real discussions are made by those determined people whose rank enables them to impose their will on others." This is perhaps a more down-to-earth enunciation than current decisionmaking theorists might desire. Nevertheless, it does indeed appear to have been given substance in the genesis of the fleet of *St Laurent*, her sisters and successors.

APPENDIX I

RCN Hierarchy 1947–50

Naval Board		
Chief of the Naval Staff (CNS)	Vice-Admiral H.E. Reid	until August 1947
	Vice-Admiral H.T. Grant	from September 1947
Vice-Chief of the Naval Staff (VCNS)	Rear-Admiral F.L. Houghton	from September 1947
Assistant Chief of the Naval Staff (ACNS)	Commodore F.L. Houghton	January–September 1947
ACNS (Plans) & (Air)	Commodore H.N. Lay	from April 1948 to July 1949
ACNS (Plans)	Commodore R.S. Bidwell	from July 1949
Chief of Naval Personnel (CNP)	Commodore G.R. Miles	until August 1948
	Commodore W.B. Creery (later Rear-Admiral)	from August 1948
Chief of Naval Technical Services (CNTS)	Commodore J.G. Knowlton (later Rear-Admiral)	from September 1947
Naval Staff		
Director of Naval Plans & Intelligence (DNPI)	Captain H.N. Lay	from December 1945 to April 1948
Deputy Director Plans	Commander A.H.G. Storrs	from April 1946 to April 1948
Director of Naval Plans & Operations (DNPO)	Commander A.H.G. Storrs	from April 1948 to August 1948
	Commander J.V. Brock (later Captain)	from August 1948 to July 1950
Technical Services		
Naval Constructor in Chief (NCC)	Constable Captain A.N. Harrison	to July 1948
	Constable Captain R. Baker (later Constructor Commodore)	from July 1948

Source: The above data have been obtained from the various relevant issues of *The Canadian Navy List*, published annually until 1964 by the King's, later the Queen's, Printer.

APPENDIX 2

Events in the Decision Process

		Character of Decision		
		political	military	technical
End 1946	Vice-Admiral Grant's speech drawing attention to ASW	X	X	
1947				
January	Commander Storrs's paper "Future Planning"	X	X	
March	DNPI paper "Planning of Post War Navy"	X	X	
July	DWT paper "Canadian Naval Requirements in War and Peace"	X	X	
September	Prime Minister St Laurent's address to UN re an alliance	X		
October	Destroyer conversion to ASW planned		X	X
1948				
January	Contract for RNC Icebreaker to US design	X		X
March	D/DNAD Memo "Policy for Future Development of the Defence Forces in Canada"		X	X
	Extension of Western European Union; Brussels Pact; Discussion re NATO	X		
April	VCNS re adoption of US standards		X	X
May	Letter to USN re US designs			
	CNS to minister re Naval construction	X	X	X
July	Arrival of Constable Captain Baker			X
September	Chiefs of Staff Committee seeking approval for naval program	X		
October	Baker's analysis of AS Escorts		X	X
	Cabinet Defence Committee approval for naval program	X	X	
	Review of machinery			X
	Acceleration of construction		X	X
1949				
January	NCC queries staff requirements and produces preliminary sketch design		X	X
	Board approval		X	
February	Development of design in UK			X
March	Submission to cabinet	X		
April	Contractual arrangements initiated	X		X
	NATO founded	X		
May	Final sketch design		X	X
June/July	Contracts placed	X		X
September	Proposed final draft staff Requirements approved		X	
October	White Paper: *Canada's Defence Program 1949–50*	X	X	

Chapter 11

CANADA AND THE COLD WAR AT SEA, 1945–68

Joel J. Sokolsky

The dawn of the Cold War was a Mahanian dream. American seapower was, Admiral Chester Nimitz noted, "more absolute than ever possessed by the British ... so absolute that it is sometimes taken for granted."[1] The dream seemed to become a nightmare when this superior seapower was not only taken for granted but also dismissed as irrelevant. "How could enough time be allowed for seapower to take its effect, where war was characterized by strategic bombing by nuclear weapons?" asked one of the leading military thinkers of the age. Nations, their land and air forces, as well as their economies, would "disappear in the first blow."[2]

If such doubts could be raised about the United States Navy (USN), what could be said to justify the posture of the Royal Canadian Navy in the Cold War? In the nuclear age, what need could there be for the anti-submarine warfare (ASW) expertise perfected by the RCN in the Second World War and emphasized in the post-1945 period? Was the development of a largely ASW maritime force by the RCN during the Cold War an anachronism? Had Canada's senior naval officers convinced the government of the virtues of such a force based on cherished memories of the Battle of the Atlantic rather than on sound strategic concepts? And even if traditional ASW operations made some sense, would it not have been better for the RCN to build a more "balanced fleet" to cover a wider range of contingencies?

Such criticism of the Cold War RCN reflects a tendency to cling to Mahanian views of seapower. Mahan saw seapower as a decisive force in history and the destruction of the enemy fleet as the primary means by which that force was manifest. But even while he was writing, his views were being challenged. Fred T. Jane argued that the influence of seapower depended upon larger strategic and political considerations and that what history showed was merely how states made use of the sea to influence the political or military situation ashore. Seapower was defined as the ability of states to secure, deny, and exploit the sea for military purposes,[3] and the destruction of the enemy's naval forces was just one means by which these tasks were accomplished; it was not the sole object of naval forces. Thus the acquisition by the USN of an atomic delivery capability first from aircraft carriers in the early 1950s and soon afterwards with the deployment of Polaris nuclear ballistic missile submarines (SSBN), simply represented a new way in which the seas were exploited to influence the situation ashore. The advent of the carrier and the SSBN underscored "the modern strategic role of seapower formerly manifested in the silent blockading squadrons and amphibious operations of the Royal Navy."[4]

In the strategic and political environment of the post-war era, naval forces were also employed in their traditional roles to support limited wars and to exert political suasion through gunboat diplomacy. As with nuclear deterrence, the objectives in these non-nuclear usages have been less the destruction of rival maritime forces and more the exertion of power, either latently or directly, ashore.[5]

The continuing relevance of seapower in the nuclear age—in deterrence, limited war, and gunboat diplomacy for example—have, however, been of no more than tangential interest to the RCN. As a primary ASW force its task has been to secure use of the sea against Soviet forces dedicated to denying that use in the context of a possible major war in Europe between the North Atlantic Treaty Organization (NATO) and the Warsaw Pact. But during much of the Cold War, the USSR did not possess a large modern high seas fleet. In the event of war, the United States and her allies would not have had to wage major battles at sea. Thus the RCN of this time, designed to contribute to collective security at sea in the interest of Canada's own national security, did so when the seas were in many respects NATO's "forgotten front."[6] From a Mahanian perspective, this absence of a comparable, rival fleet could justify raising questions about the relevance of the RCN in the Cold War. Yet in the larger political and strategic perspective, bearing in mind that the ultimate objective of seapower is to influence the situation ashore, the post-war RCN was anything but an anachronism.

The reason for this was that NATO was, from the very beginning, conceived of as a maritime alliance. It was not the Soviet navy as such that made this so but the continued existence of large Soviet land and air forces in Eastern Europe. Expectations that it might be necessary to sustain conventional forces in a land/air war, of whatever duration, lie at the base of NATO's maritime posture and planning. Of course, in the unprecedented strategic environment of the Cold War, the maritime policies of the USN and its NATO allies were beset with inherent uncertainties. Would the allies make their ships available? Would they do so in time? Could convoys really be organized? If they could, would the harbour facilities be adequate? Would the first use of nuclear weapons make control of the sea lines of communication (SLOC) a useless tactical asset? By the same token, precisely because the exact nature of the collective response could not be known in advance, allied naval leaders were compelled to provide for as wide a range of contingencies as possible, including the traditional convoying of merchant ships laden with reinforcements and supplies.

As much as they could serve as a guide to national naval policies, the strategies adopted by NATO were to shape the RCN in the Cold War. In their wide-ranging nature, in particular because they went beyond the projection of nuclear power ashore, these strategies would provide the RCN with a credible role in the nuclear age.

Planning for the post-war RCN began in 1943 with a view to creating a "balanced" task force "rather than an escort force solely for the protection of shipping and thereby providing a capability for a wider range of naval activities." This meant a fleet of at least five cruisers, two light fleet carriers, and three destroyer flotillas.[7]

These plans were gradually scaled down. In November 1945, the US Naval attaché at the Ottawa Embassy was told by Vice-Admiral G.C. Jones, chief of the naval staff, that given projected defence budgets, the post-war RCN would only have 10,000 officers and enlisted men. By cutting the shore establishment "down to a minimum," Jones estimated that the RCN could maintain in active commission a fleet of two cruisers, two escort carriers, and two destroyer flotillas.[8] Statements by the minister at this time indicated that there would be twelve destroyers, eighteen frigates, and twelve escort minesweepers.[9] It was a drastic reduction from the wartime navy, a navy of about 100,000 people and 470 vessels, mostly devoted to convoy escort.

While the goal was to create a balanced fleet, of whatever size, it seemed evident even by then that the RCN would posture its forces for co-operation with its wartime ally the United States Navy as well as continue the traditional links with the Royal Navy. It would appear, though, that there was a recognition within the RCN that in terms of seapower in the nuclear age, the USN was going to be the dominant force. Therefore, while the British traditions remained strong, the navy was anxious to forge closer ties to the USN. Included in the above-mentioned report by the US naval attaché in Ottawa was the view that "all the ranking officers of the Royal Canadian Navy ... are definitely pro-US rather than pro-British. They have a high regard for officers of the US Navy ... and ... an equally high respect for the US fleet and our methods of operation. More and more do they resent control by the Royal Navy and it is obvious to the naval attaché that they would welcome a continuance of their close ties with the US Navy."[10]

No doubt the US attaché saw things the way he wanted to. For the RCN, as for other services, the level of co-operation with the US would be less a function of professional preference than the result of international events and the Canadian government's response to them. Quite soon after the war the Canadian government made it clear that it did not see on the horizon a threat sufficient to maintain even the modest balanced fleet proposed in 1945. In January 1947, the government cut 50 million dollars from the naval estimates and reduced manpower ceilings to 7500. The cabinet also decided to keep only one escort carrier, *Magnificent* (which was better suited to cold weather operations).[11] By 1948, the fleet numbered forty-four vessels including one carrier, two cruisers, eighteen frigates and destroyers, and nine minesweepers.[12]

For the RCN, the key factor in maintaining itself and in increasing its size was the onset of the Cold War and the decision of the Canadian government to support the American containment policy with regard to the Soviet Union. The navy would now have a mission in support of national foreign policy objectives. While in later years the RCN was to suffer at the hands of succeeding Liberal governments, at this time the internationalist group led by Lester B. Pearson and fully supported by Louis St Laurent adopted a world view which in a sense rescued the RCN from oblivion in the nuclear age.

This view was based upon Canadian support for what became known as the Pax Americana. A Pax Americana was not what Canadians had had in mind at the end of the war, but as John Holmes notes, Canadian leaders were becoming increasingly "concerned with the dangers of international communism largely because it posed a threat to world order." Given this perception, Ottawa realized that "for the time being the United States alone could provide the sinews for a pax and must therefore remain strong." Thus, "Canadian actors saw themselves as acting collectively as loyal and responsible allies and associates in a good cause."[13] And they did so, according to Holmes, not out of some blind sense of servitude or resignation to American policies but based upon a clear understanding of Canadian national security interests. Canada's position as a western ally was determined, within the rigid bipolar structure of the international system, by geographic fact, historical linkages, the Canadian political and economic structure, and public attitudes.

For the navy, this broad foreign policy orientation meant a reversal of its immediate post-war decline. In late 1948 the authorized RCN manpower levels rose to 9047. At the same time, eighteen River Class

HMCS *Canada*, an auxiliary patrol ship during the First World War, at St John's, Newfoundland. Originally completed as a fisheries protection cruiser in 1904, she also served as a naval training ship for Department of Marine and Fisheries seamen before the founding of the RCN. From the collection of Captain John Roue RCN (Ret'd).

More evidence of the RCN's origins: patrol craft at Halifax during the First World War. They include the drifters HMCS *Givenchy* (trawler) and HMCS *Cartier* (patrol vessel). *Cartier* was built in 1910 for the Department of Marine and Fisheries.

The Canadian government customs cruiser *Margaret* was taken over by the navy a few months after she left the builder's ya[rd] in 1914. From the collection of Captain John Roue RCN (Ret'd).

Originally built as a luxury yacht and purchased from its American owner for the RCN in 1915, HMCS *Hochelaga* perform[ed] patrol duties on the Atlantic coast. Her captain was dismissed from the service after he turned away on sighting the Germ[an] submarine U-156. From the collection of Captain John Roue RCN (Ret'd).

…urchased for the RCN in the United States in 1915, the fast yacht *Winchester* was fitted with torpedo armament and …mmissioned as HMCS *Grilse*. From the collection of Captain John Roue RCN (Ret'd).

…awler minesweepers moored at the entrance to the North West Arm, Halifax. From this advanced position the vessels could …ickly reach the harbour mouth for sweeping operations. In the foreground are *TR 1* and *TR 16,* two of the Admiralty trawlers …ilt in Canada and subsequently loaned to the RCN by the British government. From the collection of Captain John Roue …N (Ret'd).

Trawlers and drifters of the east coast patrols (1914–18) under way in Halifax harbour. These ships were built in Canada Admiralty design for the RN and RCN and served in many parts of the world, some serving into the Second World War.

The corvette HMCS *Sackville*, which took part in the battle for ONS 18 and ON 202, in 1943. She was taken in hand by the Canadian Naval Corvette Trust in the 1980s and restored as the Canadian National Naval Memorial.

HMCS *Sackville* as seen at the naval review of 1985, after restoration to her wartime appearance. She is the only surviving corvette of the Second World War.

Rear Admiral L.W. Murray, then Commanding Officer Atlantic Coast (he would become Commander-in-Chief, Canadian Northwest Atlantic in May 1943), presenting an award to a member of HMCS *St Croix*'s ship's company in late 1942. Lieutenant Commander A.H. Dobson, RCN, who is looking on, went down with his ship during the battle for ONS 18 and ON 202.

Lieutenant Commander A.H.G. Storrs, RCNR, who commanded HMCS *Drumheller* in 1943, rose to the rank of Rear Admiral and later was Commissioner of the Canadian Coast Guard.

Lieutenant Commander A.F. Pickard, RCNR, who commanded the corvette HMCS *Chambly* during the battle for ONS and ON 202. He later rose to the rank of Captain.

HMCS *Esquimalt* in pack ice. Red Bay, Newfoundland, 1944. These spring conditions give an indication of what both U-boa and surface ships had to contend with in Canadian coastal waters. Photo by T.C. Manuel in the collection of Michael Hadl

...-190 after her surrender in May 1945, at St John's, Newfoundland. On 16 April 1945 this U-boat torpedoed and sank HMCS *Esquimalt* five miles east of Chebucto Head, Nova Scotia. The submarine remained undetected until 29 April. After capture she became HMC Submarine U-190 and was sunk off Halifax in "Exercise Scuppered" on 21 October (Trafalgar Day) 1947. Maritime Command Museum, Halifax, courtesy of G.R. Benham, copy in the collection of Michael Hadley.

"The Last Round-up." At the end of the Second World War minesweepers, corvettes, and frigates sailed to Sorel, Quebec, for acceptance by the War Assets Disposal Corporation. Commander Martin Doyle, who supplied the photograph, was the Supply Co-ordinator of the program.

Minesweepers destoring, Shelburne, Nova Scotia. 2 November 1945. Photo by Bagg.

Minesweepers alongside, destoring. J 255 is HMCS *Red Deer*.

...nada's navy at the half-century mark. Three "Bay" class wooden minesweepers precede the fleet carrier HMCS *Bonaventure*, ...lowed by "Restigouche" and "St Laurent" class destroyer escorts of the Third and Fifth Canadian Escort Squadrons, during ... naval review of 1960. Among the other vessels are postwar conversions of "River" class frigates in the Seventh and Ninth ...nadian Escort Squadrons.

"Mr. International Navy," Rear Admiral Richard B. Colbert USN. This photograph was taken while he was President of the Naval War College, Newport, Rhode Island, from 1969 to 1971.

The destroyer escort HMCS *St Laurent,* the lead ship of the first class of major warship designed and built in Canada, and HMCS *Ottawa* of the same class, photographed in silhouette off the west coast of Canada, 10 February 1960.

HMCS *Ottawa*, *Assiniboine* and *Saguenay*, photographed off Hawaii, July 1960.

HMCS *Provider* (Operational Support Ship laid down 1 May 1961, commissioned 28 September 1963) replenishing HMCS *Bonaventure* and the modernized "River" class frigate HMCS *Cap de la Madeleine,* during the annual fleet exercise, "Maple Spring," 1965.

HMCS *Margaree*, of the "St Laurent" class, laid down at Halifax Shipyards 12 September 1951 and commissioned 5 October 57, did her major refit at Canadian Vickers, Montreal in 1978-9 and was modernized in the DELEX program of 1979-82. re she is seen in Halifax Harbour in 1985.

Two Canadian "Oberon" class diesel submarines moored beyond a British "Porpoise" class diesel submarine, HMS *Seali...* wearing the flag of the Royal Navy's Flag Officer, Submarines, during his visit to Halifax for the naval review of 1985. T... Canadian submarines HMCS *Ojibwa*, *Onondaga*, and *Okanagan* were built at Chatham Dockyard, England, and commission... between 1965 and 1968.

HMCS *Skeena*, a "St Laurent" class destroyer escort modernized as a helicopter destroyer in the DELEX (destroyer life extension) program of 1979-82 after an extensive refit in 1977-8. Seen at the naval review of 1985 in Halifax harbour, she carries a variable depth towed sonar array at the stern and is fitted with the "Bear Trap" for helicopter landing, both Canadian innovations.

HMCS *Iroquois*, lead ship of the "DDH 280" class, the first class of Canadian ships to be built as Helicopter Destroyers. Powered by gas turbines, the ship incorporates the CCS 280 electronics system developed by RCN design teams, as well as "Bear Trap" and variable depth sonar.

HMCS *Algonquin*, of the "DDH 280" class. In the background can be seen HMCS *Restigouche* and HMCS *Annapolis*. T "Improved Restigouche" and "Annapolis" class ships were logical developments of the "St Laurent" class. In 1985, wh this photograph was taken, even the DDH 280 class were fairly old ships.

frigates and nineteen Bangor Class minesweepers were saved from the scrap metal dealer; many were refitted for active duty.[14]

The North Atlantic Treaty Organization, an alliance which Canada played a major role in establishing, gave direction to the general rearmament. As Brian Cuthbertson has noted: "Once the Canadian government committed forces to Europe and made Europe a strategic frontier of Canadian defence, then the maintenance of secure sea communications across the Atlantic was a *sine qua non*,"[15] especially since Canada's allies were planning to secure the sea lines of communication to Europe in the event of war. At this time the naval tasks of national sovereignty protection, continental defence of North America, and NATO were nearly indistinguishable. Thus, that a predominately ASW navy was superimposed upon the small balanced fleet was "natural and logical." In the 1950s, as Cuthbertson observes, "Canadian naval policy and experience meshed into NATO strategy with an ease not present in other areas of defence activity."[16]

As a task for the RCN, the NATO ASW convoy escort role does indeed appear to have been logical given the role of seapower in the nuclear age and the maritime character of the NATO alliance. But did the navy have to become almost exclusively a NATO ASW force? Not only was this force superimposed upon the fleet, but as a 1968 DND historical study put it: "in the ensuing years, non anti-submarine warfare units such as cruisers, fighter aircraft and minesweepers have been phased out so that the RCN could concentrate on becoming highly specialized in the techniques of its chosen field."[17] NATO provided the navy with a sound strategic objective, the defence of Europe in its maritime dimensions. This in turn afforded it the opportunity to relate its capabilities, existing and potential, to a specific maritime task: ASW and convoy escort. Without NATO, the navy would have had a difficult time justifying even its ASW assets let alone other maritime capabilities associated with a more balanced fleet. It would appear, based upon now declassified US and Canadian documents, that the RCN's leadership perceived its salvation in the NATO role.

The first meeting of NATO's North Atlantic Ocean Regional Planning Group (NAORPG),[18] held in Washington in October 1949, was attended by Vice-Admiral H.T.W. Grant, chief of the naval staff, and Air Vice Marshall H.L. Campbell, RCAF.[19] Of the five sub-planning groups established, Canada only sought and obtained membership in subgroup B, "Atlantic Ocean Lines of Communication." Others in the group were France, the Netherlands, the UK, and the US. At the request of Admiral Grant, the phrase "offensive anti-submarine operations" was omitted from the group's terms of reference.[20] This seemed to indicate a Canadian preference to restrict its interests to open-ocean ASW and avoid the more offensive operations being contemplated by the USN, such as direct attacks on Soviet naval facilities.

Grant apparently did seek Canadian membership in a briefly proposed northern area subgroup which would have dealt with the SLOC between the Atlantic ocean lines of communication and Northwest Europe.[21] In the end, two subgroups were created, one dealing with the sea lines of communication to Northwest Europe and the other with those between the Atlantic and Western Europe and West Africa. Canada was not made a member of either, again apparently reflecting a Canadian preference to restrict its commitments to the central ocean areas. Subgroup B emphasized planning for the protection of transatlantic shipping from submarines and aerial attacks.

Canada did obtain representation in the bodies which were to deal with the overall direction of the allied maritime effort. As the representative of a contributing country, the Canadian chief of the naval staff would sit on the NAORPG Chief of Staff Committee. Below this was to be a "co-ordinating committee." This was not an executive body but rather a liaison group to co-ordinate operations of the subgroups and oversee the exchange of information between them.[22] Grant had proposed that membership in the co-ordinating committee be the same as that of subgroup B—the group that Canada was in. There was some objection to this, but it was eventually accepted (thus excluding Iceland, Portugal, and Denmark from the committee).[23]

Amid this early planning for a co-ordination of NATO maritime policies came the Korean War. Since there were no substantial naval forces in opposition, the Canadian destroyers allocated to United Nations forces supported the ground war through blockade, shore bombardment, and the provision of escorts for amphibious forces and carriers. Some Canadian officers, such as Jeffry Brock, commanded combined allied task forces for specific operations, and the navy came through the experience with its reputation and self-confidence much enhanced.

It was, of course, an experience that would not be repeated. For the RCN, as for the armed forces in general, its most important impact was felt in Europe. Convinced that the Korean attack was the prelude to a global communist offensive centred in Europe, the US pressed its NATO allies to increase their standing forces. At the meeting of the North Atlantic Council Deputies held on 4 August 1950, it was agreed that each deputy would report back to the council by 28 August on the steps being taken to increase total combat forces "readily available" by 1 July 1951.[24]

The need to meet formal NATO obligations provided the RCN with an even more solid justification to request significant increases than mere membership in the alliance. Under Minister of National Defence Brook Claxton, an Accelerated Defence Programme was initiated in 1950. In a memorandum to Claxton, dated 2 August 1950, Vice Admiral Grant drew attention to Canada's commitment to NATO's North Atlantic Ocean Regional Planning Group made the previous October.[25] Grant stressed that NAORPG faced a shortage of anti-submarine vessels which Canada could ease. He also noted that the three destroyers sent to Korea and the three which had to be kept available for relief, refits, and time on passage were all "already committed to the Atlantic on D-day under the approved NAORPG emergency plan and without them Canada's contribution in the Atlantic would be almost negligible in the early stages of a war." Grant recommended that the *Uganda* be recommissioned for the training of officers and that the *Ontario* be sent to relieve the three destroyers in Korea early in 1951. (He added that "it would be desirable, of course, to obtain General McArthur's reaction.")

Grant wanted ships brought out of reserve and commissioned with full wartime complements. This would expand the action fleet from one carrier, a cruiser, five destroyers, four frigates, and two minesweepers to a force of one carrier, two cruisers, eleven destroyers, six frigates, and seven minesweepers, in addition to one arctic patrol vessel and various auxiliary ships. Claxton was reminded that the "Mobilization Plan requires a second operational carrier at the earliest possible time. This is required to balance our naval forces as they expand. It is obvious that if naval air war operations are to be sustained for more than a few weeks, the second carrier is essential." Grant therefore recommended that the government look into the possibility of borrowing a second carrier similar to *Magnificent* from the Royal Navy. This vessel could be "kept in reserve in Canada on the east coast where it can be used for harbour training purposes, or ... kept in reserve in the UK earmarked for the RCN in hostilities." Finally, Grant requested construction of four additional anti-submarine destroyers and minesweepers.[26]

In its report to the North Atlantic Council, Canada said that by 1 July 1951 it would have refitted four anti-submarine destroyers and in the following years would recommission one cruiser, three destroyers, one frigate, and two minesweepers. In addition, accelerated shipbuilding projects included seven anti-submarine escorts, fourteen minesweepers, five "gate vessels," and an icebreaker. In the area of naval aviation, the thirty-five Firefly anti-submarine aircraft were to be replaced by seventy-five Avengers with a further purchase of twelve Sea Fury fighters. Authorized personnel strength was to increase from 9600 to 13,440 with other improvements to harbour defences, ammunition stocks, and training facilities.[27]

Thus began a major naval rearmament program to meet the exigencies of the Cold War and the need for collective deterrence. Although approval for a second carrier was never obtained. The target strength of the RCN by 1954 was raised to 20,000; fourteen destroyer escorts were under construction. By 1957 the fleet composition was as follows:

Carriers	1
Cruisers	1
Destroyers/frigates	34
Minesweepers	7
Submarines	0
Other	30
Auxiliary	56
Total	129[28]

In 1952, the RCN had bought another British light fleet carrier, *Powerful*, renamed *Bonaventure* and commissioned in 1957. Replacing *Magnificent*, *Bonaventure* received *Banshee* fighters and Grumman *Tracker* ASW aircraft. Long-range land-based naval aviation was supplied by the RCAF initially with Lancasters and later with Argus aircraft. During the 1950s, successful tests were made for the landing of ASW helicopters on platform-fitted escort vessels. In the 1960s the RCN acquired its own submarines.

In order to bolster collective defence, NATO not only increased its standing forces but also created three peacetime major combined commands: Allied Command Europe (ACE), under a Supreme Allied Commander (SACEUR); Channel Command, under an allied Commander-in-Chief (CINCHAN); and an Atlantic Command (ACLANT), replacing the North Atlantic Ocean Regional Planning Group. This organization placed Canada's NATO commitments in a recognized framework and enabled the navy to focus on its alliance objectives.

The position of Supreme Allied Commander, Atlantic (SACLANT) was not filled until 1952 because of a dispute which arose between the United Kingdom and the United States over which country would get the post. Winston Churchill, prime minister once again, was determined to secure it for the Royal Navy. Canada, including the RCN, apparently sided with the United States in supporting the appointment of an American admiral. In January 1952, Churchill himself came to Ottawa to lobby with Prime Minister Louis St Laurent and External

Affairs Minister Lester B. Pearson for the appointment of a British SACLANT. He hoped to enlist their support in his subsequent negotiations with President Truman and Secretary of State Dean Acheson. In a letter to Acheson written shortly after Churchill's Ottawa visit, Pearson wrote: "I am no present or former 'naval person,' but I can't think it matters very much one way or the other at this time." However, he did say that the "naval people" in Ottawa "feel differently and I suppose they know." Thus the Canadian government, although sympathetic to the desire of the "old gentleman," did not support his position.[29]

Under ACLANT Canada was given responsibility for a large area of the North Atlantic stretching out from its eastern coastal waters reaching to almost mid-ocean (approximately 40° longitude) and southward from Nova Scotia to approximately 40° latitude). Almost identical to the Canadian Northwest Atlantic theatre established in 1943, this Canadian Atlantic Sub-Area (CANMARLANT) was now part of Western Atlantic Area of ACLANT. The senior naval officer at Halifax, Flag Officer Atlantic Coast (FOAC), served as Commander (CANCOMARLANT). He shared the command with the RCAF Air Commander Atlantic (CANCOMAIRLANT). The two services used the same operational headquarters and in 1959 all anti-submarine facilities in eastern Canadian waters were officially co-ordinated under the control of the FOAC. In the Pacific as well, the RCN flag officer was to take charge over all air and sea ASW forces.[30]

When the first SACLANT, Admiral Lynde McCormick, USN, visited Ottawa as part of his initial tour of NATO capitals in 1952, he appears to have been told by the government that Canada would make its major contribution to the allied convoy protection posture. "Big Role Awaits Canada in Keeping Sea Lanes Open," announced the *Toronto Evening Telegram*. "Canada to Play Big Role in Atlantic Command," echoed the *Montreal Gazette*.[31] McCormick reported to the NATO Standing Group that he was looking to Canada to help with the shortages in carrier task forces, hunter-killer groups, and convoy escort carriers.[32]

The RCN was only able to contribute a single escort carrier which did take part in subsequent NATO exercises such as the first, Mainbrace. For the most part, the navy emphasized its surface escort capabilities which also participated in NATO exercises in which convoy escort was tested. For example, in the May 1956 exercise New Broom V, a NATO merchant ship convoy of US amphibious force ships escorted by Canadian and American aircraft carriers and destroyers sailed from Norfolk, Virginia, to Gibraltar. The convoy was "attacked" by American and British submarines which themselves were attacked by Canadian and American hunter-killer groups and shore-based ASW aircraft.[33]

Canadian forces also participated in exercises in the Eastern World War Atlantic region of ACLANT, such as Sea Enterprise in 1955 involving SACLANT and CINCNORTH with ships from the US, Norway, and the UK.[34]

The RCN was now developing close ties with the USN. Canadian ships still flew the white ensign and belonged to "Her Majesty," but the old relationship with the Royal Navy was bound to become more distant when an American admiral served as SACLANT and when the RCN was so deeply involved in the seaward defence of North America. Although a NATO area, the eastern seaboard for all intents and purposes became the responsibility of Canadian and US forces.

As in continental air defence this was an exclusively bilateral exercise in collective security, but no formal joint command arrangements comparable to the North American Air Defence Command (NORAD) were established. The measures that the RCN undertook to provide continual surveillance of Canadian waters, and the earmarking for forces for SACLANT, required no special organizational structure. It was enough that both countries had an interest in identifying and locating Soviet maritime forces, particularly submarines and intelligence ships, in North American waters. The USN deployed an ocean-floor sensor system as part of its global Sound Surveillance System (SOSUS), off the eastern seaboard, and the RCN had some access to the information received. In 1959, Canada took over the USN research establishment at Shelburne, Nova Scotia, and shared information from air and sea patrols with the United States.

It was the nature of seapower in the nuclear age that continental surveillance be maintained. Since there could be no certainty about the form an international crisis might take and whether it would abate or lead to war, forces had to be available at a moment's notice for deployment along the seaboard. This is what happened during the Cuban Missile Crisis of 1962. Much has been written about the effects of this crisis on Canadian-American defence relations. It is well known that Prime Minister John G. Diefenbaker hesitated in formally putting Canadian forces on alert. Most attention was focused then, and in later histories, on air rather than maritime defence. The fact is that the RCN responded quickly and effectively, well in advance of formal authorization. Within six hours of receiving the American announcement of the Cuban blockade, at 1000 EST on 24 October 1962, Rear-Admiral K.F. Dyer, CANCOMARLANT, had reorganized his command for war and placed as many naval and air units as possible on surveillance duties. Within the next twenty-four hours he had cancelled all long leaves, ordered all naval forces in the region to their war stations—

they sailed over the next few days—and recalled forces absent on a training cruise.[35]

Jeffry Brock recalls in his memoirs that because of the close working relationship between the USN and the RCN, "the action of the White House and the Pentagon in deploying a United States blockade force around Cuba, automatically impinged upon Canadian activities and particularly on the prudent disposition" of Canadian ships.[36] Failure to honour the RCN's "solemn obligations," as embodied in Canadian-American defence arrangements, would have been "too degrading and traitorous even to contemplate." Without "orders, leadership or any confidence that there would be any political backing," the RCN took measures "which had to be taken and which the Canadian people had every right to expect from those responsible for the actualities of defence."[37]

It would appear from Brock's memoirs that Dyer in Halifax worked closely with Brock, then vice-chief of the naval staff, in Ottawa:

> I set up my war room in Ottawa which was in continuous communication with both the Maritime Commander Atlantic and the Maritime Commander Pacific. I organized a very close scrutiny of Soviet fishing ship activities in and around the east coast of Canada and paid particular attention to the shadowing of the Soviet fishing headquarters ship *Atlantika*. I ordered delays in the refit dates of certain units of the fleet and also stopped the decommissioning of some of the other units. I also kept my chief informed of as much of this as I thought he would like to hear. Knowing he could not confide in the minister, I wanted to give my boss freedom from political accountability.[38]

The swiftness of the RCN's response was much appreciated by the US. After the crisis, the USN Task Group Commander Eastern Sea Frontier sent a message to Canada's Atlantic Fleet commander thanking him for outstanding support.[39] In his report on the crisis, the US Commander-in-Chief Atlantic Fleet noted that:

> the large scale movement of amphibious forces to the Caribbean required VP aircraft coverage. Canadian Argus aircraft under CANCOMAIRLANT (the RCAF commander for the Atlantic) increased their surveillance and their assistance and co-operation in ASW throughout the crisis contributed significantly to the ASW effort. Without this valuable assistance much of the Western Atlantic area would not have been adequately covered.[40]

The forces which allowed the RCN to perform such an effective role during the Cuban Missile Crisis were those which had been acquired largely to meet the NATO and North American tasks. The predominantly ASW posture of the navy made Canada's maritime forces "unbalanced" but still flexible, since ASW capabilities would be required in a multitude of scenarios involving Canada's obligations to collective security. In the 1960s, serious questions began to be raised about whether such a posture was serving national goals, particularly foreign policy objectives. A series of efforts were made to relate actual forces and capabilities to specific tasks beyond a general support for collective security, which would serve as a guide to future force requirements.

The first of these efforts was undertaken by the RCN itself. Before he assumed the post of vice-chief of the naval staff, Jeffry Brock had directed an ad hoc committee on naval objectives whose report became known as the *Brock Report*.[41] It was a thorough examination of the role of the RCN in the nuclear age and made far-reaching recommendations for the future posture of the navy.

The *Brock Report* stressed the importance of collective security to the role of the RCN, which was "to ensure that Canada in concert with friendly nations will be able to use the seas for our own purposes in peace and war." It was a "cardinal fact," that "some form of collective security is essential to Canada. Accordingly, it will be implicit that the RCN will rarely if ever operate without the support of one or more of our allies."[42]

But while the importance of co-operation with other navies was stressed, the thrust of the *Brock Report* recommendations was that Canada needed more balanced and flexible maritime forces "to support our country's external policies." The emphasis upon NATO and co-operation with the USN and the Royal Navy was correct, but the result was that "our defence policy provides planned support for our external policy only with regard to NATO: for anything else, expediency is the answer."[43] The report suggested that the RCN in particular needed a greater capability to support Canadian military operations outside the NATO theatre in "other than a European type war." This included sea-based air support for ground forces and mobile command and base facilities for external undertakings.

The report did not question the importance of nuclear weapons for maritime forces. Indeed, it recommended that Canada acquire the capability to employ nuclear weapons in its own naval forces. Physical possession of the weapons in peacetime was not needed, but the RCN should be trained to use them and arrangements should be made to deploy them quickly amongst the forces in the event of an emergency.

However, it argued that the "cutting edge" of future policy is nonnuclear force: the only kind of military force which can "rationally be employed to support policy in the more probable situations." More nuclear weapons will enhance deterrence but will also increase the reluctance to use them. "This fact in itself," the report stressed, "will tend to increase the strategic significance of control of the seas and amphibious capabilities."[44] The capacity for non-nuclear maritime operations was especially important in view of the growth of the Soviet navy. The report also drew attention to the need to reassert Canadian sovereignty in the Arctic. This would not be for military purposes but rather mainly for "research and operational evaluation."

Some of the changes the *Brock Report* recommended to composition of Canada's maritime forces were as follows:

- acquisition of six Barbel Class attack submarines by 1966;
- acquisition of six nuclear attack submarines by 1973;
- eight general purpose frigates to support land operations and maintain ASW capabilities by 1967–9;
- replacement of the *Bonaventure* carrier and Prestonian Class frigates by "Heliporter Frigates," each with fourteen ASW helicopters; these would also provide the "desired mobility of land forces," since they could each transport two hundred troops with light equipment a distance of 3000 miles in less than seven days and airlift them to the landing area on arrival. Twelve such ships would be acquired by 1975;
- no replacement for the Banshees currently on the carrier;
- the life of older ships would be extended to the 1970s as the newer ones were built;
- research vessels able to operate in the Arctic would be acquired.[45]

In many ways the *Brock Report* was prescient. It recognized that the growth of superpower nuclear arsenals would place a premium on the maintenance of conventional forces to widen the scope of deterrence. It stressed the importance of maintaining a Canadian ASW capability as part of Canada's contribution to collective security. And it foretold the emphasis upon sovereignty protection, especially in the Arctic, which would soon become a major declared role for the fleet. The proposed fleet it outlined would certainly have given the RCN more "balance," including a heretofore non-existent nuclear capability.

But the major thrust of the balancing would be to enhance the navy's capability for limited war operations for the projection of amphibious forces ashore. This was to be a major task for the twelve heliporters. Again, the report foreshadowed the development of helicopter-supported over-the-beach landing tactics which would be used by the US Marines and the British. Yet the question remains: was such a capability relevant to the likely tasks which the RCN would be required to undertake? Armed forces are needed to back up foreign policy, but what Canadian foreign policy of that day, or later, would require amphibious capabilities, especially when they were suited for non-NATO contingencies? It is true that peace-keeping operations needed some support from the RCN. However, this was logistical and did not entail the landing of Canadian troops against hostile fire from shore.

Although the challenge of limited war was something the US was then paying more attention to, it was not something that Canada had seriously to plan for. The report correctly notes that the RCN would only go to war as part of a collective effort. But other allies would not be supporting a Canadian military operation in the Third World, since Canada had no interests to protect. Rather it would be Canada which would be asked, as it was in Korea, to support its allies, most likely the United States. After the Korean conflict, however, the Canadian government had indicated its great reluctance to become involved in such conflicts and to maintain forces for other than NATO or North American contingencies.

The point is, the "unbalanced" fleet which was postured for NATO and North American roles did support Canadian foreign policy insofar as it supported collective security in that area of the world most important to Canada. It was a credible role because it would be in this area that the RCN would be most likely to back up Canadian foreign policy with force and in co-operation with allies. In this sense, the ASW specialization was not a liability to Canadian national interests; rather, it was an asset, by being an asset to Canada's closest allies. More submarines and surface ships would undoubtedly have enhanced the navy's ability to meet the coming challenges of the 1960s. A nuclear capability would have added some "balance" to the fleet (although it would hardly have affected the overall strategic situation between east and west). Still, the surface ASW orientation of the RCN, had it been continually maintained and improved during the 1960s and 1970s, would have sustained a credible and relevant force. This was not to be the case. Ironically, the quest for a balanced fleet would not, as did the *Brock Report*, stress the need for a wider range of war-fighting capabilities but rather would call for greater attention to non-military roles.

Among the military roles which were questioned in the 1960s was a relatively new one for the RCN, that of strategic ASW. The *Brock Report* had discussed the threat to Canada from Sea-Launched Ballistic Missiles. This was the gravest threat, but one which appeared most difficult to deal with since there was no defence against an SLBM or any intercontinental missile, once fired. The report noted, though, that "any progress that can be made, and demonstrated, towards early detection, identification and tracking of the launching submarine will pay dividends. This will also contribute to the protection of the deterrent in the form of the West's retaliatory strike capability."[46]

The Soviets had first tested diesel-powered Ballistic Missile Submarines (SSB's) in 1955. By 1960, Hotel and Golf class SSB's were patrolling North American waters carrying SS-N-4 SARK and SS-N-5 SERB missiles with ranges of 350 and 700 nautical miles respectively. At that time the USSR lacked an ICBM (Intercontinental Ballistic Missile) capability and these first SLBM's were the only missiles able to strike at North America. Their limited ranges, however, made detection of the platforms easier for Canadian and American ASW forces.[47] The 1960s saw a dramatic increase in Soviet sea-based capabilities with the deployment of the Yankee Class SSBN's carrying the SS-N-6 Sawfly SLBM with a range in excess of 1300 nautical miles. It was believed that the Yankees gave the Soviets the capability to hit important targets in North America, most especially US Strategic Air Command (SAC) bases and command and control facilities. Patrols of these SSBN's off the North American coast gave the Soviets coverage of a wide range of other targets.[48] By the time the Yankees were deployed, the USSR land-based nuclear capabilities had dramatically improved with the introduction of ICBM's able to strike at targets in the US from the Soviet Union. This period also saw the consolidation of the Soviet Strategic Rocket Forces (SRF) command's control over nuclear weapons for both deterrent and warfighting purposes. Thus the SRF targeted the ICBM's against American cities and major military targets deep in US territory, while the Yankees appeared to be allocated to "soft" coastal targets, including the SAC bases near the Atlantic and Pacific coasts.[49]

While the deployment of the Yankees reduced the warning time available to the US, most analysts agreed that the Soviets did not have an effective first-strike against "soft" targets for a number of reasons. First of all, there were never enough Yankees on patrol to pose a serious threat to SAC bases or other command and control centres. Second, in order for the Yankees to take advantage of the short warning time of a close-in launch, their SLBM's would have to be fired on a depressed trajectory. No point in the continental United States is more than 1000 nautical miles from the open ocean. Thus all targets would be in range of Soviet SSBN, patrolling 200 nautical miles off shore. An SLBM fired at this distance on a "minimum energy trajectory" would take about sixteen minutes to arrive. At a "highly depressed" trajectory, a missile with a 2500 nautical mile or greater maximum range would reach its target in half the time, roughly eight minutes. This would reduce the ability of the US to get aircraft off the ground. There was no evidence that the USSR had been able to achieve the capability for such depressed trajectory launches.[50]

With the subsequent introduction of the Delta Class SSBN with SLBM ranges of over 4000 miles, the Soviets achieved a truly intercontinental sea-based capability. Nevertheless, the USN still viewed the shorter range Yankees as a threat. They could be used for strikes against naval facilities and surface forces at sea, as well as against "soft" inland targets in a situation where the longer-range Soviet SLBM's were being held back as a strategic reserve.[51] In many ways the threat posed by the Yankees was similar to the continuing threat posed by Soviet bombers even after the rise of the ICBM threat. If conflict broke out in Europe or elsewhere, with both sides holding back their ICBM's, they would have to use passive surveillance and active bomber defences to guard against a possible bomber attack directed at certain soft targets such as communications and command centres. As unlikely as this threat appeared in the missile age, the two countries could not totally dismantle their defences against the bomber, including tactical aircraft which were used for early identification. So too with the SSBN threat to North America. Canada and the United States had to maintain passive and active strategic ASW, for while there was no defence against an SLBM once fired, knowledge about Soviet SSBN movements in the seaward approaches to North America was a necessary maritime task. Such activity on Canada's part was viewed by the RCN simply as an extension of its NATO-related tactical ASW capabilities and commitments, which were concentrated in peacetime in the Western Atlantic. As DND would argue in 1984 in response to a Senate committee recommendation that Canada restrict its ASW operations out of concern for the stability of the nuclear balance, Maritime Command (MARCOM) could not restrict itself to the tactical ASW role. "Both Canada's contribution to collective security and the defence of North America require the capability to detect and if necessary neutralize hostile submarines operating in ocean areas for which Canada is responsible as well as those operating in the maritime approaches to North America."[52]

Since the navy could not claim that it would be able to protect the country from SLBM's once fired, there appeared to be no strong case for putting massive effort into strategic ASW.[53] Some analysts, such as Colin Gray, argued that if ASW against the SSBN involving bottom-based detection and long-range maritime patrol aircraft were seen by the United States "to be vital capabilities for the protection of the deterrent from SLBM," then the US "would probably wish to control these capabilities itself."[54]

The USN did take primary responsibility for meeting any SSBN threat in North American waters. But, since surveillance against the SSBN was an extension of the RCN's regular activities, it would appear that public statements to the effect that the emphasis had changed from tactical to strategic ASW really had no major impact on the posture and deployment of the forces. As Rear-Admiral J.C. Wood told a senate committee in 1982, Canada performs a surveillance role against Soviet SSBN "threatening North America" in the northwest Atlantic and northeast Pacific "in conjunction with US forces."[55]

Nevertheless, support for a strategic ASW role was weak, especially within the Liberal government and parliaments of the late 1960s. In its report on maritime forces, the House of Commons standing Committee on External Affairs and National Defence (SCEAND), recommended only "limited" co-operation with the USN in anti-SSBN activities. It was only necessary to be able to detect massive SSBN build-ups; this activity should not be carried forward to the extent that it becomes detrimental to "Canada's principle objectives given limited financial resources."[56] The 1971 White Paper, *Defence in the 70s*, was more explicit: "Although an anti-submarine warfare capability will be maintained as part of the general purpose maritime forces," it stated, "the present degree of emphasis on anti-submarine warfare directed against submarine launched ballistic missiles will be reduced in favour of other maritime roles."[57]

By the time *Defence in the 70s* was released, the navy, now Maritime Command, was encountering weakened political support for its tactical ASW role as well as for its strategic activities. Questioning of the NATO convoy role had been growing because of the view that this role was only relevant to a protracted conventional conflict in Europe and such a scenario was becoming increasingly unlikely. The SCEAND report concluded that "no need for convoy protection can be envisaged in any likely eventuality."[58] The 1971 White Paper maintained the NATO role, but it was clear that when the Trudeau government spoke of "other maritime roles" for the forces, it had non-military sovereignty protection tasks in mind. SCEAND had stressed the need to augment the forces of Maritime Command in their policing role. Not only did these forces "for commercial and other reasons" function as a "manifestation of national sovereignty," but they also would have to act unilaterally since the US and other NATO countries were the ones most likely to challenge Canadian sovereignty.[59]

Amid all the questioning of the NATO role and calls for a greater emphasis on essentially non-military policing functions was the turmoil brought about by unification. Unification, however, need not have led to the subsequent decline of Canada's maritime capabilities and its contribution to collective allied seapower. The one thing that neither unification nor even the 1971 White Paper had changed was Canada's alliance obligations. Nominally, priorities had been reordered to emphasize sovereignty protection, yet NATO and NORAD commitments were maintained. The navy had long argued that it could meet the sovereignty tasks with capabilities designed to meet the NATO and North American roles. The key factor was not unification but the Liberal government's unwillingness to maintain Canada's maritime forces at levels close to those required for a credible contribution to collective security. It was assumed that sovereignty could be assured with lower levels of spending on modern maritime forces. At sea, as elsewhere, the Trudeau government believed it could demonstrate its continued adherence to collective security by making only symbolic contributions. This view was bolstered by apparent perceptions that the NATO ASW role was in itself neither crucial nor relevant.

The remarkable aspect about this downgrading of the NATO role for Maritime Command was that it coincided with the renewed emphasis which NATO itself was placing upon its maritime forces. As the *Brock Report* had predicted in 1961, the growth of nuclear arsenals would compel the West to enhance conventional capabilities, including those dedicated to maintaining security of the seas. The Trudeau government and senior DND officials were fully aware of the changes taking place with regard to NATO's maritime posture. This change was the result of the adoption by NATO of a flexible response strategy in 1967 and the growing appreciation that the Soviet navy was increasingly acquiring the capability to challenge the West at sea.

At the beginning of 1967, SACLANT's staff, especially Admiral Richard Colbert, USN, deputy chief of plans, were pressing for a "new concept of maritime strategy" for NATO. The basic thrust was to increase NATO's ability to respond quickly and collectively at sea in the event of a crisis and to affirm the importance of the sea for NATO's overall strategy.[60] Unlike the ground and air forces along the central front, forces assigned to the naval commands were not permanently under NATO command. While the principal naval commanders as national commanders had forces directly at their disposal, NATO had to be able to move collectively at sea in a short time. Thus in 1967 SACLANT set out to persuade the North Atlantic Council to approve the creation of a standing force permanently under his command.

From 1965 to 1967, SACLANT had conducted the Matchmaker exercises which saw several allied ships carrying out an extended joint patrol with underway replenishment. This provided SACLANT's staff with a basis for evaluating the feasibility of forming a permanent NATO squadron. As a further means of increasing the immediate availability of forces, the SACLANT staff also developed the idea of a "Maritime Contingency Force" (MCF). This force would be drawn from forces already earmarked by national governments but would be available on short notice to support SACLANT's contingency plans. Taken together, the permanent squadron and the MCF were viewed as "among other things," providing "a substantial part of the answer to the Northern Flank problem." There, the growing Soviet presence might place NATO at a disadvantage in the early moments of a crisis.[61] In a November 1967 letter to a Finnish naval officer, Colbert noted that "We have a new strategy that hopefully will be adopted (at the North Atlantic Council meeting) in December ... and from SACLANT viewpoint we have made a lot of progress in selling NATO maritime strategy."[62]

At the same meeting in which the flexible response strategy was endorsed, the North Atlantic Council did agree to transform the Matchmaker naval training squadron into a Standing Naval Force Atlantic (STANAVFORLANT). This force, to be composed of destroyer-type ships, would, by virtue of being continuously operational, "enhance existing co-operation between naval forces of member countries." Colbert viewed the decision as "a great success for us in our efforts to strengthen the Alliance by reorganization and employment of existing naval forces already available in peacetime."[63]

STANAVFORLANT was activiated on 13 January 1968 at Portsmouth, England. The original composition included ships from the UK, Norway, and The Netherlands. In subsequent years anywhere from four to eleven destroyer-type ships and, occasionally, submarines would sail with the force as member nations contributed ships as part of their normal training cycles. Command of the force rotates yearly. Formally under SACLANT's ultimate command, STANAVFORLANT would come under CINCEASTLANT's (Commander-in-Chief Eastern Atlantic) operational command when it was in European waters.

As described in formal briefings for US Navy officers,[64] STANAVFORLANT had four main functions. First, it would provide training experience for joint operations enabling allied navies to improve "naval operational proficiency and NATO tactical development and evaluation." Second, by its very existence, STANAVFORLANT would give evidence of allied solidarity. Third, the force would provide NATO with a multinational ocean surveillance capability to monitor Soviet naval exercises and movements. The fourth function of STANAVFORLANT would be to provide SACLANT with an immediately available combined force to be deployed "to the scene of any possible contingency to reaffirm the solidarity of the NATO alliance and provide a visible deterrent." STANAVFORLANT would move "quietly to a threatened area or just out of sight over the horizon" and thus be ready to respond to higher political and military direction while at the same time exercising the right of freedom of the seas. The force could also provide the initial elements around which a "more powerful and versatile NATO force could be formed" if tensions continued to escalate.

SACLANT was anxious to have a Canadian ship participate in the STANAVFORLANT "on a continuing basis." Indeed, in early 1968 a request was made of Canada to provide the commander of the force for 1969. There was apparently some concern at DND that participation would be permanent. In a letter to Rear-Admiral Robert W. Trimbell, Admiral Colbert, then serving on the staff of SACLANT, stressed that while the force itself was to be a permanent NATO formation, individual ships would serve for only a four-month period. Another Canadian concern had been "the distance that Canadian ships might be relative to their Emergency Defence Plan (EDP) stations if they were attached to the STANAVFORLANT. Colbert noted that nations might withdraw their forces at any time. "Therefore," he continued, "assuming the availability of strategic warning as is now accepted within NATO, Canadian ships operating remote from the CANLANT area—say in the Eastern Atlantic—could be recalled at the first indication of such warning and be available to proceed to their EDP station."[65]

Canada would be primarily involved in changes to the allied maritime posture in the Atlantic. But changes were also taking place in the Mediterranean. There the commands were reorganized. On 5 June 1967, the position of Commander-in-Chief Allied Forces Mediterranean was abolished. All allied maritime forces, with the exception of the Sixth Fleet, were placed under a new Commander, Naval Forces South (COMNAVSOUTH), subordinate to the Commander-in-Chief South (CINCSOUTH). His first task in a war would be to "neutralize" the immediate naval threat to the Sixth Fleet. Subordinate to COMNAVSOUTH was another new command, Maritime Air Mediterranean (MARAIRMED), created by the Defence Planning Committee (DPC) in November 1968. This command brought together the land-based maritime air units of the US, Britain, Italy, Greece, and Turkey. In April 1969, the DPC authorized the creation of a Mediterranean naval-on-call force. In May 1973 a Standing Naval Force Channel (STANFORCHAN) was created, consisting of nine counter-measure vessels from Belgium, Denmark, Germany, and the UK.

Senior allied staff officers had begun openly to alert allied governments of the growing Soviet threat. Colbert, for example, prepared a briefing on the "Soviet World-wide Maritime Challenge," which was presented in all NATO capitals.[66]

In March 1968, Colbert himself briefed then Minister of National Defence Leo Cadieux and senior DND officials in Ottawa. In a subsequent letter to Vice-Admiral Sir Peter Hill-Norton of the Royal Navy, Colbert reported that "the minister of defence of Canada was most emphatic in his views that our story needed to be gotten across to the public in various NATO nations." Writing to then Canadian chief of the defence staff, J.V. Allard, Colbert praised the minister, saying that "I was particularly impressed by the views expressed by Minister Cadieux on the need for telling our story to the people."[67]

However strongly Mr Cadieux felt about the Soviet maritime threat, this concern did not carry over into the new Liberal administration of Pierre Trudeau. Based on the defence review and policy statements which emerged in the late 1960s and early 1970s, it would appear that the government saw no need to alert the Canadian people about NATO's new maritime posture. As a participant in allied councils and combined commands, though, the Canadian government was fully informed of these changes and the reasons for them.

On 24 January 1968, SACLANT presented to the North Atlantic Council his appreciation of the "World-wide Soviet Maritime Challenge." As a result, Secretary General Manilo Brosio directed that a study be undertaken on NATO's maritime posture. The chairman of the military committee then asked SACLANT to undertake this study, who in turn selected a group of allied naval officers to examine: (a) the relative strength of the maritime forces of NATO and the Soviet Bloc, world wide, and (b) the maritime strategic doctrines of the two sides.[68]

The *Brosio Study*[69] was presented to the secretary general on 19 March 1969. It was a wide-ranging study which examined not only the respective strengths of the two opposing allied maritime forces but also the economic and political contexts in which each was developed. Included as well was one particular conflict scenario, a limited one along the northern flank. The scenario was run for the forces existing at the time of the study and run again using estimated forces for a 1977 time frame. The study concluded that while present maritime forces could contain the Soviet surface, subsurface, and aerial threat, the prospects were not good for later years. Even at that time, it was estimated that it would take several weeks to secure the Norwegian sea in order to project force ashore and move merchant shipping safely. By 1977, ASW operations would not be sufficient to prevent Soviet submarines from reaching the sea lanes, and escort forces could not contain the air threat.

While all hypothetical scenarios and war gaming can only be

speculative, the results of the *Brosio Study* appeared to confirm, for the first time in a NATO assessment, that the Alliance would have to wage a major campaign at sea if it were to use the seas to support its position ashore. In the "comprehensive" study, *Allied Defence in the Seventies,* presented to the DPC in December 1970, attention was directed to the maritime threat facing NATO. The DPC called for "better maritime surveillance and anti-submarine forces, more maritime patrol aircraft and seaborne missile systems and the replacement of overaged ships."

The US Navy was particularly anxious to have its allies contribute more to NATO's maritime posture. The number of ships in the American fleet had been declining and, although the newer vessels were more potent, the USN viewed its global commitments as stretching its capabilities in the event of war. It might not be possible for the USN to meet its NATO and other responsibilities simultaneously. Thus, in 1970, the Chief of Naval Operations Elmo Zumwalt asked the US Naval War College to develop a plan to improve the ASW capabilities of the NATO allies. The *Newport Study* was undertaken with the assistance of US naval officers from several allied commands. It was completed in April 1971.

In a letter to Zumwalt, dated September 1971, Admiral Colbert (by then SACLANT chief of staff) reported that he was working with Admiral Horacio Riverio, CINCSOUTH, on implementing the recommendations of the *Newport Study*. He wanted the US defence department to support their efforts by persuading the allies to "carry a heavier burden at sea." Colbert called for the "elimination" of what he referred to as the McNamara policy of "downgrading NATO navies." It was also important to establish with the US Joint Chiefs of Staff the fact that "the shift in the balance of the threat has been to seaward [and] that the Military Assistance Program allocations to strengthen allied naval forces need to reflect this."[70]

The US and NATO were also concerned about the state of allied plans for the organization and control of merchant shipping in the event of war. Despite the emphasis on airlift and pre-positioning begun in the 1960s, NATO still felt it necessary to make provisions for the massive movement of American reinforcements and resupplies by sea, in convoy if necessary.

In 1972, the office of the Assistant Secretary of Defense for Program and Analysis released a major study which looked at American requirements and capabilities to meet a NATO sealift. *The Sealift Procurement and National Security*[71] study found that US government-owned fleets and privately owned US merchant fleets would be unable to provide the necessary bottoms for such a sealift. It concluded, however, that the difference would be made up by NATO-flag shipping which would be made available to the US during a crisis.

The problem was not the lack of adequate shipping but rather timely acquisition. During the 1970s, the US and NATO engaged in several measures to ensure that adequate allied-flag shipping could be quickly brought to US ports for the movement of American military cargo. In September 1973, the Department of Defense and the Commerce Department entered into a new agreement with NATO "to increase the availability of NATO flag shipping in the event of a major deployment of forces to Europe." Emphasizing that the sealift problem was "not so much a matter of total capacity as early availability," Secretary of Defense James Schlesinger reported to Congress in 1974 that three hundred "suitable" NATO-flag ships (some roll-on, but mostly break-bulk), "which normally frequent US East and Gulf coast ports would be 'earmarked' in peacetime to facilitate their acquisition in a contingency." These ships would be directed to American ports "in response to specific US deployment requirements."[72] In latter years, NATO's Planning Board for Ocean Shipping refined its procedures. In 1977, a new NATO shipping organization, the Civilian Sealift Group, was created. This was a group of representatives from major NATO shipping companies who would assist the United States in marshalling some six hundred NATO-flag vessels earmarked for a reinforcement sealift.

In enhancing its plans to acquire merchant shipping for the US, the alliance continued to plan for and test convoy procedures. To some extent the growing range of Soviet offensive weaponry made close convoy protection ineffective by itself. Yet this only meant that convoys would need extended protection ranging out several hundred miles. The principle, however, that merchant ships could be better protected if they moved together was maintained. In 1973, the US Joint Chiefs of Staff issued another version of its *Allied Guide to Masters* (ACP 148(b)) to allied merchant ship masters. The guide outlined steps to be taken in the event of war, naval control of shipping procedures, and convoy organization and tactics. It also set forth basic defensive measures to be taken in the event of air, submarine, and surface attack including missile and nuclear strikes. SACLANT also continued to conduct a convoy commodore course.

During the major NATO exercise Strong Express in 1972, involving a conventional conflict along the northern flank, six convoys were organized. Several of these convoys moved from German and Danish ports across the North Sea, while a western Atlantic convoy of ten ships sailed to Europe from Halifax and Boston escorted by Canadian and American destroyers. A NATO-wide naval control of shipping organization provided convoy operational briefings through the exercise.[73]

Thus Canada began to downgrade its NATO maritime roles, including convoy escort, simultaneous with an upgrading of the importance of those roles by the alliance. Yet, characteristic of the Trudeau government's approach to collective security, it did not withdraw from any alliance commitment nor even eliminate those roles which it was apparently no longer willing to fund adequately. Here is part of the origin of the commitment-capability gap which would grow through the 1970s. To be sure, ambiguities and uncertainties about the role of seapower in NATO strategy remained, as they did in all other aspects of the allied posture. But it was evident that if the alliance intended to maintain conventional deterrence, especially as a hedge against early nuclear use, it would have to upgrade its maritime forces. The Canadian government supported the need to build up conventional forces. At sea, however, as elsewhere, it was prepared to let others assume the burden for backing up its foreign policy with adequate armed forces.

Given the condition of Canada's maritime forces by the early 1980s, it was not surprising that the 1985 celebrations of the navy's seventy-fifth anniversary emphasized the great days of the past rather than the present or the future. Among the eras deserving of fond remembrance was that of the Cold War. While lacking the drama of the world war battles of the Atlantic, the role of the RCN in the early days of the nuclear age was a credible and relevant one. The advent of nuclear weapons had done much to change the nature of the strategic environment, but the kinds of maritime forces Canada could and did contribute to collective security were still needed.

As the Cold War drew to a close, the strategic environment had changed again. The achievement by the Soviets of nuclear parity with the US made nuclear war less likely. But the old problem of providing for the defence of Europe against superior Soviet conventional land and air forces remained, and therefore seapower was still important. It was even more important given the growth in Soviet maritime capabilities. In North America, as well, the need to maintain adequate maritime forces persisted and grew as the Soviets extended their maritime reach. The influence of history had again placed a premium on seapower. Canada's maritime forces were no longer in a position to meet the challenge as they had done in 1962. It was therefore not the RCN of the Cold War which was an anachronism in the nuclear age but the MARCOM of later years.

Chapter 12

INTERNATIONAL NAVAL CO-OPERATION AND ADMIRAL RICHARD G. COLBERT: THE INTERTWINING OF A CAREER WITH AN IDEA

John B. Hattendorf

INTRODUCTION

Most of us who serve in navies or devote our days to writing and thinking about naval power take almost for granted the concept that navies are an expression of national power and therefore, in modern terminology, reinforce nationalism. We become almost hypnotized with the idea that there is a continuum from national policy to naval strategy and tactics. Indeed, that is the powerful thought that lies at the foundation of Mahan's writings and Corbett's analysis. Yet it is not the only way to view the matter. There is an even older thought: the idea that there is an essential commonality among those who go down to the sea in ships. Richard Colbert has been one of a very few senior admirals in the United States Navy to champion this other view. At the first International Sea Power Symposium in 1969, an occasion which brought together for the first time many heads of free world navies, Colbert outlined his own view:

> The experience of this conference has strongly confirmed what all of us already knew by instinct and experience: that the common aspects of so many of the problems we each face in operating at sea creates a strong fraternal bond. This unites all of us in blue suits who share similar professional concerns.
>
> We recognize that there are political problems and interests which sometimes limit our co-operation. But it is equally clear that the broad interests of the world community we serve are enhanced by bringing our common perspective to bear on common problems. Much can be done on a Navy-to-Navy basis.[1]

An acquaintance of Colbert's in the Italian Navy defined the concept even more sharply when he wrote, "probably the underlying philosophy lies in the *Idea of Considering Navies of the World as a Social System* to a degree separated or divorced from the states they defend."[2] In other words, it is possible to discern a kind of global brotherhood of naval officers, indoctrinated with a concept of international naval co-operation and nurtured by close, personal relations.

In a sense it seems an idealistic concept founded on a belief in peace and friendship on a global scale that should be the basis for all human relations.[3] Yet at the same time, Colbert's notion can be viewed as a realistic, pragmatic strategy for the free world as the United States and its allies face Soviet naval power.[4] As some of his contemporaries noted, Colbert was not a theoretician given to working out new concepts in abstract form, but once someone else had formed a concept, he was superb at developing it further and bringing it to fruition.[5] It is in this sense that Colbert was accurately described in an honorary degree citation as "Sailor-Statesman of the Navy, creator, innovator, educator."[6]

In the thirty-six years of his naval career, Colbert slowly but increasingly became interested in concepts and ideas relating to international naval co-operation. By the time of his death in 1973, he had reached the rank of full admiral and had truly earned the title which Admiral Elmo Zumwalt gave him: "Mr International Navy."[7]

EARLY CAREER

Colbert came from an unusual family background. He was born in Brownsville, Pennsylvania, on 12 February 1915, the son of Charles F. Colbert, jr, and Mary Louis Benford Colbert. His father, a prominent leader in the coke, coal, and alloy business, was president of the Pittsburgh Metallurgical Company. Colbert attended Shady Side Academy, an established college preparatory school in Pittsburgh. During his years there, he developed a passionate desire to become a naval officer, despite his father's fond hope that he would join the family business. Young Colbert decided to test out his desire and, with his father's help, obtained a berth on board the steamship *Robert Luckenbach* for the summer of 1931, on a voyage from New York to Seattle and back via the Panama Canal. It was an eventful trip which gave Colbert the experience of a hurricane and of hard work at sea. At the end of it, having firmly established his love for ships and the sea, the sixteen-year-old boy wrote his diary: "I can honestly say I have never enjoyed a summer as much as this one."[8]

After proving himself at sea, the next hurdle was to obtain an appointment to the naval academy following his graduation from school in June 1933. It was no easy task. Starting more than a year in advance, his father began writing letters to friends, business associates, local politicians, and his congressman asking their help. Disappointingly, they all replied that no appointments were available that had not already been promised to other equally good candidates.[9] Finally, in desperation, a friend of the family and the chancellor of Syracuse University, Charles W. Flint, wrote to President-elect Franklin D. Roosevelt asking his assistance. Roosevelt gave Flint the formula which eventually won the boy his commission: "The only chance for young Colbert," Roosevelt wrote, "is to find some other Congressman or Senator who has a vacancy and who would be willing to have him move into the district or state in which the vacancy exists for the purpose of establishing a residence there, even though it be a temporary one."[10] In the end, Colbert did not have to look too far afield. Congressman Harry A. Estrep of Pennsylvania's 35th District appointed Colbert to the US Naval Academy in the class of 1937. This early incident is illuminating because it reveals the Colbert family's ease in approaching influential people, a skill which Richard Colbert often used later in life.

Colbert was a Naval Academy midshipman from 1933 to 1937; his class started with 440 and graduated 331. On graduation, he stood only 247 in the class. He was neither a great scholar nor an athlete, but he clearly stood out as a leader and as someone well trained in the social graces. He commanded the Third Battalion of Midshipmen in the first third of his senior year and again for the final third of the year, when the best and most successful leaders of the class were chosen. Throughout his academy years, he was busy in extracurricular activities, particularly social ones. On one occasion during the Midshipman's Practice Cruise in 1936, Colbert was selected from among the other midshipmen on board the flagship USS *Arkansas* to receive distinguished civilian guests. "I seem to be getting a name for being a Majordomo," he wrote to his father.[11] Indeed, he served on the hop committee and the Christmas card committee, was co-director of the musical clubs show, and, finally, served as chairman of the most important social event of his four years at Annapolis, the Ring Dance.[12] Those experiences and social training helped Colbert develop his approach and style, so important later in his life.

While social events were prominent, one can find even in his midshipman days the first traces of his interest in foreign affairs.[13] He reflected this in a speech he prepared for the academy's public speaking group, the Quarterdeck Society, in January 1935. The prize-winning speech, entitled "The War Peril," reflected for the first time

Colbert's appreciation of foreign opinion. In his speech, he declared that there was one great overwhelming fear in Europe, the fear of a war that, no matter where it started, would spread and destroy the Western world. "America cannot afford to be indifferent to this universal opinion of Europe," Colbert concluded.[14] It was a thought that echoed throughout his career.

Upon graduation from Annapolis in June 1937, Colbert went to his first sea assignment, the commissioning crew of the new aircraft carrier USS *Yorktown*. In 1939, he was reassigned, this time to the Asiatic Fleet, where he received orders to the flush-deck four-piper USS *Barker*. Colbert served in the *Barker* for five years, rising from junior ensign to Lieutenant Commander and commanding officer. The ship saw duty in Southeast Asian and Australian waters as well as escort duty in the Atlantic and as part of the carrier USS *Core*'s successful hunter-killer group. His years in *Barker* brought him the first experience of co-operation with other navies. In early 1942, *Barker* was one of the ships in ABDA-Float (American British Dutch Australian) the allied naval command under Admiral Thomas C. Hart, USN, then under Vice-Admiral C.E.L. Helfrich, Royal Netherlands Navy. *Barker* served in the striking force along with British, Dutch, and Australian ships in the unsuccessful attempts to intercept the Japanese invasion fleet off Bali and Banka Island in February 1942. The experience of those actions impressed Colbert, who was then the ship's communications officer. Despite the current view of historians who see the Java Sea campaign as a mismanaged affair, Colbert often discussed with his colleagues how relatively smoothly he believed the ship-to-ship communications between ships of different navies had functioned in that critical situation.[15]

Despite the defeat of ABDA command, Colbert's memory of his experience stayed with him and convinced him not only of the practicality of multinational forces but also of the real advantage that multinational arrangements had for securing the seas. Looking back in 1966, he argued against those who wished to replace NATO with a series of bilateral treaties, saying that such treaties had not worked in "slow-motion" wars such as the Second World War. They could not be responsive to the complex, fast-moving events that could lead to nuclear war. Thinking of the events leading up to the Second World War naval engagements in the Dutch East Indies, Colbert commented that those were "desperate times, and I saw this lesson first hand. It was a bitter lesson."[16] Through that experience, Colbert came to believe that there was greater potential for success through the combined efforts of many nations than through following only the individual interests of single nations.

From *Barker*, Colbert went on to command the destroyer *Meade* in both the Atlantic and the Pacific, remaining in command of her until the end of the war. Promoted to commander, Colbert was assigned at the end of the war to the Bureau of Naval Personnel, where he worked on plans for the post-war naval reserve. During that period, he also served as a social aide in the Truman White House. He kept up his interest in foreign affairs through membership in the United Nations Club, but in these years he had not settled down fully to concentrate on international issues.

MATURATION OF A CONCEPT

The real turning point in Colbert's career came in 1948, when he was selected as aide and flag secretary to Admiral Richard L. Conolly, USN, commander-in-chief US Naval Forces Eastern Atlantic and Mediterranean, based in London. Commenting on his new orders, Colbert told a friend, "Am not sure whether I like it or not. I guess I will find out."[17] He did, and Conolly's ideas and approach came to have a marked influence on Colbert.

Conolly was a superb negotiator, and Colbert accompanied him in meetings with naval leaders in most of the western European and Mediterranean nations and learned much from the way Conolly handled problems and dealt with other leaders. One incident in particular seemed to summarize Conolly's approach and influenced Colbert's way of thinking. During a cruise in the Mediterranean on board his flagship in 1949, USS *Columbus*, Conolly arranged a table-top war game in which he posed the problem of an allied naval command in the Mediterranean; it was one of the first steps in the arduous process of creating what would become the NATO Mediterranean naval command. In order to examine carefully the issue of whether the command headquarters should be afloat or ashore, and what forces should participate, Conolly gathered together senior officers from a number of countries. Each co-operated but clearly showed his national bias. Conolly finished the exercise not with solutions but by making all who participated feel that they were part of a team dealing with a common problem.[18] That was a theme basic to Richard Colbert's way of thinking.

By all accounts, Colbert's association with Conolly provided the basic insight upon which he built his later work. At the same time, there was a parallel and personal development which helped to shape his international outlook further. At a New Year's ball in 1949, Colbert met Prudence Ann Robertson, daughter of E.J. Robertson, the managing director of Lord Beaverbrook's newspapers *The London Daily Ex-*

press, The Evening Standard and two Scottish newspapers. A Canadian who had gone to live in London after the First World War, E.J. Robertson nurtured Colbert's instinctive feeling for international co-operation as the most viable means of achieving world peace, and Colbert returned his interest with admiration and devotion. At the end of Colbert's tour of duty in London, he and Prudence Robertson were married at St Paul's Church, Knightsbridge. Throughout their married life, Colbert felt that England was his second home; at the same time, he learned from his wife how to be sensitive to differences in points of view between Europeans and North Americans.[19]

COLBERT IN WASHINGTON

Leaving England in December 1950, Colbert accompanied Admiral Conolly to his new position as president of the Naval War College, then Colbert moved on to his own new assignment in the political-military affairs division of the office of the chief of naval operations.

Shortly after Colbert's arrival, the division received a new director, Rear Admiral Bernard L. Austin. Colbert obviously liked the work in his new assignment under Austin, much of which was dealing with foreign issues and with other nationalities.[20] During this period Admiral Austin became concerned with the problem of providing instruction for naval officers from nations who wanted training in the United States. There had already been a move to put service education on a more systematized basis through the establishment of the NATO Defence College in Paris, but this was not sufficient to meet all the demand. In the late 1940s and early 1950s, there were many requests made to the US Navy for use of its service schools, but no regularized arrangements had been made. In light of this, Austin directed Colbert to make a staff study of the best way in which a course could be developed for foreign naval officers.[21] This work was the seed from which much would grow later in Colbert's career.

While Colbert was at work on this and other projects, he came to the attention of Admiral Forrest Sherman, the Chief of Naval Operations. Sherman selected Colbert to become his aide later in the year, undoubtedly on Admiral Conolly's recommendation. Before that could become a permanent assignment, however, Sherman needed an experienced and knowledgeable aide on temporary assignment with him for overseas trips. One important assignment came in 1950-1, when Sherman was a member of an inter-allied committee negotiating how the new NATO military commands would be structured. After each negotiating session, Sherman would relax with his aides and unwind by discussing the events of the day. Through this method Sherman taught Colbert about national sensitivities and current issues as well as successful methods of international negotiation.[22]

In July 1951, another issue arose in which Admiral Sherman used Colbert's experience and expertise. Some years earlier, while with Admiral Conolly, Colbert had been closely involved in the staff work leading to the US proposal for obtaining American naval base rights in Spain. As early as 1948, Franco had said that he would make bases available, but President Truman and the National Security Council had initially rejected the proposal.[23] Despite qualms about associating their country with fascist Spain, Sherman and Conolly, among others, believed that NATO's southern flank would be vulnerable without friendly bases in Spain. As the only member of the joint chiefs to take this view, Sherman went ahead, having finally persuaded Truman that it was an important strategic issue.[24] With Colbert at his side, Sherman travelled to Spain for talks with Franco. As was his custom, Sherman had negotiated privately with Franco, and afterwards he filled in the details and the rationale behind all his agreements in discussion with his aide. Continuing on from Spain to Naples for further talks with European leaders, Admiral Sherman suddenly died of a heart attack before he could prepare any written reports of his conversations. Colbert was the US naval officer with the most thorough knowledge of what Sherman and Franco agreed upon[25] and thereby Colbert became a direct link in the chain that led to the US Navy's use of Rota, Spain, as a naval base.

COLBERT AT THE NAVAL WAR COLLEGE

Upon completion of his tour of duty in Washington, Commander Colbert reported to the heavy cruiser USS *Albany* as executive officer. During his two years on board, the *Albany* served as flagship for Commander, Battleship-Cruiser Force, Atlantic, and was deployed to the Mediterranean. Colbert distinguished himself as an exceptionally capable administrator, a good shipmate,[26] and, as one of his commanding officers recalled, "the best executive officer any ship had had (or the good fortune to have)."[27]

Upon completion of his sea duty, Colbert had to choose between assignment as either head of an academic section at the Naval Academy or a student at the Naval War College. Seeking advice, Colbert wrote to his old boss, Admiral Conolly, then retired. Conolly gave him the sound advice which was to prove remarkably true. "In regard to the possibilities for duty," Conolly wrote, "I would say by all means take the Naval War College if you have the opportunity ... I have always considered it a turning point in a naval career."[28] In the autumn of

1955, Colbert reported to the Naval War College as a student in the naval warfare course. Recently promoted to captain, Colbert stayed on for two more years as a staff member.

The background for Colbert's new assignment stretched back to the early 1950s when he had done his staff study on training foreign naval officers under Admiral Austin in the political-military affairs branch. In 1955–6, the president of the Naval War College was Vice Admiral Lynde McCormick, who had taken up the college presidency after having been the first Supreme Allied Commander, Atlantic. In this role, McCormick had commanded several NATO exercises, including Mainbrace, the largest allied peacetime exercise up to that time. These experiences taught McCormick the fundamental need for developing better understanding among NATO navies. His experience paralleled that of Admiral Arleigh Burke.

During 1955, Burke's first year as Chief of Naval Operations, he began to lay the groundwork for closer co-ordination between the US and other NATO navies. At the same time, he saw the need for similar co-ordination with friendly navies in Asia, Africa, and throughout the Americas. In addition, he wanted to create a way in which naval officers from nations which had fought against the United States during the Second World War could shed their unspoken sense of inferiority following defeat and become full-fledged allies.

One of the options Burke saw was the chance to offer a year's study at the Naval War College, modelled upon the lines of the curriculum already in place for the first year of the naval warfare course. Burke made contact with the leaders of several allied navies, who were generally enthusiastic about this idea. By the spring of 1956, twenty-three navies had accepted Burke's invitation, with Admiral McCormick's full co-operation to implement the course at the Naval War College.

At the time these plans were coming to fruition, Colbert was just finishing his first year as a student in the naval warfare course. When Burke selected Colbert to head up the new course, there was some jealousy on the part of others at the college. But Burke had full confidence in Colbert, having known him while he was in the political-military affairs division where his office had been directly across the hall from Burke's.[29]

Colbert's first task was to choose a name for the course. He was firmly opposed to the idea of using the word "foreign" in the name, wanting instead to select a name which would reflect a positive and mutual goal. After about a month, he selected the name Naval Command Course for Free World Naval Officers.[30]

The purpose of the course was multifaceted. Basically it was to prepare officers for higher command responsibilities within their own navies, while at the same time familiarizing them with US Navy doctrines, methods, and practices. But its purpose was much broader than that, as Professor August Miller reflected after his first year's experience under Colbert's direction:

> At the Naval War College in an atmosphere of complete freedom of thought and expression, the foreign officers both symbolize and interpret their own navies and their countries not only to Americans but to each other; and on the basis of this free inquiry it can be readily recognized that such an open exchange of ideas will help to allow friendly nations to co-operate and to operate with one another in maximum efficiency in time of world stress.[31]

Colbert himself was well satisfied with the course and privately wrote to a friend, "all goes well—almost too smoothly. The capability of the students' is far beyond our expectations—they really look like the 'future CNO's [Chiefs of Naval Operations] of the Free World' as Admiral Burke describes them."[32]

Colbert took great pains with the course, designing an appropriate curriculum and nurturing close personal contacts among the students. The social side of the course was an essential element, and the Colberts spent a large sum of their own money to ensure that all went well, not only with cocktail parties but also with flowers for sick family members or small farewell gifts. For all of this, Burke consistently gave Colbert full credit for the course's success. As he wrote to Colbert privately a decade later, "the idea was good, but a lot of good ideas come a cropper, and this one did not because of you. You were the man who started it properly, who nursed it and nurtured it along the proper lines."[33]

Yet in this period, Colbert's ideas were very much in the process of development. The experience of being the director of the naval command course for its first two classes very clearly became the foundation upon which his later career was built. At this stage, however, he did not seem to have a clear vision of what could practicably be done with the co-operation he was then nurturing.

EXPERIENCE IN INTER-ALLIED AND INTER-AGENCY
NAVAL ASSIGNMENTS

After three years at the Naval War College, Colbert left for Washington where he was assigned to the staff of the Joint Chiefs of Staff in the Long Range Plans and Basic War Plans Branch. In 1960, Colbert became commanding officer of the Sixth Fleet's general stores ship, USS

Altair, based in Barcelona, Spain. This proved a formative and influential phase of his career, which reinforced some of his experience with the Naval Command Course. The ship spent much time at sea in support of the operations of the Sixth Fleet and developing an early approach to vertical replenishment at sea by helicopter; Colbert's experimentation with this new idea was a major contribution to its use and led to its becoming a standard and routine operation for ships at sea. While engaged in these operations, Colbert was also intensely concerned with his ship's relationship to its home port and in developing co-operation with the Spanish navy. This, he thought, was a key element in the alliance system.

When word reached him that the very small US naval facility at Barcelona might be abolished and the fleet supported by a more "cost-effective," larger base, Colbert objected strongly. His reasoning reflected his growing belief in the importance of personal relationships across national and cultural boundaries. He pointed out to his superiors that it was important for the US Navy's sailors and their families to develop a close relationship with the people of the country in which their base was located, through an appreciation and recognition of their host's customs and way of life. *Altair's* home port in Barcelona gave such an opportunity. "It would appear," Colbert wrote, "that every opportunity should be grasped by the US Navy to establish and maintain more small unobtrusive United States representation of this type in friendly countries, rather than closing them and concentration at installations which already are criticized as large and conspicuous overseas bases."[34]

Colbert was selected for his major command while still in command of *Altair*. He had asked for assignment to "a cruiser out of Boston," and the Bureau of Naval Personnel had obliged by giving him command of the guided missile heavy cruiser USS *Boston*. Under Colbert's command, *Boston* deployed to the Mediterranean and, for a brief period, served as the flagship for Commander Sixth Fleet. Admiral David L. McDonald later recalled that "Colbert and his crew in the *Boston* went out of their way to make their ship a most outstanding Flagship."[35]

It was while in command of *Boston* that Colbert decided he wanted to develop his experience further in political-military affairs. In 1962, Colbert became interested in the possibility of obtaining one of the two military billets on the State Department's Policy Planning Council, then headed by Walt W. Rostow. The council had been established in 1947 by Secretary of State General George C. Marshall to be a long-range planning and advisory staff whose task would be to analyze major foreign policy problems. Among its functional responsibilities the council was particularly charged with co-ordinating political-military policy and inter-agency planning.

Rostow wanted to fill his military billets with the best qualified officers. Because he did not want to accept just any officer that the Department of Defense might assign, Rostow wanted to have a competition that would produce "real Rhodes Scholarship type of thinking." During his search, Rostow interviewed Colbert in November 1962 and later received from him what Rostow described as "a very moving letter." Rostow recalled that Colbert wanted to have the experience which the Policy Planning Council assignment would give him, but Colbert was aware that the Navy's personnel bureau did not think it was good for his career. However, Colbert persisted in applying, believing that military and naval officers needed to have a deep knowledge of the problems of diplomacy. In his letter to Rostow, Colbert remarked that at the Naval War College he had been closely involved with officers from other countries and the experience had had a marked effect on his attitude. Above all, he wanted to build upon the sense of fraternity that he had experienced.[36]

In 1962, Assistant Secretary of Defense for International Security Affairs Paul H. Nitze was particularly interested in getting high-calibre military and naval officers into other agencies of the government, particularly the State Department. A dozen years earlier, Nitze had headed the Policy Planning Council and knew well its importance and its role. The Navy had never sent an officer to the Policy Planning council, but Nitze's assistant, Captain Elmo R. Zumwalt, jr, USN, shared Nitze's view and also wanted to see the Navy increase its influence. Both Zumwalt and Nitze believed that an assignment to the State Department would be career-broadening. Colbert, too, shared this belief, but the detailing officers in the Bureau of Naval Personnel consistently told him that such an assignment would irreparably damage his career. Colbert's ability obviously impressed Rostow, while within the Department of Defense, Zumwalt as Nitze's aide "pulled the necessary levers" and got Colbert the assignment he wanted.[37]

Colbert's work ranged widely and deeply in foreign policy issues during his two years with the Policy Planning Council, including work on topics such as multilateral forces, Vietnam, the Inter-American Military Force, a US-Australian squadron, and nuclear arrangements east of Suez in the face of a Chinese communist nuclear threat.[38] The Inter-American Military Force was an idea which specifically reflected Colbert's ideas; it was a subject on which he wrote a number of papers. Colbert had in mind a force that, though primarily naval, included army and air components. As he visualized it, the force would be of modest size involving a few thousand people drawn from seven or eight countries in Latin America, with United States participation limited to no more than 15–20 per cent of the total force. In Colbert's view "it would be important that the US not be any more than just a partner in the project."[39] Colbert envisaged that its primary mission would be ocean surveillance and sea control, but it could also be a peacekeeping force, thus providing a place for the participation of armies. An important aspect of this force was its training; significantly, Colbert envisaged that it would be provided by the force itself at a base set up in some convenient place in Latin America. This would have an advantage in keeping the force's training independent of the United States and limiting the number of officers who would be brought into the United States for training.[40]

In 1964, at the end of his state department duty, Colbert began to be involved in developing the concept for the Multi-Lateral Force, a concept which he believed might be attractive to NATO countries whose navies had surface ships but no aircraft carriers. Colbert believed it would form a much less costly alternative to American nuclear submarines, by placing Polaris missiles in merchant ships, manned by mixed NATO crews with joint responsibility among all NATO nations for nuclear deterrence. This proposal, which implied that the nuclear nations would delegate a certain amount of their sovereignty to an Allied committee, was never implemented.

The idea of mixed manning was tried out. Colbert was one of the small group with Rostow that recommended to Secretary Nitze that the US Navy demonstrate the feasibility of manning a single ship with officers and men from different nations. The short-term experiment was successfully carried out by the USS *Claude V. Ricketts* in 1964–5.[41]

Reflecting on their time together in the State Department, Colbert and his colleague Colonel Robert N. Ginsburg, USAF, wrote:

> To participate in the work of the Council ... can be an exhilarating experience for the military man who follows the path and precepts of George C. Marshall. For the Council's work is almost daily vindication of the dedicated military officers' unuttered creed. It is not, he knows, the man that is important, nor is it the idea, nor the military service or branch of government, nor the government itself. It is only the Republic and its perpetuation that really matter.[42]

While Colbert was off in the depths of the State Department, some of his fellow officers thought he had been forgotten by the Navy, but it was not so. In May 1964, he was one of five of his classmates selected for Rear Admiral. And to show the importance of his work, the Navy promoted him while still on the Policy Planning Council, rather than waiting for him to assume his naval command.

Then in June 1964, he reported as Commander, Cruiser-Destroyer Flotilla Six, based at Charleston, South Carolina. The fifty or so ships under his command gave him the responsibility, as one friend commented, equivalent to the commander-in-chief of a smaller navy. A year later, Colbert became deputy chief of staff and assistant chief of staff for policy, plans, and operations to the Supreme Allied Commander, Atlantic (SACLANT), Admiral Thomas H. Moorer.

Colbert's first assignment after he reported to SACLANT was to establish the Iberian-Atlantic Command. When Moorer became SACLANT in April 1965, he had pointed out that NATO had agreed several years before to establish a command covering the sea approaches to the Straits of Gibraltar, but that neither the money nor the men necessary to carry this task out had been authorized. Moorer told the NATO Military Committee that he wished either to have the directive cancelled or receive the resources necessary to do the job. The committee agreed to provide what was needed and this task, in turn, was given to Colbert. In short order, Colbert brought IBERLANT (Iberian Atlantic) into being. In Moorer's words, "this action not only significantly enhanced the capability of NATO to deal with naval operations in the area, but also significantly increased the morale, prestige and overall interest of our Portuguese allies. I give Admiral Colbert all of the credit for this important move."[43]

Simultaneously, Colbert began to develop a proposal to create a Standing Naval Force, Atlantic. For three years NATO had run an exercise called Matchmaker in which ships of various allied navies joined in an exercise for a six-month period. In late November 1966, Colbert, as a result of a discussion with Admiral Moorer, prepared a concept paper which proposed a permanent Matchmaker force that could serve as a naval contingency force for the Allied Command, Atlantic.[44] In May 1967, the NATO defence committee agreed in principle to establish a standing naval force, and this was approved in a ministerial meeting in December 1967. The force was activated in January 1968. In Colbert's view, this was only the beginning. He had already written that:

> With this as a prototype conceivably we can follow suit with similar forces in time in the Mediterranean, the Indian Ocean, the Western Pacific, and very importantly Latin American. As the Soviet Union continues to expand its sea power world wide, I can think of

no more pragmatic and meaningful counter to their activities than the US participating as partners with friendly countries in their various areas.[45]

In Colbert's mind, the crisis that led up to the June 1967 Arab-Israeli war would have been the ideal proving ground for a multinational standing naval force. "If a few of the maritime nations had formed a squadron of destroyers and contested the closure of the Gulf of Aquaba—perhaps by escorting an Israeli ship through—in support of the principle of freedom of the seas and innocent passage, the situation there might have been pacified and the Arab-Israeli war, such as it was, averted for a time or altogether."[46]

PRESIDENT OF THE NAVAL WAR COLLEGE

After the activation of the Standing Naval Force, Atlantic, and its first visit to the United States in the spring of 1968, Colbert was unexpectedly selected to be president of the Naval War College. Promoted to vice admiral in a sudden jump over some ten of his classmates, Colbert was delighted to be returning to Newport. "It is a dream come true—a dream that I would never have mentioned to anyone, for fear of being precocious,"[47] he remarked.

As president of the Naval War College, Colbert made a remarkable imprint on the institution. He was largely responsible for implementing new plans to expand the scope of the college's academic programs as well as to improve its physical plant. Like other colleges, the Naval War College had several academic chairs named for distinguished naval men in specific subject areas. Colbert continued the policy of that time by inviting distinguished civilian academics to hold these positions for a short time. He also wanted to increase the number of academic areas they represented.

In particular Colbert took special interest in two of the civilian academic chairs which had been proposed by his senior academic advisor, Professor Frederick H. Hartmann. Colbert's interest in these particular positions reflected his deep-seated appreciation for different cultural outlooks. First he brought to fruition the proposal to establish the Claude V. Ricketts Chair of Comparative Cultures. He appointed an anthropologist, John M. Roberts of Cornell University, to hold this chair in 1969–70.[48] Secondly, and for similar reasons, he supported an unsuccessful proposal to establish a chair in Oriental Studies. Explaining his view, Colbert wrote, "There are some leading contemporary thinkers who believe that the twenty-first century will be the Asian Century." With this increased awareness of the importance of the Far

East in world power politics, economically, socially, and strategically, such a scholar "would be able to add perspective to every point on the Asian scene where we as a nation have been and remain very much involved."[49]

Then after expanding the civilian faculty, he and his staff established a number of military chairs which were designed to extend the concept of the civilian academic chairs and ensure that the best qualified officers in each area of professional naval interest were brought to the college as instructors in those areas.

In developing the curriculum, Colbert continued along the lines of his predecessors, but he stressed the historical importance which the Naval War College had placed on international law since its founding in 1885. In the pages of the *Naval War College Review*, Colbert asked rhetorically, "Why should the Naval War College alone amongst service colleges, place such emphasis on the study of international law?" The answer was obvious to Colbert, for at sea, "international law is the only law." But also, "the inter-relationship of legal, political, economic and social factors which are operative on a global scale and increasing significance of our international commitments require a clear understanding of the rules governing the relations between states."[50]

In the specific area of international naval co-operation, Colbert took four major initiatives at the Naval War College. He established the first of several exchange visits between the presidents of the US Naval War College and the Royal Naval College, Greenwich,[51] supplemented by a week-long visit of forty US Naval War College students to Greenwich in 1970. Second, he proposed the establishment of a Naval Staff Course for middle-grade free-world naval officers, complementing the Naval Command Course, but at a lower level and emphasizing the participation of smaller navies which did not have comparable educational facilities. Colbert particularly had in mind that this course would primarily develop the professional and managerial skills for the student officers to use in their own navies, emphasizing the naval decisionmaking process, naval planning, and the broad understanding of the roles of sea power. At the same time, it could familiarize the students with the methods, practices, and doctrines of the US Navy while developing an international bond among the graduates.[52]

Third, Colbert built on the long-standing desire of the Naval Command Course graduates to have a reunion in Newport, combining it with the successful rise of so many of them to flag rank. He wished to use it as a means to create at the senior flag officer level "areas of mutual interest, co-ordination, and co-operation that could pay substantial dividends for the future."[53] The result was the International Sea Power Symposium in November 1969, the first in a series of meetings bringing together the chiefs of navies and other naval leaders to discuss, in an academic setting, current naval issues of mutual concern.[54] Out of the conference came much constructive and valuable thinking which led to the development of further regional discussions on the implication of Soviet maritime expansion. But most importantly for Colbert, senior naval officers at the conference became aware of their common outlook. As Canadian Rear-Admiral Harry Porter wrote to Colbert after the meeting, "I have come away from it with an increased realization of the brotherhood of the sea and comforting knowledge that most naval officers share the same problems, the same aspirations, and the same feelings about the importance of sea power on countries and mankind as a whole."[55]

The last of Colbert's contributions at the Naval War College consisted of projects which he designed as practical contributions to promote international naval co-operation. For example, he gave to the students in the Naval Command Course the mission of designing a "Free World Frigate," a modern, efficient, and economical ship of frigate or corvette size. The basic idea in Colbert's mind was to have officers from a variety of friendly nations "design" a ship that could provide the basis for commonality and standardization in multinational naval forces, such as the Standing Naval Force, Atlantic. Eventually he hoped to see a squadron of such escort ships with the same hull design, using components from many nations, each flying a different national flag. The resulting design found support from key leaders in the United States such as Admirals Elmo Zumwalt and Isaac C. Kidd, jr, but nothing came of it. Colbert was deeply disappointed that it seemed impossible to break down nationalistic barriers in building warships.[56]

Colbert's final effort at the Naval War College was developed from a point in Zumwalt's "Project Sixty," the action plan for his term as chief of naval operations. Colbert created the detailed plan of action Zumwalt used to persuade allied navies to improve and expand their anti-submarine warfare capabilities, better to counter the growing Soviet Navy.[57]

FINAL ASSIGNMENTS

In June 1971, Colbert left the Naval War College to become chief of staff to the Supreme Allied Commander, Atlantic. He was delighted with the prospect of continuing his work with NATO. "It will be like 'going home,'" he wrote.[58] Taking a circuitous route from Newport to Norfolk, Colbert prepared himself for his new position and laid the groundwork for the second International Sea Power Symposium in 1971 by visiting the chiefs of navies in Italy, Greece, Turkey, Belgium,

West Germany, the United Kingdom, and Portugal. On this, Colbert acted as Admiral Zumwalt's personal representative as well as the prospective SACLANT chief of staff.[59]

Later at the SACLANT headquarters, Colbert was deeply involved in the daily work of allied naval co-operation. A year later, he was promoted to Admiral and appointed Commander-in-Chief, Allied Forces Southern Europe. During his final years as a NATO officer, both in Norfolk and Naples, Colbert rounded out his series of practical initiatives to support international co-operation by recommending additional multilateral naval forces for the Indian Ocean and the Mediterranean. Recognizing, too, the deep expertise needed by naval officers who work within alliances, Colbert drafted a proposal to establish a NATO postgraduate school to train recently commissioned officers under the guidance of the NATO international staff.[60] Within the US Navy, Colbert recommended that a NATO career pattern should be laid out for selected officers, who would then be fully aware of NATO procedures, problems, and programs. His plan was rejected, but too often, he believed, US naval officers who came to NATO on short tours of duty without enough international experience were engrossed in the path their careers would take them within the US Navy and lacked much of the expertise, knowledge, and sensitivity to alliance problems which extended experience would bring. "Techniques for dealing with foreign personnel require more thoughtfulness, understanding, and patience," Colbert wrote, characteristically putting the issue in terms of personal relationships. In an international setting, a tactless remark or insensitivity to another viewpoint, he believed, was often far more difficult to repair than they would be within a single nation's staff.[61]

As Commander-in-Chief, Allied Forces Southern Europe in 1972–3, Colbert's principal concern was to reduce the tension between Greece and Turkey. Under his leadership, the Naval On-Call Force, Mediterranean was started and expanded with the hope of developing it into a standing naval force using Greek, Turkish, Italian, British, and US ships. Colbert had more success in his initiatives to develop co-operation between the French navy and NATO, working out a treaty allowing annual exercises. Through the combined efforts of Colbert and French Admiral J. Guillou, a large Franco-American naval exercise took place off the coast of the United States in 1973.[62]

During Colbert's tenure as commander-in-chief, he discovered that he had an incurable case of cancer, but he remained at his post until a week before his death at the age of fifty-eight, on 2 December 1973. As Admiral Guiseppe Pighini, Commander, Allied Naval Forces Southern Europe under Colbert, put it, he was "a man dedicated to his duty till the last breath of life."[63]

Colbert's highest duty, as he saw it, was clearly revealed in a letter he wrote to Chaplain Henry Duncan, only a few months before he died:

> I am a realist and know that I am on borrowed time. I am convinced that the Lord has decided to give me some extra time to do some things in this, my last command, which might better insure a safer world. That is the gist of my prayers. All I ask is just a bit more time to carry on and establish some concepts—multinational NATO forces which will strengthen our Free World against what I am convinced is a desperate threat, despite all the talk of detente.[64]

REFLECTION ON A CAREER

Richard Colbert's entire naval career was developed around a gradually growing and strengthening commitment to international naval co-operation. He never worked out or developed his thoughts on this subject in any complete way, but as one reflects on his various statements and the innovations he made during his career, one can discern a philosophy that bears much of enduring value. It was a philosophy grounded in a sense of the need for co-operation, close personal ties, loyalty, camaraderie, and social grace in day-to-day life. He was a friendly outgoing man with an understated style—a man who assumed that cordial co-operative behaviour was the best way to accomplish things.[65] In the life of a career naval officer, this meant leadership and personal responsibility. Colbert reflected these concepts in a letter he wrote near the end of his career to a young officer just taking up his first command. Referring specifically to Admiral Zumwalt's innovative reforms in the US Navy, Colbert advised: "Old Navy or New, long hair or short, it seems to me what ultimately makes the difference in readiness and effectiveness is the sense of camaraderie and respect that come from personal involvement and identification on the part of all hands. I fear that a lot of Navy men never got the underpinning message behind many of the recent innovations: the emphasis on personal responsibility."[66]

This point was an essential aspect of his philosophy, not only in shipboard command but also in forming bonds with other countries and other navies. The key was personal responsibility and, through it, personal relationships. In opening the first International Seapower Symposium, he stressed "the pure professional naval competence which each of us can bring ... [to] provide threads of a cloth which might well be woven into a durable and serviceable fabric."[67]

Colbert believed that the highest professional naval competence arose from two equally important sources: practical experience and war college education. "War colleges have always been the storehouses of the military arts," Colbert said, "but nowadays they must prepare officers to function outside the confines of purely operational expertise, in an era of transition, of apparent detente, of new structuring of international politics."[68]

The international courses played an essential role in this. Colbert believed that through such courses which stressed "undiluted, the small, close, intimate nature"[69] of the relationship built during a year's study together. It was nothing that could be mass produced but was created slowly and surely over time by a delicate formula: a small group, one officer only from each country interacting with the entire group of carefully selected students and well-chosen staff, teaching a curriculum that takes into account the foreign officers' diverse backgrounds, and letting them develop together where they would not be overwhelmed or at a disadvantage as they came to understand something of life not only in a foreign country but in one so very different from their own.[70] The result of this, Colbert found, was that it created a bond. "Once one has become part of that special fraternity," he wrote, "neither time nor distance can dissolve the unique ties it forms among its members."[71]

These kinds of ties were the basis, he believed, for the kind of partnership among nations which is urgently needed in the modern world. After the Second World War, the United States responded to the urgent and practical needs of her allies with the Truman Doctrine, the Marshall Plan, and other forms of assistance. But these led to domination. With full economic recovery from the war, these policies were no longer appropriate. "Domination leads to dependence," Colbert believed, "while true "partnership" encourages the independence, pride and dignity of our sovereign allies."[72]

Further developing this idea, Colbert saw that there was an alternative to previous US foreign policy, one which encouraged and supported regional co-operation and partnership in various areas. The growth of Soviet maritime power presented a challenging problem "which no one country is able to resolve itself."[73] In this situation Colbert saw many advantages in a policy and strategy founded on partnership among allied and friendly nations. This could best be achieved through multilateral naval forces designed for major regions of the globe. The advantages of such forces were clear to him: the cost, financially and politically was low, and they avoided the internal political dissent caused by massive or overwhelming commitment by the United States, while at the same time increasing the effectiveness of such a force by being the symbolic and real expression of several nations united in common effort. Moreover, the general maritime interests of the free world could be served by multilateral naval forces which could give rationale and justification for navies in countries where they were under attack.[74] In all of this, Colbert clearly perceived the forms of naval expertise which regional and small navies provided which complemented the expertise within larger navies concentrating on global-scale naval operations.

In a career intertwined with ideas of international, naval co-operation, Richard Colbert sought to achieve four important objectives:[75]

First, he believed that naval officers were particularly competent in solving international problems. For navies, the sea is the same good friend or cruel foe all over the world. Because of this, naval officers have naturally developed a similar way of thinking and can easily discuss mutual problems, apart from national prejudices. With this in mind, Colbert sought out successful senior naval officers as responsible representatives of different free world societies and tried to motivate them to learn through each other's perspective the value of freedom. He did this in the Naval Command Course by creating an academic environment of mutual respect and candor where the American political system and way of life, and that of each country represented, was openly discussed.

Secondly, through the International Sea Power Symposium, he sought to establish a forum where the highest naval leaders could exchange with their professional peers knowledge, concepts, views, and opinions about naval technology, tactics, strategy, and the importance of sea power. Through this, he hoped to foster deeper understanding through an appreciation of different national perspectives.

Third, in all his proposals for international co-operation, he hoped to establish among naval officers a deeper awareness of the need for mutual reliance as a key element in every nation's national interest.

Fourth, he sought to establish rapport across cultural boundaries and to develop personal knowledge and understanding for different national views as expressed by naval officers. In doing this, Colbert wanted to create a group of knowledgeable naval leaders who could ensure that the effectiveness of multinational forces would not be jeopardized by any failure to understand one's own ally.

Although Richard Colbert was an officer in the United States Navy, his vision was clearly wider than the ordinary officer's. His vision has certainly touched the officers and men of Canadian ships who have served in the Standing Naval Force, Atlantic; the senior flag officers who have attended the International Sea Power Symposia, and the twenty-four Canadian officers who have attended courses at the Naval War College.[76]

In all of his objectives, the unifying theme is the mutual experience of the naval profession, which reaches beyond cultures and nations to establish its own fraternity. Few naval officers have seen this vision so clearly as Richard Colbert and few have done so much to foster it. Those who would follow in his wake must share his notion that no measure of international leadership can replace trust and understanding among allies and a sound appreciation of common goals.

Chapter 13

ECONOMIC CONSIDERATIONS IN THE DEVELOPMENT OF THE CANADIAN NAVY SINCE 1945

Dan W. Middlemiss

INTRODUCTION

Most observers of post-Second World War Canadian defence policy would agree that Canada has acquired a small, highly specialized navy, one which over the years has been increasingly hard-pressed to carry out adequately its national and alliance responsibilities. Given these realities, the question then arises: Why does Canada have the type of navy and naval policy it has? On this issue, opinions differ, sometimes widely, depending on which aspects of policy are being addressed: commitments, specific roles, contributions, or capabilities. Most assessments have been framed in the context of changing external strategic and doctrinal requirements, or domestic political imperatives, or both. Few have been rooted in an appreciation of the role which economic considerations have played in the development of the post-war Canadian navy.

That such considerations have received little attention is not surprising given the similar neglect of Canadian defence economics as a whole.[1] Nevertheless, because economics deals with the allocation of scarce resources among competing demands, it would appear to have direct relevance to the types of issues which concern Canadian politicians and military planners in formulating defence policy in general and naval policy in particular. Indeed, economic considerations constitute an important dimension of naval policymaking. For example, in determining the overall size of the defence budget, planners must decide what proportion of the nation's defence resources should be provided to the navy. Once the level of the navy's budget is established, planners must then decide how to allocate the navy's budget among various expenditure categories: personnel, operations, maintenance, and equipment. Finally, planners must consider the impact of naval expenditures, particularly with respect to the domestic economy. What are the socioeconomic consequences of closing naval bases? To what extent should naval spending be used to support an indigenous shipbuilding industry or to achieve other economic objectives of the government?

Thus it is possible to distinguish conceptually three broad types of economic considerations—those relating to the levels, allocations, and impact of naval expenditures[2]—which influence Canadian naval policy. But theory and conceptual clarity is one thing; the practical world of policymaking is quite another. To bridge the gap between theory and practice, we must determine which economic considerations have exerted what kind of influence upon Canadian naval policy under what conditions and during which time periods.[3] This analytical task is complicated by the fuzziness of the subject-matter itself, for in practice the distinction between economics and politics is not a clear one. What on the surface may be viewed as a matter of "objective" economics upon closer analysis often reveals itself to be a matter of "subjective" political choice. As Gavin Kennedy notes, decisions about a particular defence posture have economic consequences, and economics can isolate "the tyranny of choice" involved in deciding the levels and allocations of defence expenditures. Ultimately, however, the decisions are political rather than economic in nature.[4] Stated differently, economic considerations can help determine what can be afforded for defence, the most cost-effective methods to achieve different defence goals, and the "opportunity costs" of the decisions taken, but political considerations largely determine what will be afforded for defence, the ends sought, the priorities among them, and the means selected to attain them.

This study is an attempt to identify, analyze, explain, and evaluate the role of economic considerations in the development of the post-1945 Canadian navy. It seeks to establish the relationships among the various types of economic factors themselves, as well as among the political, military, and economic considerations which have influenced Canada's naval policy over time. In the course of this examination, several important questions will be addressed. To what extent has the navy been a "burden" on the Canadian economy, the federal budget, and the defence budget itself? Has the navy truly been the "Cinderella" service of the Canadian armed forces? If so, why? What constitutes "budgetary constraint" in the context of the Canadian navy, and what are the consequences of such restraint? Has the navy's role stability and specialization been the cause or the effect of this restraint? How, and to what extent, has Canadian naval policy been influenced by largely "non-defence" domestic and external considerations?

FUNDING LEVELS: THE "CINDERELLA" SERVICE?

Following the Second World War, the Canadian navy has not been a major burden on the economy or the federal treasury. Furthermore, it has been a consistent loser in the Department of National Defence's (DND) inter-service budgetary allocation process, leading one observer to label it the "Cinderella" service.[5]

Over the period 1947–84,[6] Canada's gross national product (GNP)—the usual measure of the nation's wealth—increased 3080 per cent, and total federal expenditures increased 3264 per cent; during the same period, spending on the Canadian navy increased by a more modest 1684 per cent.[7] Comparable increases for the more recent unification years (1969–84) are: GNP 437 per cent; total federal expenditures 352 per cent; and navy spending 207 per cent (Table 1). Expressed as a percentage of GNP and total federal expenditures, spending on the Canadian navy has actually *decreased* over the 1947–84 period (figures for 1969–84 are in brackets) by 44 per cent (43 per cent) and 47 per cent (63 per cent) respectively. From this we may conclude that neither the state of the Canadian economy nor the federal treasury have of themselves impeded the funding of the Canadian navy. A relatively prosperous domestic economic climate has not necessarily produced an equally prosperous Canadian navy.

What of the relationship between total DND expenditures and navy spending? A comparison of the pre- and post-unification periods reveals that total DND spending for the 1947–68 and the 1969–84 periods increased by 352 per cent and 353 per cent respectively, while navy spending for these two periods increased by 334 per cent and 207 per cent respectively. This would seem to suggest that the navy's funding levels closely matched those of DND as a whole. However, appearances can be deceiving. Expressed as a percentage of DND expenditures, Navy spending *decreased* by 4 per cent and 32 per cent for the 1947–68 and the 1969–84 periods respectively. When annual changes in spending levels are compared for the 1947–84 period, the correlation between DND and navy expenditures becomes even less clear. For example, these level changes are positively correlated (that is, varied in the same direction as increases or decreases) in 28 of the 37 years. Of the 23 positive correlations for *increases*, the navy's percentage changes exceeded DND's in 16 years, while of the 5 positive cor-

TABLE 1: GNP/expenditures comparison

Fiscal year ending 31 March	Gross national product[1] ($000s)	Total federal expenditure[2] ($000s)	Total DND expenditure[3] ($000s)	Total navy expenditure[4] ($000s)
1946	11,885,000	5,136,229	2,140,794	241,783
1947	13,473,000	2,634,227	387,612	64,883
1948	15,509,000	2,195,626	195,999	43,728
1949	16,800,000	2,175,892	268,805	44,700
1950	18,491,000	2,448,616	384,879	73,400
1951	21,640,000	2,901,242	782,457	99,900
1952	24,588,000	3,732,875	1,415,474	182,400
1953	25,833,000	4,337,276	1,882,418	260,300
1954	25,918,000	4,350,522	1,805,915	289,000
1955	28,528,000	4,275,363	1,665,969	304,200
1956	32,058,000	4,433,128	1,750,112	340,800
1957	33,513,000	4,849,035	1,759,426	326,700
1958	34,777,000	5,087,411	1,668,463	295,000
1959	36,846,000	5,364,040	1,424,741	273,000
1960	38,359,000	5,702,861	1,516,572	255,800
1961	39,646,000	5,958,101	1,517,531	245,500
1962	42,927,000	6,520,646	1,626,104	272,000
1963	45,978,000	6,570,342	1,571,044	269,400
1964	50,280,000	6,872,402	1,683,471	298,000
1965	55,364,000	7,218,275	1,535,635	272,500
1966	61,828,000	7,734,796	1,548,447	275,000
1967	66,409,000	8,779,681	1,640,378	305,700
1968	72,586,000	9,824,081	1,751,598	281,600
1969	79,815,000	10,738,956	1,760,796	377,200
1970	85,685,000	11,921,595	1,788,428	373,900
1971	94,450,000	13,183,144	1,817,876	401,100
1972	105,234,000	14,840,865	1,895,175	415,600
1973	123,560,000	18,340,000	1,932,246	402,300
1974	147,528,000	22,551,000	2,231,983	431,000
1975	165,343,000	29,213,000	2,511,873	457,800
1976	191,857,000	33,978,000	2,973,680	393,200
1977	210,189,000	39,011,000	3,371,199	424,900
1978	232,211,000	42,902,000	3,770,980	522,100
1979	264,279,000	46,923,000	4,108,027	580,000
1980	297,556,000	52,364,000	4,389,289	556,500
1981	339,797,000	62,378,000	5,077,076	680,600
1982	358,302,000	67,474,000	6,027,729	781,500
1983	390,310,000	78,276,000	6,991,964	953,300
1984	428,500,000	88,615,000	7,972,241	1,157,300

Sources: 1 *Economic Review* 1984, and Stats Can (calendar year)
2 Public accounts
3 Public accounts
4 Table 2

relations for *decreases*, the navy's changes exceeded DND's in 2 years. Of the 9 negative correlations (that is, variations in opposite directions), the navy's percentage changes were *decreases* in 7 years, 4 of which occurred in the post-unification period. Perhaps all that should be concluded from this is that DND's funding levels have not been reliable indicators of the navy's spending levels. Sometimes the navy has done relatively better; other times it has fared less well.

Quite a different picture of the navy's funding fortunes emerges from an examination of DND's inter-service budgetary allocations. Table 2 indicates that the navy has consistently placed third compared to air force and army in budgetary allotments since the Second World War. While the service funding figures for the 1968–75 period appear to indicate a departure from the overall post-war pattern, this was not the case. With the arrival of unification, DND's accounting methods were changed to reflect the new command and program activity structure of the Canadian Armed Forces (CAF). Thus, certain expenditures which previously had been charged to each of the three services were redirected to different program activity categories (that is, communications services and personnel support, the latter including training). As well, a new integrated geographic command, Canadian Forces Europe (CFE), was created. Because CFE comprised major land and air combat forces, certain expenditures on those forces which had been charged to the army and air force prior to 1968 were now omitted from Forces Mobile Command and Air Command budgets. Maritime Command (MARCOM) expenditures, on the other hand, continued to reflect roughly the same costs formerly charged to the navy. Because DND does not break down CFE expenditures between land and air elements, the figures in Table 2 *understate* quite substantially the actual spending on the army and air force in relation to that on the navy.

Notwithstanding this necessary caveat about the comparability of post-1968 service figures, it is instructive to note that, following the introduction of DND's new funding formula in 1976, the navy again reverted to its traditional last place position in the inter-service budgetary allocations. Clearly, from the standpoint of funding levels, the navy *has* been the "Cinderella" service.

But the data in Table 2 do not necessarily demonstrate that economic considerations have been the sole, or the main, or even a significant, determinant of the navy's funding levels over time. For example, our earlier analysis has discounted the argument that naval spending has been a major burden on the domestic economy, the federal treasury, and the defence budget. Moreover, there is considerable historical evidence to suggest that these levels reflect political and military

TABLE 2: Total Army, Air Force, and Navy Expenditures

Fiscal year ending 31 March	DND expenditure ($000s)	Army expenditure ($000s)	Air Force expenditure ($000s)	Navy expenditure ($000s)
1946	2,140,794	949,667	949,343	241,783
1947	387,612	219,359	99,280	64,883
1948	195,999	84,825	58,258	43,728
1949	268,805	101,900	90,200	44,700
1950	384,879	135,800	136,400	73,400
1951	782,457	407,300	230,600	99,900
1952	1,415,474	424,100	602,000	182,400
1953	1,882,418	516,100	768,100	260,300
1954	1,805,915	436,400	915,000	289,000
1955	1,665,969	454,400	814,700	304,200
1956	1,750,112	461,400	798,200	340,800
1957	1,759,426	459,500	863,100	326,700
1958	1,668,463	424,700	813,800	295,000
1959	1,424,741	432,900	797,500	273,000
1960	1,516,572	400,800	728,400	255,800
1961	1,517,531	402,200	751,600	245,500
1962	1,626,104	442,300	781,400	272,000
1963	1,571,044	443,000	713,900	269,400
1964	1,683,471	452,700	700,800	298,000
1965	1,535,635	433,600	656,000	272,500
1966	1,548,447	451,700	636,300	275,000
1967	1,640,378	458,500	645,600	305,700
1968	1,751,598	230,900	253,700	281,600
1969	1,760,796	334,300	287,300	377,200
1970	1,788,428	321,300	312,600	373,900
1971	1,817,876	307,100	314,200	401,100
1972	1,895,175	291,800	322,900	415,600
1973	1,932,246	349,800	343,600	402,300
1974	2,231,983	414,900	400,000	431,000
1975	2,511,873	416,900	403,300	457,800
1976	2,973,680	470,300	765,600	393,200
1977	3,371,199	563,300	893,900	424,900
1978	3,770,980	619,100	984,700	522,100
1979	4,108,027	607,500	1,144,700	580,000
1980	4,389,289	698,500	1,352,700	556,500
1981	5,077,076	774,200	1,561,400	680,600
1982	6,027,729	927,200	1,670,800	781,500
1983	6,991,964	974,400	2,099,000	953,300
1984	7,972,241	1,079,000	2,330,800	1,157,300

Sources: 1945–67 Public accounts
1968 National finances
1969–84 DND supplied figures

judgments concerning the appropriate amounts of resources for the navy in relation to Canada's overall defence objectives and missions.

Shortly after the end of the Second World War, Canada rapidly demobilized its navy, which on V-E day had comprised 374 combat vessels, more than 566 auxiliary craft, and some 90,000 regular personnel. While the actual size, composition, and deployment of the fleet had yet to be determined, it was apparent from the outset that the government had limited designs for the post-war Canadian navy. The goal was a "good workable little fleet," as Mr Abbott, minister of naval services, put it:[8] one which emphasized quality over quantity and could be readily expanded if necessary. The stress on smallness was later justified on several grounds: first, the premise that the navy would only be used in close co-operation with Canada's great power allies;[9] second, the continued emphasis on coastal defence and protection of allied shipping;[10] third, and most important, the higher priority accorded air defence roles.[11]

These political and military considerations constituted powerful rationales for the early roles and posture of the post-war Canadian fleet and hence for the funding levels considered appropriate for the navy. There were few apparent indications during these formative years that the navy was underfunded or operating under budgetary constraints in terms of its ability to carry out its assigned tasks and responsibilities. Indeed, from an economic perspective, it could be argued that the amounts provided for naval expenditures were a cost-effective means of achieving Canada's defence objectives. Whether this was true or remained true during and after the Korean War is another matter. To assess this we must examine the relationship between the navy's funding levels and its internal spending allocations.

SPENDING ALLOCATIONS: A NAVY UNDER BUDGETARY CONSTRAINT?

Given the Canadian government's evident preference for a small peacetime navy—a predilection both occasioned and sustained by the higher priority attached to air roles and the decision to specialize in anti-submarine warfare (ASW) maritime roles so as to contribute effectively (and without unnecessary duplication) to the North Atlantic Treaty Organization (NATO)—the navy's funding levels may be viewed as appropriate responses to domestic and external political-military requirements. Indeed, inasmuch as the Canadian navy has numbered an average of 87 ships of all types since 1968 (the 1985 total is 84)— almost exactly the same size as it was in 1954 (85) and virtually the same distribution among major, minor, and auxiliary ship classes— one might be tempted to conclude that the optimum size, composition, and roles of the navy were determined during the Korean War.[12] However, such a conclusion would be both simplistic and unwarranted insofar as it ignores the considerable efforts of navy planners to build and operate a larger and somewhat more diversified fleet during and after the Korean War. That these planners failed in their endeavours can be attributed to the influence of several economic factors, the impact of which can be seen in the changing dynamics of the navy's own budgetary allocation process.

The Korean War unquestionably provided the catalyst for a dramatic expansion of the Canadian navy. As part of DND's accelerated defence program, the navy was to receive rearmed, refitted, and recommissioned ships, as well as many newly constructed ships, including ASW frigates and escorts, minesweepers, gate vessels, and an arctic patrol vessel. The goal was a fleet of about 100 ships equipped and manned to carry out harbour and coastal defence in addition to ASW and convoy escort roles.[13] This represented a substantial increase in the size of the navy from its 1950 total of 52 ships.

However, owing to construction delays, enormous cost escalations, and personnel training bottlenecks, the various ship construction programs were delayed, and the fleet size goal was not attained until 1956. In fact, the expansion reached its peak of 129 ships in 1958 (a post-war high), and the last of the 14 new ASW destroyer escorts was not commissioned until 1960.[14] Throughout this period of expansion—the "golden years" of the post-second World War navy—budgetary pressures had already begun to erode the navy's ability to sustain a fleet of this size and composition. From the late 1950s onwards, the navy waged a steadily losing battle to maintain the fleet structure it had somewhat fortuitously acquired as a result of the Korean build-up. In the process, the navy also had to reduce its operations both at home and abroad and refocus its role more directly on ASW. This part of the navy's history is truly one of difficult policy choices dictated by budgetary constraint.

But the first signs of this constraint came earlier. Echoing its wartime plans for the post-war fleet,[15] the navy wanted another light aircraft carrier. As the chief of the naval staff explained in August 1950: "The Mobilization Plan requires a second operational carrier at the earliest possible time. This is required to balance our naval forces as they expand. It is obvious that if naval air war operations are to be sustained for more than a few weeks the second carrier is essential."[16]

This proposal for a more balanced fleet, one which was to resurface later, was never acted on for reasons of cost. Claxton stated the government's case thus: "If we had more money to spend on defence and if we did not have to do other things with greater priority I would like to have an aircraft carrier on the west coast as well."[17] Similar reasons put to rest suggestions that the navy acquire submarines: "The submarine is a very specialized type of vessel and its crew require special training. It is simply not economical for a navy with a strength of approximately 10,000 to divide its forces so that there are one or two units of each type."[18]

Despite a 167 per cent increase in naval spending between 1951 and 1954, and continued increases over the next two years, not everything was possible for the rapidly expanding navy. Indeed, by 1957, the costs of manning and operating the still growing number of ships within a budget already headed towards a steady, twelve-year (1957–68) decline, had begun to squeeze the navy's operations and force structure. Mounting personnel costs were particularly troublesome. During the 1950–57 period, regular navy manpower had risen from 9259 to 19,111. As G.M. Dillon has shown, starting in 1955 personnel expenditures began to increase steadily while capital expenditures began an equally steady decline.[19] This marked the beginning of an intra-budgetary trade-off for the navy which was to persist, largely uninterrupted, until the mid-1970s.

The effects of this changing pattern of resource allocation within a downwardly fluctuating overall budget soon manifested themselves. Cost-saving measures were explored, and the first victim was *Labrador* which, although only commissioned in July 1954, was transferred to the Department of Transport in April 1958.[20] As a result the navy lost its independent icebreaking capability in the Arctic and, with it, one of its national defence missions. Other force structure and role changes were forthcoming. Between 1957 and 1960, the navy paid off its two cruisers on cost-effectiveness grounds in response to the new threat posed by Soviet missile-firing submarines.[21] While the economies of this measure were welcomed, the navy was inexorably moving to a more specialized ASW posture.

This can be discerned from other changes in the fleet's composition. The navy continued to build new ASW escort vessels—which reached a post-war peak total of 43 in 1964—and began to equip some destroyers with ASW helicopters. The aircraft carrier *Bonaventure*'s jet fighters were retired and replaced by ASW aircraft–Grumman Tracker S-2's in the early 1960s. To extend the range of the fleet to cope with the missile submarine threat, the navy acquired the first of its underway replenishment ships, *Provider*, in 1963.

The *Brock Report* of July 1961 represented one attempt to stem the tide towards an ASW-specialized fleet. The report's emphasis on the need for a more versatile, balanced, general-purpose fleet was justified on two principal grounds. The first was political and stressed the navy's role in relation to Canada's broader defence and foreign policy objectives:

> Because there was no change in the roles and tasks of the Canadian forces to meet the changing conditions of the 1950s, they have tended to develop along specialized lines solely in response to their NATO content. Consequently, our defence policy provides planned support for our external policy only in regard to NATO; for anything else expediency must provide the answer ...
>
> Because of the more or less mutually exclusive nature of the NATO roles of our forces, Canadian defence policy is open to the criticism of not providing a balanced and flexible support for our country's external policy.[22]
>
> Accordingly, for limited war, intervention or policing action the basic maritime requirement is for general purpose, versatile forces which can co-operate with the other services or with forces from other nations.[23]

The second argument stressed cost-effectiveness factors. The report argued that "present ASW forces amount to putting too many eggs in too few, highly vulnerable baskets" and advocated a "small cheap and many" concept which would "yield benefits in greater effectiveness per unit of cost."[24] As a result the report concluded: "we can no longer afford to send sonars to sea at the present high cost per unit. Expensive anti-submarine ships can only be justified if they have additional required capabilities."[25]

To gain these additional capabilities, the report recommended the acquisition of: conventionally powered submarines; general purpose frigates; helicopter frigates; research vessels; and small, unconventional sonar-carrying platforms such as hovercraft, hydrofoils, midget submarines, and unmanned craft.[26]

The Diefenbaker government appeared receptive to the broad thrust of the *Brock Report*. On 11 April 1962, the minister of national defence announced Ottawa's approval of the acquisition of eight new general-purpose frigates along with three British-built *Oberon*-class submarines.[27] Ironically, this movement towards a more general-purpose capability for the navy ultimately was scuttled by the same type of cost-effectiveness argument, albeit applied differently, which had animated the *Brock Report*.

After the change to a Liberal government in April 1963, the new defence minister, Paul Hellyer, initiated a review of Canadian defence policy "to determine the best and most effective contribution we can make to the collective defence of the free world and to the maintenance of peace in the years ahead." To facilitate the review:

> All major procurement programmes are being reconsidered. In particular, any procurement programme which would tend to limit future policy or interfere with the exercise of future options is being carefully reviewed.
>
> One of these programmes is the General Purpose Frigate Programme. It is a project involving the expenditure of large sums of money. For this reason all present and likely future options have to be carefully considered before proceeding.[28]

These were ominous words for the navy and, despite a forthright defence of the navy's aspirations for a broader, general purpose capability by the chief of the naval staff,[29] on 24 October 1963 Hellyer announced the cancellation of the general-purpose frigate program.[30] While Hellyer defended this decision on the grounds of the near doubling of the estimated costs of the program, he later interjected a novel twist to the cost-effectiveness argument in support of the government's stance: "To proceed with this project would have had an important influence on future policy and would have severely restricted the options available to us. We concluded that this particular combination of weapons systems would not be the most effective solution in respect of any policy we might adopt."[31]

From this perspective, and in direct contrast to the professional advice of senior naval planners, the prospect of adding more versatility to the fleet would have *limited* the tasks, capabilities, and policy options of the navy. An interesting, if somewhat puzzling, point of view to say the least!

The twisted logic of this rationale suggests that economic considerations were now exerting an important influence on naval policy. Certainly the rising costs of modern warships played a role. But later Hellyer was more candid about other budgetary constraints. A continuing concern was the growing imbalance between rapidly mounting personnel, operations, and maintenance (POM) expenditures on the one hand and shrinking capital (especially equipment) expenditures on the other.[32] Another was the government's overall fiscal position. Large and growing federal deficits coupled with rising statutory expenditures caused by social welfare programs compelled Ottawa to take steps to restrict the growth of defence spending, which represented the largest area of discretionary, or "controllable," federal spending.[33]

Such considerations accentuated developments already taking place in the Canadian navy. For instance, continuing the previous government's austerity program—which had resulted in a reduction of the forces' total manpower, the retirement of the navy's *Banshee* jet fighters, reduction of fuel consumption, and deferrals of other military maintenance, construction, and equipment programs in the early 1960s[34]—in December 1963 Hellyer announced several additional cost-saving measures including: taking ten auxiliary vessels out of service; closing some naval supply, ammunition depots, and repair facilities; and closing seven naval reserve divisions (out of twenty-one) and both naval air reserve squadrons to reduce the naval reserves from a strength of 4000 to 2700 personnel.[35]

The results of Hellyer's defence policy review, and its associated cost-effectiveness studies, were elaborated upon in the government's March 1964 White Paper on defence. While indicating the government's intention to add some flexibility to the fleet via "a modest additional sea-lift" capability—which was eventually achieved through the commissioning of the two new fleet replenishment ships, *Protecteur* (1970) and *Preserver* (1971)—the main emphasis of the White Paper from a naval standpoint was the government's clearly stated intention to retain ASW as the main role of the navy as derived from Canada's NATO commitments.[36] The economic reasoning behind this renewed ASW emphasis for the navy was instructive: Canada had a large capital and training "investment" in this specialized role.[37] Therefore, while the most appropriate, cost-effective size and "mix" of the fleet had yet to be determined, the ASW *role* itself was considered the most cost-effective contribution the navy could make to allied defence, especially in conditions of overall funding restrictions imposed on DND. The stability and continuity of the navy's specialized ASW role were thus reinforced directly by economic considerations: funding level constraints and internal resource allocation pressures.

Even within this optimized role, the navy was encountering budgetary difficulties. The White Paper noted that consideration was being given to the procurement of two or three nuclear-powered submarines for ASW purposes. These were never obtained, presumably because of their extremely high capital and support costs.[38] Furthermore, although a new construction program was announced on 22 December 1964 for four sophisticated destroyer escorts of the DDH-280 class, the navy was quickly losing other ships from its fleet. For example, while the number of major warships peaked at 44 in 1964, this figure dropped rapidly to only 24 ships in 1969 as older vessels were retired. Another economy measure led to the dropping of three (of seven) ships from the Improved-*Restigouche* destroyer modernization program in 1968; these three were later placed in reserve status in 1974. The reduction in numbers of minor ships was even more dramatic: peaking at 40 vessels in 1957, this category (which included minesweepers, gate vessels, arctic patrol vessels, loop and cable layers, coastal defence craft, launches, and training ships) plummeted to 10 ships in all by 1966, remaining there until 1975. Finally, the number of auxiliaries peaked at 58 in 1959 and remained steady at this figure until 1964; the number then began a steady decline to the current total of 34. Thus, between 1958 and 1968, the navy lost one-third of its fleet and with it much of its general purpose capability (see Appendix A).

The arrival of Pierre Trudeau as the new leader of the Liberal party and then as prime minister in 1968 brought the prospect of a major reorientation of Canadian defence policy. The previous emphasis on Canada's NATO commitments was to be downgraded while sovereignty protection was to be elevated to Canada's top defence priority, in keeping with the general domestication of Canadian foreign policy.[39] To determine how this new focus affected the specific roles and posture of the forces, the government embarked on an extensive review of Canada defence policy, the results of which were outlined in broad terms in the August 1971 White Paper on defence.

Cost-effectiveness considerations pervaded the document. The White Paper noted that: "With the limited resources available for Canadian defence needs, it is desirable to have versatile forces and multi-purpose equipment rather than a high degree of specialization. Multiple tasking is also necessary in order to make the most efficient use of available resources."[40] Significantly, while noting there was "no obvious level for defence expenditures in Canada," the government believed "a judgement must be made on proposed defence activities in relation to other Government programs." Given the government's perception of a generally benign international environment, this political "guns-versus-butter" trade-off meant that the "available resources" for defence would "continue to be curtailed, as reflected in continuing manpower cutbacks and constraints on equipment acquisition"; DND's budget would "remain within approximately 1 per cent of the present ceiling."[41]

What did all this mean for the navy? According to the White Paper, MARCOM henceforth would give a higher priority to surveillance and control tasks for the protection of Canadian national interests and lower emphasis to ASW directed against ballistic missile-carrying submarines.[42] In general, the government was following the direction of the earlier *Brock Report* in advocating a return to a more versatile, general purpose, and flexible fleet. Recognizing that this new policy would take "a long time" to implement, the government was nonethe-

TABLE 3: MARCOM Expenditure Allocations ($000s)

Fiscal year ending 31 March	Total MARCOM expenditure ($000s)	Personnel[1]	Per cent	Operating[2]	Per cent	Capital	Per cent
1969	377,153	174,112	46	116,095	31	86,946	23
1970	373,937	170,853	46	106,694	29	96,390	26
1971	401,132	185,791	46	111,648	28	103,693	26
1972	415,629	206,354	50	121,103	29	88,172	21
1973	402,269	219,571	55	125,449	31	57,249	14
1974	431,016	232,146	54	146,899	34	51,971	12
1975	457,752	290,587	63	130,770	29	36,395	8
1976	393,211	252,108	64	106,057	27	35,046	9
1977	424,948	276,495	65	98,601	23	49,852	12
1978	522,094	303,444	58	140,753	27	77,897	15
1979	580,000	341,238	59	118,938	21	119,824	21
1980	556,513	354,260	64	136,490	25	65,763	12
1981	680,649	384,716	57	201,717	30	94,216	14
1982	781,530	435,827	56	241,283	31	104,420	13
1983	953,294	501,602	53	282,015	30	169,677	18
1984	1,157,279	533,245	46	291,892	25	332,142	29

Sources: DND-supplied figures
1 military and civilian personnel costs
2 operating and maintenance costs

less determined to apply it to new equipment acquisitions, modifications to existing equipment, and the training of maritime forces.[43]

In broad terms, then, the 1971 White Paper constituted a blueprint for the long-run development of the navy. Ironically, given NATO's 1967 adoption of a "flexible response" strategy, and its stress on preserving a conventional option for the defence of Europe (and the attendant requirement to protect sea lines of communications for the reinforcement and resupply of land and air forces in that theatre), Canada's apparent intention to downgrade its NATO maritime roles in the 1970s was diametrically opposed to emerging trends in alliance maritime policy.[44]

In practical terms, however, the reversal in Canada's naval policy was more apparent than real. Indeed, for the navy the Trudeau era amounted to "constraint as usual." Once again, economic factors played a large part in determining the navy's fortunes. Table 3 reveals some interesting features of the navy's funding levels and allocations during the 1969–84 period. While fluctuating slightly, the navy's overall expenditure levels remained fairly stable from 1969 to 1977, averaging about $408 million over these nine years; total funding then began a steady increase to 1984. More significantly, the intra-budgetary trade-off between personnel and capital expenditures continued unabated. Personnel expenditures rose gradually from 1969 to 1974 and then increased abruptly to 65 per cent of MARCOM's budget in 1977. Capital expenditures experienced a more rapid decline from 26 per cent of MARCOM's budget in 1971 to only 8 per cent in 1975, a post-war low. Personnel expenditures remained high from 1978 to 1982 and since then have begun to decrease steadily as a percentage of MARCOM spending. Capital spending remained relatively low after 1975 and only began to increase significantly as the navy embarked on several refit and modernization programs, dockyard expansion, and most recently, the new six-ship Coastal Patrol Frigate (CPF) construction program. Operations and maintenance expenditures remained steady from 1969 to 1974 and decreased substantially from 1975 to 1979 as the navy had to reduce its operations in response to the dramatic increase in fuel costs caused by the 1973 OPEC crisis. Operating expenses stabilized at slightly higher levels as a percentage of MARCOM's budget after 1980.

These budgetary constraints prevented the navy from realizing the general-purpose capability aspirations of the 1974 White Paper. True, some additional versatility was acquired with the completion of the four-ship, DDH-280 destroyer construction program in 1973, but these ships remained dedicated to NATO ASW roles. Moreover, the navy lost some flexibility with the disposal of the aircraft carrier *Bonaventure* in 1970, after a sixteen-month, $17 million refit. The carrier was too costly to operate, and its crew was needed to man the new DDH-280s.[45] Moreover, the navy had found it more cost-effective to carry out its ASW role with helicopter-equipped destroyers. The navy retired the last of its minesweepers in 1967, and, while there are plans now for new mine countermeasures vessels, acquisition approval has been delayed in the light of more urgent re-equipment priorities. Finally, despite the large increase in the numbers of minor war vessels in the mid-1970s, much of this was actually a "paper shuffle." Seven auxiliary vessels (tugs and tenders) were reclassified as reserve training ships and one gate vessel was reclaimed from an earlier loan to the Department of Transport. Seven second-hand vessels were also acquired from the RCMP, including six small patrol craft.[46]

Other maritime equipment programs, actual and planned, also show an emphasis on the navy's specialized ASW role. After DND's budgetary freeze was lifted in 1973, the navy modernized its *Sea King* ASW helicopters and gained additional ASW capability in the form of eighteen *Aurora* long-range patrol aircraft. Significantly, additional civilian surveillance capabilities were eliminated from the *Aurora* owing to cost considerations; the aircraft became optimized in the ASW role, despite the government's earlier projection for a more multipurpose airplane.⁴⁷ The new CPF's are also ASW-specialized ships, and the navy will acquire six additional, follow-on ships of this class. Finally, the navy plans to replace its ASW submarines and helicopters. From this we may conclude that the government has abandoned the 1971 blueprint for a more versatile, general purpose capability for the navy. Budgetary pressures and cost-effectiveness considerations over a long period have forced the navy to concentrate its limited resources on what it does best, namely its traditional specialized ASW role. New acquisitions, as forecast in the 1987 White Paper, will enhance that role, and give it a new underwater dimension.

During the 1970s and 1980s, the navy has gone to great lengths to retain its capacity to carry out ASW. But once again economic factors have made this a difficult proposition. In 1971, the *Bras d'Or* experimental ASW hydrofoil was laid up to await disposal largely on cost-effectiveness grounds: the ship was too small and limited as an ASW platform to justify the costs of a refit and further sea trials.⁴⁸ On 10 October 1973, Minister of National Defence James Richardson announced a "modernization and renewal program" for the Canadian Forces to be financed by a new, five-year funding formula. While the intention was to update and replace the forces' equipment, including *Sea King* improvements and the acquisition of new long-range patrol aircraft for the navy, certain "money saving adjustments" resulted in four older destroyers being placed in reserve for disposal by the end of 1974, a reduction of the *Tracker* fleet from 33 to 16 aircraft (along with the elimination of their ASW equipment), and the retirement of the ASW training submarine *Rainbow*.⁴⁹ Sizeable cost increases in the DDH-280 program also meant less money for other purposes.

Meanwhile, unexpectedly high inflation rates outpaced the new funding formula, thereby forcing additional economies on the navy in 1974 and 1975. As part of an across-the-board cut in DND spending in 1974, MARCOM's budget was reduced by about 10 per cent. This resulted in reduced operations and training for the navy. As well, Arctic surveillance flights were eliminated to save fuel; Canadian participation in a NATO training exercise was cancelled; personnel were reduced; forward bases were closed; six *Argus* maritime patrol aircraft were eliminated; and ship and aircraft operations were reduced to 82 per cent of normal minimum requirements.⁵⁰

At the same time as rising personnel and operating costs were reducing the funds available for the navy's badly needed re-equipment programs, years of similar capital underfunding in the army and air force placed the navy in the unenviable position of competing against higher priority procurement programs. While a contract was awarded for new long-range patrol aircraft in July 1976, only eighteen *Aurora*s would be acquired, about half the number desired by some senior naval planners and by DND itself. Again, cost considerations in relation to higher priority projects were responsible for the acknowledged reduction in capability.[51] Similarly, although the government announced its intention on 22 December 1977 to begin the first phase of the CPF program—as part of the force level of twenty-four fully capable surface warships approved by Cabinet in 1977[52]—the contract was not awarded until 29 June 1983, and the total program is now not expected to be completed until 1992 or 1993, several years behind the original schedule. As noted earlier, other navy re-equipment programs—CPF phases 2 and 3, submarines, fleet replenishment ships, mine countermeasures craft, and a *Sea King* replacement—had been delayed or deferred, owing to cash-flow problems and competition from other DND procurement programs, until the 1987 White Paper. Even the programs announced in 1987 will depend on the ultimate willingness of government to exceed spending estimates.

In the meantime, the navy has had to make do with less. In some instances, the navy has resorted to costly, short-term expedients in an effort to preserve its already shrinking ASW capabilities. The Destroyer Life Extension (DELEX) program is a case in point. Because of the age and growing obsolescence of most of its destroyer fleet, combined with delays in the CPF program, DND opted to extend the life of its sixteen steam-driven destroyers. The 213.8 million-dollar DELEX program will keep all sixteen ships seaworthy and will effect some improvements to the combat capabilities of ten ships. Similarly, the 1.6 billion-dollar Tribal Update and Modernization Program (TRUMP), and the 42.4 million-dollar Submarine Operational Update Program (SOUP) will improve the capabilities of the four DDH-280 destroyers and three *Oberon* submarines.

Notwithstanding the improvements to the fleet's ASW capabilities, DELEX, TRUMP, and SOUP are clearly "stop-gap" measures necessitated by the chronic capital shortages of the navy over the past decade or so. Moreover, they are expensive steps and only partly redress the problems posed by the growing hull-age of the fleet. Given the usually accepted figure of 20 years as the "normal" operational lifetime of destroyers,[53] then 16 of 20—80 per cent—of the navy's destroyer fleet is over-age. This compares unfavourably with the 1983 average of 39 per cent of all NATO destroyers classed as over-age.[54] In the past, Canada paid off its destroyers at an average age of 20 years, but in 1985 the average age of the navy's destroyers is 23 years, a figure which will rise to 27 years by the time the first CPF is commissioned.[55] This fleet-age issue is symptomatic of a larger problem confronting the modern Canadian navy. Despite refits and modernization measures, in the absence of capital funds to sustain an ongoing ship replacement program, the navy has found it increasingly expensive to operate and maintain its aging fleet at operationally acceptable levels. The recent spate of embarrassing breakdowns of the navy's destroyers attests to this fact. The navy is rapidly reaching the point where it is no longer cost-effective to maintain and operate older ships rather than replace them with new vessels.

Evidence of the navy's coping approach to its budgetary constraints—reflecting an exemplary "must do, can do" attitude—can be found elsewhere as well. For example, in 1985, with 9400 regular force personnel, the navy is operating virtually the same size fleet as it did in 1954 and 1969 but with 45 per cent and 49 per cent *less* regular manpower respectively. But the combination of very high sea-to-shore ratios—exceeding 70 per cent in some instances, compared to the 40 to 50 per cent ratio considered desirable in the 1950s[56]—coupled with the operation of old, obsolescent ships, must obviously have a deleterious, albeit unquantifiable, effect on the navy's morale.[57]

Notwithstanding its efforts to cope with budgetary constraint, the navy has not been able to carry out its alliance commitments and national responsibilities at the same levels of operation, and arguably with the same effectiveness, as it has in the past. This "commitment—capability gap" has been recognized both inside and outside government circles. Taking first Canada's predominantly ASW NATO responsibilities, the trend over time has been for the navy to earmark a decreasing number of ships and aircraft to the Supreme Allied Commander, Atlantic (SACLANT), as the following figures indicate:[58]

1952: 24 ships
1954: 36 ships
1955: 43 ships
1957: 40 ships, 50 aircraft
1960: 30 ships, 3 squadrons
1963: 30 ships, 40 aircraft
1968: 19 ships
1982: 15 ships, 14 aircraft
1985: 15 ships, 14 aircraft

Because of the reduced number of ships and aircraft, combined with age-obsolescence problems, there is a mounting scepticism that the navy, as it is currently postured, can carry out its various responsibilities. This is especially so given the additional duties acquired after Canada declared its 200-mile fishing zone in 1977. For example, despite the reinstatement of northern surveillance flights after a parliamentary outcry in 1974, the number of NORPATS has been reduced from 36 to about 20 per year. DND candidly admitted its sovereignty surveillance and control shortcomings in 1984: "In summary, the effectiveness of Canadian sea denial operations is a function of time and money. It is judged that existing assets are adequate to meet normal peacetime requirements, but the department does recognize that the current force inventory would be inadequate to sustain extensive sea denial operations in the waters over which Canada claims jurisdiction."[59] Professional navy opinion has also rendered a sobering assessment of the navy's ability to fulfil its NATO ASW commitments in a wartime environment.[60] In this regard, it is worth recalling the words of a previous defence minister: "I cannot see any possibility of material reductions in the size of our regular forces if we are to be able to maintain the commitments to which I have previously referred."[61] But the navy *has* shrunk in size and capability, while its commitments have expanded.

Nor is this "commitment—capability gap" likely to be narrowed by the prospect of additional funding for the navy in the foreseeable future. As a much-celebrated, leaked DND planning document recently noted regarding Canada's maritime capabilities:

> Canada's maritime forces are no longer capable of fulfilling simultaneously national requirements and international commitments. This situation results from financial constraints over the past decade which led to the failure to make timely provision for the modernization or replacement of obsolescent ships and other major combat systems. The major concern stems from the projection that there will only be 12 seaworthy surface combatants remaining in service by the early 1990s ... over the same period, insufficient funds will leave shortfalls in respect of the replacement or modernization of the Oberon Class submarines, the destroyer borne helicopters, certain major weapons and sensor systems, and shore training facilities to keep abreast with the rising Soviet threat. The projected decline in Canada's maritime capabilities can only be checked by a substantial increase in funds to permit the systematic implementation of replacement programs.[62]

In its 1984 response to senate recommendations for new maritime equipment to rectify this projected deficiency, DND noted that:

> the calculation of the incremental funding required to acquire new equipment ... is based on the assumption that current budgetary plans contain provision for the replacement or updating

(or both) of all equipment currently possessed by MARCOM. In fact, current funding levels fall some billions of dollars short of the level that would be necessary over the next 15 years to afford all of the maritime capital programmes that have been identified within the department based on the existing number of major weapons platforms.[63]

In short, the legacy of years of capital starvation and budgetary constraint is likely to remain with the navy for a long time to come.

SPENDING IMPACT: A DOMESTIC IMPERATIVE?

Considerations relating to the economic impact of defence expenditures have played an important and continuing role in the development of post-Second World War Canadian naval policy. Historically, there have been two main and largely inter-related dimensions to these considerations. On the one hand, the navy has sought to foster the development of a domestic industrial capacity to satisfy the navy's ongoing and emergency requirements for ship construction, repair, and maintenance. On the other hand, navy planners have been politically astute enough to recognize the attraction of "selling" their naval spending programs on the basis of local and regional employment and industrial development opportunities. Of course, the importance of both sets of considerations have long been recognized by both federal politicians and DND itself.

Whether policies based on such economic considerations have produced the most cost-effective navy for Canada is open to argument. Moreover, at times the "industrial preparedness," mobilization-potential rationale of the first of these considerations, appeared to be at odds with alliance "short war/nuclear war" doctrine. Nevertheless, studies have shown that: defence expenditure per job created is lowest for ship repairs,[64] and defence spending has a disproportionately large economic impact in the "defence sensitive" shipbuilding and repair industry of Nova Scotia and British Columbia.[65] Such findings constitute a powerful political argument for an equitable regional distribution of naval spending in Canada's labour-intensive shipbuilding and repair industry. However, they also suggest the vulnerability of this industry—and by extension, DND's naval industrial preparedness policy—to prolonged periods of low naval expenditures.

Although the minister of naval services in 1945 noted the need for "close liaison" between heavy industry (such as shipbuilding) and the defence departments concerning new weapons developments,[66] it was not until the Korean War, when the navy was furnishing "about half the work being done in Canadian shipyards,"[67] that the government began to articulate this need as part of a coherent "industrial preparedness" policy. C.D. Howe, minister of the new Department of Defence Production (DDP), outlined the objectives of this policy as follows: "to provide our forces with the best of modern equipment; to build up our mobilization reserves; to provide facilities capable of all-out production should an emergency develop ... to strengthen the economic fabric of our country."[68]

In implementing this policy, DDP stressed specialization and financial assistance. DDP officials were aware of the economies of scale to be derived from concentrating Canada's limited productive capacity in a few specific industries: namely aircraft, electronics, and shipbuilding. Accelerated depreciation allowances and capital assistance grants directed to these industrial sectors would encourage specialization. As applied to the shipbuilding industry, the new policy was not without certain "costs," many of which are still in evidence today. As C.D. Howe explained in 1951:

> These are new types of ... vessels of which no prototypes are yet afloat. This means that certain capital assistance is necessary, and that some delays and difficulties at the shipyards may be expected from time to time. Although Canadian shipbuilding costs are somewhat higher than European costs, it has been government policy to maintain key personnel and essential equipment in all our major Canadian yards for strategic reasons.[69]

Although it had taken considerably longer than expected to implement this preparedness policy in the shipbuilding industry—the 14-ship ASW destroyer escort program, originally scheduled for completion on 30 June 1954, was not completed until 1960—an important naval production infrastructure had been established as a result of the Korean rearmament program. Following the war, a different challenge faced the government. Having nurtured the Canadian shipbuilding industry through its Korean rebirth, Ottawa was now confronted with the problems of preserving it in peacetime. Whereas in 1951 DDP's main objective had been the rapid re-establishment and expansion of this industry to meet the heavy demands of war, by the mid-1950s the problem became one of the "maintenance and stabilization" of the industry to provide a sustained rate of growth and stable employment for the many Canadians involved in shipbuilding.[70] Indeed, by 1959, the steadily dropping level of employment in the industry (as the destroyer construction program was coming to an end) was a source of concern to the Diefenbaker government.[71]

However, so persuasive were the political arguments for ensuring not only the survival of the shipbuilding industry but also the equitable distribution of construction contracts among the various shipyards on both coasts, that no one in the government, or the navy, apparently thought to question whether this was the most efficient way to allocate limited resources, or whether the preparedness rationale was undermined by existing NATO doctrine which stressed the importance of "forces-in-being" rather than industrial mobilization potential. The absence of such questioning, therefore, suggests that political-economic considerations had begun to supplant purely military considerations in the development of Canadian naval policy.[72]

While different defence ministers continued to give lip-service to the necessity of distributing naval shipbuilding work as equitably as possible, and of "keeping alive" the expertise of this industry,[73] as the navy's funding levels began to shrink in the 1960s, cost considerations compelled the navy to seek cheaper offshore procurement at the expense of domestic production. For example, regarding the prospective acquisition of three British-built *Oberon* submarines in 1963, the chief of the naval staff acknowledged that while these submarines could be constructed in Canada they "would cost a great deal more."[74] Paul Hellyer also stressed the importance of production sharing arrangements with the British government in the decision to purchase the submarines abroad.[75]

The subject of production sharing is an important one from the standpoint of the development of the Canadian shipbuilding industry and its ability to service the needs of the navy. During the 1958–63 period, the earlier pattern of bilateral economic defence collaboration between Canada and the United States was formalized in the Defence Production and Development Sharing Arrangements (DPDSA).[76] However, unlike the arrangements facilitating cross-border trade in other defence products, protectionist attitudes and measures in *both* countries significantly restricted the access of the Canadian shipbuilding industry to the lucrative US defence market. For example, the Burns and Tollefson amendments to the annual US Defence Appropriations act "prohibit purchase of any naval vessel from foreign sources as well as the subcontracting of 'major components' of naval ship hulls or superstructures to foreign yards."[77] As a result, from 1959 to 1984, the value of Canadian shipbuilding exports to the United States has amounted to only 810.6 million dollars as compared to total Canadian defence exports under the DPDSA of 9,617.9 million dollars, or 8 per cent of the total. This compares unfavourably with combined aerospace-electronics exports representing 71 per cent of the total (Table 4).

TABLE 4: Canadian Defence Exports to US by Industry Sector, 1959–84
($ Canadian Millions)

	1959–81	1982	1983	1984	Total 1959–84
Aerospace	2,657.8	260.3	422.0	415.5	3,755.6
Armament	557.4	34.4	52.8	75.5	720.1
Electrical and electronics	1,890.6	412.0	357.2	450.2	3,110.0
General Purchasing	125.9	41.2	16.4	27.0	210.5
Shipbuilding	483.4	123.9	105.8	97.5	810.6
Vehicles	307.0	156.1	253.2	294.8	1,011.1
Total	6,022.1	1,027.9	1,207.4	1,360.5	9,617.9

Source: Defence Programs Bureau, Department of External Affairs.

As a consequence of these DPDSA restrictions, the Canadian shipbuilding industry has been largely denied the opportunity afforded other defence industrial sectors of sustaining its productive capacity via exports to the US during the "lean" years of the navy's capital funding. As a result, the shipbuilding industry has lost much of its earlier naval design and engineering expertise as well as its ability to compete against foreign industry on cost grounds.[78]

To the extent that this is true, it would appear that over the past decade successive Canadian governments have abandoned the earlier industrial preparedness policy, at least as it pertains to the navy. As one former senior naval officer charged in 1976: "I see our navy being starved to death because Canada has abdicated its responsibility of maintaining a self-sufficient industrial base from which to produce the necessary equipment."[79]

However, this may already be changing. Beginning with the *Aurora* program in 1976, the government has begun to use defence procurement as an economic policy instrument to obtain a high percentage of contractually stipulated "industrial benefits." By demanding production offsets in offshore procurement programs and "Canadian content" criteria in domestic and/or semi-indigenous procurement programs, Ottawa is hoping to restore employment opportunities in, and enhance the technological capacity of, the Canadian defence industry.[80] The CPF program is a hybrid example of both the offsets and Canadian content approaches. By virtue of the 21,420 million dollars (1983–84) in industrial benefits and 30,230 person-years of employment expected to be generated by the CPF contract, the government hopes to "establish a long-term capability in the Canadian shipbuilding industry to handle future naval ship requirements of the Canadian Forces"; "facilitate the export of Canadian designed and built ships as well as other high technology products";[81] and "create large scale economic and regional development benefit for Canadian industry."[82]

Whether this new approach will succeed in recapturing lost skills and developing a self-sustaining Canadian naval shipbuilding industry remains to be seen. In the meantime, there is already evidence that the Saint John Shipbuilding and Dry Dock Company is encountering problems with the CPF program.[83] Furthermore, DND will face a difficult choice between domestic and alliance considerations when it considers whether or not to participate in the ship construction phase of the NATO Frigate Replacement Program in the next year or two. If Ottawa decides to participate, it would likely undermine the current policy of supporting the development of an indigenous Canadian shipbuilding industry.[84]

Hard decisions lie ahead, but the domestic economic imperative will remain an important consideration in Canadian naval policy.

CONCLUSIONS

While it is difficult to make categorical conclusions about the role of economic considerations in the development of the post-war Canadian navy, some general observations appear to be justified.

First, given the generally healthy state of the Canadian economy since 1945, there is no compelling macroeconomic reason why Canada could not have supported a larger and more general-purpose navy. The crucial determinants of the navy's size and composition have been political and military in nature. Second, within the overall funding levels established for the navy as a result of political-military decisions about defence commitments and priorities, economic considerations have played a significant role in shaping the navy's resource allocation decisions. The operative principle here has been that of budgetary constraint. Escalating personnel, operations, and equipment costs within a generally stable overall budget have forced the navy to introduce a series of cost-saving measures. Over time, the cumulative effect of these economies has been to: reduce the size of the fleet; reinforce the specialized nature of its role; and impair its ability to carry out its national and international commitments. Third, while domestic employment and industrial development considerations have played a part in navy policy, their importance waned somewhat in the 1960s but may now be regaining their former salience. In turn, the deterioration of Canada's naval shipbuilding industry may have inhibited the growth of the navy in the past and may constrain procurement options in the near future.

Thus, the interaction among political, military, and economic considerations in the development of the modern Canadian navy has been complex and has varied with time and circumstance. But if one overriding conclusion stands out, it is this: for the Canadian navy, what politics has proposed, economics has disposed.

APPENDIX A

Composition of Canada's Naval Fleet Since 1946–47

Year	Total ships	Major warships	Per cent	Minor warships	Per cent	Auxiliary ships	Per cent
1946–7	44	22	50	17	39	5	11
1947–8	44	21	48	15	34	8	18
1948–9	46	23	50	14	30	9	20
1949–50	52	23	44	12	23	17	33
1950–1	70	23	33	14	20	33	47
1951–2	72	23	32	17	24	32	44
1952–3	80	23	29	25	31	32	40
1953–4	85	24	28	26	31	35	41
1954–5	97	29	30	33	34	35	36
1955–6	102	32	31	35	34	35	34
1956–7	113	32	28	40	35	41	36
1957–8	129	36	28	37	29	56	43
1958–9	120	39	33	23	19	58	48
1959–60	119	42	35	19	16	58	49
1960–1	120	43	36	19	16	58	48
1961–2	120	43	36	19	16	58	48
1962–3	120	43	36	19	16	58	48
1963–4	120	44	37	18	15	58	48
1964–5	104	39	38	14	13	51	49
1965–6	102	34	33	10	10	58	57
1966–7	96	32	33	10	10	54	56
1967–8	87	25	29	10	11	52	60
1968–9	87	24	28	10	11	53	61
1969–70	88	25	28	10	11	53	60
1970–1	87	24	28	10	11	53	61
1971–2	87	24	28	10	11	53	61
1972–3	88	26	30	10	11	52	59
1973–4	88	27	31	10	11	51	58
1974–5	87	27	31	12	14	48	55
1975–6	89	26	29	24	27	39	44
1976–7	88	26	30	25	28	37	42
1977–8	88	26	30	26	30	36	41
1978–9	88	26	30	26	30	36	41
1979–80	89	26	29	26	29	37	42
1980–1	89	26	29	26	29	37	42
1981–2	86	26	30	25	29	35	41
1982–3	86	26	30	24	28	36	42
1983–4	84	26	31	24	29	34	40
1984–85	84	26	31	24	29	34	40

Source: Hobson, *Composition of Canada's Naval Fleet.*

Chapter 14

CANADIAN NAVAL RESPONSIBILITIES IN THE ARCTIC

Harriet Critchley

Throughout the Canadian navy's seventy-five-year history, naval responsibilities have been driven by clearly established priorities in Canada's foreign and defence policies. When expressed in oceanic terms, alliance commitments and the allocation of naval resources indicate that the first priority has traditionally been assigned to the Atlantic, with the Pacific taking a distant second priority and the Arctic an even more distant third. This prioritization is reflected today in the assignment of twelve destroyers, three submarines, and two replenishment ships to the east coast, four destroyers and one replenishment ship to the west coast, and no ships to the Arctic region.

The situation is so pronounced and of such long standing that one would be hard put to describe the priorities as "competing" in any meaningful way—except, perhaps, in the minds of those who argue the need for a change. Such arguments are being put forward with increasing insistence as we near the end of the twentieth century and look to the future. This paper will concentrate on the various factors and arguments that concern retaining or changing the priority attached to naval responsibilities in the Arctic.

"Sovereignty" is unquestionably the overriding factor in any *Canadian* discussion of foreign or defence policy with respect to the Arctic. The phrase "Arctic sovereignty" is instantly familiar to most Canadians, yet the use of the phrase "Atlantic sovereignty" or "Pacific sovereignty" would likely be greeted with utter perplexity by those same people. Although the phrase is so familiar and so frequently used, the meaning attached to it is often nebulous. The legal concept of sovereignty is quite precisely linked to the notion of a state's authority over territory: "a state occupies a definite part of the surface of the earth, within which it normally exercises, subject to the limitations imposed by international law, jurisdiction over persons and things to the exclusion of the jurisdiction of other states."[1] This jurisdiction extends beyond the land and water within the territory to the airspace over the territory and to certain areas of sea which form part of the state's domain either as inland waters or territorial sea. The state exercises its authority by passing legislation, making regulations, and acceding to agreements with other states.

The legal concept of sovereignty is, however, only part of the amalgam subsumed in the phrase "Arctic sovereignty." One analyst has used the idea of "technological sovereignty" to distinguish another set of components of the amalgam: the range of state services which will ensure that the maintenance of legal sovereignty is factual and effective.[2] The concern expressed by some that Canada must "protect" its sovereignty in the Arctic by increasing federal government capabilities or services north of 60° is, in the terms used here, a concern for technological sovereignty. The range of state services required for the exercise of technological sovereignty is extremely broad, including such areas as health, environmental preservation, economic development, national security, and defence, to name just a few.

There are aspects of both legal and technological sovereignty involved in our concern for "Arctic sovereignty." Canadian legal sovereignty over the *land* in Canada's arctic region has not been disputed by any other sovereign state since 1930, when Norway recognized Canadian sovereignty over the Sverdrup Islands. There are also clear precedents in international law for establishing sovereignty in largely uninhabited lands—where the level of state activity is low and intermittent—which indicate that there is no basis for disputing Canadian sovereignty over the archipelago.[3] There is, in short, no dispute concerning Canada's sovereignty over the land territory in Canada's Arctic region, and the likelihood of such a dispute arising in the future is extremely remote. The same is not true, however, for Canadian sovereignty over the waters in that region.

The status of the waters in Canada's Arctic region has been and continues to be controversial. This is the only aspect of Canada's legal sovereignty in the Arctic which is in dispute, and the dispute is primarily between Canada and the United States. From at least 1968 to the present, the United States has held the view that the Northwest Passage is an international strait. As such, the coastal state (Canada) has no jurisdiction whatsoever over those waters and the airspace above them.

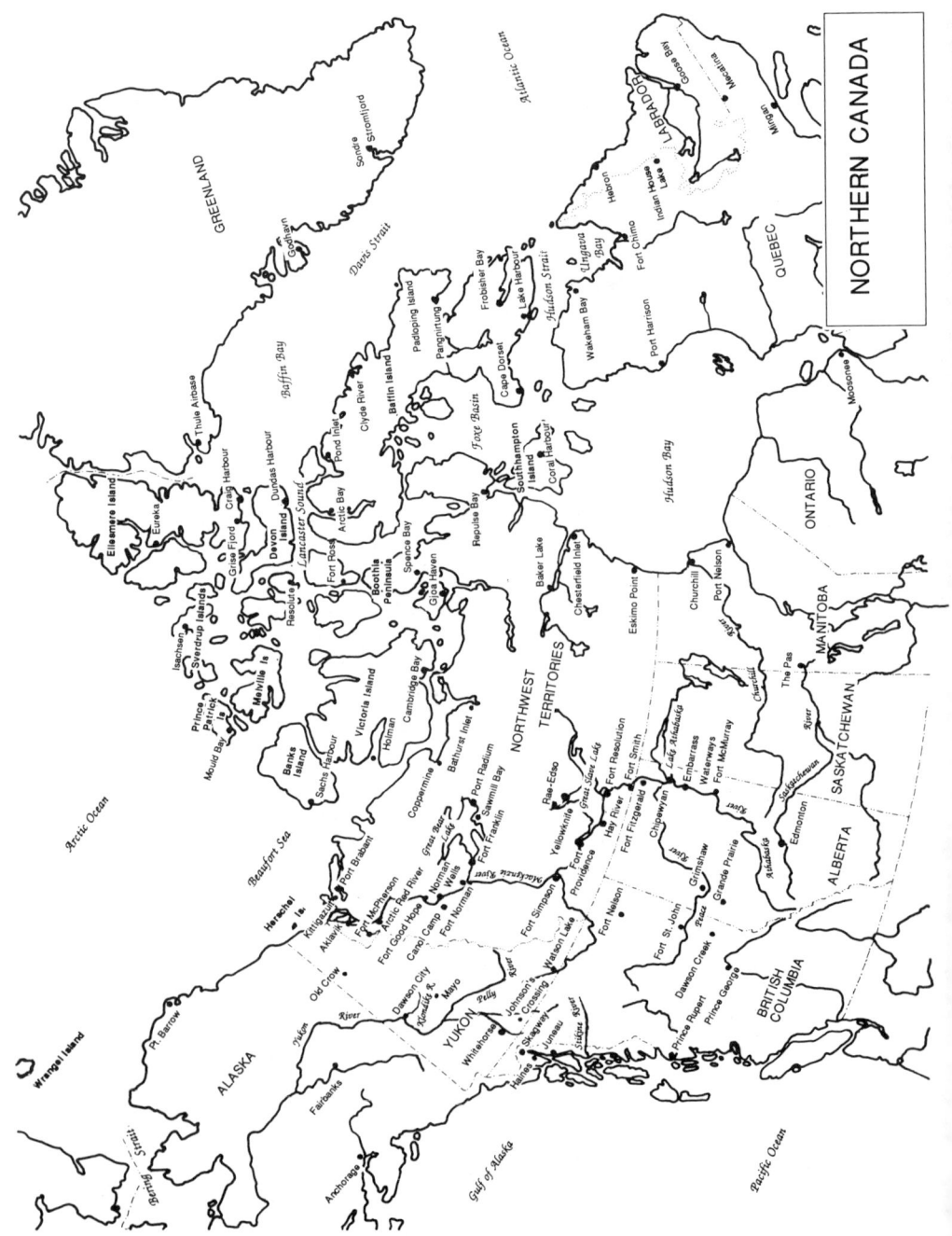

Successive Canadian governments have made statements and taken actions to assert at least partial sovereign jurisdiction over those waters.

In 1970, as a direct reaction to the voyages of the US oil tanker *Manhattan* through some of the Northwest Passage waters, the Arctic Waters Pollution Prevention Act (AWPPA) was passed. The act was proclaimed in 1972; in it, Canada asserted a functional jurisdiction (that is, jurisdiction solely for the purpose of guarding against pollution in coastal and maritime waters) throughout all of the waters of the Arctic archipelago and extending out one hundred nautical miles from the archipelago.[4] The assertion of functional jurisdiction is not identical with sovereign jurisdiction, in which case the waters in question would have been declared as internal waters or territorial sea. This declaration was not made in 1970. However, in separate legislation, which was also passed in 1970, the width of Canada's territorial sea was extended from three to twelve miles.[5] This legislation had the effect of enclosing within the territorial sea the eastern end of the Northwest Passage at Barrow Strait,[6] thereby asserting at least a partial sovereign jurisdiction over the passage.

In that same period, three authoritative statements made by government officials expressed the Canadian *view* that the waters in and around the arctic archipelago were internal waters.[7] In all three statements, an outright sovereign claim was avoided. In addition, some Canadian scholars of international law questioned whether the Northwest Passage fulfilled one criterion of the two-part international legal definition of an international strait. One scholar in particular reached the conclusion that it did not: "it is clear beyond doubt that the Northwest Passage has never been 'a useful route for international maritime traffic' as the Corfu Channel had been and is not a strait 'used for international navigation' envisaged by the 1958 Territorial Sea Convention."[8] If by definition the passage is not an international strait and it is enclosed by strips of territorial sea, then Canada has sovereign jurisdiction over it.

Further confusion about the status of the waters in Canada's Arctic region came about as a result of the multilateral negotiations at the Third United Nations Conference on the Law of the Sea (UNCLOS III). The Canadian delegation succeeded in introducing a clause into the negotiating document which gives functional jurisdiction to coastal states with respect to controlling marine pollution in ice-covered and ice-infested waters.[9] This clause closely parallels the preamble of the AWPPA; the fact that it survived negotiations to become Article 234 of the 1982 Law of the Sea Convention indicates strongly that Canada's claim of functional jurisdiction in Arctic waters has international sanction. Another result of the UNCLOS III negotiations was the establishment of Exclusive Economic Zones (EEZ's) which extend two hundred nautical miles outward from the coastline of states, and in which these states are to have a triple functional jurisdiction. The EEZ, a new phenomenon in international law of the sea, was such a popular concept at UNCLOS III that a number of states put the concept into practice before the negotiations were concluded. Canada, for example, declared its two hundred mile zone in the Arctic in March 1977. This zone overlaps completely the one hundred mile zone created by the AWPPA, and it extends another one hundred miles outward from the archipelago. In the new zone, Canada has jurisdiction to manage resources within the area and the right to control marine scientific research and to monitor and control marine pollution. However, as these EEZ's are not part of the coastal state's territorial waters, Canada does not have sovereign jurisdiction over its Arctic zone.

Throughout the period 1968–85, the Canadian government followed an oblique approach to the question of the status of Arctic waters: the *view* that these waters were within Canada's sovereign jurisdiction was clearly enunciated, but the sovereign *claim* was not asserted. Instead, the government assumed a series of administrative responsibilities and functional jurisdictions that approximated an assertion of at least partial sovereignty.

The government's approach changed in mid-1985 after the voyage of the USCG *Polar Sea* through the Northwest Passage. In September, it was announced that Canada would draw straight baselines from the northern mainland along the outer edge of the Arctic archipelago and back to the mainland. Further, the waters within the area so circumscribed—including the Northwest Passage—would be declared internal Canadian waters in January 1986. Finally, legislation would be introduced to extend the application of Canadian civil and criminal law to this offshore zone. In making this announcement, the government was asserting full Canadian sovereignty in the Arctic region in unmistakable terms.[10]

These actions have not resolved the dispute between Canada and the United States over the status of the waters—particularly the status of the Northwest Passage—and bilateral negotiations on the matter have yet to yield a positive result. The dispute is usually referred to as a dispute over whether *the* Northwest Passage is *an* international strait. While one may conclude that a single, clearly definable passage exists, recently published research, based on analysis of actual vessel navigation of the passage over the past eighty-odd years, shows that there are *five* main routes of "the" passage.[11] In the past, the choice of route depended upon vessel draft and varying ice conditions. As these constraints to navigation are more than likely to persist in the future, one can assume that use of the five main routes will continue. Together, these routes include most of the waters north of the Canadian mainland and south of the Queen Elizabeth Islands![12] If, therefore, "the" passage is an international strait, Canada would have no jurisdiction whatsoever over all of those waters and the airspace above them. In short, the threat to Canada's legal sovereignty with respect to the waters in its Arctic region is real and substantial.

The government's oblique approach to legal sovereignty over Arctic waters appears to be responsible for the importance attached to various aspects of technological sovereignty. In the 1950s the concern was for effective occupation of the land territory, but in the past two decades the Canadian government has clearly indicated that its concern stems from a requirement to protect extremely fragile ecosystems in a hostile environment: an environment where, owing to severe climatic conditions, ice infestation, and ice cover, the hazards to vessel navigation are exceptional. This concern has brought about new regulations governing the design specifications of ships to ensure the hulls can withstand the rigours of ice navigation. It has also led to the establishment of new aids to navigation, the regular promulgation of ice forecasts, and icebreaker escort. Rather than attempt to *exclude* vessels in general or the vessels of particular states from these waters, the government has applied standards and procedures to *allow* for safe navigation, and it has done so in a non-discriminatory fashion.

The federal agency which has primary responsibility for ensuring safe navigation in Canada's waters is the Coast Guard. In Arctic waters, the responsibility includes the provision of icebreaker escort, ice pilots, and other navigation aids, ice surveillance, and a vessel reporting system. While these services also constitute highly visible, and therefore important, components of technological sovereignty, some observers point to the limited enforcement capability inherent in Canada's civilian, unarmed Coast Guard. As the ability of state agencies to enforce regulations and laws is the key component to technological sovereignty, and as armed forces' equipment and personnel are used to enforce Canadian regulations off the east and west coasts, those observers then suggest a similar enforcement role for the armed forces in Arctic waters.

The Canadian Armed Forces' (CAF) primary responsibility is national security and defence. The means of meeting that responsibility are listed as commitments in the 1971 White Paper on defence: a policy document that has been in effect for most of the period under consideration here. *Defence in the 70s* lists the protection of sovereignty as one of the CAF's four commitments; the other three are the defence of

North America, contributing to NATO, and peacekeeping. Although the four commitments can be seen as a continuum, and the protection of Canadian sovereignty "is simply the basic element of the total defence effort,"[13] the specific tasks assigned to the armed forces to meet the sovereignty protection commitment in the Arctic have been regarded as worthy and interesting but essentially "non-military" or "non-defence" by many in the CAF and in the Department of National Defence (DND). One example of such "non-defence" tasking is the use of long-range patrol aircraft, which are configured for antisubmarine surveillance over open water, for the visual observation of offshore drilling rigs in Arctic waters to enforce pollution regulations. On the other hand, major equipment plans and purchases for the CAF during the 1970s and early 1980s (such as the Aurora maritime patrol aircraft, the CF-18, Leopard tanks, and the Canadian Patrol Frigate program) buttressed the conclusion that fulfilling NATO and NORAD commitments was the crux of Canada's national security policy. In short, national defence and sovereignty protection in the Arctic could be viewed as two separate goals; the latter goal—and the tasks associated with it—holds the distinct potential to detract from the capability of meeting the first goal.

This view of competing goals is changing as the increasing strategic significance of the Arctic has become more apparent to a wider selection of Canadians. The September 1985 statement on Arctic sovereignty included explicit reference to national defence and defence tasks as an integral part of the exercise of sovereignty in the Arctic. However it was also noted that "Canada, in the past, had not developed the means to ensure our sovereignty over time ... [and] when we looked for ways to exercise our sovereignty we found that the Canadian cupboard was nearly bare."[14] This is an accurate statement of the very modest capabilities of Canada's land and air forces,[15] but at the very least, it is an understatement where the capabilities of the naval forces are concerned. None of Maritime Command's (MARCOM) ships is ice-strengthened: none can operate in ice-covered or even moderately ice-infested waters. As a result, the only "Arctic" activities of MARCOM ships are occasional visits to ports in southwestern Greenland and annual voyages (Operation NORPLOY) from Halifax along the coast of Labrador and into Hudson Bay. Even these activities are constrained to the few months of the year when the waters are ice-free. In short, Canada's naval vessels are effectively barred at any time of the year from almost all of the Arctic waters over which Canada asserts a sovereign jurisdiction.

This observation begs the question: what are the requirements for a naval capability in those waters? While there is a clear requirement to provide for safe navigation—especially in the future if commercial navigation increases as a result of increased oil and natural gas exploration in the high Arctic—this is a Coast Guard responsibility and the plans to construct the Polar 8 icebreaker should yield sufficient capability to carry out that task. The navy renounced the "icebreaker business" some time ago because that activity was consuming resources required for naval defence tasks. Is it desirable to reverse that decision now? Would the navy of the 1990s have the resources available to acquire and man the icebreakers without decreasing its current strength and activity levels in naval defence or stretching out even further the already embarrassingly long acquisition phase for replacing older destroyers and submarines? How would such a reversal affect the ability to meet the increased demand for naval defence in the Pacific? How would such a reversal affect Canada's total defence effort, including NATO and NORAD tasks, when there is a widely recognized gap between the country's commitments and its current capabilities to fulfil them? Those questions do not yield clear answers easily, not to mention positive answers to the matter of naval responsibility for safe navigation in Arctic waters. In fact, the Senate Sub-committee on National Defence argued quite forcefully to the contrary in its report on maritime defence: "The sub-committee sees no compelling reason to acquire ice-breakers for MARCOM ... the sub-committee sees no purpose in altering the present arrangement whereby Canada's ice-breaking fleet is operated by the Coast Guard."[16]

While a requirement for naval forces to provide for *safe navigation* is not at all apparent, other developments over the past decade do raise the question of a requirement for naval forces to provide for *naval defence* in Arctic waters. Developments in submarine design, advances in the accuracy of submarine-launched ballistic missiles, and advances in ASW technology are several of the major factors that are changing the strategic value of the Arctic.[17] Two matters are of particular interest: the Soviet Union's deployment to the Northern Fleet of all Typhoon Class ballistic missile submarines, which are designed to surface through ice; and the adoption by the Soviet navy of a "bastion" strategy with respect to the deployment of its Northern Fleet submarines.[18] The possibility—indeed probability—of increased ballistic-missile and attack submarine deployments in the Arctic by the Soviet navy and the consequent ASW anxieties on the part of the US Navy raise the spectre of superpower undersea naval rivalry in, or adjacent to, a whole new area of Canada's sovereign waters.

These developments have caused two changes in the approach to the question of naval responsibilities in the Arctic. What had been judged in the past as a very modest requirement for an Arctic naval capability has changed, and Canada's Arctic naval capability requirements could now increase anywhere from moderately to substantially. Secondly, any response will constitute the means to meet simultaneously the goal of sovereignty assertion and the goal of national defence: goals that in the past may have been viewed as conflicting in terms of Armed Forces' resource use are now essentially identical—or at least highly complementary—for Canada's Arctic waters.

Canada will likely choose from five types of responses to the increase in superpower naval rivalry in the Arctic. The first type of response is for Canada to do nothing. While this option has the attraction, to a government that is committed to deficit reduction, of adding no new expenditures to the federal budget, "doing nothing" would clearly signal to other states a Canadian lack of interest in Arctic matters. Such a signal is hardly an accurate reflection of our historic interest in the region or of the value attached to it as a vital component of the Canadian identity. It also contradicts directly the current government's vigorous assertion of sovereignty in the Arctic.

The second type of response might be styled as passive unilateral. These are initiatives that Canada alone could take, including: the secondment of naval personnel on a regular basis to Coast Guard icebreakers for training in Arctic navigation;[19] the construction of new Coast Guard icebreakers in a manner that would allow them to be equipped with helicopters and containerized weapons on a contingency basis;[20] and increasing the frequency of MARCOM ship visits and patrols in the Labrador Sea, Davis Strait, Baffin Bay, and Beaufort Sea. Another initiative which fits this type of response is the construction and operation of an undersea detection grid at those narrow archipelagic waterways which could serve as transit routes for submarines between the Arctic and the Atlantic oceans. Such an "undersea DEW Line" would perform a function quite similar to that performed by the actual DEW Line: early warning, and therefore deterrence, of any attempt to transit the area for hostile purposes. Rather than detecting long-range bombers however, this grid would concentrate on the detection of submarines. Submarines of both the ballistic missile and attack types can only perform their functions effectively when their exact location is not known to a potential enemy. When their location is known, the submarines themselves become targets. Therefore, whenever possible, it is in the interest of the command structure to have the submarines avoid areas which contain such detection installations. In short, the very installation of such a system would deter submarines from operating in those waters. As similar installations—for example, the sound surveillance system off the Atlantic coast—are operated by naval communications personnel, it would be highly likely that the Arctic system will utilize the same people. The data received by such a system could be transmitted to Canadian or allied surface navies for action in open water south of the detection grid. The government has recently announced, in the White Paper on defence, its intention to deploy such a fixed sonar system in the Canadian Arctic.[21]

While the "undersea DEW Line" has been advocated by some observers—including this writer—as a cost-effective response that would allow the appropriate authorities to gather better information on the exact dimensions of the problem before committing expensive resources to its solution, other observers prefer a more activist approach. In what might be termed "the active unilateral response," Canada would require its own fleet of attack submarines which have a prolonged under-ice capability. Knowledgeable analysts agree that the most effective ASW platform in ice-covered and heavily ice-infested areas are nuclear-powered attack submarines. These submarines can be used in conjunction with an undersea detection grid or as ASW platforms on their own. It appears that this activist unilateral response has recently been adopted by the Canadian government. It plans to acquire ten to twelve nuclear-powered attack submarines for ocean surveillance and control in the Atlantic, Pacific, and Arctic.[22] Although it is expected that most of these seagoing activities will be in the Atlantic and Pacific oceans, they will involve patrols in the Arctic as well. Such a response certainly complements the government's vigorous assertion of Arctic sovereignty and its apparent commitment to increasing Canada's defence capability. However, this response also raises important questions. What is the cost, in the financial and human terms, of acquiring and manning such a fleet? What effect would such an acquisition have on the performance of other naval tasks and the planned replacement program for the navy's older destroyers? Finally, given the rather uncertain quality of information about the level of superpower submarine activity in these Arctic waters, is it not premature to commit to a particular activist response at this time? Is it not prudent first to gather more accurate information on the nature of the problem?

The fourth type of response is bilateral. The idea of sharing the defence of Arctic waters with the United States in a combined naval command and with combined resources has received considerable attention recently. As is the case with the "undersea DEW Line" mentioned above, this idea is borrowed from our experience in bilateral continental air defence. Of course, the object would be to detect and defend against intrusions of the Soviet Union's submarines in our Arctic waters, rather than the Soviet Union's long-range bombers in our airspace. This response option has many of the attractions and problems of NORAD: access to intelligence information has to be balanced with guaranteed long-term participation at the highest command and decisionmaking levels to insure the continued fulfilment of Canada's national security interests; the budgetary advantages of cost-sharing, resource-sharing, and cross-training must be matched by the clear recognition of complete sovereignty in Canadian Arctic waters; the flexibility available for planning the Canadian contribution to such a bilateral naval defence structure has to be compared with the flexibility inherent in unilateral decisionmaking. The creation of an "undersea NORAD" for Arctic waters is a response option that should be considered, but only when informed by the country's nearly three decades of experience in NORAD. Before concluding any such bilateral arrangement, both Canada and the United States should be confident that it would serve the best long-term interests of both states.

The fifth type of response is multilateral. An increase in superpower naval rivalry in Arctic waters affects the security of Canada's European NATO allies as well. Deployment of Soviet submarines in Arctic waters presents a new threat—or at least a threat from a new ocean area—to the potential European targets of Soviet submarine-launched ballistic missiles and to the naval defence of alliance sea lines of communication.[23] As such deployments and operations increase, they will complicate NATO defence planning, planning under the direction of Supreme Allied Commander Atlantic (SACLANT), and activities of the Standing Naval Force Atlantic (STANAVFORLANT). Some observers suggest that this problem can be addressed by the creation of an Arctic NATO command with headquarters located variously in northern Scotland, Iceland, or the Canadian High Arctic, in order to foster a co-ordinated alliance response to the problem. These suggestions also deserve careful consideration and detailed discussion, but a necessary prerequisite is agreement within NATO that the Arctic *is* an alliance concern and is within NATO's mandated jurisdiction. Canada may be the ideal NATO member to initiate such discussions. Depending on the outcome, a multilateral response may have advantages for Canada over a unilateral, or even a bilateral, approach in spite of the time and effort that would be required to reach such an agreement.

This brief summary of the five types of responses to increased superpower naval deployments in the Arctic gives an indication of the wide range of actual responses that are available to Canada. As several of the types of options are not mutually exclusive, the various permutations and combinations yield even more actual responses. With the exception of the "do nothing" type of response, all of the options involve increased responsibilities for Canada's navy in Arctic waters; as well, they all simultaneously address threats to legal sovereignty, problems with technological sovereignty, and the recently developed requirement to provide for naval defence in the Arctic. Although the pace and degree of change varies depending on the response chosen, one matter is clear: as Canadians contemplate defence policy for the next decade and the next century, naval responsibilities in the Arctic will merit much more than the "distant third" priority that they have traditionally enjoyed.

Chapter 15

SHIPS: MANAGING THE NEED

J.M. Treddenick
and
C.G. Galigan

INTRODUCTION

Long before the days when naval officers found it necessary to confront uncomfortable (and decidedly non-nautical) concepts such as program budgeting and cost-effectiveness, and long before dilettante economists dabbled in defence matters, Lord Jellicoe laid out four alternative model fleets for the post-First World War Canadian navy. His proposals are summarized in Table 1, but, suffice to say, none was ever implemented.

In our own day, serious students of naval affairs continue to make similar proposals. Prominent among recent contributions have been those of the Senate Subcommittee on National Defence, Vice-Admiral Timbrell and Vice-Admiral Fulton.[1] And of course there are the fleets actually programmed and planned by the Department of National Defence (DND). But which of these model fleets can be realized; which, if any, is likely to be realized; and which are to be consigned to the same fate which befell those of Lord Jellicoe?

This paper represents an attempt to construct a simple framework within which questions of this sort might be approached. Its fundamental argument is that alternative fleet proposals must be assessed on an integrated evaluation of affordability, costs, and capability: in short, the "need" for a particular fleet configuration must be both defined and managed within a context of economic reality. In the first section various approaches to need definition are described and assessed. The second section includes a description of our methodology and suggests measures of costs and effectiveness for a number of model fleets. In the third section we evaluate the affordability of these

TABLE 1: Lord Jellicoe's Model Fleets for Canada, 1919[2]

Fleet units	Fleet 1	Fleet 2	Fleet 3	Fleet 4
Battle cruisers			1	2
Light cruisers		3	5	7
Flotilla leaders		1	1	1
Destroyers			6	12
Destroyer parent ships			1	1
Submarines	8	8	8	16
Submarine parent ships		1	1	1
Aircraft carriers			1	2
Fleet minesweepers			2	4
Local defence destroyers	4	4	4	4
P-boats	8	8	8	8
Trawler minesweepers	4	4	4	4
Annual cost (£ millions)	1.0	2.0	3.5	5.0

fleets against projected resource availability constraints and we assess their desirability in terms of cost-effectiveness measures. A final section offers some conclusions and proposals with regard to need definition and management.

APPROACHES TO NEED DEFINITION

Defining a nation's need for warships is the type of problem which has irresistible appeal to amateur strategists. In reality, however, it is a complex problem, one which is infinitely arguable in detail and one requiring great professional experience and expertise in its resolution. But the actual process of defining the need—the steps one must go through—is seen by many planners and analysts to be one of elegant rationality and simplicity. One begins with the national interest as it emerges from the specifics of geography, politics, and economics and more generally from the world role the nation defines for itself. Possible threats to this national interest are identified and evaluated in terms of magnitude and probability. Countering those threats in the maritime environment requires the provision of naval capabilities of appropriate scale and diversity, possibly modified by the availability of naval capabilities provided by allied nations facing common threats. Given the prevailing technology of naval warfare, the required capabilities can then be translated into a specific fleet configuration. Any difference between the required fleet and the existing fleet defines the required shipbuilding program while the cost of that program generates the naval capital budget.

The underlying naiveté of this approach is easily sensed. Nevertheless, there can be no question of its necessity. This type of analysis has to be done, done well, and redone by as varied a group of analysts as possible, both within and outside the naval establishment. Its essential elements—national interest, threats, capability requirements, and fleet structure—must be clearly defined and their relationships one to the other fully understood. Most importantly, the sets of assumptions, upon which alternative fleet proposals critically depend, should be subjected to rigorous and skeptical examination.

Even when meticulously done, however, requirements exercises of this nature, if they go no farther than generating model fleets, become the stuff of pipe dreams. Invariably the proposals which emerge from such exercises are described by military planners in terms of "the minimum absolute requirement." But this is "pie-in-the-sky" planning; it is a "needs-first" approach to fleet design which degenerates to the preparation of wish lists by creators who doom themselves to the frustration of unrealized expectations.

The difficulty is that, in a world of infinite desires and finite resources, no naval program can be paramount. Tradeoffs must be made. Within the naval budget choices must be made between ships and more sailors, more intensive operations, or better training, all of which contribute to naval capability. Within the defence budget, tradeoffs must be made between ships and aircraft or tanks. Within the federal budget, choices must be made between ships and non-defence programs, and within society as a whole, choices must be made between ships and personal consumption or business investment. Choosing to build ships therefore implies that other valued needs are foregone. Selecting an appropriate model fleet requires that the contribution of that fleet to the national interest must in some way be weighed against the value of those other needs which are displaced. In short, any exercise in model fleet construction is incomplete and probably futile if it fails to include cost considerations. Unfortunately, most proposals based on the straight requirements approach are guilty of this omission. At best, questions of cost are included as an afterthought; generally they are treated as a problem distinct and separate from the problem of requirements.

That fleet building is expensive of course escapes no one's attention. The question of costs must ultimately be confronted, for costs define the reality of what is possible; model fleets designed without regard to costs are likely to remain unfulfilled dreams. But there is a real danger that the cost side of the equation may be overemphasized. Thus governments may establish a shipbuilding budget on the basis of vague notions of what may be affordable, regardless of what may be appropriate in terms of need. Given this budget and the costs of shipbuilding, the type and quantity of potential fleets which can be accommodated by this budget are constrained. The budget arrived at by the controllers of the purse strings is invariably described in terms of "the maximum affordable." What is affordable becomes what is needed. This cost-first approach is, however, not without its advantages. It certainly simplifies the decisionmaking process, particularly in the sense that the difficult relationships between national interests and ship needs become largely irrelevant and may therefore be conveniently avoided.

It takes little familiarity with the recent history of Canadian defence policymaking to realize that the idea of affordability has dominated equipment expenditure decisions. More than any other factor, preconceptions of what can be afforded have constrained and will likely continue to constrain naval development in this country. Separating the questions of national interest and affordability has been tried in Canada, with unfortunate results. The defence budget, which of course establishes the framework of constraints within which fleet development must take place, remained roughly constant in the region of 1.5 to 1.9 billion dollars over the two decades after 1953, the last year of the Korean War and the peak year of the deployment to Europe. But twenty years of constant budgets and rising inflation took their toll. Declining real expenditures and the need to reallocate higher proportions of declining resources to personnel, operations, and maintenance combined to reduce investment in equipment to ridiculously low levels. Only after 1973, when the drastic implications of this policy could no longer be ignored, was the budget allowed to increase sufficiently to provide some modest real growth. But the damage had been done. Ships were neither modernized nor replaced in sufficient numbers to prevent fleet capabilities from declining. Moreover, as we shall demonstrate, this decline in fleet capabilities is almost certain to continue unless present and future affordability notions are significantly revised.

An approach to defining needs which emphasizes cost and affordability at the expense of requirements is of course as hopelessly invalid as the pipe-dream of establishing requirements without due attention to costs. In the former case, costs and affordability tend to assume an absoluteness of their own. In reality, however, short of pre-empting the entire productive capacity of the nation, there is no upper limit on what can be afforded for ships should the requirement for them be sufficiently highly valued relative to the value of society's other needs. Neither is there a lower limit. Should the value of ship requirements be sufficiently low, no expenditures on ships would be entirely rational.

The extremes of "minimum absolute requirements" and "maximum absolute affordability" are unlikely to coincide. However, there does exist, at least theoretically, a more rational approach to need definition. Ideally, a nation's defence expenditures should be established at that level where an increment in such expenditures just increases national welfare (however that may be measured) by an amount equal to the amount of national welfare given up by removing an equal amount of expenditures from the civilian sector of the economy. In this way the nation's welfare level is maximized within the constraint of its productive capacity. Once the optimal level of defence expenditure is thus established, the allocation of defence resources among alternative defence activities can then be arrived at through similar reasoning. Resources allocated to fleet building, for example, should be established at that level where an increment in such expenditures contributes an amount of defence capability given up by not allocating that amount of expenditure to other defence activities. Every defence activity would thus be funded, within the defence budget, up to the point where the last dollar (or the last million or billion dollars) spent on it would generate the same increment in defence capability. If this particular allocation of resources is not achieved, then it is obvious that a reallocation of resources among defence activities would increase total defence capability. What would emerge from reallocations of this nature is a balance and mix of forces which maximize defence capabilities. Optimal ship needs fall naturally out of this type of reasoning.

This approach to defining ship needs will be immediately recognized as the economists' pipe dream. Definitional and measurement problems aside, the relationship between national welfare and defence capability simply cannot be determined objectively, nor can the relationship between defence capability and individual defence activities. Individuals will hold differing views on these relationships; as a result, there cannot exist one "correct" defence budget or one "correct" shipbuilding program. We are left then, as always, to the rough and tumble of political and bureaucratic struggle to sort out these important allocational decisions. But, operational or not, this approach, based on ideas of economic rationality, at least suggests how arguments for particular model fleets may be more advantageously structured and managed.

Not without a certain amount of chagrin in some quarters, ideas of allocational rationality have indeed crept into defence decision-making in Canada. The Defence Program Management System (DPMS), the formal mechanism of defence resource allocation in the Department of National Defence, is itself based on just this philosophical thrust. First, allocational decisions, particularly with regard to capital acquisition, are supposed to be based on the contribution which each candidate project is likely to make to defence capabilities. Secondly, allocational decisions are supposed to take a long-term view in the sense that projects are approved not only on the basis of resources currently required and available but also on the basis of implied future resource requirements and their likely availability. Thirdly, the costs of each project, which are weighed against its potential contribution to defence capabilities, are supposed to be exhaustive, in the sense that total acquisition, operating, and maintenance costs are evaluated over the life of the equipment under consideration. Approved projects are then programmed into the defence plan in some order which supposedly reflects their costs, the anticipated availability of resources, and their importance to the defence effort.

While admirable in intent and while in our opinion it has served the government and DND well, the DPMS suffers from some important deficiencies. First, the DPMS decision process has evolved into what is clearly recognizable as a priority setting exercise. The term "priority" is of course heavily loaded with connotations of rationality and good sense. But closer examination suggests that what results from priority-setting is the satisfying of each major defence requirement in some sort of sequential ordering. One major requirement is fully funded within resource availability constraints while others must await their turns until resources become available. More cynical observers might see the queuing order being established based on the service element which has been the longest without a major project. In any event, no concern appears to be given to the possibility that at some point an extra million or billion dollars spent on the approved project may yield less defence capability than would be obtained by allocating those expenditures to the first units of other projects. Such a process does not conform to the ideal of rational resource allocation outlined above. From a defence-wide perspective what is likely to result is a permanent procession of unbalanced forces: air capabilities may become completely modernized while the equipment inventories of the other elements are left to deteriorate, both physically and technologically. When the turn of the next element does come up, years of neglect will require even larger expenditures than otherwise might be expected just to restore its original capability level.

This tendency to concentrate resources on a few major need areas at a time is reinforced within the DPMS by a focus on the individual capital project as the unit of decisionmaking. Each equipment project has a well-defined lifespan, from an initial statement of requirements through several screening and approval levels to the delivery of the last unit. Success in managing each project is measured in terms of completing the project within the cost, performance, delivery schedules, and economic benefits criteria established in the contract. Once a major project is completed, the departmental staffing, decisionmaking, and project management resources are then shifted to the next major project. Because each project is by nature unique, large, and complex, considerable resources of this type are required; because they are scarce, these resources must be rationed in terms of both quantity and time. The result is a certain intensity of effort and attention directed at a series of projects in turn, a process which adds to the start-stop nature of Canadian weapons acquisition. Moreover, this start-stop experience for specific projects will generate future echo effects as systems reach the end of their physical and operational lives. But because different weapons systems have different useful lifetimes, and because they are put in place sequentially, it is a mathematical certainty that a bunching of future replacement requirements will occur, with all that would imply for the potential overloading of the financial and administrative capacity of the DPMS.

There would appear to be real advantages to adopting a less time-intensive approach to acquiring defence equipment. The first advantage would be that in any given year the capital budget would be less concentrated on one or a few major projects and would be spread more evenly over all environments. More balanced capabilities on a force-wide basis would be achievable since it would no longer be necessary to allow some capabilities to run down as one was being refurbished. A second advantage is that it would be possible to economize on staffing, decision-making, and project management resources as longterm investment planning resulted in such tasks becoming more routine. A third advantage in eliminating the start-stop process of weapons acquisition would be to encourage domestic producers to stay in the weapons market for the long haul. Under the existing situation, DND is usually faced with the choice of buying abroad and attempting to arrange offsetting economic benefits for domestic industry or rebuilding the infrastructure necessary to support domestic production. In both cases, the costs of acquiring weapons systems are unnecessarily increased. With respect to warship acquisition, where political considerations render domestic production the only feasible alternative, recent experience has found that as a result of years of inactivity, domestic capacity for naval shipbuilding had largely withered away, resulting in tremendous start-up costs for any new shipbuilding program.

Yet a third difficulty with the DPMS is that while it does purport to consider full life-cycle costs when making procurement decisions, it ignores two extremely important cost areas: physical depreciation and technological updating. If military equipment, particularly ships, is to retain its capability, then provision must be made to replace continuously that portion of the equipment which becomes physically depreciated with use and time and also to update the technology of the equipment at a rate which approximates the rate of technological implementation of allies and potential adversaries. These depreciation and technological updating costs are likely to be large over the life of the equipment, both in absolute terms and relative to original procurement costs. This realization serves to underscore the fact that annual gross investment in fleet development will only add to fleet capabilities if it exceeds the annual cost of physical depreciation and technological updating. Doing less diminishes fleet capabilities.

Thus far we have discussed alternative conceptual approaches to defining and managing ship needs. On the assumption that defining and managing ship needs cannot be independent of the decisionmaking process through which these needs must be satisfied, we have also outlined certain impediments which, in our opinion, the DPMS places on a desirable need-management system. Out of all of this it should be possible to formulate a procedure which will yield realistic choices for selecting model fleets.

First, from the requirements approach it is clearly essential that hard thinking be done with respect to the relationships between national interests, threats, and required naval capabilities. Dreaming about alternative model fleets which could conceivably provide those capabilities should be encouraged, and seemingly radical proposals should not be dismissed out of hand. For each alternative, realistic implementation dates should be ascertained. It is then necessary to describe each alternative both in terms of its ability to meet perceived threats and in terms of its potential contribution to general defence capabilities over the entire period to the target date.

Second, full costing of the alternatives over the period to the target date should be done. Such costing would have to include not only acquisition, operating, and maintenance costs but also, and more importantly, the full annual costs of physical and technological deterioration. Realistic time-phasing of these costs to the target date must then be determined and accompanied by measures of their potential impact on the capital budget, the defence budget, and the economy as a whole. In constructing these expenditure time profiles no concession to start-stop funding should be made. Rather, for the reasons already cited, a more time-extensive approach to fleet development should be encouraged; continuous replacement and addition should become the philosophical underpinning of the fleet-building process.

A third feature of the need-management procedure should be the requirement to present alternative model fleets and their associated expenditure time paths in a format which encourages argument in terms of incremental capabilities and incremental costs. Such a format permits the decisionmaker to weigh the worth of extra capability against its cost.

In the next section, some computational experiments based on this suggested approach to ship need definition and need management are discussed. These experiments are applied to recently proposed model fleets for the Canadian navy; accordingly they proceed on the assumption that the first step in the process, the requirements phase, has already been done. The objective is to produce some ideas about what is possible for the development of the Canadian fleet. Our work concentrates on the second and third steps.

NEED-MANAGEMENT: MEASURES OF EFFECTIVENESS AND COSTS

To illustrate our need management procedure we begin with the five alternative model fleets described in Table 2. For purposes of comparison, Fleet 1, the currently existing fleet, is included as a base case. Fleet 2 corresponds to the fleet planned by DND for the late 1990s. Fleet 3 is based on the proposal made by the Senate Subcommittee on National Defence. Fleet 4 is intended to represent the fleet suggested in the 1976 Defence Structure Review. Finally, Fleet 5 is based on Admiral Timbrell's 1983 proposal to the Senate Subcommittee. For each fleet we have selected a target year of 2010, a year which is sufficiently distant to permit a realistic expectation of full implementation; not entirely coincidentally, it is also the year which will mark the centenary of the Canadian navy.

Because it is not the number or mix of ships in each model fleet which is the important variable of concern but rather the total capability of each fleet, and because the alternative model fleets must be made comparable for analytical purposes, each model fleet in Table 2 has been rated in terms of what we call Combat Equivalence Units (CEU). To measure the CEU level of each fleet, a ship of the new FFH type has been arbitrarily assigned a CEU of unity. The CEU values of other ship types, both existing and proposed, have been assigned CEU values relative to the FFH value based on their principal function, age and relative cost. For example, the existing fleet of DDES and DDHS, with the exception of the DDH-280 class, have been assigned an average 1985 CEU of 0.5. The DDH-280s have been assigned an average value of 0.75.

Through physical depreciation and technological obsolescence, the

TABLE 2: Alternative Model Fleets, Target Year 2010

Fleet units	Fleet alternatives				
	1	2	3	4	5
Destroyer: DDE/DDH (River Class)	16	0	0	0	0
Destroyer: DDH (Tribal Class)	4	4	0	0	0
Frigate: FFH (City Class)	0	12	16	24	36
Submarine: SS	3	3	10	3	10
Operational support ships: AOR	3	3	3	3	4
Fast patrol boats: FPB	0	0	12	0	0
Minesweeper: MS	0	0	9	0	0
Mine hunters: MH	0	0	4	0	0
Combat Equivalance units	12.5	16.5	21.8	25.5	40.4

CEU value of a ship will decline over time unless it is continuously maintained physically and kept up to date technologically. In our analysis it has been assumed that a typical naval vessel has a useful operational life of twenty-five years and therefore depreciates each year on a fixed line basis of 4 per cent of its original value. Our best guess with respect to the technology of naval warfare is that it changes at a rate of approximately 10 per cent per year. But because only about one-half of a ship's components, principally the combat systems, is subject to such a high rate of technological change, a rate of 5 per cent has been employed in our analysis. It also follows that the price of a new FFH (or one CEU) necessarily increases at a rate of 5 per cent per annum, net of any inflationary effects.

To illustrate our use of the CEU measure, consider the hypothetical case of an FFH delivered at the end of 1985. By the end of 1986, using annual physical and technological rates of depreciation of 4 per cent and 5 per cent respectively, the CEU value of this ship would have declined to (1-.04-.05) or 0.91. By the end of 1987 this value would have declined to (1-.08-.01) or 0.82. Alternatively, the 1985 CEU rating of unity could have been preserved had total maintenance and technological updating equal to 9 per cent of the original cost been undertaken in 1986 and 9.25 per cent in 1987.[3] Under these assumptions it is evident that even to maintain the capability level of an existing fleet, increasing expenditures for physical maintenance and technological improvement will be required. Note that these expenditures take no account of any purely inflationary price increases.

It is not a requirement that expenditures for physical depreciation and technological updating necessarily be applied to the actual ship on whose behalf they were incurred. In practice they could be applied to the modernization of other ships or even the construction of new ships; the important consideration is that *total* fleet capability is maintained or increased by these expenditures. Similarly, a particular fleet configuration does not represent the only possible way of achieving a given fleet CEU level. A particular CEU level could be obtained through various combinations of ship types, ages and technological characteristics, including many older, less technologically advanced ships, or a few newer and more advanced ships, or combinations of each. Assessing the tradeoff opportunities among the various combinations yielding the same capability level is obviously beyond our competence and is better left to experienced naval professionals. We must assume, however, that in formulating their model fleets, the proposers have at least implicitly done this sort of analysis.[4]

Our needs-management exercise next requires that an implementation scheme be devised such that each model fleet achieve its target capability level in the year 2010. Many alternative schemes are possible, but in our view the preferable approach is to implement each model fleet such that total fleet CEU levels grow by a fixed percentage each year, the actual growth rate being determined by the difference between the target year CEU level and the 1985 CEU level. This constant growth rate scheme has the attractive advantage of allowing a slower build-up of administrative and financial resources during the planning and implementation periods. The alternative time-paths of fleet capability development resulting from this procedure are indicated in Figure 1. Because the currently existing fleet is assumed to retain its capability level over the planning period, its development path is indicated by a horizontal line at its initial capability level of 12.5 CEU's.

Each fleet alternative offers a particular capability level measured in CEUs, but with the exception of the existing fleet, these levels are only partially available before the target year. Capability therefore has a time dimension, and it becomes necessary for planning purposes to account for the total capability provided by each fleet over the entire period. The measure we employ is the CEU-year; total CEU-years are obtained for each fleet by multiplying the CEU level achieved in each year by the number of years that level is maintained. For example, in the simplest case, Fleet 1 is assumed to maintain a constant CEU level of 12.5 over the entire 25-year period and therefore provides a total capability of (25 x 12.5) or 312.5 CEU-years. Ratings for the four alternative model fleets, which require more complicated calculation because of the exponential growth of their CEU levels, are indicated in Table 3.[5]

Having obtained the capability development paths, we can now ascertain the expenditure time profiles required to implement them.

Figure 1

CAPABILITY IMPLEMENTATION
FOR ALTERNATIVE FLEET MODELS
1985 – 2010

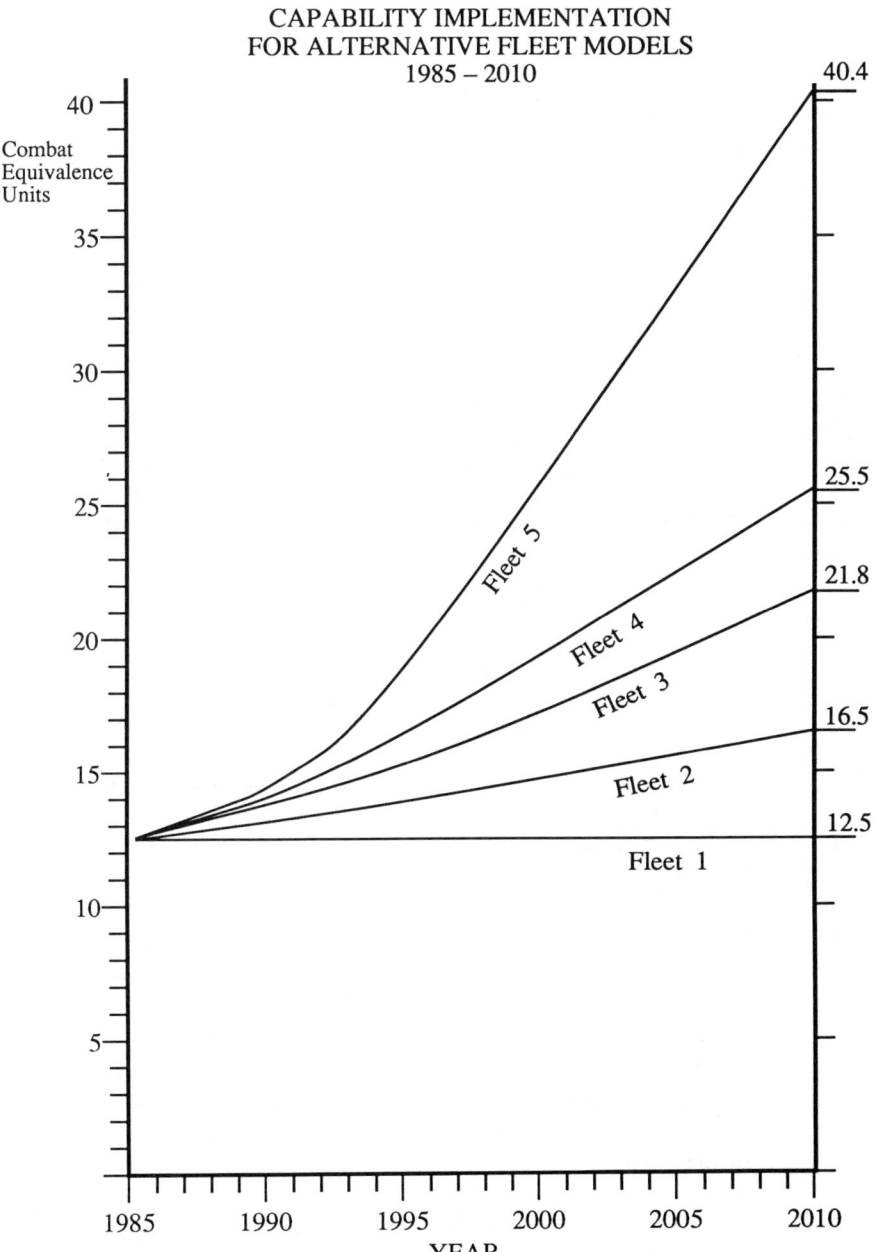

TABLE 3: Alternative Model Fleet Total Capabilities

Fleet	CEU rating in 2010	Total CEU-years 1986–2010
1	12.5	312.5
2	16.5	357.9
3	21.8	406.9
4	25.5	439.3
5	40.4	558.1

Annual expenditures must include the procurement costs of added ships (in CEU's), the cost of maintaining the original physical capability of the fleet achieved in the previous year, and the cost of technologically updating the fleet achieved in the previous year. Procurement costs have been assumed to be 0.5 billions of 1985 dollars per CEU, the estimated 1985 costs of the new Canadian FFH, and are assumed to grow at a rate of 5 per cent per year to account for annual improvements in technology. Post-1985 acquisitions therefore will be more costly but will also be more technologically advanced. It should be noted again that no account is taken of purely inflationary cost increases and that all expenditures are calculated in terms of 1985 dollars. Actual outlays in a particular year will, of course, have to include any inflation premium.

Expenditure time profiles for each alternative model fleet, including expenditures required to maintain and update the existing fleet, have been computed as shown in Figure 2 and are summarized in Table 4. The first column of Table 4 indicates total actual expenditure requirements over the period 1986–2010. These totals have a certain importance, but it is not strictly correct to compare alternative fleets on the basis of simple totals. Because each fleet implies a different time-phasing of expenditures, and because we are therefore really discussing alternative future naval development budgets, it is necessary to convert each alternative expenditure flow to an equivalent lump sum at a common date such that the different time flow of expenditure may be compared logically. One means of accomplishing this conversion is to discount each expenditure flow by an appropriate rate of interest to obtain this present value in the base year. Thus, using a rate of 10 per cent (approximately the current government borrowing rate), the total discounted present values of the expenditure flows are obtained as indicated in the second column of Table 3.[6] The final column of the table shows the estimated expenditures required for each alternative fleet in the last year of the planning period.

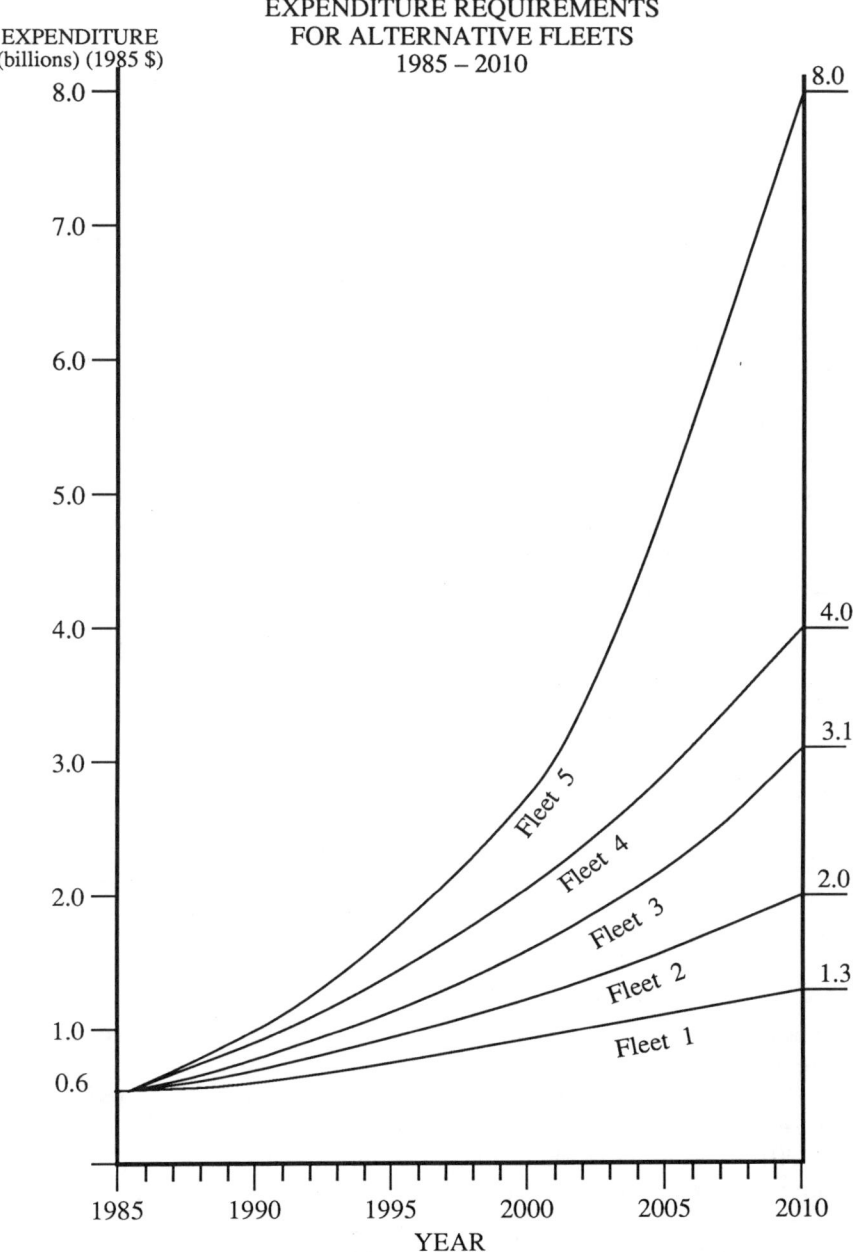

Figure 2

EXPENDITURE REQUIREMENTS
FOR ALTERNATIVE FLEETS
1985 – 2010

TABLE 4: Alternative Model Fleet Expenditure Implications, 1986–2010
(billions of 1985 dollars)

Fleet	Total actual expenditures	Total present value expenditures	Expenditures in 2020
1	21.2	6.6	1.3
2	28.8	8.2	2.0
3	38.7	10.1	3.1
4	45.8	11.4	4.0
5	74.0	16.3	8.0

NEED-MANAGEMENT: AFFORDABILITY AND CHOICE

On the basis of the expenditure requirements and effectiveness measures obtained in the previous section, it is possible to construct some educated speculations about the affordability and choice implications of the five alternative model fleets.

Assessing the affordability of the fleets must be done within the context of a hierarchy of economic constraints. For our purposes, four such constraint levels may be identified. They include, in descending order, the nation's productive capacity, the defence budget, the capital budget component of the defence budget, and the allocation of the capital budget between shipbuilding and other defence capital projects. This hierarchy of constraint may be stylized as follows:

I	national productive capacity	
II	civilian expenditure	defence budget
III	capital	personnel, operations, and maintenance
IV	shipbuilding	other defence capital projects

Changes at any of these constraint levels would have important implications for the affordability of the contemplated fleets.

At the outset it is necessary to have some idea about the pattern of total resource availability to the economy over the planning period 1986–2010. While less than ideal for our purposes, Gross National product (GNP) has been selected as the appropriate measure. On the basis of observed experience over the past twenty-five years, it has been assumed to grow at an average annual rate of 4 per cent. It should be pointed out, however, that this growth rate is decidedly optimistic given the performance of the Canadian economy over more recent years. Nevertheless, given an assumed growth rate of 4 per cent, the 2010 GNP is estimated to be 1160 billions of 1985 dollars. This figure compares with a 1985 GNP of 462.8 billions of dollars.

Next we require some estimate of share of GNP that can be expected to be allocated for defence purposes. It is tempting to select some particular percentage, such as the current 2 per cent or the NATO average of 3.3 per cent, but we have resisted doing so on the grounds that this procedure clearly does not represent the way in which provision for defence is made in this country. In recent years, the government has decided to increase the defence budget by some particular real growth rate for a stipulated period of time. In our experiments, two alternative growth rates have been applied: 3 per cent, which has been accepted as a NATO goal and which has proven to be approximately achievable and sustainable in Canada, and 6 per cent, a rate which seems to be wildly optimistic but one which has been frequently cited as the rate necessary to re-establish Canadian defence capabilities. Applying these rates of growth yields defence expenditures in 2010 of 18.8 and 38.6 billions of 1985 dollars respectively, expenditures which would represent 1.6 and 3.3 per cent of the estimated GNP in that year.[7] In 1985, the defence budget amounted to 9.6 billions of dollars, representing 2.07 per cent of GNP.

At the next constraint level we need to know how much of each year's defence expenditures will be made available for capital acquisition. To determine this availability we have simply assumed that DND's goal of allocating 30 per cent of the defence budget to capital will be realized in 1986 and will be sustained until 2010. As a result, DND capital expenditures are estimated to rise to 5.7 or 11.6 billions of 1985 dollars in 2010, depending upon whether a 3 or 6 per cent real defence expenditure growth rate is assumed.[8] The 1985 provision for capital acquisition was approximately 2.5 billions of dollars or 26 per cent of the defence budget.

Finally, it is necessary to determine what will be available in the defence capital budget for maintaining and improving fleet capabilities. Perhaps somewhat optimistically, we have assumed that in every year of the planning period one-quarter of the capital budget will be allocated to shipbuilding, ship maintenance, and technological updating of existing ships. This assumption yields ship expenditures of 1.4 or 2.9 billions of 1985 dollars in 2010, again depending on the defence growth rate assumed. The important figure for planning fleet development, however, is not the target year expenditure availability but rather total expenditure availability over the entire

TABLE 5: Expenditure Projections to 2010 (billions of 1985 dollars)

	Assumed defence growth rate	
	3 per cent	6 per cent
Gross National Product (GNP)	1160.0	1160.0 per cent
Defence expenditures	18.8	38.6 per cent
Defence capital expenditures	5.7	11.6 per cent
Shipbuilding expenditures	1.4	2.9 per cent
Total shipbuilding expenditure (1986–2010)	25.3	39.3 per cent
Total present value of shipbuilding expenditures (1986–2010)	8.0	10.8 per cent
Defence expenditures/GNP	1.6 per cent	3.3 per cent

TABLE 6: Estimated Expenditure Requirements and Availability, 1986–2010 (billions of 1985 dollars)

	Total present value expenditures	Total actual expenditures
Expenditure availability (3 per cent)	8.0	25.3
Expenditure availability (6 per cent)	10.8	39.3
Expenditure requirements		
Fleet 1	6.6	21.2
Fleet 2	8.2	28.2
Fleet 3	10.1	38.7
Fleet 4	11.4	45.8
Fleet 5	16.3	74.0

planning period—more correctly for our purposes, the total present value of annual expenditure availability. Our estimates for these figures are 25.3 or 39.3 billions of 1985 dollars for total expenditures and 8.0 and 10.8 billions of 1985 dollars for the total present value of annual expenditures. These expenditure projections for both defence growth rate assumptions are summarized in Table 5.

A preliminary assessment of the affordability for the alternative model fleet can be obtained by comparing the expenditure requirements time path for each fleet with the estimated time path of expenditure availability. The information required to make these comparisons is summarized in Table 6. Expenditures are presented in terms of both total present values and total actual expenditures. Because alternative time paths are under consideration, the relevant measures are the total present values; total actual expenditures are given for information purposes only.

It is immediately apparent from Table 6 that, under the assumption of 3 per cent annual growth in defence expenditures, a fleet capability only slightly above that currently provided by the existing fleet would be achievable by the year 2010. With a total present value of expenditure availability of 8.0 billion dollars (25.3 billion in total actual availability), it is estimated that, at most, a fleet consisting of twelve modern frigates, three submarines, and three operational support ships could be achieved. The prospect for fleet development is more promising, as would be expected, with expenditure availability estimated using the assumption of 6 per cent annual growth in defence expenditures. In this case the expenditure requirements for Fleets 1, 2, and 3 can all be accommodated within the higher expenditure availability envelope. But Fleet 4, the core of which is twenty-four FFH or similar types, requires expenditures which exceed those estimated to be available, even with the assumption of 6 per cent growth. Note that Fleet 5 requires a total present value of 16.3 billions of dollars compared to expenditure availability of 8.0 and 10.8 billions under the 3 and 6 per cent growth assumptions. In actual expenditure terms, the implementation of Fleet 5 would require almost three times the expenditure availability under the 3 per cent growth assumption and almost twice that available under the 6 per cent growth assumption.

It is of some interest to compare the actual time paths of expenditure requirements and expenditure availability. Taking Fleet 4 as an example, Figure 3 depicts expenditure requirements rising from 0.6 billions of dollars in 1985 to 4.0 billions in 2010. (The expenditure requirements to maintain the capability level of Fleet 1, the existing fleet, over the period 1985–2010 are shown for comparison.) It is clear from the diagram that by 1990 the expenditures required to develop Fleet 4 begin to exceed expenditures available under the 3 per cent growth assumption.[9] In the target year 2010, requirements exceed availability by 2.6 billion dollars. Under the assumption of 6 per cent growth, expenditure requirements for Fleet 4 exceed expenditure availability by 1995. In this case the shortfall in 2010 is reduced to 1.1 billion dollars.

Even though expenditure requirements exceed estimated expenditure availability for some model fleets, it is not at all implied that these fleets cannot be afforded in any absolute sense. Obviously all that is required, should a particular fleet capability be deemed sufficiently important, is that total defence expenditures be increased in each year to cover the shortfall. Assessing the desirability of additional funding of this nature would involve determining its impact both on the total defence budget and on the economy itself. To give some idea of these impacts, Table 7 indicates the revised total defence expenditures necessary in 2010 to meet the requirements for each fleet. The impact on

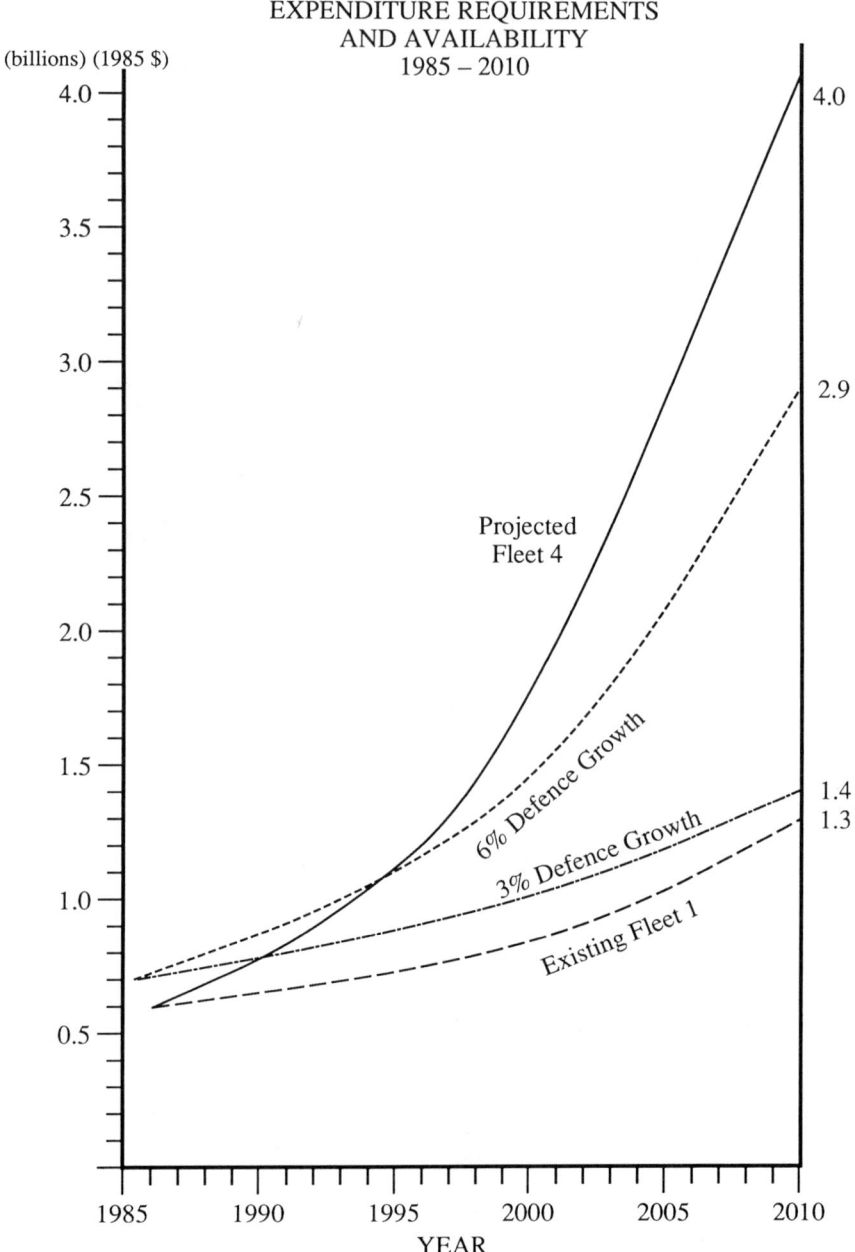

Figure 3

EXPENDITURE REQUIREMENTS AND AVAILABILITY 1985 – 2010

TABLE 7: Defence Expenditure Requirement in 2010, including Fleet Expenditure Shortfalls (billions of 1985 dollars)

	3 per cent growth		6 per cent growth	
	$	percent GNP	$	percent GNP
Projected defence expenditure	18.8	1.6	38.6	3.3
Fleet 1	18.8	1.6	38.6	3.3
Fleet 2	19.4	1.7	37.6	3.3
Fleet 3	20.6	1.8	38.9	3.4
Fleet 4	21.5	1.9	39.7	3.4
Fleet 5	25.5	2.2	43.8	3.8

the economy is indicated in terms of the revised percentage of GNP which these new defence budgets would represent. For example, to provide completely for the implementation of Fleet 4 would require total defence expenditures in 2010 to rise from the anticipated 18.8 to 21.4 billion dollars (with corresponding increases in all previous years in the planning period) under the 3 per cent growth assumption. This increase in expenditures would see the defence budget rising from 1.6 to 1.8 per cent of GNP in 2010. Under the assumption of 6 per cent defence growth, defence expenditures would rise from 38.6 to 39.8 billion dollars, or from 3.3 to 3.4 per cent of GNP.

A further consideration in assessing the affordability and desirability of the alternative model fleets is the comparison of the effectiveness provided by each relative to its cost. Specifically, a rational decisionmaker would want to know how total capability, measured in CEU-years, is improved as we move from Fleet 1 to Fleet 2, from Fleet 2 to Fleet 3, and so on, and how much required expenditures increase as we do so. Based on the effectiveness measures given in Table 3 and the expenditure requirements given in Table 4, the relationship between total effectiveness and total cost is depicted in Figure 4. The critical decision variables are not, however, total effectiveness and total expenditures, nor the ratio of total effectiveness to total expenditures. Rather, they are the ratio of "incremental" effectiveness to "incremental" expenditure, or in graphic terms, the slope of the curve in Figure 4. Thus the important questions must focus on how much extra effectiveness can be achieved by increasing expenditures by, say, 1 billion dollars.

Estimates of incremental effectiveness, incremental expenditures, and the ratio of the two are given in Table 8. As can be observed, moving from Fleet 1 to Fleet 2 yields an increase in effectiveness of 45.4 CEU-years but requires an increase in the total present value of expenditures of 1.6 billion 1985 dollars, for a gain of 28.4 CEU-years per

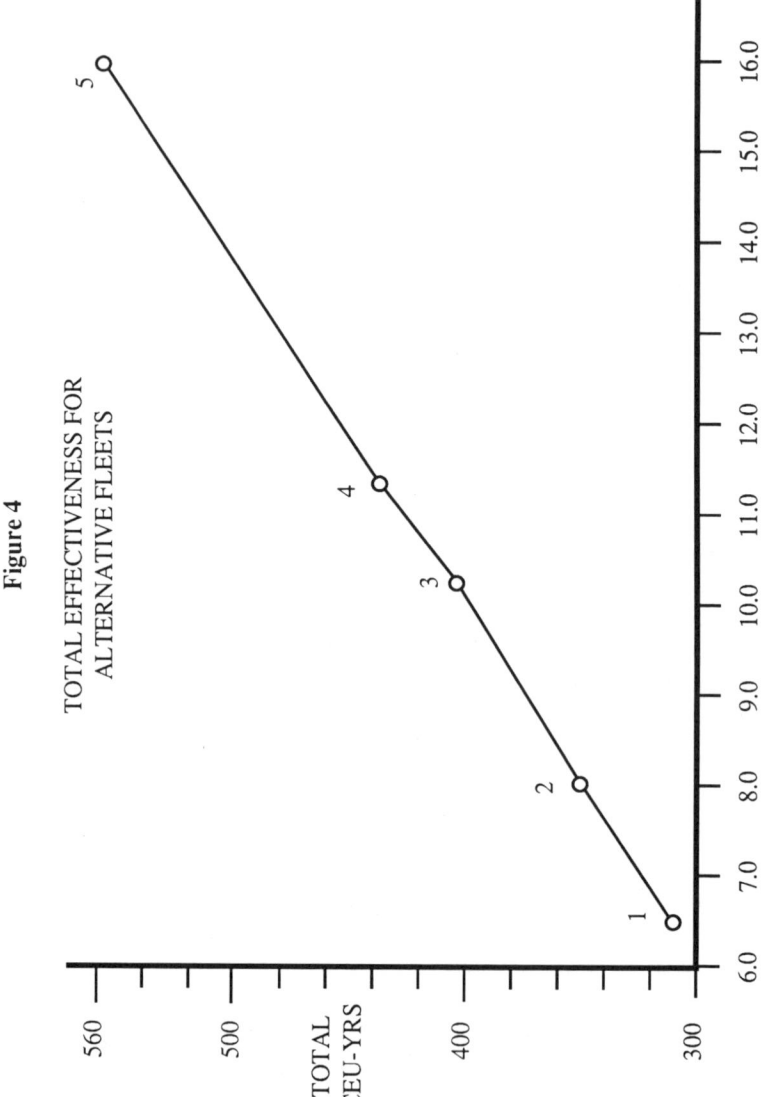

Figure 4

TOTAL EFFECTIVENESS FOR ALTERNATIVE FLEETS

TABLE 8: Effectiveness per Billion 1985 Dollar Expenditure of Alternate Proposed Fleets

Fleet	Incremental effectiveness (CEU-years)	Incremental expenditure ($billion)	Incremental effectiveness per $billion
1	—	—	—
2	45.4	1.6	28.4
3	49.0	1.9	25.8
4	32.4	1.3	24.9
5	118.8	4.9	24.2

billion dollars of expenditure. From Fleet 2 to Fleet 3 the effectiveness gain is reduced to 25.8 CEU-years per billion dollars. Moving to Fleet 4 and Fleet 5 implies reductions to 24.9 and 24.2 additional CEU-years for each additional billion dollars. What has emerged here is a situation of slightly decreasing returns (or slightly increasing costs). In other words, as fleet capabilities are expanded, effectiveness increases slightly less than proportionately to expenditures.

Information of this sort could be very useful to the decisionmaker. It puts him in the position of being able to assess whether an additional 24.2 CEU-years of effectiveness, for example, is in fact worth a billion dollars. Or could that billion dollars be allocated to some other defence activity to obtain a greater increment of effectiveness, assuming of course that effectiveness is comparable across different defence activities.

It should be clear, however, that the sort of information presented in Table 8 indicates only the "cost" of additional effectiveness; it says nothing about the "worth" of the additional effectiveness, a judgment which remains subjective and which must be considered in light of alternative expenditure opportunities facing political and military decisionmakers.

CONCLUSIONS

To anyone concerned with the growth and wellbeing of the Canadian navy, the results of this ship need-management exercise must be less than comforting. Even though our assumptions have been optimistic on the expenditure availability side and decidedly conservative on the requirements side, our analysis indicates that it will likely be possible to increase fleet capability only marginally above that of the existing fleet between now and the year 2010. If, in the rather unlikely scenario where defence expenditures are permitted to grow at a real rate of 6 per cent per year, and that rate is sustained until 2010, it would be possible to increase fleet capability by almost 75 per cent. Even under these conditions, however, the goal of a fleet built around twenty-four modern, state-of-the-art frigates would appear to be elusive. Fleets of the size proposed by Vice-Admiral Timbrell appear impossibly remote.

Our results must of course be tempered with healthy skepticism and recognized as being notional rather than definitive in intent. After all, we are attempting to project developments over a long time, when in a world of dramatic economic, political, and technological change, it is dangerous to predict what will happen tomorrow. Nevertheless, the way in which the Canadian navy will appear in twenty-five years is being conditioned by decisions taken today. Therefore, it is our contention that analysis of this nature should be done not so much to indicate where we are going but to indicate at least where it is possible to go.

Clearly there is room for improvement in our analysis. All of our assumptions are open to argument and revision. Particularly we are uncomfortable with the lack of substance in the CEU measure of capability. A better approach would be to present senior naval planners with an extensive menu of model fleet alternatives and require them to assign capability levels to each one. It should then be possible to repeat the exercise outlined in this paper and obtain improved expenditure growth paths and improved cost-effectiveness measures. The exercise would also be improved if better data on physical and technological depreciation rates for ships were available.

If one idea emerges with some force from this study it is the necessity for continuous funding of fleet maintenance and development. In the face of relentless physical and technological deterioration of ships, periodic bursts of expenditures for shipbuilding and updating is just not appropriate to the maintenance and growth of fleet capability levels.

It is, of course, one thing to argue the desirability of continuous funding and another much more difficult thing to accomplish it. Our suggestion would be to use the type of analysis described in this paper to build a case for a model fleet which could be soundly supported on the grounds of effectiveness, cost, and affordability. Next, a concerted effort could be made within the naval establishment and the broader naval community to achieve consensus on the appropriateness of this model and its target date. Efforts should then be directed to publicizing and rationalizing this fleet to such an extent that its desirability for Canadian national interests becomes an accepted conventional truth. With professional and public support, the case for a long-term funding program could then be forcefully argued in the councils of government. To protect this funding it would then be desirable to attempt to have the naval capital budget treated as an individual estimates vote separate from the current total DND capital vote. Even more preferable, and not beyond the realm of the possible, would be to convince the government that the fleet-building needs of this country are so important that their provision should be made statutory rather than subject to an annual vote. In any event, should some similar long-term commitment to continuous and appropriate funding not be forthcoming, it is likely that there will be little to celebrate in twenty-five years' time.

Chapter 16

CANADA AND MARITIME DEFENCE:
PAST PROBLEMS, FUTURE CHALLENGES*

R.B. Byers

Canada's current maritime defence policy and posture can be analyzed from a number of perspectives. Irrespective of the analysis, it is difficult, if not impossible, to avoid sobering and pessimistic assessments of inadequacy. Canada's maritime forces lack the capability to fulfil the roles and missions declared to be in the security interests of Canada. Of even greater concern is that the situation will deteriorate even further, at least into the 1990s.

The Conservative government committed itself, in principle, to review defence policy and upgrade capabilities. Prior to 1987 the government of Prime Minister Brian Mulroney had not clarified how it would rectify the shortcomings and inadequacies of Canada's defence policy and posture. The problems, which are longstanding, deep-rooted, and extend to all three services, have been particularly acute in the maritime environment. For twenty years successive Liberal governments declared that Canada had a credible defence posture and met its obligations to the Western Alliance. Many defence analysts and strategists disputed this assessment. Yet the large majority of Canadians have remained blissfully unaware of or unconcerned about the gap between the mythology of defence articulated by Liberal governments and the reality of Canada's defence policy and posture.

The May 1983 Senate report, *Canada's Maritime Defence*, aptly summed up the extent of the problem for Canada's maritime forces:

---

* This article represents a pre-1987 White Paper assessment of "Canada and Maritime Defence." For the author's views on *Challenge and Commitment: A Defence Policy for Canada*, including the priority allocated to maritime issues, see "The 1987 Defence White Paper: An Analysis," *Canadian Defence Quarterly*, Vol. 17, No. 2 (Autumn 1987).

"MARCOM, [Maritime Command], which is responsible for the country's seaward defences, cannot meet its commitments to the protection of Canadian sovereignty, to the defence of North America—much less to NATO."[1] The evidence presented to the Senate committee reflected a general consensus that the maritime forces—hereafter referred to as the navy—no longer constituted a viable military force in terms of the requirements of contemporary seapower. Both serving and retired admirals supported this position. Canada's navy had deteriorated to the point where the maritime commitment to NATO constituted a "phantom" commitment.

The deterioration of naval capabilities should be placed within the context of the decline of overall military capabilities since the mid-1960s. The most tangible indicators of military power, such as force levels, economic resources, and quantity of equipment, show that the Canadian Armed Forces (CAF) are less well off currently than twenty years ago, but commitments have been increased. In effect, a commitment-capability gap exists. All three elements—land, sea and air—have been adversely affected, but the navy's position is substantially worse than that of the army or the air force.

This paper examines the factors which have contributed to the commitment-capability gap and addresses the challenges which face the Conservative government and the Department of National Defence (DND) if the situation is to be rectified. Four areas of concern are particularly important: the economic; the political; the organizational/professional; and the policy. Within this framework the major future challenges for the navy involve sea denial-anti-submarine warfare (ASW) linkages; the nuclear threat at sea; and force structure developments.

THE ECONOMIC CONTEXT[2]

Allocations of resources for defence indicate clearly that successive governments have underfunded the defence sector for more than twenty years. Since the early 1950s, defence expenditures have not kept pace with the overall growth in federal expenditures. In the mid-1960s the Department of National Defence faced major financial difficulties. The government adopted a formula-funding approach to defence which, in one form or another, has been utilized ever since. The viability of formula-funding for defence is questionable. Versions adopted during the 1960s and early 1970s were insufficient to augment capabilities. However, as a result of the 1975 Defence Structure Review and the 1978 decision to adopt NATO's proposal that defence spending targets be set at 3 per cent real growth through to 1983–4, this situation was partially rectified. The Mulroney government has retained the formula-funding approach, but at a lower level than projected Liberal defence spending.

Four observations are important. First, spokesmen for the Mulroney government initially discussed defence spending in terms of 6 per cent real growth in order to overcome the deficiencies which face the CAF. Real growth between 1986 and 1990 is likely to average less than 2 per cent. Second, the projected 15-year equipment program to the year 2000 for DND cannot be met without increased allocations to the capital component of the budget. Third, increases recommended by the Lafond Committee in order to rebuild Canada's navy would represent a 7 per cent real increase in the defence budget; defence as a percentage of GNP would increase to about 2.2 per cent.[3] Fourth, the Mulroney government has adopted the position that the economics of defence is *the major* defence issue: that is, the government has retained the Liberal orientation. This is a false perspective for reasons discussed later in this paper.

Thus for the navy the prospects for significant increases in resources remain bleak. Most observers would agree with C.R. Nixon, former deputy minister of national defence, that "the central problem of Canada's defence situation over the past fifteen, if not twenty, years is that budgets have been inadequate to maintain the size of Canadian Forces which would be required to give substantive effect to [the country's] declared policy."[4]

However, Maritime Command appears to have fared less well than either Mobile Command or Air Command. Given the unified force structure, comparisons are difficult, but since the three commands and Canadian Forces Europe constitute the major operational combat commands, the allocation of resources by command give some sense of funding priorities. Budgetary figures[5] for the last decade indicate that Air Command has been funded at a substantially higher level than either MARCOM or Mobile Command. In 1975-6 Air Command was allocated 25.7 per cent of the defence budget, while Mobile Command received 15.8 per cent and MARCOM 13.2 per cent. This distribution pattern has since remained relatively constant. In 1986-7 the figures were 28.1, 14.7, and 19.5 per cent. Furthermore, the land and air forces assigned to Canadian Forces Europe accounted for approximately 10.2 per cent of total defence services program in 1986-7.

The distribution of the capital budget by command further illustrates the navy's problem. For the period from 1967-8 through to 1983-4, MARCOM capital expenditures averaged 3.1 per cent of the total budget while Air Command (or its equivalent) averaged 5.2 per cent and Mobile Command 3.3 per cent. Because navies are more expensive to equip and maintain than either air forces or armies, this data suggests that the navy has been more adversely affected by inadequate financial resources. Changes in the distribution of service personnel within the CAF also support this conclusion. In the early 1960s the RCN constituted some 16.6 per cent of total service personnel (21,000 of 126,000). In 1986, 11.2 per cent of the CAF was classified as naval personnel (9616 of 86,036) with an additional 4973 (5.87 per cent) air force personnel assigned to Maritime Air Group.

THE POLITICAL CONTEXT

The economic problems faced by the CAF and the implications for the navy illustrate the impact of underfunding on Canadian national security. The political considerations involved explain why this occurred.

The Trudeau era is history, but the Trudeau legacy continues to influence Canada's defence policy and posture, since the Mulroney government appears to be continuing in the Liberal tradition. Like any other sphere of public policy, defence is politics, and at the core of politics is the allocation of resources. During much of the Trudeau era—primarily the period prior to 1975—defence as public policy was almost non-existent in Canada. Politicians in Ottawa responsible for the allocation of resources did not consider defence and defence-related considerations to be significant.

Beyond this level of generalization, judgments about defence become both more complex and more personal in nature: more complex in that the lack of political priority allocated to defence stemmed from a number of sources; more personal in that individual policymakers—elected and appointed—must be held accountable for the decisions (or lack thereof) which affected Canada's defence policy and posture.

The ultimate political responsibility in Canada's political system resides with the collegial nature of cabinet decisions. The prime minister, along with the ministers of national defence, finance, and external affairs, are the key cabinet members involved with defence. The prime minister can set the tone and agenda for the priorities adopted by the government but in many instances cannot do so unilaterally or without regard for cabinet colleagues or other individuals who influence policy decisions. All policymakers, the prime minister included, are circumscribed and constrained when policy decisions are ultimately agreed upon by cabinet. Yet, Mr Trudeau had a profound influence on Canada's defence policy and posture. After becoming prime minister, Mr Trudeau was determined to adopt a more collegial foreign and defence policy process at the cabinet level. This accounted, in part, for the wide-ranging and relatively open debate among cabinet ministers during the 1968-9 foreign and defence review.[6]

By the mid-1970s the international political and strategic environment, along with East-West relations, had begun to deteriorate. This changed international situation convinced some advisors to urge Mr Trudeau to reassess Canada's defence policy and issue a new defence White Paper.[7] He rejected this advice on the grounds that the policy statements based on the 1968-9 review remained appropriate. Mr Trudeau's personal opposition was likely the major explanation for the unwillingness of successive ministers of national defence through to 1984 to support a review of defence policy. In addition, senior DND officials were concerned that a defence review would circumscribe the re-equipment program that was approved by the 1975 Defence Structure Review.

Compared with the Pearson era, the policy framework of the Trudeau era downgraded the importance of national and international security. Mr Trudeau's relatively benign view of the Soviet threat placed considerable emphasis on East-West accommodation. With detente, military power declined in importance and less emphasis was placed on the need to ensure deterrence credibility. This period was short-lived, but Mr Trudeau failed to appreciate sufficiently the links between defence and foreign policy. As such the political utility of Canada's defence commitments were suspect. The prime minister appeared to reject the proposition that a direct relationship existed between adequately meeting defence commitments and the extent to which Canada had a voice within the Western Alliance.

Other significant factors affected Canada's defence environment. Both external affairs and national defence assumed less importance during the early Trudeau era. This was compounded by a number of relatively weak ministers, especially in the defence portfolio. Because defence issues remained a low priority for both the prime minister and his government, the defence portfolio assumed less importance. The Mulroney government has rectified this situation by allocating increased importance to the defence portfolio. With the publication of a defence White Paper, overall policy guidance should exist for DND.

During most of the Trudeau era, parliament provided no political counterweight to the government. Neither the Conservatives nor the New Democrats formulated defence policy options, and defence issues were not debated in the House of Commons. Through their acquiescence, the political parties agreed with the government's approach. The Standing Committee on External Affairs and National Defence (SCEAND) made no meaningful contribution, except to review

NORAD. Only when the Senate Committee on Foreign Affairs established the subcommittee on National Defence did this situation change.

Public attitudes and policymakers' perceptions of these attitudes also affected the political context for defence. Public apathy toward defence issues prevailed during the 1970s. No public debate took place and the public appeared satisfied with the way defence issues were handled. The media for the most part was ill-informed or ignored defence-related matters. The role and influence of interest groups in the defence sector was minimal.

Given the political environment of the late 1960s and the 1970s, it was not surprising that defence-related issues and the CAF were of secondary concern. The situation would have been even worse were it not for pressure from Canada's allies. The Mulroney government, however, has stated that defence is a public policy priority and has indicated that Canada would make a more credible and sustainable contribution to Western security than before.[8] Yet it still remains unclear how this will be implemented.

Within this environment, the navy fared worse than the army and the air force. John Anderson, as assistant deputy minister (policy), pointed out that "Canadians who live in the major centres of population tend to be in the central part of the country, and tend to forget just how dependent on the sea they are, how much coastline they have, and what a major interest they have in being protected at sea."[9] Psychologically, the navy and the oceans have not been part of the Canadian political or military tradition, at least for most central Canadians, including most elected politicians.

THE ORGANIZATIONAL/PROFESSIONALISM CONTEXT

Unification of the CAF had a more profound and negative impact on the Canadian navy than it did on either the army or the air force. While many senior army and air force officers opposed unification, the navy emerged as the main opposition within DND. The political opposition to unification was primarily attributed to the "Admirals Revolt," and both Admiral Brock and Admiral Landymore assumed prominent roles in the attempt to save the identity of the RCN.[10]

For the navy, unification remained a constant reminder of the RCN's demise. Pressure from retired service personnel greatly influenced the establishment by the Clark government of the Fyffe Committee on Unification in 1979. Senior retired naval officers argued for a return to a tri-service organization for defence with individual service identity, but the *Fyffe Report* did not heed this advice.[11] After the 1980 election, the resurrected Trudeau government had no inclination to alter fundamentally Canada's organization for defence.

Despite Liberal reluctance to alter the status quo, proponents of service identity continued to press their case. Commodore Robert Hendy RCNR (ret'd) argued before the Lafond Committee that as a result of unification "the navy has been forced to strike its battle ensign, had its uniform ridiculed, its senior officers retired and long held traditions disparaged."[12] During the 1984 election campaign the Conservatives supported distinctive uniforms for each of the three services, and as a government they moved quickly to implement this campaign promise.

A return to navy blue will not, however, resolve the other negative effects of unification's organizational changes for the navy, which, compared with the army and air force, lost political and bureaucratic influence and power as a result of these changes. Assessments are subjective, but the selection of only one naval officer among the nine Chiefs of Defence Staff (CDS) appointed since unification would support this view.

The position of the CDS can be crucial in the overall direction and evolution of the Canadian forces. Contrary to the claims of unification, the integrated defence structure did not eliminate inter-service rivalry.[13] In competing for scarce resources, each of the three services still had to make a claim for capital equipment. General Jacques Dextraze, who was CDS between 1972 and 1977, commented on the problems relating to priorities and individual service requirements: "I certainly fought, when I was Chief of the Defence Staff for the requirements of all branches of the services to be recognized. I know the naval requirement was a heavy one. Of course, we started with the air force and the army. I should have said the army and the air force; being an army man I suppose, I put the army first."[14]

The extent to which senior naval officers were able to make a case for the navy is important. Testimony before the Lafond Committee indicated that policymakers in National Defence Headquarters (NDHQ) often lacked sufficient appreciation of the operational requirements of the various commands. Not surprisingly, senior naval officers have argued forcefully for the location of the service heads at NDHQ in Ottawa, rather than in the field as operational commanders.[15] This issue should be addressed by the Mulroney government.

Of further significance is whether naval issues within NDHQ have been adequately articulated and promoted by senior naval planners and commanders to the government and to the attentive public. Has a real case been made for the Canadian navy? Who has made the case? This is part of a larger problem. Observers of Canada's defence scene have referred to the lack of an independent analytical capability to assess strategic issues affecting the country's defence policy and posture.[16] This is true for both the private and the public sector. DND has acknowledged the deficiencies of its strategic planning process and is in the process of taking steps to rectify "major shortcomings" in such areas as strategic assessment, defence posture assessments, capabilities planning guidance, and force development guides.[17]

Irrespective of overall assessments, does the Canadian officer corps, and more particularly the senior officer corps, place enough emphasis on developing the necessary expertise to assess the strategic issues which affect Canadian policy? Neither the officer corps as a body nor its naval component attach much importance to strategic analysis. Yet Canada's officer corps historically has prided itself on a high degree of military professionalism. Despite all the problems of the Trudeau era, senior retired personnel have drawn solace in the professionalism of the Canadian Forces. But while operational professionalism is essential, it is not sufficient for an effective multidimensional approach to the profession of arms. Canada's officer corps does not exhibit the multidimensional character incorporating all the major attributes of the profession of arms which affect and interact with security-related issues.[18] This judgment pertains to all three services but appears to be particularly applicable to the navy.

In the past, senior naval officers at both NDHQ and MARCOM failed to appreciate sufficiently the strategic environment. They have had to be concerned with force structures and the continued operation of outmoded equipment. However, the relationships between seapower and Canada's maritime interests, within a naval environment in which nuclear weapons assume a central role, have been downplayed or ignored. Unless and until the navy is able to place greater emphasis on strategic analysis, policymakers in Ottawa will fail to grasp the importance of seapower for Canadian national security.

THE POLICY CONTEXT

Canada's defence activities and postures have been affected by the interrelationships between two major approaches to defence: collective self-defence within the Western Alliance, and the pursuit of Canadian security interests, particularly Canadian sovereignty. In terms of a new defence White Paper, these two approaches should constitute the major policy perspectives. The overall objectives of the White Paper should reflect the basic continuity of defence policy regarding NATO, NORAD, peacekeeping, Canadian sovereignty, and arms limitation.

Despite continuity of objectives, the implementation and interpretation of Canadian defence policy has been marked by ambivalence, confusion, inconsistency, and dissent. The shifting priorities between roles, missions, and capabilities demanded by a commitment to military interdependence have all too often clashed with sovereignty-related objectives. At the risk of overstatement, the 1964 defence White Paper emphasized collective self-defence, while the 1971 defence White Paper placed greater emphasis on the need to pursue sovereignty interests, especially surveillance and control.

Both documents reflected the relative shift in priorities concerning maritime defence policy and posture. In 1964 the government indicated that military interdependence was the order of the day for the RCN, and continued emphasis on anti-submarine warfare (ASW) was the appropriate priority for the navy. Yet, despite the recommendations of the 1961 *Brock Report*[19] concerning force structure requirements, the 1964 White Paper made no commitment to augment naval capabilities. At the outset of the Trudeau era, however, the navy was told to place greater emphasis on roles and missions related to sovereignty and independence. The 1971 White Paper stated that "Canada's maritime forces must be reoriented with the long term objective of providing a more versatile general purpose capability."[20]

In retrospect, neither White Paper dealt adequately with Canada's maritime interests or the importance of seapower for Canadian and Western security. No attempt was made to articulate clearly the roles and missions for the navy. The dilemmas posed during the Trudeau era by the shift in emphasis from a navy based on sea denial roles and missions to one tasked with naval presence roles and missions constituted the most significant policy development for the Canadian navy in the post-1945 era. The declaration that Canada's maritime forces would emphasize a naval presence navy with some (limited) sea denial emphasis ran contrary to the traditional Canadian approach to naval operations.

Emphasis on naval presence meant that sovereignty-related missions would become the primary maritime objective, the short war scenario in Europe would be the probable outcome of an East-West conflict, and Canada's maritime contribution to the Western Alliance could be symbolic. A sea denial emphasis, however, would have meant that maritime contributions to Western security would be as important as sovereignty requirements, Canada's maritime contribution should enhance deterrence credibility, the long war scenario could prevail, and in the future Canada could require an independent sea denial capability.[21]

The long-term implications should have been more clearly stated at the beginning of the Trudeau era: a sea denial navy can perform naval presence roles and missions, but a navy structured on naval presence tasks cannot operate within a high threat sea denial environment. Unfortunately, neither naval spokesmen nor other senior DND officials were able to convince the government to address this dilemma more openly. For example, the 1968–9 SCEAND review did not focus on maritime requirements. Nevertheless, the SCEAND report of 26 March 1969 led to the establishment of a subcommittee on Maritime Forces which reported to the House in mid-1970. The *Penner Report* clearly opted for the naval presence option and also argued for the importance of sovereignty and enforcement of extraterritorial jurisdiction, thereby downgrading the importance of ASW. In reaching its conclusions, the committee discounted convoy requirements, limited nuclear war at sea, naval support for UN peacekeeping, and military surface operations in the Arctic.[22]

After publication of the 1971 White Paper, neither the defence minister nor other government officials addressed directly the shift in naval policy other than to confirm government priorities and agree with the main policy recommendations of the *Penner Report*.[23] A SCEAND review focussed almost exclusively on issues related to sovereignty and the protection of Canada. Though its report did not explicitly address naval issues, the Navy League of Canada and the Naval Officers Association of Canada (NOAC) presented briefs discussing the manner in which the government handled naval issues. The Navy League brief noted that "the White Paper seems deficient in defining a precise military role for the maritime forces ... One cannot quarrel with the importance ... of sovereignty ... but it must be recognized that a military force, to be operative, must be capable of military action to counter encroachments upon Canada's interests." The brief argued that "in terms of 'surveillance' Canada might have an adequate capability but in terms of 'protection' a more extensive defence system is required."[24] In a similar manner, the NOAC presentation argued that "the White Paper does *not* define 'general purpose role' and without realistic role definitions, it is impossible to establish the proportions of the whole that would be assigned to each function."[25]

The inability of defence officials and senior naval officers to present a strategically coherent and cogent case for ASW affected maritime priorities during the Trudeau era. The government accepted the 1970 *Penner Report* judgment that the navy's ASW rationale was suspect. The report adopted the view that the Nuclear-Powered Ballistic Missile Submarine (SSBN) equipped with Sea-Launched Ballistic Missiles (SLBM's) "has fundamentally changed the nature of antisubmarine warfare from that of World War II and the immediate postwar period when Canada began to specialize in ASW."[26]

Several points regarding the ASW debate of the late 1960s and early

1970s[27] are worth noting. First, the DND rationale for ASW specialization was deemed to have become "in more recent years ... more vague."[28] Not surprisingly, the *Penner Report* rejected attempts by navy spokesmen to make an undifferentiated case for ASW based on the submarine qua submarine as a threat. Second, the traditional tactical ASW role for convoys against the attack submarine threat—point ASW—was discounted, given the acceptance of the short war scenario in Europe by Supreme Allied Commander Europe (SACEUR) and DND officials. Third, the navy argued that ASW operations against Soviet SSBN's—strategic ASW—were necessary, given their presence off North America.

The confusion and ambivalence within DND regarding implementation and interpretation of Canada's new defence policy was compounded by the NDHQ's reorganization into an integrated (civil-military) structure and the financial crisis resulting from the defence budget freeze. Only at the time of the 1975 Defence Structure Review did DND officially clarify links between new defence roles and specific defence objectives and tasks. The review linked the four major roles in *Defence in the 70s* to 15 objectives and 55 operational and 11 miscellaneous tasks; of the 55 operational tasks at least 22, in one form or another, were maritime-specific. The review's objectives by themselves offered no explicit guidance with regard to priorities for the navy. The *Lafond Report* expressed dismay with the approach adopted by DND, recommending that this situation be clarified and priorities be clearly established. The report recommended that greater emphasis be allocated to sea denial roles and missions and that capabilities be augmented with the view to make a more credible maritime contribution to NATO.[29] In effect, the debate had come full circle—from sea denial to naval presence and back to sea denial—but the fifteen-year interval had taken its toll.

However, it should be noted that DND and the navy had established priorities which did not conform—either in substance or in inclination—to those of the 1971 White Paper. Officials within DND were less than enthusiastic about quasi-military and non-military roles. DND supported the White Paper priorities in principle but made sure that, to the extent possible, military tasks remained at the operational core of defence activities. A review of the annual DND reports for the post-1971 period indicate an emphasis on roles and missions related to collective self-defence. By the early 1980s the military and political-strategic environment had deteriorated, and the assumptions of the 1971 White Paper were no longer valid. Even the Liberals came to accept the view that Canadian security was primarily a function of

Western security, and that Canada should make more of a contribution to collective self-defence.

For the Canadian navy, DND's response of 26 March 1984 to the *Lafond Report* clarified the extent to which the interpretation of government policy had evolved since the early 1970s. The DND statement indicated clearly that sea denial roles and missions now constituted the basis of Canada's maritime defence policy. The Canadian navy had been tasked with two primary missions: (a) "defending, in conjunction with US and NATO forces, the maritime approaches to North America and the sea areas vital to NATO"; and (b) "conducting in conjunction with US forces, surveillance to detect, track and identify submarine forces threatening North America."[30]

If adequate capabilities existed to fulfil these primary missions, then DND claims that secondary missions related to sovereignty and other tasks would be met. The extent to which the Mulroney government would incorporate these missions as central to maritime defence policy remained unclear as of late 1986.

FUTURE CHALLENGES

Canada's maritime interests and the importance of seapower have been clearly articulated by senior DND officials. Mr Anderson stressed the importance of the geopolitical links within the Western Alliance and other democracies which constitute "scattered bastions linked by oceanic highways." Thus "the ability of the western alliance to move naval and mercantile shipping despite any Soviet opposition has become increasingly critical to credible deterrence and effective conventional defence."[31] Admiral N. Brodeur noted the necessity for the West to retain naval superiority since "NATO's war can be lost at sea, but the Warsaw Pact's war cannot."[32] However, deterrence remains the cornerstone of Western security policy, and in the words of the chief of DND's operational research and analysis, Dr George Lindsey: "All of us hope, and many believe, that strategic nuclear deterrence will continue to prevent World War III, nuclear or conventional, limited or unlimited."[33]

However, the operationalization of deterrence has become one of the most controversial security issues of the 1980s.[34] Both Moscow and Washington committed themselves to maintaining strategic stability and reducing the risks of nuclear war at the time of the 1979 SALT II treaty. Yet no consensus emerged on the requirements for deterrence. Canadian governments, committed to the principles of mutual deterrence and strategic stability, have been unwilling to become publicly involved in the strategy debate within the West or between East and West.

The central challenge for Canadian maritime defence policy is to ensure that Canada's maritime forces are tasked and structured to enhance the credibility and stability of deterrence. The links between deterrence and primary naval missions are crucial. Canada's primary missions require the navy to operate within the context of military interdependence where nuclear deterrence and nuclear weapons assume central importance. This poses both policy and operational problems which were not adequately addressed by either the Lafond Committee or by DND's 1984 response to the *Lafond Report*.

The first issue of substance concerns the relationship between the sea-based deterrent and ASW. Current American strategic doctrine has an important countervailing component based on nuclear warfighting principles and the further acquisition of such assets. Yet, assured destruction considerations remain important and thus a hybrid doctrine exists. For the United States Navy (USN), the strategic logic of the strategy places greater emphasis on strategic ASW as a naval mission than was the case when Mutual Assured Destruction (MAD) formed the core of American doctrine.[35]

Even though most analysts agree that a strategic ASW capability is neither technologically nor operationally feasible (in the foreseeable future), the USN continues to place considerable emphasis on augmenting ASW capabilities which could be tasked for such missions. Give the Maritime Strategy of the USN, political and bureaucratic pressure could be felt by American administrations to place even greater emphasis on strategic ASW missions.

Canada's maritime defence policy diverges from the strategy adopted by the United States. DND statements regarding naval missions and force structure developments implicitly indicate a continuing commitment to MAD. In terms of force structure developments, DND according to the proceedings of the Lafond Committee, did not intend to acquire "nuclear submarines or nuclear weapons, nor to develop anti-submarine capabilities solely or primarily for strategic purposes."[36] The acquisition of nuclear-powered attack submarines (SSN's) indicates some departure from this position, but presumably the SSN's are not intended for "strategic purposes."

This position of maintaining a commitment to the retention of the viability of the Soviet sea-based deterrent in order to enhance mutual deterrence constitutes sound policy and a prudent approach to seapower. In light of the range profile of the SS-N-8/18/20 SLBM's, there is no need for Soviet SSBN's to operate in ocean space outside of the North Norwegian Sea, the Barents Sea, the Sea of Okhotsk, and possibly parts of the Arctic. The logical extension of DND's position is for the Canadian government to urge the superpowers officially to recognize the need to retain the viability of the sea-based deterrent and to establish SSBN sanctuaries as part of a confidence-building regime.

However, DND's position on ASW requires clarification. Admiral J.C. Wood has maintained that it is necessary for the navy to "conduct, in conjunction with US forces, surveillance over Soviet strategic submarine forces threatening North America."[37] The purpose of this mission is to "determine their location and deployment patterns to ensure timely detection of any changes in those patterns which would give warning of Soviet intention to attack." This is deemed important since Yankee Class SSBN's "must deploy to launch positions and ocean areas for which Canada has been assigned and accepted responsibility, in order to strike targets in North America."[38] Furthermore, naval planners are concerned with the threat posed by Soviet developments of sea launch cruise missiles (SLCM's).

Of these two threats, the Yankee Class is relatively insignificant. During the 1970s the Yankee Class constituted the major component of the Soviet sea-based deterrent. Since then, however, the Delta Class and now the Typhoon Class have become operational and Yankee Class SSBN's are being converted to SSN's. By the mid-1990s it is unlikely that Yankee Class SSBN's will remain operational. In addition, given the military value of the Delta and Typhoon Class SSBN's, coupled with the range of their SLBMs, it is not likely that they will be deployed into those areas of ocean space currently patrolled by Yankee Class SSBN's. The SLCM threat, however, poses more complex strategic issues. The Soviet Union has tested successfully the SS-NX-21 with an estimated range of 3000 kilometres. This system could be deployed on new classes of Soviet SSN's, including the Akula, Mike, and Sierra Class. Yankee Class SSBN's are reported to be reconfigured with the SS-NX-24 SLCM.

The roles of SLCM's remain controversial, but as Soviet deployments proceed, the military threat to North America could be substantial. Nevertheless, SLCM's are not first-strike systems and presumably would be held in strategic reserve. If so, they would constitute nuclear war-fighting systems to be employed if deterrence failed. Thus, for DND to advocate a strategic surveillance/warning mission against SLCM's does not appear to be strategically viable, nor does it constitute a cost-effective use of scarce resources.

In terms of MARCOM's current operational planning, the strategic surveillance missions require the capability to detect, locate, identify, and trail Soviet SSBN's/SSGN's (Guided Missile Nuclear Submarine) in the North Atlantic: all the stages for ASW except the final stage—destruction. NDHQ has been reluctant to advocate full-scope ASW for the navy on at least two grounds. First, full-scope ASW could require the acquisition of nuclear systems, particularly SSN's, and possibly nuclear weapons. Second, strategic ASW constitutes a destabilizing naval mission. The ASW situation is further complicated by an unduly restricted interpretation of "strategic" as distinct from "tactical" ASW. Changes in Soviet and American seapower capabilities require a more differentiated categorization of ASW into three different types: strategic, theatre, and tactical. Strategic ASW could entail missions against SSBN's in those regions classified as SSBN operating areas/havens. Tactical ASW could continue to be categorized as point defence ASW of both military and merchant assets. Theatre ASW could be defined as area defence to cope with Soviet submarine intrusions into NATO operating regions. Theatre ASW would not destabilize the strategic environment, as the operational requirements for Soviet SSBN's to patrol within NATO regions are minimal, even though this is not the case for SSGN's equipped with SLCM's. Should these distinctions be adopted by the navy, then it would be appropriate to assess the extent to which theatre ASW missions would require the navy to develop full-scope ASW capabilities within clearly defined geographical regions.

A second challenge which has not been addressed sufficiently by either the Canadian government or by DND, including the navy, is the relationship between primary naval missions and nuclear weapons, especially theatre/tactical nuclear weapons for war-fighting purposes. This issue is of particular importance since Canada's maritime forces must operate in a military environment at sea that is becoming increasingly reliant on naval nuclear weapons for general purpose roles, including sea denial.

The extent of the problem can be summarized briefly by the case of the USN. The USN has more than 340 major combatants of which 85 per cent are nuclear capable. In addition to 5700 SLBM's, the United States currently deploys some 2700 tactical nuclear weapons for general purpose naval missions, numbers that will increase substantially during the next decade. Thus even greater emphasis will be placed on nuclear deployments for sea control/sea denial missions. The same trend is occurring within the Soviet navy. Nuclearization at sea is continuing at an accelerated rate.[39]

Current and future deployments of theatre/tactical nuclear weapons at sea confer military-strategic advantages on the Soviet navy at the expense of Western security.[40] The use of nuclear weapons for these purposes is disadvantageous to Western naval assets given the size and structure of NATO—especially American—naval forces. Finally, the larger number of Soviet naval platforms would suggest that the Soviets can deploy a far larger number of theatre/tactical nuclear weapons should the current trends continue.

Most naval analysts and defence planners agree that the extent of nuclearization at sea means that the prospect of any conflict at sea remaining conventional is unlikely. The naval strategic environment has changed considerably since the late 1960s when the *Penner Report* argued that the problems of limited nuclear war at sea were not important. The pending large-scale deployments of SLCM's, in conjunction with Soviet land-based naval assets, would most likely extend a nuclear war at sea beyond ocean space.

Given the inter-operability of American and Canadian naval forces, current Canadian nuclear weapons policy places the Canadian navy in a disadvantageous position should deterrence fail. The logical extension of the current maritime strategic environment would indicate that Canada may have to acquire nuclear weapons in order to fulfill primary naval missions. This issue, unfortunately, has not been analyzed and discussed within the public domain. However, many senior naval commanders would prefer to de-emphasize reliance on nuclear weapons for general purpose naval missions. Furthermore, new conventional technologies and weapons might be nearly as effective as nuclear weapons in performing sea denial missions, which suggests that the reliance on theatre/tactical weapons at sea might be overrated. Thus on military-strategic grounds, Canadian security and the role of the navy would be enhanced if our allies and the Soviets could be convinced to place less reliance on such weapon systems.

Here the question of naval arms limitation becomes particularly important. Both the United States and the Soviet Union advocate deep cuts in nuclear arsenals. US President Reagan's view of the Strategic Defense Initiative is based on the premise that the nuclear threat and nuclear weapons can, hopefully, be eliminated. Canadian government policy advocates reductions in the nuclear capabilities of both superpowers. Unfortunately, not one of today's arms limitation negotiations has responsibility for addressing the deployment of theatre/tactical weapons at sea. These types of nuclear weapons, with the exception of SLCM's, have been omitted from the arms limitation agenda. Canada could make a positive contribution to arms limitation and also enhance Western security if the government were to initiate the necessary steps to advocate the review of these types of nuclear weapons within the appropriate arms limitation context. It is also important, from the defence perspective, to ascertain the degree to which the reduction/elimination of theatre/tactical nuclear weapons could be offset by conventional naval capabilities. Unfortunately, the Mulroney government has not been willing to consider this issue from either the defence or arms limitation perspective. Yet it is essential for the Canadian government and the Canadian Forces to pursue those arms control issues that directly affect Canadian security and the operational ability of the CAF. *Canadian content*, essential in Canada's arms limitation policy, should be directly related to these concerns.[41]

Current American and NATO naval policy pose a third challenge. "SACLANT's strategy calls for a 'bottling-up' of the main Soviet fleet in the northern reaches of the Atlantic and the Mediterranean."[42] Canada's lack of capabilities would make it politically and militarily irresponsible to commit existing Canadian surface forces to this mission. Current operational plans appear to acknowledge this problem.

Dr Lindsey has stated that a third Battle of the Atlantic "would almost certainly involve the full participation of nearly all the Canadian maritime forces."[43] The USN and the RN would be utilized to execute (if this were possible) the forward strategy. Admiral Wood has suggested that the forward strategy would take into account that some Soviet breakout must be anticipated because some Soviet submarine assets "would be free to harass the sea lines of communication."[44] The possible deployment of Backfire-B naval aircraft with air-to-surface missiles over the North Atlantic must be considered. Canada's responsibility would be to fill in the gaps. This indicates that the Canadian navy would operate independently in a high threat environment. A point defence ASW capability must be complemented by a viable anti-air capability, otherwise Canadian naval forces would be vulnerable.

A fourth challenge concerns the Arctic as a special case. Most DND officials, including naval officers, have argued that the direct military threat to the north is minimal. Surface/subsurface naval missions in the Arctic are being contemplated, as Professor Critchley points out in Chapter 14, but as of late 1986 they had not been advocated as a vital military necessity by DND. Continuing pressure from the non-governmental sector to increase Canada's military presence in the North for sovereignty purposes has had some effect on policy. The Polar Star voyage of mid-1985 reinforced these arguments and on 12 September 1985 the government announced policy initiatives including augmented military operations to protect Canadian sovereignty interests. Canadian sovereignty in the North must be protected, in part, by the CAF, and this could best be accomplished by establishing a base in the eastern Arctic. A military subsurface capability may eventually be required, since the government acknowledges that Soviet submarines are being deployed under the ice pack.[45] However, there has been insufficient data on which to base a strategic judgement.[46] If there is a military threat an icebreaker operated by the navy is obviously an inadequate response. Future developments remain both controversial and to some extent unclear. The acquisition of SSN's would give MARCOM considerable flexibility, but it seems likely the Arctic will be more of a transit route than a regular patrol area. SSN's would, however, be more important for sea control and sea denial purposes.

Regardless of government-approved maritime force structures, re-equipping the Canadian navy will be a lengthy and costly process. The navy of the mid- to late 1990s will be a function of a number of factors: the degree of support from the Canadian people for defence as public policy; the political support and direction offered by the Canadian government, including realistic and timely policy statements on defence; the management of DND in a manner which makes the most effective use of limited resources; and the professionalism of the naval officer corps.

The current government-approved force structure model, based primarily on peacetime rather than wartime requirements, has never been fully costed. Unless and until force structure developments are placed within a realistic, long-term framework, the CAF will be forced to meet commitments with inadequate capabilities. Defence dollars must be spent for defence, and Canada's defence policy and posture must enhance deterrence stability. The real challenge is a political, military, organizational, and economic one to bridge the commitment-capability gap and avoid the mistakes of the Trudeau era.

Chapter 17

THE FUTURE OF NAVAL WARFARE

G.R. Lindsey

MAJOR HISTORICAL DEVELOPMENTS IN NAVAL WARFARE IN THE LAST SEVENTY-FIVE YEARS

Some historians dislike, even resent, the use of history to forecast the future. Others do not object to the practice, though they do not choose to take part themselves. This difference is to be found amongst maritime historians and among those attempting to forecast matters such as the future of sea power.

During the seventy-five years from 1910 to 1985, the history of sea power has developed at an uneven pace. Steady technological progress during the quarter century prior to 1914 allowed the First World War to be fought at sea with highly developed, fast, armoured warships armed with efficient long-range guns, with submarines good enough almost to win the first Battle of the Atlantic, and with wireless permitting instant communication over extremely long distances. The next twenty years saw more naval disarmament than development, but advances were made with aircraft carriers and naval aircraft. Many warships saw service in both world wars. The major technological improvements made during the Second World War were in detection equipment (radar and sonar), many aspects of naval aviation, more capable submarines, and the development of the vehicles needed for amphibious assault and for maintenance of a large fleet far from its permanent bases and sources of supply. The forty years since the Second World War, which represent over one-third of the age of mechanical propulsion, have brought some fundamentally new developments as well as steady improvements to most of the inherited technologies. The most significant of the new technologies include guided missiles, nuclear weapons, nuclear propulsion, helicopters, and ocean surveillance satellites. The older technologies have been substantially improved in the case of aircraft, aircraft carriers, sonar, radar, and communications.

Turning from technology to strategy, the profound effect of Mahan's writings (between 1884 and 1911) should be noted. Although based on the history of the age of sail, his theories were applied to naval planning in the age of steam. Up to the First World War, and consistent with Mahanian philosophy, priorities in naval building programs went to battleships and the associated craft needed to protect them. Between 1914 and the Battle of Jutland in May 1916, the main attention of the British and German navies was devoted to strategies for a major fleet engagement. In fact, Jutland was the only major fleet engagement between Tsushima in 1905 and the Pacific battles of 1942, and there have been none since 1944, so that history provides plenty of theory and planning but only limited actual experience regarding great surface battles in the twentieth century.

Key developments in the naval strategy of the First World War were the economic blockade of the Central Powers by the Allies and, even more important, the campaign by Germany in 1917 and 1918 to cut the sea lines of communication of the Allies by unrestricted submarine warfare. Although historical lessons were available to them from the days of sail, the Allies were slow to turn to convoy for the defence of merchant shipping. By a narrow margin it allowed them to overcome the U-boat menace. Another campaign of note centred on the Allied effort to open the Dardanelles in 1915, resulting in a failure of warships to force passage through minefields covered by shore batteries and the failure of a large amphibious assault to overcome determined resistance on land.

Naval planning between the wars discounted the capability of the submarine for economic blockade, though giving considerable attention to the threat of surface warships for the same purpose. Another mistake, for which historical evidence was not available, was to neglect the vulnerability of surface ships to air attack and, consequently, the superiority of aircraft carriers to battleships as means to establish command of the sea.

The naval history of the Second World War demonstrated above everything else the striking power of aircraft against surface ships. Although surface ships could defend themselves to a certain extent with multiple anti-aircraft armament, the best protection came from friendly fighter aircraft, whether land-based or embarked on carriers. In many ways the experience of the First World War was repeated with regard to submarine warfare. Axis submarines came very close to cutting the supply lines of their maritime Allied opponents, but they were defeated by both convoys (defended by escort ships equipped with radar and sonar) and aircraft, both land-based and embarked. American submarines succeeded in interdicting the Japanese maritime communications in the Western Pacific, while maintaining their own, owing in part to the face that the Japanese considered submarines as weapons to be used against warships rather than merchant ships. Having been expelled from the European mainland, and facing strong Axis forces in Africa and the Pacific Islands, the Allies were obliged to develop the technique of large-scale amphibious assault on heavily defended coasts. And in the vast reaches of the Pacific Ocean the US Navy had to develop a mammoth fleet train able to sustain forces thousands of miles from their main bases.

Aircraft carriers played central roles in most of these operations, the large attack carriers being the key elements in establishing sea control and in projecting power ashore, while smaller escort carriers proved valuable for anti-submarine warfare beyond the range of land-based air. Battleships could not exercise their previous role as the main element of sea control, though they proved useful for shore bombardment during amphibious assault. Cruisers and destroyers had important roles in the fight for sea control and in anti-aircraft defence, but most of the responsibility for anti-submarine defence fell on aircraft and on smaller escort vessels of the corvette and frigate classes.

Radar, barely at the stage of operational use at the beginning of the Second World War, went through rapid and highly successful development for practical application at sea, in the air, and on land. A warship able to detect other ships out to the horizon in conditions of bad visibility had a decisive advantage over an opponent without this capability. Gunfire became far more accurate, where range and fall of shot were measured by radar. However, the most potent application of radar at sea was against submarines, which needed to spend a lot of time on the surface. British anti-submarine aircraft were able to detect surfaced U-boats charging their batteries at night; they could approach to close range before illuminating the target with a powerful "Leigh Light" and attacking with depth charges. But when the U-boats fitted the "Metox" receiver they were able to detect the airborne radar at long range and dive if it approached them. A continuing battle of measure and countermeasure was waged, both technical and tactical, including radar, radio navigation, and communications.

The ability to intercept wireless communications and to decypher messages was of great importance for many major activities in the Second World War, not least for the defence of convoys against submarine attack. As with the other types of electronic warfare, measure begat countermeasure. Careful precautions were taken not to exploit information in such a way that the enemy could deduce its source. The secrecy was preserved for many years after the war. The sequel is a continuing effort to intercept transmissions, using satellites as well as receivers on land, sea, and in the air, to create unbreakable cyphers, and to break them, using the most powerful computers available.

The chronology of sonar is somewhat different from that of radar. Developed in the First World War, it was expected to keep submarines relatively ineffective in a future war. Such was not the case with the ships' hull-mounted sonar, which was unable to detect a submarine on the surface, beneath a refracting layer, in shallow water, or when the ship was nearly over its target. The most important advances in sonar came after the Second World War, when great improvements were achieved. Hull-mounted active sonars were made far more powerful and accurate. Dipping sonar was provided for helicopters. The greatest strides were made with passive sonar, especially in submarines, in air-dropped sonobuoys relaying their signals to fixed-wing aircraft, helicopters, and surface ships, and in fixed sonar systems mounted on the sea bottom. More recently, passive sonar has reached new levels of performance with towed arrays: long strings of hydrophones towed behind a surface ship or submarine.

Subsequent to the Second World War there has been a dearth of active naval engagements. There were, however, military campaigns which could not have taken place but for sea control and the existence of secure sea lines of communication, and there were situations in which naval presence and capability had great influence. Such events are examples of seapower, whether or not violence was done at sea. In fact, the future history of seapower may focus on capabilities and implicit threats rather than on active naval engagements. Capabilities and implicit threats depend on vehicles and weapons, but in peacetime the real capabilities of the vehicles and weapons must be surmised from their technical characteristics and their performance in routine operations at sea and in exercises, which is not as informative or convincing as is the history of performance in battle. It may, however, be the only history we will have.

- The United Nations action in Korea in the early 1950s and the long campaigns by the French (1947–54) and then the United States (1964–73) in Indo-China were only possible because of the complete sea control exercised by the Western countries. North Korea and North Vietnam were unable to interfere with the heavy and continuous sealift coming from halfway around the world, nor did China or the USSR make any such attempt.
- After the initial setbacks on the ground in 1950, the UN forces redressed the situation in Korea with the highly successful

amphibious landing at Inchon, using the equipment and tactics of the Second World War. Subsequent ground operations in Korea were aided by naval gunfire support and air attacks from carriers.
- Helicopters aided the Anglo-French landings in Egypt in 1956.
- The attempt by the Soviet Union to establish nuclear-armed ballistic missiles in Cuba in 1962 was countered by American sea power, able to exert sea denial to prevent the passage of Russian ships. Success also depended on the American superiority in strategic nuclear weapons, but seapower allowed effective non-violent action.
- Right from the beginning of the American involvement in Vietnam, carrier aircraft were used against land and air targets, and marines were employed in land battles. North Vietnamese harbours were mined, coastal shipping was controlled, and light naval craft patrolled in the rivers.
- The British campaign in the Falkland Islands in 1982 began with a phase to achieve sea control, followed by an amphibious landing and subsequent land operations supported by naval power. The opposition to the British naval forces, almost entirely from land-based air, and quite effective, made use of modern anti-ship cruise missiles. The British forces included light carriers with short takeoff and vertical landing (STOVL) aircraft and helicopters but no airborne early warning.

Apart from all these operations and capabilities to contest command of the sea with surface ships and aircraft, the United States, and later the USSR, Great Britain, and France developed submarines with nuclear propulsion and ballistic missiles with nuclear warheads that could be launched from these submarines while submerged. Hence appeared a new form of sea power. It had been preceded to a certain extent by the placing of nuclear armed bombing aircraft on large attack carriers, thus providing a sea-based strategic nuclear capability. But this capability was limited by the range of the aircraft, the detectability of the carrier, and the vulnerability of both aircraft and carrier. In contrast, the submarine-launched missiles had ranges of thousands of miles and could not be intercepted, while the submarine could remain invisible and invulnerable for months on end. As intercontinental ballistic missiles (ICBM) were made more accurate, retaliatory forces depending on land-based ICBM's and bomber aircraft became increasingly vulnerable to a surprise first strike, whereas submarines at sea were not so threatened.

Nuclear propulsion also offered a tremendous improvement to the capability of attack submarines. Able to cruise submerged at high speed, and no longer obliged to come to the surface or to refuel, submarines became far less vulnerable to surface ships or aircraft.

Nuclear propulsion has been tried in a few surface ships, notably large aircraft carriers and icebreakers, but the advantages are less evident than for submarines, and the costs are high. Gas turbines have had much more general application for warships, producing more power for the machinery weight and space than steam turbines, and better able to deliver maximum power on short notice. Gas turbines have had even more influence on aircraft propulsion, whether to power rotating machinery (as in turboprop aircraft and helicopters), or to produce thrust directly (as in turbojet aircraft).

Guided missiles other than torpedoes made their first appearance in the form of anti-ship glider bombs launched from German land-based bomber aircraft. These were soon followed by large gravity bombs, also radio-controlled from the launching aircraft. It was possible to engage the glider bombs by anti-aircraft fire, but gravity bombs fell too quickly. A battleship was sunk, and another battleship, several cruisers, and other warships were badly damaged by these weapons off the Italian coast in 1943.

The Japanese Kamikaze aircraft, while carrying a human pilot, resembled anti-ship guided cruise missiles in all other respects. These inflicted heavy losses on American warships in 1944 and 1945, including carriers and battleships; 2300 Kamikaze sorties sank 34 ships and damaged 288. The American countermeasures were remarkably similar to those of carrier battle groups today and to those the British used in the Falkland Islands in 1982: positioning radar picket ships in an outer screen, maintaining a combat air patrol overhead, and using massed anti-aircraft fire.

Since the Second World War, myriads of guided missiles have been developed, a substantial proportion of them for maritime use. A surface ship makes an ideal target for a homing missile, being large and metallic, offering a sharp contrast to the background of sea and sky, and being slow moving with a limited capability to manoeuvre. An anti-ship cruise missile can approach at low altitude, making detection difficult and late, or can approach at high altitude before attacking the ship in a fast, steep dive. Although engagement by anti-aircraft weapons may be possible, the target is much more difficult than a larger, slower, and more vulnerable aircraft. Anti-ship cruise missiles can be given far greater range and a bigger explosive warhead than the heaviest guns, and they can be launched from small surface ships, aircraft, or submerged submarines. In 1967 the Israeli destroyer *Eilat* was sunk by Soviet-built Styx anti-ship missiles fired from horizon range by a Komar fast patrol boat of the Egyptian navy. An Indian motor torpedo boat used a Styx to sink a Pakistani destroyer in 1971, and Israeli surface-launched Gabriel missiles had considerable success in the Yom Kippur war of 1973. In 1982 several British warships were sunk or badly damaged by Exocet anti-ship missiles launched from Argentine aircraft and from shore, and ships are being damaged today in the Persian Gulf by air-launched missiles.

Guided missiles can also be used to defend ships against aircraft, or against missiles. They are better than guns at all but very close range. In 1968 an American cruiser brought down two Vietnamese aircraft at a range of sixty-five miles, using Talos surface-to-air missiles. Missiles can be used against land targets, though guns are most cost-effective when they have adequate range, and missiles can deliver anti-submarine torpedoes through the air to a point in the water close to their target.

Torpedoes, which are a form of guided missile, began the Second World War as gyro-controlled straight running weapons. By 1943 passive acoustic homing guidance was in use and was employed with considerable success by German U-boats for the attack of escort warships. In subsequent decades, both passive and active acoustic guidance has been designed into anti-submarine torpedoes, and torpedoes launched by a submarine can receive guidance signals through trailing wires. Nuclear warheads can also be fitted in naval tactical missiles for use against surface or land targets, aircraft, or submarines.

Another major change in naval operations has been made possible since 1945 by new technology. Helicopters, capable of vertical takeoff and landing, can be operated from a ship of frigate size. And following a long-range detection of a submarine, they can relocate (using dipping sonar or sonobuoys) and attack (using torpedoes) at a range well beyond the reach of shipborne weapons. With other equipment, helicopters can be used for surveillance against ships and aircraft (using radar), for attack of surface targets (using missiles), for delivery of troops in an amphibious assault, for search and rescue, and for transfer of stores and personnel between ships or between ships and shore.

Knowledge of the location of the enemy's ships has always been a matter of prime importance in naval warfare or in situations of tension. Prior to the advent of radar this depended on visual sighting, unlikely to be obtained beyond a range of twenty to thirty miles, except for the occasions on which information could be drawn from wireless intercepts. The first use of embarked aircraft was twofold: to fly scouting missions well beyond the visual horizon of the fleet, and to report the fall of shot from their own ships in bombardment operations or naval engagements. The dispatch of large numbers of carrier aircraft to attack an enemy fleet with bombs or torpedoes was always preceded by visual sighting reports, usually made by reconnaissance aircraft. Modern airborne radar has extended the capabilities of reconnaissance aircraft, especially in conditions of poor visibility. But an even greater breakthrough has been made by reconnaissance satellites, able to sweep over all the oceans of the earth. Photographs give the most detailed information, but only in good visibility, whereas satellites using active radar can detect larger ships at any time. To be tactically useful, the information must be relayed to the weapons systems with little delay.

Satellites are making other important contributions to naval capabilities, too. Worldwide communications make increasing use of satellite relays, submerged strategic submarines as well as surface ships use navigation satellites to fix accurate positions, weather predictions are improved by the data collected by meteorological satellites, and electronic intelligence on the emissions from ships' radars and wireless is collected by satellite.

FUTURE TECHNOLOGICAL DEVELOPMENTS

What major technological developments will emerge in the future? It seems clear that we are seeing the last battleships, with armour and big guns. The anti-ship missile has superseded the gun as the major surface weapon, and armour is unlikely to defeat a missile which can strike anywhere on the superstructure. A few old battleships will be retained for shore bombardment, with some of their gun turrets replaced by missile launchers.

The future of cruisers, destroyers, and frigates will depend on which anti-air, anti-surface, and anti-submarine weapons can be mounted on a small- to medium-sized hull. At present, area air defence requires a ship of cruiser size, because of the need of radar and fire control equipment, missile launchers, and magazines. A beginning has been made in the design of multipurpose launchers, able to store and to fire anti-air, anti-surface, and anti-submarine missiles. Vertical launchers will permit simultaneous engagements on different azimuths. Phased array radars have many advantages over the older, mechanically scanning types, especially for simultaneous engagements, but may always need to be large and mounted well above the waterline, which implies a large ship. And, having invested in the large ship, it may prove cost-effective to fit it with several weapons systems. The minimum size of an anti-submarine escort will probably be determined by the need for a helicopter landing platform and hangar.

Helicopters may be somewhat reduced in size or replaced by remotely piloted vehicles. The towed sonar array is likely to become a standard fitting for anti-submarine escort ships. All warships will have a point defence weapon with some capability against anti-ship missiles.

Anti-submarine warfare is at present almost totally dependent on the ability of acoustic sensors to detect submerged submarines. Active hull-mounted sonar may have reached a plateau of performance, representing what can be accomplished with high power and sophisticated beam forming and signal processing. Passive sonar has made the greatest strides in the last decade, owing largely to improved signal processing and to long arrays of hydrophones towed behind the ship. But passive detection depends on the noise output of submarines, which is being reduced significantly. An additional problem is that the performance of sonar is limited by background noise in the sea, which is increasing. It is quite probable that in the next decade or two the performance of passive sonar will either reach a plateau or deteriorate. Attention may turn to the development of new types of active systems, possibly using towed arrays or sonobuoys. It is likely that more use will be made of fields of long-life moored sonobuoys, whether active or passive.

There is no doubt that submarines have an assured naval future, especially as strategic missile boats and as attack boats for use against both surface ships and other submarines. Improvements will be made in deeper diving and quieter propulsion. Closed cycle propulsion may be provided by fuel cells or some other non-nuclear means. As anti-submarine aircraft become more effective, submarines will likely be fitted with anti-aircraft weapons. A low-flying helicopter, in particular, should be quite vulnerable to a small infrared homing missile. Although it would be easier to launch the missile in the right direction after a periscope observation, the noise transmitted into the water by the helicopter's rotors might give sufficient indication of its position to permit release of an instrumented raft that would float to the surface, seek and acquire the target, and launch a homing missile.

The future of aircraft carriers will be determined by the success in building high-performance short takeoff and landing (STOL) fighter, attack, reconnaissance, and anti-submarine aircraft. Although an attack carrier can accommodate a few high-performance CTOL attack bombers, fighters, airborne early warning aircraft, fixed-wing anti-submarine aircraft, and helicopters in a 50,000-ton hull, cost-effectiveness favours 70–90,000 tons and a bigger air complement. But a much smaller hull (15–25,000 tons) can handle helicopters and STOL aircraft. HMS *Invincible*, displacing 20,000 tons fully loaded, has a normal complement of five STOVL Sea Harriers and nine heavy helicopters, used effectively in the Falkland Islands in 1982. However, greater payload and endurance than that of the Harrier would be most desirable. For a smaller carrier there are attractions in using a small waterplane twin hull rather than a standard displacement hull. Two fully submerged pontoons provide the buoyancy, below the level of surface waves, and can be far apart to give excellent lateral stability. The superstructure is kept well above wave height by streamlined vertical struts, the only structure needing to meet the stresses of the waves.

Another major choice concerns the defence of the carrier. The USSR has put several types of missiles on its large air capable ships, whereas other countries have left defence to the carrier's own aircraft and to escorting cruisers and destroyers. In fact, American attack carriers now operate in carrier battle groups, similar to the former battle fleet. With the cost of the escort force exceeding that of the carrier, it is doubtful that any navy below the status of a superpower will be equipping itself with new carrier battle groups. Yet a smaller carrier with STOL fighters capable of air defence would still require a screen for defence against submarines and anti-ship missiles. If the air defence screen is to be provided by fighter aircraft operating from the carrier, and if attacking aircraft are to be intercepted beyond the range of their anti-ship missiles, then the fighters must have adequate speed, range, and endurance to reach their targets or else carry the radar, fire control, and long-range air-to-air missiles allowing them to engage targets at a considerable range. Either of these requirements imply a large airframe. Note, for example, that the long range CTOL F-14 with its long range Phoenix missiles weighs about three times as much as the STOVL Sea Harrier.

Remotely piloted flying vehicles are likely to come into use for such purposes as reconnaissance and surveillance, providing an elevated platform for radar or cameras whose information can be relayed to a ship, and for electronic countermeasures and delivery of anti-ship missiles or anti-submarine torpedoes, for which purpose the vehicle might be expendable. Remotely piloted underwater vehicles will be employed for mine clearance and possibly for deployment of deep sonar.

Cruise missiles, already in widespread use as anti-surface ship weapons, are now making an appearance in a strategic nuclear role and for tactical employment against targets on land. Protected in capsules, sized to fit into standard torpedo tubes, with their own self-contained guidance, and able to take either nuclear or conventional warheads, a few could be carried on virtually all submarines and surface warships.

Whereas it is quite simple to give an anti-ship cruise missile more range than the thirty-five miles available to radar or eyesight directed from the superstructure of a surface ship, and not difficult to exceed the range of radar in an aircraft (to perhaps two hundred miles), guidance of the long-range missile would then require information from a third party, normally an aircraft. In the future it is probable that reconnaissance satellites will be able to provide this information by relaying reports of the targeted ship's position directly to the launching vehicle.

Electronic warfare will continue to become more and more important for naval operations. It will be used to gather intelligence from enemy radiations, whether for communications, sensors, or guidance of missiles, and also to disrupt all of these activities on the part of the adversary. It will be a major defence against enemy missiles, whether guided by radar or optical techniques.

The Strategic Defense Initiative (SDI), a top priority American research and development program intended to provide defence against ballistic missiles, will be attempting to produce sensors and fire control devices able to detect, track, and destroy small objects at ranges of hundreds or thousands of miles moving at speeds of four miles a second. It seems highly probable that techniques attaining even a reasonable fraction of such capabilities could be used to intercept aircraft or anti-ship missiles at ranges of a few miles moving at speeds of less than half a mile per second. It should be much easier to put a large power supply and heavy apparatus in a warship or even in large aircraft than into a space vehicle. Therefore, except for systems that can only work in the high vacuum of outer space, applications to the defence of surface ships could prove easier and make their appearance earlier than for defence against intercontinental ballistic missiles (ICBM's).

It is also possible that defence against ballistic missiles, especially against SLBM's, could require sea-based platforms, either for sensors or for weapons. Whereas the location of the opponent's ICBM's will probably be known (perhaps only approximately if they are land-mobile), this is less likely to be true of his SSBN's. On the other hand, it may be possible to station sensors and weapons much closer to the launch position of the SLBM's. The best opportunity to defend against SLBM's could be during their boost phase or mid-course over the sea, from sea-based platforms, or possibly by counterattack on the launching submarine after it has revealed its position but before it has launched all of its missiles.

It is by no means impossible that the research phase of SDI will never be translated into a deployed defence against intercontinental ballistic missiles but that some of the techniques will be converted to other uses such as tactical defence of ships against anti-ship missiles.

STRATEGIC NUCLEAR DETERRENCE, SEA CONTROL, SEA DENIAL, AND POWER PROJECTION

Strategic nuclear deterrence, as currently practised by the SSBN's of four major navies, is sure to continue for many years, unless the missiles ever have to be launched. In fact the major preoccupation of navies possessing SSBN's is likely to be the preservation of these as the invulnerable means for assured retaliation should their country (or perhaps an ally) be subjected to a strategic nuclear attack. If the means of detecting and attacking submarines should improve, even more attention will be paid to the defence of the SSBN's. This can be done by making their machinery extremely quiet, making them able to dive deep, sending them into remote areas (perhaps under ice cover), providing them with torpedo countermeasures, having protective escort vehicles (probably SSN's), or establishing defended bastions or sanctuaries into which hostile anti-submarine weapons cannot penetrate. The SLBM's will be made ever more accurate and, if ballistic missile defences are built, will be given penetration aids.

Sea control will continue to be an objective, but it will only be possible over limited areas of the oceans. Land-based air, land-based missiles, fast patrol craft equipped with anti-ship missiles, coastal submarines, and minefields will all be able to contest sea control out to a considerable distance from their shores, unless and until they are neutralized by air attack, assault, and occupation. Over the open ocean it will be difficult to exercise effective control in areas within range of a modern force of attack submarines and maritime strike aircraft.

If there is ever another great sea battle between major surface fleets, it will involve carrier battle groups on one or both sides. It will resemble some of the Second World War battles in the Pacific theatre, except that submarines will play a more important part, and most of the striking power will be vested in anti-ship missiles rather than air-delivered bombs and torpedoes.

Sea denial is and will continue to be easier than sea control. A weaker force will be able to deny control of the seas adjacent to its shores, but perhaps without being able to exercise unconstrained use of the same area itself. In fact, as surface ships become more vulnerable to aircraft and submarines, it will become increasingly difficult to ensure the safety of merchant shipping anywhere.

Apart from the threat of nuclear bombardment, projection of power across the sea depends on sea control and sealift if there are friendly ports at the receiving end. But if landings must be forced against armed opposition, a specially equipped amphibious fleet will be required. It is probable that future technology will develop unorthodox craft adapted for this purpose, such as air cushion vehicles or surface effect ships, able to approach the shore quickly and beach in shallow water or even skim over low ground. Air support and helicopter landings will be provided from the larger ships. However, few countries will be able to afford such forces.

DEFENCE OF SHIPPING

It is for the problem of defence of shipping that history may contain the best advice for the future. Neglect of the lessons of the past nearly cost the Allies the first Battle of the Atlantic, until they finally adopted convoys. Many of the characteristics of the second Battle of the Atlantic bore striking resemblance to those of the first. Forty years later many of the former situations apply. Merchant ships are faster, but so are the submarines. Sonar is better, but it is used by both submarine and anti-submarine escort. Anti-submarine aircraft are better, including the helicopters carried on various classes of ship, and they have sonobuoys, but submarines do not have to come to the surface. The changes, on balance, favour the submarine. But for all the advantages of airlift, most countries are utterly dependent on sea trade for their economy, and many would be equally dependent on military sealift in time of war.

An interesting debate among those responsible for protection of shipping in NATO turns on the relative merits of escorted convoys and of so-called "sanitized lanes." The latter would attempt to clear a transoceanic route of submarines and keep hostile aircraft and surface raiders away, leaving merchant ships to traverse it independently. It is probable that this tactic would be the most effective in the case of a short route, traversed by heavy merchant traffic, with numerous warships and aircraft available for anti-submarine and anti-air defence. But if such circumstances do not prevail it will probably be better to move merchantmen (or troopships) in convoys escorted by warships equipped for anti-submarine and anti-aircraft defence. Excellent results were obtained in both world wars for the safe delivery of shipping across the English Channel. But over more extended routes, even along the British coast, it proved impossible to maintain effective "sanitized lanes."

In the past, submarines had to close their targets to a distance within the range of straight-running torpedoes. In the future they will have longer-range homing torpedoes or anti-ship missiles of still longer range (probably but not certainly limited by line of sight). In the past aircraft had to overfly or dive on their targets with bombs or launch straight-running torpedoes. In the future they will launch anti-ship missiles from long range (again, probably but not necessarily limited by line of sight from high altitude). The ships could be defended by counterattacking the launching platform (the submarine or the aircraft) or by destroying or deflecting the missile in flight. Attack of the launching platform will require long-range anti-submarine or anti-aircraft weapons, unless it can be done from an outer screen of defensive ships. Destruction of an anti-ship missile in flight may be possible up to the last seconds before impact, but probably only by special self-defence weapons mounted on the target ship or one close to it and capable of coming into action rapidly. Since the anti-ship missile depends on a radar or infrared sensor and an automatic guidance system, defence may be possible by deception, rather than destruction, but the jammers or decoys will probably have to be in the target ships. There will be advantages in fitting anti-missile weapons on merchant ships as well as warships, perhaps in modules quickly changeable from one ship to another. For this there is a certain historical precedent in the case of the guns fitted on merchant ships in the two world wars, with their complement of marine anti-aircraft gunners.

In both battles of the Atlantic it was usual to sail fast merchant ships and fast passenger ships carrying troops independently. It was difficult for a U-boat to position itself within torpedo range. But a nuclear-powered submarine will be faster than a fast merchant ship, and the range of an anti-ship missile is far greater than that of a torpedo. Moreover, the submarine may have the benefit of reports of the ship's position as observed by a reconnaissance satellite, so that evasive routing will not be as useful as in the past. When a convoy is escorted by ships equipped with helicopters, and when land-based air support is available, there is hope of detecting and attacking the submarine beyond his weapon range. But the speed of an undefended ship will not provide much protection in the future.

Long before the days of submarines and aircraft, merchant ships were threatened by surface attack. This could be by armed merchant cruisers, not recognizable as warships until they pressed their attack. Thirteen of these sank or captured 108 Allied ships in the First World War, in addition to destroying another 21 by mines. In the Second World War, 10 German armed merchant cruisers accounted for 133 Allied ships, mines accounted for ten more. In 1914, the German light cruisers *Emden* and *Karlsruhe* sunk a large number of Allied ships in the Pacific and South Atlantic. Germany started the Second World War with three 20,000 ton "pocket battleships" particularly adapted for commerce raiding. The *Admiral Graf Spee* sank nine ships before being defeated in the Battle of the River Plate in 1939, and the *Admiral Scheer* sank eleven in a single cruise in 1941. The battle-cruisers *Scharnhorst* and *Gneisenau* sank 22 ships in two months in the North Atlantic in 1941, but the battleship *Bismarck*, intent on commerce raiding, was sunk after a hunt involving most of the heavy ships of the Royal Navy. German battleships formed a serious threat to the convoys sent to northern Russia in 1942 and 1943, until the *Scharnhorst* was sunk at sea and the *Tirpitz* immobilized in harbour.

The Allied merchant shipping sunk in the Second World War by surface warships and merchant raiders totalled about one and a half million tons. Although small compared to the fourteen and a half million tons sunk by U-boats, it generated a disproportionate offsetting effort on the part of Allied heavy warships. But the commerce raiders depended on surprise, preying on lone or inadequately escorted merchant ships, and they hoped to avoid engagement with equal or superior forces. They roamed widely, depending on U-boats or prepositioned tankers for fuel and supplies. The most successful, *Atlantis*, was at sea for twenty months before she was sunk in 1941, having captured or destroyed twenty-two Allied ships in the South Atlantic, Indian, and Pacific oceans. But today, with modern airborne and satellite-borne ocean reconnaissance, the presence of a surface raider at sea would be likely to be discovered soon after leaving port.

TACTICAL NUCLEAR WARFARE AT SEA

As on land, the threat of nuclear weapons exerts certain constraints on conventional naval operations, although the probability that they will actually be used may be very low. For example, a task force or convoy can reduce the losses to nuclear attack by adopting a wide spacing between ships, but this will reduce the effectiveness of anti-submarine and anti-air defence.

In a contest between a maritime alliance (dependent on command of the surface of the sea to maintain its communications) and a continental adversary (able to survive with land communications only), it seems unlikely that the former would initiate or welcome the use of tactical nuclear weapons at sea. Although nuclear warheads would increase the lethality of anti-aircraft and anti-submarine weapons, they would ensure that one hit or even one not-so-near miss on a surface ship would destroy it. One well-placed nuclear weapon would damage several ships unless they were widely separated. Nuclear attack on naval bases or commercial seaports would probably render them unusable for considerable periods. However, nuclear attack on seaports would be difficult to distinguish from strategic attack on the homeland and would probably signal the final escalation to all-out nuclear exchange.

As long as a state of strategic nuclear deterrence applies, which is likely for a long time, the fear of escalation will probably prevent recourse to tactical nuclear weapons at sea. However, if escalation to the strategic use of nuclear weapons appeared imminent, a preemptive attack on the opponents' SSBN's and attack carriers could be delivered with specially armed land-based ballistic missiles as well as nuclear armed anti-ship and anti-submarine missiles, using barrage fire to cover considerable areas of the ocean when the location of the target was imprecisely known.

MINE WARFARE

Marine mines defeated the attempt to force the Dardanelles in 1915, destroyed many surface ships in shallow waters in both world wars, practically cut Japan off from international or even coastal sea communication in 1945, and posed serious obstacles to assault ships in Wonsan in North Korea in 1950 and to merchant ships in Haiphong in North Vietnam in 1972. The Dover Strait barrage prevented passage by U-boats in 1917–18. But mines were less successful in the open ocean, where the great North Sea Barrage of 1917, involving 70,000 mines intended to prevent the passage of U-boats, failed to accomplish its task.

The marine mines of the future will be far more sophisticated. They will be actuated by sound and by pressure as well as the older mechanism of contact or magnetic field. They will lie on the bottom, or be buried in the bottom, as well as being moored by cables which can be cut by sweepers. They will have sensors with computers able to distinguish ships from submarines and able to refuse the triggering attempts of sweepers and then detonate when a ship crosses on a later occasion. Instead of remaining stationary, they will be able to launch torpedoes to home on a passing ship or submarine emitting an appropriate acoustic signature.

Mine countermeasures will also be much more sophisticated, including high-definition sonars able to hunt mines on the bottom, remotely piloted vehicles able to disarm or destroy mines, and helicopters, lighter-than-air ships, air cushion vehicles, and surface effect ships able to tow minesweeping apparatus at high speed but to avoid destruction when mines are detonated.

Mines will be an effective weapon for economic blockade. They can be laid quickly and unobtrusively by submarine, aircraft, or surface ship, and they have the psychological advantage that the intended victims can be warned, after which they can be said to be destroying themselves if they do not heed the warning.

THE PLANNERS' DILEMMA

Planners responsible for the future structure of the naval forces of their countries face serious dilemmas today. They may feel able to choose the weapon systems best able to cope with various specific contingencies, but it is by no means clear what contingencies are most likely to arise. And in the case of the major navies, what they prepare is likely to influence what contingencies do arise. Twice in this century nations prepared for a short war and found themselves in a long one. Today the superpowers have armed for a nuclear war in the hope, so far achieved, that they will not have to fight one.

The record of the naval planners prior to 1914 and 1939 was not impressive. They failed to foresee the effectiveness of submarine blockade. They greatly underestimated the vulnerability of ships to air attack, the potential of the aircraft carrier, and the need for amphibious operations. Given an unlimited budget, modern technology could probably devise a navy capable of undertaking any specified task. But the cost of the more capable elements soon passes the limits of feasible peacetime budgets. Certain elements such as large attack carriers and nuclear-powered submarines are beyond the reach of all but the most wealthy countries. Multipurpose ships of cruiser or destroyer size are affordable only in limited quantities. Cheaper vessels can be quite effective for a particular role, such as frigates for anti-submarine escort, conventionally powered submarines, small fast attack craft, or land-based strike aircraft for coastal defence, or vehicles for mine countermeasures.

With the huge cost of the most capable ships, only the superpowers or major alliances will be able to field balanced fleets able to deal with all contingencies. For the smaller members of alliances, their choice will be driven in part by the overall needs of the alliance and in part by their own national requirements. Every maritime nation will have some requirements for maritime functions important in peacetime, which it will wish to make the responsibility of its naval forces. In most cases these may demand less capability than a wartime role and may represent a diversion from training for war.

The nuclear-powered strategic submarine carrying long-range ballistic missiles armed with multiple nuclear warheads is likely to remain confined to the few largest navies. But sea-launched cruise missiles embarked on small ships and attack submarines may become accessible to many countries. If any of these should acquire nuclear warheads, they would then command a strategic capability of considerable import.

Thus it is possible to foresee five different types of naval forces for the future. One would be composed of the largest and most capable ships, submarines, and aircraft, provided by a superpower or composed from the major units of an alliance. It could be used to assert sea denial or control, conduct amphibious operations, or otherwise project power. A second would be assembled for a limited tactical role, such as the protection of sea communications over a particular route, and would be made up from units such as escort ships and maritime patrol aircraft largely provided by maritime nations of middle status. A third would be of national composition, possibly for harbour defence or minesweeping, possibly in relation to disputes over coastal jurisdiction, or possibly for peacetime duties such as control of contraband or fishing activity. Some of the ships and aircraft used for these activities should be easily convertible from peace to war in the second role.

The other two forces would be for strategic deterrence, or possibly for strategic attack. One would consist of SSBNs, operating far from any fleet, kept as safe as possible from attack, and conserved as a threat of retaliation should the nation be subjected to nuclear attack. This type of force is likely to be retained by the US and the USSR for a long time. But a second type of strategic nuclear capability is conceivable in the future, accessible to smaller powers and based on nuclear-armed sea-launched cruise missiles carried by attack submarines and warships of destroyer or frigate size.

The power and influence of a middle- or small-sized maritime nation, and Canada falls into at least one of these categories, will depend on its ability to play a part in one or more of these five types of naval force.

PAST PARTICIPATION AND THE POSSIBLE FUTURE OF CANADIAN MARITIME FORCES

During the first half of the seventy-five year history of the Canadian navy, its training, equipment, and employment were patterned on those of the Royal Navy. Although Canada operated anti-submarine carriers, cruisers, and destroyers and undertook offensive operations in European waters, the emphasis was on smaller types of warship and on the role of convoy protection. The building and manning of 60 frigates, 107 corvettes, and 66 minesweepers, for example, represented a significant contribution to defence of Allied shipping in the

Second World War. Also, at the time when radar was a new device, Canada undertook the extensive training of radar officers, many of whom served in the largest warships of the Royal Navy. However, the radar and sonar equipment fitted in RCN ships tended to be inferior to what was made available to some of the Allied navies.

After the Second World War, RCN destroyers participated in the Korean War, and an aircraft carrier embarking both anti-submarine and fighter aircraft was in operation until 1970. Between 1945 and 1963, 24 destroyers of about 2400 tons and 20 small minesweepers were built in Canada. Construction of three 8000-ton operational support ships commenced between 1961 and 1967, but the only other warships laid down up to 1985 were four 3600-ton *Tribal* class destroyers. Six *City* class frigates are now under construction, with a further six planned. The four *Tribals* are to be modified to acquire improved anti-air and anti-missile capability, together with facilities to enable them to serve as command ship for an anti-submarine escort force.

In the 1960s and 1970s, Canada made some important technological innovations, including variable depth sonar and the equipment and procedures needed to operate a heavy anti-submarine helicopter from the deck of a destroyer. Canada also pioneered the development of an anti-submarine hydrofoil, although the technically successful prototype *Bras d'Or* was not put into production. In addition to ship-based ASW, Canada took a leading role in development and operation of Long Range Maritime Patrol Aircraft, including the Argus, built in Canada, and the Aurora. These aircraft have been used for reconnaissance in the Arctic as well as for anti-submarine patrol in the Atlantic and Pacific. Canada has been to the fore in the development and operational employment of anti-submarine sonobuoys, dropped from aircraft, laid by ships, or moored in long-life fields, and is active in the study of the operational use of towed sonar.

As is the case for other navies, the future of Canada's frigate-type warships will be largely dependent on the ability to mount anti-air, anti-missile, anti-surface, and anti-submarine weapons on the same medium-sized hull. Multipurpose missile launchers may make this possible, but the space and weight of the radar and sonar needed for fire control may drive the size of the ship into the class of large destroyer, especially if the air defence is to cover a large area around the ship. Another factor will be the size of the anti-submarine weapon, currently one or two large helicopters but possibly replaced in the future by a smaller helicopter, some other form of VTOL (Vertical Take-off and Landing) aircraft, a remotely piloted vehicle, or a long-range anti-submarine rocket. The anti-submarine role will continue to be the most important for Canadian maritime forces, but the future of the surface fleet will be in doubt unless every warship can be armed for defence against attack by aircraft and anti-ship missiles.

If VTOL aircraft continue to be the most effective shipborne anti-submarine weapon, a vessel specifically designed to carry several of these could prove appropriate for Canada. It would be considerably larger than a frigate, could use the small waterplane twin hull design to provide good lateral stability, and might do double duty as an operational support ship for a group of frigates equipped with sonar and air defence systems.

It seems unlikely that the Canadian navy will be equipped to participate in strategic nuclear deterrence or power projection, both important roles for the major navies. Without ballistic missile submarines, large attack carriers, and amphibious assault vessels, a small navy can play no more than a peripheral part in such operations. Canadian surface ships will not have the speed to form part of the escort of a carrier battle group. However, Canadian anti-submarine forces, whether ships, aircraft, or submarines, can help to protect the approaches to the bases from which American strategic submarines operate and can conduct surveillance of the movements of foreign shipping.

If the coming years bring radical change to the roles of Canadian maritime forces, it is likely to be in activities close to the shores of Canada. Such have not been necessary in the past, except for the period in the Second World War when German U-boats operated in the Gulf of St Lawrence and close to Nova Scotia and Newfoundland. The two threats most likely to stimulate coastal defence in the future would be mining of Canadian harbours (and the approaches to these) and hostile activity in the waters of the Canadian Arctic. There are good military reasons to expect mining, which could provide a cheap and effective interference with crucial shipping, especially if Canada is inadequately prepared to conduct mine countermeasures.

While it is possible that Soviet attack submarines would use passages through the Canadian Arctic islands to get from their home bases in the Kola Peninsula to the North Atlantic sea lanes, or to the approaches to the seaports of North America, there seems little reason for Soviet missile submarines to patrol close to the Canadian coast. Thus, the military requirement is to be able to prevent transit through a limited number of narrow passages. This must start with the installation of systems able to detect and identify penetration by submarines, which may be submerged under thick ice cover. In wartime, a capability to destroy the intruder would be required, and if he were under the ice the usual anti-submarine operations of surface ships, helicopters, and air-dropped sonobuoys would be prevented. Diesel-electric submarines would have a limited capability to operate under ice cover, a limitation which could be alleviated by an auxiliary closed-cycle propulsion system or a small nuclear reactor, or completely solved by using an SSN with full-scale nuclear propulsion. Alternatively, in wartime it should be possible to deny passage of enemy submarines by means of a detection and identification barrier linked to a controlled minefield.

Capabililties for coastal defence of Canadian waters may be determined by considerations other than security. Concerns over sovereignty in the Canadian Arctic could produce demands for surveillance of all types of foreign intrusion in peacetime. The North Warning System will provide this for aircraft, and surface ships could be monitored by maritime patrol aircraft. But continuous surveillance for intrusion by submarines would require underwater detection barriers and, if tracking were demanded, nuclear-powered submarines. One may doubt whether the present concerns over sovereignty will be sustained at the level that will warrant the heavy cost of a fleet of SSN's. If they are not, then the case for SSN's will depend on their value for the traditional Canadian role of protection of shipping in the North Atlantic, supplemented by surveillance of the approaches to American submarine bases. While undoubtedly useful for these roles, and uniquely so when their quarry is under ice, they are in competition with the other proven anti-submarine systems, including fixed-wing aircraft, helicopters, surface ships, and conventionally powered submarines.

NOTES

INTRODUCTION: THE CANADIAN NAVY IN THE MODERN WORLD

1 Vancouver: University of British Columbia Press 1982.
2 London: Allen Lane 1976.
3 B.D. Hunt, *Sailor Scholar: Admiral Sir Herbert Richmond, 1871–1946* (Waterloo, Ontario: Wilfrid Laurier University Press 1982).
4 R.A. Preston, *Canada's RMC: A History of the Royal Military College* (Toronto: University of Toronto Press 1969). Dr Preston is now preparing a detailed study of Canadian precommissioning education.
5 D.M. Schurman, *The Education of a Navy: The Development of British Naval Strategic Thought, 1867–1914* (London: Cassell 1965); *Julian Corbett, 1854–1922: Historian of British Maritime Strategy from Drake to Jellicoe* (London: Royal Historical Society 1982).
6 See, for instance, Hamline A. Caldwell Jr, "Tactical ASW," *Journal of Defence and Diplomacy* 4, No. 4 (April 1986): 44–8. He concludes: "Antisubmarine warfare is no easier than infantry warfare and shares many of its philosophical and tactical elements. Thought to the contrary during the past two or three decades was an abberation." The entire field of coastal and shallow water anti-submarine operations is ripe for historical investigation. Roger Sarty's account in his collection, for instance, is only the second attempt ever made to examine operational aspects of RCN history in the First World War, yet many of the problems are still relevant seventy years later. I am grateful to Marc Milner for bringing the above reference to my attention.
7 Marc Milner, "Royal Canadian Navy Participation in the Battle of the Atlantic Crisis of 1943," *RCN in Retrospect* 158–74; Jürgen Rohwer and W.A.B. Douglas, "'The Most Thankless Task' Remembered: Convoys, Escorts and Radio Intelligence in the Western Atlantic, 1941–43," ibid. 187–234.
8 See Harold Leavitt, *Managerial Psychology* 4th ed. (Chicago: University of Chicago Press 1978) 259–68. The quotations and citations in this section are all taken from E.C. Ball and Marc Garneau, "Technology and the Canadian Navy, 1953–1985," a paper read at the "Canadian Navy in the Modern World" conference, Halifax, NS, Octoer 1985.
9 Lieutenant (N) D.G. Brassington, "The Canadian Development of VDS," *Maritime Warfare Bulletin*, 75th Anniversary Edition, October 1985, 45–65; Captain C. Dalley, "The Marriage of the Small Ship and the Large Helicopter," ibid. 66–75; Captain (N) D. Macgillivray and Lieutenant (N) G. Switzer, "Canadian Contributions to Tactical Data Systems and Data Link Development," ibid. 76–96; E.C. Brady, "Gun Armament Systems in Post-war Canadian Destroyers," *Canadian Defence Quarterly* 5, No. 1 (Summer 1975): 13–20.
10 A more recent study by Rear-Admiral S.M. Davis has placed a slightly different emphasis on personnel developments in the technical field. The General List, in company with

what was called the Restricted Duty List, seemed to have three objectives: to remove allegedly undue Branch loyalties; to give a whole range of technical officers a better chance at senior appointments; and, to ensure that some—the Restricted Duty Officers—would advance within the narrow confines of specialization. S.M. Davis to W.A.B. Douglas, 25 February 1987.
11 See, for instance, Captain Thomas Pullen, "What Price Canadian Sovereignty?" *Proceedings*, United States Naval Institute 113 (September 1987): 66–73; idem, "Why We Need a Polar 8," *Canadian Geographic*, 107, No. 2 (April / May 1987), 84–6.

CHAPTER ONE: NAVAL MASTERY

1 P.M. Kennedy, *The Rise and Fall of British Naval Mastery* (London and New York 1976, 2nd ed. 1982).
2 Ibid., 9.
3 Ibid., xv.
4 Ibid.
5 A.T. Mahan, *The Influence of Sea Power upon History, 1660–1783* (Boston 1890). Among the many studies of Mahan, one might note W.E. Livezey, *Mahan on Sea Power*, 2nd ed. (Norman, OK 1981); D.M. Schurman, *The Education of a Navy: The Development of British Naval Strategic Thought, 1867–1914* (London 1965), Chapter 4; M. Hanke, *Das Werk Alfred T. Mahans: Darstellung und Analyse* (Osnabrück 1974); R. Seager, *Alfred Thayer Mahan* (Maryland 1977).
6 Kennedy, *British Naval Mastery*, xvi, 7, and passim.
7 Ibid., Chapters 2–5; G.S. Graham, *Sea Power and British North America 1783–1820* (Cambridge, MA 1941); G.S. Graham, *Empire of the North Atlantic* (Toronto 1950); P. Padfield, *Tide of Empires: Decisive Naval Campaigns in the Rise of the West*, 2 vols. to date (London 1979, 1982).
8 For example, see R. Pares, "American versus Continental Warfare, 1739–63," *English Historical Review* 51, No. 203 (1936): 429–65; M. Howard, "The British Way in Warfare: A Reappraisal" (1974 Creighton Lecture, London 1975).
9 Cited in Kennedy, *British Naval Mastery* 106.
10 See note 7 above.
11 For details, see M. Beloff, *Imperial Sunset*, Vol. 1, *Britain's Liberal Empire 1897–1921* (London 1969), Chapters 2–4; G.L. Monger, *The End of Isolation: British Foreign Policy 1900–1907* (London 1963), Chapter 1; Kennedy, *The Realities behind Diplomacy: Background Influences on British Foreign Policy 1865–1980* (London 1981), Chapter 1; B. Porter, *The Lion's Share: A Short History of British Imperialism, 1850–1983* (2nd ed., London 1985), Chapters 3 and 4.
12 Quoted in G. Barraclough, *An Introduction to Contemporary History* (Harmondsworth, England 1967), 100.
13 Quoted in Kennedy, *British Naval Mastery*, 191.
14 N. Mansergh, *The Commonwealth Experience* (London 1969), 134.
15 I find the most incisive commentary on the Canadian position in Beloff, *Imperial Sunset*, Vol. 1, Chapter 4, but there is also good detail in D.C. Gordon, *The Dominion Partnership in Imperial Defense, 1870–1914* (Baltimore, Maryland 1965), Chapters 8 and 11; and especially R.A. Preston, *Canada and "Imperial Defense": A Study in the Origins of the British Commonwealth's Defense Organizations, 1867–1919* (Durham, NC 1967), passim.
16 Preston, *Canada and "Imperial Defense,"* Chapter 13; A.J. Marder, *From the Dreadnought to Scapa Flow: The Royal Navy in the Fisher Era*, Vol. 1, *The Road to War 1904–1914* (London 1961), 151–85.
17 Cited in M. Howard, *The Continental Commitment* (London 1974), 51–2.
18 Preston, *Canada and "Imperial Defense,"* 336ff.; B.M. Gough, "The Royal Navy's Legacy to the Royal Canadian Navy in the Pacific," in J.A. Boutilier (ed.), *The RCN in Retrospect, 1910–1968* (Vancouver 1982), 1–11.
19 G.N. Tucker, *The Naval Service of Canada*, 2 vols (Ottawa 1952), Vol. 1, 124.
20 D.C. Gordon, "The Admiralty and Dominion Navies, 1902–1914," *Journal of Modern History* 33, no. 4 (1961): 407–22; Preston, 378–86, 420–29.

21 Cited in Beloff, *Imperial Sunset*, Vol. 1, 156.
22 Tucker, *The Naval Service of Canada*, Vol. 1, Chapters 8–9; Preston, *Canada and "Imperial Defense,"* 455ff.; Gordon, *The Dominion Partnership*, Chapter 11.
23 J.H. Rose, A.P. Newton, and E.A. Benians (eds), *The Cambridge History of the British Empire*, Vol. 6, *Canada and Newfoundland* (Cambridge 1930), 740.
24 For the naval-strategical context of the world war, see Kennedy, *British Naval Mastery*, Chapter 9. Tucker, *The Naval Service of Canada*, Vol. 1, Chapters 10–13, covers the RCN during the war.
25 Kennedy, *British Naval Mastery*, passim, Howard, "The British Way in Warfare," passim, and L. Dehio, *The Precarious Balance* (London 1963) all argue along those lines.
26 E.A. Benians, J. Butler, C.E. Carrington (eds), *The Cambridge History of the British Empire*, Vol. 3, *The Empire-Commonwealth, 1870–1919* (Cambridge 1959), 641. For details of the campaigning see G.W.L. Nicholson, *Canadian Expeditionary Force 1914–1919* (Ottawa 1962); A.F. Duguid, *Official History of the Canadian Forces in the Great War 1914–1919*, Vol. 1 (Ottawa 1935). Also useful is S. Harris, "From Subordinate to Ally: The Canadian Corps and National Autonomy 1914–1918," *Revue Internationale d'Histoire Militaire* 54, Edition Canadienne (1982): 109–30. All further references to this journal are to this special Canadian issue.
27 *Cambridge History of the British Empire*, Vol. 6, *Canada*, 748.
28 Ibid., 637. See also M. Bliss, "War Business as Usual: Canadian Munitions Production, 1914–18," in N.F. Dreisziger (ed.), *Mobilization for Total War: The Canadian, American and British Experience, 1914–1918, 1939–45* (Waterloo, Ontario 1981), 45–55; D. Carnegie, *The History of Munitions Supply in Canada 1914–1918* (London 1925).
29 Tucker, *The Naval Service of Canada*, Vol. 1, Chapters 10–13; Preston, *Canada and "Imperial Defense,"* 498–9.
30 Tucker, *The Naval Service of Canada*, Vol. 1, 237 and passim. See also H.F. Pullen, "The Royal Canadian Navy between the Wars," in Boutilier, *The RCN in Retrospect*, 62–73.
31 Kennedy, *Realities behind Diplomacy*, Chapters 5–6; Howard, *The Continental Commitment*, Chapter 4.
32 Quoted in J. Eayrs, *In Defence of Canada*, 4 vols (Toronto 1964–80), Vol. 1, 172.
33 Ibid., Vols. 1 and 2, is the standard account here.
34 C. Barnett, *The Collapse of British Power* (New York 1972), Chapters 3–5. For a more sympathetic view, see N. Hillmer, "Defence and Ideology: The Anglo-Canadian Military 'Alliance' in the 1930s," *International Journal* 33, no. 3 (1978): 588–612; Mansergh, *The Commonwealth Experience*, Chapter 10; R.F. Holland, *Britain and the Commonwealth Alliance 1918–39* (London 1981), Chapters 5–10.
35 Kennedy, *British Naval Mastery*, Chapter 10, for a summary.
36 Which may be why much of the earliest literature on "appeasement" hardly mentioned the role of the Dominions: see the discussion in R. Ovendale, *"Appeasement" and the English-Speaking World* (Cardiff 1975), 4–9. The present position is that there is now a wealth of books and articles upon the Dominions and Appeasement: see the references in Ovendale, *"Appeasement" and the English-Speaking World*, Holland, *Britain and the Commonwealth Alliance*, Barnett, *The Collapse of British Power*, Mansergh, *The Commonwealth Experience*, Eayrs, *In Defence of Canada*, and Hillmer, "Defence and Ideology."
37 Kennedy, "Strategy versus Finance in Twentieth-Century Britain," in Kennedy, *Strategy and Diplomacy 1870–1945: Eight Essays* (London 1983), 100ff., for the literature.
38 See Hankey's worried memo that, since the American neutrality policy would prevent Britain from drawing upon supplies from that country, so vital in 1914–17, "the dominions, including Canada especially, ... can render immense assistance in supplementing our own hard-pressed and harassed resources." Holland, *Britain and the Commonwealth Alliance*, 194.
39 Howard, *The Continental Commitment*, 5 Chapter 5; Barnett, *The Collapse of British Power*, Chapter 5. For the build-up of the German Army, see A. Seaton, *The German Army 1933–45* (London 1982), Chapters 3 and 4.
40 Holland, *Britain and the Commonwealth Alliance*, Chapter 10; J.L. Granatstein and R. Bothwell, "A Self-Evident National Duty: Canadian Foreign Policy 1935–9," *Journal of Imperial and Commonwealth History* 3 No. 2 (1975): 213–33; J. English and N. Hillmer,

"Canada's Alliances," in *Revue Internationale d'Histoire Militaire*, No. 54 (1982): 37. Eayrs is altogether more critical in his essay "'A Low Dishonest Decade': Aspects of Canadian External Policy, 1931–1939," in H.L. Keenleyside et al., *The Growth of Canadian Policies in External Affairs* (Durham, NC 1960), 59–80.

41 Holland, *Britain and the Commonwealth Alliance*, 41.
42 There is a good coverage in Ovendale, *"Appeasement" and the English-Speaking World*, 223ff. See also J.L. Granatstein, *Canada's War: The Politics of the Mackenzie King Government, 1939–1945* (Toronto 1975), 5–17.
43 See R. Bothwell, "'Who's Paying for Anything These Days?': War Production in Canada 1939–45," in Dreisziger, *Mobilization for Total War*, 59–69; and L.R. Aronson, "From World War to Limited War: Canadian-American Industrial Mobilization for Defence," in *Revue Internationale d'Histoire Militaire*, No. 54 (1982): 208–45, for the relevant literature.
44 G. St John Barclay, *The Empire Is Marching: A Study of the Military Effort of the British Empire 1800–1945* (London 1976), 214. An early work is C.P. Stacey, *The Canadian Army 1939–1945: An Official Historical Summary* (Ottawa 1948). More generally, Stacey, *Arms, Men, and Government: The War Policies of Canada, 1939–1945* (Ottawa 1971); and W.A.B. Douglas and B. Greenhous, *Out of the Shadows: Canada in the Second World War* (Toronto 1977).
45 G.W.E. Nicholson, *The Canadians in Italy* (Ottawa 1955), passim.
46 Stacey, *The Canadian Army*, 1.
47 Tucker, *The Naval Service of Canada*, Vol. 2, 21.
48 W.G. Lund, "The Royal Canadian Navy's Quest for Autonomy in the North West Atlantic," in Boutilier, *The RCN in Retrospect*, Chapter 9; and see also W.A.B. Douglas, "Alliance Warfare, 1939–1945: Canada's Maritime Forces," in *Revue Internationale d'Histoire Militaire*, No. 54 (1982): 162ff.
49 References are in M. Milner, "Royal Canadian Navy Participation in the Battle of the Atlantic Crisis of 1943," in Boutilier, *The RCN in Retrospect*, Chapter 10, as well as his book *North Atlantic Run: The Royal Canadian Navy and the Battle for the Convoys* (Toronto 1985).
50 See the breakdown of the C escort groups in Milner's "Royal Canadian Navy Participation," 169–71.
51 The best survey here is W.A.B. Douglas, "Conflict and Innovation in the Royal Canadian Navy, 1939–1945," in G. Jordan (ed.), *Naval Warfare in the Twentieth Century 1900–1945* (London and New York 1977), 210–32; but see also Tucker, *The Naval Service of Canada*, Vol. 2, Chapter 4; and Eayrs, *In Defence of Canada*, Vol. 3, 81ff.
52 Kennedy, *British Naval Mastery*, Chapter 11.
53 Douglas, "Conflict and Innovation," 211.
54 Ibid. Eayrs, *In Defence of Canda*, Vol. 2, passim.
55 On which, see generally D. Morton, "The Military Problems of an Unmilitary Power," *Revue Internationale d'Histoire Militaire*, No. 54 (1982): 1–30.
56 Most studies of the RCN after 1945 seem to be about organization, not policy, although Eayrs, *In Defence of Canada*, Vols. 3 and 4, covers both. See also the two survey articles by J.D.F. Kealy in *Marine-Rundschau* 65 (1968): 313–32, and 75 (1978): 426–39.
57 Eayrs, *In Defence of Canda*, Vol. 3, 101. Although it is now difficult to get exact figures of the allocations to each branch (because of the 1968 amalgamation of the services), it seems clear from the personnel lists that the navy remains at the end of the line.
58 For a good American example, see E.R. May, *"Lessons" of the Past: The Use and Misuse of History in American Foreign Policy* (Oxford 1973), Chapters 2 and 3.
59 J. Bovey, "The Destroyers' War in Korea, 1952–53," in Boutilier, *The RCN in Retrospect*, Chapter 14; T. Thorgrimsson and E.C. Russell, *Canadian Naval Operations in Korean Waters 1950–1955* (Ottawa 1965).
60 Eayrs, *In Defence of Canada*, Vol. 4, 272.
61 G. Kennedy, *Defense Economics* (London 1983), 55, 61.
62 *Jane's Fighting Ships 1984/85* (London 1984), 125.
63 *The Military Balance 1984–85* (London: International Institute for Strategic Studies 1985), table on 140.
64 See especially A.K. Cameron, "The Royal Canadian Navy and the Unification Crisis," in

Boutilier, *The RCN in Retrospect*, Chapter 19; D.P. Burke, "The Unification of the Armed Forces," in *Revue Internationale d'Histoire Militaire*, No. 54 (1982), 302–27, with good references to further literature.

CHAPTER TWO: STRATEGY AND MARITIME LAW

1 Useful introductory and general reference works covering these developments would include: R.C. Amacher and R.J. Sweeney (eds), *The Law of the Seas: US Interests and Alternatives* (1976); R.P. Barston and P. Birnie (eds), *The Maritime Dimension* (1980); K. Booth, *Navies and Foreign Policy* (1977) and also "The Military Implications of the Changing Law of the Sea" (unpublished manuscript 1978); Sir J. Cable, *Gunboat Diplomacy* (1971); J.L. George (ed.), *Problems of Sea Power as We Approach the Twenty-First Century* (1978); M. Howard (ed.), *Restraints on War* (1979); P. Nitze and L. Sullivan (eds), *Securing the Seas: The Soviet Naval Challenge and Western Alliance Options* (1979); D.P. O'Connell, *The Influence of Law on Sea Power* (1975); G.H. Quester (ed.), *Sea Power in the 1970s* (1975); G.P. Smith, *Restricting the Concept of Free Seas* (1980); C. Till et al., *Maritime Strategy and the Nuclear Age* (1982). Also, Adelphi Papers Nos. 122–4, *Power at Sea (*IISS, 1976); republished in part in J. Alford (ed.), *Sea Power and Influence: Old Issues and New Challenges* (1980).
2 See Mark W. Jones's *Sea Power and The Law of the Sea* (1976); also, W.E. Butler, *The Soviet Union and the Law of the Sea* (1971).
3 B.D. Hunt, "British Policy on the Issue of Belligerent and Neutral Rights, 1919–1939," in C. Symonds (ed.), *New Aspects of Naval History* (1981), 279–90.
4 Ibid., 284n18.
5 W.N. Medlicott, *The Economic Blockade* (1952), Vol. 1, 5.
6 As quoted in Hunt, "British Policy," 286.
7 O'Connell, *The Influence of Law*, 50–1.
8 H.S. Levie, "The Falklands Crisis and the Laws of War," in A.R. Coll and A.C. Arend (eds), *The Falklands War: Lessons for Strategy, Diplomacy and International Law* (1985).
9 *International Legal Materials* 16, No. 6 (November 1982): 1261–1354.
10 U. Jenisch, "The Law of the Sea: Will it Float?" *NATO's Fifteen Nations* (December 1982–January 1983); B.H. Oxman, "The Third UN Conference on the Law of the Sea: The Tenth Session" (1981), *American Journal of International Law* (1982): 9–10.
11 See J.E. Harf, M.E. Denham, M.O. Lombardi, "The President, the Congress and National Security: The Case of the Law of the Sea," unpublished paper presented at the annual meeting, Section in Military Studies, ISA (Monterey, CA 1983).
12 B. Buzan, "A Sea of Troubles: Sources of Dispute in the New Ocean Regime," Adelphi Paper No. 143 (Spring 1978): 3.
13 K. Booth, "Military Implications," 13.
14 P.V. Lyon and B.W. Tomlin, *Canada as an International Actor* (1979), 180.
15 *Canadian Year Book of International Law*, 12 (1974), 277–9; *Third United Nations Conference on the Law of the Sea* (Ottawa: Department of External Affairs 1973), pp. 32.
16 See A.E. Gotlieb, "Canadian Diplomatic Initiatives: The Law of the Sea," in M.G. Fry, *Freedom and Change: Essays in Honour of Lester B. Pearson* (1975), 139–40, 144–7.
17 See E.J. Dosman, *The Arctic in Question* (1976), 34–42.
18 R.D. McConchie and R.S. Reid, "Canadian Foreign Policy and International Straits," in B. Johnson and N.W. Zacker (eds), *Canadian Foreign Policy and the Law of the Sea* (1977), 171.

CHAPTER THREE: HISTORICAL STRATEGY AND ITS USES IN LARGE AND SMALL NAVIES

1 Alfred Thayer Mahan (1840–1914), historian and naval publicist; Sir Julian Corbett (1854–1922), naval historian and savant, and official historian of the Royal Navy in the First World War; Sir Herbert Richmond (1871–1946), Admiral and naval historian; Vere Harmsworth, Professor of Naval and Imperial History and latterly Master of Downing College in the University of Cambridge; Bernard Brodie (1910–79), historian, strategic thinker and Rand Corporation expert; Theodore Ropp (1911–   ), professor

of history at Duke University, adviser on naval policy, and member of the board of directors of the Smithsonian Institution.
2 R.C. Anderson, FSA (1883–1973). Marine historian and sometime Hon. President of the Society for Nautical Research.
3 Personal recollection.
4 Sir Karl R. Popper (1902–   ), author of *The Poverty of Historicism* (London 1957).
5 Elias Canetti (1905–   ), Nobel Prize-winning author for *Crowds and Power* (London 1962), 231, where he describes how historians venerate the survivors of this world. He is not enamoured of historians; see his *The Human Province* (New York: Continuum 1978).
6 John Campbell, *Lives of the British Admirals* (London 1817).
7 William James, *The Naval History of Great Britain from the Declaration of War by France in 1793, to the Accession of George IV* (London 1860).
8 Gerald S. Graham, *The Politics of Naval Supremacy* (Cambridge 1965). Graham is Professor Emeritus and was once Rhodes Professor of Imperial and Naval History at King's College, University of London.
9 There was more than that to Mahan. For the influences on his pedagogical purposes see D.M. Schurman, *The Education of a Navy: the Development of British Naval Strategic Thought* (London 1965), 64–74; see also D.M. Schurman, "Mahan Revisited," in *Särtryck ur Kungl Kriegsvetenskapsakademiens Bihäfte-Militärhistorisk Tidskrift 1982*, 30–1, and 32–40.
10 See, for example, A.T. Mahan, *The Influence of Sea Power Upon History, 1660–1783* (Boston 1890), passim.
11 See *Britain and the British Seas* (London 1900); for a good discussion of Mahan and Mackinder see Paul M. Kennedy, *The Rise and Fall of British Naval Mastery* (London 1976), 183–202.
12 (London 1910).
13 (London 1893).
14 (London 1900).
15 See Donald M. Schurman, *Julian S. Corbett, 1854–1922: Historian of British Maritime Policy from Drake to Jellicoe* (London 1981), 47–8.
16 Schurman, "Mahan Revisited," especially 38.
17 J.M. Ellicott, "Three Cranks and What They Turned," USNI *Proceedings* (1924): 1625.
18 Schurman, *Corbett*, 69.
19 Ibid. 67.
20 A point I made in the preface to the *Ecucation of a Navy*.
21 "Mahan: Evangelist of Sea Power" (Princeton 1943), 415–45.
22 Schurman, "Mahan Revisited," 29.
23 See especially Corbett, *The Successors of Drake* (London 1900) 407–9; see also his *England in the Seven Years War*, 2 vols (London 1907), 157, 354.
24 S.R. Roskill, *The War at Sea*, 3 vols (London 1954–61), see especially Vol. 1, 1–15.
25 S.R. Roskill, *The Strategy of Sea Power* (London 1962).
26 For instance, see his *Imperial Defence and Capture at Sea in War* (London 1932).
27 S.E. Morison (1887–1976), Harvard professor and official historian of the United States Navy in the Second World War.
28 John B. Hattendorf (194?–   ), Ernest J. King Professor of Naval History at the US Naval War College.
29 John B. Hattendorf, with John D. Hayes (eds.), *The Writings of Stephen B. Luce (US Naval War College, 1975)*; see also articles by Hattendorf and Anthony S. Nicolosi in the Centennial edition of the US Naval War College *Review* (Newport September–October 1984).
30 His Honour, George F.G. Stanley (1907–   ), Lt Governor of the Province of New Brunswick; historian and author of *Canada's Soldiers* (Toronto 1974), and once department head and dean at the Royal Military College of Canada.
31 Charles Stacey (1906–   ), military historian; author of *Canada and the Age of Conflict* (Toronto 1977–81), and official historian of the Canadian Army in the Second World War.
32 Barry D. Hunt (1937–   ), soldier and professor of naval history; author of *Sailor-Scholar: Admiral Sir Herbert Richmond, 1881–1946* (Waterloo, Ontario 1982), and also author of a major assessment of the naval writings of the past century; see his "The Out-

standing Naval Strategic Writers of the Century," in the Centennial Issue of the US Naval War College *Review* (Newport, September–October 1984).
33 See for instance James Boutilier (ed.), *The RCN in Retrospect* (Vancouver 1982).
34 That is, France, Italy, or even the Federal Republic of Germany.
35 Mahan did not understand this. See *The Influence of Sea Power upon History* (Boston 1890), 134–8; also Kennedy's *Mastery*, 73, where he touches upon it lightly.
36 Kennedy, *Mastery*, 215; see also his strong article, "The Development of German Operations Plans against England, 1896–1914," *English Historical Review* 89, No. 350 (January 1974).

CHAPTER FOUR: MARCOM EDUCATION

1 Morris James, "A View of the RN," *Encounter* 40, No. 3 (March 1973): 15–27.
2 Charles Owen, *No More Heroes: The Royal Navy in the Twentieth Century: Anatomy of a Legend* (London: George Allen and Unwin 1935), 37–9.
3 Quoted in [Great Britain], Department of Education and Science, *The Sea in Education* (London: Her Majesty's Stationery Office, Education pamphlet No. 44 1964), 3.
4 Michael Lewis, *England's Sea Officers: The Story of the Naval Profession* (London: Allen and Unwin 1939), 82–106; Michael Lewis, *The Navy of Britain* (London: Allen and Unwin 1948), 192–4, 250–4.
5 Julian S. Corbett, "Education in the Navy, 1," *Monthly Review* 8, No. 3 (1902): 36–7.
6 Admiral Lord Chatfield, *It Might Happen Again: [Autobiography]*, Vol. 2 (London: Heinemann 1947), 54.
7 Captain S.W. Pack, *Britannia at Dartmouth* (London: Alvin Redman 1967), 242–3.
8 Sir J.A. Ewing, Director of Naval Education, quoted in *How to Become a Naval Officer, and Life at the Royal Naval Colleges at Osborne and Dartmouth* (London: Cleve, Matthews and Seagrove 1910), 40.
9 Pack, *Britannia at Dartmouth*, 184.
10 *How to Become a Naval Officer*, 47.
11 Great Britain, House of Commons, Sessional papers, Cd. 6703, *Reports of the Committee Appointed to Enquire into the Education and Training of Cadets, Midshipmen, and Junior Officers of His Majesty's Fleet* (London 1913), 23, 170ff.
12 Charles Langbridge Morgan, *The Gunroom* (London: A & C Black 1919); Clio, "On the Education of Naval Officers," *The Naval Review* 40 (May 1952): 148–52.
13 Kenneth G.B. Dewar, *The Navy from Within* (London: Gollancz 1939), 46, quoted by Arthur J. Marder, *The Anatomy of British Sea Power* (New York: Knopf 1940), 388. Dewar, when commanding the Flagship *Royal Oak* in 1927, complained in a legitimate confidential letter to the Flag-Admiral that the officer's behaviour threatened the discipline on his ship. Dewar was court-martialled for an act to the prejudice of good order by his forwarding a letter written by his second-in-command. Dewar was found guilty but was promised reassignment. The Flag-Admiral was retired without promotion. Two years later Dewar was promoted and retired. In his book Dewar recommended reforms in naval education that eventually came about.
14 Clio, "On the Education of a Naval Officer"; Charles Owen, *No More Heroes: The Royal Navy, Anatomy of a Legend* (London: Allen, Unwin 1975), 196–7; J.M. Kenworthy, *Sailors, Statesmen, and Others: An Autobiography* (London: Rich and Cowan 1933), 32–3.
15 Great Britain, Parliament, House of Commons, *Parliamentary Debates*, Vol. 248 (26 February 1931): 2295–6.
16 G.B., Civil Service Commission, Army, Navy, and Air Force Examinations, 1926. The list of schools seen there in 1954.
17 G.B., Civil Service Commission, interviews for Army Entrance Examinations, 1925; ibid., Annual Files on Army, Navy, and Air Force Examinations, 1925–39.
18 Admiral Lord Chatfield, *The Navy and Defence: Autobiography*, Vol. 1 (London: Heinemann 1942), 252.
19 Peter Karsten, *The Naval Aristocracy: The Golden Age of Annapolis and the Emergence of Modern American Navalism* (New York: Free Press 1972), xiii, 7–16, 107–16, 392.
20 Lewis, *The Navy of Britain*, 194; Lewis, *England's Sea Officers*, 276.

21 Owen, *No More Heroes*, 196–7.
22 P. Willet Brock, "Commander E.A.E. Nixon and the Royal Naval College of Canada, 1910–1922," James A. Boutilier (ed.), *The RCN in Retrospect* (Vancouver: University of British Columbia Press 1982), 33–43; Richard H. Leir, "'Big Ship Time': The Formative Years of RCN Officers Serving in RN Capital Ships," ibid. 74–95.
23 Gilbert Tucker, *The Naval Service of Canada: Its Official History*, Vol. 2, *Activities on Shore During the Second World War* (Ottawa: King's Printer 1952), 260–7.
24 P. Willet Brock, "Commander E.A.E. Nixon and the Royal Naval College of Canada, 1910–1922," in Boutilier, *RCN in Retrospect*, 35–6.
25 Tucker, *Naval Service of Canada*, Vol. 2, 260; DHist, Lawrence interview with Captain Grant.
26 Pack, *Britannia*, 36–7, 55, 217–18, 233.
27 Tucker, Naval Service of Canada, Vol. 2, 260–7.
28 Richard A. Preston, *Canada's RMC* (Toronto: University of Toronto Press 1969), 328.
29 Louis Audette, "The Lower Deck and the Mainguy Report of 1949," in Boutilier, *RCN in Retrospect*, 245–6.
30 Rear Admiral E.R. Mainguy, et al., *Report on Certain "Incidents" ... on HMC Ships, Athabaskan, Crescent, and Magnificent* (Ottawa, October 1949), 57.
31 Recruitment to RMC from residential private schools. Sample classes at time of registration:

Date of entry	Total enrolment	From private schools	Percentage
1908	36	20	56
1919	47	32	68
1928	34	25	46
1933	58	14	28
1939	50	7	14
1948	100	22	22
1958	65	3	5

32 See Michael Lewis, *England's Sea Officers: The Story of the Naval Profession* (London: Allen and Unwin 1948) (first published in 1939); Michael Lewis, *The Navy of Britain* (London: Allen and Unwin 1948); Samuel P. Huntington, *The Soldier and the State: The Theory and Politics of Civil-Military Relations* (Cambridge: Belknap Press 1957); Morris Janowitz, *The Professional Soldier: A Social and Political Portrait* (Glencoe, IL: Free Press 1960).
33 Lieutenant-Commander J.C. Marks, "Memo to CNP: RMC. Brief on obligatory active force service," n.d., NAC, RG 24, v. 18102.
34 General Foulkes to Chiefs of Staff, "Production and Training of Officers [to supplement CSC and ROTP]," 5 January 1954, RCAF, 801–142 v. 272.
35 Ibid.
36 "The Report of the Ad Hoc Committee on Personnel Structure," 1957, 68 (hereafter *Tisdall Report*).
37 Ibid. 72.
38 Brigadier Rothschild, DROPT, Report to the CSC Advisory Board, 10/11 October 1958, DPED; and information from Admiral Landymore.
39 RMC Faculty Council, 11 July 1957.
40 Joint Services Universities Canservocolls Committee, 7/58, 13 February 1958, DHist 113.3M3.009(D4).
41 Ibid. 26/58, 10 July 1958.
42 Canadian Service Colleges Advisory Board, 10/11 October 1958, DPED.
43 Peter Newman, *The True North: Not So Strong and Free: Defending the Peaceable Kingdom in the Nuclear Age* (Toronto: McClelland and Stewart 1983), 80.

44 Richard A. Preston, "Broad Pennants on Point Frederick," *Ontario History* 50 (1958): 81–90.
45 R.A. White, "Change and Fealty to Tradition in Today's Royal Military College of Canada," *Canadian Defence Quarterly* 1 (Winter 1971): 35–41.
46 *Tisdall Report*, 57, 69.
47 RMC, *Commandant's Report*, 1962–3, 9.01.
48 Canadian Army, *The Professional Officer* (23 August 1963), Annex C, 15, 18, and Appendix 1.
49 House of Commons, *Reports of the Special Committee on Defence*, 1964–5, Table 2, 15.
50 D.J. Goodspeed, *The Armed Forces of Canada, 1867–1967: A Century of Achievement* (Ottawa: Queen's Printer 1967), 231–8.
51 Jean J. Allard, *Mémoires du Général Jean J. Allard en collaboration avec Serge Bernier* (Ottawa: Editions de Montagne 1985), 400–1. (Translation published by University of British Columbia Press 1988.)
52 Ibid. 337.
53 Ibid. 334–5, 342–3.
54 Ibid. 376, 384.
55 Chief of Personnel Development Study, 1976, 25.
56 Allard, *Mémoires*, 382, 400–2.
57 Ibid. 403–4.
58 Ibid. 403; Officer Development Board, *Report* (Ottawa, March 1969) [Vol. 1], Part 1, 100–2, Part 2, 144.
59 Officer Development Board, *Report* [Vol. 1] Part 1, 22.
60 Rear Admiral R.W. Murdoch, *Draft Report on the Study of Professionalism in the Canadian Forces* (Ottawa: Canadian Forces Headquarters 1971), 13, 66–7.
61 Officer Development Board, *Report*, 45, 46.
62 RMC Faculty Board Minutes, 5 April 1977.
63 CPD Study, October 1976, Annex E, CMC Cost Analysis by Dr H.A.H. Bailey, 13.
64 CPD Study, Annex C, 1–2.
65 CPD Study, 76.
66 Colonel W.G. Svab, COl, 202 Workshop Depot to DGLEM, NDHQ, 16 May 1975, DND HQ, 4840–1 Vol. 6, Production of Officers, General.
67 Vice-Admiral D.S. Boyle, Commander Maritime Command to ADM(Per) NDHQ, 20 August 1975, DND HQ 4840–1 Vol. 6, Production of Officers, General.
68 Brigadier General J.E. Vance, to DGLEM, 20 June 1975, DND HQ 4840–1 Vol. 6, Production of Officers, General.
69 ADM(Per) Academic Task Force, *Report on Academic Development at the Canadian Military Colleges* Mar[ch] [19] 77, 3.
70 ADM(Per) Military Development Task Force, *Report on Military Development at the Canadian Military Colleges* March 1977, v.
71 Academic Task Force, 66–7.
72 Advisory Board, April 1978, Item 12, 51, 62, Annex A, 16, DPED.
73 CMC Advisory Board, March 1980, Annex F.
74 Captain(N) W.J. Broughton, "Maritime Engineering Classification: Get Well Project," *Maritime Engineering Journal* (August 1984): 1–27.

CHAPTER FIVE: THE END OF PAX BRITANNICA AND THE ORIGINS OF THE RCN

1 *Colonial Conference of 1902, Summary of Proceedings* (Ottawa: King's Printer 1902), 4, 31–2, and O.D. Skelton, *Life and Letters of Sir Wilfrid Laurier*, 2 vols (Toronto: Oxford University Press 1921), Vol. 2, 294.
2 Captain Stephen W. Roskill, *The Strategy of Sea Power* (London: Collins 1962), 83–9.
3 Some duties were not so humanitarian, including putting down slave risings, bombarding villages of innocent native peoples, and coercing Irish peoples who refused to pay their rates.
4 *Naval Chronicle*, Vol. 32, 243.

5 "Our policy," said Castlereagh, "has been to secure the Empire against future attack. In order to do this we had acquired what in former days would have been thought romance—the keys of every great military position" (*Hansard*, first series, Vol. 32, 1104).
6 Quoted in James Morris, "A View of the Royal Navy," *Encounter*, 40 (March 1975): 25.
7 Arthur J. Marder, *The Anatomy of British Sea Power: A History of Naval Policy in the Pre-Dreadnought Era, 1880–1905* (New York: Alfred A. Knopf 1940), Chapters 7 and 8 review the subject of the "two-power standard." For all this book's considerable merits it really does not examine the Admiralty's decisionmaking and decisions. It is anatomy of the body without examining how the brain functioned.
8 Quoted in Paul Kennedy, *The Realities behind Diplomacy: Background Influences on British External Policy, 1865–1980* (London: Fontana 1981), 26.
9 The first Admiralty War Plan dates from 1907. See Lieutenant Commander P.K. Kemp (ed.), *The Papers of Admiral Sir John Fisher* (London: Navy Records Society, Vol. 106, 1964), 318–468. Fisher had a hand in this as did Captain G.A. Ballard, Captain Edmond J.W. Slade, and perhaps Captain Maurice Hankey, RMA, but it also bears the arguments of Sir Julian Corbett. For a review of how various British boards and committees reorganized defence planning in this period, see Barry D. Hunt, *Sailor-Scholar: Admiral Sir Herbert Richmond 1871–1946* (Waterloo, Ontario: Wilfrid Laurier University Press 1982), Chapter 1.
10 Admiral of the Fleet Lord Fisher, *Memories* (London: Hodder and Stoughton 1919), 5.
11 See especially, Gilbert Norman Tucker, *The Naval Service of Canada: Its Official History; Volume 1: Origins and Early Years* (Ottawa: King's Printer 1952), Chapters 6 and 7. The text of The Naval Service Act 1910 (9–10 Ed. VII, Chapter 43) is in ibid. 377–85.
12 W.A.B. Douglas, "Canadian Naval Historiography" *The Mariner's Mirror* 70, No. 4 (November 1984): 349–62.
13 Nigel D. Brodeur, "The Naval Service of Canada: The End of the Beginning," paper presented to The Royal Canadian Navy in Retrospect Conference, Royal Roads Military College, Victoria, British Columbia, March 1980, a shorter version of which appeared in James A. Boutilier (ed.), *The RCN in Retrospect, 1910–1968* (Vancouver: University of British Columbia Press 1982), 13–32. Richard Howard Gimblett, "'Tin-Pots' or Dreadnoughts? The Evolution of the Naval Policy of the Laurier Administration, 1896–1911," MA thesis, Trent University 1981.
14 Thomas R. Melville, "Canada and Sea Power: Canadian Naval Thought and Policy, 1860–1911," PH.D. thesis, Duke University 1981.
15 See especially, Richard A. Preston, *Canada and "Imperial Defense"* (Durham, NC: Duke University Press 1967) and Donald C. Gordon, *The Dominion Partnership in Imperial Defense, 1870–1914* (Baltimore: Johns Hopkins University Press 1965).
16 On tradition, Vice-Admiral H.G. DeWolf recalled in 1985: "We grew up with the Royal Navy. As I recall, we were told to go to England and imbibe the spirit of the Royal Navy. We did. When war came along, my experiences convinced me that everything I had learned in my early days with the Royal Navy was sound. I don't think I made any mistakes because of anything I had been taught by the RN. On the other hand, the Royal Navy always regarded us as part of their navy. They were always inclined to look upon our ships or our squadrons as theirs. They didn't seem to grasp the fact that we were developing a service of our own. I think that was simply a lack of knowledge on the part of some individual officers rather than the Admiralty itself. For instance, when the war started they sent over an Admiral to take charge in Halifax. When he arrived, he found we already had somebody in charge. That sort of thing had to be dealt with very tactfully. In the early days, a lot of the officers in the Navy came from the Maritimes or BC and many had British backgrounds. So starting with that, plus the training we received in the UK, there was sometimes the feeling in Canada that we weren't very Canadian, that we were more British than Canadian. We'd spent so much time over there and picked up so much of their way of life that we were perhaps a little bit different than our contemporaries in Canada. I think that was a fair criticism. Now, of course, we had the greatest admiration for the Royal Navy, but we gradually learned that anything they could do we could do as well. On the material side, we learned the hard way during the war that there

was too much stuff lost coming across the Atlantic so we gradually shifted to the USN as a source of supply or to our own sources. From this grew closer ties with the USN." *Maritime Warfare Bulletin, Commemorative Edition 1985*, 24.

17 Quoted in Donald M. Schurman, *Julian S. Corbett, 1854–1922: Historian of British Maritime Policy from Drake to Jellicoe* (London: Royal Historical Society Studies in History Series, No. 26, 1981), 100. See also Samuel F. Wells, jr, "British Strategic Withdrawal from the Western Hemisphere, 1904–1906," *Canadian Historical Review* 49, No. 4 (December 1968): 335–56.

18 In 1898 Lieutenant-General Sir Percy Lake and Captain Reginald Custance RN examined the defences of Lakes Ontario and Erie. They developed plans so that in the hoped-for expectation that the Americans would cross the border first (and would thus be labelled the agressors!), Canadian forces could mount a counterattack. Schurman, *Corbett*, 110. By 1905 the Admiralty had concluded that Canada was indefensible (see note 23 below).

19 Fisher to Viscount Knollys, [late August 1904], Portsmouth, in Arthur J. Marder (ed.), *Fear God and Dread Nought: The Correspondence of Admiral of the Fleet Lord Fisher of Kilverstone*, 2 vols. (London: Jonathan Cape 1952, 1956), Vol. 1, 327.

20 Wells, "British Strategic Withdrawal," 338. However, in the previous year, 1903, the newly created Committee for Imperial Defence had been pressing on Canada to develop a general scheme of defence and suggesting that plans for this ought to have London's expert criticism and advice. For a discussion of this and related points including the Committee for Imperial Defence's agreement with the Canadian Minister of the Militia, Dr Frederick Borden, that the General Officer Commanding the Canadian Militia should be a Canadian officer, see Gordon, *Dominion Partnership*, 176–7.

21 Quoted in Arthur J. Marder, *From the Dreadnought to Scapa Flow: The Royal Navy in the Fisher Era, 1904–1919, Vol. 1: The Road to War, 1904–1914* (London: Oxford University Press 1961), 40.

22 Wells, "Britain's Strategic Withdrawal," 346–7.

23 Wells, "Britain's Strategic Withdrawal." Also, Ottley–Battenburg memo on Defence of Canada 1905, and related documents, Adm. 1/7807, Public Record Office, Kew, England (National Archives of Canada Reel B3634).

24 Wells, "Britain's Strategic Withdrawal," 349.

25 Quoted in ibid., 340.

26 Minto to Lord Morley, 3 April 1906, quoted in Ronald Hyam, *Britain's Imperial Century, 1815–1914* (New York: Barnes and Noble 1976), 122.

27 Brian Tunstall, "Imperial Defence, 1870–1897," in *Cambridge History of the British Empire* Vol. 3 (Cambridge: Cambridge University Press 1959), 583.

28 Lord Haldane, *Before the War* (London: Cassell and Co. 1920), 7–8; also Admiral Sir H.W. Richmond, "National Policy and Naval Strength, XVIth to XXth Century," Raleigh Lecture (London 1923), 3.

29 London's war plans included, at the War Office at least, deliberate concealment from the Dominion premiers of its strategic aims on the eve of the 1914 war, that is, that overseas contingents should come to the help of the mother country rather than the other way round. See on this and related matters John Gooch, *The Plans of War: The General Staff and British Military Strategy, c. 1900–1916* (London: Routledge and Kegan Paul 1974), Chapters 5 and 6, and, by the same author, *The Prospect of War: Studies in British Defence Policy, 1847–1942* (London: Frank Cass 1981), esp. Chapter 3, "Great Britain and the Defence of Canada, 1896–1914."

30 Admiralty Memorandum ... 1902, in A.B. Keith (ed.), *Selected Speeches and Documents in British Colonial Policy, 1763–1917* 2 parts (London: Oxford University Press 1966), Part 2, 230–9.

31 Donald C. Gordon, "The Admiralty and Dominion Navies, 1902–1914," *Journal of Modern History* 33, No. 4 (December 1961): 409.

32 General S. Graham, *Empire of the North Atlantic: The Maritime Struggle for North America* 2nd ed. (Toronto: University of Toronto Press 1958), 291.

33 Gordon, "Admiralty," 409ff.

34 In Skelton, *Laurier*, Vol. 2, 297.
35 Tunstall, "Imperial Defence," 595–97; also *Parliamentary Papers*, 1911, 54, (Cmd. 5746–2), 1–3.
36 *Nineteenth Century*, February 1889, quoted in Admiral Sir Herbert Richmond, *Statesmen and Sea Power* (Oxford: Clarendon Press 1946), 273.

CHAPTER SIX: HARD LUCK FLOTILLA

This paper could not have been completed in its present form without the material gathered and narratives written by the members of the Naval Historical Section, which, in 1966, combined with the Army and Air Force Historical Sections to form the Directorate of History at National Defence Headquarters in Ottawa. I must express my appreciation to the late E.C. Russell, formerly the naval historian, and to J.D.F. Kealy, the late Thor Thorgrimsson, Hartley Brown, and Philip Chaplin of his staff. Philip also read a draft of the manuscript and caught many slips, a service for which I am most grateful.

1 Gilbert Norman Tucker, *The Naval Service of Canada: Its Official History.* Vol. 1: *Origins and Early Years* (Ottawa 1952).
2 B.M. Ranft, "The Naval Defence of British Sea-Borne Trade 1860–1905" (PH.D. Oxford University 1967), A.J. Marder, *From the Dreadnought to Scapa Flow: The Royal Navy in The Fisher Era, 1904–1919.* Vol. 1: *The Road to War, 1904–1914* (London 1961), 358–67.
3 See, for example, Colonial Defence Committee, No. 399M, "Defence of Halifax against Torpedo Attack," 27 February 1908, National Archives of Canada (hereafter NAC), Record Group (hereafter RG) 7 G-21, box 234, file 343(8).
4 Richard Howard Gimblett, " 'Tin-Pots' or Dreadnoughts?: The Evolution of the Naval Policy of the Laurier Administration, 1896–1911" (MA thesis, Trent University 1981).
5 Roger Sarty, "Silent Sentry: A Military and Political History of Canadian Coast Defence 1860–1945" (PH.D. diss., University of Toronto 1982), 172–3, 221–2.
6 Ibid. 275–6.
7 Ibid. 276–7; Gaddis Smith, *Britain's Clandestine Submarines 1914–1915* (New Haven, CN 1964), 76–7, 101, 103, 108–10; NAC, RG 24, box 4020, files 62-12-1, 62-12-2.
8 Tucker, *Naval Service*, vol. 1, 219.
9 Perley, memorandum, 2 July 1915, Graham Green to Borden, 12 August 1915, NAC, Manuscript Group (hereafter MG) 26 H, Sir Robert Borden papers, Vol. 76, p. 39492; Kingsmill to minister, 11 August 1915, extracts from file 62-13-4 in Directorate of History (hereafter DHist), Naval Historical Section files (hereafter NHS), 1440-11.
10 Historical Records Officer to Senior Canadian Naval Officer (London), 12 January 1944, DHist, NHS 1700–1903.
11 United States, Navy Department, Office of Naval Records and Llibrary, Historical Section, *German Submarine Activities on the Atlantic Coast of the United States and Canada* (Washington 1920), 15–23; NHS, "Ships and Vessels of the RCN on the Atlantic Cost in the Great War 1914–1918," 17 July 1963, 16–21; "Information Regarding Marine Defences of Defended Ports ... in Canada," 1 July 1917, NAC, RG 24, box 3809, file 10-11-1 lists the vessels then in commission.
12 NHS, "Ships and Vessels," 22-4; extracts from file 65-7-2 in DHist, NHS 1440-11; Borden to Blount, telegram, 30 March 1917, NAC, MG 26H, reel C-4314, p. 35454; Anderson, minute, 4 February 1917, Great Britain, Public Record Officer (hereafter PRO), Adm 116/1400 case 620.
13 "Information regarding Marine Defences," 1 April 1918, NAC, RG 24, box 3810, file 10-11-1; NHS, "Ships and Vessels"; see also Fraser McKee, *The Armed Yachts of Canada* (Erin, Ontario 1983), Chapters 2–3.
14 David M. Trask, *Captains and Cabinets: Anglo-American Naval Relations, 1917–1918* (Columbia, MO 1972), Chapter 2.
15 C. Ernest Fayle, *Seaborne Trade.* Vol. 3: *The Period of Unrestricted Submarine Warfare* (London 1924), 134, 139–40, 313.
16 Long to Governor General, telegram, 7 July 1917, Transports Sydney to Naval Ottawa, signal 7991, 3 August 1917, Graham Green to Chambers, 20 July 1917, NAC, RG 24, box 5645, file 48-48-1, Vol. 1; the final reports of the naval control of shipping staffs are in

NAC, RG 24, box 3981, file 49-2-40; for a detailed account of the byzantine Canadian command structure on the Atlantic coast see NHS, "RCN Shore Establishments on the Canadian East Coast, 1910–1919," 1961; Commander-in-chief, North America and West Indies, general letter, 1 October 1918, PRO, Adm 137/504, f. 427.
17 Patrick Beesly, *Room 40: British Naval Intelligence 1914–18* (London 1982), 120; NAC, RG 24, box 4031, file 65-7-3, quote from Long to Governor General, telegram, 22 June 1917.
18 Kingsmill to minister, 1 August 1917, NAC, RG 24, box 4031, file 65-7-3.
19 NAC, RG 24, box 3832, file 17-10-3; Kingsmill to secretary of the Admiralty, November 1917, PAC, RG 24, box 3831, file 17-10-1, Vol. 1.
20 Admiralty to Colonial Office, 3 January 1918, NAC, RG 24, box 3831, file 17-10-1, Vol. 1.
21 Deputy minister, Department of the Naval Service to under secretary of state, Department of External Affairs, 8 March 1918, enclosing "Memorandum on Organization of Atlantic Patrols," ibid.
22 Ibid.: NHS, "Ships and Vessels," 30–1.
23 NAC, RG 24, box 5662, file 58-53-30; deputy minister, Department of the Naval Service to under secretary of state, Department of External Affairs, 23 May 1918, Admiralty to Naval Ottawa, signal 793, 4 July 1918, NAC, RG 24, box 4031, file 66-7-6.
24 Commander-in-chief, North America and West Indies, general letter, 1 April 1918, PRO, Adm 137/504, f. 331.
25 Hose to secretary, Department of the Naval Service, 25 March 1918, PAC, RG 24, box 3832, file 17-10-4; Sarty, "Silent Sentry," 327–8.
26 PAC, RG 24, box 4027, file 62-18-2, Vols. 1–3; extracts from file 47-19-4, DHist, NHS 1440-6, "Halifax 1905–20."
27 On the east coast air patrols see J.D.F. Kealy and E.C. Russell, *A History of Canadian Naval Aviation 1918–1962* (Ottawa 1965), 1–10; S.F. Wise, *Canadian Airmen and the First World War: The Official History of the Royal Canadian Air Force*. Vol. 1, (Toronto: University of Toronto Press 1980), 603–8.
28 Commander-in-chief, North America and West Indies, general letter, 3 May 1918, PRO, Adm 137/504, f. 348; Hose to Kingsmill, 20 April 1918, NAC, RG 24, box 3833, file 17-10-7, vol. 1.
29 Hose to secretary, Department of the Naval Service, 22 May 1918, Submarine chaser division commander to Admiral Superintendent Halifax, 19 June 1918, NAC RG 24, box 4031, file 65-7-6.
30 Hose to secretary, Department of the Naval Service, 1 August 1918, ibid.; Department of the Naval Service, *Navy List*, August 1918.
31 Kingsmill to minister, 21 February 1918 forwarding Hose, memorandum, nd., NAC, RG 24, box 3831, file 17-10-1, Vol. 1; Notes from file 47-2-4, DHist, NHS 1440-6, "Halifax 1905–20"; *Trawler 30* log, 12 June 1918, NAC, RG 24, vol. 7953.
32 Washington to Naval Ottawa, signal, 2 May 1918, same to same, signal, 16 May 1918, PAC, RG 24, box 4021, file 62-13-2, vol. 3.
33 USN, *German Submarine Activities*. Unless noted otherwise, all descriptions of U-boat operations are derived from this source. William Bell Clark, *When the U-Boats Came to America* (Boston 1929) contains some additional information.
34 Robert M. Grant, *U-Boat Intelligence 1914–1918* (London 1969), 152.
35 Washington to Naval Ottawa, signal 27, 5 July 1918, NAC, RG 24, box 3773, file 48-38-1, vol. 3.
36 Grant, *Intelligence*, 153–4; Navinet Halifax to Naval Ottawa, signal 922, 26 July 1918, NAC, RG 24, box 4021, file 62-13-2, vol. 3.
37 Report of attack on *Dornfontein*, NAC, RG 24, box 4023, file 62-13-10, vol. 5; Transports Saint John to Naval Ottawa, signal 515, 3 August 1918, PAC, RG 24, box 4021, file 62-13-2, vol. 4.
38 Signals, 4-6 August 1918, NAC, RG 24, box 4021, file 62-13-2, vol. 4.
39 Patrols Sydney to Naval Ottawa, signal, 5 August 1918, NAC, RG 24, box 4031, file 65-7-6; Newcombe to Captain of Patrols, 13 August 1918, DHist, NHS 8000, "Niobe" (the account of the movements of the Canadian and American patrol vessels is primarily based upon this report); logs of *Canadian Drifter (CD) 14*, NAC, RG 24, Vol. 7155; *CD 15*, ibid., Vol. 7157; *CD 19*, ibid., 7158; *CD 33*, ibid., vol. 7171; *St Eloi*, ibid., 7919.

40 Report of attack on *Luz Blanca*, NAC, RG 24, box 4023, file 62-13-10, vol. 4.
41 Sydney-Ottawa signals, 5–7 August 1918, NAC, RG 24, box 4031, file 65-7-6; NHS, "RCN Shore Establishments," 27–8.
42 In addition to the First World War logs in the 7000 series of volumes in NAC, RG 24, see the final reports of the Canadian control of shipping staffs, NAC, RG 24, box 3981, file 49-2-40; notes from file 57-4-30, DHist, NHS 8000, "Trawlers and Drifters," vol. 2.
43 USN, *German Submarine Activities*, 11; Washington to Naval Ottawa, signals 101 and 104, 6 August 1918, Admiralty to Naval Ottawa, signal 42, 8 August 1918, NAC, RG 24, box 3773, file 48-48-1, vol. 4; Grant, *Intelligence*, 154.
44 Report of attack on *Triumph*, NAC, RG 24, box 4023, file 62-13-10, vol. 4; signals, 21–3 August 1918, NAC, RG 24, box 4023, file 62-13-2, vols. 4–5.
45 Quote from McKnight to Captain of Patrols, 17 September 1918, DHist, NHS 1440–6, "Halifax 1905–20"; also see exracts from file 47-5-1, DHist, NHS 8000, "Stadacona (Ship Afloat)."
46 Quote from extracts from file 47-23-164, DHist, NHS, "Halifax 1905–20"; Kingsmill, memorandum, 7 August 1918, DHist 81/520/1000-973, vol. 1.
47 Signals, 10–12 August 1918, NAC, RG 24, box 4031, file 65-7-6; notes from file 57-4-30, DHist, NHS 8000, "Trawlers and Drifters," vol. 2; Signals, 27 August–8 September 1918, NAC RG 24, box 4021, file 62-13-2 vol. 5.
48 Naval Ottawa to Transports Sydney, signal 44, 6 August 1918, NAC, RG 24, box 4031, file 65-7-6; *Laurentian* log, 11 August 1918, NAC, RG 24, vol. 7450; Notes from file 57-4-31, DHist, NHS 8000, "Trawlers and Drifters," vol. 2.
49 Director of Operations Division to Director of the Naval Service, 29 August 1918, Department of the Naval Service, "Drifters Built in Canada," 3 March 1919, NAC, RG 24, box 4031, file 65-7-6; NHS, "Ships and Vessels," 35–7.
50 Naval Ottawa to Navyard Halifax, signal 974, 19 August 1918, Storey to Director of the Naval Service, 20 August 1918, NAC, RG 24, box 4031, file 65-7-6.
51 Naval Ottawa-Patrols Sydney signals, 3–5 September 1918, ibid.
52 Navinet Halifax to Naval Ottawa, signal 732, 14 September 1918, NAC, RG 24, box 4021, file 62-13-2, vol. 5; NAC, RG 24, box 3970, file 47-30-2, vol. 2.
53 *Margaret* log, 14–26 September 1918, NAC, RG 24, box 7493; Notes from file 57-4-31, DHist, NHS, "Trawlers and Drifters," vol. 2; Patrols Sydney to Naval Ottawa, signal 430, 21 September 1918, Washington to Naval Ottawa, signal 410, 31 October 1918, NAC, RG 24, box 3773, file 48-48-1, vol. 4.
54 Ballantyne to Wemyss, 11 September 1918, NAC, RG 24, box 3831, file 17-10-1, vol. 1; G.J. Desbarats diary, 16 September 1918, NAC, RG 30E89, vol. 5.
55 Hose to secretary, Department of the Naval Service, 24 September 1918, NAC, RG 24, box 4032, file 65-7-12.
56 Naval Ottawa to Britannia, signal 2023, 29 August 1918, NAC, RG 24, box 5651, vol. 2; Newcombe to Captain of Patrols, 13 August 1918, DHist, NHS 8000, "Niobe."
57 Hose to secretary, Department of the Naval Service, 21 October 1918, NAC, RG 24, box 4032, file 65-7-12; Kingsmill to minister, 5 November 1918 forwarding Gibbs to Director of the Naval Service, 28 October 1918, Ballantyne to Kingsmill, 5 November 1918, NAC, RG 24, box 4029, file 65-1-1.
58 Report of attack on *Erik*, NAC, RG 24, box 4023, file 62-13-10, vol. 4; Clippings from *The Standard* (St John, NB) in NAC, RG 24, box 4021, file 62-13-2, vol. 4.
59 Grant, *Intelligence*, 155; *German Submarine Activities*, 99; see also report of attack on *Kingfisher*, NAC, RG 24, box 4023, file 62-13-10, vol. 4; quote from Arthur Hezlett, *The Submarine and Sea Power* (London 1967), 94–5.

CHAPTER SEVEN: INSHORE ASW IN THE SECOND WORLD WAR

1 See my *U-Boats against Canada: German Submarines in Canadian Waters* (Montreal and Kingston: McGill-Queen's University Press 1985).
2 Nazi party newspaper *Völkischer Beobachter: Kampfblatt der national-sozialistischen Bewegung GroBdeutschlands* in describing the Quebec conference, September 1944.
3 Joseph Schull, *The Far Distant Ships: An Official Account of Canadian Naval Operations in the Second World War* (Ottawa: Queen's Printer 1952).

4 Karl Dönitz, *Memoirs: Ten Years and Twenty Days*. Trans. R.H. Stevens (London: Weidenfeld and Nicolson 1959) 195. Originally *Zehn Jahre und Zwanzig Tage* (Bonn: Atheneum-Verlag 1958).
5 War Diary, Commander U-boats (KTB/BdU), 2 January 1942, Bundesarchiv-Militärarchiv, Freiburg i.B., Federal Republic of Germany (hereafter BA-MA): PG 30302/3. Unless otherwise noted, this and other German sources are rendered by my translation.
6 See for example, W.A.B. Douglas and Brereton Greenhous, *Out of the Shadows: Canada in the Second World War* (Toronto: Oxford University Press 1977); Marc Milner, *Canadian Naval Force Requirements in the Second World War*, OREA Extra-Mural Paper No. 20 (Ottawa: Operational Research and Analysis Establishment, Department of National Defence 1981); also note 1 above, 19.
7 *Ubootshandbuch der Ostküste Kanadas*, Bd. 1 [covers Cape Breton, Nova Scotia, Bay of Fundy], Marinedienstvorschrift Nr. 299, (Berlin: Oberkommando der Kriegsmarine 1942); Bd. 2 *Neufundland und Belle Isle Strasse* (Berlin 1942); Bd. 3 *St Lorenz-Golf* (Berlin 1943).
8 Interview with Admiral Godt, Kiel, Germany, July 1982.
9 From U-1232's daily one-page newspaper *Der Zirkus* (Nr. 1, Jg. II, 3 January 1945). Sole extant copies in possession of the U-boat's former commanding officer, Dr Kurt Dobratz. On isolated occasions the Nazi party newspaper *Völkischen Beobachten* spoke explicitly of the "Canadian Navy" (14 September 1942; 25 September 1942), or the "Canadian Coast" (10 November 1942).
10 As used herein, the terms "Canadian Zone" and "Canadian waters" refer to the operational area under control of commander-in-chief, Canadian Northwest Atlantic (formerly Commanding Officer, Atlantic Coast). It is broadly depicted in "RCN Operational Plotting Sheet: East Coast of Canada" (Ottawa: Department of Mines and Technical Surveys 1942) which spans longitudes 50° to 69° West. Contemporary Canadian hydrographic chart L/C 4001 "Gulf of Maine to Strait of Belle Isle" reflects the actual area.
11 For a survey of Allied ASW equipment see Anthony J. Watts, *The U-Boat Hunters* (London: Macdonald and Jane's 1976).
12 For purposes of discussion I have standardized the description to conform to a basic Type VII C *Atlantikboot*. For details see Eberhard Rössler, *The U-Boat: The Evolution and Technical History of German Submarines*. Trans. Harold Erenberg (London: Arms and Armour Press 1981). Originally *Geschichte des deutschen Ubootbaus* (Munich: J.F. Lehmanns Verlag 1975).
13 Based on U-boat War Diaries (available in BA-MA). Significantly, aerial reconnaissance on the outbound leg from Europe forced U-548 to transit 65 per cent submerged.
14 For a brief account of German Search Radar (radar warning or observation devices) in the High Frequency war see Rössler (note 12 above), 196–8. Naval Intelligence produced a revealing précis, "G.S.R. and Radar in German U-Boats: Development and Tactical Use," *RCN-RCAF Monthly Operational Review* (November 1944): 24–6. See also note 29 below.
15 A/Captain D.K. Laidlaw, RCN(T), Director of Operations Division, to CNS, "Protection of Shipping in Canada's Coastal Zone," 21 November 1944. Directorate of History, National Defence Headquarters, Ottawa (hereafter DHist): NSS 1048-48-31.
16 Commander-in-chief Portsmouth, DTG 221530/February 19 44, in "TAS Signals 1940–45," DHist: 81/520/1000-973, vol. 8.
17 War Diary (KTB/U-553), 3 August 1942, BA-MA: RM 98/V. PG 30590b.
18 Marinedienstvorschrift, *Handbuch für U-Bootskommandanten*, M. Dv. Nr. 906 (Berlin: Oberkommando der Kriegsmarine 1942). (BA-MA.)
19 The weather station was established by U-537 in October 1943. See also Alec [W.A.B.] Douglas, "The Nazi Weather Station in Labrador," *Canadian Geographic* 101, No. 6 (December 1981/January 1982): 42–7; W.A.B. Douglas and Franz Selinger "Oktober 1943–Juli 1984: Eine Marine-Wetterstation auf Labrador," *Marine Rundschau*, No. 5 (March 1982): 256–62.
20 Though not sunk, HMCS *Magog* was so severely damaged that she was eventually

scrapped.
21 Marinedienstvorschrift (M.Dv.Nr. 87), *Anleitung zum Erkennen und Schätzen der GröBe von Handelsschiffen auf See* (Berlin: Oberkommando der Kriegsmarine 1938); unveränderter Nachdruck, 1943. BA-MA: RMD 4/87.
22 See RADM G.C. Jones, COAC, Halifax, "Control of Navigational Aids: West Coast," 20 July 1942, DHist: 181. 002 (D 68 A), folder 2. Also DHist: 83/662. The monthly "Report of Proceedings, Staff Officer Operations" throughout the war reveals the high number of collisions and groundings despite full navigational facilities.
23 For an evaluation of hunts to exhaustion see *RCN-RCAF Monthly Review*, December 1943, DHist: 182.013 (D 26).
24 For a discussion of this problem see my *U-boats*, 30–2, and Marc Milner, *North Atlantic Run: The Royal Canadian Navy and the Battle for the Convoys* (Toronto and London: University of Toronto Press 1985), 60.
25 In 1941 U-111 observed that chart folios for large submarines operating off Belle Isle contained not a single nautical chart, List of Light Signals, or Sailing Direction for the Canadian and American coasts. He and his successors of 1942 depended on the large-area small-scale German chart G 1870 (scale 1:8 million). At other times they had recourse to British Admiralty charts. But the War Diary of U-1231 notes during the St Lawrence operations of November 1944 that "English charts are very skimpy with regard to [pilotage] data," KTB/U-1231, BA-MA: RM 98/v. PG 30869-879a, Case 16/2.
26 Of the victims to merchants, U-756 was rammed and sunk by SS *Unicoi*, while U-132 was destroyed by the explosion of an ammunition ship in convoy SC 107.
27 Interview with Admiral Hartwig, Kiel, Germany, July 1982.
28 Milner, *North Atlantic Run*, 79, observes that "from August 1940 to February 1942 only four U-boats are known to have been detected on the surface with the aid of radar, and of this number only one was attacked."
29 For details of the following see Helmut Giessler, *Der Marine-Nachrichten-und Ortungsdiensts, Technische Entwicklung und Kriegserfahrung*, Wehrwissenschaftliche Berichte, Herausgegeben vom Arbeitskreis für Wehrforschung, Bd. IV (Munich: J.F. Lehmanns Verlag 1971). For the full range of "Naval Operating Manuals" (Marinedienstvorschriften) see the collection in BA-MA: RMD 4/291; RMD 4/960-968, RM 7/106.
30 RCAF, "Radar Anti-Submarine Measures in Gulf of St Lawrence," NS 1037-2-6 (Staff), 22 May 1944, DHist: 1650-239/16 B, vol. 1.
31 NL-9 consisted of seven vessels screened by the three corvettes HMCS *Arrowhead*, *Shawinigan*, and *Trail*. *Carolus* sank 9 October 1942.
32 War Diary (KTB/U-69), BA-MA: RM 98/175.
33 There were, of course, some exceptions. The War Diary of U-43 notes during the St Lawrence operations in October 1942 that aircraft attacks seemed to have been initiated by possible radar contact. Significantly, its GSR search receiver had given no warning.
34 War Diary (KTB/U-43), 18 October 1942, BA-MA: RM 98/116.
35 War Diary (KTB/BdU), August 1944, BA-MA: RM87/42.
36 Canadian asdic occasionally proved unable to locate known wrecks, such as that of the British submarine HMS/M P-514 rammed and sunk in error by HMCS *Georgian* (46° 32' 30" N, 53° 33' W), and that of HMCS *Esquimalt* sunk by U-190 off the Sambro lightship.
37 See "Description of Method Used by HMCS Saint John in Attacking Bottomed Contacts" [derived from experience in the Western Approaches], DHist: "Torpedo: A/S General," 81/520, 1000-973, vol. 1.
38 Interview with Kurt Petersen, Commanding officer of U-541, July 1982, and subsequent correspondence.
39 The term "Zaunkönig" means "wren" or "hedge-sparrow." "GNAT" is an Allied acronym for German naval acoustic torpedo.
40 *Shawinigan* was torpedoed from 2500 meters. Admiralty advised commands in April 1943 of the new torpedo. Operational Research in Ottawa prepared a provisional evaluation on 20 September 1943. See "Notes on Homing Torpedoes from the Operational Standpoint." Both documents in DHist: "TAS Signals 1940–50," 81/520/1000-973, vol. 4.

41 DHist: 8000-Grandmère. See Admiral L.W. Murray's response to "Report of Attack."
42 Samuel Eliot Morison, *The Battle of the Atlantic, September 1939–May 1943*. Vol. 1 of *History of United States Naval Operations in World War II* (Boston: Little, Brown and Company 1960), 330.
43 See, for example, "Notes on the 'Cat' Gear," *RCN-RCAF Monthly Review* (January 1944): 24–26, DHist: 182.013 (D6). Also DHist: "TAS Signals 1940–45," 81/520/1000-973, vol. 8 (C-in-C, WA to AIG 32). See also *United States Anti-Submarine Bulletin* November 1943, "Counter-Measures against German Acoustic Torpedo," 15–18, and December 1943, 17–8 (DHist).
44 Quoted in Hirschmann's translation with kind permission of Werner Hirschmann, who offered the documents to the author in June 1985.
45 Interview with Admiral J.C. Hibbard, Victoria, BC, May 1985.
46 See RCN Operational Research Report No. 31, "Anti-U-Boat Operations of the Royal Canadian Navy 1940–1944," DHist: 1650-239/16 B, vol. 2; and Naval Intelligence Division, Admiralty, NID 04045/44, BR 1907 (103), *Interrogation of U-Boat Survivors: Cumulative Edition*, June 1944, DHist: Document 80/582, Item 64.
47 See *United States Fleet Anti-Submarine Bulletin* (September 1944): 41–42 (DHist).
48 Interview with Kurt Petersen, CO of U-541.
49 Letter to the author, from Werner Hirschmann, former engineer officer aboard U-190 (which sunk HMCS *Esquimalt*), 2 July 1985.
50 James B. Lamb, *The Corvette Navy: True Stories from Canada's Atlantic War* (Toronto: Macmillan 1979).
51 Letter from Hirschmann.

CHAPTER EIGHT: INSHORE ASW

1 I am deeply indebted to my friend and colleague Dr Roger Sarty for sharing his pioneering research on Canadian plans and responses to the inshore submarine threat.
2 See S.F. Wise, *Canadian Airmen and the First World War: The Official History of the Royal Canadian Air Force*, Vol. 1 (Toronto: University of Toronto Press 1980), chapter 8.
3 Admiral Sir R. Bacon and F.E. McMurtrie, *Modern Naval Strategy* (London: Frederick Muller 1940), 148–9.
4 "The Efficiency of the Asdic in Coastal Waters," UBW (45) 4, U-Boat Warfare Committee, British Cabinet, n/d, commander-in-chief CNA's covering letter 4 April 1945, National Archives Canada (NAC), RG 24, 11580, D 23-2-1.
5 Willem Hackman, *Seek and Strike: Sonar, Anti-Submarine Warfare and the Royal Navy 1914–54* (London: Her Majesty's Stationery Office 1985), 139–46.
6 W.A.B. Douglas, *The Creation of a National Air Force: The Official History of the Royal Canadian Air Force*, Vol. 2 (Toronto: University of Toronto Press 1986), chapters 12 and 14. See also M. Milner, *North Atlantic Run: The Royal Canadian Navy and the Battle for the Convoys* (Toronto: University of Toronto Press 1985), Chapters 5 and 6.
7 HMS *Pelican*, Report of Proceedings, 7 May 1943, NAC, RG 24, 11026, CND 7–16.
8 Two sinkings were made by No. 1 Group aircraft during the battle for SC 107 in late October, early November 1942, see Douglas, *Creation of a National Air Force*, Chapter 14.
9 Director of Naval Operations to Assistant Chief of the Naval Staff and the Chief of the Naval Staff, 15 August 1940, Directorate of History (DHist), NS 8000, HMCS *Captor*.
10 "Defence of Shipping in the Gulf of St Lawrence, Plan GL," 25 April 1941, DHist, NHS 1650-239/16B, vol. 1.
11 Captain (D), Halifax, Monthly Report for May 1942, DHist, NS 1000-5-13, Vol. 11.
12 "AS Warfare Operational Research Report, Canadian Atlantic Coast Area," Report No. 3, 21 April 1943, NAC, Accession 83–84/167, NSS 1670-3-2, Vol. 1, claims no losses from convoys off Nova Scotia during 1942, but at least one ship, *Pacific Pioneer*, was lost from ON-113 in July 1942, see Milner, *North Atlantic Run*, 127.
13 Douglas, *Creation of a National Air Force*, Chapter 13.
14 See scheme in Appendix A to a revision of the Gulf Plan for 1942 in DHist 1650-239/16B, vol. 1.
15 M. Hadley, *U-Boats against Canada: German Submarines in Canadian Waters* (Kingston and

Montreal: McGill-Queen's University Press 1985), 101–2, 117–19 and 125–7.
16 Douglas, *Creation of a National Air Force*, Chapter 13.
17 "AS Warfare Operational Research Report, Canadian Atlantic Coast Area," Report No. 2, 22 March 1943, NAC, Accession 83-4/167, NSS 1670-3-2, vol. 1.
18 "AS Warfare Operational Research Report, Canadian Atlantic Coast Area," Report No. 3, 21 April 1943.
19 Secretary of the Naval Board Memorandum, "Defence of the Gulf of St Lawrence," 27 February 43, DHist 1650-239/16B, vol. 1.
20 *Atlantic Convoy Instructions*, Operations Section, Article 101, DHist 83/761.
21 "Hints on Escort Work," Part I in DHist 81/700, balance of parts in NAC, RG 24, 11938, NSS 8440–2, vol. 1, and Naval Staff comments on copies in NAC, RG 24, 3901, NSS 1037-2-9, vol. 1.
22 "Gulf of St Lawrence. GL 43," 25 May 1943, NAC, RG 24, 11579, NSD 16-59-19.
23 RCN "Daily States" for 1943, DHist, NHS 1650-DS.
24 Staff Officer (AS), Gaspé to NOIC, Gaspé, 2 November 1943, NAC, RG 24, 12009, G 23-4-1.
25 Wilfrid Eggleston, *Scientists at War* (Toronto: Oxford University Press 1950), 147.
26 Director of AS Memorandum, 22 December 1943, DHist, Naval Historian's Auxiliary Ship files, *Culver*.
27 Commander-in-chief, CNA to various, 27 June 1943, NAC, RG 24, 11696, NSDH 1003-6-15; Eggleston, *Scientists at War*, 147.
28 Hackman, *Seek and Strike*, 144; "History of the Anti-Submarine Measures Division of the Tenth Fleet," Chronology, Operational Archives Branch, Naval Historical Centre, Washington, DC; *United States Fleet Anti-Submarine and Escort of Convoy Instructions* (FTP 223A), January 1944, DHist 79/532; "Sound Ranging Chart of the North Atlantic Ocean," US Hydrographic Officer, May 1942, NAC, RG 24, 11026, CNA 7-16-4.
29 Douglas, *Creation of a National Air Force*, Chapter 16.
30 Ibid.
31 Ibid.
32 Quote from Commodore Reid as cited in ibid.
33 "A Comparison of AS Hunts in Canadian and British Coastal Waters," RCN Operational Research Report No. 35, 27 August 1945, NAC, RG 24, 11463, Reports.
34 Commander-in-chief, Western Approaches to various, 142141A/12/43, NAC, RG 24, 11580, D 23-2-1.
35 Douglas, *Creation of a National Air Force*, Chapter 16.
36 *RCN-RCAF Monthly Operational Review*, May 1943, DHist 181.013 (D6).
37 Ibid. December 1944.
38 *U.S. Fleet Anti-Submarine Bulletin*, November 1944, DHist.
39 Admiralty, *Monthly Anti-Submarine Report*, February 1944, DHist library.
40 Captain (D), Halifax, minute on SO(AS), Gaspé's Report on Asdic Conditions in the Gulf, 17 December 1943, NAC, RG 24, 11026, CNA 7–16.
41 "Review of the Asdic Oceanographic Conferences," January 1944, by J.P. Tully, NAC, RG 77, Accession 85–6/044; PN-2; Atlantic Oceanographic Research Group (AORG), St Andrews, NB, to Commodore Superintendent, HMC Dockyard, Halifax, 16 May 1944, NAC, RG 24, 11696, NSDH 1003-6-15.
42 "Review of the Asdic Oceanographic Conferences," April 1944, by J.P. Tully, NAC, RG 77, Accession 85–6/044, PN-3; "Asdic Ranging Conditions in the Halifax Approaches," National Research Council, National Research Laboratories Report, PSA 1, 18 August 1944 NAC, RG 24, 11463, Bathythermography-General.
43 Lt(AS) R.A. Nairn, *Springhill*, to commander-in-chief, CNA, 12 December 1944 NAC, RG 24, 11026, CNA 7-16-4.
44 Douglas, *Creation of a National Air Force*, Chapter 17.
45 Joint RCN/RCAF Anti-Submarine Committee, Minutes, 2 November 1944, DHist, 181.009 (D3188); "Escort Group W.13," DHist, NHS 1650-239/16B, vol. 2: Captain (D), Halifax, 17 December 1943 NAC, RG 24, 11575, D 1-18-1.
46 Secretary of the Naval Board Memorandum, 15 November 1944, NAC, RG 24, 11026, CNA 7–16.
47 Ibid., and Naval Staff Minutes, 23 October 1944, DHist.

48 Admiralty, *Monthly Anti-Submarine Report*, August 1944, DHist Library.
49 Commodore (D), Western Approaches Minute on Senior Officer EG 11 to Commodore (D), WA, "Submarine Warfare in the Channel," 17 July 1944, NAC, RG 24, 11938, NS 8100-1, vol. 1.
50 Admiralty 092030Z/9/44, NAC, RG 24, 11580, D 23-2-1.
51 Senior Officer, EG-27, Report of Proceedings, 22 January 1945, DHist, NHS 8440, EG-27, vol. 1.
52 See Captain (D), Halifax, Monthly Reports in DHist NS 1000-5-13.
53 Commander of the Port to commander-in-chief, CNA, 23 January 1945 NAC, RG 24, 11695, NSDH 1003-6-2, vol. 1.
54 "Bottom Sediments and Their Effect on Shallow Water Echo Ranging in Canadian Atlantic Waters," NRC, National Research Laboratories Report, PSA 3, 30 November 1944 NAC, RG 24, 11026, CNA 7–16.
55 Naval Staff Minutes, DHist.
56 "Submarine Warfare in the Channel," SO EG-11 to Commodore (D) Western Approaches, 17 July 1944, and related correspondence, NAC, RG 24, 11938, NS 8700-1, vol. 1.
57 Joint RCN/RCAF Anti-Submarine Committee, Minutes 25 January 1945, DHist 181.009 (D3188).
58 Appendix A to ibid. 29 March 1945.
59 "Conference between Task Group 22.9 and Canadian Anti-Submarine Forces on 19th January 1945," Report of CTG 22.9 to commander-in-chief, US Fleet, 21 January 1945, NAC, RG 24, 11938, NS 8100-1 vol. 1.
60 "Refraction Errors in Estimating Submarine Depths in Canadian Atlantic Waters," NRC, National Research Laboratories Report, PSA 4, 22 January 1945, and Minutes of Conference on Bathythermography at NSHQ, 18–22 December 1944, NAC, RG 24, 11026, CNS 7–16: Naval Staff Minutes, 23 October 1944 DHist.
61 Naval Staff Minutes, DHist.
62 See especially the minutes of the Joint RCN/RCAF Anti-Submarine Committee, DHist 181.009(D3188).
63 Captain (D), Halifax to CinC, CNA, 25 March 1945, PAC, RG 24, 11575, D 1-18-1.
64 Senior Officer, EG-28, to Captain (D), Halifax, 11 March 1945 and Captain (D), Halifax to SO EG-28, 17 April 1945, NAC, RG 24, 11575, D 1-18-1.
65 "A Comparison of AS Hunts in Canadian and British Waters," NAC, RG 24, 11463, Reports.

CHAPTER NINE: CANADA AND THE WOLF PACKS, SEPTEMBER 1943

1 F.H. Hinsley, E.E. Thomas, C.F.G. Ransom, R.C. Knight, *British Intelligence in the Second World War: Its Influence on Strategy and Operations*, 3 Vols. (London: Her Majesty's Stationery Office [HMSO] 1978–81), Vol. 2, 548.
2 Ibid., 561 and Appendix 19: "The Breaking of the U-boat Enigma (Shark)," 747–52; Heinz Bonatz, *Seekrieg im Äther: Die Leistungen der Marine-Funkaufklärung, 1939–1945* (Herford: Mittler 1981), 239–56; Ralph Erskine and Frode Weirud, "Naval Enigma: M4 and Its Roots," *Cryptologia*, 11, No. 4 (October 1987), 235–44. They show that M4 was being used in the M3 mode, and therefore was easier to break.
3 S.W. Roskill, *The War at Sea*, Vol. 2, *The Period of Balance* (London: HMSO 1956), 367–8; Sir Peter Gretton, *Crisis Convoy: The Story of the Atlantic Convoy HX.231* (London: Davies 1974), 20; Hinsley, et al., *British Intelligence*.
4 Roskill, *Period of Balance*; S.E. Morison, *History of US Naval Operations in World War II*, Vol. 10, *The Atlantic Battle Won* (Boston: Little, Brown & Co. 1956), 16, 19–20.
5 Hinsley, et al., *British Intelligence*, 563; Roskill, *Period of Balance*, 367; Admiralty, Naval Staff, Pink Lists, 1 March 1943 and 1 April 1943; Public Record Office (PRO): Cab 86/3, AU (43) 90, 22 March 1943, para. 1(c).
6 Kriegstagebuch des Befehlshabers der U-Boote—War Diary, Commander, U-boats— (KTB/BdU) 24 May 1943; Karl Dönitz, *10 Jahre und 20 Tage* (Munich: Bernard & Graefe 1980), 333–4.

7 Ibid. 397–414.
8 Philip M. Morse and George E. Kimball, *Methods of Operational Research* (London: Chapman and Hall 1951), 43–4; David Syrett and W.A.B. Douglas, "Die Schliessung des Grönland-Luftlochs im Atlantik, 1942–1943," Part 1, *Marine Rundschau* 83, No. 1 (January 1986).
9 J. Rohwer and G. Hümmelchen, *Chronology of the War at Sea, 1939–1945*, Vol. 2 (London: Ian Allan 1974), 331–2; PRO ADM 199/2021, Anti-U-boat Division, Admiralty: Analysis of the Bay Operations, 14 June–21 September 1943.
10 Hinsley, et al., *British Intelligence*, Vol. 3, 220; KTB/BdU, July 1943.
11 Rohwer/Hümmelchen, *Chronology, 346;* ADM 199/599, Director, Trade Division, Admiralty, Threats in the Bay Area, 20 July 1943, ADM 199/2021.
12 Operational Archives US Navy History Division, Washington, Convoy folders for UGF/UGS/GUF/GUS convoys 1943; Daily Situation Maps Atlantic, July 1943.
13 Hinsley, et al., *British Intelligence*, Vol. 1, 638.
14 Ibid. Vol. 3, 211–2; ADM 1/12589, American Operational Research Group: Direct Routing and the Offensive against the U-boats.
15 Adm 199/599, Convoy Organization: Size, Cycles, Routing; ibid., Pink Lists, 1 June, 1 July, 1 August, 1 September 1943; ibid., NSHQ to commander-in-chief CNA, 1742Z, 29 September 1943, Group Organization of Canadian Escort Forces.
16 W.A.B. Douglas, *The Official History of the Royal Canadian Air Force*, Vol. II, *The Creation of a National Air Force* (Toronto: University of Toronto Press 1986) 561–7; Syrett and Douglas, "Die Schliessung,"; PRO AIR 25/254, HI No 15 Group RAF, Operations Record Book.
17 ADM 223/16, Admiralty appreciation of U-boat situation, 1 August 1943, and Submarine Tracking Room, U-boat situation, Autumn 1943, 121–7.
18 ADM 223/21, Admiralty Intelligence Summaries, Autumn 1944.
19 These dispositions have been reconstructed by J. Rohwer from the following sources:
   (a) KTB/BdU, 23 August–24 September 1943
   (b) USN Operational Archives, Daily Situation Maps Atlantic
   (c) ADM 199, Reports of Proceedings, Commodores of Convoys (HX, SC, ON, ONS, SL, HG, OS, MKF, MKS, KMS, XK, UGF, UGS, GUF, GUS);
   (d) Ibid., Reports of Proceedings, Senior Officers, Escort Groups (same convoys)
   (e) National Archives, Washington, SRH 008, Op 20 G Study, "U-boat Operations," Part B: Chapters 9 and 10, 167–87, "U-boat Defensive and Anti-Submarine Activities, May 1943–June 1944."
20 KTB/BdU, 15 September 1943; PRO DEFE 3/721, Enigma Intercepts, ZTPGU 16929, 0943/18/9/43.
21 USN Operational Archives, Report of Operations, Commander Task Group 21.12, 5–26 September 1943.
22 DEFE 3/721, ZTPGU 16869A, 0548/14/9/43.
23 ZTPGU 16869, 0123/13/9/43; ZTPGU 16880, 1937/13/9/43.
24 ADM 199/2022, Naval Staff, Anti-U-boat Division, 15 November 1943, Analysis of U-boat operations in the vicinity of Convoys ONS-18 and ON-202, 19–24 September 1943 (hereafter AU Analysis).
25 ZTPGU 16961A, 1931/19/9/43; ZTPGU 16972A, 2255/19/9/431; ZTPGU 16974, 2150/18/9/43.
26 ZTPGU 16961B, 0648/20/9/43.
27 ZTPGU 17174, 1137/25/9/43; KTB/BdU 20 September 1943.
28 Ibid., ZTPGU 17178, 1133/25/9/43.
29 ZTPGU 16880, 1937/13/9/43.
30 RCN *Navy Lists*. The Captain of *Chambly*, A.F. Pickard, had been her navigating officer when she sank a U-boat during the battle for SC-42 in September 1941. See J. Rohwer and W.A.B. Douglas, "The 'Most Thankless Task' Revisited: Convoys, Escorts and Radio Intelligence in the Western Atlantic, 1941–1943," in J.A. Boutilier (ed.), *The RCN in Retrospect, 1910–1968* (Vancouver: University of British Columbia Press 1982), 187–234. *Sackville*, the last remaining corvette, was dedicated as the Canadian national naval memorial in 1985; Ernest M. Chadwick, first lieutenant and later captain of

Gatineau in 1943, and also a noted artist, painted *Sackville* for this occasion.
31 Eberhard Rössler, *The U-boat: The Evolution and Technical History of German Submarines*, Trans. Harold Ehrenberg (Annapolis: US Naval Institute Press 1981), first published as *Geschichte des Deutschen U-bootbaus* (Munich: J.F. Lehmanns Verlag 1975), 143–71.
32 The convoy battle has been reconstructed by W.A.B. Douglas from the following sources:
 (a) DEFE 3/721, Enigma Intercepts
 (b) ADM 199/353, 497–590, Convoys ON-202 and ONS-18, Reports of Proceedings
 (c) ADM 199/583, 636–40, Convoy ON-202, Commodore's Report of Proceedings
 (d) ADM 199/2022, AU Analysis
 (e) ADM 223/16, 92–99, OIC analysis of ONS-18 and ON-202
 (f) AIR 24, Operations Record Books 86 and 120 Squadrons RAF
 (g) National Defence HQ, Ottawa, Directorate of History, (DHist) 31/520/8280, ONS-18 and ON-202, and related files
 (h) DHist 79/446 Translation of the KTB/BdU
 (j) DHist, Operations Record Book 10(BR) Squadron RCAF
 (k) DHist, 181.003, RCAF Submarine attack records
 (m) National Archives of Canada (NAC), RG 24, ships' logs
 (n) National Archives Collection, Washington, RG 242, National Archives Microfilm Publication T1022, Records of the German Navy, 1850–1945, U-boat KTBS.
33 KTB U-270; *Gatineau* log.
34 KTB U-270 and U-238; *Gatineau* log; ADM 199/353, 565–8.
35 KTBS U-238, U-731, U-338; *Gatineau* and *Kamloops* logs; ADM 199/353, 551–4.
36 Ibid. 507.
37 ORB 120 Squadron.
38 ADM 199/353, 508.
39 Ibid.; *Drumheller* log; ORB 120 Squadron; KTBS U-386 and U-338.
40 KTB U-386; ADM 199/353, 508.
41 KTB U-386.
42 KTBS U-305, U-338, U-645; *Drumheller* log; ORB 120 Squadron.
43 KTBS U-305, U-952.
44 KTB/BdU; KTBS U-260, U-270, U-641, U-952.
45 KTBS U-270, U-377, U-641, U-952.
46 KTBS U-270, U-377, U-378, U-731; *Sackville* log.
47 ADM 199/353, 508. Commander Evans omitted to report that the MAC ship flew off several Swordfish when the fog lifted. When they returned they had to land in fifty yards visibility, with the aid of lighted bats and a fog buoy streamed astern of the carrier. Ibid. 588.
48 Ibid.
49 *Chambly, Sackville, Morden* logs.
50 J. Rohwer, *Axis Submarine Successes, 1939–1945* (Annapolis: US Naval Institute Press 1983) originally published as *Die U-booterfolge der Achsenmächte, 1939–45* (Munich: J.F. Lehmanns Verlag 1968), 172; KTB U-422; *Chambly, Morden* logs; ADM 199/353, 575–80; AU Analysis.
51 ADM 199/353, 511.
52 ORB 10(BR) Squadron; KTB U-270; AU Analysis.
53 ORB 10(BR) Squadron; KTBS U-377, U-402; AU Analysis.
54 ADM 199/353, 588-9; AU Analysis.
55 KTBS U-260, U-275, U-305, U-378, U-584, U-641, U-666, U-731; ADM 199/353, 508–9.
56 KTB U-952; AU Analysis. The location of U-275 60 miles on the starboard bow of the convoy according to the Anti-U-boat Division analysis is patently wrong.
57 KTBS U-260, U-666, U-731; *Gatineau, Morden* logs; for an attempted reconstruction of events by the escort commander see ADM 199/353, 517–20; for an account by one of the survivors, see *Royal Canadian Navy, Monthly Review*, No. 31 (August 1944).
58 KTBS U-238, U-260, U-302; *Chambly, Gatineau* logs; AU Analysis.
59 DHist 81/520/8280, ONS-18, Minutes of conference held at St John's, Newfoundland, 26 September 1943, 16.

60 KTB U-238; *Drumheller* log; ADM 199/353, 513.
61 KTBs U-238, U-305, U-641, U-731, U-758, U-952.
62 KTB U-952.
63 Ibid.; *Chambly* log.
64 KTB/BdU; KTB U-758. This U-boat released a new deceptive device, the "Bolde 5," which created realistic echoes distinguishable from a submarine only to a very sensitive and well-trained ear.
65 ORB 10(BR) Squadron; KTBs U-305, U-422.
66 DHist 81/520/8280, ONS-18, Minutes of conference, 26 September 1943.
67 ADM 199/353, 516.
68 Ibid.
69 *Chambly* log; Minutes of conference, 26 September.
70 ADM 199/353, 542.
71 J. Rohwer, *The Critical Convoy Battles of March 1943: The Battle for HX.229/SC.122*, translated from the German edition of 1975 by Derek Masters and A.J. Barker (Annapolis: US Naval Institute Press 1977), 36.
72 Evaluation of "Zaunkönig" firings in action (September 1943–May 1945). Information from the Library of Contemporary History, Stuttgart, for the federal office of military technology and procurement; MS IV 2/04/101 a 505/622, prepared by J. Rohwer. Source: U-boat torpedo firing reports.
73 Oberkommando der Kriegsmarine, Seekriegsleitung–Supreme Naval Command, Naval War Staff (OKM, Skl)/Chef MND III: xB-Bericht Nr 39/1943, Vol. 30, September 1943.
74 ADM 223/16, OIC/SI 713, 30 September 1943; ADM 1/16582, Special Report on the German Acoustic Torpedo and the Various Counter-Measures Against It, 31 March 1944.
75 ADM 223/18, OIC Special Intelligence Summary, 20 and 27 September, 4 and 11 October 1943.
76 Ibid.; ADM 199/354, 578, 583, 584. Reports of Proceedings, convoys ON-203, ON-204, ONS-19, HX-258; ADM 199/1491, Anti-U-boat Division, Analysis of attacks on and by U-boats, Convoy SC-143, 119-26.
77 Rohwer/Hümmelchen, 358; Sir Peter Gretton, *Convoy Escort Commander* (London: Cassell 1964); KTB/BdU 15–20 October 1943.
78 Syrett/Douglas, "Die Schliessung"; Eberhard Rössler, *Die deutschen U-Boote und ihre Werften*, vols. 1, 2 (Munich: Bernard and Graefe 1979, 1980).
79 J. Rohwer, "Die Einfluss der alliierten Funkaufklärung auf den Verlauf des Zweiten Weltkrieges," *Vierteljahrshefte für Zeitgeschichte*, 27, No. 3 (1972): 325–69.

CHAPTER TEN: THE "ST LAURENT" DECISION

1 J. Boutilier (ed.), *The RCN in Retrospect, 1910–68* (Vancouver: University of British Columbia Press 1982), illustration facing 115.
2 D. Macintyre, *U-Boat Killer* (London: Weidenfeld and Nicholson 1956), 79.
3 Gieves, the foremost naval tailor in England, outfitted generations of British and Commonwealth naval officers with their uniforms, and ensured legal custom by the generous toleration of overdue accounts owed by impecunious sailors. Gieves became virtually synonymnous with naval uniforms, and a symbol of the British connection.
4 J. Lamb, *The Corvette Navy* (Toronto: Macmillan 1977).
5 J.D. Harbron, "Royal Canadian Navy at Peace 1945–49: The Uncertain Heritage," *Queen's Quarterly* 73, No. 3 (Autumn 1966): 311.
6 This speech is recorded in part in J. Eayrs. *In Defence of Canada*, Vol. 3 (Toronto: University of Toronto Press 1977), Document 4.
7 Mr St Laurent, speaking to the UN General Assembly in September 1947, asserted that the UN charter, currently hamstrung by the veto procedure, caused the Security Council to be "frozen in futility and divided by dissension."
8 As noted in Escott Reid, *Time of Fear and Hope: The Making of the North Atlantic Treaty 1947–49* (Toronto: McClelland and Stewart 1977), 40.
9 *Debates of the House of Commons*, Vol. 6 (1948): 5784.

10 Ibid. 5785.
11 Canada, Department of National Defence, (Ottawa: King's Printer 1949), 14 (White Paper based on Report of the Department of National Defence tabled on 19 October 1949).
12 These observations are from the noted authority and recent Nobel prize-winner H.A. Simon, *the New Science of Management Decision* (New York: Harper and Row 1960), 1.
13 N.P. Mouzelis, *Organization and Bureaucracy* (London: Routledge and Kegan Paul 1967), 124.
14 Y. Dror, "Muddling Through: 'Science' or Inertia," *Public Administration Review* 24, No. 3 (1964): 155.
15 G.T. Allison, "Conceptual Models and the Cuban Missile Crisis," *Political Science Review* 63, No. 3 (September 1969).
16 Here Allison uses the classic aphorism "Where you stand, depends on where you sit," ibid. 71.
17 It appears that September 1947 is a good "focal" date, since there were several significant appointments at that time.
18 While the RCN organization at headquarters was being adjusted during the period 1947-8, the changes appear to have been primarily in matters of title and emphasis. It will become evident that, in most instances, there was continuity of the individuals involved.
19 Thus endeavouring to give substance to John Ruskin's assertion that "Take it all in all, a Ship of the Line is the most honourable thing that man, as a gregarious animal, has ever produced."
20 J.V. Brock, *The Dark Broad Seas* (Toronto: McClelland and Stewart 1981). The author observes, "There was that old residue of resentment amongst the Naval College RCN officers about my acceptance into 'their Navy' from the RCNVR as a Commander with sufficient seniority to put me in line for early promotion. Their resentment was always well disguised but it was there nevertheless" (195). Storrs (now Rear Admiral) in a private communication to the author, observed that "colleagues at the Commander and senior Lieutenant Commander level were quite outspoken at times. So one felt a certain sensitivity, probably to a degree greater than was really warranted, and was inclined to walk carefully."
21 Chiefs of Staff Committee, "Appreciation of World Strategical Situations," CSC 5-1, 16.
22 From Minutes of Chiefs of Staff Committee, 9 December 1946.
23 Memorandum to ACNS from A/DNPI "RCN Future Planning," NSS 1650-26, 17 January 1947.
24 Memorandum to DCNS from DNPI "Planning of Post War Navy," NSS 1650-26, 14 March 1947 (Without, apparently, giving credit to Storrs' paper.)
25 Memorandum to DNPI from DWT "Canadian Naval Requirements in War and Peace," TS 11400-25, 5 July 1947.
26 Naval Board Minutes No. 229-2, 23 October 1947, Directorate of History, National Defence Headquarters, Ottawa (DHist).
27 Naval Board Minutes No. 234-8, 10 January 1948.
28 Memorandum to DNAD from D/DNAD, "Policy for future development of the Defence Forces in Canada," National Archives of Canada (NAC) RG 24 NSS 1400-25, 22 March 1948.
29 Memorandum from VCNS to ACNS, DNAD, D/DNAD of 29 April 1948. (Somewhat ambiguously this also bears a note, presumably from Sec/VCNS "Sir, Propose NFA" to which VCNS responds "yes," the date being 5 May 1948, RG 24, NSS 1400-25.)
30 Letter from naval secretary to naval member Canadian Joint Staff, Washington, 20 May 1948, RG 24, NSS 1400-25. (Note that in April 1948 Captain Lay had been promoted and moved from DNPI to the newly created post of assistant chief of naval staff (Plans) and (Air).)
31 Memorandum for the minister, from CNS TS 11600-25 of 26 May 1948, RG 24 NSS 1400.
32 Naval Staff paper appended to Memorandum to Minister, ibid.
33 Minutes of Chiefs of Staff Committee 29 September 1948 RG 2, Series B2, C-10-9-D-M-40.

34 Extract from Minutes of Cabinet Defence Committee to review "Service Programs for Fiscal Year 1949–50," File 11400-25 of 8 October 1948. Naval Board Minutes No. 231.3 of 1 October had noted that Preliminary Estimates 1949–50 "contained necessary funds to begin implementation of a proposed new construction program."
35 Cabinet Defence Committee Minutes of 8 October 1948.
36 Memorandum to Staff from NCC "Proposed AS Escort Vessel" NSS 8200–17 of 12 October 1948.
37 Written in a communication relating to the "History of the Royal Corps of Naval Constructors" and kindly made available by Mr D.K. Brown RCNC. Admiralty, Bath.
38 Naval Board Minutes No. 263–4 of 19 October 1948.
39 Naval Board Minutes No. 430–5 of 26 October 1948.
40 Naval Board Minutes No. 264–6 of 29 October 1948.
41 Memorandum to CNTS from RG 24, NCC NSS 8200-17 of 14 January 1949.
42 Naval Board Minutes No. 275–8 of 19 January 1948. Approval had the minor caveat that "installation of bunks was subject to the feasibility of accommodating the proposed War Complement of these ships."
43 Memorandum to CNTS from NCC "Interim Report of Progress" re visit to UK. RG 24 NSS 8200–17 of 18 February 1949.
44 Submission to the "Governor General in Council" from the minister of national defence, RG 24 NSS 8200-6 of 26 March 1949.
45 Memorandum to CNTS from NCC, "Sketch Design of AS Escort Vessel," RG 24 NSS 8200-17, 28 May 1949.
46 Brock, *The Dark Broad Seas*, 196–7.
47 It appears to have no confirmation from either Rear Admiral Storrs or Sir Rowland Baker in the communications noted earlier.
48 Noted in copies of Cabinet Minutes dated 2 June 1949, 20 July 1949 and 26 July 1949 in File RG 24 NSS 8200-17.
49 Naval board Minutes No. 305-5 of 15 December 1949.
50 Naval Staff Minutes No. 464–2 of 6 September 1949.
51 Memorandum to Cabinet Defence Committee, RG 24 NSS 1650-26/NSS 2200-50 of 17 August 1950.
52 Baker noted, in the private communication to which reference has been made (note 36); "Regarding the Escort Vessel ... I was again very lucky because the UK Whitby's were slow off the mark—the British did not have a design complete with working drawings, nor did the USN have a design which would meet the RCN Staff Requirement."
53 Naval Board Minutes No. 302–3 of 9 November 1949.
54 Private communication to the author, November 1984.

CHAPTER ELEVEN: CANADA AND THE COLD WAR AT SEA, 1945–68

1 As quoted in Geoffrey Till, et al., *Maritime Strategy and the Nuclear Age* (New York: St Martin's Press 1982), 56.
2 Bernard Brodie, *A Guide to Naval Strategy* (New York: Praeger 1965), 225.
3 Fred T. Jane, *Heresies of Sea Power* (London: Longmans Green and Company 1906), 1. This definition is a composite of a number of definitions found in the classical and modern literature. See especially Michael MccGwire, "Maritime Strategy and the Super Powers," *Power at Sea II: Super-Powers and Navies*, Adelphi Paper, No. 123 (London: International Institute for Strategic Studies 1976), 15; Till, et al., *Maritime Strategy*, 13; Sir Herbert Richmond, as quoted in ibid. 13; Brodie, *Guide to Naval Strategy*.
4 John J. Clark, "Merchant Marine and the Navy: A Note on the Mahan Hypothesis," *Journal of the Royal United Services Institute* 112, No. 636 (May 1967): 164.
5 See, for example, Jonathan Howe, *Multicrises, Sea Power and Global Politics in the Missile Age* (Cambridge, MA: MIT Press 1973); B. Blechman and S. Kaplan, *Force Without War: US Armed Force as a Political Instrument* (Washington, DC: Brookings Institution 1978); B. Dismukes and James McConnell (eds.), *Soviet Naval Diplomacy* (New York: Pergamon 1979); Edward N. Luttwak, *The Political uses of Sea Power*, Studies in International Affairs, No. 23 (Baltimore: Johns Hopkins University Press 1974); James Cable, *Gunboat Diplomacy* (New

York: St Martin's Press 1981); MccGwire, "Maritime Strategy," 15; Dov Z. Zakheim, "Maritime Presence, Projection and the Constraints of Parity," *Equivalence, Sufficiency, and the International Balance* (Washington, DC: National Defense University 1978), 109.
6 See, for example, Kenneth Myers, *North Atlantic Security: The Forgotten Flank:* Washington papers, Vol. 6, No. 62 (Beverly Hills and London: Sage Publications 1979); Paul Nitze, Leonard Sullivan, and the Atlantic Council Working Group on Securing the Seas, *Securing the Seas: The Soviet Naval Challenge and Western Alliance Options* (Boulder, CO: Westview Press 1979); James L. George (ed.), *Problems of Sea Power as We Approach the Twenty-First Century* (Washington, DC: American Enterprise Institute 1978).
7 Brian Cuthbertson, *Canadian Military Independence in the Age of the Superpowers* (Toronto: Fitzhenry and Whiteside 1977), 123–4.
8 Operational Archives of the US Navy (OA), Washington Navy Yard, Washington, DC, Strategic Plans Division Record, OPNAV, Vol. 1, 1912–47, Series 3, Records of the Naval Members of the PJBD Canada-United States, 1940–47, Memo, US Naval Attaché, Ottawa, to the chief of naval intelligence, 5 November 1945 (hereafter Naval Attaché Memo, 1945).
9 As quoted in Sharon Hobson, *The Composition of Canada's Fleet* (Halifax: Centre for Foreign Policy Studies, Dalhousie University 1986), 15.
10 Naval Attaché Memo, 1945.
11 Department of National Defence, Directorate of History (DHist), SGR II 223, J.D.F. Kealy, "The Development of the Canadian Navy, 1945–1967," 3.
12 Hobson, *Composition of Canada's Fleet*, 6.
13 John W. Holmes, *The Shaping of Peace: Canada and the Search for World Order, 1943–1957*, Vol. 2 (Toronto: University of Toronto Press 1982), 29.
14 Kealy, "Development of the Canadian Navy," 4.
15 Cuthbertson, *Canadian Military Independence*, 127.
16 Ibid. 128.
17 Kealy, "Development of the Canadian Navy," 4.
18 The account of the first meeting of the North Atlantic Ocean Regional Planning Group (NAORPG) held in October 1949 is taken from records of that meeting and subsequent report to the NATO Standing Group. Several documents are cited; all are located at the US Navy Operational Archives and are found in the Immediate Files of the CNO (OP-00), 1949, box 8. The documents used here are as follows: "North Atlantic Ocean Regional Planning Group, First Meeting, Monday 31 October 1949" (NAORPG, 1st Meeting); "NAORPG, First Meeting, Record of Action Taken at the Second Session, 2 November 1949" (NAORPG, 2d Session): "NAORPG, First Meeting, Record of Action Taken at the Second Session-Corrected" (2d Session-Corrected); "NAORPG, First Meeting, Record of Action taken at the Fourth Session, 9 November 1949," (NAORPG 4th Session); "NAORPG, Note by the Secretary NAORP Group to the Standing Group, 9 November 1949, (NAORPG Note).
19 OA, NAORPG, 1st Meeting.
20 OA, NAORPG, 2d Session, 2.
21 OA, NAORPG, 2d Session, Corrected, 6.
22 OA, NAORPG, Report, Appendix A, p. 2.
23 OA, NAORPG, 2d Session, Corrected, 8.
24 National Archives of Canada (NAC), Claxton Papers, MG 32, B5, Vol. 94, Folder, Accelerated Defence Program (Claxton Papers, Accelerated Programme), "Memorandum for Cabinet, Increases over Present Strength of Total Combat Forces to Become Effective by 1 July 1955."
25 Ibid., "Memorandum to the Minister-Accelerated Defence Programme, Accelerated Shipbuilding Programme," 31 July 1950.
26 Ibid., "Memorandum to the Minister-Accelerated Defence Programme, Accelerated Shipbuilding Programme," 31 July 1951.
27 Ibid., Department of National Defence, "Planned Increases over Present Strengths to be Completed by 1 July 1950."
28 Hobson, "Composition of Canada's Fleet," 1.
29 Harry S. Truman Library, Independence, M., Papers of Dean Acheson, Memorandum

and Correspondence, 1952, Letter from Lester B. Pearson, 15 January 1952, 3. Pearson also mentioned that Churchill was anxious to have "Rule Britannia" restored as the official hymn of the RCN. Having switched to "the more appropriate song, 'Vive la Canadienne'," Canada could not go along. It was agreed, however, that "Rule Britannia" would be played whenever a British Admiral came aboard a Canadian ship. "In return," Pearson noted, "we expect the British to reduce their demands for economic help from, say a billion dollars, to $999 million!" Ibid.
30 Kealy, "Development of the Canadian Navy," 7.
31 Library of Congress, Manuscript Division (LCMD), The Papers of Admiral Lynde McCormick (MP), box 4, (Trips), Canada File.
32 LCMD, MP, box 6, File 7, "SACLANT Initial Trip to Atlantic Command Nations, 24 February–20 March 1952, Informal Report to the Standing Group, 1 April 1952."
33 John Winton, *Convoy: The Defence of Sea Trade* (London: Michael Joseph 1983) 327.
34 OA, Command File, post 1 January 1946, (CF), Report of the Commander-in-Chief Atlantic Fleet for the period 1 July 1955–30 June 1956, 23. Hereafter, all such reports will be CINCLANTFLT Report.
35 DHist, 80/381, "Operations Cuba."
36 Jeffry V. Brock, *The Thunder and the Sunshine* (Toronto: McClelland and Stewart 1983), 108–9.
37 Ibid. 108, 110.
38 Ibid. 110–11.
39 DHist, "Operations Cuba."
40 OA, CP, CINCLANTFLT Report, April 1963, 30.
41 DHist, *The Report of the Ad Hoc Committee on Naval Objectives*, July 1961 (hereafter, Brock Report).
42 Ibid. 69–70.
43 Ibid. 15.
44 Ibid. 34–5.
45 Ibid. see section 3, 103ff.
46 Ibid. 71.
47 See Kenneth R. McGruther, *The Evolving Soviet Navy* (Newport, RI: Naval War College Press 1978), 27, 99.
48 See James A. Winnerfeld and Carl H. Builder, "ASW: Now or Never," United States Naval Institute *Proceedings* (USNIP) 97, No. 9 (September 1971); Robert P. Berman and John C. Baker, *Soviet Strategic Forces Requirements and Responses* (Washington, DC: Brookings Institution 1982), 58.
49 Michael R. MccGwire, "Naval Power and Soviet Oceans Policy," in United States, Congress, Senate, Committee on Commerce, Committee Print, *Soviet Oceans Development*, 94th Congress, 2d Session (Washington, DC: GPO, October 1976), 179; Bermand and Baker, *Soviet Strategic Forces*, 58.
50 Harold A. Feiveson and John Duffield, "Stopping the Sea-based Counterforce Threat," *International Security* 9, No. 1 (Summer 1984): 196; Alton H. Quanbeck and Archie L. Wood, *Modernizing the Strategic Bomber Force: How and Why* (Washington, DC: Brookings Institution 1976), 44.
51 Carl H. Clawson, jr, "The Wartime Role of Soviet SSBNs-Round Two," *USNIP* 106, No. 3 (March 1980): 68.
52 Canada, Senate, Special Committee on National Defence, Hearings, 32nd Parliament, 2nd Session, Issue No. 8, 17 April 1984, 8A:9. This strategic ASW role should be distinguished from a forward strategic ASW strategy whereby the USN would send its attack submarines into Soviet SSBN "bastions" near the USSR in order to undertake the underwater equivalent of a counterforce's strike. Some arms controllers view such an approach inherently destabilizing because Mutual Assured Destruction (MAD) is said to rest heavily upon the known invulnerability of SSBN's. General improvements in ASW capabilities, especially the newer USN attack submarines, have enhanced the potential for both tactical and strategic ASW, regardless of where they might be carried out. The US Navy has been careful in its public statements not to draw attention to the nuclear damage limiting potential of its ASW forces. According to one analyst, the USN went along with

the mutual assured destruction approach to deterrence which stressed the need to preserve the invulnerability of SSBN's; "All ASW was described as tactical ASW ... This permitted procurement of ASW forces in accordance with MAD guidelines but left the option open to employ them in a damage limiting/warfighting mode if deterrence failed" (Hamlin Caldwell, "The Empty Silo-Strategic ASW," *United States Naval War College Review* 34, No. 5 (September/October 1981): 7).

53 See, for example, G.R. Lindsey, "Canadian Maritime Strategy: Should the Emphasis be Changed?," paper submitted to the House of Commons Standing Committee on External Affairs and National Defence (August 1969), 36.
54 Colin Gray, *Canada's Maritime Forces*, Wellesley Paper 1 (Toronto: Canadian Institute of International Affairs 1973), 22.
55 As quoted in R.B. Byers, "Canadian Maritime Policy and Force Structure Requirements," *Canadian Defence Quarterly* 12, No. 4 (Spring 1983): 12.
56 Canada, House of Commons, Standing Committee on External Affairs and National Defence, 28th Parliament, 2nd Session, *Tenth Report Respecting Maritime Forces* (Ottawa: Queen's Printer 1970), 17 (hereafter *Tenth Report*).
57 Canada, Department of National Defence, *Defence in the 70s* (Ottawa: Information Canada 1971), 28.
58 *Tenth Report*, 19.
59 Ibid. 17.
60 US Naval War College, Naval Historical Collection, Newport, RI (NHC), The Richard G. Colbert Papers (CP), Series I, box 17, folder 330, letter from Colbert to Capt. J.A. Merin, 17 February 1967; letter to C.J. Zimmerman, 1 March 1967. (References to the Colbert Papers use the list found in the Register. Because many items have been removed for security reasons the citations given here may not correspond with the exact location of the documents at present.)
61 Ibid., box 18, folder 331, Letter to Walter Rostow, 4 May 1967.
62 Ibid., box 19, folder 336, Letter to Capt Gillow, FN, 1 Nobember 1967.
63 Ibid., box 19, folder 336, Letter to Rear Admiral J.H. Adams, USN, 20 December 1967.
64 The Colbert Papers contain two declassified briefing notes on STANAVFORLANT: Series I, box 18, folder 337, "Naval War College Look at the Standing Naval Force Atlantic," enclosure to a letter to Rear Admiral L. Gies, 18 February 1969; Series II, box 21, folder 39, "SNFL Briefing for CINCLANT/CINCLANTFLT Officers," undated.
65 Ibid., box 19, folder 368, Letter to Rear Admiral R.W. Trimbell, 4 April 1968.
66 Ibid., Series II, box 21, folder 38, "The Soviet World-wide Maritime Challenge," a briefing prepared by headquarters, Supreme Allied Command Atlantic.
67 Ibid., Series I, box 19, folder 368, Letter to VADM Sir Peter Hill-Norton, 25 March 1968; Letter to General J.V. Allard, 3 April 1968.
68 See ibid., Series II, box 21, folder 38 for the steps leading up to the initiation of the Brosio Study.
69 The full title of the Brosio Study is Supreme Allied Commander Atlantic, *Report of Study: Relative Maritime Strategies and Capabilities of NATO and the Soviet Bloc* (Norfolk, VA: March 1969). (Much of this study remains classified. The author was allowed to read the study in its entirety on the understanding that only general summary references would be made to its contents.)
70 NHC, CP, Series I, box 18, folder 348, Letter to Elmo Zumwalt, 3 September 1971.
71 United States, Department of Defense, Office of the Assistant Secretary of Defense, Program and Analysis, *Sealift Procurement and National Security* (SPANS) (Washington, DC, 9 August 1972).
72 United States, Department of Defense, *Annual Report for FY 1975 and FY 1975-1980 Defense Program* (Washington, DC: GPO 1974), 165.
73 "Exercise Strong Express in Retrospect," *International Defense Review* (December 1972): 661.

CHAPTER TWELVE: INTERNATIONAL NAVAL CO-OPERATION AND ADMIRAL RICHARD G. COLBERT

1 Naval Historical Collection, Naval War College, Manuscript Collection 30: Richard G. Colbert papers. (Hereafter, Colbert Papers), Series 2, box 19, folder 62: Concluding Remarks to Sea Power Symposium, 20 November 1969. Printed version in Naval War College brochure "First Seapower Symposium," 17–18.
2 Colbert Papers, Series 1, box 19, file 382: Commander Falcon Accame, Italian Navy, to Colbert, 10 November 1971.
3 Letter from Captain Henry A. Ceulemans, Belgian Navy (ret.) to Hattendorf, 27 August 1985.
4 Letter from Admiral Thomas H. Moorer, USN (ret.) to Hattendorf, 27 August 1985.
5 Letter from Captain Allan P. Slaff, USN (ret.) to Hattendorf, 6 September 1985; NHC, Oral History 9: Captain Clarence O. Fiske, USN (ret.), 68.
6 Colbert Papers, Series 4, box 21, folder 1: Citation, Honorary Doctor of Education, Salve Regina College, Newport, Rhode Island, 12 September 1970.
7 Elmo R. Zumwalt, jr, *On Watch* (New York: Quadrangle Books 1976), 141–2.
8 Colbert Papers, Series I, box 1: "Diary of Richard G. Colbert, *SS Robert Luckenbach*. NY–Seattle, via Panama Canal," 15 July–8 Sepbember 1931.
9 Colbert Papers, Series 1, box 1, folders 1–7.
10 Colbert papers, Series 1, box 1, file 6: Franklin D. Roosevelt to Charles W. Flint, 25 January 1933.
11 Colbert papers, Series 1, box 2, file 27: RGC to Charles Colbert, 17 June 1936.
12 Letter from Rear Admiral John R. Wadleigh, USN (ret.) to Hattendorf, 19 August 1985.
13 Colbert papers, Series 1, box 1, file 19: RGC to Charles Colbert, 5 March 1935.
14 Colbert papers, Series 1, box 1, file 18: "The War peril," speech.
15 Letter from Captain Robert S. Guy, USN (ret.) to Hattendorf, 27 August 1985. For details of these actions, see F.C. Van Oosten, *The Battle of the Java Sea* (Annapolis: Naval Institute Press 1976), 29–33.
16 R.G. Colbert, "International Co-operation for Peace," *Vital Speeches* 33, No. 4 (1 December 1966): 127.
17 Colbert papers, Series 1, box 2, file 43: RGC to Lt G.W. Beck, jr, USN, 8 March 1948.
18 Letter from Captain Robert S. Guy, USN (ret.) to Hattendorf, 27 August 1985.
19 Letter from Mrs Prudence Colbert Mackall to Hattendorf, 23 September 1985.
20 Letter from Rear Admiral E.M. Eller, USN (ret.) to Hattendorf, 20 August 1985.
21 Naval Historical Collection, Oral History Number 1, "The Reminiscences of Vice Admiral Bernard L. Austin, USN (ret.)," [Annapolis: Naval Institute 1971], 417; Letter from Captain Robert C. Penniston, USN (ret.) to Hattendorf, 14 August 1985. Colbert's original 1951–2 study has not been found.
22 Letter from Captain Guy to Hattendorf, 27 August 1985.
23 Gaddis Smith, *Dean Acheson* (New York: Cooper Square 1972), 367–9.
24 Clark G. Reynolds, "Forrest Percival Sherman," in Robert M. Love, sr, *The Chiefs of Naval Operations* (Annapolis: Naval Institute Press 1980), 230–2.
25 Interview with Captain Wilbur Holmes, USN (ret.), 27 August 1985.
26 Rear Admiral John F. Davidson, USN (ret.) to Hattendorf, 23 August 1985.
27 Vice-Admiral Robert H. Rice, USN (ret.) to Hattendorf, 27 August 1985.
28 Colbert papers, Series 1, box 3, file 76: Admiral Richard L. Conolly to Colbert, 12 December 1954.
29 J.B. Hattendorf, B.M. Simpson III, and J.R. Wadleigh, *Sailors and Scholars: The Centennial History of the Naval War College* (Newport: Naval War College 1984), 230; Conversation Admiral Arleigh Burke, USN (ret.) to Hattendorf, 27 September 1985.
30 Letter from Captain Guy to Hattendorf, 27 August 1985.
31 August C. Miller, jr, "An International Mission for the Naval War College," US Naval Institute *Proceedings* 83, No. 12 (December 1957): 1364.
32 Colbert Papers, Series 1, box 4, file 85: RGC to Captain A.O. Vorse, 22 August 1956.
33 Ibid., Series 1, box 7, file 158: Arleigh Burke to RGC, 25 July 1967.
34 Ibid. Series 2, box 20, file 69: Draft "Factors bearing on the Proposed US Navy withdrawal from Barcelona, Spain."
35 Letter from Admiral David L. McDonald, USN (ret.) to Hattendorf, 26 August 1985.
36 Telephone conversation, Walt W. Rostow to Hattendorf, 16 September 1985.

37 Letter from Admiral Elmo R. Zumwalt, jr, USN to Hattendorf, 27 August 1985.
38 W.W. Rostow, *The Diffusion of Power 1957–1972* (New York: Macmillan 1972), 400, 426–7, 505, 510.
39 Colbert papers, Series 1, box 6, file 129: RGC to Captain A.B. de Vasconcelles, 4 January 1965.
40 Ibid. file 134: RGC to Commander T.E. Fortson, 4 July 1965; RGC to Colonel R.N. Ginsburgh, 14 July 1965.
41 Letter from Vice Admiral W.W. Behrens, USN (ret.) to Hattendorf, 20 September 1985 and telephone conversation 12 November 1985.
42 Richard G. Colbert and Robert N. Ginsburgh, "The Policy Planning Council," US Naval Institute *Proceedings* 92, No. 4 (April 1966): 81.
43 Letter from Admiral Thomas H. Moorer, USN (ret.) to Hattendorf, 27 August 1985.
44 Colbert papers, Series 2, box 49: Memo C-3 to C-OO, 28 November 1966.
45 Ibid., Series 1, box 7, file 161: RGC to W.W. Rostow, 27 December 1967.
46 Ibid., box 16, file 365: RGC to Captain W.P.B. Barber, RN, 18 July 1967.
47 Ibid., file 302: RGC to Vice Admiral C.K. Duncan, 2 August 1968.
48 Colbert papers, Series 2, folders 1–3.
49 Ibid., Series 1, file 312: RGC to "John," 18 June 1971, serial 1855.
50 Richard G. Colbert, "Challenge" *Naval War College Review* (January 1969): 1.
51 Colbert papers, Series 2, box 17, file 375: Admiral E.R. Zumwalt to Rear Admiral Colin C. Dunlap, 8 September 1970.
52 Ibid., Series 1, file 310: President Naval War College to Chief of Naval Operations, 4 February 1971; file 351: RGC to Captain David F. Emerson, 20 December 1971.
53 Letter from Admiral Thomas H. Moorer to Hattendorf, 27 August 1985; Quote from Colbert Papers, Series 2, box 19, file 46: RGC Memo to Captain Stansfield Turner, aide to the secretary of the navy.
54 The Eighth International Sea Power Symposium met at the Naval War College, 20–3 October 1985.
55 Colbert papers, Series 2, box 19, file 57: Rear Admiral H.A. Potter to Colbert, 27 November 1969.
56 Ibid., Series 1, box 13, file 265: RGC to Scott Terrill, 10 April 1973. For detailed information on the design, see Naval Historical Collection, Ms Coll. 57: Harrison T. Loeser Papers.
57 President, Naval War College Letter to CNO, OO/rbm, Serial 0015, 2 April 1971 forwarding "The Newport Study: A Plan to Persuade Allies to Improve and Expand Their ASW Capabililties," Love, *Chiefs of Naval Operations*, 372–5.
58 Colbert papers, Series 1, box 10, file 222: RGC to W.W. Rostow, 12 April 1971.
59 Ibid., file 313: Trip Report 12–29 July 1971.
60 Ibid., file 318: RGC to Zumwalt, 21 December 1971; box 12, file 257: RGC to Vice-Admiral T. Lewin, RN 10 January 1973.
61 Ibid., Box 12, file 250: RGC to Zumwalt, 2 November 1971.
62 Letter from Admiral Giuseppe Pighini, Italian Navy (ret.) to Hattendorf, 23 September 1985; Admiral J. Guillou, French Navy (ret.) to Hattendorf, 12 January 1986.
63 Pighini to Hattendorf, 23 September 1985.
64 Captain Henry C. Duncan, USN, "A Tribute to Admiral Richard Colbert," Arlington Cemetery, 5 December 1973.
65 Letter from Professor Vincent Davis to Hattendorf, 28 August 1985.
66 Colbert papers, Series 1, box 13, file 279: RGC to Commander Spencer Johnson, 3 August 1973.
67 R.G. Colbert, "Address to First International Seapower Symposium," *Naval War College Review* (February 1970): 2.
68 R.G. Colbert, "War College Education and the Future," US Naval Institute *Proceedings*, 99, No. 11/849 (November 1973): 109.
69 Ibid.
70 Colbert papers, Series 1, box 13, file 271: RGC to Zumwalt, 14 June 1973.
71 Ibid., file 270: RGC to Lieutenant (JG) August C. Miller, III, 1 June 1973.
72 Colbert papers, Series 2, box 2: "Draft of Remarks Prepared for E.R. Zumwalt at ACLANT

Flag Symposium, 3 November 1970" by RGC and Commander McNulty; Series 3, box 21, file 14. "Closing Remarks to NCC," 2 June 1970.
73 Colbert papers, Series 2, box 18, file 41: Unpublished draft article, "The Indian Ocean Enigma."
74 Ibid., Series 3, box 20, file 20: Remarks to NCC, not dated.
75 The following is based largely on letter from Commander Humberto Cancio, jr, Cuban Navy (ret.) to Hattendorf, 2 October 1985, and letter from Rear Admiral Christer Kirkegaard, Royal Swedish Navy (ret.) to Hattendorf, 1 October 1985.
76 The Canadian officers who have attended the Naval Command College at the Naval War College are: Commodore William P. Hayes, Captain J.H.G. Bovey, Commander John C. Smyth, Commander David A. Avery, Captain Henry W. Vondette, Commodore Constantaine Cotaras, Rear-Admiral Fred J. Mifflin, Major-General Alan Pickering, Captain Robert F. Gladman, Rear-Admiral Peter Cairns, Captain Lawrence Dzioba, Colonel Geoffrey Craven, Captain Basil Moore, Captain Wilfred Lund, Captain J.T.O. Jones, Brigadier-General M. Scott Eichel, Commander Vilnis U. Auns, Commander Douglas J. McClean, Captain Steen K. Jessen, Commander Ronald Perks, and Commander James Dickson. The Canadian Officers who have attended the intermediate level, Naval Staff College, at the Naval War College are: Lieutenant-Colonel James K. Millar, Captain Chris Dalley, and Major Joseph P. Vermette.

CHAPTER THIRTEEN: ECONOMIC CONSIDERATIONS IN THE DEVELOPMENT OF THE CANADIAN NAVY SINCE 1945

1 See D.L. Meredith and J.M. Treddenick, "The Economics of Defence: A Neglected Area of Research in Canada," Paper prepared for the conference on "The Canadian Military: Directions for Future Research," York University, 20–1 November 1982; and R.B. Byers, "Canadian Defence and Defence Procurement: Implications for Economic Policy," In Denis Stairs and Gilbert R. Winham, research co-ordinators, *Selected Problems in Formulating Foreign Economic Policy* Vol. 30 (Toronto: University of Toronto Press 1985), 132.
2 Meredith and Treddenick, "Economics of Defence," discuss these three aspects in general terms.
3 For a broader but related discussion, see K. Booth, *Navies and Foreign Policy* (London: Croom Helm 1977), Chapter 8.
4 Gavin Kennedy, *Defence Economics* (London: Duckworth 1983), 2.
5 G.M. Dillon, *Canadian Naval Policy Since World War II: A Decision-Making Analysis* (Halifax: Centre for Foreign Policy Studies, Dalhousie University 1972), 18.
6 Fiscal year 1947 was selected as the starting point for comparison because it was the first complete, non-wartime year.
7 Unless otherwise indicated, the year figures refer to the fiscal year ending on 31 March of the year cited, while expenditure figures refer to the actual "budget year" amount unadjusted for price inflation.
8 Canada, Parliament, House of Commons, *Debates*, II [hereafter *Debates*] 22 October 1945, 1368.
9 Abbott, *Debates*, V, 19 August 1946, 5021; Claxton, *Debates*, VI, 24 June 1948, 5780.
10 Claxton, *Debates*, VI, 24 June 1948, 5785.
11 Ibid.
12 For an excellent, detailed analysis, see Sharon Hobson, *The Composition of Canada's Naval Fleet, 1946–85* (Halifax: Centre for Foreign Policy Studies, Dalhousie University 1986).
13 Honourable Brooke Claxton, *Canada's Defence Programme, 1951–2* (with Revisions to 30 June 1951), and Hobson, *Composition of Canada's Naval Fleet*, 3–3 to 3–8.
14 Hobson, *Composition of Canada's Naval Fleet*, 25.
15 James Eayrs, *In Defence of Canada*, Vol. 3, *Peacemaking and Deterrence* (Toronto: University of Toronto Press 1972), 81.
16 National Archives of Canada (NAC), Claxton Papers, MG 32, B5, Vol. 94, "Memorandum to the Minister: Accelerated Defence Programme—Recommendations for the Increase

in Strength of the RCN," Vice-Admiral H.T.W. Grant, Chief of the Naval Staff, 2 August 1950.
17 Claxton, *Debates*, IV, 8 June 1950, 3380. See also Claxton, *Debates*, V, 21 May 1954, 4990–1 for a similar explanation.
18 Claxton, *Debates*, IV, 9 June 1950, 3431.
19 See, Dillon, *Canadian Naval Policy*, Table 4, 28.
20 Pearkes, *Debates*, II, 5 December 1957, 1903.
21 Pearkes, *Debates*, III, 8 August 1958, 3222.
22 Canada, Department of National Defence, Chief of Naval Staff, *Report of the Ad Hoc Committee on Naval Objectives* (July 1961), 15 [hereafter *Brock Report*].
23 Ibid. 57.
24 Ibid. 67.
25 Ibid. 83.
26 Ibid. 84–7.
27 Harkness, *Debates*, III, 11 April 1962, 2835.
28 Hellyer, Canada, Parliament, House of Commons, Special Committee on Defence, *Proceedings* [hereafter Special Committee on Defence], 27 June 1963, 14.
29 Vice-Admiral Rayner, Special Committee on Defence, 15 October 1963, 410–29.
30 Hellyer, *Debates*, IV, 24 October 1963, 3937.
31 Hellyer, Special Committee on Defence, 5 November 1963, 665–7.
32 Ibid. 684.
33 Honourable P.T. Hellyer, Address to the Rotary Club of Sherbrooke, Quebec, 4 February 1964.
34 Hobson, *Composition of Canada's Naval Fleet*, 33.
35 Hellyer, *Debates*, VI, 5 December 1963, 5455–6.
36 Canada, Department of National Defence, *White Paper on Defence* (Ottawa: Queen's Printer 1964), 23–4.
37 Ibid. 23.
38 Ibid. Similar cost considerations later led a parliamentary committee to forgo a recommendation to acquire such submarines. See Canada, Parliament, House of Commons, Standing Committee on External Affairs and National Defence, *Tenth Report to the House Respecting Maritime Forces*, No. 34 (12 February 1970), 38–9.
39 Prime Minister P.E. Trudeau, "A Defence Policy for Canada," *Statements and Speeches*, No. 69/7, 3 April 1969, and "The Relation of Defence Policy to Foreign Policy," *Statements and Speeches*, No. 69/8, 12 April 1969.
40 Canada, Department of National Defence, *Defence in the 70s* (Ottawa: Information Canada 1971), 16.
41 Ibid. 41.
42 Ibid. 19, 28.
43 Ibid. 28.
44 See Joel J. Sokolsky, "Canada and the Cold War at Sea, 1945–1968," this volume.
45 The retirement of *Bonaventure* released badly needed personnel for retraining to man the four new DDH-280 destroyers. See Gerald Porter, *In Retreat: The Canadian Forces in the Trudeau Years* (Toronto: Deneau and Greenberg, nd), 43–6.
46 Hobson, *Composition of Canada's Naval Fleet*, 52.
47 Michael Tucker, *Canadian Foreign Policy: Contemporary Issues and Themes* (Toronto: McGraw-Hill Ryerson 1980), 157, 162–3.
48 J.H.W. Knox, "An Engineer's Outline of RCN History: Part II," in James A. Boutilier (ed.), *The RCN in Retrospect, 1910–1968* (Vancouver: University of British Columbia Press 1982), 329–30.
49 Honourable James Richardson, Statement on "A Modernization and Renewal Program for the Canadian Forces," 10 October 1973.
50 Porter, *Canadian Forces in the Trudeau Years*, 53–60.
51 Canada, Senate, Special Committee of the Senate on National Defence, *Proceedings*, No. 8, 17 April 1984, "Departmental Review Senate Sub-Committee on Defence Report Canada's Maritime Defence" [hereafter Departmental Review], Appendix ND-8A, 12.

52 Ibid.
53 See Pearkes, *Debates*, v, 3 July 1959, 5430, and 6 July 1960, 48; also *The Military Balance, 1983–1984* (London: International Institute for Strategic Studies 1983), 140.
54 *The Military Balance, 1983–1984*, 144.
55 Hobson, *Composition of Canada's Naval Fleet*, 53-4.
56 Claxton, *Debates*, IV, 26 June 1950, 4122–23; I, 6 September 1950, 322; I, 22 October 1951, 281; and IV, 28 June 1952, 3892. For 1983 ratios, see Canada, Senate, Standing Senate Committee on Foreign Affairs, Sub-Committee on National Defence, *Report: Canada's Maritime Defence* (Ottawa: Supply and Services Canada 1983), 74 [hereafter *Senate Report*].
57 *Senate Report*, 4.
58 Claxton, *Debates*, IV, 24 June 1952, 3639; Honourable Brooke Claxton, *Canada's Defence Programme, 1954–1955*; Honourable Ralph Campney, *Canada's Defence Programme, 1955–56*; Pearkes, *Debates*, II, 5 December 1957, 1898; Pearkes, House of Commons, Special Committee on Defence Expenditures, 3 June 1960, 230–1; Hellyer, Special Committee on Defence, 27 June 1963, 13–14; and Hobson, *Composition of Canada's Naval Fleet*.
59 Departmental Review, 8.
60 See the comments summarized in *Senate Report*, 33–40.
61 Pearkes, *Debates*, VII, 3 August 1960, 7524.
62 "Supplement to DND Strategic Overview, 1984/85: An Analysis of the Capital Equipment Program" (nd), 4.
63 Departmental Review, 11.
64 D.H.J. Norman, "An Input-Output Evaluation of the Effect of Defence Expenditure on the Canadian Economy," *DRAE Project Report No. PR10* (Ottawa: Defence Research Analysis Establishment, DND June 1972), 69.
65 J.M. Treddenick, "Regional Impacts of Defence Spending," in Brian MacDonald (ed.), *Guns and Butter: Defence and the Canadian Economy* (Toronto: Canadian Institute of Strategic Studies 1984).
66 Abbott, *Debates*, II, 26 October 1945, 1546.
67 Claxton, *Debates*, I, 31 August 1950, 101.
68 Honourable C.D. Howe, "Address to 65th Annual Meeting of the Vancouver Board of Trade," 29 January 1952, 3. NAC, Howe Papers, 89–2, folder 60.
69 Howe, *Debates*, v, 14 June 1951, 4071–2; see also Howe, *Debates*, v, 7 May 1953, 4954.
70 Howe, *Debates*, VI, 29 June 1956, 5520.
71 Crouse, *Debates*, I, 23 January 1959, 268.
72 The 1961 *Brock Report* was an exception in this regard, inasmuch as it advocated a strengthening of conventional naval capabilities and adding more versatility to the fleet. In addition, it clearly justified maintaining a healthy shipbuilding industry on the grounds of national security. It also suggested that a viable industry would lead to lower ship construction costs for the navy via an "equitable distribution of yard overhead costs" (52). Although there was a "make-work" element here, it was clearly rooted in the *military* requirement for an in-place, industrial shipbuilding capacity for the Canadian navy.
73 Harkness, *Debates*, III, 12 April 1962, 2895, and Hellyer, *Debates*, IV, 24 October 1963, 3937.
74 Rayner, Special Committee on Defence, 9 July 1963, 118.
75 Hellyer, *Debates*, v, 12 November 1963, 4610.
76 For background see my "Economic Defence Co-operation with the United States 1940–63," in Kim Richard Nossal (ed.), *An Acceptance of Paradox: Essays on Canadian Diplomacy in Honour of John W. Holmes* (Toronto: Canadian Institute of International Affairs 1982).
77 *Production Sharing Guidebook* (Ottawa: US Division, Defence Programs Bureau, Department of External Affairs, nd), 20.
78 Porter, *Canadian Forces in the Trudeau Years*, 74–5.
79 Vice-Admiral J.C. O'Brien cited in ibid. 68.
80 Byers, "Canadian Defence and Defence Procurement," 184.

81 DND, "Canadian Patrol Frigate Project: Background Information on Industrial Benefits," 29 June 1983, 1.
82 DND, Background Information: Canadian Patrol Frigate Project," 5.
83 *Defence Newsletter* 4, No. 1 (January 1985): 33–4.
84 Sharon Hobson, "Shipbuilding and Defence," *Seaports and the Shipping World* (December 1984): 41, 58.

CHAPTER FOURTEEN: CANADIAN NAVAL RESPONSIBILITIES IN THE ARCTIC

1 J.L. Brierly, *The Law of Nations* (Oxford: Oxford University Press 1963), 162.
2 Donat Pharand, *Northwest Passage: Arctic Straits* (Dordrecht: Martinus Nijhoff 1984), 112.
3 These precedents are the *Eastern Greenland* case, decided by the Permanent Court of International Justice in 1933 (Permanent Court of International Justice, Series A/B No. 53) and the *Clipperton Island Arbitration* in 1931 (*American Journal of International Law* 26:390).
4 Arctic Waters Pollution Prevention Act, Chapter 48, 18–19, Elizabeth II (Statutes of Canada 1970).
5 Act to Amend the Territorial Sea and Fishing Zones Act, Chapter 68, 18–19, Elizabeth II (Statutes of Canada 1970).
6 The main channel of the western end of the Passage (Prince of Wales Strait) was already enclosed under the three-mile-territorial sea principle.
7 Statement by the prime minister (Pierre Trudeau), *House of Commons Debates* (15 May 1969): 8720. Statement by the minister for external affairs (Mitchell Sharp), *House of Commons Debates* (17 April 1970): 6015. Statement by the minister for external affairs (Allan MacEachen) in Standing Committee on External Affairs and National Defence, *Proceedings*, No. 22 (22 May, 1976): 6.
8 Donat Pharand, *The Law of the Sea of the Arctic* (Ottawa: University of Ottawa Press 1973), 61.
9 *Revised Single Negotiating Text*, Part 3, Section 9, Article 43 (A/CONF 62 WP 8/Rev., 1, 6 May 1976).
10 Statement by the secretary of state for external affairs (Joe Clark) *House of Commons Debates* (10 September 1985): 6462–4.
11 Pharand, *Northwest Passage* 38–58.
12 Ibid. See Figure 2 on the map sheet attached to the inside back cover.
13 Canada, Senate Standing Committee on Foreign Affairs, Sub-committee on National Defence, *Canada's Maritime Defence* (Ottawa: Supply and Services Canada 1983), 27.
14 *House of Commons Debates* (10 September 1985): 6462–3.
15 This subject is discussed in detail in a forthcoming article. See W. Harriet Critchley, "Defence and Policing in Arctic Canada," in F.W. Griffiths (ed.), *Politics of the Northwest Passage* (Montreal: McGill-Queen's University Press 1987).
16 Canada, Senate Standing Committee on Foreign Affairs, Subcommittee on National Defence, *Canada's Maritime Defence*, 51.
17 W. Harriet Critchley, "Polar Deployment of Soviet Submarines," *International Journal* 39 (Autumn 1984): 828–65.
18 Geoffrey Till, "Strategy in the Far North," and David Hobbs, "New Military Technologies and Northern Waters," in C. Archer and D. Scrivener (eds), *Northern Waters: Security and Resources Issues* (London: Croom Helm 1986), 69–80, 91–5.
19 Canada, Senate Standing Committee on Foreign Affairs, Subcommittee on National Defence, *Canada's Maritime Defence* 52.
20 Ibid. 92.
21 Canada, National Defence, *Challenge and Commitment: A Defence Policy for Canada* (Ottawa: Canadian Government Publishing Centre, Supply and Services 1987), 51.
22 Ibid. 52–5.
23 W. Harriet Critchley, "Polar Deployment of Soviet Submarines," *The Globe and Mail* (Toronto), 6 April 1987.

CHAPTER FIFTEEN: SHIPS: MANAGING THE NEED

1 The model fleets proposed by the Senate Subcommittee and by Vice-Admiral Timbrell are described in Canada, Standing Committee on Foreign Affairs, Subcommittee on National Defence, Report, *Canada's Maritime Defence* (Ottawa: Supply and Services Canada 1983), 55–59. Vice-Admiral Fulton's proposal is described in Vice-Admiral J.A. Fulton, "A Canadian Fleet Model," in Brian MacDonald (ed.), *High Tech and High Seas* (Toronto: The Canadian Institute of Strategic Studies 1987).
2 Gilbert Norman Tucker, *The Naval Service of Canada: Its Official History*, Vol. 1 (Ottawa: King's Printer 1952), 312.
3 Note that the additional .25 per cent accounts for the technological deterioration in 1987 of the technolgical updating which took place in 1986. In this context the term "maintenance" applies specifically to replacement and repair of equipment such that it retains its original capability; it does not apply to more general housekeeping activities or routine maintenance which are undertaken to preserve the working order of equipment.
4 It must be particularly assumed that, of all fleet combinations yielding equal capability levels, the least-cost fleet is selected.
5 The exponential growth path provides for a certain level of CEU in each year, increasing from the baseline of 12.5 in 1986 to the target level of, for example, 25.5 for Fleet 4 in 2010. Summing these annual figures provides the total CEU year capability.
6 The total discounted present values of the alternative expenditure streams may be thought of as the 1985 costs of alternative annuities which, at 10 per cent interest, would just yield the expenditure streams necessary to acquire and maintain the capabilities of each fleet.
7 It appears to be only a matter of coincidence that a 6 per cent growth rate of defence expenditures produces a defence: GNP ratio in 2010 equal to the current average for all NATO nations.
8 Of course, if the capital portion of the defence budget was permitted to rise above 30 per cent, say through proportionate reductions in other components of the budget or through appropriate increases in the total defence budget, then shipbuilding affordability would certainly be increased. However, we are pessimistic that such increases would be forthcoming. Indeed, given recent experience, we are even pessimistic that the goal of 30 per cent can be maintained.
9 But note that expenditures on Fleet 4 may continue beyond 1990 if the excess of expenditure availability prior to that date can be applied in succeeding years. However, as the present value totals indicate, expenditure availability will eventually fall short of requirements for this fleet.

CHAPTER SIXTEEN: CANADA AND MARITIME DEFENCE

1 Canada, Standing Senate Committee on Foreign Affairs, Report of the Subcommittee on National Defence, *Canada's Maritime Defence* (Ottawa: Minister of Supply and Services 1983), 2 (hereafter the *Lafond Report*).
2 The data in this section is drawn primarily from R.B. Byers, "Canadian Defence and Defence Procurement: Implications for Economic Policy," in Denis Stairs, et al. (eds), *Selected Problems in Formulating Foreign Economic Policy*, Royal Commission on the Economic Union and Development Prospects for Research Volume No. 30, 1985.
3 *Lafond Report*, 16.
4 Cited by Peter C. Newman, *True North: Not Strong and Free* (Toronto: McClelland and Stewart 1983), 19.
5 Data provided by John Willis of the Centre for International and Strategic Studies, York University. National Defence, 1986–7 Estimates, Part 3, Expenditure Plan, Minister of Supply and Services Canada 1986.
6 Bruce Thordarson, *Trudeau and Foreign Policy* (Toronto: Oxford University Press 1972), remains the best study of the review process and outcome.
7 Interview, 29 November 1984.
8 R.B. Byers, "Canadian Security and Defence: The Legacy and the Challenges," *Adelphi*

Papers 214 (London: International Institute for Strategic Studies Winter, 1986): Canada, Department of National Defence, *Challenge and Commitment: A Defence Policy for Canada* (Ottawa 1987), 49–68, 89–90.

9 Senate of Canada, Standing Senate Committee on Foreign Affairs. Proceedings of the Subcommittee on National Defence, Issue No. 22, 2 March 1982, 22–30 (hereafter the Lafond Committee).

10 On unification, see David P. Burke, "Hellyer and Landymore: The Unification of the Canadian Armed Forces and an Admiral's Revolt," *American Review of Canadian Studies* 8, No. 2 (Autumn 1978): 3–25; and R.B. Byers, "Structural Change and the Policy Process in the Department of National Defence," *Canadian Public Administration* 16, No. 2 (Summer 1973): 220–42.

11 Task Force on Review of Unification of the Canadian Armed Forces, 15 March 1980 (hereafter *Fyffe Report*).

12 Lafond Committee, Issue No. 43, 22 March 1983, 43A: 15–16.

13 For organizational issues, see Peter C. Kasurak, "Civilianization and the Military Ethos: Civil-Military Relations in Canada," *Canadian Public Administration* 25, No. 1 (Spring 1982): 108–29; and J.E. Neelin and L.M. Pederson, "The Administrative Structure of the Canadian Armed Forces: Overcentralized, Overly Staff-Ridden," *Canadian Defence Quarterly* 4 No. 2 (Autumn 1974): 33–9.

14 Lafond Committee, Issue No. 39, 3 March 1983, 39:9.

15 Ibid. 19, 28. Also see the *Fyffe Report* and the report of the Review Group on the Report on the Task Force on Unification of the Canadian Forces, 31 August 1980.

16 For example see John Gellner, "Strategic Analysis in Canada," *International Journal* 33, No. 3 (Summer 1978): 493–505; and Lafond Committee, Issue No. 25, 23 March 1982, 23:6, 23:7.

17 Auditor General of Canada, *Report of the Auditor General of Canada to the House of Commons* (Ottawa: Minister of Supply and Services, December 1984), 12-4-5.

18 See R.B. Byers and Colin Gray (eds), *Canadian Military Professionalism: The Search for Identity*, Wellesley Paper No. 2 (Toronto: Canadian Institute of International Affairs 1973).

19 *The Report of the Ad Hoc Committee on Naval Objectives* (Ottawa: Naval Headquarters 1961).

20 Canada, *Defence in the 70s* (Ottawa: Information Canada 1971), 28.

21 See R.B. Byers, "Canadian Maritime Policy and Force Structure Requirements," *Canadian Defence Quarterly* 12, No. 4 (Spring 1983): 9–17.

22 House of Commons, Standing Committee on External Affairs and National Defence (SCEAND), Report of the Subcommittee on Maritime Forces, 26 June 1970, 32:50, 32:62 (hereafter the *Penner Report*).

23 SCEAND, Issue No. 1, 24 February 1972, 1:10.

24 SCEAND, Issue No. 13, 11 May 1972, 13:24, 13:27.

25 Ibid. 13:46.

26 *Penner Report*, 32:42.

27 See R.B. Byers, "Canadian Defence: The ASW Dilemma," *Survival* 18, No. 4 (July/August 1976): 154–61.

28 *Penner Report*, 32:30.

29 *Lafond Report*, 39, 40. See pp. 101–9 for list of DND roles, objectives, and tasks.

30 Lafond Committee Issue No. 8, 17 April 1984, 8A1:4.

31 Ibid., Issue No. 22, 2 March 1982, 22:6, 22:7.

32 Ibid., Issue No. 23, 9 March 1982, 23:6.

33 Ibid., Issue No. 22, 7 March 1982, 22:13.

34 See R.B. Byers (ed.), *Deterrence in the 1980s: Crisis and Dilemma* (London: Croom Helm 1985).

35 For example, see Admiral James D. Watkins, US Navy, "The Maritime Strategy," *Proceedings*, US Naval Institute, Special Supplement, (January 1986).

36 Lafond Committee, Issue No. 8, 17 April 1984, 8A:8, 8A9.

37 Ibid., Issue No. 23, 9 March 1982, 23:11.

38 Ibid., Issue No. 8, 17 April 1984, 8A:9.

39 For a discussion of this and related seapower issues, see R.B. Byers (ed.), *The Denuclearisation of the Oceans* (London: Croom Helm 1986).

40 For an elaboration of this issue and its implications for Canada, see the author's contribution in Brian Macdonald (ed.), *High Tech and the High Seas* (Toronto: Canadian Institute of Strategic Studies 1985).
41 Byers, *Canadian Security and Defence*, 23–6.
42 Lafond Committee, Issue No. 23, 9 March 1982, 23:12. See also note 35. See also Watkins, "The Maritime Strategy."
43 Ibid., Issue No. 22, 2 March 1982, 22:15, 22:16. Dr Lindsey's comments referred to a non-nuclear conflict, but the same situation would prevail in a nuclear war.
44 Ibid., Issue No. 23, 9 March 1982, 23:13.
45 Canada, House of Commons, *Hansard*, 12 September 1985.
46 For an assessment of this issue, see W. Harriet Critchley, "Polar Deployment of Soviet Submarines," *International Journal* 39, No. 4 (Autumn 1984): 828–65. See also R.B. Byers and Michael Slack (eds.), *Strategy and the Arctic*, The Polaris Papers 4 (Toronto: Canadian Institute of Strategic Studies 1986).

CHAPTER SEVENTEEN: THE FUTURE OF NAVAL WARFARE

Background Reading

Robert Berman and Bill Gunston, *Rockets and Missiles of World War III* (London: Hamlyn 1983).
Jan S. Breemer, *US Naval Developments* (Annapolis, MD: Nautical and Aviation Publishing Co. 1983).
James Cable, *Britain's Naval Future* (London: Macmillan 1983).
Vice Admiral M.W. Cagle, *The United States Navy of Tomorrow* (New York: Dodd, Mead 1975).
James George (ed.), *Problems of Sea Power as We Approach the Twenty-First Century* (Washington: American Enterprise Institute for Public Policy Research 1978).
Adm. S.G. Gorshkov, *The Seapower of the State* (Annapolis, MD: Naval Institute Press 1979).
Gregory K. Hartmann, *Weapons that Wait* (Annapolis, MD: Naval Institute Press 1979).
Rear Admiral J.R. Hill, *Anti-Submarine Warfare* (Shepperton, Surrey, England: Ian Allan 1984).
Admiral Lord Hill-Norton, *Seapower* (London: Faber and Faber 1982).
Hubert Moineville, *Naval Warfare Today and Tomorrow* (Oxford: Basil Blackwell 1983).
Paul Nitze and Leonard Sullivan, *Securing the Seas: The Soviet Challenge and Western Alliance Options* (Boulder, CO: Westview 1979).
Bryan Perrett, *Weapons of the Falklands Conflict* (Poole, England: Blandford 1984).
E.B. Potter (ed.), *Seapower: A Naval History* (Annapolis, MD: Naval Institute Press 1981).
Antony Preston, *Navies of World War 3* (Greenwich, CN: Bison Books 1984).
Bryan Ranft and Geoffrey Till, *The Sea in Soviet Strategy* (Annapolis, MD: Naval Institute Press 1983).
Clark G. Reynolds, *Command of the Sea: The History and Strategy of Maritime Empires*, Vol. 2. *Since 1815* (Malabar, Florida: R.E. Krieger 1983).
Captain S.W. Roskill, *The War at Sea 1939–1945*, 3 vols. (London: Her Majesty's Stationery Office 1954–61).
James L. Stokesbury, *Navy and Empire* (New York: William Morrow 1983).
Geoffrey Till, *Maritime Strategy and the Nuclear Age*, 2nd ed. (New York: St Martins 1984).
Geoffrey Till (ed.), *The Future of British Sea Power* (London: Macmillan 1984).
B.W. Watson and P.M. Dunn (eds), *Military Lessons of the Falkland Islands War* (London: Arms and Armour 1984).

CONTRIBUTORS

CONTRIBUTORS

Rod Byers is Senior Research Fellow and past Director of the Centre for International and Strategic Studies, and Professor of Political Science, at York University, Toronto. Educated at the Royal Military College of Canada, he served in the Royal Canadian Navy from 1956 to 1964 before embarking on postgraduate studies at the University of Saskatchewan. He received his MA in 1965 and his PH.D. from Carleton University in 1971. Among many publications he has edited *The Denuclearisation of the Oceans* (London: Croom Helm 1986) and has written *Canadian Security and Defence: The Legacy and the Challenge* (Adelphi Paper No 214, London 1986). He is also the author of *The Canadian Annual Review of Politics and Public Affairs, 1985* (Toronto: University of Toronto Press 1988).

Harriet Critchley is Director, Strategic Studies Programme, and Associate Professor of Political Science at the University of Calgary. Educated in Canada and the United States, she received her doctorate from Columbia University and was a post-doctoral fellow at the University of British Columbia before taking up her present position in 1980. Active in the Canadian Institute of International and Strategic Studies, she has written widely in the field of strategic studies and circumpolar politics, and has served as a consultant to both the Departments of External Affairs and National Defence. Her most recent article is "The Arctic" in *International Journal* (Autumn 1987).

S. Mathwin Davis joined the Royal Corps of Naval Constructors during the Second World War and served in HMS *Rodney*, being present at the *Bismarck* action. Coming to Canada in 1947, he joined the Naval Reserve in 1950 and the Royal Canadian Navy in 1953. He served as a Constructor Officer in Ottawa, Halifax, and Montreal and was leader, in 1959, of the RCN's Nuclear Submarine Survey Team, which first proposed that Canada should build its own nuclear submarines. From 1960 to 1965 he was Director General – Ships, responsible for the design or construction of all warships currently (1988) in the Canadian Fleet. After unification he became Assistant Deputy Chief Engineering and finished his naval career as Commandant (1969–74) of the National Defence College. Upon retirement, he enrolled at Queen's University as a National Defence Fellow and obtained his PH.D. in Public Administration. Subsequently, he was a Distinguished Visitor at the Public Service Commission's Executive Staff Development Centre. Latterly he has been an Adjunct Professor in the School of Public Administration at Queen's University. He has post-graduate degrees in public administration, international affairs, war studies, and education and, in 1986, was a NATO Defence Fellow, and also holder of a Post-Doctoral Fellowship in Military History.

Colin G. Galigan, BA, MA, has combined a military career as a Logistics/Finance officer with academic training as an economist. He is an Alberta native who joined the Canadian Armed Forces in 1969. After graduation from the Royal Military College, he served in a number of finance-related positions in the field and at National Defence Headquarters. He returned to RMC to pursue graduate studies in economics. Most recently he has been an associate research fellow with the Centre for Studies in Defence Resources Management. His main research interests lie in defence economics and in particular the assessment of defence expenditure impacts upon the economy. He is a member of the International Defence Economics Association.

Barry Morton Gough, B.ED., MA, PH.D., FR Hist S, is a native of Victoria, British Columbia, and Professor of History, Wilfrid Laurier University, Waterloo, Ontario. He has devoted his professional career to writing and teaching Canadian history with a special emphasis on maritime affairs. He is the award-winning author of the trilogy, *The Royal Navy and the Northwest Coast*, *Distant Dominion*, and *Gunboat Frontier*, all published by the University of British Columbia Press. He is President of the Canadian Nautical Research Society. He is researching and writing the history of the North American and West Indies Station based on Halifax, 1815–1914, and a descriptive and analytical study, in two volumes, on the rise and fall of the Pax Britannica.

Michael L. Hadley, CD (BA, UBC; PH.D., Queen's), Professor of Germanic Studies at the University of Victoria, and Captain (N)(Retd) is the author of books and articles on German literature and thought. As a naval historian he has published in both German and Canadian journals. His book *U-Boats Against Canada: German Submarines in Canadian Waters* (1985) won both the Keith Matthews Prize of the Canadian Nautical Research Society and the John Lyman Prize of the North American Society for Oceanic History. He has had both seagoing and shore commands in the Canadian navy, including the naval reserve unit HMCS *Malahat*; fluent in German, he served briefly as liaison officer aboard the German training ship *Deutschland*. As guest of the C-in-C, Fleet, Federal German Navy, he has lectured on schnorkel-submarine operations at the Fleet Historical and Tactical Conference in Kiel, Germany. A past president of the Canadian Association of University Teachers of German and the Maritime Defence Association of Canada, he is currently Chairman of the Defence Minister's Academic Advisory Board on the Canadian Services Colleges.

John B. Hattendorf is the Ernest J. King Professor of Maritime History at the US Naval War College in Newport, Rhode Island. He spent nearly eight years in uniform as a naval officer. At sea, he served on board destroyers in both the US Atlantic and Pacific fleets and ashore, at the Naval Historical Center, Washington, DC, and on the staff of the Naval War College. He took his AB degree in history at Kenyon College, his AM degree at Brown University, and his D.Phil. at the University of Oxford. Hattendorf's publications include *The Writings of Stephen B. Luce* (1974); *On His Majesty's Service: The Diary, Letters and Reports of J.H. Wellings, Assistant U.S. Naval Attaché, London, 1940–41* (1983); *Sailors and Scholars: The Centennial History of the Naval War College* (1984); an annotated edition of Charles Nordhoff, *Man of War Life* (1985); *A Bibliography of the Writings of Alfred Thayer Mahan* (1986); *England in the War of the Spanish Succession* (1987), and with Robert S. Jordan he has edited and contributed to *Maritime Strategy and the Balance of Power: Britain and America in the 20th Century* (forthcoming). He is a series editor for *Classics of Sea Power*. Hattendorf has been elected a Corresponding Member of the Royal Swedish Society of Naval Science and, in Britain, the Society for Nautical Research.

Barry Hunt was educated at the Royal Military College (BA, MA), the University of Western Ontario, King's College (University of London, England), and Queen's University (PH.D.). From 1960 to 1967 he served with the Royal Canadian Regiment in Canada and with the Royal Fusiliers of the British Army in the United Kingdom and Germany. Since 1967, he has been a civilian member of the RMC faculty, where he is currently Professor and Head of the Department of History. In 1974–5 he was Visiting Professor at the University of Western Ontario, and in 1980–1 at the US Navy Postgraduate School, Monterey, California. In 1986–7, he attended the National Defence College of Canada. Dr Hunt is the author of several articles on naval history and maritime strategy, and of the biography *Sailor-Scholar: Admiral Sir Herbert Richmond, 1871–1946* (1982). He has also co-edited *War Aims and Strategic Policy in the Great War* (1977), and *War and Diplomacy across the Pacific, 1919–1952* (1988).

Paul Kennedy was born in Wallsend, England, in 1945. He took first-class Honours in History at the University of Newcastle in 1966, and his D.Phil. at Oxford in 1970. Between 1966 and 1969 he also acted as Research Assistant to Sir Basil Liddell Hart. From 1970 to 1983 he was successively Lecturer, Reader, and then Professor of History at the University of East Anglia; since 1983, he has been Dilworth Professor of History at Yale. He is a Fellow of the Royal Historical Society, and a former Fellow both of the Alexander von Humboldt Foundation and the Institute for Advanced Studies at Princeton. He is the author and editor of eleven books, including *The Rise of the Anglo-German Antagonism, Strategy and Diplomacy 1860–1945*, and, recently, *The Rise and Fall of the Great Powers*.

George Lindsey, who earned degrees in mathematics and physics from Toronto, Queen's, and Cambridge, served in the Royal Canadian Artillery in the Second World War with the British and Canadian Army Operational Research Groups, and joined the Canadian Defence Research Board in 1950. Since then he has worked in operational research, systems analysis, and strategic studies, for RCAF Air Defence Command, SACLANT Antisubmarine Research Centre (La Spezia), and the Operational Research and Analysis Establishment of the Canadian Department of National Defence. He was Chief of ORAE for twenty years before retiring in 1987. He has written on a number of subjects, including nuclear and maritime strategy, defence technology, air defence, and the Arctic. He is an active participant in the research program of the Canadian Institute of Strategic Studies.

Danford W. Middlemiss was educated at the University of Toronto (BA 1967; MA 1968; PH.D. 1976). From 1973 to 1976 he was engaged in Canadian maritime enforcement studies with the Institute of International Relations at the University of British Columbia. From 1976 to 1981 he was Director of the Centre for Strategic Studies at the University of Alberta. Since 1981, he has been an Associate Professor with the Department of Political Science, Dalhousie University. He has published articles on the economic aspects of Canadian defence policy and has testified on numerous occasions before various parliamentary committees on the maritime and other aspects of Canadian defence. He is co-author of a forthcoming textbook on Canadian defence policy. He is currently Director of the Centre for Foreign Policy Studies at Dalhousie University.

Marc Milner has published widely on the Canadian navy and the Second World War. His *North Atlantic Run* (1985), a study of RCN operations in the mid-Atlantic, 1941–3, was particularly well received. He served on the staff of the Directorate of History at National Defence Headquarters, and contributed to the maritime air section of the official history of the Royal Canadian Air Force and a forthcoming official history of Canadian naval operations in the Second World War, before taking up his present appointment as Associate Professor of History at the University of New Brunswick, where he has a chair in military history. His contribution to this book reflects his ongoing interest in the field.

Richard A. Preston is W.K. Boyd Professor Emeritus at Duke University and Honorary Professor of History at the Royal Military College of Canada. Born in England, he taught at University College, Cardiff, the University of Toronto, RMC, and Duke. He was Director of Canadian Studies at Duke from 1973 to 1979 and was awarded the Donner Medal for the promotion of Canadian Studies in the United States and the Northern Telecom International Gold Medal. Among his publications are: *Canada's RMC*, *Canada and Imperial Defence*, and *The Defence of the Undefended Border*. Forthcoming is *To Serve Canada: A History of the Royal Military College since the Second World War*. During the Second World War he served with the Royal Air Force.

Professor Dr Jürgen Rohwer, Director of the Library of Contemporary History in Stuttgart, Federal Republic of Germany, is one of the world's leading authorities on the history of navies during and since the Second World War. Editor of *Marine Rundschau* from 1958 to 1986, and of the *Jahresbibliographie der Bibliothek für Zeitgeschichte* since 1959, his publications include *Decisive Battles of World War II* (English edition 1965), *Axis Submarine Successes 1939–1945* (English edition 1983), *Chronology of the War at Sea 1939–45* (2 volumes, English edition 1972–4), and *The Critical Convoy Battles of March, 1943* (English edition 1977). He has published important articles in *Brassey's Defence Annual*, *US Naval Institute Proceedings* and *Naval Review*, *Revue Maritime*, *Rivista Maritima*, *Navigator* (Rio de Janeiro), and *Defence Journal* (Karachi). Active in many national and international professional organizations, he has played a major part in bringing together historians from different parts of the world and of different political persuasions. He made major contributions to *The RCN in Retrospect* (1982) and to the International Commission of Military History's Canadian meeting at Montreal, Quebec, in August 1988.

Roger Sarty is a native of Halifax, Nova Scotia, and did his graduate work at Duke University and the University of Toronto. Since 1981 he has been an historian at the Directorate of History, National Defence Headquarters, Ottawa. After assisting in the production of W.A.B. Douglas's *The Creation of a National Air Force: The Official History of the Royal Canadian Air Force, Volume II* (Toronto 1986), he joined the team that is now preparing an operational history of the Royal Canadian Navy in the Second World War. Dr Sarty has published a number of papers on Canadian maritime defence and a monograph on British and American coast defence in the nineteenth century. He has also prepared an historical study of fortifications at Halifax for Parks Canada.

Donald M. Schurman was born in Sydney, Nova Scotia, and earned his BA and MA from Acadia University and a second MA and his PH.D. from Cambridge University. During the Second World War he was part of #6 Bomber Group, Bison (429 Squadron). He has taught at the University of Alberta, the Royal Military College of Canada, Queen's University, and the University of Singapore. From 1980 to 1987 he was Professor and Head, Department of History, RMC. From 1961 to 1987 he was Official Historian of the Diocese of Ontario (Anglican). He is a member of the Council of the Navy Records Society, was Ecumenical Visitor to the Russian Orthodox, the Armenian, and the Coptic Church of Ethiopia in 1983, and to the Patriarchiates of Cyprus, Syria, and Jerusalem in 1987. In 1986 he was a delegate to the UN Conference on Peace and Conflict Resolution Studies at Suva, Fiji. His publications include *The Education of a Navy* (1965), with Gunn, Matthews, and Wiebe, *The Complete Letters of Benjamin Disraeli* Volumes 1 and 2 (1982), and *Julian Stafford Corbett, 1854–1922* (1982). He was named Distinguished Professor at RMC in 1986 and retired in 1987.

Joel J. Sokolsky is an Assistant Professor of Political Science at the Royal Military College of Canada. A native of Toronto, he received his MA from the Johns Hopkins School of Advanced International Studies (SAIS) in Washington, DC. He earned his PH.D. with the Department of Government of Harvard University, where he wrote his doctoral thesis on NATO maritime strategy.

Dr Sokolsky has taught at SAIS and Dalhousie University. His areas of interest include international security relations, American foreign and defence policy, and Canadian foreign and defence policy. Coauthor of *Canada and Collective Security: Odd Man Out*, he has also published articles on Canadian defence and foreign policy and naval strategy. Dr Sokolsky has been the recipient of a number of scholarships, including the Department of National Defence Security Studies Scholarship and a NATO Fellowship.

John Treddenick is an economist with particular interests in the economics of defence. He was born in Winnipeg in 1938 and attended the Royal Military College of Canada (BA 1960) and Queen's University

(PH.D. 1969). Commissioned in the RCN in 1960, he served in HMC ships *Stadacona, Margaree,* and *Saskatchewan*. In 1963 he transferred to the RCNR and served in HMCS *Cataraqui* while pursuing graduate studies. Since 1967 he has been a member of the faculty of RMC. His teaching and research interests are in the fields of defence economics and quantitative analysis. In 1979 he spent a year with the Centre for Defence Studies at the University of Aberdeen and is Honorary Visiting Fellow in Defence Studies at that university. He is a graduate of the NATO Defense College, Rome, and is currently a member of its faculty.

INDEX

Abbott, Douglas G., 260
Acheson, Dean G., 217
Aircraft, types
  Avro Lancaster, 216
  Backfire-B (Tupolev Tu-22), 332
  Blohm and Voss BV-222 "Wiking," 183
  Bristol Beaufighter, 161
  British Aerospace Sea Harrier, 343
  Canadair CL 28 Argus, 216, 219, 269, 352
  Consolidated B-24 Liberator, 145, 160, 162, 171, 172, 173, 175, 176, 177, 181, 183
  Consolidated Canso/Canso 'A', 162, 183
  Consolidated PBY Catalina, 145
  Curtiss HS 2L, 120
  DeHavilland Mosquito, 161
  Dornier Do-217, 161
  Douglas B-18A Digby, 145
  Fairey Firefly, 215
  Fairey Swordfish, 166, 175, 177
  Grumman AS3 Avenger, 215
  Grumman CS2F Tracker, 216, 269
  Grumman F-14 Tomcat, 343
  Hawker Sea Fury, 215
  Heinkel He-177, 161
  Lockheed CP 140 Aurora, 268, 270, 276, 286, 352
  Lockheed Hudson, 183
  McDonnell F2H3 Banshee, 216, 221
  Sikorsky CHSS Sea King, 268, 269, 270
Albrecht, Oberleutnant zur. *See* Fritz
Allard, General Jean V., 78–82
Allied Forces Southern Europe, 249
Anderson, John, 321, 327
Arbick, Commander J. H., RCN, 197
Arctic Waters Pollution Prevention Act, 283, 284
Asdic. *See* Sonar
Ashe, Commander G. P. B., RCN, 155
Atlantic Oceanographic Research Group, 153
Austin, Rear Admiral Bernard L., USN, 238

Bahr, Kapitänleutnant Rudolf, 173, 180
Baker, Constructor Commodore R., RCN(R), 195, 198, 199, 200, 201, 204, 205, 207
Ballantyne, C. C., 122, 124
Bathythermography (BT), 149, 150, 153, 154, 155

Befehlshaver der Unterseeboote (BdU), 127–28, 130–31, 140, 160, 164–65, 174
Belligerent rights, 37–39, 41
Beobachtungsdienst (B-Dienst), 129, 136, 159, 161, 165, 182
Bermuda, 19, 97, 104, 108
Bletchley Park, 159, 166
Bliss, Commander P. M., RN, 152–53
Borden, Sir Robert L., 20, 104
Boyle, Vice-Admiral D. S., RCN, 84
Brand, Captain E. S., RCN, 65
Bridgman, Commander C. E., RNR, 167
Britannia, HMS, 64–66
Brock, Rear-Admiral J. V., RCN, 194, 200, 202, 205, 207, 214, 219, 321
Brock, Rear-Admiral P. W., RN, 67–68
Brock Report, 1961, 220–22, 226, 262, 263, 266, 324
Brodeur, Rear-Admiral Nigel D., RCN, 94, 327
Brodie, Bernard, 50, 52
Brosio, Manilo, 229, 230
Browning, Vice-Admiral M. E., RN, 108
Brussels Pact, 191, 196
Burke, Admiral Arleigh, USN, 240–41
Burnett, Commander P. W., RN, 166, 168–69, 171

Cabinet Defence Committee, 198, 203
Cabinet War Committee, 190
Cadieux, Léo, 229
Campbell, Air Vice-Marshall H. L., RCAF, 213

Canadian Armed Forces (CAF), 27, 30, 258, 285, 286, 317, 318, 319, 321, 332, 333
Air Command, 258, 318
Canadian Forces Europe (CFE), 258, 318
Maritime Air Group, 319
Maritime Command, 3, 12, 14, 35, 61–89, 219, 224, 226, 258, 266, 268, 286, 287–88, 317–18, 323, 329, 333
Mobile Command, 258, 318
Canada's Maritime Defence (1983 Senate Report), 316
Canadian Atlantic Sub-Area (CANMARLANT), 217
Canadian Coastal Zone, 144, 148
Canadian Industrial Preparedness Association, 200
Canadian Maritime Commission, 200
Chadwick, Lieutenant Ernest M., RCN, 168
Chamberlain, Joseph, 26, 91, 98
Chambers, Rear-Admiral B. M., RN, 108
Churchill, Sir Winston S., 100, 105, 216, 217
Ciphers and codes (includes Ultra and Enigma machine), 159, 166–67, 180, 182, 184
Civilian Sealift Group, 231
Clark, C. Joseph, 321
Claxton, Brooke, 69, 215, 261
Coast Guard, 285, 287, 288
Coke, Vice-Admiral Sir Charles H., RN, 108, 109
Colbert, Admiral Richard B., USN, 7, 226, 227, 228, 229, 230, 233–53
Collège Militaire Royal (CMR),

73, 75
Colonial Naval Defence Act of 1865, 99
Combat Equivalence Units (CEU's), 300–304, 311, 313, 314
Command and control systems, 9–10
Committee of Imperial Defence, 96, 98, 100
Conolly, Richard L., USN, 237, 239
Convoys, First World War, 107, 112, 117, 121
Convoys, Second World War
  BX-141, 136, 140, 154, 157
  CS-52, 145
  HC-12, 115, 116, 117, 121
  HX-181, 136
  HX-229, 159
  HX-252, 163
  HX-253, 164
  HX-255, 166
  HX-256, 166, 167
  HX-258, 183
  HX-259, 183
  HX-262, 183
  HX-263, 183
  HX-264, 183
  KMS-24/09-92, 164
  MKF-22, 165
  MKS-22/SL-135, 164
  NL-9, 134
  ON-113, 139
  ON-115, 129
  ON-198, 163
  ON-199, 164
  ON-200, 165, 166
  ON-201, 166
  ON-202, 6, 165, 166, 167, 168, 171, 172, 175, 176, 178, 179, 182
  ON-203, 182, 183
  ON-206, 183
  ON-207, 183
  ON-208, 183
  ONS-5, 145
  ONS-16, 163
  ONS-17, 165, 166
  ONS-18, 6, 163, 165, 166, 167, 168, 171, 172, 175, 178, 179, 182
  ONS-19, 183
  ONS-20, 183
  ONS-21, 183
  ONS-154, 28
  QS-15, 139, 147
  QS-33, 147
  SC-42, 139
  SC-107, 28
  SC-122, 159
  SC-140, 164, 166
  SC-143, 183
  SC-145, 183
  SC-247, 116
  SH-194, 138, 157
  SQ-36, 140, 147
  TO-8, 166
  UC-4, 167
  UGS-16, 166
  UGS-17, 166
  UT-1, 164
Cooper, Colonel P. S., 76
Corbett, Sir Julian S., 4, 37, 50–52, 64, 233
Creery, Rear-Admiral W. B., RCN, 189, 207
Cuban Missile Crisis, 193, 218, 220
Curio, Oberleutnant Oskar, 177, 179
Cuthbertson, Brian, 213

Dardanelles, 349
Declaration of London, 1909, 38–39

Defence Planning Committee (DPC), 228, 230
Defence Production and Development Sharing Arrangements (DPDSA), 275
Defence Program Management System (DPMS), 296–99
Department of Defence Production (DDP), 187, 274
Department of Marine and Fisheries, 4
Department of National Defence, 8, 11, 12, 48, 75, 81, 87, 224, 226, 228, 256, 258, 261, 266, 268, 269, 270, 272, 273, 277, 286, 292, 296, 297, 300, 307, 317–18, 321, 323, 326–29, 332–33
Department of Supply and Services, 8
Department of the Naval Service, 93, 109
Department of Transport, 262, 268
Destroyer Life Extension (DELEX), 270
Dewar, Admiral K. G. B., RN, 66
DeWolf, Vice-Admiral H. G., RCN, 188, 189
Dextrase, General J. A., 322
Diefenbaker, John G., 218, 263, 275
Dobson, Lieutenant-Commander A. H., RCN, 169, 173
Dönitz Admiral Karl, 5, 28, 126, 130, 131, 135, 139, 144, 160, 161, 163, 165, 168, 180, 182, 183
Dreadnought shipbuilding race, 5, 19, 20, 92, 93

Dyer, Rear-Admiral K. F., RCN, 218, 219

Evans, Commander Martin B., RN, 166, 168, 171–73, 175–81
Exclusive Economic Zone (EEZ), 44, 45, 284
Exercises, 217–18, 226, 231

Fisher, Admiral Sir John, 19, 20, 64, 93–100, 103
Fisheries Protection Service, 94
Foulkes, Lieutenant-General Charles, 75
France, 23, 24, 92, 93, 96, 99, 101, 338
Fulton, Vice-Admiral J. A., RCN, 292
Fyffe Committee, 321

Geneva Naval Conference, 1927, 38
Gibbs, Commander G. P., RN, 123, 124
Gimblett, Richard Howard, 94
Ginsburg, Colonel Robert N., USAF, 244
Godfrey, Air Vice-Marshall A. E., RCAF, 180
Godt, Admiral Eberhard, 127
Graf von Spee, Admiral, 20, 102
Grant, Vice-Admiral H. T. W., RCN, 190, 195–96, 205, 207, 213–15
Grant, Captain J. M., RCN, 68
Grant, Vice-Admiral W. L., RN, 108, 111–12, 114, 117, 121
Gray, Colin, 224

Guillou, Admiral J., 249
Guimond, Major-General Bernard J., 81

Haldane, Lord, 98
Hartmann, Professor Frederick H., 246
Hartwig, Admiral Paul, 132, 136, 138, 140, 147, 149
Hatcher, Captain J. O., RN, 109
Hayes, Commodore W. P., 76
Helfrich, Vice-Admiral C. E. L., 236
Hellyer, Paul, 32, 78, 79, 263–65, 275
Hendy, Commodore Robert, RCNR, 322
Hepp, Kapitänleutnant Horst, 170, 177–79, 181
Hibbard, Rear-Admiral J. C., RCN, 188
High Frequency Direction Finding (HF/DF), 28, 127, 152, 167, 170, 177, 181, 182
Hill-Norton, Vice-Admiral Sir Peter, RN, 229
Hodgson, Paymaster Lieutenant J. S., RCNVR, 189
Holmes, John W., 212
Horton, Admiral Sir Max, RN, 139, 171
Hose, Rear-Admiral Walter, RCN, 109, 111, 117–18, 122–23
Houghton, Rear-Admiral F. L., RCN, 189, 197, 207
Howe, C. D., 274
Hydrophones, 113, 169

International Seabed Authority (ISA), 45
International Sea Power Symposium, 233, 247, 248, 250, 252
Italy, 23, 92–93
Ites, Oberleutnant Otto, 181

Jane, Fred T., 209
Janowitz, Morris, 67, 71
Japan, 19, 21, 23, 24, 93, 94, 101, 336, 339
Jellicoe, Lord, 189, 292
Jones, Vice-Admiral G. C., RCN, 211

Kennedy, Gavin, 255
Kenworthy, Commander J. M., RN (later Lord Strabolgi), 66
Kidd, Admiral Isaac C., jr, USN, 248
King, William Lyon Mackenzie, 8, 23–26, 31, 189, 190
Kingsmill, Admiral C. E., RCN, 108, 109, 117, 119, 203
Knowlton, Rear-Admiral J. G., RCN, 205, 207
Korean War, 1950–53, 30, 78, 214–15, 222, 260, 261, 273–74, 295, 337–38, 349, 352

Lafond Committee, 322, 326–28
Laidlaw, Captain D. K., RCN, 155
Laurier, Sir Wilfrid, 19, 20, 31, 91, 94, 104, 124, 189

Lamb, James, 142, 188, 189
Landymore, Rear-Admiral W., RCN, 75–76, 79–80, 321
Law of the Sea Convention, 1982, 283
Lay, Rear-Admiral H. N., RCN, 188, 196, 202, 207
Leigh Light, 164, 177, 336
Leir, Rear-Admiral R. H., RCN, 67
Leonard, Dr A. C., 85
Lewis, Michael, 64, 67, 71, 80
Lowe, Percy, 75

Macdonald, Angus L., 190
Macintyre, Captain Donald, RN, 188
Mahan, Admiral A. T., USN, 4, 16, 17, 29, 50–53, 55, 93, 209, 210, 233, 335
Mainguy Report, 1949, 7, 70, 73–74
Maritime Engineering (MARE), 79, 86–88
Maritime Officer Production Study (MOPS), 85
Maritime Surface and Subsurface, 79, 85, 87–88
Marshall, George C., 242
McCormick, Admiral Lynde, USN, 217, 240
McDonald, Admiral David L., USN, 242
Miller, August, 241
Missiles
    Exocet, 340
    intercontinental ballistic (ICBM), 223–24, 338, 344
    phoenix, 343
    polaris, 244
    sea-launched ballistic (SLBM), 223–35, 325, 328–30, 344–45
    styx, 339–40
    submarine launched cruise, 329–31
Mitchell, Lieutenant-Commander J. E., RCNVR, 157
Moorer, Admiral Thomas H., USN, 245
Morison, Admiral S. E., USN, 52
Mulroney, Brian, 316, 318, 319, 321, 327
Murray, Rear-Admiral L. W., RCN, 144, 153, 155–58

Nairn, Lieutenant R. A., RCNVR, 154
National Defence Headquarters (NDHQ), 84, 322–23, 326, 330
National Research Council, 149, 150, 153, 155
National Security Council, 239
Naval Board, 194, 200–203, 205
Naval Command Course for Free World Naval Officers, 240, 242, 247–48, 252
Naval Officer Training Centre (NOTC), 86
Naval Officers Association of Canada (NOAC), 325
Naval Officers Training Course, 87
Naval Service Act, 1910, 4, 189
Naval War College (US), 238–41, 243, 246–48, 252
Navy League of Canada, 18, 325
Netherlands, The, 56
New Zealand, 5, 18, 99, 100
Newcombe, Commander P. F., RN, 116–17
Newfoundland Royal Naval

Reserve, 110
Nimitz, Fleet Admiral Chester W., USN, 209
Nitze, Paul H., 243–44
Nixon, C. R., 318
North American Air (Aerospace) Defence Command (NORAD), 218, 226, 286, 287, 290, 321, 323
North Atlantic Council, 201, 214–15, 226–27, 229
North Atlantic Ocean Regional Planning Group (NAORPG), 213–15
North Atlantic Treaty Organization (NATO), 7, 31, 32, 34, 36, 78, 102, 191–92, 196, 198, 203, 210–11, 213–14, 216–17, 220, 222, 224–32, 236–38, 240, 244–45, 249, 260, 263, 265–72, 275, 286–87, 290, 307, 317, 323, 326–27, 330, 332, 346
Northwest Passage, 46–47, 281, 283, 284
Norway, 56–57

Officer Candidate Training Plan, 87–88
Operational Intelligence Center, 159, 167
Operational research, 139
Operations
 Musketry, 161
 Norploy, 286
 Observant, 140
 Otter, 151
 Overlord, 189, 215
 Paukenschlag, 130
 Percussion, 161, 164
 Salmon, 151
 Seaslug, 161

Otto, Oberleutnant Paul, 169, 170, 174

Paradis, Major-General J. J., 83, 85
Pearson, Lester B., 47, 212, 217, 320
Penner Report, 1970, 325, 326, 221
Pickard, Leiutenant-Commander A. F., RCNR, 169, 178
Piers, Rear-Admiral D. W., RCN, 76
Pighini, Admiral Guiseppe, 249
Porter, Rear-Admiral H. A., RCN, 248
Prentice, Captain J. D., RCN, 148, 154–55
Pressey, Commander A. R., RCN, 149
Pullen, Rear-Admiral H. F., RCN, 166
Pullen, Captain T. C., RCN, 13
Puxley, Captain W. L., RN, 157

Quebec Conference, 1943, 189–90

Radar, 9, 126, 133–34, 147, 149, 181, 334, 336, 340–42
 German search receiver (GSR), 128, 133–34, 160–61, 166, 169, 182, 336
Rankin, Lieutenant-Commander A. H., RCN, 169, 174
Raymond, Captain D. L., RN, 155
Reagan, Ronald, 36, 45, 331
Regular Officers Career Development Plan, 88
Regular Officer Training

Program (ROTP), 71–73, 75, 77, 81, 84, 87–88
Reid, Vice-Admiral H. E., RCN, 151–52
Richardson, James A., 82, 269
Richmond, Admiral Sir Herbert, RN, 34, 39, 52
Riverio, Admiral Horacio, 230
Roberts, John M., 246
Ropp, Theodore, 50, 52
Rostow, Walt W., 242–44
Rowley, Major-General Roger, 81
Royal Air Force
  Coastal Command, 145, 147, 161–62, 183
  Squadrons
    No. 120, 171
    No. 179, 164
Royal Australian Navy, 5, 20, 30, 80, 99, 100
Royal Canadian Air Force, 27, 30, 31, 132, 134, 138, 146, 151, 216
  Eastern Air Command, 6, 147, 162
  Squadrons
    No. 10, 167, 176
    No. 113, 147
    No. 119, 136
    No. 407, 166
Royal Canadian Air Force Staff College, 58, 68–70, 72–73
RCN-RCAF Monthly Review, 152
Royal Canadian Navy
  Canadian Northwest Atlantic Command, 144, 153
  Cornwallis, HMCS (shore establishment), 157
  Flag Officer Atlantic Coast (FOAC), 217
  Mid Ocean Escort Force, 6
  Naval Service Headquarters (NSHQ), 150, 155
  Western Local Escort Force (WLEF), 146, 148
Royal Commission on Bilingualism and Biculturalism, 82
Royal Corps of Naval Constructors, 195
Royal Military College of Canada, 59, 68–69, 72, 74–76, 85
Royal Naval Canadian Volunteer Reserve, 104, 105, 110
Royal Naval College, Dartmouth, 63, 65–68, 72
Royal Naval College, Greenwich, 65–66, 68, 70
Royal Naval College of Canada, 68, 194
Royal Naval College, Osborne, 65
Royal Naval Engineering College, Keyham, 69, 73
Royal Naval Engineering College, Manadan, 63, 67
Royal Roads Military College, 68–70, 72, 75–76, 86, 88

St Laurent, Louis S., 212, 216
Salisbury, Lord, 38, 42
Sampson, Rear Admiral William Thomas, USN, 95
Schlesinger, James R., 231
Second Language Training, 82, 86, 88–89
Seeley, Sir John R., 18
Selborne, Lord, 64, 97
Senate Committee on Foreign Affairs, 321
Senate Sub-Committee on National Devence, 287, 292, 300

INDEX 407

Sherman, Admiral Forrest P., USN, 238, 239
Ships, icebreaking
  American
    Polar Sea, 36, 48, 364
    Polar Star, 332
    Wind class, 197
  Canadian
    Labrador, 262
    Polar class 8, 48, 287
Ships, merchant and fishing
  Agnes B. Holland, 115
  Anastasios Pateras, 139
  Atlantika, 219
  Bayou Chico, 136
  Bergsdalen, 124
  Caribou, 136, 137
  Carolus, 134
  Chatham, 138
  Culver, 149, 150
  Destiny, 170
  Dinaric, 139
  Dornfontein, 115, 124
  Ekholi, 150
  Empire MacAlpine, 166, 175, 177
  Erik, 118, 124
  F. Q. Barstow, 116
  Gladys M. Hollett, 115
  Hainault, 139
  Herbert L. Pratt, 114
  James Gordon Bennett, 179
  Lancer, 170
  Lusitania, 108
  Luz Blanca, 116, 117, 118, 124
  Manhattan, 36, 47, 283
  Mauretania, 167
  Nelson A., 115
  Newby Hall, 122
  Northern Foam, 175, 177
  Oregon Express, 179
  Orkan, 183
  Pacific Pioneer, 140
  Port Jemseg, 179
  Queen Elizabeth, 167
  Rathlin, 169, 170, 173, 180
  Samtucky, 156
  Skjelbred, 179
  Steel Voyager, 179
  Sydland, 118
  Theodore Dwight Weld, 170
  Triumph, 118
  Waleha, 178
  Watuka, 151
  Willie G., 124
Ships, naval
  American
    Albany, 239
    Altair, 242
    Arkansas, 235
    Barker, 236, 237
    Bogue, 165–66
    Boston, 242
    Card, 166
    Claude V. Ricketts, 244
    Columbus, 237
    Core, 236
    DeLong, 112
    Meade, 237
    Mojave, 138
    San Diego, 114
    Santee 166
    Submarine chasers, 112, 118
    Tingey, 112, 116
    Yorktown, 120, 236
  British
    Bermuda, 164
    Egret, 161, 164
    Fencer, 183
    Icarus, 168, 171, 175, 179
    Invincible, 342
    Itchen, 169, 172–74, 177–78, 181
    Keppel, 168, 172–73, 175–76, 178

Lagan, 168–70, 173
Le Tiger, 158
Minotaur, 190
Nabob, 190
Narcissus, 168, 173–74, 177
O'rchis, 168
Pelican, 145
Polyanthus, 168, 170, 173, 174, 178
Puncher, 190
Salisbury, 140
Sheffield, 164
Stonecrop, 164
Stork, 164
Towy, 177
Tracker, 183
Wallflower, 164
Wanderer, 164

Canadian
Acadia, 107
Algonquin, 203
Arleux, 106
Arras, 106
Athabaskan, 161, 164,
Bangor, 131, 148–49, 213
Bonaventure, 216, 221, 262, 268
Bras d'Or, 269, 352
Canada, 107
Canadian Patrol Frigate, 11, 268–70, 276–77, 286, 352
Cartier, 107, 113, 118–19
Chambly, 169, 175, 178–79, 181
Charlottetown, 131, 136
Clayoquot, 131, 136–37, 141, 156
Corvette class, 129, 131, 148, 149
DDH-280 class destroyer escorts, 8, 9, 265, 268–70, 300, 352
Drifters (anti-submarine), 110, 112, 113
Drumheller, 168, 172, 173, 178, 179
Drummondville, 139
Esquimalt, 131, 136, 157
Festubert, 115
Gatineau, 168–70, 172, 177–78
Grandmère, 137
Grilse, 122
Hochelaga, 107, 118–20
Kamloops, 168, 170
Kentville, 138
Lady Evelyn, 107
Magnificent, 70, 190, 212, 215–16
Magog, 131, 137, 153
Margaret, 107
Morden, 169, 175, 177, 181
Niobe, 6, 104
Norsyd, 134
Ontario, 215
Preserved, 265
Prestonian, 138, 221
Protecteur, 265
Provider, 262
Racoon, 131
Rainbow, 6, 102
Restigouche II, 8, 265
Sackville, 169, 174–76
St Croix, 169, 172, 173, 174, 178
St Eloi, 116
St Laurent II, 8
Shawinigan, 136, 137, 153
Shearwater, 111
Sioux, 203
Skeena, 139
Springhill, 154
Stadacona, 107
Swansea, 151

Trawler 22, 118, 119
Trawler 30, 113
Trawler 32, 118–19
Uganda, 69, 190, 215
Valleyfield, 128, 131, 151
Warrior, 190
German
  Admiral Graf Spee, 348
  Admiral Scheer, 348
  Atlantis, 348
  Emden, 347
  Frederick Douglas, 170, 173
  Gneisenau, 348
  Karlsruhe, 347
  Leipzig, 6
  Narvik class destroyers, 161
  Scharnhorst, 348
  Tirpitz, 348
Other nations
  Belgrano (Argentina), 42
  Eilat (Israel), 339
  Komar class (Egypt), 340
  Lobelia (France), 169, 177, 178
  Roselys, 169, 175, 176
  Renoncule (France), 169, 175, 177, 180
Singapore, 54–56
Slade, Captain Edmond, RN, 95
Small, Squadron Leader N. E., RCAF, 147
Smith, Lieutenant E. C., RCNVR, 169, 181
Sonar (asdic), 9, 127, 129, 132, 135, 137, 138, 140, 141, 144, 148, 154, 156, 334, 337, 340, 342
Sonobuoys, 340, 342
Sound Surveillance System (SONUS), 218
Soviet Strategic Rocket Forces (SRF), 223

Spain, 239, 242
Standing Committee on External Affairs and National Defence (SCEAND), 225, 320, 325
Standing Naval Force Atlantic (STANAVFORLANT), 227, 228, 245, 246, 248, 252, 290
Standing Naval Force Channel (STANFORCHAN), 228
Stewart, Lieutenant Donald M., RCNVR, 168
Storrs, Rear-Admiral A. H. H., RCN, 168, 194, 196, 202, 204, 205, 207
Story, Vice-Admiral W. O., RN (ret'd), 108, 117, 123
Strategic Arms Limitation Treaty II (SALT II), 327
Strategic Defense Initiative (SDI), 331, 344
Submarine Tracking Room, 159, 161, 165, 182, 184
Submarines
  Ballistic missile nuclear-powered (SSBN), 210, 223–25, 325–26, 328–30, 349
  Canadian
    CC-1, 111
    CC-2, 111
    Oberon class, 263, 270, 272, 275
    Rainbow II, 269
  German
    Deutschland (became U-155), 106, 121–22
    schnorkel-equipped, 128–29, 152
    U-53, 106
    U-69, 128, 134, 137, 138
    U-94, 181
    U-107, 151

410   INDEX

U-111, 128, 135
U-117, 115, 118, 120, 124–25
U-123, 128
U-132, 135, 139, 147
U-134, 164
U-140, 114, 115
U-151, 113
U-155, 161
U-156, 114–18, 120–21, 124–25
U-165, 147
U-170, 165
U-190, 138, 142, 157
U-214, 164
U-215, 158
U-229, 154–65, 174, 176
U-233, 151
U-238, 165, 170, 175, 177–80
U-260, 164–66, 173–74, 177–78
U-270, 163, 165, 168–70, 173–73, 176, 182
U-275, 165, 177
U-305, 163, 165–66, 173–75, 178–81
U-338, 164–66, 170, 172–73
U-341, 165, 167
U-377, 165, 174–76
U-378, 165, 174
U-386, 164–66, 171–73, 181
U-387, 165
U-402, 165, 168, 178
U-413, 165
U-422, 165, 175, 180
U-448, 165
U-460, 154–66
U-515, 165
U-517, 132, 136, 138, 140, 147
U-523, 164
U-533, 129
U-536, 140–41, 165
U-537, 151
U-539, 151, 156
U-541, 134–35, 140–41, 153
U-543, 151
U-548, 128, 151
U-580, 151
U-584, 165, 175, 178
U-603, 165
U-621, 164
U-634, 164
U-641, 165, 174, 179–80
U-645, 163, 165–66, 173
U-666, 165
U-669, 165–66
U-731, 165, 170, 171–72, 175–77
U-753, 147
U-754, 136
U-758, 165, 168, 179–80
U-760, 164
U-802, 134–35, 140, 151, 153
U-806, 140–41, 156
U-845, 141–51
U-854, 156
U-856, 151
U-952, 165, 173, 174–74, 177, 179
U-1221, 140
U-1222, 151
U-1223, 153
U-1228, 153
U-1231, 141
U-1232, 127, 135, 136, 138, 140–41, 154–57
Guided Missile Nuclear-powered (SSGN), 329
Nuclear-powered (SSN), 13, 328–30, 333, 345, 354

INDEX   411

Soviet, 223–24, 287, 329
Support groups, 141, 153–54,
  157, 158, 159, 164, 167, 171,
  173, 175
Supreme Allied Commander
  Atlantic (SACLANT), 34,
  216–18, 226–29, 231, 240,
  245, 248, 249, 271, 290, 332
Supreme Allied Commander
  Europe (SACEUR), 216, 326
Svab, Colonel W. G., 84
Sweden, 57–58

Territorial Sea Convention,
  1958, 283
Timbrell, Rear-Admiral R. W.,
  RCN, 292, 300, 314
Tisdall, Rear-Admiral E. P., 74,
  75, 77, 84
Todd, Commander G. F.,
  RCNVR, 189
Torpedo-Anti-Submarine
  (TAS), 129
Torpedoes, German, 137–38,
  160, 163, 168–69, 172–74,
  177, 182
Tribal Update and
  Modernization Program
  (TRUMP), 270
Trudeau, Pierre Elliott, 31, 47,
  82, 226, 229, 232, 266–67,
  319–20, 322, 323–25, 333
Truman, Harry S., 317
Tully, J. P., 153

Unification of armed forces, 3,
  7, 10, 79–86, 226, 321
Union of Soviet Socialist
  Republics, 13, 18, 30, 35–36,
  92–93, 99, 101, 195–96, 203,
  210, 212, 214, 218, 221,
  223–24, 226, 229, 251, 272,
  287, 289–90, 320, 326–32,
  343, 351, 353
United Nations, 42, 46, 78, 214,
  337
United Nations Conference on
  the Law of the Sea (UNCLOS),
  35–36, 43–47, 283–84
United States Navy, 7, 21, 39,
  41, 77, 80, 94–95, 99, 101,
  107, 150, 153, 155–56, 209,
  211–12, 214, 218, 230–31,
  241–42, 287, 328, 332
University Reserve Training
  Programme (URTP), 71
University Training Plan,
  Officers (UTPO), 85

Vance, Lieutenant-General
  J. E., 84

Walker, Captain F. J., RN, 167
War Office, 96–98
Warsaw Pact, 210, 327
Wemyss, Lord, 122
Western Union, 191, 196
White papers on defence, 320,
  323
  1949, 191
  1964, 265, 324
  1971, 225–26, 266–68, 285,
    324–26
  1987, 13, 270, 289
Winn, Commander Rodger, RN,
  130, 161, 163, 166, 182
Wood, Vice-Admiral J. C., 225,
  329, 332
Wood, Rear Admiral Spencer
  S., USN, 112
Woods Hole Oceanographic
  Institute, 149–50

Young, Colonel J. D., 85

Zumwalt, Admiral Elmo, USN,
  230, 234, 243, 248, 250